HTML, XHTML, and CSS Bible

3rd Edition

Brian Pfaffenberger, Steven M. Schafer, Charles White, Bill Karow

WILEY

Wiley Publishing, Inc.

HTML, XHTML, and CSS Bible, 3rd Edition

Published by
Wiley Publishing, Inc.
10475 Crosspoint Boulevard
Indianapolis, IN 46256
www.wiley.com

Copyright © 2004 by Wiley Publishing, Inc., Indianapolis, Indiana

Published simultaneously in Canada

ISBN: 0-7645-5739-4

Manufactured in the United States of America

10 9 8 7 6 5 4 3 2 1

No part of this publication may be reproduced, stored in a retrieval system or transmitted in any form or by any means, electronic, mechanical, photocopying, recording, scanning or otherwise, except as permitted under Sections 107 or 108 of the 1976 United States Copyright Act, without either the prior written permission of the Publisher, or authorization through payment of the appropriate per-copy fee to the Copyright Clearance Center, 222 Rosewood Drive, Danvers, MA 01923, (978) 750-8400, fax (978) 646-8600. Requests to the Publisher for permission should be addressed to the Legal Department, Wiley Publishing, Inc., 10475 Crosspoint Blvd., Indianapolis, IN 46256, (317) 572-3447, fax (317) 572-4355, e-Mail: brandreview@wiley.com.

For general information on our other products and services or to obtain technical support, please contact our Customer Care Department within the U.S. at (800) 762-2974, outside the U.S. at (317) 572-3993 or fax (317) 572-4002.

Wiley also publishes its books in a variety of electronic formats. Some content that appears in print may not be available in electronic books.

Library of Congress Cataloging-in-Publication Data: Available from Publisher

Trademarks: Wiley, the Wiley logo, and related trade dress are trademarks or registered trademarks of John Wiley & Sons, Inc. and/or its affiliates, in the United States and other countries, and may not be used without written permission. All other trademarks are the property of their respective owners. Wiley Publishing, Inc., is not associated with any product or vendor mentioned in this book.

WILEY is a trademark of Wiley Publishing, Inc.

About the Authors

Bryan Pfaffenberger is the author of more than 75 books on computers and the Internet, including the best-selling *Discover the Internet*, from IDG Books Worldwide. He teaches advanced professional communication and the sociology of computing in the University of Virginia's Division of Technology, Culture, and Communication. Bryan lives in Charlottesville, Virginia, with his family and an extremely spoiled cat.

Steven M. Schafer is a veteran of technology and publishing. He programs in several languages, works with a variety of technologies, and has been published in several technical publications and articles. He currently is the COO/CTO for Progeny, an open source–based service and support company. Steve can be reached by e-mail at sschafer@synergy-tech.com.

Chuck White is a Web development professional who has written numerous articles and books on Web development, including *Mastering XSLT* and *Developing Killer Web Apps with Dreamweaver MX and C#*, and tutorials for IBM DeveloperWorks. His first published work on CSS was for *Web Techniques* magazine in 1997, and he has been working with large and small Web sites since 1996. He is currently a Web software engineer for eBay.

Bill Karow, in addition to writing several computer books, has served as a contributor or technical editor on more than 30 other books. Formerly in charge of systems development for Walt Disney Entertainment, Bill now serves as a computer consultant in the Orlando area when he's not out riding his bicycle. He also has the distinction of having stood atop many of the buildings at Walt Disney World, fanfare trumpet in hand (with their permission, of course).

Credits

Acquisitions Editor
Jim Minatel

Development Editor
Marcia Ellett

Production Editor
Gabrielle Nabi

Technical Editor
Wiley-Dreamtech India Pvt Ltd

Copy Editor
TechBooks

Editorial Manager
Mary Beth Wakefield

**Vice President & Executive
Group Publisher**
Richard Swadley

**Vice President and Executive
Publisher**
Bob Ipsen

Vice President and Publisher
Joseph B. Wikert

Executive Editorial Director
Mary Bednarek

Project Coordinator
Erin Smith

Proofreading and Indexing
TechBooks Production Services

*To Miri, I'll desperately miss
my late-night company.*
Steve

Acknowledgments

A book such as this is hard work, and only a small portion of that work is performed by the authors. As such, the authors would like to thank the following:

The management team at Wiley Publishing for continuing to support large, tutorial-reference books so folks like you (the reader) can benefit.

Jim Minatel, for putting together the plan, assembling the team, and making us all behave.

Bryan Pfaffenberger, the original author of the 1st and 2nd Editions of this book, for providing a solid outline and organization for us to follow.

John Daily, who compiled the referential information in Appendixes A and B, for stepping up and providing the critical attention to detail necessary for such work.

Marcia Ellett, for continuing to be one of the best development editors around—keeping us all on track and organized—and for providing crucial insights and feedback throughout the process.

Wiley-Dreamtech India Pvt Ltd. for providing the technical editing—ensuring that the information is accurate and pertinent, as well as providing additional useful insights.

TechBooks, for ensuring that our text is easy to read and understand, despite our best efforts.

The production crew who packaged the raw material into this nice package you now hold.

And last, but definitely not least, our friends and family who give us the love and support that enables us to do this in the first place.

Contents at a Glance

Contents

Part I: Understanding (X)HTML — 1

Part III: Controlling Presentation with CSS   267

Chapter 24: Defining Pages for Printing 387

Part IV: Advanced Web Authoring   399

Chapter 25: JavaScript 401

Chapter 26: Dynamic DHTML 429

Chapter 31: Introduction to XML 505

Chapter 32: XML Processing and Implementations 523

Part V: Testing, Publishing, and Maintaining Your Site   547

Chapter 33: Testing and Validating Your Documents 549

Chapter 34: Web Development Software 555

Part VI: Principles of Professional Web Design and Development   601

Chapter 39: The Web Development Process 603

Chapter 40: Developing and Structuring Content 617

Introduction

The World Wide Web has come a long way from its humble beginnings. Most Internet historians recognize Gopher as the precursor to the Web. Gopher was a revolutionary search tool that allowed the user to search hierarchical archives of textual documents. It enabled Internet users to easily search, retrieve, and share information.

Today's World Wide Web is capable of delivering information via any number of medium—text, audio, video. The content can be dynamic and even interactive.

However, the Web is not a panacea. The standards that make up the HTTP protocol are implemented in different ways by different browsers. What works on one platform may not work the same, if at all, on the next. Newly Web-enabled devices—PDAs, cell phones, appliances, and so on—are still searching for a suitable form of HTML to standardize on.

This turmoil makes a book like this difficult to write. Although standards exist, they have been implemented in different ways and somewhat haphazardly. In addition, there are more technologies at work on the Web than can be easily counted. One book cannot hope to cover them all.

This book attempts to cover a broad subset of available technologies and techniques, centering on the HTML 4.01 standard, along with a mix of newer, upcoming standards such as XML and XHTML.

Who Should Read This Book?

This book is geared toward a wide audience. Those readers who are just getting started with HTML and Web content will benefit the most as this book provides a decent learning foundation as well as ample reference material for later perusal. Experienced users will find the chapters covering new standards and technologies to be the most useful, and will also appreciate having a comprehensive reference for consultation.

Although the Web is technical in nature, we have done our best to boil down the technology into simple and straightforward terms. Whether you are a computer scientist or a computer neophyte, you should be able to understand, adopt, and deploy the technologies discussed herein.

Book Organization, Conventions, and Features

The Wiley "Bible" series of books uses several different methods to present information to help you get the most out of it. The book is organized according to the following conventions.

Organization

This book is organized into logical parts. Each part contains related chapters that cover complementary subjects.

Part I, *Understanding (X)HTML*, is your introduction to the HTML protocol.

Part II, *HTML and XHTML Authoring Fundamentals*, continues coverage on the basics of the HTML protocol and familiarizes you with the basic HTML elements.

Part III, *Controlling Presentation with CSS*, covers Cascading Style Sheets—covering how CSS works and introducing its various elements.

Part IV, *Advanced Web Authoring*, delves into more advanced topics such as scripting, Dynamic HTML, and XML.

Part V, *Testing, Publishing, and Maintaining Your Site*, covers more details about the tools and methodology for creating and publishing your content to the Web.

Part VI, *Principles of Professional Web Design and Development*, covers more philosophical topics about developing structured, accessible content and how to protect your content online.

Part VII, *Appendixes*, provides reference material on HTML tags, CSS conventions, and language codes.

Conventions and features

There are many different organizational and typographical features throughout this book designed to help you get the most from the information.

Tips, Notes, and Cautions

Whenever the authors want to bring something important to your attention, the information will appear in a Tip, Note, or Caution. These elements are formatted like this:

Caution This information is important and is set off in a separate paragraph with a special icon. Cautions provide information about things to watch out for, whether these things are simply inconvenient or potentially hazardous to your data or systems.

Tips generally are used to provide information that can make your work easier—special shortcuts or methods for doing something easier than the norm.

Notes provide additional, ancillary information that is helpful, but somewhat outside the current discussion.

Code

It is often necessary to display code (HTML tags, JavaScript commands, script listings) within the text. This book uses two distinct conventions, depending on where the code appears.

Code in Text

A special font is used to indicate code within normal text. This font looks like this:
`<body onLoad="JavaScript:displaygraphics();">`.

Code Listings

```
Code listings appear in specially formatted listings, in a different font,
similar to these lines.
```

Feedback

Wiley Publishing, Inc., and the authors of this book value your feedback. We welcome ways to improve the content presented here, such as being informed of errors and omissions. You can visit `www.wiley.com` for information on additional books and ways to provide feedback to the publisher.

Understanding (X)HTML

Introducing the Web and HTML

This chapter addresses the questions most people have when they're getting started with HTML/XHTML, such as what is the difference between HTML and XHTML, and when do Cascading Style Sheets (CSS) come into play? If you're already familiar with the basic concepts discussed here, you can get started with practical matters in Chapter 2. Still, I encourage you to at least skim this chapter, making sure you understand the very important distinction between structure and presentation (see *What Is CSS?*) and how HTML, XML, and XHTML are related (see *What Is XHTML?*).

What Is the World Wide Web?

The World Wide Web—the Web, for short—is a network of computers able to exchange text, graphics, and multimedia information via the Internet. By sitting at a computer that is attached to the Web, using either a dialup phone line or a much faster broadband (Ethernet, cable, or DSL connection), you can visit Web-connected computers next door, at a nearby university, or halfway around the world. And you can take full advantage of the resources these computers make available, including text, graphics, videos, sounds, and animation. Think of the Web as the multimedia version of the Internet, and you'll be right on the mark.

How Does the Web Work?

The computers that make all these Web pages available are called *Web servers*. On any computer that's connected to the Web, you can run an application called a Web browser. Technically, a Web browser is called a *Web client*—that is, a program that's able to contact a Web server and request information. When the Web server receives the requested information, it looks for this information within its file system, and sends out the requested information via the Internet.

They all speak a common "language," called HyperText Transfer Protocol (HTTP). (HTTP isn't really a language like the ones people speak. It's a set of rules or procedures, called *protocols,* that enables computers to exchange information over the Web.) Regardless of where these computers reside—China, Norway, or Austin, Texas—they can communicate with each other through HTTP.

The following illustrates how HTTP works (see Figure 1-1):

✦ Most Web pages contain *hyperlinks,* which are specially formatted words or phrases that enable you to access another page on the Web. Although the hyperlink usually doesn't make the address of this page visible, it contains all the information needed for your computer to request a Web page from another computer.

✦ When you click the hyperlink, your computer sends a message called an *HTTP request.* This message says, in effect, "Please send me the Web page that I want."

✦ The Web server receives the request, and looks within its stored files for the Web page you requested. When it finds the Web page, it sends it to your computer, and your Web browser displays it. If the page isn't found, you see an error message, which probably includes the HTTP code for this error: 404, "Not Found."

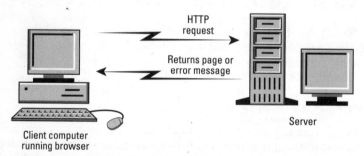

Figure 1-1: The client requests the page. Then the server evaluates the request and serves the page or an error message.

What Is Hypertext?

You probably noticed the word "hypertext" in the spelled-out version of HTTP, Hypertext Transfer Protocol. Originated by computing pioneer Theodore Nelson, the term "hypertext" doesn't mean "text that can't sit still," although some Web authors do use a much-despised HTML code that makes the text blink on-screen. Instead, the term is an analogy to a time-honored (but physically impossible) science fiction concept, the hyperspace jump, which enables a starship to go immediately from one star system to another. Hypertext is a type of text that contains hyperlinks (or just *links* for short), which enable the reader to jump from one hypertext page to another. You may also hear the word *hypermedia.* A hypermedia system works just like hypertext, except that it includes graphics, sounds, videos, and animation as well as text.

In contrast to ordinary text, hypertext gives readers the ability to choose their own path through the material that interests them. A book is designed to be read in sequence: Page 2 follows page 1, and so on. Sure, you can skip around, but books don't provide much help, beyond including an index. Computer-based hypertexts let readers jump around all they want. The computer part is important because it's hard to build a hypertext system out of physical media, such as index cards or pieces of paper.

The Web is a giant computer-based hypermedia system, and you've probably already done lots of jumping around from one page to another on the Web—it's called *surfing.* If one Web page doesn't seem all that interesting once you visit, you can click another link that seems more related to your needs (and so on). The Web makes surfing so easy that you'll need to give some thought to keeping people on your sites—keeping them engaged and interested—so they won't surf away!

Where Does HTML Fit In?

Hypertext Markup Language (HTML) enables you to mark up text so that it can function as hypertext on the Web. The term *markup* comes from printing; editors mark up manuscript pages with funny-looking symbols that tell the printer how to print the page. HTML consists of its own set of funny-looking symbols that tell Web browsers how to display the page. These symbols, called *elements,* include the ones needed to create hyperlinks.

The invention of HTML

HTML and HTTP were both invented by Tim Berners-Lee, who was then working as a computer and networking specialist at a Swiss research institute. He wanted to give the Institute's researchers a simple markup language, which would enable them to share their research papers via the Internet. Berners-Lee based HTML on Standard Generalized Markup Language (SGML), an international standard for marking up text for presentation on a variety of physical devices. The basic idea of SGML is that the document's *structure* should be separated from its *presentation:*

✦ *Structure refers* to the various components or parts of a document that authors create, such as titles, paragraphs, headings, and lists. For example, you're reading an item in an *unordered list,* as it is termed in SGML (most people use the more familiar *bulleted list*). In SGML, you mark up this item as a bulleted list, but you don't say anything about how it's supposed to look. That's left up to whatever device displays or prints the marked-up file.

✦ *Presentation* refers to the way these various components are actually displayed by a given media device, such as a computer or a printer. For example, this book displays this bulleted list item with an indentation and other special formatting.

What's so great about separating structure from presentation? There are several very important advantages:

✦ *Authors usually aren't very good designers.* It's wise, especially in large organizations, to let writers compose their documents, and let designers worry about how the documents are supposed to look. That's particularly true when an organization has a corporate look or style, such as Apple Computer's standard typeface, which you'll see in all of its documents. The designers make sure that every document produced within the organization conforms to that style. So SGML doesn't contain any features that control presentation.

✦ *If markup consists of structure alone, the document's appearance can be changed quickly.* All that's necessary is to change the presentation settings on whatever device is displaying the document.

✦ *Documents containing only structural markup are much easier and cheaper to maintain.* When presentation markup is included along with structural markup, the document becomes an unmanageable mess, and maintenance costs skyrocket.

✦ *If a document contains only structural markup, it is more accessible to people with limited vision or other physical limitations.* For example, a document marked up structurally might be presented by a Braille printer for those with limited vision, or by a text reader for those with limited hearing.

Sounds great, right? Still, from the beginning, HTML didn't make the structure versus presentation distinction as clearly as SGML purists would have liked. And as HTML developed and the Internet became a commercial network, Web authors demanded more tools to make their documents look attractive on-screen. The companies that make Web browsers responded by introducing new, nonstandardized HTML elements that contained presentation information. By 1996, many Web experts were worried that HTML standards were spiraling out of control. The newly founded World Wide Consortium, hoping to keep at least some kind of standard in place, tried to standardize existing practices, including the use of presentation and structure. The result was the W3C's HTML 3.2 standard, which is still widely used. But organizations found that HTML 3.2 exposed them to excessive maintenance costs. The SGML purists were right: Structure and presentation should have been kept separate.

A short history of HTML

To date, HTML has gone through four major standards, including the latest 4.01. In addition to the HTML standards, Cascading Style Sheets and XML have also provided valuable contributions to Web standards.

The following sections provide a brief overview of the various versions and technologies.

HTML 1.0

HTML 1.0 was never formally specified by the W3C because the W3C came along too late. HTML 1.0 was the original specification Mosaic 1.0 used, and it supported few elements. What you couldn't do on a page is more interesting than what you could do. You couldn't set the background color or background image of the page. There were no tables or frames. You couldn't dictate the font. All inline images had to be GIFs; JPEGs were used for out-of-line images. And there were no forms.

Every page looked pretty much the same: gray background and Times Roman font. Links were indicated in blue until you'd visited them, and then they were red. Because scanners and image-manipulation software weren't as available then, the image limitation wasn't a huge problem. HTML 1.0 was only implemented in Mosaic and Lynx (a text-only browser that runs under UNIX).

HTML 2.0

Huge strides forward were made between HTML 1.0 and HTML 2.0. An HTML 1.1 actually did exist, created by Netscape to support what its first browser could do. Because only Netscape and Mosaic were available at the time (both written under the leadership of Marc Andreesen), browser makers were in the habit of adding their own new features and creating names for HTML elements to use those features.

Between HTML 1.0 and HTML 2.0, the W3C also came into being, under the leadership of Tim Berners-Lee, founder of the Web. HTML 2.0 was a huge improvement over HTML 1.0. Background colors and images could be set. Forms became available with a limited set of fields, but nevertheless, for the first time, visitors to a Web page could submit information. Tables also became possible.

HTML 3.2

Why no 3.0? The W3C couldn't get a specification out in time for agreement by the members. HTML 3.2 was vastly richer than HTML 2.0. It included support for style sheets (CSS level 1). Even though CSS was supported in the 3.2 specification, the browser manufacturers didn't support CSS well enough for a designer to make much use of it. HTML 3.2 expanded the number of attributes that enabled designers to customize the look of a page (exactly the opposite of HTML 4). HTML 3.2 didn't include support for frames, but the browser makers implemented them anyway.

Note   A page with two frames is actually processed like three separate pages within your browser. The outer page is the *frameset.* The frameset indicates to the browser, which pages go where in the browser window. Implementing frames can be tricky, but frames can also be an effective way to implement a Web site. A common use for frames is navigation in the left pane and content in the right.

HTML 4.0

What does HTML 4.0 add? Not so much new elements—although those do exist—as a rethinking of the direction HTML is taking. Up until now, HTML has encouraged interjecting presentation information into the page. HTML 4.0 now clearly deprecates any uses of HTML that relate to forcing a browser to format an element a certain way. All formatting has been moved into the style sheets. With formatting information strewn throughout the pages, HTML 3.2 had reached a point where maintenance was expensive and difficult. This movement of presentation out of the document, once and for all, should facilitate the continued rapid growth of the Web.

Tip   Use the W3C's MarkUp Validation Service, available at `http://validator.w3.org/`, to check your HTML against most of the versions mentioned in this chapter.

XML 1.0

Extensible Markup Language (XML) was originally designed to meet the needs of large-scale electronic publishing. As such, it was designed to help separate structure from presentation and provide enough power and flexibility to be applicable in a variety of publishing applications. In fact, many modern word processing programs contain XML components or even export their documents in XML-compliant formats.

CSS 1.0 and 2.0

Cascading Style Sheets (CSS) were designed to help move formatting out of the HTML specification. Much like styles in a word processing program, CSS provides a mechanism to easily specify and change formatting without changing the underlying code. The "cascade" in the name comes from the fact that the specification allows for multiple style sheets to interact, allowing individual Web documents to be formatted slightly different from their kin (following department document guidelines but still adhering to the company standards, for example). The second version of CSS (2.0) builds on the capabilities of the first version, adding more attributes and properties for a Web designer to draw upon.

HTML 4.01

HTML 4.01 is a minor revision of the HTML 4.0 standard. In addition to fixing errors identified since the inception of 4.0, HTML 4.01 also provides the basis for meanings of XHTML elements and attributes, reducing the size of the XHTML 1.0 specification.

XHTML 1.0

Extensible HyperText Markup Language (XHTML) is the first specification for the HTML and XML cross-breed. XHTML was created to be the next generation of markup languages, infusing the standard of HTML with the extensibility of XML. It was designed to be used in XML-compliant environments, yet compatible with standard HTML 4.01 user agents.

So who makes the rules?

Every organization has its own rule-making body. In the case of the Web, the rule-making body is the World Wide Web Consortium (W3C). The W3C is composed of representatives from a number of high-tech companies who want to have a say in the standards. The W3C tries to balance the interests of the academy, the companies producing the Web browsers (notably Netscape and Microsoft), and the technology. The W3C pulls together committees with representatives from interested members and puts the specifications in writing for HTTP and HTML, as well as a host of additional Web standards, including CSS. If the W3C weren't maintaining all these standards, the Web wouldn't be as easy to use; in fact, it might not have become anywhere near as popular as it is. You can visit their Web site at `http://www.w3c .org`.

Buzz and scrambling

How does the W3C decide when a new technology must be standardized or a new version of an existing technology must be developed? Newsgroups and mailing lists exist where leading figures in the relevant field talk about the shortcomings of an existing version or the idea of a new technology (that's the buzz). If a ground swell of support seems to exist for a new technology or a new version, the W3C begins the process of specifying it.

Something else, however, carries more weight and more urgency than discussion by agitators and activists. This is ongoing development by software developers (that's the scrambling). In reality, the W3C is mostly involved in trying to standardize the proprietary extensions developed by software developers, such as Netscape and Microsoft. If the W3C didn't do this, within two versions of their browsers, HTML might not run the same (or at all) on both systems. The W3C reins them in to some degree. Neither wants to produce a browser that lacks support for recommended HTML elements, so even if Netscape introduced a new element, Microsoft will incorporate that element in the subsequent version of their own browser—after an official recommendation by the W3C (and vice versa).

Committees and working drafts

When a new technology or a new version of an existing technology is required, the W3C convenes a committee of interested parties to write the specification. The committee publishes its work on an ongoing basis as a working draft. The point of publishing these working drafts is this: Software developers who want to implement the new technology or the new features of the new version can get a jump on things and build their product to incorporate the new features. When the specification is finalized and developers are ready to use it, products that implement it are on the market.

There is also the issue of books. You want books on new technologies to be in the bookstores the day the recommendation is finalized. For this to happen, authors must write the books using the working drafts—a moving target—as the reference materials. Working drafts have changed during the writing of this book. Sometimes this works and sometimes it doesn't. If the specification changes radically from the working draft to the final version, the book will be inaccurate.

Voting process

Democracy: You just can't get away from it. When a working draft reaches a point where the committee is pleased and believes it is complete, the working draft is released to the public as a proposed recommendation. Members of the W3C have up to six weeks to vote on it—votes can take the form of any one of three choices: yes, yes if certain changes are made, or no. At the conclusion of the voting process, the W3C can recommend the specification officially, make the requested changes and recommend the specification with the changes, or discard the proposal.

What Is CSS?

In 1997, the World Wide Web Consortium released the first HTML 4 recommendation, the first to embody a serious effort to separate structure from presentation. The W3C envisioned a transitional period, in which Web authors would continue to use some presentation features in their pages, but the end point was clear: Any Web page that wanted to conform strictly to HTML would have to omit presentation-related coding.

To see for yourself how difficult maintaining HTML 3.2 code can be, consider the following HTML:

```
<li><FONT SIZE="+1" FACE="comic sans ms" FAMILY="sans-serif"
COLOR="#0000FF"><P><A name="do"></a><B>What does <i>Stay In
Touch</i> do?</B></P></FONT>
<FONT SIZE="-1" FACE="comic sans ms" FAMILY="sans-serif"
COLOR="#000000"><P><i>Stay In Touch</i> allows you to harness
the power of the World Wide Web to communicate with people
who visit your web site. Using <i>Stay In Touch</i> list
management service you can set up a sign-in page on your web
site today and customize it to match the rest of your web
site. Your visitors can sign into your site when they visit,
then you can send mail to your visitors based on a number of
criteria: the interest they indicate, the publications they
read, etc. To see an example of this, go to the Demo and view
the Send Mail option.</P></FONT>
<li><FONT SIZE="+1" FACE="comic sans ms" FAMILY="sans-serif"
COLOR="#0000FF"><P><A name="security"></a><B>How secure is my
list?</B></P></FONT>
<FONT SIZE="-1" FACE="comic sans ms" FAMILY="Sans Serif"
COLOR="#000000"><P>Only you have access to your list. Access
to your list is available exclusively from secure pages
residing on our server. You have enough to worry about. The
security of your list needn't be one of those
things.</P></FONT>
```

Figure 1-2 shows what this HTML code looks like in a full page on a PC, while Figure 1-3 shows what that same page looks like on a Mac (notice that the font is slightly different).

The maintenance nightmare

From looking at the HTML and then seeing the HTML interpreted by the browser, you can pretty much tell what part of the text is instructions to the browser and

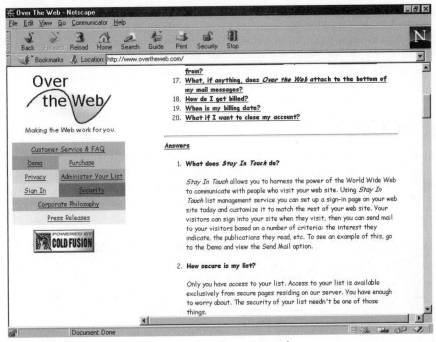

Figure 1-2: How a PC browser displays the HTML code.

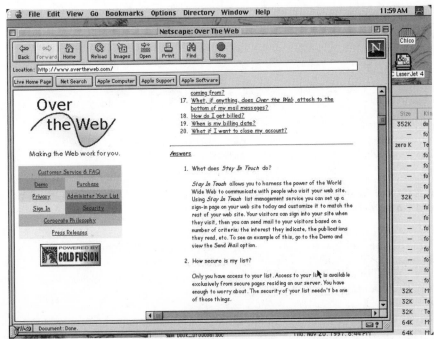

Figure 1-3: The previous text displayed in a browser on a Mac.

what part is the content. But would you feel comfortable making changes to the content—say, adding another bulleted set of questions and answers? Probably not. With all those codes embedded within the text, you might mess something up. And you probably wouldn't want someone else who didn't know what all those codes meant doing it either.

The worst maintenance nightmares occur when you want to change the look of your pages throughout your Web site. Because the presentation code has to be included in every page, you have to change every page to change the look of your site.

Consider the site map shown in Figure 1-4. Every screen should have the same formatting: same font, same heading sizes, same alignment, same text color, and same background color. With HTML 3.2, you could do this only by inserting all the needed presentation code on every single page.

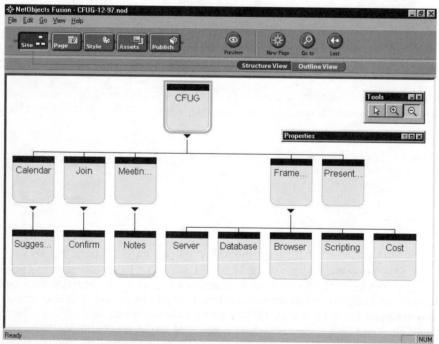

Figure 1-4: Map of a Web site.

HTML 4.01 enables you to return to the ideal of separating structure and presentation. What does this mean to you and your ability to maintain a site? It's simple. HTML that contains nothing but structural code is vastly simpler and cheaper to maintain.

Consider the following code. It produces the same results as the previous example in the browser. Notice there is no formatting. All the HTML you see is related to the structure.

```
<li>What does <i>Stay In Touch</i> do?</li>
<p><i>Stay In Touch</i> allows you to harness the power of
the World Wide Web to communicate with people who visit your
web site. Using <i>Stay In Touch</i> list management service,
you can set up a sign-in page on your web site today and
customize it to match the rest of your web site. Your
visitors can sign into your site when they visit. Then you
can send mail to your visitors based on a number of criteria:
the interest they indicate, the publications they read, etc.
To see an example of this, go to the Demo and view the Send
Mail option.</p>
<li>How secure is my list?</li>
<p>Only you have access to your list. Access to your list is
available exclusively from secure pages residing on our
server. You have enough to worry about. The security of your
list needn't be one of those things.</p>
```

Note   The use of the italic tags (`<i>`) in the preceding code is arguably "formatting" and is used to simplify the example while conforming to the visual style of the text *"Stay In Touch."* When using HTML 4.01 and CSS it might be better to use span tags (`<span>`) to refer to a CSS class instead of directly specifying the italic text attribute. See Chapter 16 for more information on styles and span tags.

How comfortable would you be updating the previous HTML? How about if you needed to add another set of questions and answers? Already, you can see that using HTML 4.01 makes a world of difference.

There's only one problem. The simpler, HTML 4.01-compliant code looks just terrible on-screen; with no presentation information in the code, the browser falls back on its default presentation settings.

Enter CSS

By themselves, strictly conformant HTML 4 documents are ugly. Web authors would never have accepted HTML 4 if the W3C had not also developed Cascading Style Sheets (CSS). In brief, CSS enables Web authors to specify presentation information without violating the structure versus presentation distinction. The information the browser must know to format the previous text is stored separately, in a *style sheet*. The style sheet lists the presentation styles that the browser should use to display the various components of the document, such as headings, lists, and paragraphs. The style sheet is kept separate from the marked-up text. It can be stored in a special section of the HTML document itself, away from the document's text, or in a separate file entirely.

The idea and the name come from the publishing industry, where style sheets are still used today. And they're cutting costs wherever Web documents are created and maintained.

Think back to the problem of updating a Web site's look, discussed earlier. Without CSS, you'd have to make changes to the presentation code in each and every page.

Thanks to CSS, all you have to do is make changes to the single, underlying style sheet that every page uses, and the entire site's appearance changes.

What does "cascading" mean?

In Cascading Style Sheets, the term "cascading" refers to what computer people call the *order of precedence*—that is, which style information comes first in the style pecking order. Here's the order:

✦ *Element-specific* style information comes first. This is style information that's embedded within the HTML. But wait—doesn't this violate the structure versus presentation rule? Yes, but sometimes it's necessary. If element-specific information is given, it takes precedence over page-specific and global styles.

✦ *Page-specific* style information is kept in a special section of the document, called the *head,* that's separate from the text. It defines the way a particular page looks. If page-specific information is given, it takes precedence over global styles.

✦ *Global styles* are specified in a separate style sheet file. They come into play unless conflicting element- or page-specific styles are given.

See Figure 1-5 for a summary of these points.

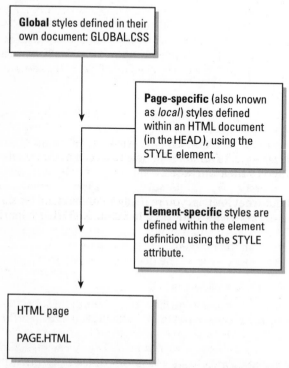

Figure 1-5: The cascading model of style definitions.

HTML 4.01 almost eliminates the need to have an HTML expert perform site maintenance. This means HTML 4.01 helps reduce the cost of maintaining your Web site. When was the last time you heard anything about reducing costs being associated with the Web?

What Is XHTML?

Combined with CSS, HTML 4.0 was a major advance, so one might expect even better versions of HTML in the future, right? Not according to the World Wide Web Consortium. Apart from a minor update (HTML 4.01) in 1999, HTML 4.0 is the last version of HTML. That's because it has been replaced by XHTML, which is the version of HTML you're going to learn in this book.

Actually, there's very little difference between HTML and XHTML. It's a matter of making a few changes to your HTML 4.0 code to make sure it's XHTML-conformant. But there's a much deeper reason for this change. To understand why HTML has become XHTML, you must learn a little about XML, another World Wide Consortium standard.

As you've learned, HTML is based on SGML, an international standard for markup languages. Actually, SGML isn't a markup language in itself. It's a language that's useful for *creating* markup languages. You can use it to make up codes for just about anything you want. For example, an accounting firm could use SGML to mark up the structure of accounting documents; one code could be used to mark daily totals, while a different code could be used to mark monthly totals. To keep a record of all these newly created codes, as well as to specify them for presentation devices, a special file, called a *document type definition (DTD)*, is used. HTML 4.01 is defined in a document type definition, written in SGML.

SGML isn't equally loved by all. To many, SGML is outmoded, overly complex, and too difficult to learn. So the World Wide Consortium decided to create a new version of SGML that would be simpler and easier to learn. The result is the Extensible Markup Language (XML). Like SGML, XML enables people to define new markup languages that are exactly suited to their purposes.

Now that you know a little about what XML is, you're ready to understand what XHTML is. Just as HTML is a markup language defined in SGML, XHTML is a markup language defined in XML.

Creating an HTML Document

Creating an HTML document is relatively easy. One of the nice properties of HTML is it is just text. The content is text and the tags are text. As a result, you can write your HTML in any text editor. If you are running any variety of Windows, you can use Notepad, which comes installed with Windows. If you have a Mac on your desk, you can use SimpleText. If you work in UNIX, you can use emacs, vi, jove, pico, or whatever you normally use to edit text. Essentially, any text editor or editor capable of producing text-only documents can be used to create HTML documents.

Writing HTML

What else do you need to know to write your HTML? Presumably, by now, you know the following:

- ✦ What your purpose is (at least generally)
- ✦ You need to write your content from your focused message
- ✦ You mark up your content with HTML tags
- ✦ You can write your page with a text editor that is already installed on your computer

Obviously, you need to know the elements. But before discussing those, here are a few guidelines about how you should and shouldn't use HTML.

Name your files with a Web-friendly extension

When saving an HTML file you should always give it a .html or .htm extension. (The former, .html, is generally preferred.) This correctly identifies the file as having HTML content so that Web browsers and servers correctly handle it.

Other Web files have their own extensions—for example, most PHP files use .php, graphic files use .jpg, .gif, or .png, and so on. This book suggests appropriate extension(s) as each technology is discussed.

Format your text

If you are already writing HTML pages, you may need to break your bad habits. You probably already think in terms of getting the browser to make your page look the right way. And you use HTML to make it do this. You may even use goofy conventions such as 1-pixel-wide clear image files (usually GIFs) and stretch them to indent your paragraphs.

With HTML 4, you needn't out-maneuver the browser. Browsers that support the HTML 4 standards display your pages as you define them—no more of that arrogant printer stuff! And fortunately, with HTML 4, you can define the way you want your pages to look outside of the content, so your HTML won't be all cluttered with tags.

Structure your document

So, if you are not supposed to use HTML to format your pages, how should you use HTML?

HTML defines your document's structure. Then, outside the main body of the document (or even in a separate file, if you prefer), you define the appearance of each element of the structure (just like the publisher and the printer in the previous example).

With few exceptions, you want all your paragraphs to be formatted the same—uniform margins, indents, fonts, spacing between lines, and color.

So, within the main body of your document, you type your text for each paragraph and mark up your document to indicate where each paragraph begins and ends. Then, in a separate location and only once, you define how you want all your paragraphs to look. Existing ways to override this universal definition are discussed later.

The most important concept to remember—and this is a big change for you if you've already been writing HTML 3.2 or earlier versions—is that the HTML only defines the *structure* of your document. The *formatting* of your document is handled separately.

What is so great about this? First, your text doesn't get all cluttered up with tags. And second, you can define the look for your entire site in one place. You simply have every page in the site (even if some pages in your site are being written by people you have never met) point to the style sheet (the place where you put all those style definitions).

Don't I Need a Web Server?

Later chapters will show you how to upload your documents to a dedicated and public Web server where others can see them. In the meantime, you can simply use your computer's hard drive and a local browser to dabble privately with HTML.

Note   Server-side technologies such as PHP require an actual Web server.

Simply put the document on your hard drive and direct your browser at the file. For example, in Windows you can double-click an HTML file in Windows Explorer (or any other file manager) to open it in the default browser (normally Internet Explorer). Most browsers also have an Open File option under their main File menu.

Create additional files, directories, and subdirectories on your local hard drive as needed to hold additional pages or levels of a site.

Tip   Apache, the Web's most popular HTTP server, is available for several architectures and best of all, it's free to use. If you need a local Web server for testing purposes, visit the Apache Web site (http://httpd.apache.org/) for more information or to download a copy for your machine. For more information on Apache, see Wiley's *Apache Server 2 Bible, 2nd Edition*, by Mohammed J. Kabir.

Summary

This chapter covered the basics of HTML and the Web. Before actually creating Web documents, it is important to understand the evolution of the technologies behind the Web, and the direction they will take in the future. The next few chapters discuss the basic elements of HTML documents and get you on your way to creating your own Web content.

✦ ✦ ✦

What Goes Into a Web Page?

HTML has come a long way from its humble beginnings. However, despite the fact that you can use HTML (and its derivatives) for much more than serving up static text documents, the basic organization and structure of the HTML document remains the same.

Before we dive into the specifics of various elements of HTML, it is important to summarize what each element is, what it is used for, and how it affects other elements in the document. This chapter provides a high-level overview of a standard HTML document and its elements. Subsequent chapters will cover each element and technology in detail.

Specifying Document Type

One attribute of HTML documents that is frequently overlooked is the Document Type Definition (DTD). This definition precedes any document tags and exists to inform client browsers of the format of the following content—what tags to expect, methods to support, and so forth.

The `<!DOCTYPE>` tag is used to specify an existing DTD. The DTD contains all the elements, definitions, events, and so on associated with the document type. A `DOCTYPE` tag resembles the following:

```
<!DOCTYPE HTML PUBLIC "-//W3C//DTD HTML 4.01//EN"
   "http://www.w3.org/TR/html4/strict.dtd">
```

This tag specifies the following information:

- ◆ The document's top tag level is HTML (`html`).
- ◆ The document adheres to the formal public identifier (FPI) "W3C HTML 4.01 Strict English" standards (`PUBLIC "-//W3C//DTD HTML 4.01//EN"`).

✦ The full DTD can be found at the URL `http://www.w3.org/TR/` `xhtml1/DTD/xhtml1-strict.dtd`.

The Overall Structure: HTML, Head, and Body

All HTML documents have three, document-level tags in common. These tags, `<html>`, `<head>`, and `<body>`, delimit certain sections of the HTML document.

The `<html>` tag

The `<html>` tag surrounds the entire HTML document. This tag tells the client browser where the document begins and ends.

```
<html>
... document contents ...
</html>
```

Additional language options were declared within the `<html>` tag in previous versions of HTML. However, those options (notably `lang` and `dir`) have been deprecated in HTML version 4.0. The language and directional information is routinely contained in the document type declaration (`<!DOCTYPE>`).

The `<head>` tag

The `<head>` tag delimits the heading of the HTML document. The heading section of the document contains certain heading information for the document. The document's title, meta information, and, in most cases, document scripts are all contained in the `<head>` section. A typical `<head>` section could resemble the following:

```
<head>
  <link rel="stylesheet" type="text/css" href="/styles.css">
  <title>Title of the Document</title>
  <meta name="description" content="Sample Page">
  <meta name="keywords" content="sample, heading, page">
  <script language="JavaScript">
    function NewWindow(url){
    fin=window.open(url,"",
    "width=800,height=600,scrollbars=yes,resizable=yes");
    }
  </script>
</head>
```

Cross-Reference Most `<head>` level tags are covered in detail in Chapter 3. JavaScript scripting is covered in more detail in Chapters 15 and 28.

Most of the content within the <head> section will not be visible on the rendered page in the client's browser. The <title> element determines what the browser displays as the page title—on Windows machines, the document title appears in the browser's title bar, as shown in Figure 2-1.

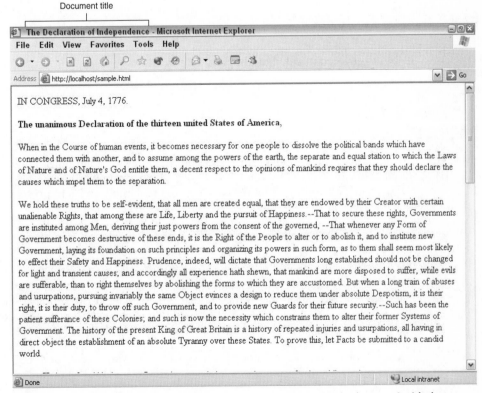

Figure 2-1: In Windows, the document's `<title>` appears in the browser's title bar.

The main, visual content of the HTML document is contained within `<body>` tags.

Note that with HTML version 4.0, most attributes of the `<body>` tag have been deprecated in favor of specifying the attributes as styles. In previous versions of HTML, you could specify a bevy of options, including the document background, text, and link colors. The `onload` and `onunload` attributes of the `<body>` tag, as well as global attributes such as `style`, are still valid. However, you should specify the other attributes in styles instead of within the `<body>` tag, such as in the following example:

```
<html>
<head>
 <title>Document Title</title>
 <style type="text/css">
  body { background: black; color: white}
```

```
   a:link { color: red }
   a:visited { color: blue }
   a:active { color: yellow }
 </style>
</head>
<body>
... document body...
</body>
</html>
```

Cross-Reference   Styles are covered in detail in Chapters 16 and 24.

Styles

Styles are a relatively new element for HTML, but they have revolutionized how HTML documents are coded and rendered. Styles are the main basis behind the "extensible" in XHTML—they allow Web authors to create new styles to present their content in a variety of custom, but consistent formats.

At their root, styles are simply an aggregation of display attributes, combined to achieve a particular result. Those familiar with styles in word processing will have little trouble understanding HTML styles.

Note   Styles are typically presented in the context of cascading, as in the Cascading Style Sheet (CSS) standard. The CSS standard defines a method where several styles sheets (lists of style definitions) can be applied to the same document—repeated style definitions supercede previously defined styles, hence the *cascade*. You'll find more information on styles, style sheets, and CSS in Chapter 16.

For example, suppose you needed to highlight particular text in a document that needed to be deleted. The text needs to be displayed in red and as strikethrough. You could surround each section of text with `<font>` and `<del>` tags. However, that approach has two distinct disadvantages:

✦ The `<font>` tag has been deprecated and should not be used.

✦ If you later change your mind about the color or decoration (strikethrough), you would have to find and change each set of tags.

Instead, define a style for the elements that contains the desired text attributes. The following HTML code snippet defines such a style and uses it to highlight a sentence later in the document:

```
<html>
<head>
  <style>
```

```
      .redline { color: red; text-decoration: line-through; }
   </style>
 </head>
 <body>
 <h1>An Early Draft of the Declaration of Independence</h1>
 <p>When in the Course of human events, it becomes necessary
 for one people to dissolve the political bands which have
 connected them with another, and to assume among the powers
 of the earth, the separate and equal station to which the
 Laws of Nature and of Nature's God entitle them, a decent
 respect to the opinions of mankind requires that they should
 declare the causes which impel them to the separation. <span
 class="redline">This document declares those
 causes.</span></p>
 </body>
 </html>
```

This code results in the output shown in Figure 2-2.

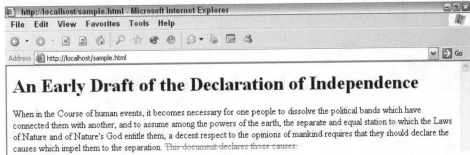

Figure 2-2: The "redline" style is applied to applicable text via the `<span>` tag.

 Note
Styles can also be applied directly to many HTML tags using the style attribute. For example, to apply the red and strikethrough attributes to an entire paragraph, you could use the following code:

```
<p style="color: red; text-decoration: line-
through;"> sample paragraph </p>
```

However, using styles in this manner removes many of the easily modified advantages gained by using styles.

If you later needed to change the text attributes, one edit in the `<style>` section of the document would affect the change throughout the document. But what if you had several documents that used the style? You would still have to edit each document to make the style change. Luckily, HTML's style implementation allows for external style sheets that can be applied to multiple documents—then you only have to change the external style sheet.

The following code defines `site-styles.css` as an external style sheet in the current HTML document:

```
<html>
<head>
<LINK rel="stylesheet" href="site-styles.css"
type="text/css">
</head>
<body> ...
```

The contents of the `site-styles.css` document would be the definitions that you would have placed between the <style> tags. For the preceding redline example, the contents of this file could simply be the following:

```
.redline { color: red; text-decoration: line-through; }
```

Cross-Reference There are many more attributes that can be applied to text and other objects via styles. You'll find more details on styles in Chapter 16.

Block Elements: Markup for Paragraphs

As with most word processors, HTML includes several tags to delimit, and hence, format paragraphs of text. These tags include the following:

✦ `<p>`—Formatted paragraphs

✦ `<h1>` through `<h6>`—Headings

✦ `<blockquote>`—Quoted text

✦ `<pre>`—Preformatted text

✦ `<ul>`,`<ol>`, `<dl>`—Unnumbered, ordered, and definition lists

✦ `<center>`—Centered text

✦ `<div>`—A division of the document

Each of the block elements results in a line break and noticeable space padding after the closing tag. As such, the block elements only work when used to format paragraph-like chunks of text—they cannot be used as inline styles.

More detail about each of these tags is covered in the following sections.

Cross-Reference You'll find more details on block elements and their formatting in Chapter 4.

Formatted paragraphs

The paragraph tag (`<p>`) is used to delimit entire paragraphs of text. For example, the following HTML code results in the output shown in Figure 2-3:

```
<p>The quick brown fox jumped over the lazy dog. The quick
brown fox jumped over the lazy dog. The quick brown fox
jumped over the lazy dog. The quick brown fox jumped over the
lazy dog.</p>
<p>The quick brown fox jumped over the lazy dog. The quick
brown fox jumped over the lazy dog. The quick brown fox
jumped over the lazy dog.</p>
```

Figure 2-3: Paragraph tags break text into distinct paragraphs.

As with most tags, you could define several formatting elements (font, alignment, spacing, and so on) of the `<p>` tag. For example, you can center a paragraph by adding an `align` attribute to the `<p>` tag:

```
<p align="center"> The quick brown fox jumped over the lazy
dog. The quick brown fox jumped over the lazy dog. The quick
  brown fox jumped over the lazy dog.</p>
```

However, such formatting has been deprecated in favor of specifying formatting via style sheets. The following is an example of using style sheets to achieve the same results as the align attribute:

```
<html>
<head>
<style type="text/css">
p.center {text-align: center}
</style>
</head>
<body>
<p class="center"> The quick brown fox jumped over the lazy
dog. The quick brown fox jumped over the lazy dog. The quick
  brown fox jumped over the lazy dog.</p>
</body>
</html>
```

Using either of the preceding methods results in the paragraph being center-justified in the browser.

Headings

HTML supports six levels of headings. Each heading uses a large, usually bold character-formatting style to identify itself as a heading. The following HTML example produces the output shown in Figure 2-4:

```
<!DOCTYPE HTML PUBLIC "-//W3C//DTD HTML 4.01//EN"
    "http://www.w3.org/TR/html4/strict.dtd"> <html>
<body>
<h1>Heading 1</h1>
<h2>Heading 2</h2>
<h3>Heading 3</h3>
<h4>Heading 4</h4>
<h5>Heading 5</h5>
<h6>Heading 6</h6>
<p>Plain body text: The quick brown fox jumped over the lazy dog.</p>
</body>
</html>
```

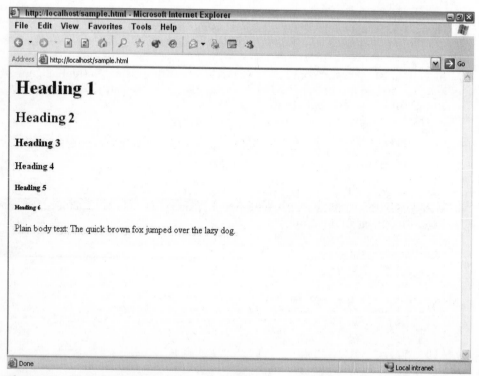

Figure 2-4: HTML supports six levels of headings.

The six levels begin with Level 1, highest, most important, and go to Level 6, the lowest, least important. Although there are six predefined levels of headings, you probably will only find yourself using three or four levels in your documents. Also, because there is no limit on being able to use specific levels, you can pick and choose which levels you use—you don't have to use <h1> and <h2> in order to be able to use <h3>. Also, keep in mind that you can tailor the formatting imposed by each level by using styles.

Cross-Reference   Styles are covered in Chapter 16.

Quoted text

The <blockquote> tag is used to delimit blocks of quoted text. For example, the following code identifies the beginning paragraph of the Declaration of Independence as a quote:

```
<body>
<p>The Declaration of Independence begins with the following paragraph:</p>
<blockquote>
When in the Course of human events, it becomes necessary for
one people to dissolve the political bands which have
connected them with another, and to assume among the powers
of the earth, the separate and equal station to which the
Laws of Nature and of Nature's God entitle them, a decent
respect to the opinions of mankind requires that they should
declare the causes which impel them to the separation.
</blockquote>
</body>
```

The <blockquote> indents the paragraph to offset it from surrounding text, as shown in Figure 2-5.

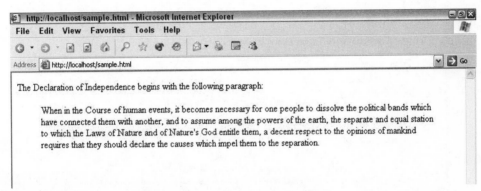

Figure 2-5: The <blockquote> tag indents the paragraph.

List elements

HTML specifies three different types of lists:

✦ Ordered lists (usually numbered)

✦ Unordered lists (usually bulleted)

✦ Definition lists (list items with integrated definitions)

The ordered and unordered lists both use a list item element (`<li>`) for each of the items in the list. The definition list has two tags, one for list items (`<dt>`) and another for the definition of the item (`<dd>`).

The following HTML code results in the output shown in Figure 2-6.

```
<html>
<body>
<ol>A basic ordered list
  <li>First ordered item
  <li>Second ordered item
  <li>Third ordered item
```

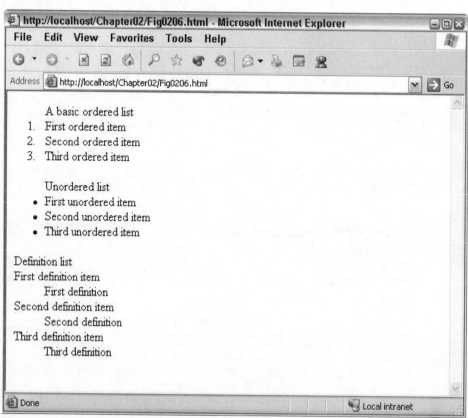

Figure 2-6: A sample list in HTML.

```
</ol>
<ul>Unordered list
  <li>First unordered item
  <li>Second unordered item
  <li>Third unordered item
</ul>
<dl>Definition list
  <dt>First definition item
  <dd>First definition

  <dt>Second definition item
  <dd>Second definition

  <dt>Third definition item
  <dd>Third definition
</dl>
</body>
</html>
```

Because of the amount of customization allowed for each type of list, you can create many substyles of each type of list. For example, you can specify that an ordered list be ordered by letters instead of numbers. The following HTML code does just that, resulting in the output shown in Figure 2-7.

```
<html>
<body>
<ol style="list-style: lower-alpha;">A basic ordered list (lower-case alpha)
  <li>First ordered item
  <li>Second ordered item
  <li>Third ordered item
</ol>
</body>
</html>
```

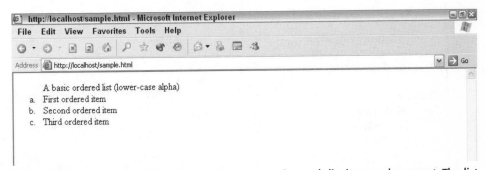

Figure 2-7: Using various list styles, you can customize each list in your document. The list shown uses the `list-style lower-alpha`.

Note   Older versions of HTML allowed various list options to be specified in the list tag(s). However, current versions of strict HTML and XHTML formats specify that all list options be contained within styles.

Preformatted text

Occasionally, you will want to hand format text in your document or maintain the formatting already present in particular text. Typically, the text comes from another source—cut and pasted into the document—and can be formatted with spaces, tabs, and so on. The preformatted tag (`<pre>`) causes the HTML client to treat white space literally and not to condense it as it usually would.

For example, the following table will be rendered just as shown below:

```
<pre>
+---------------+--------------------+
| name          | value              |
+---------------+--------------------+
| newsupdate    | 1069009013         |
| releaseupdate | Wed, 8/28, 8:18pm  |
| rolfstatus    | 0                  |
| feedupdate    | 1069009861         |
+---------------+--------------------+
</pre>
```

Divisions

Divisions are a higher level of block formatting, usually reserved for groups of related paragraphs, entire pages, or sometimes only a single paragraph. The division tag (`<div>`) provides a simple solution for formatting larger sections of a document. For example, if you need a particular section of a document outlined with a border, you can define an appropriate style and delimit that part of the document with `<div>` tags, as in the following example:

```
<html>
<head>
  <style>
    .bordered { border-style: solid; }
  </style>
</head>
<body>
<p>This is a normal paragraph.</p>
<div class="bordered"><p>This is a paragraph delimited with
the defined div style which includes a border.</p></div>
</body>
</html>
```

This code results in the output shown in Figure 2-8.

Cross-Reference For more information on how to format blocks of text with the `<div>` tag, see Chapter 16.

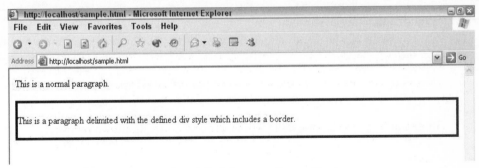

Figure 2-8: <div> tags are used to delimit large sections of text.

Inline Elements: Markup for Characters

The finest level of markup possible in HTML is at the character level; just as in a word processor, you can affect formatting on individual characters. This section covers the basics of inline formatting.

Basic inline tags

Inline formatting elements include the following:

- ✦ Bold (`<b>`)
- ✦ Italic (`<i>`)
- ✦ Big text (`<big>`)
- ✦ Small text (`<small>`)
- ✦ Emphasized text (`<em>`)
- ✦ Strong text (`<strong>`)
- ✦ Teletype (monospaced) text (`<tt>`)

For example, consider the following sample paragraph, whose output is shown in Figure 2-9.

```
<html>
<body>
<p>This paragraph shows the various inline styles, such as
<b>bold</b>, <i>italic</i>, <big>big text</big>, <small>small
text</small>, <em>emphasized text</em>, <strong>strong
text</strong>, and <tt>teletype text</tt>.</p>
</body>
</html>
```

Note that several inline tags, such as strikethrough (`<strike>`) and underline (`<u>`) tags, have been deprecated in the current specifications. Even the font tag (`<font>`)

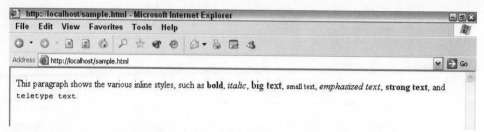

Figure 2-9: Inline elements can affect words or even individual characters.

has been deprecated in favor of spanning styles (see the *Spanning* section later in this chapter). As for the strikethrough and underline tags, they have been replaced by delete (`<del>`) and insert (`<ins>`), which are used for revisions (delete for deleted text, insert for inserted text).

Cross-Reference   More information on inline elements is contained in Chapter 4.

Spanning

Spanning tags (`<span>`) are used to span inline styles across multiple characters or words. In effect, the `<span>` tag allows you to define your own inline styles. For example, if you need to specify text that is bold, red, and underlined, you could use code similar to the following:

```
<html>
<head>
<style>
  .emphasis { color: red; text-decoration: underline;
      font-weight: bold; }
</style>
</head>
<body>
<p><span class="emphasis">This text is emphasized</span>,
 while this text is not.</p>
</body>
</html>
```

The `<span>` tag allows you to apply the stylistic formatting inline, exactly where you want it.

Special Characters (Entities)

Some special characters must be referenced directly instead of simply typed into the document. Some of these characters cannot be typed on a standard keyboard, such as the trademark symbol (^{TM}) or copyright symbol (©); others could cause the HTML client confusion (such as the angle brackets, < and >). Such characters are commonly referred to as "entities."

Entities are referenced by using a particular code in your documents. This code always begins with an ampersand (&) and ends with a semicolon. Three different ways to specify an entity exist:

✦ A mnemonic code (such as `copy` for the copyright symbol)

✦ A decimal value corresponding to the character (such as `#169` for a copyright symbol)

✦ A hexidecimal value corresponding to the character (such as `#xA9` for a copyright symbol)

Note that if you use the decimal or hexadecimal methods of specifying entities, you need to prefix the value with a number sign (#).

The following are all examples of valid entities:

✦ —A non-breaking space (see later)

✦ <—The less-than symbol, or left-angle bracket (<)

✦ ©—The copyright symbol (©)

✦ &—An ampersand (&)

✦ ——An em dash (—)

 Cross-Reference You'll find more information on entities in Chapter 9.

Inappropriate Entity Use

One particular entity, the nonbreaking space, is often used and abused to add white space to HTML documents. For example, to add a larger gap between paragraphs, the following code is often used:

```
<p> </p>
```

This code results in a blank paragraph—without the space, most browsers will not render the paragraph because it is empty.

However, that is not the intent of this entity—it is meant to keep words from being split between rows of text. Using it to add white space is not recommended. Instead, use styles as directed in the various sections of this book.

Organizational Elements

Two HTML elements help organize information in a document: tables and forms. Tables allow you to present data in column and row format, much like a spreadsheet. Forms allow you to present (and retrieve) data using elements common to GUI interfaces—elements such as text boxes, check boxes, and lists.

Tables

HTML tables are very basic, but can be very powerful when used correctly. At their base level, tables can organize data into rows and columns. At their highest level, tables can provide complicated page design—much like a page in a magazine or newspaper, providing columns for text and sections for graphics, menus, and so on.

Tables have three basic elements and, hence, three basic tags:

✦ The table definition itself is defined and delimited by `<table>` tags.

✦ Rows of data are defined and delimited by `<tr>` (table row) tags.

✦ Table cells (individual pieces of data) are defined and delimited by `<td>` (table data) tags. Table cells, when stacked in even rows, create table columns.

For example, consider the following code, which results in the output shown in Figure 2-10:

```
<html>
<body>
<table border="1">
  <tr><td>Name</td><td>Age</td></tr>
  <tr><td>Angela</td><td>35</td></tr>
  <tr><td>Branden</td><td>29</td></tr>
  <tr><td>Doug</td><td>23</td></tr>
  <tr><td>Ian</td><td>31</td></tr>
  <tr><td>Jeff</td><td>34</td></tr>
  <tr><td>John</td><td>33</td></tr>
  <tr><td>Keith</td><td>39</td></tr>
  <tr><td>Michael</td><td>25</td></tr>
  <tr><td>Steve</td><td>38</td></tr>
  <tr><td>Steven</td><td>40</td></tr>
</table>
</body>
</html>
```

This example is very straightforward because the table is very simple. However, due to the number of options you can use in formatting table elements and the fact that you can nest tables within tables, the tables in your HTML documents can get very complicated (and very powerful). To illustrate this point, compare Figures 2-11 and 2-12. Figure 2-11 shows a page as it normally appears in the browser. However, if you turn on the table borders you can see how several tables (and nested tables) are used to provide the document layout, as shown in Figure 2-12.

Cross-Reference   Tables are covered in detail in Chapter 10. Using tables for page layout is covered in Chapter 11.

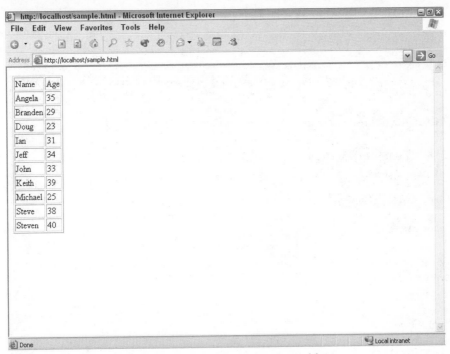

Figure 2-10: Eleven rows and two columns of data in a table.

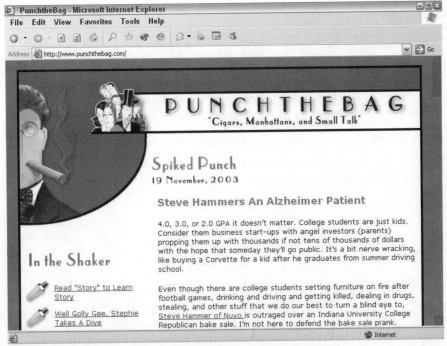

Figure 2-11: This document uses invisible tables to achieve its layout.

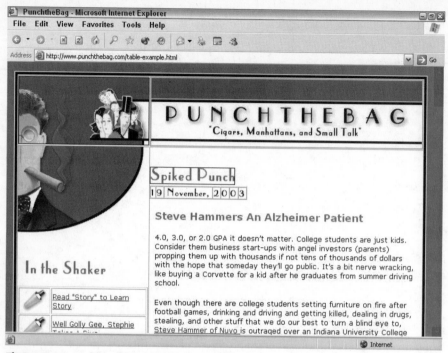

Figure 2-12: Making the table borders visible shows just how many tables are involved in laying out the page and how they help constrain the layout.

Forms

HTML forms provide a method to use standard GUI elements to display and collect data. HTML forms provide the standard litany of GUI elements, including text boxes, check boxes, pull down (also referred to as drop-down) lists, and more. In addition to providing basic GUI elements, HTML forms also provide a rudimentary method of collecting data and passing that data to a data handler for validation, storage, comparison, and so on.

A typical HTML form resembles the following code, the output of which is shown in Figure 2-13.

```
<html>
<body>
<form>
  <!-- Text field -->
  <b>Name:</b> <input type="text" name="name" size="40">
  <br><br>
  <!-- Radio buttons -->
  <b>Age:</b>
       <input type="radio" name="age"> < 20
       <input type="radio" name="age"> 21 -- 30
       <input type="radio" name="age"> 31 -- 40
       <input type="radio" name="age"> 41+
```

```
      <br><br>
      <!-- Select list -->
      <b>What is your favorite ice cream?</b>
        <select name="icecream">
          <option name="chocolate">Chocolate
          <option name="strawberry">Strawberry
          <option name="vanilla">Vanilla
        </select>
      <br><br>
      <!-- Check boxes -->
      <b>How may we contact you for more information?</b><br>
      <input type="checkbox" name="phone">Phone<br>
      <input type="checkbox" name="mail">Mail<br>
      <input type="checkbox" name="email">Email<br>
      <input type="checkbox" name="no">Do not contact me<br>
    </form>
    </body>
    </html>
```

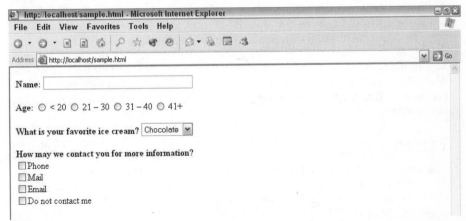

Figure 2-13: Form elements provide standard GUI controls for displaying and collecting data.

The preceding example form is very simple, it shows only some basic elements, and has no handler to process the data that is collected by the form. Real-world forms can be quite complex and usually require validation scripts to ensure the data collected is valid. However, this simple form illustrates the amount of control you can assert over data and format using HTML.

Cross-Reference   Forms are covered in detail in Chapter 13.

Linking to Other Pages

The main advantage to the World Wide Web is the ability to link to other documents on the Web. For example, if you had a page that detailed local zoning laws, you might want to include a link to a local government site where additional information could be found. A link typically appears as underlined text and is often rendered in a different color than normal text.

For example, a link might appear in a browser as follows:

```
More information can be found here.
```

The word here is linked to the other document—when the user clicks the word, the user's browser displays the specified page.

Create links by using the anchor tag, <a>. At its simplest level, this tag takes one argument—the page to link to—and surrounds the text to be linked. The preceding example could be created with the following code:

```
More information can be found
<a href="http://www.whitehouse.gov">here</a>
```

The href, or Hypertext REFerence attribute of the anchor tag, specifies the protocol and destination of the link. The example specifies http:// because the destination is a Web page to be delivered via the HTTP protocol. Other protocols (such as ftp:// or mailto:) can also be used where appropriate.

Additional attributes can be used with the anchor tag to specify such things as where the new document should be opened (for example, in a new browser window), the relationship between the documents, and the character set used in the linked document.

You can also use a variant of the anchor tag to mark specific places in the current document. A link can then be placed elsewhere in the document that can take the user to the specific place. For example, consider this HTML code:

```
For more information see <a href="#Chapt2">Chapter 2</a>
. . . More HTML . . .
<a name="Chapt2">Chapter 2</a>
```

In this example, the user can click the Chapter 2 link to move to the location of the Chapter 2 anchor. Note that the href link must include the hash symbol (#), which specifies that the link is an anchor instead of a separate page.

 Cross-Reference More information on links and anchors can be found in Chapter 7.

Images

One of the great innovations the World Wide Web and HTTP brought to the Internet was the ability to serve up multimedia to clients. The precursors to full-motion video and CD quality sound were graphical images, in the Web-friendly Graphics Interchange Format (GIF) and Joint Photographic Experts Group (JPEG) formats.

You can include images in HTML documents by using the image tag (`<img>`). The image tag includes a link to the image file as well as pertinent information used to display the image (for example, the image size). A typical image tag resembles the following:

```
<img src="/images/tmoore.jpg" alt="A picture of Terri"
width="100" height="200">
```

The preceding example would result in the image `tmoore.jpg` being displayed at the location in the document where the tag appears. In this case, the image is in the `images` directory of the current server and will be displayed without a border, 100 pixels wide by 200 pixels high. The `alt` attribute is used to provide a textual equivalent for browsers that cannot display graphics (or whose users have configured them not to).

Images can also be used as navigation aids—allowing the user to click certain parts of an image to perform an action, display another document, and so on. For example, a map of the United States could be used to help a user select their state—clicking a state would bring up the applicable page for that state. Navigational images are commonly referred to as *image maps* and require a separate map of coordinates and geometric shapes to define the clickable areas.

You'll find more information on images in Chapter 6.

Comments

Although HTML documents tend to be fairly legible, there are several advantages to adding comments to your HTML code. Some typical uses for comments include aiding in document organization, document specific code choices, or marking particular document sections for later reference.

HTML uses the tag `<!-` to begin a comment and `->` to end a comment. Note that the comment can span multiple lines, but the browser will ignore anything between the comment tags. For example, the following two comments will both be ignored by the browser:

```
<!-- This section needs better organization. -->
```

and

```
<!-- The following table needs to include these columns:
  Age
  Marital Status
  Employment Date
-->
```

)ts

HTML is a static method of deploying content—the content is sent out to a client browser where it is rendered and read, but it typically doesn't change once it is delivered. However, there is a need in HTML documents for such things as decision-making ability, form validation, and, in the case of Dynamic HTML (DHTML), dynamic object attribute changes. In those cases (and more), client-side scripting can be used.

Cross-Reference For more information on client-side scripting, see Chapter 15.

Client-side scripting languages, such as JavaScript, have their code passed to the client browser inside the HTML document. It is the client's responsibility to interpret the code and act accordingly. Most client-side scripts are contained in the `<head>` section of the HTML document, within `<script>` tags, similar to the following example:

```
<html>
<head>
  <script language="JavaScript">
    function MiscWindow(w,h,url){
      opts = "width="+w+",height="+h;
      opts = opts+",scrollbars=no,resizable=yes";
      fin=window.open(url,"",opts);
    }
  </script>
</head>...
```

In most cases, the document needs to include events to run the script(s). These events can be embedded in elements (via onmouseover or similar attributes), tied to links, called via form elements, or run upon the document being loaded or unloaded (via onload and onunload attributes in the `<body>` tag).

Note There are methods to run scripts automatically, that is, without a corresponding event. However, such methods are typically thought of as bad form—it is much better practice to always tie a script's execution to an event.

Putting it All Together

As you can see, the standard HTML document is a fairly complex beast. However, when taken piece by piece, the document becomes just like any other HTML document. The following HTML listing shows how all of these pieces fit together.

```
<!DOCTYPE HTML PUBLIC "-//W3C//DTD HTML 4.01//EN"
  "http://www.w3.org/TR/html4/strict.dtd"> <html>
<head>
  <meta   ... meta tags go here ... >
  <title>  title of the page/document goes here</title>
```

```
<LINK rel="stylesheet" href="external style sheet name"
    type="text/css">
<style>
   ... any document specific styles go here ...
</style>
<script>
    ... client-side scripts go here ...
</script>
<body>
   ... body of document goes here, paragraphs modified by
 block elements, characters, words and sentences modified by
 in line elements ...
</body>
</html>
```

All HTML documents should have a `<DOCTYPE>` specification, `<html>` and `<body>` tags, and at least a `<title>` within the `<head>` section. The rest of the elements are strictly optional, but help define the documents' purpose, style, and ultimately its usability, as you will see in the following chapters.

Summary

You have seen what basic elements make up an HTML document. Although the amount of elements may seem daunting at first, you will quickly learn what purpose each element serves, how it affects other elements in the document, and how to best use each element to construct the best HTML document for your purpose. As you read about the elements in more detail—within the next few chapters—try to match their capabilities against your needs.

From here, you should read Chapters 3 through 24 to extend your understanding of the various elements of HTML. Alternatively, jump to specific chapters that cover elements that interest you, or that you don't completely understand. (Follow the various cross-references in each section in this chapter to find the relevant chapter to the specific element you wish to learn more about.)

✦　　✦　　✦

Starting Your Web Page

Now that you know more about the background of HTML and the types of elements involved in an HTML document, it's time to delve into the particulars of each element. This chapter covers more specifics of the basic elements and starts to show how easy it is to manipulate HTML to create impressive documents.

Basic Rules for HTML Code

Creating HTML documents is actually quite easy—HTML documents are simply text files embedded with HTML commands. You can create the documents with any editor capable of exporting raw text. In addition, HTML browsers are very forgiving about white space—additional tabs, line feeds, or spaces don't matter.

As you create your first few HTML files, it is important to start using some good coding habits, habits that will serve you well as you code more complex pages later on. For example, consider the practices outlined in the following sections.

Use liberal white space

Insert liberal line breaks to separate code sections, and use spaces to indent subsequent elements. Both of these will help you read and understand your code. Consider the following two code samples:

```
<!DOCTYPE HTML PUBLIC "-//W3C//DTD HTML 4.01//EN"
   "http://www.w3.org/TR/html4/strict.dtd">
<html>
<head>
<title>The Declaration of Independence</title>
<meta name="description" content="Our Nation's
Declaration of Independence"><meta name="keywords"
content="declaration, independence,
```

```
revolutionary, war, July, 4, 1776">;</head><body><h1>The
Declaration of Independence</h1><p>IN CONGRESS, July 4,
1776.</p><p>The unanimous Declaration
of the thirteen united States of America,</p><p>When in the
Course of human events, it becomes necessary for one people
to dissolve the political bands which have connected them
with another, and to assume among the powers of the earth,
the separate and equal station to which the Laws of Nature
and of Nature's God entitle them, a decent respect to the
opinions of mankind requires that they should declare the
causes which impel them to the separation.</p> <p>We hold
these truths to be self-evident, that all men are
created equal, that they are endowed by their Creator with
certain unalienable Rights, that among these are Life,
Liberty and the pursuit of Happiness. . .
```

and

```
<!DOCTYPE HTML PUBLIC "-//W3C//DTD HTML 4.01//EN"
    "http://www.w3.org/TR/html4/strict.dtd">
<html><head><title>The Declaration of
Independence</title><meta name="description" content="Our
Nation's Declaration of Independence">
<meta name="keywords" content="declaration, independence,
revolutionary, war, July, 4, 1776">
</head><body>
<h1>The Declaration of Independence</h1><p>IN CONGRESS, July
4, 1776.</p>
<p>The unanimous Declaration of the thirteen united States of
America,</p><p>When in the Course of human events, it becomes
necessary for one people to dissolve the political bands
which have connected them with another, and to assume among
the powers of the earth, the separate and equal station to
which the Laws of Nature and of Nature's God entitle them, a
decent respect to the opinions of mankind requires that they
should declare the causes which impel them to the
separation.</p><p>We hold these truths to be self-evident,
that all men are created equal, that they are endowed by
their Creator with certain unalienable Rights, that among
these are Life, Liberty and the pursuit of Happiness. . .
```

As you can tell, the second example is much easier to read and, hence, easier to troubleshoot.

Use well-formed HTML

Well-formed HTML means that your documents need to have the following characteristics:

✦ Contain a `<DOCTYPE>` tag.

✦ Elements must be nested, not overlapping. This means that you need to close elements in the opposite order of how they were opened. For example, the following example is wrong:

```
<p>The last word is <b>bold</p></b>
```

Note how the bold and paragraph tags overlap at the end of the block. Instead, the bold tag should have been closed first, as in the following example:

```
<p>The last word is <b>bold</b></p>
```

✦ Element and attribute names must be in lowercase. XHTML is case-sensitive; the tag <HR> is different from the tag <hr>. All the tags in the XHTML Document Type Definitions (DTDs) are lowercase—so your documents' tags need to be, as well.

✦ All non-empty elements must be terminated. For example, the following is not allowed:

```
This is one paragraph<p>This is another paragraph<p>
```

Instead, each open paragraph tag needs to be closed.

✦ All attribute values must be quoted. For example, consider the two following tags:

```
<table border=0>
```

and

```
<table border="0">
```

The first tag is incorrect because the attribute value is not quoted. The second is correct because the attribute is correctly quoted.

✦ You cannot use minimized attributes, that is, attributes without values. For example, consider the two following tags:

```
<input type="checkbox" checked>
```

and

```
<input type="checkbox" checked="checked">
```

The first tag has a minimized attribute; the checked attribute is named but has no value.

✦ Any empty tag must have a closing tag or the opening tag must end with a slash (/). For example, consider the <hr> tag, which doesn't have a closing tag. As such, it should always appear with an ending slash, <hr />.

Comment your code

Well-written code should speak for itself. However, there are plenty of instances when including comments in your code is warranted. For example, in Chapters 22 and 23, you will learn how to use nested tables to create complex textual layouts. However, such constructs often result in code such as the following:

```
      </table>
    </table>
  </table>
```

Without comments, the nested tables are hard to follow. However, adding a few comments allows you to more easily keep track of the nested elements' purpose:

```
     </table> <!-- /Top heading -->
    </table> <!-- /Main body -->
  </table> <!-- /Floating page -->
```

Creating the Basic Structure

The basic structure for all HTML documents is the same and should include the following minimum elements and tags:

✦ `<DOCTYPE>`—The declared type of the document

✦ `<html>`—The main container for HTML pages

✦ `<head>`—The container for page header information

✦ `<title>`—The title of the page

✦ `<body>`—The main body of the page

These elements fit together in the following template format:

```
<!DOCTYPE HTML PUBLIC "-//W3C//DTD HTML 4.01//EN"
   "http://www.w3.org/TR/html4/strict.dtd">
<html>
<head>
  <meta ... meta tags go here ... >
  <title>title of the page/document goes here</title>
  <LINK rel="stylesheet" href="external style sheet name"
     type="text/css">
  <style>
     ... any document specific styles go here ...
  </style>
  <script>
     ... client-side scripts go here ...
  </script>
</head>
<body>
   ... body of document goes here, paragraphs modified by
block elements, characters, words and sentences modified by
in line elements ...
</body>
</html>
```

The following sections provide more detail on each of the various elements.

Declaring the Document Type

The `<DOCTYPE>` declaration defines what format your page is in and what standard(s) it follows. This is done by specifying what DTD the document adheres to. For example, the following `<DOCTYPE>` definition specifies the strict HTML 4.01 DTD:

```
<!DOCTYPE HTML PUBLIC "-//W3C//DTD HTML 4.01//EN"
    "http://www.w3.org/TR/html4/strict.dtd">
```

Cross-Reference The format and options of the `<DOCTYPE>` tag are covered in more detail in Chapter 2. You can find a list of valid, public DTDs on the W3C Web site at: `http://www.w3.org/QA/2002/04/valid-dtd-list.html`.

This book will cover the strict HTML 4.01 DTD unless otherwise noted.

Specifying the Document Title

The `<head>` element of an HTML document contains several other elements including the document title. The document title is delimited between `<title>` tags and can include any character or entity. For example, consider the following `<head>` section that includes a copyright symbol:

```
<title>This Page Copyright &copy; 2003</title>
```

This title shows in the title bar of Internet Explorer, as shown in Figure 3-1.

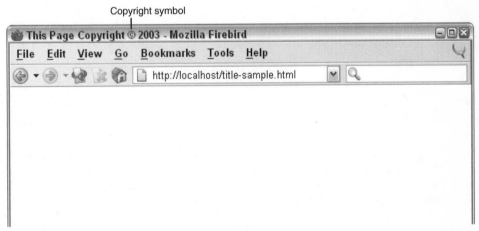

Figure 3-1: Entities are rendered correctly in document titles.

Although it is useful to have the title of your document in the title bar of the client's browser, the title is used in several other locations, as well—it is used as the default shortcut/favorite name in most browsers, it is linked to in most search engines, and so on. As such, you should always include a title for your documents, and make it as descriptive (but concise) as possible.

Providing Information to Search Engines

The `<head>` section of your document can also include `<meta>` tags. These tags are not rendered as visible text in the document—they are used to pass information and commands to the client browser.

As its name implies, the `<meta>` tag contains *meta information* for the document. Meta information is information about the document itself, instead of information about the document's contents. Most of a document's meta information is generated by the Web server that delivers the document. However, by using `<meta>` tags, you can supply different or additional information about the document.

The amount of information you can specify with `<meta>` tags is quite extensive. If you use the `HTTP-EQUIV` parameter in the `<meta>` tag, you can supply or replace HTTP header information. For example, the following `<meta>` tag defines the content type of the document as HTML with the Latin character set (ISO-8859-1):

```
<meta http-equiv="Content-Type" content="text/html; charset=ISO-8859-1">
```

In addition, you can control some aspects of how the client browser treats the document. You can specify how long the document should be cached (if cached at all), refresh the browser with a different page after a delay, and so forth. For example, the following two `<meta>` tags tell the browser not to cache the current page (`pragma, no-cache`) and to refresh the browser window with a different page after 3 seconds (`refresh`):

```
<meta http-equiv="pragma" content="no-cache">
<meta http-equiv="refresh"
content="3;URL=http://www.example.com/newpage.html">
```

Note   For a comprehensive list of HTTP 1.1 headers, see the HTTP 1.1 definition on the W3C Web site: `http://www.w3.org/Protocols/rfc2616/rfc2616.html`.

Always include at least a minimum amount of information in your documents to aid search engines in correctly categorizing your documents. Two important pieces of meta information are a description of the document and keywords relating to its content. The description and keywords information is provided by the following two `<meta>` tags:

```
<meta name="description" content="The latest movie news">
<meta name="keywords" content="movie, movies, production,
  genre, sci fi, horror, drama, comedy, anima, manga, news,
  chat, bbs, discuss, review, recent">
```

Search engines such as Google (`www.google.com`) will also list the provided description and keywords in the site's entry.

Setting the Default Path

When defining links and references in your HTML document, be as exact as possible with your references. For example, when referencing a graphic with an `<IMG>` tag, you should make a habit of including the protocol and the full path to the graphic, as shown in the following line of code:

```
<img src="http://www.example.com/images/sailboat.gif">
```

However, it isn't very practical to type the full path to every local element that is referenced in your document. As such, a document residing on the `example.com` server could reference the same graphic with the following code:

```
<img src="images/sailboat.gif">
```

But, what happens if the document is relocated? The images directory might no longer be a subdirectory of the directory where the document resides. The image might be on a separate server altogether.

To solve these problems, you could use the `<base>` tag. The `<base>` tag sets the default document base—that is, the default location for the document. Using the preceding example, a document in the root directory of the `example.com` server would have a `<base>` tag similar to the following:

```
<base href="http://www.example.com/document.html">
```

Any absolute references in the document (those with full protocol and path) will continue to point to their absolute targets. However, any relative reference (those without full protocol and path) will be referenced against the path in the `<base>` tag.

Creating Automatic Refreshes and Redirects

Meta tags can also be used to refresh a document's content or redirect a client browser to another page. Refreshing a document is useful if it includes timely, dynamic data, such as stock prices. Redirection comes in handy when a document moves—you can use a redirect to automatically redirect a visitor to the new document.

To refresh or redirect a document, use the http-equiv "refresh" option in a `<meta>` tag. This option has the following form:

```
<meta http-equiv="refresh" content="seconds_to_wait; url">
```

For example, suppose that a page on your site (`example.com`) has moved. The page used to be on the root of the server as `bio.html`, but now the page is in a `bio` directory as `index.html` (`/bio/index.html`). However, you want visitors who previously bookmarked the old page to be able to get to the new page. Placing the following document in the server's root (as `bio.html`) would cause visitors to automatically be redirected to the new page after a three-second wait:

```
<!DOCTYPE HTML PUBLIC "-//W3C//DTD HTML 4.01//EN"
   "http://www.w3.org/TR/html4/strict.dtd">
<html>
<head>
  <title>My Bio has Moved!</title>
  <meta http-equiv="pragma" content="no-cache">
  <meta http-equiv="refresh" content="$3$;
     URL= http://www.example.com/bio/index.html">
</head>
<body>
<p>My bio has moved. You will be redirected to the new page
in 3 seconds, or you can click the link below.</p>
<a href="http://www.example.com/bio/index.html">My new
bio.</a>
</body>
</html>
```

To refresh the current page, simply place its absolute URL in the refresh tag.

Tip

Using the `pragma no-cache` meta tag along with the `refresh` tag is always a good idea. This helps keep the browser from caching the document and displaying the cached copy of the document instead of the updated document. Because different browsers treat the `no cache pragma` differently, it is also a good idea to add an `expires` meta tag, as shown below:

```
<meta http-equiv="expires" content="0">
```

This tag causes the document to be immediately expired in the cache and, hence, not cached at all.

Page Background Color and Background Images

One of the easiest changes you can affect on your Web pages is to change the background color of your document. Most browsers use a white background, and specifying a different background color or a background image can easily make your document distinct.

Specifying the document background color

If you code your HTML against the transitional format of HTML, you can use the `bgcolor` attribute in the `<body>` tag. However, using that attribute is not recommended for the following reasons:

✦ The attribute is not valid for strict HTML and might impair the validation of your document.

✦ If you want to change the background color of your documents, you must change each individual body tag in each document.

A better practice is to use appropriate styles, typically in an external

The document background color is set using the `background-colo` example, to set the background color to blue, you would use the follo definition:

```
<style>
   body { background-color: blue; }
</style>
```

Cross-Reference For more information on styles, refer to Chapters 15 and 16.

Specifying the document background image

Besides setting the background of the document to a solid color, you can also specify an image to use as the document background. As with the background color attribute for the body tag, there is also a background image attribute (`background`) for the body tag. However, as with the background color attribute, it is not a good idea to use that attribute.

Instead, use the background-image property in the body style, as shown here:

Figure 3-2: The grid in the background of the document is courtesy of an image, `grid.jpg`.

```
<style>
  body { background-image: url(path_to_image); }
</style>
```

For example, the following style results in `grid.jpg` being placed as the document's background:

```
<style>
  body { background-image: url(grid.jpg); }
</style>
```

The effect is shown in Figure 3-2.

 Note   When you change the background color to a dark color, or use a dark image, you should also change the text color so it will contrast with the background. For example, the following style sets the body background to black and the body text color to white:

```
<style>
  body { background-color: black; color: white; }
</style>
```

Summary

This chapter described the basic elements you need in all HTML documents. You learned some basic guidelines for coding with HTML and how to add header information to your documents, such as a title and meta information for search engines. You also learned how to set a document's base path and redirect a user to another page. Lastly, you saw how to quickly make a document distinctive by changing its colors.

The next few chapters cover various formatting elements in more detail.

✦   ✦   ✦

HTML/XHTML Authoring Fundamentals

Lines, Line Breaks, and Paragraphs

Just as the Web is made up of individual pieces—documents or pages—those individual pieces are made up of smaller elements themselves. Just like a textual document created with a word processor, HTML documents comprise paragraphs and other block elements. This chapter examines block elements in detail.

Line Breaks

As mentioned in previous chapters, HTML is very forgiving of white space—perhaps a bit too forgiving. Instead of simply reproducing the white space contained within the code, client browsers follow the rules of HTML, condensing white space and only inserting formatting via tags.

For example, consider this code example:

```
<!DOCTYPE HTML PUBLIC "-//W3C//DTD HTML 4.01//EN"
  "http://www.w3.org/TR/html4/strict.dtd">
<html>
<head>
  <title>Excerpt From Hamlet</title>
</head>
<body>
Scene I. Elsinore. A platform before the Castle.

[Francisco at his post. Enter to him Bernardo.]

Ber.
Who's there?

Fran.
Nay, answer me: stand, and unfold yourself.
```

```
Ber.
Long live the king!

Fran.
Bernardo?

Ber.
He.

Fran.
You come most carefully upon your hour.

Ber.
'Tis now struck twelve. Get thee to bed, Francisco.

Fran.
For this relief much thanks: 'tis bitter cold,
And I am sick at heart.

Ber.
Have you had quiet guard?

Fran.
Not a mouse stirring.
</body>
</html>
```

This text, when rendered by a browser, resembles that shown in Figure 4-1. Note how the formatting has been completely changed due to the browser condensing all the white space—only rendering one space where line breaks and multiple spaces appear.

This has advantages and disadvantages, linked to the following two points:

✦ You can format your code almost however you like without worrying about affecting the formatting in the client browser.

✦ You cannot rely upon visual formatting—using multiple spaces, tabs, and line breaks—to format your HTML documents.

Instead of using plain text, you must use HTML tags to break your document into discrete paragraphs.

Paragraphs

In HTML, paragraphs are delimited by the paragraph tag, <p>. The paragraph tag controls the line spacing of the lines within the paragraph as well as the line spacing between paragraphs. The default spacing is single space within the paragraph, and double-space between paragraphs.

Each paragraph in your document should start with an opening paragraph tag (<p>) and end with a closing paragraph tag (</p>). This ensures that each paragraph in the document has the same formatting. For an example of using paragraph tags, consider the following code and its output, shown in Figure 4-2:

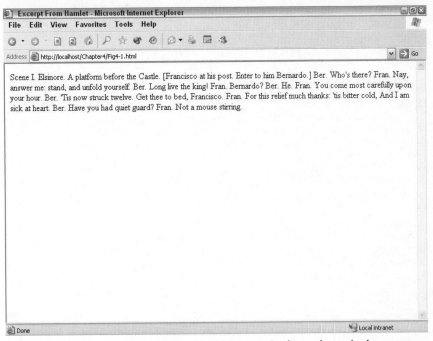

Figure 4-1: HTML browsers condense white space in the code to single spaces.

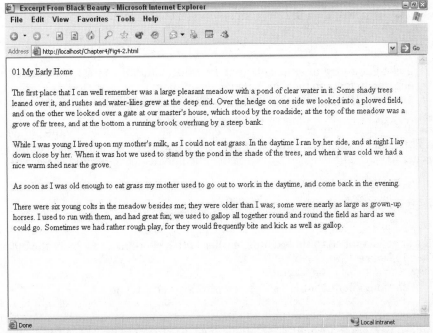

Figure 4-2: Paragraph tags control the spacing of lines within and between paragraphs in a document.

```
<!DOCTYPE HTML PUBLIC "-//W3C//DTD HTML 4.01//EN"
   "http://www.w3.org/TR/html4/strict.dtd">
<html>
<head>
  <title>Excerpt From Black Beauty</title>
</head>
<body>
<p>01      My Early Home</p>
<p>The first place that I can well remember was a large
pleasant meadow with a pond of clear water in it. Some shady
trees leaned over it, and rushes and water-lilies grew at the
deep end. Over the hedge on one side we looked into a plowed
field, and on the other we looked over a gate at our master's
house, which stood by the roadside; at the top of the meadow
was a grove of fir trees, and at the bottom a running brook
overhung by a steep bank.</p>
<p>While I was young I lived upon my mother's milk, as I
could not eat grass. In the daytime I ran by her side, and at
night I lay down close by her. When it was hot we used to
stand by the pond in the shade of the trees, and when it was
cold we had a nice warm shed near the grove.</p>
<p>As soon as I was old enough to eat grass my mother used to
go out to work in the daytime, and come back in the
evening.</p>
<p>There were six young colts in the meadow besides me; they
were older than I was; some were nearly as large as grown-up
horses. I used to run with them, and had great fun; we used
to gallop all together round and round the field as hard as
we could go. Sometimes we had rather rough play, for they
would frequently bite and kick as well as gallop.</p>
</body>
</html>
```

Tip   It is a good idea to visually format your text within the HTML code—inserting line and paragraph breaks where you want them to appear. Doing so facilitates formatting the text with tags and identifying where tags are missing.

As with most tags, you can use styles to control the spacing used by the paragraph tag. For example, using the following styles will cause the paragraph's internal line spacing to be double-spaced by increasing the line height to double its normal size:

```
<style type="text/css">
  p { line-height: 200%; }
</style>
```

If this style is applied to the example earlier in this section, it results in the output shown in Figure 4-3.

Cross-Reference   For more information on styles, refer to Chapters 16 and 17.

Standard paragraph formatting is left-justified, as shown in Figures 4-2 and 4-3. You can control the justification by using a style that modifies the text-align attribute.

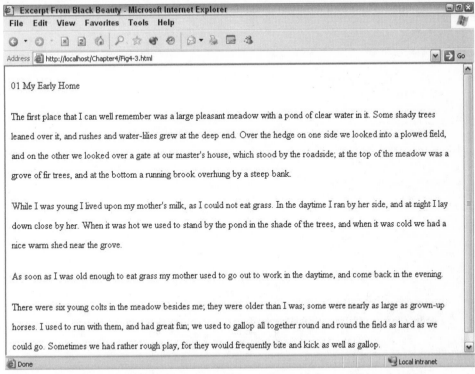

Figure 4-3: You can control the spacing within a paragraph by modifying the `line-height` attribute of the `<p>` tag.

For example, to set the standard paragraph justification to center, you would use a style similar to the following:

```
p { text-align: center; }
```

Manual line breaks

Occasionally, you will want to manually break a line without ending the paragraph. For example, consider the example earlier in this chapter from William Shakespeare's *Hamlet*:

```
Fran.
You come most carefully upon your hour.

Ber.
'Tis now struck twelve. Get thee to bed, Francisco.

Fran.
For this relief much thanks: 'tis bitter cold,
And I am sick at heart.
```

Since the text is from a play, it follows a particular style:

```
Actor_name
Dialogue
```

If you use a paragraph tag to cause each line break, you'll end up with output similar to the following:

```
Fran.

You come most carefully upon your hour.

Ber.

'Tis now struck twelve. Get thee to bed, Francisco.

Fran.

For this relief much thanks: 'tis bitter cold,
And I am sick at heart.
```

Instead, you should use a line break tag (<br>) where you need a line break in a paragraph. The preceding text would be coded as follows:

```
<p>Fran.<br />
You come most carefully upon your hour.</p>
<p>Ber.<br />
'Tis now struck twelve. Get thee to bed, Francisco.</p>
<p>Fran.<br />
For this relief much thanks: 'tis bitter cold,
And I am sick at heart.</p>
```

Note   Typically, you would use several different styles of paragraph tags to delimit the different elements. For example, when formatting a script for a play, you would have a class for the actor and another for the dialogue. An example follows:

```
<p class="actor">Fran.</p>
<p class="dialogue">For this relief much thanks:
'tis bitter cold,<br />
And I am sick at heart.</p>
```

That way, you could easily control (and change) the format of each element separately.

Nonbreaking Spaces

Just as you will want to break some text into discrete chunks, at other times you will want to keep text together. For example, you wouldn't want words separated in dates (December 25, 2003), awkward phrases that include letters and numbers (24 hours), or in some company names ("International Business Machine Corporation").

Suppose you were to use the phrase "12 Angry Men." You would not want a browser to split the "12" and "Angry" across two lines, as shown here:

```
A good example of this technique appears in the movie "12 Angry Men."
```

In cases where you do not want the client browser to break text, you should use a non-breaking space entity ( ) instead of a normal space. For example, when coding the "12 Angry Men" paragraph, you would use something similar to the following code:

```
<p>A good example of this technique appears in the movie
"12 Angry Men."</p>
```

 Cross-Reference For more information on special characters (entities, and so on), refer to Chapter 9.

The browser will then be forced to keep the phrase together, treating it as one cohesive word.

 Tip Nonbreaking spaces have long been used to force formatting on the client browser. For example, to indent a line by three spaces, HTML coders would use something like the following:

```
   Indented by three spaces
```

Before robust CSS styles, this was the only way to "space fill" text. However, now that there are a myriad of ways to achieve this result using styles, this technique becomes sloppy and should not be used. Instead, create an appropriate style and use it to achieve the same results.

Soft Hyphens

Occasionally, you will want to allow a browser to hyphenate long words to better justify a paragraph. For example, consider the following code and its resulting output in Figure 4-4:

```
<p style="text-align: justify;">The morbid fear of the number 13, or
triskaidekaphobia, has plagued some important historic figures like Mark Twain
and Napoleon.</p>
```

In cases where you want a client browser to be able to hyphenate a word if necessary, use the soft hyphen entity (­) to specify where a word should be hyphenated. Using the preceding example, you can hyphenate the word "triskaidekaphobia" with soft hyphens:

```
<p style="text-align: justify;">The morbid fear of the number 13, or
tris&shy;kai&shy;deka&shy;pho&shy;bia, has plagued some important historic
figures like Mark Twain and Napoleon.</p>
```

The resulting output, shown in Figure 4-5, shows how the option hyphens are used to break the word and achieve better justification results.

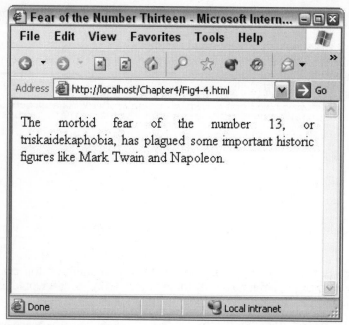

Figure 4-4: Long words can cause problems with fully justified text. Note how the first line is spread out to fill the full line width.

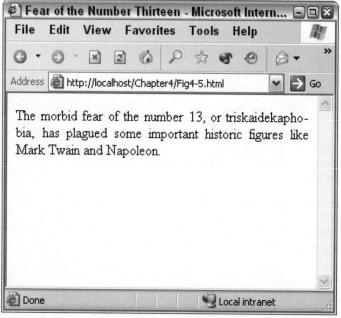

Figure 4-5: Optional hyphens are used when the browser needs to break a word.

Preserving Formatting—The <pre> Element

Sometimes you will want the client browser to interpret your text literally, including the white space and forced formatting (line breaks, and so on). In those cases, you can use the preformatted tag (`<pre>`). The preformatted tag tells the client browser that the text within the tag has been preformatted and should appear exactly as it appears in the code. The tag also causes all text within to be rendered in a monospace font.

For example, consider the following output from a MySQL database:

```
mysql> select * from settings;
+---------------+-------------------+
| name          | value             |
+---------------+-------------------+
| newsupdate    | 1069455632        |
| releaseupdate | Tue, 1/28, 8:18pm |
| status        | 0                 |
| feedupdate    | 1069456261        |
+---------------+-------------------+
4 rows in set (0.00 sec)
```

If you wanted this to appear in a browser as-is, you would have to use liberal nonbreaking spaces and line breaks, as well as specify a monospaced font, as shown in the following code:

```
<p style="font-family: courier;">
mysql> select * from settings;<br />
+---------------+-------------------+<br />
|  name       
  | value      
       |<br />
+---------------+-------------------+<br />
|  newsupdate    | 1069455632
       |<br />
|  releaseupdate | Tue, 1/28, 8:18pm |<br />
|  status       
|  0       
         |<br />
|  feedupdate    | 1069456261
       |<br />
+---------------+-------------------+<br />
4 rows in set (0.00 sec)</p>
```

Not only is this a lot of work, but it also renders the code practically illegible. A better way is to simply use the `<pre>` tag, as follows:

```
<pre>
mysql> select * from settings;
+---------------+-------------------+
| name          | value             |
+---------------+-------------------+
| newsupdate    | 1069455632        |
```

```
| releaseupdate | Tues, 1/28, 8:18pm|
| rolfstatus    | 0                 |
| feedupdate    | 1069456261        |
+---------------+-------------------+
4 rows in set (0.00 sec)
</pre>
```

As you can see in Figure 4-6, the browser does not attempt to format the text within the `<pre>` tags, and renders it in a monospace font to ensure that the formatting appears correct.

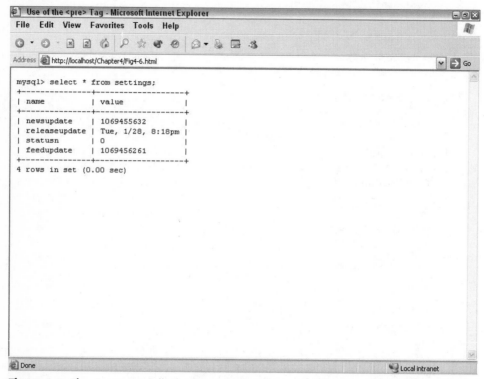

Figure 4-6: The `<pre>` tag tells the browser that the text has been preformatted and that it should be rendered verbatim.

Preformatted text is best for textual tables, or to set certain element (such as lines of code) apart from the main body of a document.

Indents

Occasionally, you will want to indent the first line of paragraphs in your documents. To do so, you can use the `text-indent` property of the paragraph tag and an applicable style. For example, if you wanted the first line of all paragraphs to be indented by half an inch, you would use a style similar to the following:

```
<style type="text/css">
  p { text-indent: .5in; }
</style>
```

Tip If you want to have different styles of paragraphs in your document—some indented, some not indented—define your style using classes. For example, the following code defines an `indent` style of the paragraph tag:

```
<style type="text/css">
  p.indent { text-indent: .5in; }
</style>
```

You would then specify the class in any paragraph tag where you wanted the indent:

```
<p class="indent">This paragraph will be
indented.</p>
```

An example of indenting the first line of paragraphs is shown in the following code and its output in Figure 4-7:

```
<!DOCTYPE HTML PUBLIC "-//W3C//DTD HTML 4.01//EN"
   "http://www.w3.org/TR/html4/strict.dtd">
<html>
<head>
  <title>First Line Indents</title>
  <style type="text/css">
     p{ text-indent: 0.5in; }
  </style>
</head>
<body>
<p>When in the Course of human events, it becomes necessary
for one people to dissolve the political bands which have
connected them with another, and to assume among the powers
of the earth, the separate and equal station to which the
Laws of Nature and of Nature's God entitle them, a decent
respect to the opinions of mankind requires that they should
declare the causes which impel them to the separation.</p>
<p>We hold these truths to be self-evident, that all men are
created equal, that they are endowed by their Creator with
certain unalienable Rights, that among these are Life,
Liberty and the pursuit of Happiness.--That to secure these
rights, Governments are instituted among Men, deriving their
just powers from the consent of the governed, --That whenever
any Form of Government becomes destructive of these ends, it
is the Right of the People to alter or to abolish it, and to
institute new Government, laying its foundation on such
principles and organizing its powers in such form, as to them
shall seem most likely to effect their Safety and Happiness.
Prudence, indeed...</p>
</body>
</html>
```

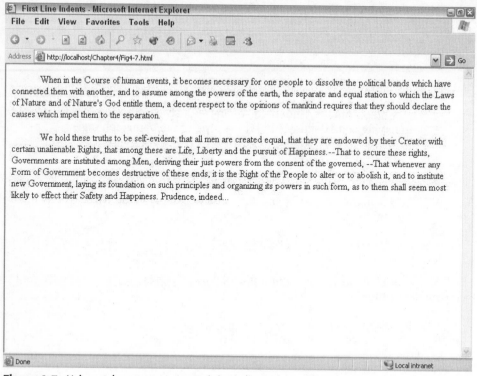

Figure 4-7: Using styles, you can control the indentation of paragraphs.

If you want to indent an entire paragraph, use the `padding-left` and, optionally, the `padding-right` attribute. These attributes add additional space to the left and right of the block element. For example, to add a half-inch indent to the left of a paragraph, you could use this style definition:

```
<style type="text/css">
    p.indent { padding-left: 0.5in; }
</style>
```

Tip   You can use the `<blockquote>` tag to easily indent a paragraph (both left and right). However, this method doesn't allow the type of control possible in defining a special style for elements you wish indented.

Headings

HTML has six predefined heading tags. Headings use `<h>` tags containing the number of the heading. The `<h1>` tag specifies the highest (most important) level of headings, while `<h6>` specifies the lowest (least important) level of headings.

As with most textual documents, HTML documents use larger fonts to specify higher-level headings. For example, consider the following example and its output, shown in Figure 4-8:

```
<!DOCTYPE HTML PUBLIC "-//W3C//DTD HTML 4.01//EN"
    "http://www.w3.org/TR/html4/strict.dtd">
<html>
<head>
  <title>Heading Tags</title>
</head>
<body>
<h1>Heading Level 1</h1>
<h2>Heading Level 2</h2>
<h3>Heading Level 3</h3>
<h4>Heading Level 4</h4>
<h5>Heading Level 5</h5>
<h6>Heading Level 6</h6>
<p>Normal body text.</p>
</body>
</html>
```

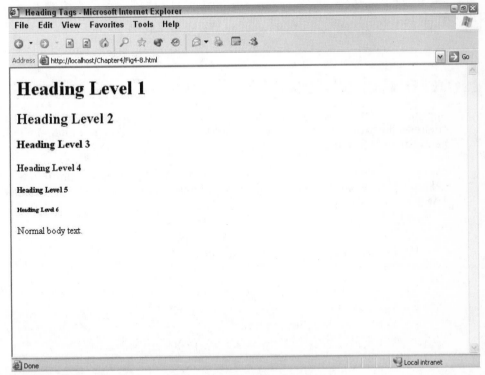

Figure 4-8: There are six, predefined heading styles in HTML.

Each heading style acts like a paragraph tag, providing an automatic line break and extra line spacing after the element. As you can see in Figure 4-8, the default spacing after a heading is one line.

You can use heading tags to delimit a wide range of text. However, their default use is to mark headings in a document, much like headings in a textual document. Also, like most tags, you can use styles to customize the size and appearance of the heading tags. For example, consider the following style code, which defines the first four heading levels in relationship to the normal paragraph font:

```
<style type="text/css">
  h1 { font-size: 18pt; font-family: Arial;
    font-weight: bold; }
  h2 { font-size: 16pt; font-family: Arial;
    font-weight: bold; }
  h3 { font-size: 14pt; font-family: Arial;
    font-weight: bold; }
  h4 { font-size: 12pt; font-family: Arial;
    font-weight: bold; }
  p { font-size: 12pt; font-family: Palatino;
    font-weight: normal; }
</style>
```

Cross-Reference Additional font elements and style guidelines can be found in Chapters 8 and 16–18.

Horizontal Rules

Horizontal rules are used to visually break up sections of a document. The `<hr>` tag creates a line from the current position in the document to the right margin and breaks the line accordingly.

For example, if you were reproducing text from a book, you might want to use rules to show a break between chapters, as shown in the following excerpt from Anna Sewell's *Black Beauty*:

```
<!DOCTYPE HTML PUBLIC "-//W3C//DTD HTML 4.01//EN"
    "http://www.w3.org/TR/html4/strict.dtd">
<html>
<head>
  <title>Excerpt of Black Beauty</title>
</head>
<body>
<p>One day he was at this game, and did not know that the
master was in the next field; but he was there, watching what
was going on; over the hedge he jumped in a snap, and
catching Dick by the arm, he gave him such a box on the ear
as made him roar with the pain and surprise. As soon as we
saw the master we trotted up nearer to see what went on.</p>
<p>"Bad boy!" he said, "bad boy! to chase the colts. This is
not the first time, nor the second, but it shall be the last.
There -- take your money and go home; I shall not want you on
my farm again."</p>
<p>So we never saw Dick any more. Old Daniel, the man who
looked after the horses, was just as gentle as our master, so
we were well off.</p>
```

```
<hr>
<p>Chapter 02      The Hunt</p>
<p>Before I was two years old a circumstance happened
which I have never forgotten. It was early in the spring;
there had been a little frost in the night, and a light mist
still hung over the woods and meadows. I and the other colts
were feeding at the lower part of the field when we heard,
quite ... </p>
</body>
</html>
```

The output of this code is shown in Figure 4-9.

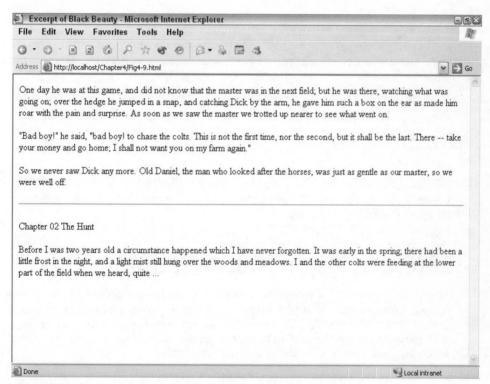

Figure 4-9: The `<hr>` tag inserts a horizontal rule in the document.

As with most tags, you can customize the look of the `<hr>` tag by using styles. For example, consider the following style:

```
<style type="text/css">
  hr { color: red; height: 5px; width: 50%; }
</style>
```

If this style were added to our last example, the results would be similar to the output shown in Figure 4-10.

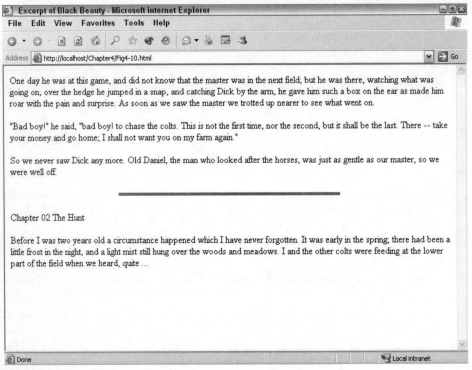

Figure 4-10: You can control various aspects of the horizontal rule, including its width, its thickness (height), and the color.

Grouping with the <div> Element

Now that you know how to format paragraphs, what about groups of paragraphs? Suppose, for example, that you wanted to indent an entire section of text and place a border around the section. Although you can accomplish the indent by using styles with paragraph tags, the unified border is harder to do. For example, consider the following code, which uses styles and paragraph tags:

```
<!DOCTYPE HTML PUBLIC "-//W3C//DTD HTML 4.01//EN"
   "http://www.w3.org/TR/html4/strict.dtd">
<html>
<head>
  <title>Paragraph Borders with Paragraph Tags</title>
  <style type="text/css">
    p.indent-highlight { padding-left: 50px;
        padding-right: 50px; border: solid 3px; }
  </style>
</head>
<body>
<p class="indent-highlight">For the first few days I could
not feed in peace; but as I found that this terrible creature
never came into the field, or did me any harm, I began to
disregard it, and very soon I cared as little about the
```

```
passing of a train as the cows and sheep did.</p>
<p class="indent-highlight">Since then I have seen many
horses much alarmed and restive at the sight or sound of a
steam engine; but thanks to my good master's care, I am as
fearless at railway stations as in my own stable.</p>
<p class="indent-highlight">Now if any one wants to break in
a young horse well, that is the way.</p>
</body>
</html>
```

The output of this code is shown in Figure 4-11. Note how each paragraph is surrounded by its own border, which is not what you wanted.

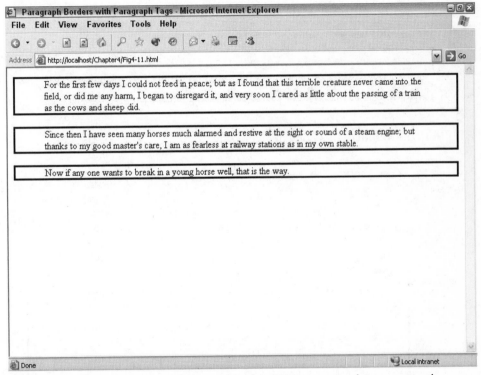

Figure 4-11: Adding some formatting, such as borders, to paragraph tags causes the formatting to distinctly appear around individual paragraphs.

This is where the division tag (`<div>`) comes in handy. The `<div>` tag is used to delimit divisions of a document, which can include several paragraphs or other block elements.

Instead of defining a style for the paragraph tag, define it as an unattached class (one without a specified element) and use it with the `<div>` tag, as in the following code:

```
<!DOCTYPE HTML PUBLIC "-//W3C//DTD HTML 4.01//EN"
    "http://www.w3.org/TR/html4/strict.dtd">
<html>
```

```
<head>
   <title>Division Borders with Division Tags</title>
   <style type="text/css">
     .indent-highlight { padding-left: 50px;
        padding-right: 50px; border: solid 3px; }
   </style>
</head>
<body>
<div class="indent-highlight">
<p>For the first few days I could not feed in peace; but as I
found that this terrible creature never came into the field,
or did me any harm, I began to disregard it, and very soon I
cared as little about the passing of a train as the cows and
sheep did.</p>
<p>Since then I have seen many horses much alarmed and
restive at the sight or sound of a steam engine; but thanks
to my good master's care, I am as fearless at railway
stations as in my own stable.</p>
<p>Now if any one wants to break in a young horse well, that
is the way.</p>
</div>
</body>
</html>
```

Note the output of this code in Figure 4-12.

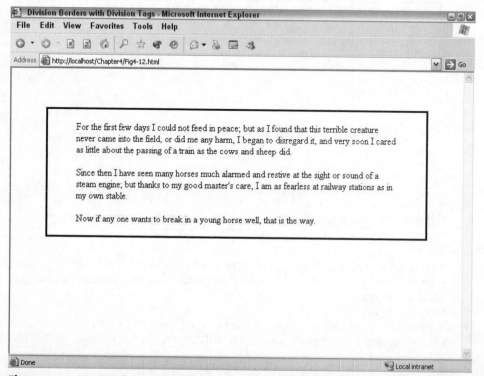

Figure 4-12: Moving the border definition to the `<div>` tag causes the border to appear around the entire division instead of around the individual pieces.

Tip

Note that the border in Figure 4-12 appears at the margins of the document, not at the indent of the paragraphs it surrounds. This is because the style specifies `padding-left` and `padding-right`, which affects the spacing between the parent element (the border) and its children (the paragraphs). To indent the border itself, you would need to specify values for `margin-left` and `margin-right`.

Keep in mind that the `<div>` tag can be used to group combinations of block elements as well—it is not limited to paragraph blocks. For example, you could easily have included a headline, horizontal rule, or other block element(s) in the paragraphs in the last example, and the border would have been rendered around them all.

Summary

This chapter covered the details of most of the block elements of XHTML—paragraphs, headings, horizontal rules, and more. The next few chapters cover more specialized elements, such as lists, images, links, and tables.

After learning about the various elements you can create in an HTML document, Part II of this book shows you how Cascading Style Sheets (CSS) contribute to creating rich, online content.

✦   ✦   ✦

Lists

HTML and its various derivatives were originally meant to be able to reproduce academic and research text. As a consequence, particular care was taken to ensure specific elements—such as lists and tables—were implemented and robust enough to handle the tasks for which they serve.

In the case of lists, HTML defines three different types of lists: ordered (commonly known as numbered) lists, unordered (commonly known as bulleted) lists, and definition lists (for term and definition pairs). This chapter covers all three types of lists and the various syntax and formatting possibilities of each.

Understanding Lists

All lists, whether ordered, unordered, or definition, share similar elements. Each HTML list has the following structure:

```
<list_tag>
  <item_tag>Item text</item_tag>
  <item_tag>Item text</item_tag>
  ...
</list_tag>
```

Note   Definition lists are slightly different in syntax because they have an item tag (`<dt>` or "definition term") and a definition description tag (`<dd>`). See the *Definition Lists* section later in this chapter for more information.

For each list you need the list opening tag, a corresponding closing tag, and individual item tags (paired; open and close).

Each type of list has its own display format:

- ✦ An ordered list precedes its items with a number or letter.
- ✦ An unordered list precedes its items with a bullet (as in this list).
- ✦ A definition list has two pieces for each item, a term and a definition.

The ordered and unordered lists have many different display options available:

✦ Ordered lists can have their items preceded by the following:

- Arabic numbers
- Roman numerals (upper- or lowercase)
- Letters (upper- or lowercase)
- Numerous other language-specific numbers/letters

✦ Unordered lists can have their items preceded by the following:

- Several styles of bullets (filled circle, open circle, square, and so on)
- Images

More information on the individual list types is provided in the following sections.

Ordered (Numbered) Lists

Ordered lists have elements that are preceded by numbers or letters and are meant to provide a sequence of ordered steps for an activity. For example, this book uses numbered lists when stepping the reader through a process. Such a list might resemble the following:

1. In Internet Explorer, open the Web page that displays the graphic you wish to use as wallpaper for your desktop.
2. Right-click the image to open the context menu.
3. Choose Set as Background to save the image and use it as your desktop wallpaper.

Ordered lists use the ordered list tag (`<ol>`) to delimit the entire list and the list item tag (`<li>`) to delimit each individual list item.

In the preceding example, the list has three elements numbered with Arabic numbers. This is the default for ordered lists in HTML, as shown in the following code, whose output is shown in Figure 5-1:

```
<!DOCTYPE HTML PUBLIC "-//W3C//DTD HTML 4.01//EN"
   "http://www.w3.org/TR/html4/strict.dtd">
<html>
<head>
  <title>Example Ordered List</title>
</head>
<body>
<ol>
```

```
   <li>In Internet Explorer, open the Web page that displays
the graphic you wish to use as wallpaper for your
desktop.</li>
   <li>Right-click on the image to open the context menu.</li>
   <li>Choose Set as Background to save the image and use it
as your desktop wallpaper.</li>
</ol>
</body>
</html>
```

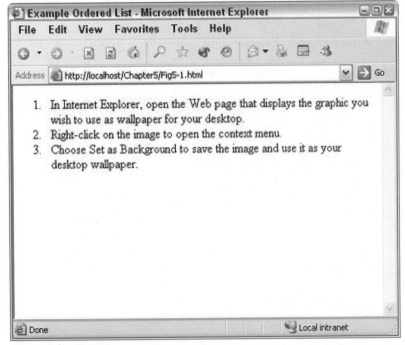

Figure 5-1: The default ordered list uses Arabic numbers for its items.

To specify a different type of identifier for each item, you would use the `list-style` attribute and define a style for the list, as shown in the following code:

```
<!DOCTYPE HTML PUBLIC "-//W3C//DTD HTML 4.01//EN"
   "http://www.w3.org/TR/html4/strict.dtd">
<html>
<head>
   <title>Example Ordered List - Letters</title>
</head>
<body>
<ol style="list-style: upper-alpha">
   <li>In Internet Explorer, open the Web page that displays
the graphic you wish to use as wallpaper for your
desktop.</li>
```

```
   <li>Right-click on the image to open the context menu.</li>
   <li>Choose Set as Background to save the image and use it
as your desktop wallpaper.</li>
</ol>
</body>
</html>
```

This code results in the list items being prefaced with uppercase letters, as shown in Figure 5-2.

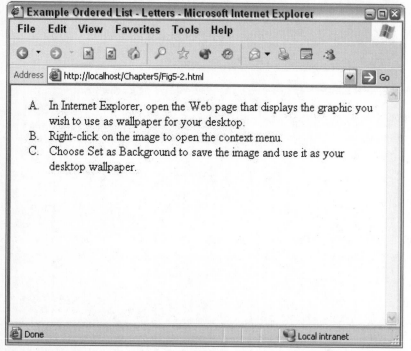

Figure 5-2: The upper-alpha value of the list-style attribute causes the ordered list elements to be prefaced with uppercase letters.

Note   Using letters or Roman numerals only makes sense for organizational lists (out-lines, and so on), not for lists that outline a series of steps—especially if the steps must be followed in order.

The list-style-type property supports the following values in CSS2:

✦ decimal

✦ decimal-leading-zero

- ✦ lower-roman
- ✦ upper-roman
- ✦ lower-greek
- ✦ lower-alpha
- ✦ lower-latin
- ✦ upper-alpha
- ✦ upper-latin
- ✦ hebrew
- ✦ armenian
- ✦ georgian
- ✦ cjk-ideographic
- ✦ hiragana
- ✦ katakana
- ✦ hiragana-iroha
- ✦ katakana-iroha
- ✦ none

Note   Some of the `list-style-types` are font-dependent—that is, they are only supported on certain fonts. If you are using a type such as `hiragana` with a Latin-based font, you will not get the results you intend.

The `list-style-types` are self-explanatory. The default type is typically decimal, but can be defined by the individual client browser. Keep in mind that your document's font and language options must support the language character sets used by the `list-type`.

Ordered lists also support the `list-style-position` property. This property controls where the number or character preceding each item appears. The property has two possible values:

- ✦ outside—The number or character appears outside the left margin of the item text.
- ✦ inside—The number or character appears inside the left margin of the item text.

The default is outside, and the difference between the two options is shown in Figure 5-3.

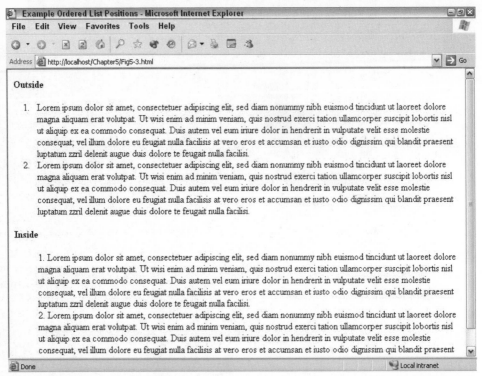

Figure 5-3: The list-style-position property controls where the list item numbers/characters appear—outside or inside the list item margins.

Changing the Start Value of Ordered Lists

Previous versions of HTML allowed the use of the `start` attribute in the `<ol>` tag to control what number or letter the list began with. For example, the following code starts a list with the decimal number 12:

```
<ol start="12" style="list-style: decimal;">
```

However, the `start` attribute of the `<ol>` tag was deprecated, and a replacement CSS style has yet to be defined. Although you can use the `start` attribute, your document will no longer validate against *strict* HTML.

If you find yourself needing consistent, yet flexible numbering, consider using the new CSS2 automatic counters and numbering feature. This feature uses the content property along with the new counter-increment and counter-reset properties to provide a flexible yet powerful automatic counter function.

The following style code will define a counter and cause any `<ol>` list to begin with an item number of 12:

```
<style type="text/css">
ol { counter-reset: list 11; }
li { list-style-type: none; }
li:before {
    content: counter(list,decimal) ". ";
    counter-increment: list; }
</style>
```

This code introduces quite a few CSS2 concepts—pseudo-elements, counters, and related properties and methods. However, it isn't as complex as it might first appear:

✦ The `ol` definition causes the counter (list) to be reset to 11 every time the `<ol>` tag is used—that is, at the beginning of every ordered list.

✦ The `li` definition sets the list style type to none—the counter will display our number; if we left the list style type set to decimal, there would be an additional number with each item.

✦ The `li:before` definition does two things: 1) causes the counter to be displayed before the item (using the `begin` pseudo-element and the `content` property) along with a period and a space; 2) increments the counter. Note that the counter increment happens first, before the display. That is the reason you need to reset the counter to one lower than your desired start.

Using the preceding styles along with the following list code in a document results in a list with items numbered 12-15:

```
<ol>
    <li>Item 12</li>
    <li>Item 12</li>
    <li>Item 12</li>
    <li>Item 12</li>
</ol>
```

Counters are a new, powerful feature of CSS2. Unfortunately, at the time of this writing, only the Opera browser fully supports counters. However, the other browsers are sure to follow suit. You'll find more information on counters and the content property in Chapter 16.

Tip The various list properties can all be defined within one property, `list-style`. The `list-style` property has the following syntax:

```
list-style: <list-style-type> <list-style-image>
        <list-style-position>
```

You can use this one property to specify one, two, or all three `list-style` properties in one declaration. For example, to define an ordered list with lowercase letters and inside positioning, you could use the following tag:

```
<ol style="list-style: lower-alpha inside;">
```

See Chapters 16 and 17 for more information on styles.

Unordered (Bulleted) Lists

Unordered lists are similar to numbered lists except that they use bullets instead of numbers or letters before each list item. Bulleted lists are generally used when providing a list of nonsequential items. For example, consider the following list of ice cream flavors:

✦ Vanilla

✦ Chocolate

✦ Strawberry

Unordered lists use the unordered list tag (`<ul>`) to delimit the entire list and the list item tag (`<li>`) to delimit each individual list item.

In the preceding example, the list has three elements each preceded with a small, round, filled bullet. This is the default for unordered lists in HTML, as shown in the following code, whose output is shown in Figure 5-4:

```
<!DOCTYPE HTML PUBLIC "-//W3C//DTD HTML 4.01//EN"
    "http://www.w3.org/TR/html4/strict.dtd">
<html>
<head>
```

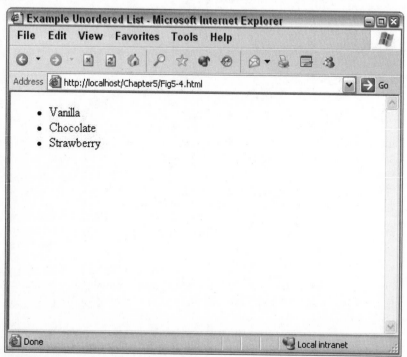

Figure 5-4: An example of an unordered list.

```
  <title>Example Unordered List</title>
</head>
<body>
<ul>
  <li>Vanilla</li>
  <li>Chocolate</li>
  <li>Strawberry</li>
</ul>
</body>
</html>
```

Unordered lists also support the `list-style-type` property, but with slightly different values:

✦ disc

✦ circle

✦ square

✦ none

The default bullet type is disc, though the client browser can define the default differently. The different bullet types are shown in Figure 5-5.

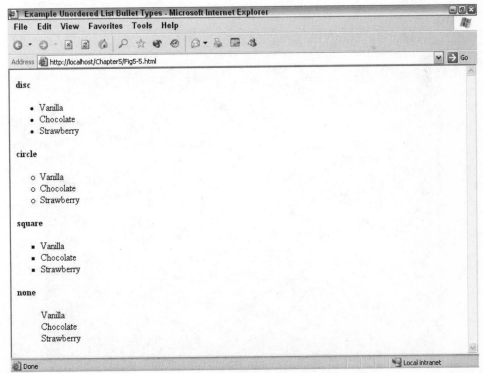

Figure 5-5: An example of the different bullet types for unordered lists.

As with ordered lists, you can define the `list-style-position` property, which in the case of unordered lists controls where the bullet appears—outside or inside the left margin of the item. For example, to move the bullet inside the item margins you would use a style with the `<ul>` tag similar to the following:

```
<ul style="list-style-position: inside;">
```

Unordered lists support one other type of bullet for each item, an image. The image for use in unordered lists must fit the following criteria:

✦ Be accessible to the document via HTTP (be on the same Web server or deliverable from another Web server)

✦ Be in a suitable format for the Web (jpg, gif, or png)

✦ Be sized appropriately for use as a bullet

To specify an image for the list, you use the `list-style-image` property. This property has the following syntax:

```
list-style-image: url(url_to_image);
```

This property can be used to add more dimension to standard bullets (for example, creating spheres to use instead of circles) or to use specialty bullets that match your content. For example, consider the two graphics shown in Figure 5-6, created in Jasc's Paint Shop Pro.

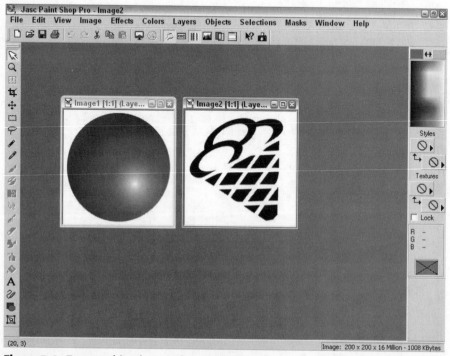

Figure 5-6: Two graphics that can be used as bullets.

Of course, the graphics must be scaled down to "bullet" size and saved in a Web-friendly format. In this case, the graphics are reduced to 10-20 pixels square and saved on the root of the Web server as `sphere.jpg` and `cone.jpg`. The following code uses the images, and the output is shown in Figure 5-7.

```html
<!DOCTYPE HTML PUBLIC "-//W3C//DTD HTML 4.01//EN"
    "http://www.w3.org/TR/html4/strict.dtd">
<html>
<head>
  <title>Example Unordered List with Image Bullets</title>
</head>
<body>
<p><b>sphere</b></p>
<ul style="list-style-image: url(sphere.jpg);">
  <li>Vanilla</li>
  <li>Chocolate</li>
  <li>Strawberry</li>
</ul>
<p><b>cone</b></p>
<ul style="list-style-image: url(cone.jpg);">
  <li>Vanilla</li>
  <li>Chocolate</li>
  <li>Strawberry</li>
</ul>
</body>
</html>
```

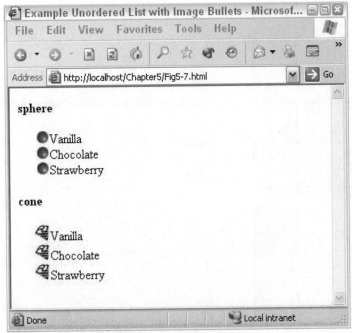

Figure 5-7: Using graphics in unordered lists.

Definition Lists

Definition lists are slightly more complex than the other two types of lists because they have two elements for each item, a term and a definition. However, there aren't many formatting options for definition lists, so their implementation tends to be simpler than that of the other two lists.

Consider this list of definitions, highlighting popular Web browsers:

Internet Explorer
Developed by Microsoft, an integral piece of Windows products.

Mozilla
Developed by the Mozilla Project, an open source browser for multiple platforms.

Netscape
Developed by Netscape Communications Corporation, one of the first graphical browsers.

Safari
Developed by Apple Computer, Inc., for Apple's OSX operating system.

The bulleted items can be coded as list terms and their definitions as list definitions, as shown in the following code. The output of this code is shown in Figure 5-8.

```
<!DOCTYPE HTML PUBLIC "-//W3C//DTD HTML 4.01//EN"
   "http://www.w3.org/TR/html4/strict.dtd">
<html>
<head>
  <title>Example Definition List</title>
</head>
<body>
<dl>
  <dt>Internet Explorer</dt>
  <dd>Developed by Microsoft, an integral piece of Windows
     products.</dd>
  <dt>Mozilla</dt>
  <dd>Developed by the Mozilla Project, an open source
     browser for multiple platforms.</dd>
  <dt>Netscape</dt>
  <dd>Developed by Netscape Communications Corporation, one
     of the first graphical browsers.</dd>
  <dt>Safari</dt>
```

```
    <dd>Developed by Apple Computer, Inc, for Apple's OSX
        operating system.</dd>
</dl>
</body>
</html>
```

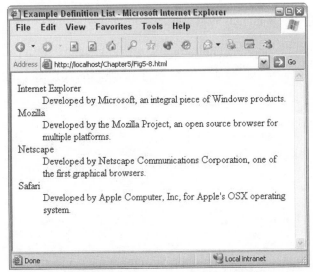

Figure 5-8: Definition lists provide term and definition pairs for each list item.

Note   To add clarity to your definition lists, you will usually want to construct styles that set the definition term in a different font or textual style. For example, you might want the definition terms to be red, bold, and italic. The following style definition accomplishes this:

```
<style type="text/css">
  dt { color: red; font-style: italic;
    font-weight: bold }
</style>
```

Nested Lists

You can nest lists of the same or different types. For example, suppose you have a bulleted list and need a numbered list beneath one of the items, as shown:

✦ Send us a letter detailing the problem. Be sure to include the following:

    1. Your name

    2. Your order number

    3. Your contact information

    4. A detailed description of the problem

In such a case, you would nest an ordered list inside an unordered one, as shown in the following code:

```
<!DOCTYPE HTML PUBLIC "-//W3C//DTD HTML 4.01//EN"
   "http://www.w3.org/TR/html4/strict.dtd">
<html>
<head>
  <title>Example Definition List</title>
</head>
<body>
<ul style="list-style: disc;">
  <li>Send us a letter detailing the problem. Be sure to
    include the following:</li>
  <ol style="list-style: decimal;"> <li>Your name.</li>
    <li>Your order number.</li>
    <li>Your contact information.</li>
    <li>A detailed description of the problem.</li>
  </ol>
</ul>
</body>
</html>
```

The output of the code is shown in Figure 5-9.

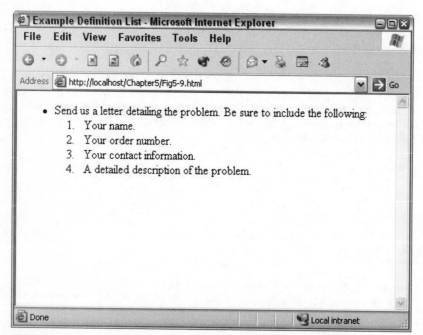

Figure 5-9: You can nest different types of lists within one another.

Note that the nested list does not span any open or close tags—it starts after the close tag of the parent's item and before any other tags in the parent list. It is also formatted (indented) to make it easier to identify in the code. Using this method, you can nest any list within any other list.

Summary

This chapter covered the ins and outs of the three different list types in HTML: numbered, bulleted, and definition. You learned how to define and format each type of list and how you can nest lists for more flexibility.

From here, if you are relatively new to HTML you should progress through the chapters in order, learning about the various elements of an HTML document. Starting in Chapter 16, you will begin learning how to effectively use CSS to format and better control your documents. If you are more experienced with HTML, read the chapters that interest you or that you need more information on and then read the Chapters in Part III (*Controlling Presentation with CSS*) to get a good handle on using CSS in HTML.

✦   ✦   ✦

Images

The Web was created as a graphical alternative to the text-only limitations of tools such as Gopher. As such, images play a pivotal role in Web documents—from being used as navigation aids and decoration, to conveying complex messages impossible with plain text. This chapter introduces the various image formats supported "natively" by most user agents and how to incorporate them into Web documents.

Image Formats for the Web

Most user agents support, to some degree, three graphics file formats: GIF, JPEG, and PNG. The GIF and JPEG formats have been supported for quite some time (since the origin of the Web), while PNG is relatively new. This section covers the basics of the image formats.

Image compression

All three of these graphics file formats use some form of compression to store your image. Why is compression important? Uncompressed images can be large—consider Table 6-1, which compares image dimensions, number of colors, and file size for some sample, uncompressed images.

As you can see, with file sizes like this, you would have to limit yourself to mighty tiny images, or two-color, such as black and white, images. Or, you could compress the files.

Compression options

When you implement file compression, you either have to throw away some information about the image or find a way to store the existing information about the image in a more intelligent manner. GIF files throw away some color information. JPEG files throw away some information about the image itself. PNG files store the information using a more intelligent algorithm.

Table 6-1
Uncompressed Image File Size Comparison by Image Dimensions and Number of Colors

Dimensions (in Inches)	Colors	File Size
1 × 1	2	9K
1 × 1	256	9K
1 × 1	16.7 million	18K
2 × 2	2	16K
2 × 2	256	24K
2 × 2	16.7 million	63K
3 × 3	2	16K
3 × 3	256	49K
3 × 3	16.7 million	139K

GIF

GIF was the earliest format in use in inline images on the Web. Version 1 browsers could open GIF images inline, but required that JPEG images be opened out-of-line. GIF uses a compression scheme—called *LZW compression*—that predates CompuServe, even though you might see it called CompuServe GIF. CompuServe implemented LZW compression, thinking it was in the public sphere and then found out it was proprietary. A lot of lawyers sorted it out.

How does GIF work? Simply put, GIF indexes images to an 8-bit palette. The system palette is 256 colors. Before you can save your file in GIF format, the utility you are using simply makes its best guess at mapping all your colors to one of the 256 colors in an 8-bit palette.

Is a reduction in color depth a problem? That depends. GIF uses dithering to achieve colors between two colors on the palette. Even with dithering, however, GIF images of a sunset have stripes of color, where a smooth gradation would be more natural. GIF images also tend to have more cartoonish colors because flesh tones aren't part of the palette. A GIF image of a drawing of something like a checkerboard, however, will look just fine.

Cross-Reference

See Chapter 38 for a lesson in creating animated GIFs. Transparent GIFs are discussed at the end of this chapter.

Note

A *system palette* is the 256 colors your monitor is able to display if you set your video board only to show 256 colors. These colors differ from a PC to a Mac.

JPEG

JPEG takes a different approach. JPEG stands for the *Joint Photographic Experts Group*, the name of the group that created the standard. With JPEG, you get to keep all your colors, but you don't get to keep all the data about the image. What kinds of images lend themselves to being compressed with JPEG? A tree. If you take a photo of a pine tree, the acorns are in specific places, but when the image is compressed and decompressed (opened on your Web page), the computer has to approximate where those acorns went, because it had to throw away some of the data. Is this a problem? Not with most photos of most pine trees. Faces also take well to JPEG because the colors are all there; faces in GIF can look unnatural because of the color loss.

Every generation 3 and higher browser can handle inline JPEGs. JPEGs are also ideal for showing gradient filled graphics (when the color changes gradually from one color to another). The same graphic would suffer enormously under the GIF compression because all those in-between colors wouldn't be there.

What suffers under JPEG compression? Text, schematic drawings, and any line art. Of course, with JPEG, you can select the level of compression (usually either as a percentage or as Maximum, High, Medium, or Low). You generally want to use the maximum compression level your image can handle without losing image quality. You won't know how much compression your image can handle without loss until you try it at different levels of compression.

PNG

The *Portable Network Graphics*, or PNG format, was developed exclusively for the Web and is in the public domain. The PNG format takes advantage of a clever way of storing the information about the image so you don't lose color and you don't lose image quality; it is a lossless format. The only drawback is, because the standard is so new, only fourth-generation and later browsers support PNG graphics. Eventually, PNG will replace GIFs for many color-rich, still image files. Only GIFs can support animation and transparency.

> **Note**　File formats that implement compression schemes that discard information about the image are called *lossy* file formats. Both GIF, which discards color information, and JPEG, which discards image information, are lossy file formats. File formats that don't discard any information about an image are called *lossless.* PNG is a lossless compression scheme.

Image color depth

In the computer world, everything is black or white, on or off. Computers operate in the base two system, so when creating colors, your choices of colors are base two numbers. A *bit* is a representation of on or off (1 or 0). One-bit color uses a two-color palette (2^1). Two-bit color uses a four-color palette (2^2). Eight-bit color uses a 256-color palette (2^8). Thirty-two-bit color uses a 16.7-million-color palette (2^{32}).

Between the two system palettes, there are 216 colors in common. This is called the *216-browser-safe palette.* By limiting your graphics to colors from this palette, you can be sure the browser won't have to guess or dither to achieve the color you want.

You might be thinking: *Two colors: that's not so bad. An artist can do a lot with two colors; think of the ways you can blend them.* Unfortunately, this isn't how computers work. When you select a color palette, you get only the colors in that palette, not any blends of colors in that palette.

When you create an image, you want to balance the quality of the image against the file size of the image. When you send an image file over the Internet to a Web page, you send either information about the palette or you send the actual palette. With GIF files, you send a color look-up table (CLUT) with the image. With JPEG files, you send a palette. As you can imagine, this makes the files considerably larger.

Enhancing downloading speed

What can you do to ensure your pages download quickly? There are a few things:

✦ Limit image file sizes.

✦ Limit the number of images.

✦ Reuse images as much as possible so images can be loaded from cache.

✦ Use frames so only part of the browser windows need to reload.

✦ Use text rather than images, where possible.

Image file sizes

You can limit image file sizes by doing the following:

✦ Using the maximum compression your image will take

✦ Using the smallest bit-depth your image can stand

✦ Minimizing the dimensions of your image on the page

Test your pages at 640 × 480, 800 × 600, and 1024 × 768 to see how they will look to different visitors. Often, an image that renders well at 1024 × 768 and doesn't dominate the page will look huge and overbearing at 640 × 480.

Number of images

How many images is the right number? You might be surprised to learn that sometimes very small images with white space between them load faster than one large image.

Take advantage of white space to contribute to your images. You can use two intelligent techniques to get more image for the byte. By changing the background color to match the background color of your images, you can keep your images smaller. By anti-aliasing the text against that background to blend the edges into the background color, you can achieve the look of one large graphic with multiple small, fast-loading images.

Reuse images

Reusing images is as simple as having a single graphic for "home" on all your pages. Have a single bullet graphic (if you can't stand to use the standard bullet) for every bullet on every page. Why does this help your pages load faster? Your browser checks to see whether an image it needs is already in cache and loads the image from cache, if it can. This reduces the number of bytes that actually needs to be downloaded.

Use frames

How can using frames speed download time? After the initial frameset loads, the browser will usually be loading one new frame at a time. Also, because the images are probably part of the banner and/or the navigational tools, the frame that does reload is less likely to be image-intensive.

Tip

By putting all or most of the images into one of your frames and the mostly text-based content into your main frame, you can save visitors from having to load the images more than once. After the initial load, subsequent loads will be faster.

Use text rather than images

You've read this elsewhere in the book. You can use tricks to make text look somewhat like an image. Instead of using a graphic with boxes and buttons for navigation, use a table with cells assigned different background colors.

Creating Graphics

If you want to create top-notch graphics, the tool of choice among professionals is Adobe Photoshop, available for the Mac and the PC (see Figure 6-1). Freeware and shareware software programs also are available that perform subsets of the functions performed by Photoshop. Photoshop LE, the lite version, ships with many scanners.

Essential functions

What should your graphics package be able to do? For existing images, such as photographs, you want to sharpen, blur, and perform some special effects on the image (for example, posterize, swirl, and mosaic). For images you create on the screen, you want to create your own custom palette (so you can send as few colors as you need). You also need some basic artist tools, such as a paintbrush, a pencil, a spray can, and a magnifying glass for magnifying part of the image to see it better.

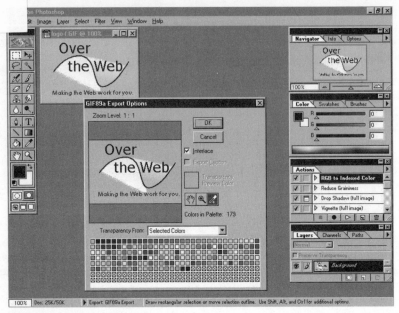

Figure 6-1: Adobe Photoshop.

Regardless of whether the image is made by hand or based on a photograph or clipart, you need the following capabilities:

+ Reduce the bit-depth of any image you want to save as GIF.

+ Index the color of the image so you can save the image to GIF.

+ Save the image as an interlaced GIF.

+ Save the image as a transparent GIF.

+ Save the image as a PNG file.

+ Save the image as a progressive JPEG, which is discussed at the end of this chapter.

Note   *Progressive JPEGs* are a nice addition to a Web page. They work the same as interlaced GIFs. Before the entire image has been downloaded, you can begin to see the image. Then the images slowly come into focus.

Free alternatives

If you aren't ready to commit to a $500 software package to get all these great functions, you can work with a number of small, free software packages and services that do many of the things previously listed for you. On the Web, you can find sites that turn your TIF file into a GIF, or make your GIF an interlaced GIF. The trade-off is the time. Finding, learning, and using a variety of small packages to solve all your imaging needs obviously takes longer than learning one package and using it on your desktop.

Capturing Graphics From Other Sites

What about taking graphics you like from another site? This is generally not an okay thing to do. Unless you have explicit permission from the creator of the images—say, you are taking graphics from a site that makes free images available or you have written permission from the owner of the site—you are essentially stealing the images from the legitimate owner. Images are intellectual property and are protected by copyright laws, and using them without permission could get you an invitation to court.

Just because an image is on a Web page doesn't mean it is in the public domain. Yes, it gets downloaded onto your own computer (into cache), and, yes, your browser gives you the ability to save the image as a local file (using the right mouse button or prolonged clicking on a Mac), but it still doesn't mean you own the image or the right to use the image. If you see something you like on another page, write to the page owner and ask if he or she owns the image and if you can use it. Chances are, the owner will be flattered by your request. Be sure that person owns the image or permission won't mean anything (if the image was stolen from somewhere else).

Progressive JPEGs and interlaced GIFs

Once upon a time on the Web, you had to wait for an image to finish loading before you knew what it was. Today, you can save your files using the progressive JPEG format or the interlaced GIF format and watch the image come into focus as it loads.

The advantage to this approach is a visitor to your site knows roughly what an image is before the entire image has downloaded. If download times are long, due to a poor Internet connection, for example, the visitor to the site can actually take a link off the page before the image has finished loading without missing anything.

Finally, these two image formats are good because the visitor participates in the download time. Instead of waiting for the page to download—sitting idly by—the visitor waits for the page to download while watching the images become clearer. This is more of a reward for waiting—and less of a sense of waiting—for the visitor.

Note   Specifying the size of the image in the image tag can also speed up the display of your Web pages. See the *Size and scaling* section later in this chapter for more information.

The sense of "coming into focus" that these types of images provide is the result of the way the images are stored. Progressive JPEGs and interlaced GIFs download only every eighth line at first, then every fourth line, then every second line, and then, finally, the odd-numbered lines. The result is the image goes from blurry to focused.

You create a progressive JPEG or an interlaced GIF by saving it into this format. In Paint Shop Pro, when you save a file as a GIF file you can choose whether you want the file to be normal or interlaced (see Figure 6-2). Freeware packages are also available that convert your regular JPEGs and GIFs into progressive JPEGs and interlaced GIFs.

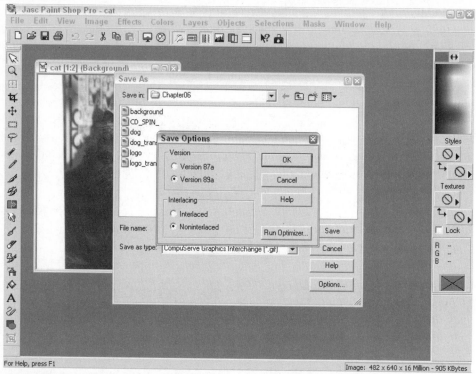

Figure 6-2: Paint Shop Pro allows you to choose whether you want your GIF to be interlaced or not.

Using Transparency

Two of the Web-supported graphics formats, GIF and PNG, support transparency, the ability for parts of images to be completely transparent. Typically, transparency is used to soften the edge of images, creating an illusion that the image is not rectangular. For example, see Figure 6-3, which shows an image with a standard opaque background and the same figure with a transparent background. The image with transparency allows the page background to show through.

Using transparency can open up the design of a document, making it more airy and less "blocky." It gives the document a more professional appearance, looking more like a published document than a Web page of the 1980s.

Different graphic editing programs handle transparency differently—some assign transparency to the background layer, some allow you to pick one color that should be transparent, some programs allow multiple colors to be transparent. Check the Help file for your editor to determine how to accomplish transparency.

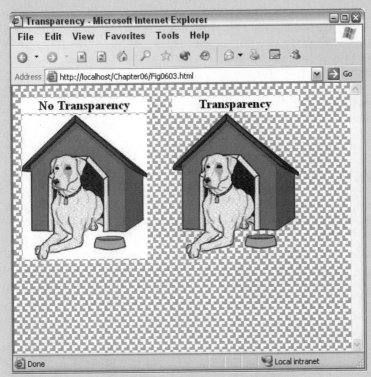

Figure 6-3: Transparency can soften an image, giving the appearance that the image is not rectangular.

Inserting an Image

Images are inserted into HTML documents using the `<img>` tag. The `<img>` tag, at a minimum, takes two attributes, `alt` and `src`.

The `alt` attribute specifies text that should be displayed in lieu of the image in nongraphical browsers (see the section "*Specifying text to display for nongraphical browsers*" later in this chapter). The `src` attribute tells the user agent what image file should be displayed. For example, if you wanted to include the graphic `cat.jpg` in your document, you could use code similar to the following:

```
<img alt="A picture of a cat" src="cat.jpg">
```

Note

The ⟨img⟩ tag has no closing tag. However, in XHTML the ⟨img⟩ tag must be closed:

```
<img alt="A picture of a cat" src="cat.jpg" />
```

The src attribute's value can be a file on the same Web server as the document, or any valid URL pointing to an image on a different Web server. Just as with the anchor tag, you can use absolute or relative URLs to specify the location of the image to display. The reasons for using either URL are the same as the reasons for using absolute or relative URLs in anchor tags.

 Cross-Reference

For more information about absolute or relative URLs, see Chapter 7.

Image Alignment

Most user agents will attempt to display the image where the ⟨img⟩ tag is inserted. For example, consider the following HTML code and the resulting display shown in Figure 6-4:

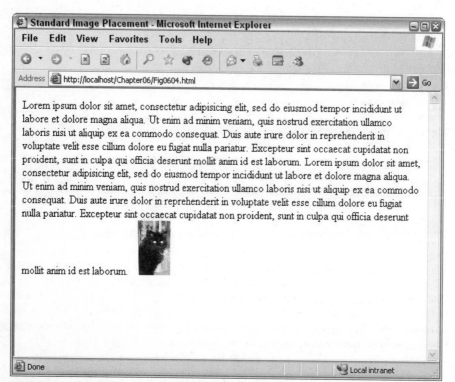

Figure 6-4: The browser displays the image at the end of the paragraph where the ⟨img⟩ tag is located.

```
<p>Lorem ipsum dolor sit amet, consectetur adipisicing elit, sed do eiusmod
tempor incididunt ut labore et dolore magna aliqua. Ut enim ad minim veniam,
quis nostrud exercitation ullamco laboris nisi ut aliquip ex ea commodo
consequat. Duis aute irure dolor in reprehenderit in voluptate velit esse
cillum dolore eu fugiat nulla pariatur. Excepteur sint occaecat cupidatat non
proident, sunt in culpa qui officia deserunt mollit anim id est laborum. Lorem
ipsum dolor sit amet, consectetur adipisicing elit, sed do eiusmod tempor
incididunt ut labore et dolore magna aliqua. Ut enim ad minim veniam, quis
nostrud exercitation ullamco laboris nisi ut aliquip ex ea commodo consequat.
Duis aute irure dolor in reprehenderit in voluptate velit esse cillum dolore
eu fugiat nulla pariatur. Excepteur sint occaecat cupidatat non proident, sunt
in culpa qui officia deserunt mollit anim id est laborum. <img alt="Picture of
a cat" src="cat.jpg"></p>
```

If the user agent cannot fit the image on the current line, it will wrap it to the next line and follow the paragraph's alignment and formatting.

Note how the default formatting (at least for Internet Explorer) of the image is to be aligned with the baseline of neighboring text. This isn't always ideal. At times, you will want to specify the alignment of the image as it relates to the text and other objects around it. Image alignment can be controlled by using the align attribute with the <img> tag. The align attribute can be set to the values shown in Table 6-2:

Table 6-2	
Align Attribute Values	
Value	**Function**
Top	Align with the top of nearby text or object
Bottom	Align with the bottom of nearby text or object
Middle	Align with the middle of nearby text or object
Left	Align to the left of nearby text or object
Right	Align to the right of nearby text or object

Figure 6-5 shows an example of each of these alignment options.

Note Most user agents render items in the order in which they appear in the document. If you are using left-aligned images, they should appear *before* the text that they should be positioned left of.

However, the align attribute has been deprecated in favor of using styles for image alignment. The following CSS properties can be used to help align images:

✦ text-align—Used in surrounding text, this property aligns the text around an image (versus aligning the image itself). See Chapter 8 for more information on using the text-align property.

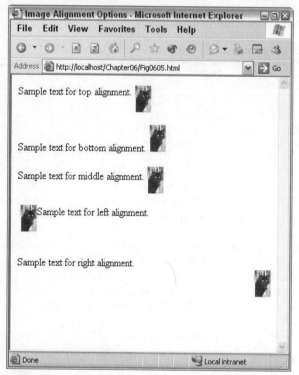

Figure 6-5: The various alignment options for images.

✦ float—Floats the image to the right or left of the user agent. Note that some user agents do not support the float property. The float property allows text and other objects to wrap next to the image.

✦ vertical-align—Aligns the image vertically with neighboring text or objects.

Note that some user agents need to process the image alignment prior to the text around it; if you are using CSS to position your images, it is usually best to position the images before neighboring text in your HTML document.

Specifying Text to Display for Nongraphical Browsers

As mentioned repeatedly in this book, it is important not to get caught up in the graphical nature of the Web, forgetting that not all user agents support graphics. In addition, some users turn off images in their browser to speed up browsing. You can use the alt attribute of the <img> tag to specify text that should be displayed when the image cannot. For example, consider the following text and the display in Figure 6-6:

```
<p><img alt="Picture of a cat" src="cat.jpg" style="float: right" width="70px">
Lorem ipsum dolor sit amet, consectetur adipisicing elit, sed do eiusmod
```

tempor incididunt ut labore et dolore magna aliqua. Ut enim ad minim veniam, quis nostrud exercitation ullamco laboris nisi ut aliquip ex ea commodo consequat. Duis aute irure dolor in reprehenderit in voluptate velit esse cillum dolore eu fugiat nulla pariatur.</p>

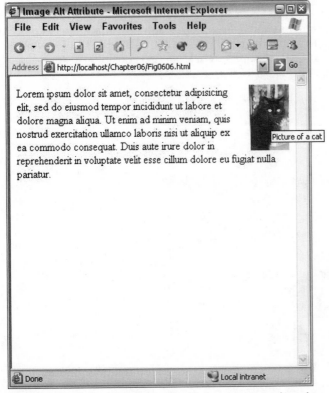

Figure 6-6: The `alt` attribute specifies text to use when the image cannot be displayed.

Some user agents display the `alt` attribute text when the user mouses over the image. This allows you to use the `alt` attribute to include additional information about an image. If you have a lot of information to convey, consider using the `longdesc` (long description) attribute as well. The `longdesc` attribute specifies a URL to a document that is to be used as the long description for the figure. Note that it is up to the user agent to decide how to enable access to the long description, if at all.

Size and Scaling

You can specify the size of an image by using the `height` and `width` attributes of the `<img>` tag. These attributes accept pixel and percentage values, allowing you to specify the exact size of an image or a size relative to the current size of the browser window.

Tip

Get in the habit of always using the `width` and `height` attributes with your `<img>` tags. These attributes allow the user agent to reserve the correct amount of space for the image while it continues to render the rest of the document. Without these attributes, the user agent must wait for the image to be loaded before continuing to load the rest of the document.

For example, suppose that you had a large, high-resolution image, but wanted to display a smaller version. Using the pixel values of the sizing attributes, you can specify a custom size of the larger image. For example, consider the following code and the resulting display in Figure 6-7:

```
<!-- Full image is 180px wide -->
<p>Full Size Image<img alt="Full size image"
   src="car.jpg"></p>
<p>Half Size Image<img alt="Half-size image"
   src="car.jpg" width="90px"></p>
```

Figure 6-7: Using percentage values, you can display an image at any percentage of its normal size.

Note

It is important to use both the correct height and width when specifying image dimensions in an `<img>` tag. If you change the proportions of the figure (by specifying a wrong width or height), you will end up with a funhouse mirror effect—the image will be stretched or shrunk in one dimension. Sometimes this can be used for effect, but usually it is accidental.

Also note that you can specify only one of the dimensions and have the user agent automatically figure out the other. However, the user agent must then wait for the entire image to load before progressing with rendering the rest of the page, so it is always better to specify both dimensions.

Image size attributes should not be used as a substitute for an appropriately sized graphic. If you need a different sized image, create the appropriate size in an image editor and use the new image instead. Although the width and height attributes can be used to display an image smaller than it actually is, the user agent must still download the entire image—the user agent must then scale the image accordingly.

Image Borders

You can use CSS styles to create borders around images. Previous versions of HTML supported a `border` attribute for the `<img>` tag, which worked similarly to the `border` attribute of the `<table>` tag. However, this attribute has been deprecated for use with the `<img>` tag. Instead, you should use styles.

CSS supports quite a few border properties, as shown in Table 6-3.

<table>
<tr><td colspan="3">Table 6-3
CSS Border Properties</td></tr>
<tr><td>*Property*</td><td>*Options*</td><td>*Use*</td></tr>
<tr><td>Border</td><td>border-width
border-style
border-color</td><td>Define a simple border around all four sides of the object, specifying the width, style, and color in one property</td></tr>
<tr><td>border-color</td><td>border-color</td><td>Set the color of the border</td></tr>
<tr><td>border-style</td><td>border-style</td><td>Set the style of the border</td></tr>
<tr><td>border-top
border-bottom
border-left
border-right</td><td>border-width
border-style
border-color</td><td>Define individual sides of the border</td></tr>
<tr><td>border-top-color
border-bottom-color
border-left-color
border-right-color</td><td>border-color</td><td>Define the color of the individual sides of the border</td></tr>
<tr><td>border-top-width
border-bottom-width
border-left-width
border-right-width</td><td>border-width</td><td>Define the width of the individual sides of the border</td></tr>
<tr><td>border-width</td><td>border-width</td><td>Define the width of the border</td></tr>
</table>

For example, to define a 4-pixel-wide border around an entire image, you can use the following code:

```
<img alt="A picture of a cat" src="cat.jpg"
style="border: 4px solid black;">
```

To define a border on just the left and right sides of an image, you would use the following:

```
<img alt="A picture of a cat" src="cat.jpg"
style="border-left: 4px solid black;
border-right: 4px solid black;">
```

Tip To simplify defining a different border on one side of an image, use the `border` property first to define a border on all sides and then the appropriate `border-side` property for the side that is the exception, overriding the previous setting for that side. For example, to create a border on all sides of an image except the right, you could specify `border-top`, `border-bottom`, `border-left`, and `border-right` properties individually. Or, you could use just `border` and `border-right`:

```
<img alt="A picture of a cat" src="cat.jpg"
style="border-left: 4px solid black;
border-right: none;">
```

Image Maps

Image maps provide a way to map certain areas of an image to actions. For example, a company Web site might want to provide a map of the United States that allows customers to click a state to find a local office or store.

There are two types of image maps, client-side and server-side. Client-side image maps rely upon the user agent to process the image, the area where the user clicks, and the expected action. Server-side image maps rely upon the user agent only to tell the server where the user clicked; all processing is done by an agent on the Web server.

Between the two methods, client-side image maps are generally preferred. They allow the user agent to offer immediate feedback to the user (like being over a clickable area) and are supported by most user agents. Server-side agents can also bog down a server if the map draws consistent traffic, hides many details necessary to provide immediate feedback to the user, and might not be compatible with some user agents.

Tip If you want an image to be clickable and take the user to one particular destination, you don't have to use an image map. Instead, embed the `<img>` tag in an appropriate anchor tag (`<a>`) similar to the following:

```
<a href="catpage.html"><img alt="Picture of a
cat" src="cat.jpg"></a>
```

Specifying an image map

A client-side image map is generally specified within the contents of a `<map>` tag and linked to an appropriate `<img>` tag with the `<img>` tag's `usemap` attribute. For example, to specify a map for an image, `travel.jpg`, you could use this code:

```
<img alt="Travel reservations" src="travel.jpg"
   usemap="#map1">
<map name="map1">
...
</map>
```

Inside the `<map>` tags you specify the various clickable regions of the image, as covered in the next section.

Specifying clickable regions

To specify an image map, a list of polygonal regions must be defined on an image and referenced in the HTML document. Three different types of polygons are supported: rectangle, circle, and free-form polygon.

✦ rect—Defines a rectangle area by specifying the coordinates of the four corners of the rectangle.

✦ circle—Defines a circle area by specifying the coordinates of the center of the circle and the circle's radius.

✦ poly—Defines a free-form polygon area by specifying the coordinates of each point of the polygon.

Note that all coordinates of the image map are relative to the top-left corner of the image (effectively 0, 0) and are measured in pixels. For example, suppose you wanted an image for a travel site with a picture of a car, plane, and hotel. When the user clicks one of the pictures, they are taken to the right page for auto rentals, airfare, or hotel reservations. Such an image would resemble the image shown in Figure 6-8.

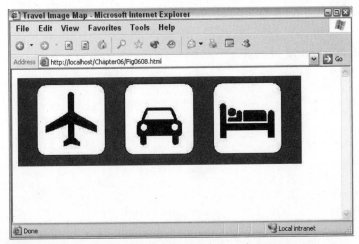

Figure 6-8: An image ready to be used as an image map.

The regions that can be used for the map are within the three icon squares (the white squares around the icons). The regions are all rectangular, uniform in size (121 pixels square), and have the following upper-left coordinates:

✦ car—35 x, 11 y

✦ plane—190 x, 11 y

✦ hotel—345 x, 11 y

Knowing the upper-left corner coordinates and the size of each rectangle, you can easily figure out the coordinates of the bottom-right corner of each rectangle.

Tip   Several tools are available to help create image map coordinates. Use your favorite search engine to find a dedicated piece of software to map regions, or examine your graphics program to see if it can create regions for you. Paint Shop Pro is an excellent Windows-based image editor that has image map tools built in.

Specifying regions using anchor tags

You can specify regions using anchor tags with shape and coords attributes. For example, to specify the three regions previously outlined, you could use the following:

```
<map name="map1">
<a href="plane.html" shape="rect" coords="35,11,156,132">
Plane Reservations</a>
<a href="car.html" shape="rect" coords="190,11,311,132">
Rental Cars</a>
<a href="hotel.html" shape="rect" coords="345,11,466,132">
Hotel Reservations</a>
</map>
```

Note that the link text helps the user determine what the clickable area leads to, as shown by the Internet Explorer ToolTip in Figure 6-9.

Specifying regions using area tags

Another way to define regions is by using <area> tags instead of anchors:

```
<map name="map1">
<area href="plane.html"
   shape="rect" coords="35,11,156,132"
   alt="Plane Reservations">
<area href="car.html"
   shape="rect" coords="190,11,311,132"
   alt="Rental Cars">
<area href="hotel.html"
   shape="rect" coords="345,11,466,132"
   alt="Hotel Reservations">
</map>
```

In the case of the `<area>` tag, using the `alt` attribute helps the user determine what the clickable area leads to, as shown by the Internet Explorer ToolTip in Figure 6-9.

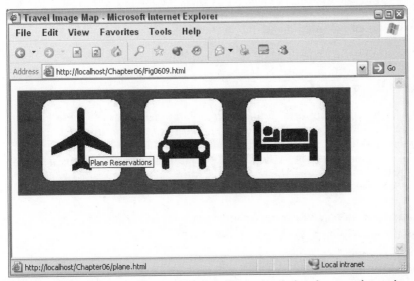

Figure 6-9: The link or `alt` text of a clickable region helps the user determine where the clicked region leads.

Putting it all together

A document with a working image map (as outlined in this section) would resemble the following code:

```
<!DOCTYPE HTML PUBLIC "-//W3C//DTD HTML 4.01//EN"
   "http://www.w3.org/TR/html4/strict.dtd">
<html>
<head>
  <title></title>
</head>
<body>
<img alt="Travel Plans" src="travel.jpg" usemap="#map1">
<map name="map1">
<area href="plane.html"
  shape="rect" coords="35,11,156,132"
  alt="Plane Reservations">
<area href="car.html"
  shape="rect" coords="190,11,311,132"
  alt="Rental Cars">
<area href="hotel.html"
  shape="rect" coords="345,11,466,132"
  alt="Hotel Reservations">
</map>
</body>
</html>
```

Note The image map example in this chapter is somewhat simplistic, using three identical rectangles for its regions. Image maps can be used for more complex purposes, such as the clickable U.S. map mentioned earlier in this chapter, allowing users to click various buildings on a map for more information, or parts on an exploded diagram of a machine.

Animated Images

The GIF format also supports rudimentary animation by showing different frames of an image one after another. The effect is similar to drawing individual frames of animation on different pages of a sketchbook and rapidly flipping the pages. Animated GIF images are not supported by all user agents and should be used sparingly due to their size—the image must store all the frames of the animation, increasing the size of the image.

Some image editors include tools to help create animated GIF images, such as Jasc Software's Animation Shop, shown in Figure 6-10.

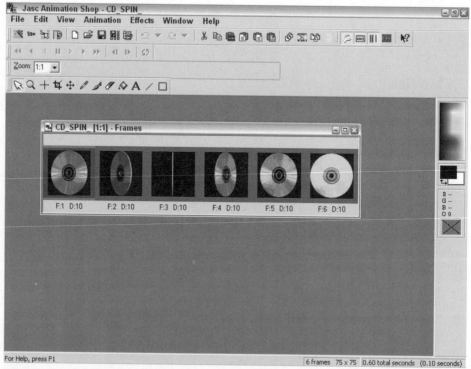

Figure 6-10: Programs such as Jasc Animation Shop can help you create animated GIFs, in this case the animation of a spinning CD-ROM.

Summary

In this chapter, you learned the basics of image formats and how you can include them in your HTML documents. You learned the benefits and drawbacks of each supported format, as well as how to include and format them in an HTML document.

Continue to read the chapters in order if you are new to HTML, learning each aspect of creating Web documents. If you are not new to HTML and you are particularly interested in media (images, video, and so on), check out Chapter 14.

✦　　✦　　✦

Links

Links are what make the World Wide Web web-like. One document on the Web can link to several other documents, and those in turn to other documents, and so forth. The resulting structure, if diagramed, resembles a web. The comparison has spawned many "web" terms commonly used on the Internet—electronic robots that scour the Web are known as "spiders," and so on.

Besides linking to other documents, you can link to just about any content that can be delivered over the Internet—media files, e-mail addresses, FTP sites, and so on.

This chapter covers the ins and outs of linking to references inside and outside the current document and how to provide more information about the relationship of your documents to others on the Web.

What's in a Link?

Web links have two basic components, the link and the target.

+ The link is the text in the main document that *refers* to another document.

+ The target is the document (or particular location in the document) to which the link leads.

For example, suppose a site on the Web reviews software. Each review includes a link to the manufacturer's Web site. Such an arrangement would resemble the diagram shown in Figure 7-1.

The link has two components: a descriptor and a reference to the target. The target is a document that can be delivered via the Internet. In the preceding example, the review might list the manufacturer's name as the descriptor and the actual Web URL would be the reference. Both are specified in the anchor tag (<a>), as follows:

```
<a href="url_of_target">descriptor_text</a>
```

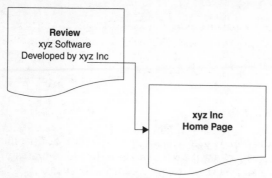

Figure 7-1: The relationship of documents on the Web via links—the user clicks the link in the review document to reach the xyz Inc. home page.

The target reference is specified via the `href` attribute, and the descriptor appears between the start and end anchor tags. For example, if the manufacturer is Acme Computers and its Web site is `acme.example.com`, the anchor tag would resemble the following:

```
<a href="http://www.example.com">Acme Computer's Web Site</a>
```

If you don't give the name of a document in the link, the Web server (in this case, `www.example.com`) will send the defined top-level document (known as an index document)—typically, this document is named `index.html` or `home.html`. If such a document doesn't exist or one has not been defined for the server, an error will be returned to the client browser.

The text "Acme Computer's Web Site" would be highlighted in the document to show it is a link. The default highlight for a link is a different color font and underlined, though you will see how to change the highlight later in this chapter.

Note According to the "strict" HTML standard, anchor links need to be placed within block elements (headings, paragraphs, and so on).

As mentioned in the introduction to this chapter, you can link to other things besides HTTP documents. All you need is the URL of the item you wish to link to, and the protocol necessary to reach the item. For example, if you wanted to link to a document on an FTP site, you could use an anchor tag similar to the following:

```
<a href="ftp://ftp.example.com/pub/example.zip">Zipped copy of the files</a>
```

Note that the protocol is specified (`ftp:` instead of `http:`), and the server name is specified (`ftp.example.com`), as is the path and filename (`/pub` and `example.zip`). A similar method can be used to link to an e-mail address (`href="mailto:someone@example.com"`). Clicking such a link will generally spawn the user's e-mail client ready to send an e-mail to the address specified.

Note The rest of this chapter concentrates on linking to other HTML documents on the Web. However, all the concepts addressed apply when linking to other content types.

Linking to a Web Page

The most popular link style on the Web is a link to another Web page or document. Such a link, when activated, causes the target page to load in the client browser. Control is then transferred to the target page—its scripts run, and so on.

To link to another page on the Internet, you simply specify the target's URL in the anchor tag. Suppose you want to link to the products page of the Acme Web site and the page is named `products.html` and resides in the `products` directory on the Acme Web server. The `href` parameter of the link would be as follows:

```
http://www.example.com/products/products.html
```

Note that the URL (`http://acme.example.com`) contains the protocol, the server name, the directory name, and the filename. Figure 7-2 shows a breakdown of the various pieces of the URL.

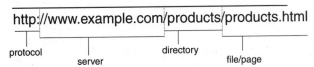

Figure 7-2: The various pieces of a URL.

In the case of this URL, the various pieces are separated by various key characters:

✦ The protocol is first, and ends with a colon (`http:`).

✦ The server name is next, prefaced with a double slash (`//www.example.com`).

✦ The directory (or directories) is next, separated with slashes (`/products/`).

✦ The filename of the page is last, separated from the directory by a slash (`products.html`).

Note The server name is actually two pieces, the server's name and the domain on which it resides. In the `www.example.com`, `www` is the server name and `example.com` is the domain.

There is a common misconception that all Web server names need to begin with `www`. Although `www` is a standard name for a Web server, the name can be almost anything. For example, the U.S.-based Web server for the Internet Movie Database (`imdb.com`) is `us.imdb.com`.

Absolute versus Relative Links

There are two types of URL styles, and therefore two link types, that you need to understand: absolute and relative. You have seen absolute links, where the URL used in the link provides the full path, including the protocol and full server address. These links are called *absolute* links because the URL itself is absolute—that is, it does not change no matter where the document in which it appears is kept.

The other type of link, a *relative* link, does not provide all of the details to the referenced page; hence, its address is treated as relative to the document where the link appears. Relative links are only useful for linking to other pages on the same Web site, because any reference off of the same site requires the remote server's name.

It's easier to understand the difference between the two types of links with an example. Suppose you are the Webmaster of `example.com`. You have several pages on the site, including the home page, a main products page, and hardware and software products pages. The home page is in the root directory of the server, while the product pages (all three) are in a products directory. The relative links back and forth between the pages are shown in Figures 7-3 and 7-4.

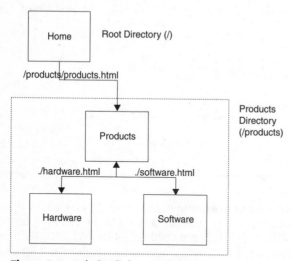

Figure 7-3: Relative links to subpages.

Note that you can use directory shortcuts to specify where the pages are:

✦ Starting a directory with a slash (/) references it as a subdirectory of the root directory.

✦ Starting a directory with a period and a slash (./) references it as a subdirectory of the current directory (the directory where the current page resides).

✦ Starting a directory with a double period and a slash (../) references it as a parent directory to the current directory.

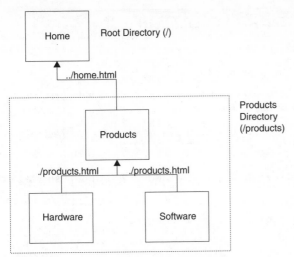

Figure 7-4: Relative links to parent pages.

Relative links are easier to maintain on sections of Web sites where the pages in that section never change relationships to one another. For example, in the case of the site shown in Figures 7-3 and 7-4, if the products pages move as a whole unit to another place on the site, the *relative* links between the product pages won't change. If the links were coded as absolute (for example, `http://www.example.com/products/hardware.html`), they would have to change.

Link Targets

Normally, links open the page they refer to in the active browser window, replacing the page currently displayed. However, you can control where the page opens using the `target` attribute in the link tag.

The `target` attribute has been deprecated in strict HTML. It appears here because most browsers still support the attribute and it can be useful. However, keep in mind that your documents will not validate against strict HTML if you use the `target` attribute.

The target attribute supports the values shown in Table 7-1.

	Table 7-1
	Target Attribute Values

Value	Description
_blank	Opens the linked document in a new browser window
_self	Opens the linked document in the same frame as the link

Continued

	Table 7-1 *(continued)*
Value	**Description**
_parent	Opens the linked document in the parent frameset
_top	Opens the linked document in the main browser window, replacing any and all frames present
name	Opens the linked document in the window with the specified name

For example, to open a linked document in a new window you would use a tag similar to the following:

```
<a href="http://www.example.com" target="_blank">
New Window</a>
```

Caution

The debate about whether you should *ever* open a new window is fierce. Most users are accustomed to all new windows being of the pop-up ad variety—and very unwelcome. However, from a user interface standpoint, new windows can be used very effectively if they are used like dialog boxes or new windows that an operating system spawns. In any case, you should make a habit of informing users when you are going to open a new window so you don't surprise them.

The last value listed for target, *name*, can also aid in the user interface experience, if used correctly. Certain methods of opening windows (such as the JavaScript window.open method) allow you to give a browser window a unique name. You can then use that name to push a linked document into that window. For example, the following code displays two links; the first opens a new, empty browser window named NEWS, and the second pushes the content at www.yahoo.com into the window:

```
<!DOCTYPE HTML PUBLIC "-//W3C//DTD HTML 4.01//EN"
   "http://www.w3.org/TR/html4/strict.dtd">
<html>
<head>
<script language="JavaScript">
function NewsWindow(){
  fin=window.open("","NEWS","width=400,height=400");
}
</script>
</head>
<body>
<p><a href="JavaScript:NewsWindow()">Open Window</a></p>
<p><a href="http://www.yahoo.com" target="NEWS">Fill Window</a></p>
</body>
</html>
```

Cross-Reference

For more information on JavaScript and the window.open method, refer to Chapter 25.

Link Titles

You can also title a link, using the `title` attribute in the anchor tag. This causes most current browsers to display the text of the title as a ToolTip when the mouse hovers over them. For example, the following link will cause Internet Explorer 6 to display "`Example.com`'s Web Site," as shown in Figure 7-5.

```
More information can be found <a
href="http://www.example.com" title=" Example.com's Web
Site">here</a>.
```

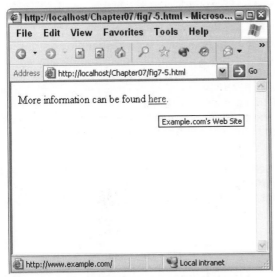

Figure 7-5: The title attribute causes a ToolTip display when the mouse hovers over the link.

You can use this feature to give the user more information on the link, before they click it.

Keyboard Shortcuts and Tab Order

In the modern world of computers it is easy to make assumptions about users, their hardware, and capabilities. Several years ago, no one would have dreamt of delivering rich, multimedia content over the Web. Today, however, it is easy to assume that everyone is using the latest browser, on a high-end computer, across a broadband connection.

However, that isn't always the case. In fact, some users who visit your site may not even have a mouse to aid in browsing. The reason could be a physical handicap, a text-only browser, or just a fondness for using the keyboard. It is important to accommodate these users by adding additional methods to access links on your page.

Keyboard shortcuts

Each link can be assigned a shortcut key for easy keyboard-only access using the accesskey attribute with the anchor tab. The accesskey attribute takes one letter as its value, the letter that can be used to access the link. For example, the following link defines "C" as the access key:

```
<a href="http://www.example.com" accesskey="C">Table of
<b>C</b>ontents</a>
```

Note that different browsers and different operating systems handle access keys differently. Some browser and operating system combinations require special keys to be pressed with the defined access key. For example, Windows users on Internet Explorer need to hold the Alt key while they press the access key. Note, also, that different browsers handle the actual access of the link differently—some browsers will activate the link as soon as the access key is pressed, while others only select the link, requiring another key to be pressed to actually activate the link.

Tip

Keyboard shortcuts won't help your users if you don't give them a clue as to what the shortcut is. In the example earlier in this section, the defined shortcut key ("C") was used in the link text and highlighted using the bold font attribute.

Tab order

It will also help your users if you define a tab order for the links in your document. As with most graphical operating systems, the tab key can be used to move through elements of the interface, including links.

Typically, the default tab order is the same as the order that the links appear in the document. However, upon occasion, you might wish to change the order using the tabindex attribute. The tabindex attribute takes an integer as its value; that integer is used to define the tab sequence in the document. For example, the following document switches the tab order of the second and third links:

```
<!DOCTYPE HTML PUBLIC "-//W3C//DTD HTML 4.01//EN"
    "http://www.w3.org/TR/html4/strict.dtd">
<html>
<head>
<title>Tab Ordered Document</title>
</head>
<body>
<p>This is the <a href="http://www.example.com"
    tabindex="1">first link</a>.</p>
<p>This is the <a href="http://www.example.com"
    tabindex="3">second link</a>.</p>
```

```
<p>This is the <a href="http://www.example.com"
    tabindex="2">third link</a>.</p>
</body>
</html>
```

Note As with most interface elements in HTML, the browser defines how `tabindex` is implemented and how tabbed elements are accessed.

Creating an Anchor

Anchor tags have another use; they can be used as a marker in the current document to provide a bookmark that can be directly linked to. For example, a large document might have several sections. You can place links at the top of the document (or in a special navigation frame) to each section, allowing the user to easily access each section.

To create an anchor in a document, you use the anchor tag with the name attribute. For example, the following code creates a `chapter01` anchor at the "Chapter 1" heading:

```
<h1><a name="chapter1">Chapter 1</a></h1>
```

To link to the anchor you use a standard link, but add the anchor name to the end of the URL in the link. To identify the name as an anchor, you separate it from the rest of the URL with a pound sign (#). For example, suppose the Chapter 1 anchor appears in the document `book.html`. To link to the Chapter 1 anchor, you could use the following code:

```
<a href="http://www.example.com/book.html#chapter1">Go to Chapter 1</a>
```

Note Because the URL in the link tag can contain the server and document names as well as the anchor name, you can link to anchors in the same document or any accessible document. If you are linking to an anchor in the same document, you can use a shortcut form of the URL, using only the pound sign and the anchor name as the URL.

In addition to using the anchor tag for bookmarks, you can link to a block element's `id` attribute. For example, if Chapter 1 appears inside an `<h1>` tag, you can set the `<h1>` tag's id attribute to Chapter1 and omit the anchor link altogether, as shown in the following code example:

```
<h1 id="chapter1">Chapter 1</h1>
```

Choosing Link Colors

It is important that links stand out from the normal content in your documents. They need to be recognizable by users. Each link has four different status modes:

✦ *Link*—The standard link in the document that is not active, nor visited (see other modes).

✦ *Active*—The target of the link is active in another browser window.

✦ *Visited*—The target of the link has been previously visited (typically, this means the target can be found in the browser's cache).

✦ *Hover*—The mouse pointer is over the link.

Each of these modes should be colored differently so the user can tell the status of each link on your page. The standard colors of each link status are as follows:

✦ *Link*—Blue, underlined text

✦ *Active*—Red, underlined text

✦ *Visited*—Purple, underlined text

✦ *Hover*—No change in the appearance of the link (remains blue, red, or purple)

Note As with other presentation attributes in HTML, the browser plays a significant role in setting link colors and text decorations. Most browsers follow the color scheme outlined in this section, but there are browsers that don't conform to this scheme.

To change the text color and other attributes of links, you can modify the properties of each type of anchor tag. For example, the following style, when used in an HTML document, sets the default visited link text to bold and yellow:

```
a:visited { color: yellow; font-weight: bold; }
```

Tip Setting the properties of the anchor tag without specifying a mode changes all of the link modes to the characteristics of the style. For example, this style sets all types of links (link, active, visited) to red:

```
a { color: red; }
```

So why would you want to change the color of links in your document? One reason would be that the normal text of your document is the same color as the default link. For example, if your text is blue, you probably want to change the default color of the links in your document to better enable users to recognize them.

It is a good idea to define all of the link attributes instead of haphazardly defining only one or two of the link status colors. The following styles define each type of link, ensuring they appear how you want in the document:

```
a:link { color: #003366;
  font-family:verdana, palatino, arial, sans-serif;
  font-size:10pt;  text-decoration: underline; }
a:visited {color: #D53D45;
  font-family:verdana, palatino, arial, sans-serif;
  font-size:10pt;  text-decoration: underline; }
```

```
a:active {color: #D53D00;
  font-family:verdana, palatino, arial, sans-serif;
  font-size:10pt;  font-weight: bold;
  text-decoration: underline; }
a:hover  {color: #D53D45;
  font-family:verdana, palatino, arial, sans-serif;
  font-size:10pt;  text-decoration: none; }
```

Note the redundancy in the styles—there are only subtle changes in each style. You should strive to eliminate such redundancy whenever possible, relying instead upon the cascade effect of styles. You could effectively shorten each style by defining the anchor tag's attributes by itself, and defining only the attributes that are different for each variant:

```
a { color: #003366;
  font-family:verdana, palatino, arial, sans-serif;
  font-size:10pt; text-decoration: underline; }
a:visited {color: #D53D45; }
a:active {color: #D53D00; font-weight: bold; }
a:hover {color: #D53D45; text-decoration: none; }
```

Link Target Details

There are a host of other attributes that you can add to your anchor tags to describe the form of the target being linked to, the relationship between the current document and the target, and more.

Table 7-2 lists these descriptive attributes and their possible values.

Table 7-2 Link Target Details		
Attribute	**Meaning**	**Value(s)**
Charset	The character encoding of the target	char_encoding for example, "ISO 8859-1"
Hreflang	The base language of the target	language_code for example, "en-US"
Rel	The relationship between the current document and the target	alternate designates stylesheet start next prev contents

Continued

Table 7-2 (continued)		
Attribute	**Meaning**	**Value(s)**
		index
		glossary
		copyright
		chapter
		section
		subsection
		appendix
		help
		bookmark
Rev	The relationship between the target and the current document	alternate
		designates
		stylesheet
		start
		next
		prev
		contents
		index
		glossary
		copyright
		chapter
		section
		subsection
		appendix
		help
		bookmark
Type	The MIME type of the target	Any valid MIME type

An example of how the relationship attributes (rel, rev) can be used is shown in the following code snippet:

```
<!DOCTYPE HTML PUBLIC "-//W3C//DTD HTML 4.01//EN"
    "http://www.w3.org/TR/html4/strict.dtd">
<html>
<head>
<title>Chapter 10</title>
</head>
<body>
<p><a href="contents.html" rel="chapter" rev="contents">Table of
Contents</a></p>
<p><a href="chapter9.html" rel="next" rev="prev">Chapter 9</a></p>
<p><a href="chapter11.html" rel="prev" rev="next">Chapter 11</a></p>
...
```

The anchor tags define the relationships between the chapters (next, previous) and the table of contents (chapter, contents).

The Link Tag

You can use the link tag to provide additional information on a document's relationship to other documents, independently of whether the current document actually links to other documents or not. The link tag supports the same attributes as the anchor tag, but with a slightly different syntax:

✦ The link tag does not encapsulate any text.

✦ The link tag does not have an ending tag.

For example, the following code could be used in chapter10.html to define that document's relationship to chapter9.html and chapter11.html:

```
<link href="chapter9.html" rel="next" rev="prev" />
<link href="chapter11.html" rel="prev" rev="next" />
```

The link tag does not result in any visible text being rendered, but can be used by user agents to provide additional navigation or other user-interface tools.

Another important use of the link tag is to provide alternate content for search engines. For example, the following link references a French version of the current document (chapter10.html):

```
<LINK lang="fr" rel="alternate"        hreflang="fr"
        href="http://www.example.com/chapter10-fr.html" />
```

Other relationship attribute values (start, contents, and so on) can likewise be used to provide relevant information on document relationships to search engines.

Summary

This chapter covered links—what they are and how to use them to reference other content on the Web. You learned how to construct a link and what attributes are available to the anchor and link tags. You also learned how to define relationships between your document and other documents, and why this is important.

From here, you should progress through the next few chapters, familiarizing yourself with the other various pieces of an HTML document.

✦   ✦   ✦

Text

Although the modern-day Web is a haven of multimedia, text is still vitally important. Only through text can some messages be succinctly communicated. Even then, diversity in text can help further clarify a message. For example, emphasizing one word with bold or italic font can change the tone and meaning of a sentence.

This chapter discusses how to format elements inside of block elements (words or sentences inside of paragraphs).

Methods of Text Control

There are various means to control the look and formatting of text in your documents. It should come as no surprise that the more direct methods—`<font>` tags and the like—have been deprecated in favor of CSS controls in HTML 4.01 and XHTML. The following sections cover the various means possible for historical and completeness purposes.

Tip Although it is sometimes easier to drop a direct formatting tag into text, resist the urge and use styles instead. Your documents will be more flexible and more standards compliant.

The `<font>` tag

The `<font>` tag enables you to directly affect the size and color of text. Intuitively, the `size` attribute is used to change the size of text, and the `color` attribute is used to change the color. The size of the text is specified by a number, from 1-7, or by signed number (also 1-7). In the latter case, the size change is relative to the size set by the `<basefont>` tag. The `<basefont>` tag has one attribute, size, which can be set to a number, 1-7.

Note Default font type and size is left up to the user agent. No standard correlation exists between the size used in a `<font>` tag and the actual font size used by the user agent. As such, the default size of the font (1-7) varies between user agents.

For example, if you wanted larger text in a red color, you could use a tag similar to the following:

```
<font size="+3" color="red">this is larger, red text</font>
```

Note that using "+3" for the size increases the text within the tag by a factor of 3 from the base font size.

Emphasis and other text tags

You can use a handful of tags to emphasize portions of text. Although these tags have not been deprecated in HTML 4.01, it is strongly recommended that you make use of CSS instead.

Table 8-1 lists the emphasis tags and their use. A sample of their use is shown in Figure 8-1.

Table 8-1 Emphasis Tags	
Tag	**Use**
<cite>	Citation
<code>	Code text
<dfn>	Definition term
<em>	Emphasized text
<kbd>	Keyboard text
<samp>	Sample text
<strong>	Strongly emphasized text
<var>	Variable(s)

The creation and adoption of these tags seems somewhat haphazard. As such, the support for the tags is not standard across user agents—you may not be able to tell the difference between text coded with <cite> or <em>, for example.

CSS text control

CSS provides several different properties to control text. Table 8-2 lists some of the more popular properties.

As you can see, CSS offers a bit more control over your text, allowing you to specify actual fonts and actual font sizes. However, the advantage to using CSS properties over hardcoded tags is not found in the list of available properties, but in the flexibility in formatting and effecting later changes. For example, suppose you were

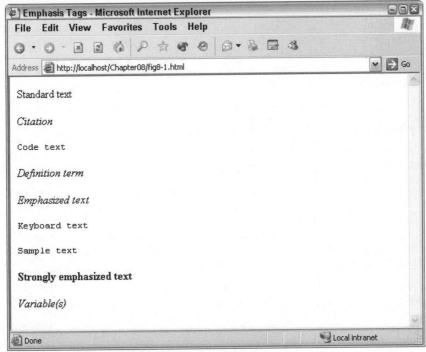

Figure 8-1: An example of text using emphasis tags.

Table 8-2
CSS Text Properties

Property	Values	Use
color	Color	Change the color of text
font	font-style font-variant font-weight font-size	Shortcut property for setting font style, variant, weight, and size
font-family	family-name	Set the font family (face)
font-size	font-size	Set the font size
font-stretch	normal | wider | narrower | ultra-condensed | extra-condensed | condensed | semi-condensed | semi-expanded | expanded | extra-expanded | ultra-expanded	Expand or compress the letter spacing

Continued

Table 8-2 *(continued)*		
Property	**Values**	**Use**
font-style	Normal | italic | oblique	Set font to italic
font-variant	Normal | small-caps	Set small-caps
font-weight	Normal | bold | bolder | lighter	Set font to bold
text-decoration	none | underline | overline | line-through | blink	Set under/overlining
text-transform	none | capitalize | uppercase | lowercase	Transform font capitalization

creating documentation for a programming language and wanted to format all reserved words a particular way—perhaps in a slightly larger, red, bold font. Using tags, the code would resemble the following:

```
<p>The <font size="+1" color="red"><b>date</b></font>
function can be used to...
```

Later, you might decide that the red color is too much emphasis, and larger, bold text is enough. You must then change every <font> tag used around reserved words.

Suppose, instead, that you used CSS, as shown in the following code:

```
<head>
  <style type="text/css">
    .reservedword { font: 14pt bold; color: red }
  </style>
</head>
<body>
<p>The <span class="reservedword">date</span> function can
be used to...
```

If you later decided to change the formatting of reserved words, you would only have to make one change to the style definition at the top of the document. (If you used an external style sheet, that one change could change an unlimited number of documents that used the sheet.)

Bold and Italic Text

Two surviving text emphasis tags are bold and italic. Their effect on text is, as expected, to make it bold or italic, as shown in the following code example and in Figure 8-2:

```
<p>This is normal text.</p>
<p><b>This is bold text.</b></p>
<p><i>This is italic text.</i></p>
```

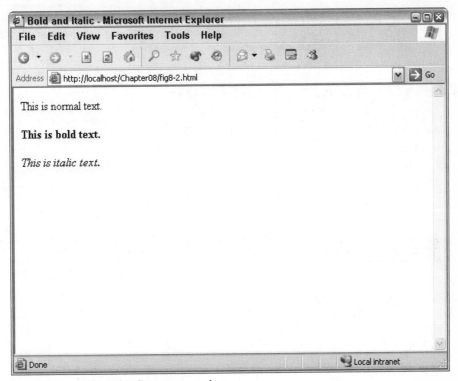

Figure 8-2: Bold and italic tags at work.

Note Not every font has a bold and/or italic variant. When possible, the user agent will substitute a similar font when bold or italic is asked for but not available. However, not all user agents are font-savvy. In short, your mileage with these tags may vary depending on the user agent being used.

For the same reasons mentioned elsewhere, it is advisable to use CSS instead of hardcoded bold and italic tags.

Monospace (Typewriter) Fonts

Another text tag that has survived deprecation is the teletype (`<tt>`), or monospaced, tag. This tag tells the user agent that certain text should be rendered in a monospaced font. Such uses include reserved words in documentation, code listings, and so on. The following code shows an example of the teletype tag in use:

```
<p>Consider using the <tt>date</tt> function instead.</p>
```

This tag is named for the teletype terminals used with the first computers, which were only capable of printing in a monspaced font.

Tip

Again, the use of styles is preferred over individual inline tags. If you need text rendered in a monospace font, consider directly specifying the font parameters using styles instead of relying upon the <tt> tag.

Superscripts and Subscripts

There are two tags, <sup> and <sub>, for formatting text in superscript and subscript. The following code shows an example of each tag, the output of which is shown in Figure 8-3.

```
<p>This is normal text.</p>
<p>This is the 16<sup>th</sup> day of the month.</p>
<p>Water tanks are clearly marked as H<sub>2</sub>O.</p>
```

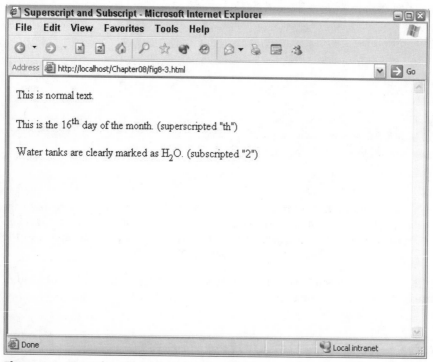

Figure 8-3: Examples of superscript and subscript.

Abbreviations

You can use the abbreviation tag (<abbr>) to mark abbreviations and, optionally, give readers the expansion of the acronym used. For example, you could use this tag with acronyms such as HTML:

```
<abbr title="Hypertext Markup Language">HTML</abbr>
```

Note that the expansion of the abbreviation is placed in the `<abbr>` tag's `title` attribute. Some user agents will display the value of the `title` attribute when the mouse/pointer is over the abbreviation.

Marking Editorial Insertions and Deletions

To further strengthen the bond between HTML documents and printed material, the insert and delete tags have been added to HTML. Both tags are used for redlining documents—that is, a visually marked-up document showing suggested changes.

For example, the following paragraph has been marked up with text to be inserted (underlined) and deleted (strikethrough). The output of this code is shown in Figure 8-4.

```
<p>Peter <del>are</del><ins>is</ins> correct, the proposal
from Acme is lacking a few <del>minor </del>details.</p>
```

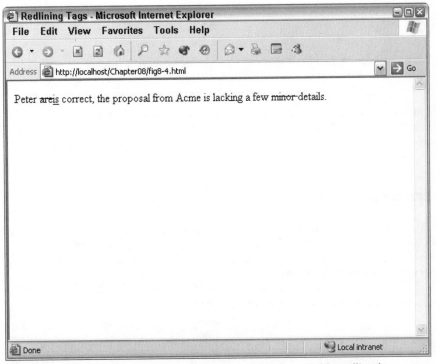

Figure 8-4: The `<ins>` and `<del>` tags can provide for suitable redlined documents.

Note that the underline tag (`<u>`) has been deprecated in favor of the `<ins>` tag.

Grouping Inline Elements with the <span> Tag

When using CSS for text formatting, you need a method to code text with the appropriate styles. If you are coding block elements, you can use the <div> tag to delimit the block, but with smaller chunks (inline elements) you should use <span>.

The <span> tag is used like any other inline tag (<b>, <i>, <tt>, and so on), surrounding the text/elements that it should affect. You use the style or class attribute to define what style should be applied. For example, both of the following paragraph samples would render the word red in red text:

```
<head>
  <style type="text/css">
    .redtext { color: red; }
  </style>
</head>
<body>
<!-- Paragraph 1, using direct style coding -->
<p>We should paint the document <span style="color: red">
red</span>.</p>

<!-- Paragraph 2, using a style class -->
<p>We should paint the document <span class="redtext">
red</span>.</p>
</body>
```

Of the two methods, the use of the class attribute is preferred over using the style attribute because class avoids directly (and individually) coding the text. Instead, it references a separate style definition that can be repurposed with other text.

Summary

This chapter covered the formatting of inline elements. You learned two distinct methods (direct tags and styles) and the various tags to supplement textual formatting. Keep in mind that you should use <div> or other block tags to format larger sections of a document.

✦   ✦   ✦

Special Characters

Although its roots are firmly grounded in plain text, HTML needs to be able to display a wide range of characters—many that cannot be typed on a regular keyboard. Language is rich with extended and accented characters, and there are many reserved characters in HTML.

The HTML specification defines many entities—specific codes—to insert special characters. This chapter introduces you to the concept of entities and lists the various entities available for use.

Note The W3C Web site is a good source of information about entities. The HTML 4 entities are listed at `http://www.w3.org/TR/html4/sgml/entities.html`.

Understanding Character Encodings

Character encoding at its simplest is the method that maps binary data to their proper character equivalents. For example, in a standard, U.S. English document character, 65 is matched to a capital A.

Most English fonts follow the American Standard Code for Information Interchange (ASCII) coding. So when a Web designer inserts a capital A, he is assured that the user will see the A.

There are, of course, plenty of caveats to that statement. The document must be encoded as English, the specified font must also be encoded as English, and the user agent must not interfere with either encoding.

Note Document encoding is typically passed to the user agent in the `Content-Type` HTTP header, such as the following:

```
Content-Type: text/html; charset=EN-US
```

However, some user agents don't correctly handle encoding in the HTTP header. If you need to explicitly declare a document's encoding, you should use an appropriate meta tag in your document, similar to the following:

```
<meta http-equiv="Content-Type" content="text/html;
charset=EN-US">
```

So what happens when any of the necessary pieces are different or changed from what they were intended to be? For example, what if your document is viewed in Japan, where the requisite user agent font is in Japanese instead of English? In those cases, the document encoding helps ensure that the right characters are used.

Most fonts have international characters encoded in them as well as their native character set. When a non-native encoding is specified, the user agent tries to use the appropriate characters in the appropriate font. If appropriate characters cannot be found in the current font, alternate fonts can be used.

However, none of this can be accomplished if the document does not declare its encoding. Without knowing the document encoding the user agent simply uses the character that corresponds to the character position arriving in the data stream. For example, a capital A gets translated to whatever character is 65th in the font the user agent is using.

Special Characters

Several characters mean special things in HTML and are used for special purposes by user agents. For example, the less than symbol (<) signals the beginning of a tag. As such, you cannot use that character in normal text. Instead, you must use an equivalent code, or entity. When the user agent renders the document, the entity is rendered as the correct character.

Entities in HTML begin with an ampersand (&), end with a semicolon (;), and contain a numeric code or mnemonic phrase in between.

Numerically coded entities can use decimal or hexadecimal numbers. Either must be preceded by a pound sign (#). Hexadecimal numbers also need to be preceded by an x. A nonbreaking space is character number 160. The following entity in decimal references this character:

```
 
```

The following entity in hexadecimal also reference character 160:

```
 
```

Mnemonic entities use a few characters to specify the entity—the characters usually are an abbreviation or mnemonic representation of the character they represent. For example, the following entity represents a nonbreaking space:

```
 
```

A few other essential entities are listed in Table 9-1.

Table 9-1 Essential Entities		
Decimal Entity	*Mnemonic Entity*	*Character*
&#34;	&quot;	Double quote mark
&#38;	&amp;	Ampersand
&#60;	&lt;	Less than symbol
&#62;	&gt;	Greater than symbol
		Nonbreaking space

Additional special-use characters are covered in the following sections.

En and Em Spaces and Dashes

There are two additional types of spaces and dashes, en and em spaces and dashes. The characters got their name from their relative size—en characters are as wide as a capital N, while em characters are as wide as a capital M.

These characters have specific uses in the English language:

✦ *En spaces* are used when you need a larger space than a normal space provides. For example, en spaces can be used between street numbers and street names (123 Main) for clarity.

✦ *Em spaces* are used to separate elements such as dates and headlines, figure numbers and captions, and so on. (Figure 2-1 A simple prompt)

✦ *En dashes* are used instead of hyphens in constructs such as phone numbers, element numbering, and so on.

✦ *Em dashes* are used grammatically when you need to divide thoughts in a sentence. (The excuse was nonsense—at least that's how it seemed to me)

Table 9-2 lists the entities for en/em elements.

Table 9-2 En and Em Entities		
Decimal Entity	*Mnemonic Entity*	*Character*
		En space
		Em space
&#8211;	&ndash;	En dash
&#8212;	&mdash;	Em dash

Copyright and Trademark Symbols

Copyright and trademark symbols are special symbols that indicate a legal relationship between individuals (or companies) and text.

The Copyright symbol (©) is used to indicate that someone has asserted certain rights on written material—text included with the symbol usually indicates which rights. For example, many written works include the following phrase as a copyright: "Copyright © 2003. All rights reserved."

The trademark and registered marks (™ and ®) are used to indicate that a particular word or phrase is trademarked—that is, marked (trademarked) or registered for unique use by an individual or company. For example, "Windows" is a registered trademark of Microsoft, and "For Dummies" is a registered trademark of Wiley.

Note Trademark and registered trademark symbols are typically superscripted after the word or phrase to which they apply. As such, you should generally use each within superscripted (`<sup>`) tags.

Table 9-3 lists the entities for Copyright, trademark, and registered symbols.

Table 9-3		
Copyright, Trademark, and Registered Entities		
Decimal Entity	*Mnemonic Entity*	*Character*
&#169;	&copy;	Copyright symbol
&#174;	&reg;	Registered trademark symbol

Note that there are fonts that include the trademark symbol (™). However, because the symbol is actually two characters, it is included as an exception, not a rule. As such, you shouldn't rely upon an entity to display the symbol, but specific small and superscript font coding such as the following:

```
<small><sup>TM</sup></small>
```

Note Use of styles is generally preferred over the use of the `<small>` tag.

Currency Symbols

There are many currency symbols, including the U.S. dollar ($), the English pound (£), the European euro (€), and the Japanese yen (¥). There is also the general currency symbol (¤). Table 9-4 lists many of the most common currency symbols.

Table 9-4		
Currency Entities		
Decimal Entity	*Mnemonic Entity*	*Character*
&#162;	&cent;	The cent symbol (¢)
&#163;	&pound;	English pound
&#164;	&curren;	General currency
&#165;	&yen;	Japanese yen
&#8364;	&euro;	European euro

Note that the dollar symbol ($) is typically ASCII character 24 (in U.S. fonts) and can be accessed directly from the keyboard.

"Real" Quotation Marks

Real quotation marks, used in publishing, cannot be typed on a standard keyboard. The quote marks available on the keyboard (" and ') are straight quotes; that is, they are small, superscripted, vertical lines.

Quote marks used in publishing typically resemble the numbers 6 and 9—that is, dots with a serif leading off of them. For example, the following sentence is set off with real quote marks:

"This sentence is a real quote."

The opening quote marks resemble the number 6, closing quote marks resemble the number 9. Table 9-5 lists the entities for real quotes.

Table 9-5		
Quote Mark and Apostrophe Entities		
Decimal Entity	*Mnemonic Entity*	*Character*
&#8216;	&lsquo;	Left/Opening single-quote
&#8217;	&rsquo;	Right/Closing single-quote and apostrophe
&#8220;	&ldquo;	Left/Opening double-quote
&#8221;	&rdquo;	Right/Closing double-quote

Arrows

A variety of arrow symbols are available as entities. Table 9-6 lists these entities.

Table 9-6 Arrow Entities		
Decimal Entity	**Mnemonic Entity**	**Character**
&#8592;	&larr;	Leftwards arrow
&#8593;	&uarr;	Upwards arrow
&#8594;	&rarr;	Rightwards arrow
&#8595;	&darr;	Downwards arrow
&#8596;	&harr;	Left right arrow
&#8629;	&crarr ;	Downwards arrow with corner leftwards
&#8656;	&lArr;	Leftwards double arrow
&#8657;	&uArr;	Upwards double arrow
&#8658;	&rArr;	Rightwards double arrow
&#8659;	&dArr;	Downwards double arrow
&#8660;	&hArr;	Left right double arrow

Accented Characters

There are many accented character entities available in the HTML standard. These characters can be used in words such as *résumé*. Table 9-7 lists the accented character entities.

Table 9-7 Accented Character Entities		
Decimal Entity	**Mnemonic Entity**	**Character**
&#192;	&Agrave;	Latin capital letter A with grave
&#193;	&Aacute;	Latin capital letter A with acute
&#194;	&Acirc;	Latin capital letter A with circumflex
&#195;	&Atilde;	Latin capital letter A with tilde
&#196;	&Auml;	Latin capital letter A with diaeresis

Decimal Entity	Mnemonic Entity	Character
&#197;	&Aring;	Latin capital letter A with ring above
&#198;	&AElig;	Latin capital letter AE
&#199;	&Ccedil;	Latin capital letter C with cedilla
&#200;	&Egrave;	Latin capital letter E with grave
&#201;	&Eacute;	Latin capital letter E with acute
&#202;	&Ecirc;	Latin capital letter E with circumflex
&#203;	&Euml;	Latin capital letter E with diaeresis
&#204;	&Igrave;	Latin capital letter I with grave
&#205;	&Iacute;	Latin capital letter I with acute
&#206;	&Icirc;	Latin capital letter I with circumflex
&#207;	&Iuml;	Latin capital letter I with diaeresis
&#208;	&ETH;	Latin capital letter ETH
&#209;	&Ntilde;	Latin capital letter N with tilde
&#210;	&Ograve;	Latin capital letter O with grave
&#211;	&Oacute;	Latin capital letter O with acute
&#212;	&Ocirc;	Latin capital letter O with circumflex
&#213;	&Otilde;	Latin capital letter O with tilde
&#214;	&Ouml;	Latin capital letter O with diaeresis
&#216;	&Oslash;	Latin capital letter O with stroke
&#217;	&Ugrave;	Latin capital letter U with grave
&#218;	&Uacute;	Latin capital letter U with acute
&#219;	&Ucirc;	Latin capital letter U with circumflex
&#220;	&Uuml;	Latin capital letter U with diaeresis
&#221;	&Yacute;	Latin capital letter Y with acute
&#222;	&THORN;	Latin capital letter THORN
&#223;	&szlig;	Latin small letter sharp s = ess-zed
&#224;	&agrave;	Latin small letter a with grave
&#225;	&aacute;	Latin small letter a with acute
&#226;	&acirc;	Latin small letter a with circumflex
&#227;	&atilde;	Latin small letter a with tilde
&#228;	&auml;	Latin small letter a with diaeresis

Continued

Table 9-7 *(continued)*

Decimal Entity	Mnemonic Entity	Character
&#229;	&aring;	Latin small letter a with ring above
&#230;	&aelig;	Latin small letter ae
&#231;	&ccedil;	Latin small letter c with cedilla
&#232;	&egrave;	Latin small letter e with grave
&#233;	&eacute;	Latin small letter e with acute
&#234;	&ecirc;	Latin small letter e with circumflex
&#235;	&euml;	Latin small letter e with diaeresis
&#236;	&igrave;	Latin small letter i with grave
&#237;	&iacute;	Latin small letter i with acute
&#238;	&icirc;	Latin small letter i with circumflex
&#239;	&iuml;	Latin small letter i with diaeresis
&#240;	&eth;	Latin small letter eth
&#241;	&ntilde;	Latin small letter n with tilde
&#242;	&ograve;	Latin small letter o with grave
&#243;	&oacute;	Latin small letter o with acute
&#244;	&ocirc;	Latin small letter o with circumflex
&#245;	&otilde;	Latin small letter o with tilde
&#246;	&ouml;	Latin small letter o with diaeresis
&#248;	&oslash;	Latin small letter o with stroke
&#249;	&ugrave;	Latin small letter u with grave
&#250;	&uacute;	Latin small letter u with acute
&#251;	&ucirc;	Latin small letter u with circumflex
&#252;	&uuml;	Latin small letter u with diaeresis
&#253;	&yacute;	Latin small letter y with acute
&#254;	&thorn;	Latin small letter thorn
&#255;	&yuml;	Latin small letter y with diaeresis

Greek and Mathematical Characters

Table 9-8 lists various Greek symbol entities.

Table 9-8
Greek Symbol Entities

Decimal Entity	Mnemonic Entity	Character
&#913;	&Alpha;	Greek capital letter alpha
&#914;	&Beta;	Greek capital letter beta
&#915;	&Gamma;	Greek capital letter gamma
&#916;	&Delta;	Greek capital letter delta
&#917;	&Epsilon;	Greek capital letter epsilon
&#918;	&Zeta;	Greek capital letter zeta
&#919;	&Eta;	Greek capital letter eta
&#920;	&Theta;	Greek capital letter theta
&#921;	&Iota;	Greek capital letter iota
&#922;	&Kappa;	Greek capital letter kappa
&#923;	&Lambda;	Greek capital letter lambda
&#924;	&Mu;	Greek capital letter mu
&#925;	&Nu;	Greek capital letter nu
&#926;	&Xi;	Greek capital letter xi
&#927;	&Omicron;	Greek capital letter omicron
&#928;	&Pi;	Greek capital letter pi
&#929;	&Rho;	Greek capital letter rho
&#931;	&Sigma;	Greek capital letter sigma
&#932;	&Tau;	Greek capital letter tau
&#933;	&Upsilon;	Greek capital letter upsilon
&#934;	&Phi;	Greek capital letter phi
&#935;	&Chi;	Greek capital letter chi
&#936;	&Psi;	Greek capital letter psi
&#937;	&Omega;	Greek capital letter omega
&#945;	&alpha;	Greek small letter alpha
&#946;	&beta;	Greek small letter beta
&#947;	&gamma;	Greek small letter gamma
&#948;	&delta;	Greek small letter delta
&#949;	&epsilon;	Greek small letter epsilon

Continued

Table 9-8 *(continued)*

Decimal Entity	Mnemonic Entity	Character
&#950;	&zeta;	Greek small letter zeta
&#951;	&eta;	Greek small letter eta
&#952;	&theta;	Greek small letter theta
&#953;	&iota;	Greek small letter iota
&#954;	&kappa;	Greek small letter kappa
&#955;	&lambda;	Greek small letter lambda
&#956;	&mu;	Greek small letter mu
&#957;	&nu;	Greek small letter nu
&#958;	&xi;	Greek small letter xi
&#959;	&omicron;	Greek small letter omicron
&#960;	&pi;	Greek small letter pi
&#961;	&rho;	Greek small letter rho
&#962;	&sigmaf;	Greek small letter final sigma
&#963;	&sigma;	Greek small letter sigma
&#964;	&tau;	Greek small letter tau
&#965;	&upsilon;	Greek small letter upsilon
&#966;	&phi;	Greek small letter phi
&#967;	&chi;	Greek small letter chi
&#968;	&psi;	Greek small letter psi
&#969;	&omega;	Greek small letter omega
&#977;	&thetasym;	Greek small letter theta symbol
&#978;	&upsih;	Greek upsilon with hook symbol
&#982;	&piv;	Greek pi symbol

Table 9-9 lists a variety of mathematical symbols.

Table 9-9
Mathematical Symbol Entities

Decimal Entity	Mnemonic Entity	Character/Symbol
&#215;	&times;	Multiplication sign
&#247;	&division;	Division sign

Decimal Entity	Mnemonic Entity	Character/Symbol
&#8704;	&forall;	For all
&#8706;	&part;	Partial differential
&#8707;	&exist;	There exists
&#8709;	&empty;	Empty set = null set = diameter
&#8711;	&nabla;	Nabla = backward difference
&#8712;	&isin;	Element of
&#8713;	&notin;	Not an element of
&#8715;	&ni;	Contains as member
&#8719;	&prod;	n-ary product = product sign
&#8721;	&sum;	n-ary summation
&#8722;	&minus;	Minus sign
&#8727;	&lowast;	Asterisk operator
&#8730;	&radic;	Square root = radical sign
&#8733;	&prop;	Proportional to
&#8734;	&infin;	Infinity
&#8736;	&ang;	Angle
&#8743;	&and;	Logical and = wedge
&#8744;	&or;	Logical or = vee
&#8745;	&cap;	Intersection = cap
&#8746;	&cup;	Union = cup
&#8747;	&int;	Integral
&#8756;	&there4;	Therefore
&#8764;	&sim;	Tilde operator = varies with = similar to
&#8773;	&cong;	Approximately equal to
&#8776;	&asymp;	Almost equal to = asymptotic to
&#8800;	&ne;	Not equal to
&#8801;	&equiv;	Identical to
&#8804;	&le;	Less than or equal to
&#8805;	&ge;	Greater than or equal to
&#8834;	&sub;	Subset of
&#8835;	&sup;	Superset of

Continued

Table 9-9 *(continued)*

Decimal Entity	Mnemonic Entity	Character/Symbol
&#8836;	&nsub;	Not a subset of
&#8838;	&sube;	Subset of or equal to
&#8839;	&supe;	Superset of or equal to
&#8853;	&oplus;	Circled plus = direct sum
&#8855;	&otimes;	Circled times = vector product
&#8869;	&perp;	Up tack = orthogonal to = perpendicular
&#8901;	&sdot;	Dot operator
&#8968;	&lceil;	Left ceiling
&#8969;	&rceil;	Right ceiling
&#8970;	&lfloor;	Left floor
&#8971;	&rfloor;	Right floor
&#9001;	&lang;	Left-pointing angle bracket
&#9002;	&rang;	Right-pointing angle bracket

Other Useful Entities

Table 9-10 lists other miscellaneous entities.

Table 9-10
Miscellaneous Entities

Decimal Entity	Mnemonic Entity	Character/Symbol
&#161;	&iexcl;	Inverted exclamation mark
&#166;	&brvbar;	Broken bar = broken vertical bar
&#167;	&sect;	Section sign
&#168;	&uml;	Diaeresis = spacing diaeresis
&#170;	&ordf;	Feminine ordinal indicator
&#171;	&laquo;	Left-pointing double angle quotation mark = left pointing guillemet
&#172;	&not;	Not sign
&#173;	&shy;	Soft hyphen = discretionary hyphen
&#175;	&macr;	Macron = spacing macron = overline = APL overbar

Decimal Entity	*Mnemonic Entity*	*Character/Symbol*
&#176;	&deg;	Degree sign
&#177;	&plusmn;	Plus-minus sign = plus-or-minus sign
&#178;	&sup2;	Superscript two = superscript digit two = squared
&#179;	&sup3;	Superscript three = superscript digit three = cubed
&#180;	&acute;	Acute accent = spacing acute
&#181;	&micro;	Micro sign
&#182;	&para;	Pilcrow sign = paragraph sign
&#183;	&middot;	Middle dot = Georgian comma = Greek middle dot
&#184;	&cedil;	Cedilla = spacing cedilla
&#185;	&sup1;	Superscript one = superscript digit one
&#186;	&ordm;	Masculine ordinal indicator
&#187;	&raquo;	Right-pointing double angle quotation mark = right pointing guillemet
&#188;	&frac14;	Vulgar fraction one quarter = fraction one quarter
&#189;	&frac12;	Vulgar fraction one half = fraction one half
&#190;	&frac34;	Vulgar fraction three quarters = fraction three quarters
&#191;	&iquest;	Inverted question mark = turned question mark
&#338;	&OElig;	Latin capital ligature OE
&#339;	&oelig;	Latin small ligature oe
&#352;	&Scaron;	Latin capital letter S with caron
&#353;	&scaron;	Latin small letter s with caron
&#376;	&Yuml;	Latin capital letter Y with diaeresis
&#710;	&circ;	Modifier letter circumflex accent
&#732;	&tilde;	Small tilde
		Thin space

Continued

Table 9-10 (continued)

Decimal Entity	Mnemonic Entity	Character/Symbol
&#8204;	&zwnj;	Zero width non-joiner
&#8205;	&zwj;	Zero width joiner
&#8206;	&lrm;	Left-to-right mark
&#8207;	&rlm;	Right-to-left mark
&#8218;	&sbquo;	Single low-9 quotation mark
&#8222;	&bdquo;	Double low-9 quotation mark
&#8224;	&dagger;	Dagger
&#8225;	&Dagger;	Double dagger
&#8240;	&permil;	Per mille sign
&#8249;	&lsaquo;	Single left-pointing angle quotation mark
&#8250;	&rsaquo;	Single right-pointing angle quotation mark

Summary

Although most of your Web documents will contain standard characters, there are times when you need accented or special characters as well. Taking character and language encoding into account, you can also fall back on HTML entities to insert these special characters.

✦   ✦   ✦

Tables

Tables are a powerful HTML tool that can be used in many ways. Developed originally to help communicate tabular data (usually scientific or academic-based data), tables are now used for many purposes, including actual page design. This chapter covers the basics of tables.

Parts of an HTML Table

An HTML table is made up of the following parts:

+ Rows
+ Columns
+ Header cells
+ Body cells
+ Caption
+ Header row(s)
+ Body row(s)
+ Footer row(s)

Figure 10-1 shows an example of an HTML table with the various parts labeled.

The table shown in Figure 10-1 is defined by the following code:

```
<!DOCTYPE HTML PUBLIC "-//W3C//DTD HTML 4.01//EN"
  "http://www.w3.org/TR/html4/strict.dtd">
<html>
<head>
  <title>A HTML Table</title>
</head>
<body>
  <table border="1">
    <caption>Table Caption</caption>
    <thead>
      <tr><td colspan="2">Table Header</td></tr>
    </thead>
```

```
            <tfoot>
              <tr><td colspan="2">Table Footer</td></tr>
            </tfoot>
            <tbody>
              <tr><th>Header Cell 1</th><th>Header Cell 2</th></tr>
              <tr><td>Body Cell 1</td><td>Body Cell 2</td></tr>
            </tbody>
          </table>
        </body>
        </html>
```

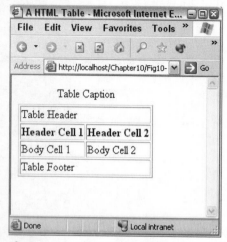

Figure 10-1: HTML table elements.

Many parts of the HTML table are optional—you only need to delimit the table (with `<table>` tags) and define rows (via `<tr>` tags) and columns (via `<td>` tags). Such a minimum table would resemble the following:

```
<!DOCTYPE HTML PUBLIC "-//W3C//DTD HTML 4.01//EN"
  "http://www.w3.org/TR/html4/strict.dtd">
<html>
<head>
  <title>A HTML Table</title>
</head>
<body>
  <table border="1">
      <tr><td>Body Cell 1</td><td>Body Cell 2</td></tr>
  </table>
</body>
</html>
```

Tip   It is possible to nest tables within one another. In fact, a particularly popular HTML technique—using tables for layout (covered in the next chapter)—depends on this ability. Tables must be nested within table cells (`<td>` tags). See the *Cells* section later in this chapter for more information on the `<td>` tag.

Table Width and Alignment

Typically, an HTML table expands to accommodate the contents of its cells. For example, consider the following code and the resulting tables shown in Figure 10-2:

```
<!DOCTYPE HTML PUBLIC "-//W3C//DTD HTML 4.01//EN"
  "http://www.w3.org/TR/html4/strict.dtd">
<html>
<head>
  <title>HTML Table Widths</title>
</head>
<body>
<p>
  Short Text Table<br />
  <table border="1">
      <tr><td>Short Text 1</td><td>Short Text 2</td></tr>
  </table>
</p>
<p>
  Longer Text Table<br />
  <table border="1">
      <tr><td>Longer Text 1</td><td>Longer Text 2</td></tr>
  </table>
</p>
</body>
</html>
```

Short Text Table

| Short Text 1 | Short Text 2 |

Longer Text Table

| Longer Text 1 | Longer Text 2 |

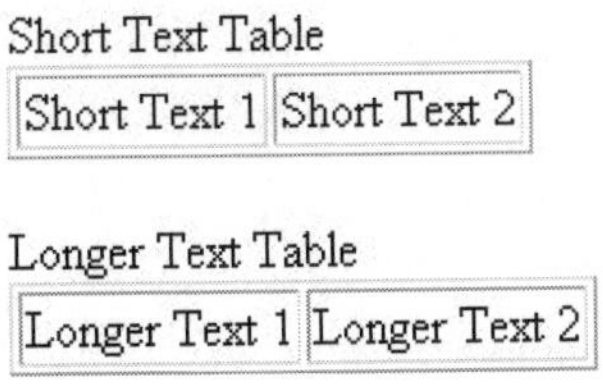

Figure 10-2: HTML tables expand to accommodate their content.

Once a table expands to the limits of its container object—whether the browser window, another table, or sized frame—the contents of the cells will wrap, as shown in Figure 10-3.

Sometimes you will want to manually size a table, either to fill a larger space or to constrain the table's size. Using the width attribute in the `<table>` tag you can set a table's size by specifying the table width in pixels or a percentage of the containing object.

For example, if you specify "50%" as in the following code, the table's width will be 50% of the containing object, as shown in Figure 10-4.

```
<!DOCTYPE HTML PUBLIC "-//W3C//DTD HTML 4.01//EN"
  "http://www.w3.org/TR/html4/strict.dtd">
```

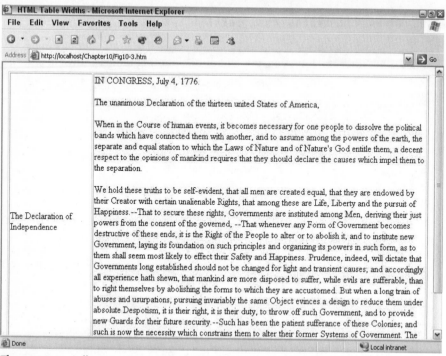

Figure 10-3: Cell contents wrap if a table cannot expand any further.

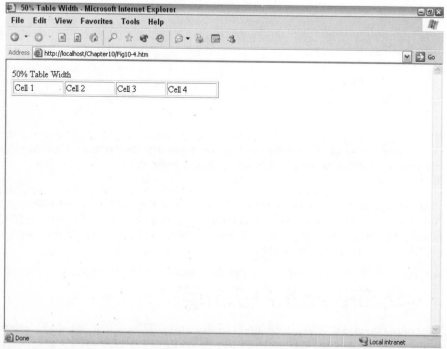

Figure 10-4: A 50% width table occupies 50% of the available width.

```
<html>
<head>
  <title>50% Table Width</title>
</head>
<body>
<p>
  50% Table Width<br />
  <table border="1" width="50%">
      <tr><td>Cell 1</td><td>Cell 2</td>
          <td>Cell 3</td><td>Cell 4</td></tr>
  </table>
</p>
</body>
</html>
```

Note Besides specifying the width of the full table, you can also specify the width of each column within the table, using width attributes in `<th>` and `<td>` tags, or specifying width within `<col>` or `<colgroup>` tags. These techniques are covered in the *"Cells"* and *"Grouping Columns"* sections later in this chapter.

Using a percentage in the width attribute allows the table to size itself dynamically to the size of its container. For example, if a table is set to 50%, the table will display as 50% of the browser window, whatever size the window happens to be.

If you need to specify the exact width of a table, you should specify the width of the table in pixels instead. For example, if you need a table to be 400 pixels wide, you would specify the table with the following tag:

```
<table width="400px">
```

However, what happens if the specified width exceeds the table's container object? If the container is scroll-bar enabled (like a browser window), horizontal scroll bars will appear to allow the user to scroll the entire table. For example, consider the table shown in Figure 10-5.

Note If the table's specified width exceeds the container's width, and the container is not scrollbar enabled, it is up to the browser to handle the table. Most browsers will resize the table to fit the width of its container.

The `<table>` tag also supports the `align` attribute, which controls where the table is positioned in the containing element. The `align` attribute supports `left`, `right`, and `center` values—the table's position is appropriately adjusted by the setting of this attribute. Note that this attribute has no visible effect on a table that occupies the full width of its container object.

Cell Spacing and Padding

There are two cell spacing options—padding and spacing—that you can control in your HTML tables. Cell spacing is the space between cells. Cell padding is the space

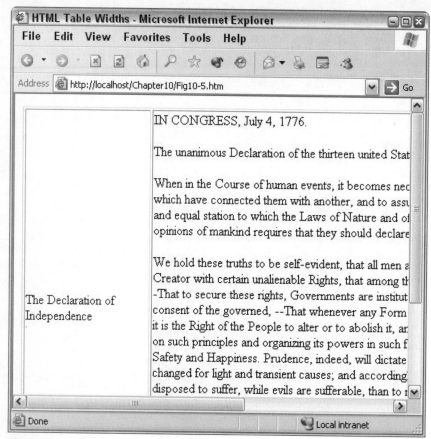

Figure 10-5: Tables too wide for their environment can get some help from scrollbars.

between the cell border and its contents. Refer back to Figure 10-1 for the relationship of cell padding and cell spacing to the table.

Cell spacing is controlled with the `cellspacing` attribute and can be specified in pixels or percentages. When specified by percentage, the browser uses half of the specified percentage for each side of the cell. The percentage is of the available space for the dimension, vertical or horizontal. This is illustrated in Figure 10-6, where the table's cell spacing is set to 20%.

Cell padding is controlled with the `cellpadding` attribute. As with cell spacing, you can specify padding in pixels or a percentage.

Tip

Keep in mind that cell spacing and cell padding can have a drastic effect on the available size for cell content. Increasing both spacing and padding decreases the cell content size.

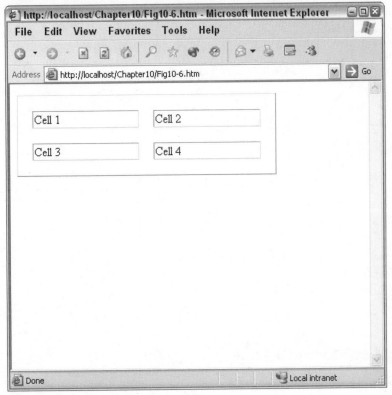

Figure 10-6: Cell spacing percentages.

Borders and Rules

The border around HTML tables and in between cells can be configured in many ways. The following sections cover the various ways you can configure table borders and rules.

Table borders

You can use the `border` attribute of the `<table>` tag to configure the outside border of the table. For example, consider the following code containing three tables and the resulting output in Figure 10-7.

```
<!DOCTYPE HTML PUBLIC "-//W3C//DTD HTML 4.01//EN"
  "http://www.w3.org/TR/html4/strict.dtd">
<html>
<head>
  <title>Table Outside Borders</title>
</head>
```

```
<body>
<p>
  No Borders<br />
  <table border="0">
      <tr><td>Cell 1</td><td>Cell 2</td></tr>
      <tr><td>Cell 3</td><td>Cell 4</td></tr>
  </table>
</p>
<p>
  Border = 1<br />
  <table border="1">
      <tr><td>Cell 1</td><td>Cell 2</td></tr>
      <tr><td>Cell 3</td><td>Cell 4</td></tr>
  </table>
</p>
<p>
  Border = 5<br />
  <table border="5">
      <tr><td>Cell 1</td><td>Cell 2</td></tr>
      <tr><td>Cell 3</td><td>Cell 4</td></tr>
  </table>
</p>
</body>
</html>
```

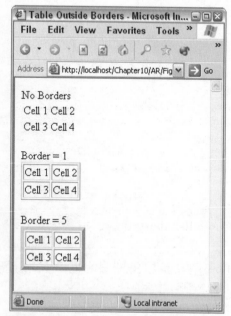

Figure 10-7: Examples of table border widths.

The border attribute's value specifies the width of the border in pixels. The default border width is 0, or no border.

Tip

Borders are an effective troubleshooting tool when dealing with table problems in HTML. If you are having trouble determining what is causing a problem in a table, try turning on the borders to better visualize the individual rows and columns. If you are using nested tables, turn on the borders of tables individually until you narrow down the scope of the problem.

To specify which outside borders are displayed, use the `frame` attribute with one of the values displayed in Table 10-1.

Table 10-1	
Values to Use with the Frame Attribute	
Value	**Definition**
Void	Display no borders
Above	Display a border on the top of the table only
Below	Display a border on the bottom of the table only
Hsides	Display borders on the horizontal sides (top and bottom) only
lhs or rhs	Display only the left side or the right side border only
Vsides	Display borders on the vertical sides (right and left) only
box or border	Display borders on all sides of the table (the default when border attribute is set without specifying frame)

Note

Not all user agents follow the defaults for table borders (no borders, or box/border when a border width is specified). If you want a table to show up with particular formatting, take care to specify all options.

Table rules

You can use the `rules` attribute of the `<table>` tag to control what rules (borders between cells) are displayed in a table. Table 10-2 shows the `rules` attribute's possible values.

Note that the width of rules is governed by the table spacing attribute. For example, setting cellspacing to a value of 5px results in rules 5 pixels wide.

Rows

Table rows are the horizontal elements of the table grid and are delimited with table row tags (`<tr>`). For example, a table with five rows would use the following pseudocode:

```
<table>
   <tr> row 1 </tr>
   <tr> row 2 </tr>
   <tr> row 3 </tr>
   <tr> row 4 </tr>
   <tr> row 5 </tr>
</table>
```

Table 10-2
Possible Rules Attribute Values

Value	Definition
none	Display no rules
groups	Display rules between row groups and column groups only
rows	Display rules between rows only
cols	Display rules between columns only
all	Rules will appear between all rows and columns

The rows are divided into individual cells by embedded `<td>` or `<th>` tags (see the next section, "*Cells,*" for more details).

Note   The row ending tag (`</tr>`) is optional. However, for clarity in your code you should consider always including appropriate ending tags.

The `<tr>` tag supports the following attributes shown in Table 10-3.

Table 10-3
Tag Attributes

Attribute	Definition
Align	Set to `right`, `left`, `center`, `justify`, or `char`, this attribute controls the horizontal alignment of data in the row. Note that if you use `char` alignment, you should also specify the alignment character with the `char` attribute described below.
Char	Specifies the alignment character to use with character (`char`) alignment
Charoff	Specifies the offset from the alignment character to align the data on. Can be specified in pixels or percentage
Valign	Set to `top`, `middle`, `bottom`, or `baseline`, this attribute controls the vertical alignment of data in the row. Baseline vertical alignment aligns the baseline of the text across the cells in the row

For an example of how baseline vertical alignment differs from bottom alignment, consider the two tables in Figure 10-8.

Bottom Alignment

Figure 10-8: Baseline alignment aligns the baseline of the text.

Baseline Alignment

If you use the alignment attributes in a `<tr>` tag, that alignment will be applied to all cells in that row. To format cell alignment individually, specify the alignment attribute(s) in individual cell tags (`<th>` or `<td>`) or in `<col>` or `<colgroup>` tags.

Note　The `bgcolor` attribute, used to set the background color for the row, has been deprecated in HTML 4.01. Instead of using this attribute, it is recommended that you use applicable styles to accomplish the same effect.

Cells

Individual cells of a table are the elements that actually hold data. In HTML, cell definitions also define the columns for the table. You delimit cells/columns with table data tags (`<td>`).

For example, consider the following code:

```
<table border="1" cellpadding="5">
  <tr>
    <td>Column 1</td><td>Column 2</td><td>Column 3</td>
  </tr>
  <tr>
    <td>Column 1</td><td>Column 2</td><td>Column 3</td>
  </tr>
</table>
```

Tip　Formatting your tables with ample white space (line breaks and indents) will help you accurately format and understand your tables. There are just as many ways to format a table in HTML as there are Web programmers—find a style that suits your taste and stick to it.

This code defines a table with two rows and three columns, due to the three sets of `<td>` tags.

You can also use table header tags (`<th>`) to define columns that are headers for the columns. Expanding on the previous example, the following adds column headers:

```
<table border="1" cellpadding="5">
  <tr>
    <th>Header 1</th><th>Header 2</th><th>Header 3</th>
  </tr>
  <tr>
    <td>Column 1</td><td>Column 2</td><td>Column 3</td>
  </tr>
  <tr>
    <td>Column 1</td><td>Column 2</td><td>Column 3</td>
  </tr>
</table>
```

Table header tags make it easy to format column headings, without having to result to character formatting. For example, the preceding code results in most user agents rendering the `<th>` cells in a bold font (the default for `<th>`). To accomplish the same formatting without header tags, you would need to include bold character formatting similar to the following:

```
<tr>
  <th><b>Header 1</b></th>
  <th><b>Header 2</b></th>
  <th><b>Header 3</b></th>
</tr>
```

Using CSS, your formatting options with `<th>` are practically limitless; simply define appropriate formatting or several formatting classes as necessary.

 Note Most user agents will not properly render an empty cell (for example, `<td></td>`). When you find yourself needing an empty cell, get in the habit of placing a nonbreaking space entity (` `) in the cell (for example, `<td> </td>`) to help ensure the user agent will render your table correctly.

Although cells represent the smallest element in a table, surprisingly, they have the most attributes for their tags. Supported attributes include those shown in Table 10-4.

 Note Previous versions of HTML also supported a `nowrap` attribute to control whether a cell's contents wrapped or not. In HTML 4.01, this attribute has been deprecated in favor of styles. See Chapters 16 and 17 for more information on styles.

Table Captions

Table captions (`<caption>`) provide an easy method to add descriptive text to a table. For example, suppose you wanted to caption a table detailing the refresh rates

Table 10-4
Cell Attributes

Attribute	Definition
Abbr	An abbreviated form of the cell's contents. User agents can use the abbreviation where appropriate (speaking a short form of the contents, displaying on a small device, and so on). As such, the value of the `abbr` attribute should be as short and concise as possible
Align	The horizontal alignment of the cell's contents—left, center, right, justify, or char (character)
Axis	Used to define a conceptual category for the cell, which can be used to place the cell's contents into dimensional space. How the categories are used (if at all) is up to the individual user agent
Char	The character used to align the cell's content if the alignment is set to `char`
Charoff	The offset from the alignment character to use when aligning the cell content by character
Colspan	How many columns the cell should span (default 1). See the *Spanning Columns and Rows* section for more information
Headers	A space-separated list of header cell `id` attributes that corresponds with the cells used as headers for the current cell. User agents use this information at their discretion—a verbal agent might read the contents of all header cells before the current cell's content
rowspan	How many rows the cell should span (default 1). See the *Spanning Columns and Rows* section for more information
Scope	The scope of the current cell's contents when used as a header—row, col (column), rowgroup, colgroup (column group). If set, the cell's contents are treated as a header for the corresponding element(s)
Valign	The vertical alignment of the cell's contents—top, middle, bottom, or baseline

of a monitor. The following code adds an appropriate caption to a table, whose output is shown in Figure 10-9.

```
<!DOCTYPE HTML PUBLIC "-//W3C//DTD HTML 4.01//EN"
  "http://www.w3.org/TR/html4/strict.dtd">
<html>
<head>
  <title>Monitor Settings</title>
</head>
<table border="1" cellpadding="3" cellspacing="2">
<caption>Supported Refresh Rates</caption>
<tr>
  <th>H Resolution</th><th>V
```

```
Resolution</th><th>Frequency</th>
</tr>
<tr>
  <td>640</td><td>480</td><td>60 to 120 Hz</td>
</tr>
<tr>
  <td>800</td><td>600</td><td>55 to 110 Hz</td>
</tr>
<tr>
  <td>832</td><td>624</td><td>55 to 106 Hz</td>
</tr>
<tr>
  <td>1024</td><td>768</td><td>55 to 87 Hz</td>
</tr>
<tr>
  <td>1152</td><td>870</td><td>55 to 77 Hz</td>
</tr>
<tr>
  <td>1280</td><td>1024</td><td>55 to 66 Hz</td>
</tr>
</table>
</body>
</html>
```

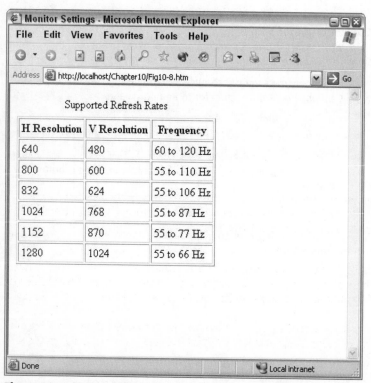

Figure 10-9: Captions ("Supported Refresh Rates" in this example) are displayed above the table.

Note that the `<caption>` tag must appear immediately after the `<table>` tag. Captions typically appear centered above the table to which they are attached—although different user agents may interpret the caption differently.

Cross-Reference You can use styles to format the caption however you like. For more information on styles, see Chapters 16 and 17.

Row Groupings—Header, Body, and Footer

Simple tables only have one section, the body, which consists of rows and columns. However, you might want to include additional information in your table by defining a table header and footer to complement the information in the body.

For example, the header could contain the header rows, the body could contain the data, and the footer totals for each column. The advantage to breaking up the table into the three sections is that some user agents will then allow the user to scroll the body of the table separately from the header and footer.

Note The HTML 4.01 specification dictates that you must use all three sections—header, body, and footer—if you use any. You cannot use only a header and body section without a footer, for example. If you don't intend to use one of the elements, you must still include tags for the section, even if the section is otherwise empty.

The table header is delimited by `<thead>` tags—otherwise, its content is exactly like any other table section, delimited by `<tr>`, `<td>`, and optionally `<th>` tags. For example, consider the following table header section:

```
<thead>
  <tr><th>Name</th><th>Hire Date</th><th>Title</th></tr>
</thead>
```

Other than being delimited by `<tbody>` tags, the table body is defined and formatted just like any other table element. The table footer is delimited by `<tfoot>` tags and is formatted like the other two sections.

Tip Although it seems counterintuitive, you should place the `<tfoot>` section *before* the `<tbody>` section in your code to allow the user agent to correctly anticipate the footer section and appropriately format the `<tbody>` section.

All three section tags support align and valign tags for controlling text alignment within the section. (The `char` and `charoff` attributes are also supported for `align="char"`.)

For an example of a table with all three sections, consider the following code and its output, shown in Figure 10-10.

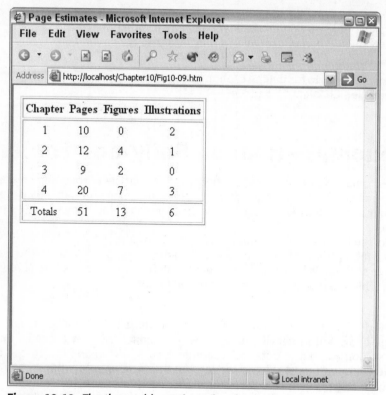

Figure 10-10: The three table sections (header, body, footer) can be set off by custom rules.

```
<!DOCTYPE HTML PUBLIC "-//W3C//DTD HTML 4.01//EN"
  "http://www.w3.org/TR/html4/strict.dtd">
<html>
<head>
  <title>Page Estimates</title>
</head>
<body>
<table border="1" cellpadding="3" cellspacing="2"
    rules="groups">
<thead align="center">
  <tr>
    <th>Chapter</th><th>Pages</th><th>Figures</th>
      <th>Illustrations</th>
  </tr>
</thead>
<tfoot align="center">
  <tr>
    <td>Totals</td><td>51</td><td>13</td><td>6</td>
  </tr>
</tfoot>
<tbody align="center">
  <tr>
```

```
    <td>1</td><td>10</td><td>0</td><td>2</td>
  </tr>
  <tr>
    <td>2</td><td>12</td><td>4</td><td>1</td>
  </tr>
  <tr>
    <td>3</td><td>9</td><td>2</td><td>0</td>
  </tr>
  <tr>
    <td>4</td><td>20</td><td>7</td><td>3</td>
  </tr>
</tbody>
</table>
</body>
</html>
```

Note how the three sections are set off by rules, but the table is otherwise devoid of rules. This is because of the `rules="groups"` attribute in the `<table>` tag. Also note how alignment attributes are used in the section tags to center the text in the table.

Background Colors

In previous versions of HTML, you could use the `bgcolor` attribute in the `<table>`, and `<tr>`, `<th>`, and `<td>` tags to set a color background for the element. This attribute has been deprecated in HTML 4.01 in favor of using styles to set the background color of table elements.

Using the deprecated method, you can set the background of a header row to yellow with code similar to the following:

```
<tr bgcolor="yellow">
  <th>H Resolution</th>
  <th>V Resolution</th>
  <th>Frequency</th>
</tr>
```

Using CSS to accomplish the same effect would resemble the following code (output is shown in Figure 10-11).

```
<tr style="background-color: yellow;">
  <th>H Resolution</th>
  <th>V Resolution</th>
  <th>Frequency</th>
</tr>
```

However, not all user agents adequately support background colors in tables. Older browsers are particularly finicky about correctly representing background colors. When in doubt, test.

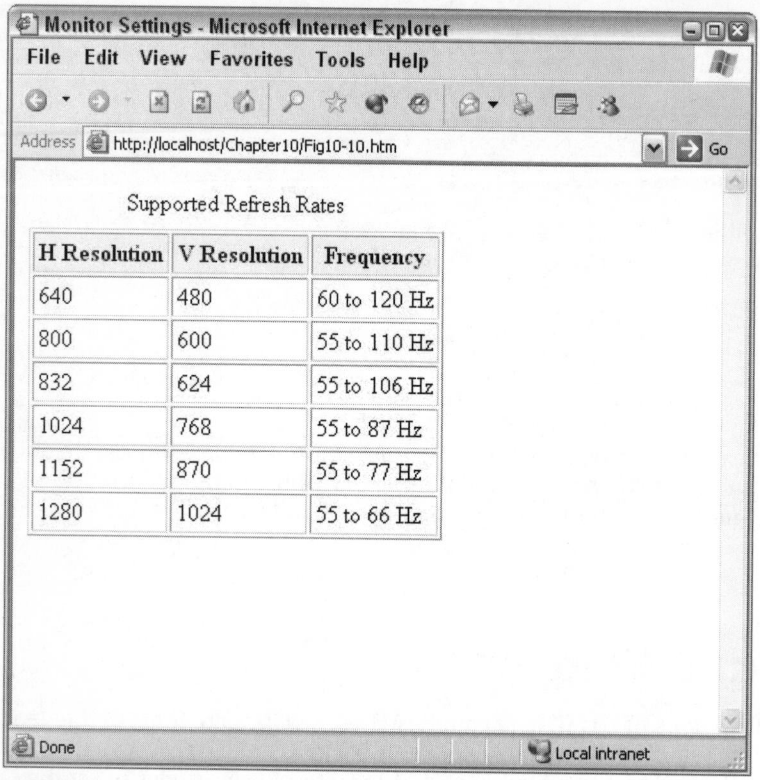

Supported Refresh Rates

H Resolution	V Resolution	Frequency
640	480	60 to 120 Hz
800	600	55 to 110 Hz
832	624	55 to 106 Hz
1024	768	55 to 87 Hz
1152	870	55 to 77 Hz
1280	1024	55 to 66 Hz

Figure 10-11: Use the background-color CSS property to control table element backgrounds.

Spanning Columns and Rows

It is possible to span data cells across multiple columns and rows using the `colspan` and `rowspan` attributes. Usually such spanning is used to provide column or row headings for groups of columns. For example, consider the following table code and the resulting output shown in Figure 10-12.

```
<table border="1" cellpadding="5">
<caption>Respondent Summary to Questions 1-4</caption>
<tr align="center">
  <th>Category</th>
  <th>Age</th><th>#1</th><th>#2</th><th>#3</th><th>#4</th>
</tr>
<tr>
  <td rowspan="3">Male<br>Respondents</td>
  <!-- Above cell spans 3 rows -->
  <td>23</td><td>A</td><td>C</td><td>F</td><td>B</td>
</tr>
```

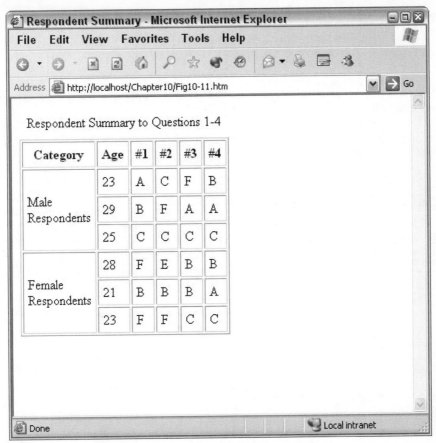

Figure 10-12: You can span cells across both columns and rows.

```
<tr>
  <!-- First cell is the span cell -->
  <td>29</td><td>B</td><td>F</td><td>A</td><td>A</td>
</tr>
<tr>
  <!-- First cell is the span cell -->
  <td>25</td><td>C</td><td>C</td><td>C</td><td>C</td>
</tr>
<!-- End of first span -->
<tr>
  <td rowspan="3">Female<br>Respondents</td>
  <!-- Above cell spans 3 rows -->
  <td>28</td><td>F</td><td>E</td><td>B</td><td>B</td>
</tr>
<tr>
  <!-- First cell is the span cell -->
  <td>21</td><td>B</td><td>B</td><td>B</td><td>A</td>
</tr>
```

```
<tr>
  <!-- First cell is the span cell -->
  <td>23</td><td>F</td><td>F</td><td>C</td><td>C</td>
</tr>
</table>
```

Note that the rows that include a previously spanned cell omit the declaration of their first cell.

You can span columns using the `colspan` attribute in a similar fashion, as shown in the following code and resulting output in Figure 10-13.

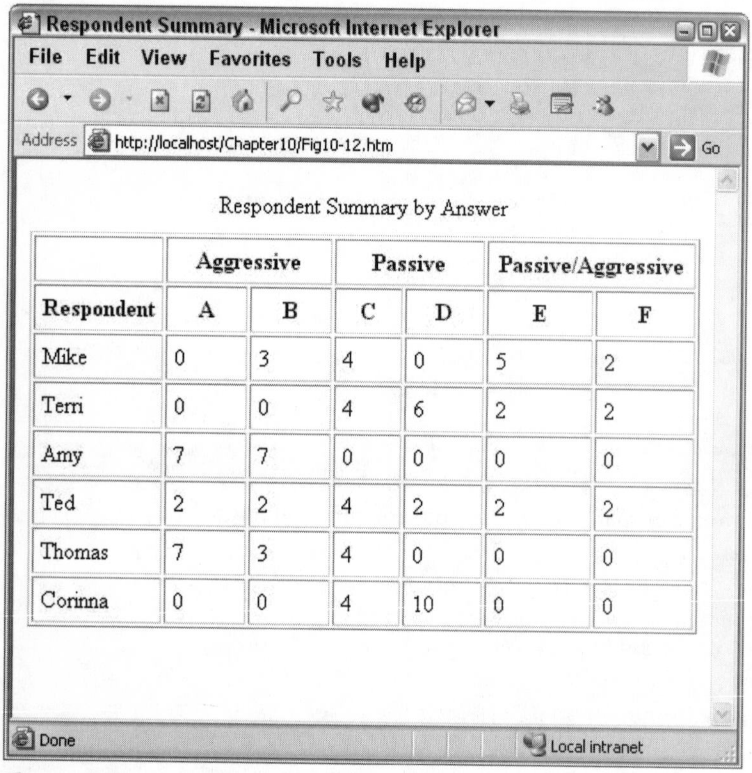

Figure 10-13: Spanning columns with the `colspan` attribute.

```
<table border="1" cellpadding="5">
<caption>Respondent Summary by Answer</caption>
<tr align="center">
  <!-- Spanning group headers -->
  <th> </th>
  <th colspan="2" width="150">Aggressive</th>
  <th colspan="2" width="150">Passive</th>
```

```
    <th colspan="2" width="150">Passive/Aggressive</th>
  </tr>
  <tr align="center">
    <!-- Individual column headers -->
    <th>Respondent</th><th>A</th><th>B</th>
    <th>C</th><th>D</th><th>E</th><th>F</th>
  </tr>
  <!-- Table data -->
  <tr>
    <td>Mike</td>
    <td>0</td><td>3</td><td>4</td>
    <td>0</td><td>5</td><td>2</td>
  </tr>
    <td>Terri</td>
    <td>0</td><td>0</td><td>4</td>
    <td>6</td><td>2</td><td>2</td>
  </tr>
    <td>Amy</td>
    <td>7</td><td>7</td><td>0</td>
    <td>0</td><td>0</td><td>0</td>
  </tr>
    <td>Ted</td>
    <td>2</td><td>2</td><td>4</td>
    <td>2</td><td>2</td><td>2</td>
  </tr>
    <td>Thomas</td>
    <td>7</td><td>3</td><td>4</td>
    <td>0</td><td>0</td><td>0</td>
  </tr>
    <td>Corinna</td>
    <td>0</td><td>0</td><td>4</td>
    <td>10</td><td>0</td><td>0</td>
  </tr>
</table>
```

You can also span columns and rows within the same table by using appropriate `colspan` and `rowspan` attributes. However, such use is not recommended without a GUI HTML editor, because the code becomes exponentially complex the more customizations you make to a table.

Cross-Reference   For more information on GUI HTML editors, see Chapter 35.

Grouping Columns

HTML 4.01 has added a few extra tags to make defining and formatting groups of columns easier. The two tags, `<colgroup>` and `<col>`, are used together to define and optionally format column groups and individual columns.

The `<colgroup>` tag is used to define and optionally format groups of columns. The tag supports the same formatting attributes as the `<tr>` and `<td>/<th>` tags (align, valign, width, and so on). Any columns defined by the ⟨colgroup⟩ will inherit the formatting contained in the ⟨colgroup⟩ tag.

To define columns in a group, use the span attribute with the ⟨colgroup⟩ tag to indicate how many columns are in the group. For example, the following HTML table code places the first three columns in a group:

```
<table>
<colgroup span="3">
</colgroup>
. . .
```

Note that additional ⟨colgroup⟩ tags can be used to create additional column groups. You must use additional column groups if the columns you are grouping are not contiguous or do not start with the first column. For example, the following HTML table code creates three column groups:

✦ Columns 1 and 2, formatted with centered alignment

✦ Columns 3–5, formatted with decimal alignment

✦ Columns 6–10, formatted with right alignment and bold text

```
<table>
<colgroup span="2" align="center">
<!-- This group contains columns 1 & 2 -->
</colgroup>
<colgroup span="3" align="char" char=".">
<!-- This group contains columns 3 - 5 -->
</colgroup>
<colgroup span="5" align="right" style="font-weight: bold;" >
<!-- This group contains columns 6 - 10 -->
</colgroup>
. . .
```

Note Column groups that do not have explicit formatting attributes defined in their respective ⟨colgroup⟩ tags inherit the standard formatting of columns within the table. However, the group is still defined as a group and will respond accordingly to table attributes that affect groups (rules="groups", and so on).

What if you don't want all the columns within the group formatted identically? For example, in a group of three columns, suppose you wanted the center column (column number 2 in the group) to be formatted with bold text? That's where the ⟨col⟩ tag comes into play, defining individual columns within the group. For example, to format a group using the preceding example (middle column bold), you could use code similar to the following:

```
<table>
<colgroup span="3">
<!-- This group contains columns 1 & 3 -->
<col></col>
<col style="font-weight: bold;"></col>
```

```
<col></col>
</colgroup>
...
```

The `<col>` tag follows similar rules to that of the `<colgroup>` tag, namely the following:

- ✦ Empty tags (those without explicit formatting) are simply placeholders.
- ✦ You must define columns in order, and in a contiguous group, using blank `<col>` tags where necessary.
- ✦ Missing or empty `<col>` tags result in the corresponding columns inheriting the standard formatting for columns in the table.

Note that in standard HTML the `<col>` tag has no closing tag. However, in XHMTL the `<col>` tag must be closed by a corresponding `</col>` tag.

Tip

Column definitions via the `<colgroup>` or `<col>` tags do not eliminate or change the necessity of `<td>` tags (which actually form the columns). You must still take care in placing your `<td>` tags to ensure proper data positioning within columns.

Summary

This chapter covered the basics of HTML tables. You learned how to define a table, what the various pieces of a table were and what each is used for, and how to format the various elements of a table.

Because of their diversity, it is impossible to cover all uses of tables. However, given enough time and imagination, each Web designer will find several uses for tables—including page design, as covered in the next chapter.

✦   ✦   ✦

Page Layout with Tables

◆ ◆ ◆ ◆

In This Chapter

Rudimentary Formatting with Tables

Real-World Examples

Floating Page

Odd Graphic and Text Combinations

Navigational Menus and Blocks

Multiple Columns

◆ ◆ ◆ ◆

Tables are one of the most flexible elements in HTML. As such, they can be used for much more than displaying tabular data. In fact, they have become one of the mainstays of document formatting and page layout for the Web.

This chapter covers how to use tables to achieve simple and complex formatting and layout results.

Rudimentary Formatting with Tables

It's not hard to see how tables can help with formatting elements on a local level. For example, consider the following code and the output shown in Figure 11-1.

```
<!DOCTYPE HTML PUBLIC "-//W3C//DTD HTML 4.01//EN"
  "http://www.w3.org/TR/html4/strict.dtd">
<html>
<head>
  <title>Simple Form</title>
</head>
<body>
<form>
<p>Name: <input type="text" size="40"></p>
<p>Age: 
<input type="radio" name="20to30" value="20to30">
 20-30 
<input type="radio" name="31to40" value="31to40">
 31-40 
<input type="radio" name="41to50" value="41to50">
 41-50 
</p>
</form>
</body>
</html>
```

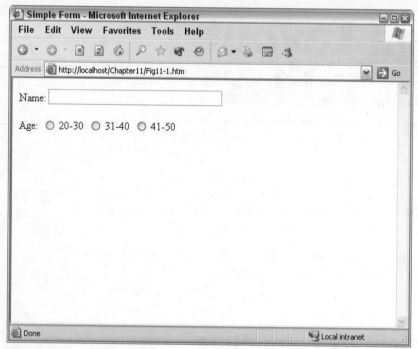

Figure 11-1: A rudimentary form using spaces for layout purposes.

A simple table can help better align the elements in this form, as shown in the following code and Figure 11-2.

```
<!DOCTYPE HTML PUBLIC "-//W3C//DTD HTML 4.01//EN"
   "http://www.w3.org/TR/html4/strict.dtd">
<html>
<head>
  <title>Rudimentary Form Alignment</title>
</head>
<body>
<form>
<table width="50%" border="1">
<tr>
<td width="25%"><p>Name:</p></td>
<td><p><input type="text" size="40"></p></td>
</tr>
<tr>
<td><p>Age:</p></td>
<td><p>
<input type="radio" name="20to30" value="20to30">
 20-30 
<input type="radio" name="31to40" value="31to40">
 31-40 
<input type="radio" name="41to50" value="41to50">
 41-50 
</p></td>
```

```
</table>
</form>
</body>
</html>
```

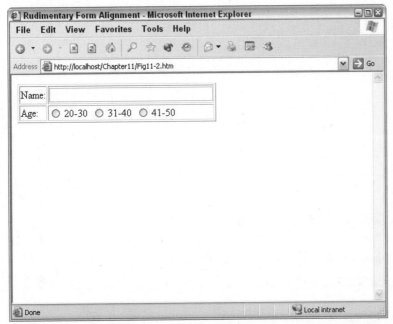

Figure 11-2: Aligning the labels and fields in a form using a simple table.

However, this serves only to line up the labels and fields in two columns. This is better than no alignment, but if you add a nested table, you can add more order to the radio buttons, as shown in the following code and Figure 11-3.

```
<!DOCTYPE HTML PUBLIC "-//W3C//DTD HTML 4.01//EN"
  "http://www.w3.org/TR/html4/strict.dtd">
<html>
<head>
  <title>Formatting with Nested Tables</title>
</head>
<body>
<form>
<table width="50%" border="1">
<tr>
<td width="25%"><p>Name:</p></td>
<td><p><input type="text" size="40"></p></td>
</tr>
<tr>
<td><p>Age:</p></td>
<td>

<table width="100%" border="1">
<tr>
```

```
<td><p><input type="radio" name="20to30"
value="20to30"></p></td>
<td><p><input type="radio" name="31to40"
value="31to40"></p></td>
<td><p><input type="radio" name="41to50"
value="41to50"></p></td>
</tr>
<tr>
<td><p>20-30</p></td>
<td><p>31-40</p></td>
<td><p>41-50</p></td>
</tr>
</table>

</td>
</table>
</form>
</body>
</html>
```

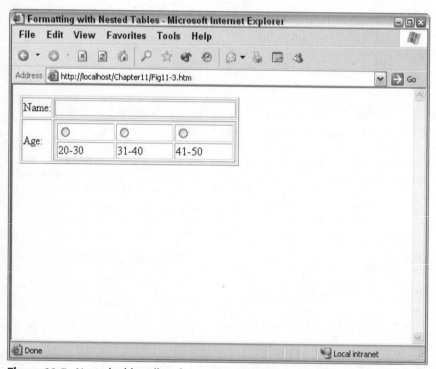

Figure 11-3: Nested tables allow for even more alignment and formatting control.

Note   Of course, in real life the tables in the examples would have even more formatting attributes to fine-tune the alignment, and the borders would be off or set
to accent the formatting.

Even though these examples are fairly small in scope, it should be easy to see the power and flexibility tables can lend to alignment, formatting, and even page layout.

Real-World Examples

You might be surprised at how many tables are hiding under the veneer of the Web pages you frequent. For example, take a look at Figure 11-4, which shows a corporate Web site.

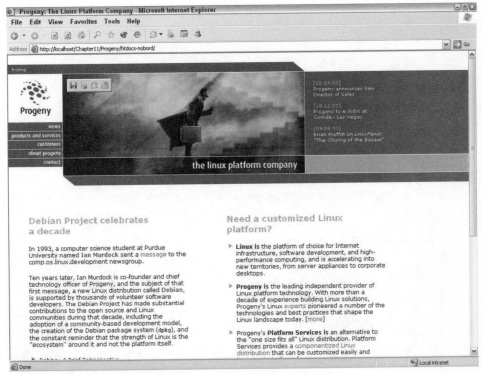

Figure 11-4: A corporate Web site that doesn't visibly use tables.

Figure 11-5 shows the same Web site with the table borders on. Note the multitude of nested tables used to achieve the layout.

Figure 11-6 shows another popular layout format, a floating page and two columns of content. Again, note that the use of tables (visible in Figure 11-7) isn't readily apparent.

The rest of this chapter shows you how to achieve some of these effects.

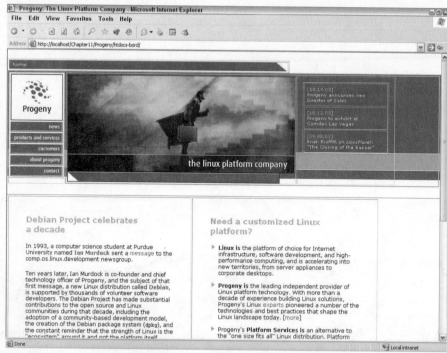

Figure 11-5: A corporate Web site with the tables made visible.

Figure 11-6: Another popular layout, floating page and multiple columns of content.

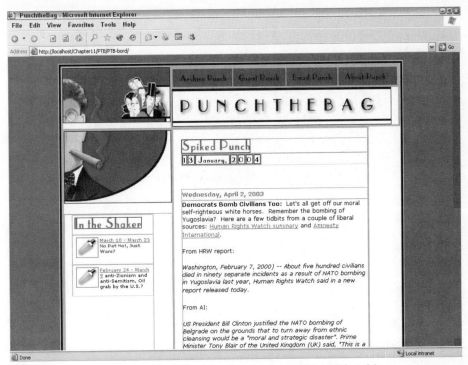

Figure 11-7: The floating page and two-column layout with visible tables.

Floating Page

The floating page layout (as shown in Figures 11-6 and 11-7) has become quite popular and is used in pages of all kinds, from corporate sites to personal Web logs. The effect is fairly easy to create using a few nested tables, as shown in the following code, the output of which is shown in Figure 11-8.

```
<!DOCTYPE HTML PUBLIC "-//W3C//DTD HTML 4.01//EN"
  "http://www.w3.org/TR/html4/strict.dtd">
<html>
<head>
  <title>Floating Table Format</title>
  <style type="text/css">
    <!-- Sets "desktop" color (behind page) -->
    body { background-color: #B0C4DE; }
  </style>
</head>
<body>

<!-- /Body container -->
  <!-- (background = border, padding = border width
       margin = centered table) -->
<table border="0" cellpadding="4px" cellspacing="0"
```

```
      style="background-color: black;
      margin: 0 auto;">
<tr>
 <td>

   <!-- Floating page -->
     <!-- (padding = page margin) -->
   <table border="0" cellpadding="5px" cellspacing="0"
    width="732px" height="900px"
    style="background-color: #FFFFFF;">
   <tr align="left" valign="top">
     <td>

        <!-- Page content -->
        <p>Content goes here.<p>
        <!-- Page content -->

     </td>
    </tr>
   </table>
   <!-- /Floating page -->

 </td>
</tr>
</table>
<!-- /Body container -->

</body>
</html>
```

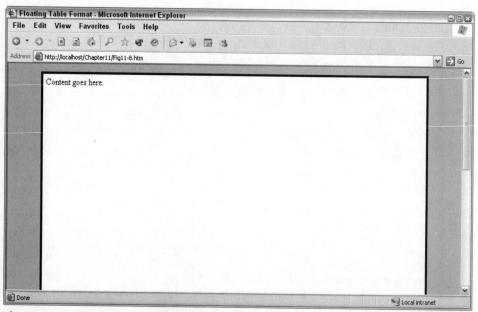

Figure 11-8: A floating page can add a bit of simple design to your documents.

Tip

Note the comments in the code delimiting the individual tables and content areas. It is a good practice to follow standard code formatting (indentation, liberal white space, and so on) *and* add sufficient comments to easily keep track of all your tables, how they are formatted, and what they accomplish.

If you want more of a drop shadow effect, you can play with the borders of the floating page, setting two adjacent borders to a nonzero value, as shown in the following code:

```
<!-- Floating page -->
  <!-- (padding = page margin) -->
<table border="0" cellpadding="5px" cellspacing="0"
  width="732px" height="900px"
  style="background-color: #FFFFFF;
  border-right: 4px solid black;
  border-bottom: 4px solid black;">
```

This code will visually increase the width of the right and bottom borders, giving the page a more realistic, three-dimensional drop shadow effect.

Tip

As you read through this chapter, keep in mind that you can combine the techniques within the same document. For example, you can put a two-column layout on a floating page by nesting a two-column table in the content area of the floating page table. Then, within one of the columns, you can evenly space out a handful of graphics by nesting another table in the column. The possibilities are endless.

Table Layout versus CSS Layout

As you'll see in Part II of this book, CSS provides plenty of controls for positioning elements in a document. Since CSS is "the wave of the future," why not learn and use CSS instead of tables for page layout purposes?

✦ Most user agents support tables, while CSS support is being slowly adopted.

✦ Tables are more forgiving when the browser window size changes—morphing their content and wrapping to accommodate the changes accordingly. CSS positioning tends to be exact and fairly inflexible.

✦ Tables are much easier to learn and manipulate than CSS rules.

Of course, each of those arguments can be reversed:

✦ CSS is pivotal to the future of Web documents and will be supported by most user agents. Using it now helps guarantee future compliance. (A lot of table attributes are being deprecated for CSS, for example.)

Continued

Continued

✦ CSS is more exact than tables, allowing your document to be viewed as you intended, regardless of the browser window.

✦ Keeping track of nested tables can be a real pain—CSS rules tend to be well organized, easily read, and easily changed.

In short, arguments can be made for both technologies and the debate can get very heated (try searching for "html table layout versus CSS layout" at www.google.com). My advice is to use whichever technology makes sense to you—use what you know or what presents your documents in the best light.

Odd Graphic and Text Combinations

You can also use tables to combine text and graphics in nonstandard layouts. For example, look at the header in Figure 11-9. The header graphic is actually several pieces, as shown in Figure 11-10.

Note   The buttons in the page's upper-right are contained in separate table cells for a variety of reasons—the most notable is to provide navigation using separate elements while still providing a cohesive graphic.

Figure 11-9: Presenting graphics and text in a nonstandard format.

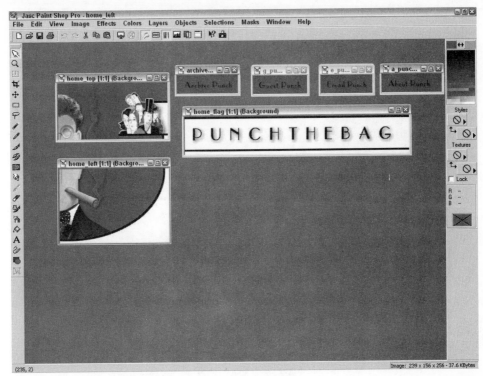

Figure 11-10: The various pieces of the header graphic.

A table with no padding and no spacing is used to put the pieces back together into a complete image while allowing text to flow to the right of the face portion. You can see the various pieces and the text in the table layout shown in Figure 11-11.

Code for this completed header is shown here:

```
<!-- Heading container -->
<table border="0" cellpadding="0" cellspacing="0">
  <tr>
  <td valign="top">
    <img border="0" src="images/home_top.gif"
      width="240" height="118">
  </td>
  <td>
<!-- Nav and main graphic -->
<table border="0" cellpadding="0" cellspacing="0">
  <tr>
  <td width="100%">
  <!-- Nav bar -->
  <table border="0" cellpadding="0" cellspacing="0"
   width="100%">
    <tr>
```

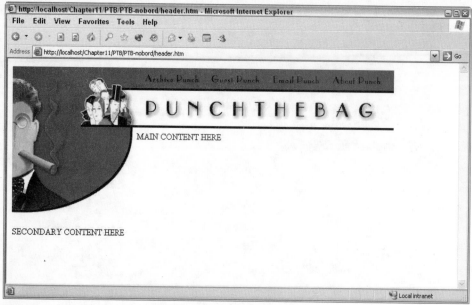

Figure 11-11: The completed layout in the table.

```
<td width="25%">
<a href="archive/index.html" onfocus="this.blur()"
onMouseOver="archive.src='images/archive_punch_on.gif'"
onMouseOut="archive.src='images/archive_punch_off.gif'"
>
<img name="archive" border="0"
src="images/archive_punch_off.gif"
width="132" height="38"></a>
</td>
<td width="25%">
<a href="guest/index.html" onfocus="this.blur()"
onMouseOver="guest.src='images/g_punch_on.gif'"
onMouseOut="guest.src='images/g_punch_off.gif'"
>
<img name="guest" border="0"
 src="images/g_punch_off.gif" width="116"
 height="38"></a>
</td>
<td width="25%">
<a href="mailto:email@example.com"
onfocus="this.blur()"
onMouseOver="email.src='images/e_punch_on.gif'"
onMouseOut="email.src='images/e_punch_off.gif'"
>
<img name="email" border="0"
 src="images/e_punch_off.gif" width="113"
 height="38"></a>
</td>
<td width="25%">
```

```
        <a href="about/index.html" onfocus="this.blur()"
        onMouseOver="about.src='images/a_punch_on.gif'"
        onMouseOut="about.src='images/a_punch_off.gif'"
        >
        <img name="about" border="0"
         src="images/a_punch_off.gif" width="131"
         height="38"></a>
        </td>
        </tr>
    </table>
    <!-- /Nav bar -->
    </td>
    </tr>
      <tr>
      <td width="100%"><img border="0"
      src="images/home_flag.gif" height="80">
      </td>
      </tr>
    </table>
    <!-- /Nav and main graphic -->
    </td>
    </tr>
    <tr>
      <td height="158" valign="top"><img border="0"
        src="images/home_left.gif" width="239"
        height="156">
        <p>SECONDARY CONTENT HERE</p>
      </td>
      <td valign="top">
        <p>MAIN CONTENT HERE</p>
      </td>
    </tr>
  </table>
  <!-- /Heading container -->
```

Using this technique you can wrap text and graphics around each other in a variety of ways. For example, if the graphic used in the preceding example descended on the right as well, you could use three columns—pieces of the graphic in the first and third, text in the middle.

Navigational Menus and Blocks

The completed page header shown in Figure 11-11 has its navigational elements in a row at the top of the page. You can construct similar, vertical layouts for your navigational elements using rowspan attributes in your tables. For example, consider the following code and the output in Figure 11-12.

```
<table border="1" width="100%">
  <tr>
    <td rowspan="4" width="65%">
      <p>Header graphic</p>
```

```
      </td>
      <td>
        <p>Nav_1</p>
      </td>
    </tr>
    <tr>
      <td>
        <p>Nav_2</p>
      </td>
    </tr>
    <tr>
      <td>
        <p>Nav_3</p>
      </td>
    </tr>
    <tr>
      <td>
        <p>Nav_4</p>
      </td>
    </tr>
  </table>
```

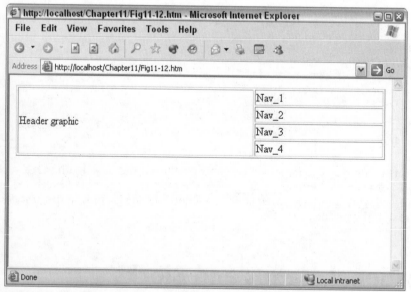

Figure 11-12: Using `rowspan`, you can create vertically stacked elements.

Note As you have no doubt realized, there are multiple ways to accomplish many of the designs shown in this chapter. For example, you could have just as easily nested a one-column table in a cell instead of using `rowspan` in the example code shown for Figure 11-12. The point is that tables are very flexible and can be used in a variety of ways to accomplish the desired layout.

Multiple Columns

As covered in Chapter 10, you can use tables to position elements in columns. This technique can be used for a variety of layout purposes:

✦ Providing navigation bars to the right or left of text (see Figures 11-4 and 11-6)

✦ Putting text into columns (see Figure 11-4)

✦ More precise positioning controls, putting text next to graphics, and so on

Columnar formatting is simple to accomplish, as shown in the following code:

```
<table border="1" cellspacing="0" cellpadding="5px"
  width="100%">
  <colgroup>
    <col width="50%">
    <col width="50%">
  </colgroup>

  <tr>
    <td colspan="2">Header graphic or navigation can go here</td>
  </tr>
  <tr>
    <td>First column content...</td>
    <td>Second column content...</td>
  </tr>
</table>
```

The output of this code is shown in Figure 11-13.

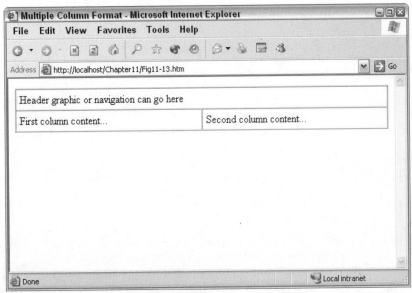

Figure 11-13: A simple two-column format.

One caveat to creating columns with tables is that the content doesn't automatically wrap from one column to the next (like in a newspaper). You must split the text between the columns manually.

Of course, the columns do not have to be the same size nor proportional to each other. You can define the columns in any size you need by using the appropriate formatting attributes. For example, if you wanted a navigation column to the left that is 200 pixels wide and a text column to the right that is 400 pixels wide, you could use this column definition:

```
<colgroup>
  <col width="200px">
  <col width="400px">
</colgroup>
```

Summary

This chapter showed you how to use tables to create various page layouts. You learned that tables, employing techniques from rudimentary formatting to graphic and text combinations, multiple columns, and navigational tools, can be used as a powerful and flexible layout tool. You will learn about more ways to format documents—using CSS—in Part II.

✦   ✦   ✦

Frames

S everal years ago, almost every document on the Web
contained frames. The frameset structure provided an
easy way to create multiple, separate scrolling areas in a user
agent window and a flexible mechanism to modify the content
of frames.

However, frames have turned out to be more of a fad. You can
have many of the benefits realized by using frames by using
the infinitely more flexible and powerful CSS formatting
methods.

That said, frames still have their uses and have even spawned
their own official Document Type Definitions (DTDs) to handle
their special tags and needs. This chapter introduces the
concept of frames and shows you how to add them to your
documents.

Frames Overview

At their simplest level, frames provide multiple separately
scrollable areas within one user window. Many non-Web
applications use the concept of separate panes to help their
organization and controls. For example, Figure 12-1 shows the
Windows Explorer, using a left pane to display folders and the
right pane to display files within the selected folder.

As you have no doubt noticed, the different panes in
applications such as Windows Explorer can be manipulated
separately from other panes. The same is true for documents
utilizing frames.

For example, take a look at Figures 12-2 and 12-3. They show
the same document except that the window in Figure 12-3 has
been scrolled to view the bottom of the text in the document.
This has caused the navigation bar to scroll as well, in this
case almost off the screen, where it can no longer be
immediately accessed.

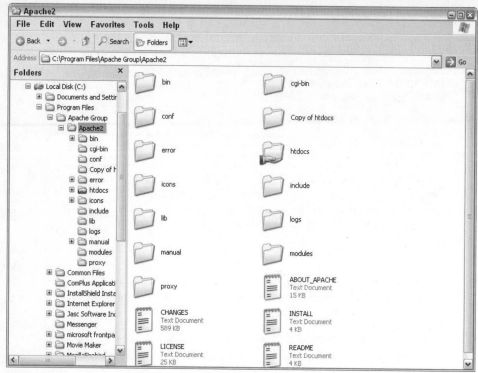

Figure 12-1: Applications such as Windows Explorer use multiple panes to display a variety of information and controls.

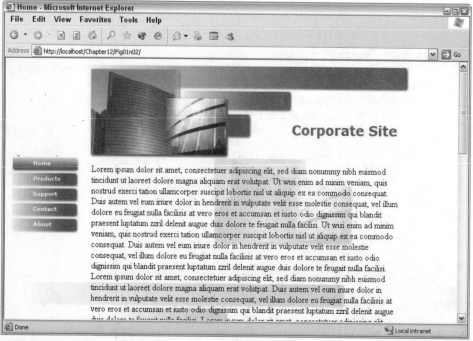

Figure 12-2: A long document uses scroll bars to allow the user to see the entire document.

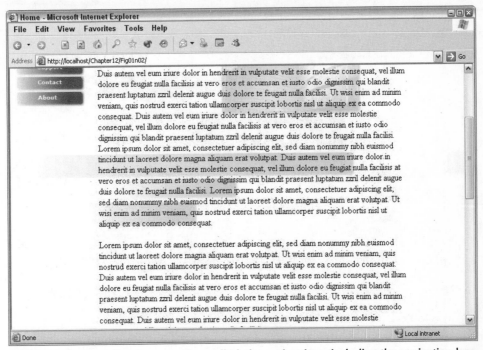

Figure 12-3: When the document is scrolled, the entire view—including the navigation bar on the left—is moved.

Now take a look at Figure 12-4. Each element—the top banner, the navigation bar, and the main content—has been placed in a separate frame. When the main content is scrolled, the banner and the navigation menu remain static within their own regions.

Framesets and Frame Documents

Frames are a bit complex to implement, as they require a separate document to define the frame layout as well as individual documents to actually occupy the frames. This section takes you through the pieces of the defining document, the frameset, and shows you how to create a frame-based layout.

Creating a frameset

A frameset is created like any other HTML document except that its content is limited to frame-related tags. The following skeletal document is an example of a frameset document:

```
<!DOCTYPE HTML PUBLIC "-//W3C//DTD HTML 4.01 Frameset//EN"
    "http://www.w3.org/TR/html4/frameset.dtd">
<html>
<head>
```

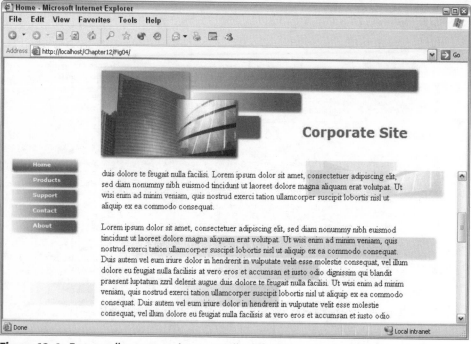

Figure 12-4: Frames allow one region to scroll while others remain static.

```
...
</head>
  <frameset attributes>
    <frame attributes></frame>
    <frame attributes></frame>
    ...
  </frameset>
</html>
```

Note the following about this code:

✦ The document uses the frameset DTD. The frameset DTD is essentially the same as the transitional DTD except for the addition of the frame-specific tags (and replacement of the `<body>` tag, covered shortly).

✦ There is no `<body>` element. Instead, the `<frameset>` tag provides the next level container under `<html>`.

✦ The `<frame>` tags, nestled inside the `<frameset>` tag, define the content for the frames and various properties of the frame itself.

✦ Other than the `<frameset>` and `<head>` sections, there is no other content in the document.

The basics of the `<frameset>` and `<frame>` tags are covered in the next two sections.

The <frameset> tag

The `<frameset>` tag defines the layout of the frames in the document. It does so by specifying whether the frames should be laid out in columns or rows and what each column's width should be.

The `<frameset>` tag has the following format:

```
<frameset cols|rows = "column_or_row_size(s)">
```

The column or row sizes can be specified as percentages of the user agent window, pixels, or an asterisk (*), which allows the user agent to assign the size. In the last case, the user agent will typically split the remaining space across the columns or rows that specify * as their width. In any case, the resulting frameset will occupy the entire user agent window. The number of entries of the `cols` or `rows` attribute also define how many frames will be used—each entry needs a corresponding `<frame>` tag within the `<frameset>`.

For example, consider these definitions:

```
<!-- Two columns, 25% of the window, the other
     75% of the window -->
<frameset cols = "25%, 75%">

<!-- Two columns, 25% of the window, the other
     75% of the window -->
<frameset cols = "25%, *">

<!-- Three rows, the first 50% of the window, the other
     two 25% of the window each -->
<frameset rows = "50%, *, *">

<!-- Two rows, the first 100 pixels high, the second is the
     size of the remaining window space -->
<frameset rows = "100px, 200px">
```

Note

In the last `<frameset>` example, the second row is defined at 200px. However, if the user agent's window is larger than 300 pixels high (the total of the rows defined), the second row will be expanded to fill the space.

The <frame> tag

While the `<frameset>` tag is responsible for defining the layout of the entire page (in terms of number of frames and their size), the `<frame>` tag is responsible for defining properties of each frame.

The `<frame>` tag has the following, minimal syntax:

```
<frame name="name_of_frame" src="url_of_content"></frame>
```

The `name` attribute gives the frame a unique name that can be referenced by URLs, scripts, and so on to control the frame's contents. The `src` attribute is used to specify the URL of the content that the frame should display.

Using only these two attributes results in a frame with minimal margins, no borders, and automatic scroll bars. More information on controlling these attributes of the frame is covered in the next few sections.

Frame margins, borders, and scroll bars

The <frame> tag supports the additional attributes shown in Table 12-1.

Table 12-1		
The <frame> Tag's Attributes		
Attribute	**Value(s)**	**Use**
frameborder	0 = no border (default) 1 = border	Whether the frame has a border or not
longdesc	url	A URL of a document to use as a long description for the frame. (Note that this is largely unsupported by user agents)
marginheight	pixels	Sets the top and bottom margins for the frame—the distance the frame's content is from its border
marginwidth	pixels	Sets the left and right margins for the frame—the distance the frame's content is from its border
scrolling	yes no auto (default)	Controls whether the frame displays scroll bars to help scroll the content displayed in the frame

As mentioned in Table 12-1, the longdesc attribute is not fully supported by most user agents. Use it if you need to specify a long description, but don't count on its functionality.

The margin attributes, marginheight and marginwidth, are self-explanatory, controlling the inside margin of the frame. They should be used to provide enough white space around the frame's content to help make the content clear.

Tip   When using images in a frame, consider setting the margins to zero so the graphic fills the frame entirely without superfluous white space.

The frameborder attribute controls whether the bounding border of the frame is visible or not. Figure 12-5 shows a frameset without borders, and Figure 12-6 shows the same frameset with borders.

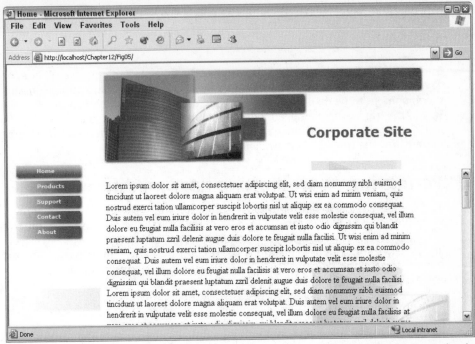

Figure 12-5: Without borders, the frame divisions are hard to distinguish, which may lend well to a seamless page design.

Figure 12-6: Frame borders can help your users understand the layout of your document and where the frame borders are so they can better manipulate them.

The `scrolling` attribute controls whether the frame will display scroll bars or not. The default setting, auto, allows the user agent to decide—if the frame contains too much content to be displayed, the user agent will add scroll bars. If the content fits within the frame, the user agent will not display scroll bars. Use the `scrolling` attribute accordingly—if you want scrollbars all the time, or don't want scrollbars no matter how the frame's content displays.

Permitting or prohibiting user modifications

The `<frame>` tag also has a `noresize` attribute that, when set, will not allow a user to modify the size of the frame. The default is to allow the user to resize the frame.

To resize a frame, the user positions the pointer over the frame division and drags the border. Figures 12-7 and 12-8 show the left frame being enlarged—as a consequence, the right frame shrinks to compensate.

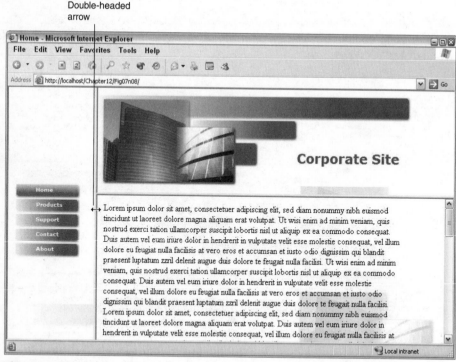

Figure 12-7: To resize a frame, the user positions the pointer over the frame border until a double arrow cursor appears.

Targeting Links to Frames

To change a frame's content, you must be able to target a frame. To do so, you must use the name attribute to uniquely identify your frames. You can then use those names in scripts and anchor tags to direct new content to the frame.

Drag border to new position

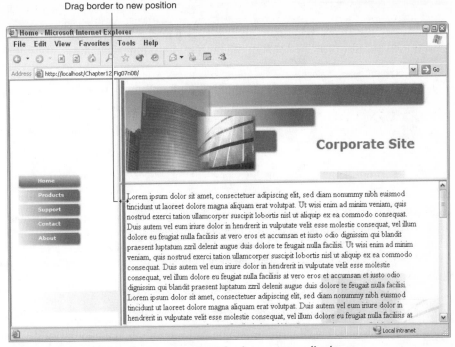

Figure 12-8: Dragging the curser resizes the frames accordingly.

Scripting languages can use the document's frame collection to target a frame. For example, JavaScript can reference the content of a frame named `news` by changing the value of the following property:

```
parent.news.location.href
```

You can use similar methods and properties to otherwise manipulate the frame content and properties.

Cross-Reference For more information on JavaScript and how it can be used to affect the properties of a document, see Chapters 25 through 27.

When you use the frameset DTD, the anchor tag (`<a>`) supports the `target` attribute, which can be used to target a frame for content. The `target` attribute supports the various values shown in Table 12-2.

Note To understand the difference between the `_parent` and `_top` values of the `target` attribute, you need to understand nested frames. Nested frames are covered in the next section.

The easiest way to direct content to a frame is to use the frame's name in the `target` attribute of an anchor. This technique is often used to control one frame independently from another, especially where one frame has a navigation control

Table 12-2
Possible Values for the Target Attribute

Value	Use
frame_name	Displays the content in the frame specified by frame_name
_blank	Open a new window to display the content
_parent	Displays the content in the parent frameset of the current frame
_self	Displays the content in the current frame
_top	Displays the content in the current window, without frames

and the other displays variable content. For example, the following code provides a handful of navigation links in the left (nav) frame, and the content is displayed in the right (content) frame. Figure 12-9 shows what this code looks like in a browser. (Only home.html is shown in the following code—other content pages would look similar.)

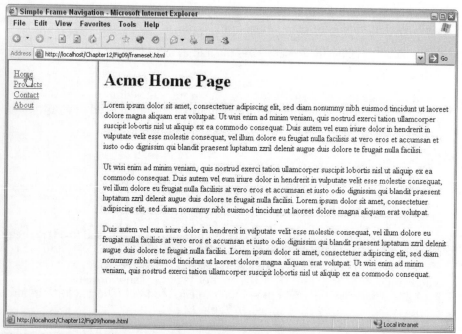

Figure 12-9: A simple frame-based navigation scheme. When the user clicks a link in the left frame, the content changes in the right frame.

frameset.html

```
<!DOCTYPE HTML PUBLIC "-//W3C//DTD HTML 4.01 Frameset//EN"
    "http://www.w3.org/TR/html4/frameset.dtd">
```

```
<html>
<head>
  <title>Simple Frame Navigation</title>
</head>
  <frameset cols = "20%,*">
    <frame name="nav" src="navigation.html"></frame>
    <frame name="content" src="home.html"></frame>
  </frameset>
</html>
```

navigation.html

```
<!DOCTYPE HTML PUBLIC "-//W3C//DTD HTML 4.01 Frameset//EN"
    "http://www.w3.org/TR/html4/frameset.dtd">
<html>
<head>
  <title>Navigation Menu</title>
</head>
<body>
  <p>
<a href="home.html" target="content">Home</a><br>
<a href="products.html" target="content">Products</a><br>
<a href="contact.html" target="content">Contact</a><br>
<a href="about.html" target="content">About</a>
  </p>
</body>
</html>
```

home.html

```
<!DOCTYPE HTML PUBLIC "-//W3C//DTD HTML 4.01 Frameset//EN"
    "http://www.w3.org/TR/html4/frameset.dtd">
<html>
<head>
  <title>Home Page Content</title>
</head>
<body>
  <h1>Acme Home Page</h1>
  <p>Lorem ipsum dolor sit amet, consectetuer adipiscing elit, sed diam nonummy
nibh euismod tincidunt ut laoreet dolore magna aliquam erat volutpat. Ut wisi
enim ad minim veniam, quis nostrud exerci tation ullamcorper suscipit lobortis
nisl ut aliquip ex ea commodo consequat. Duis autem vel eum iriure dolor in
hendrerit in vulputate velit esse molestie consequat, vel illum dolore eu feugiat
nulla facilisis at vero eros et accumsan et iusto odio dignissim qui blandit
praesent luptatum zzril delenit augue duis dolore te feugait nulla facilisi.</p>
  <p>Ut wisi enim ad minim veniam, quis nostrud exerci tation ullamcorper
suscipit lobortis nisl ut aliquip ex ea commodo consequat. Duis autem vel eum
iriure dolor in hendrerit in vulputate velit esse molestie consequat, vel illum
dolore eu feugiat nulla facilisis at vero eros et accumsan et iusto odio
dignissim qui blandit praesent luptatum zzril delenit augue duis dolore te
feugait nulla facilisi. Lorem ipsum dolor sit amet, consectetuer adipiscing elit,
sed diam nonummy nibh euismod tincidunt ut laoreet dolore magna aliquam erat
volutpat.</p>
  <p>Duis autem vel eum iriure dolor in hendrerit in vulputate velit esse
molestie consequat, vel illum dolore eu feugiat nulla facilisis at vero eros
et accumsan et iusto odio dignissim qui blandit praesent luptatum zzril delenit
```

```
augue duis dolore te feugait nulla facilisi. Lorem ipsum dolor sit amet,
consectetuer adipiscing elit, sed diam nonummy nibh euismod tincidunt ut laoreet
dolore magna aliquam erat volutpat. Ut wisi enim ad minim veniam, quis nostrud
exerci tation ullamcorper suscipit lobortis nisl ut aliquip ex ea commodo
consequat.</p>
</body>
</html>
```

Nested Framesets

You have seen how to create rows and columns using framesets. However, what if
you want a little of both? For example, consider the layout shown in Figure 12-10.

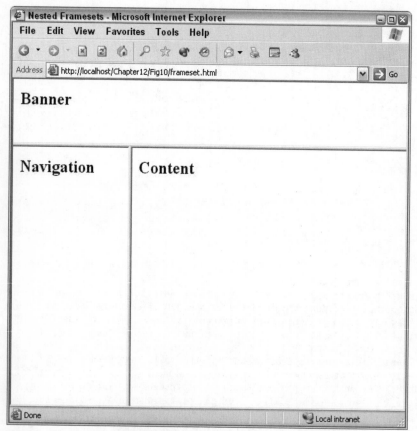

Figure 12-10: A frameset with a combination of rows and columns.

In such cases, you need to nest one frameset inside of another. For example, the
following frameset code results in the layout shown in Figure 12-10:

```
<frameset rows = "20%,*">
  <frame name="banner" src="banner.html"></frame>
```

```
<frameset cols = "30%,*">
  <frame name="nav" src="navigation.html"></frame>
  <frame name="content" src="home.html"></frame>
</frameset>
</frameset>
```

To achieve the layout, a column-based frameset is nested inside the second row of the row-based frameset. In essence, the second row of the top frameset becomes its own frameset. You could conceivably nest other framesets within this layout, but using more than two or three frames tends to clutter the document and confuse the user.

Note The _parent and _top values of the anchor tag's target attribute were mentioned earlier in this chapter. Looking at the example in this section, you can see how those two values would each affect the target.

The _parent value causes the content to load within the frameset, that is the immediate parent of the current frame. For example, using _parent in a link within the content frame would cause the specified content to load in the area defined for the column-based frameset.

The _top value causes the content to load within the top-most frameset. For example, using _top in a link within the content frame would cause the specified content to load in the area defined for the row-based frameset, effectively taking up the entire user agent window.

Inline Frames

Inline frames were conceived as a better method to allow smaller pieces of content to be incorporated in scrollable containers within a larger document. Although you can use regular framesets to create individually scrolling regions, the layout is somewhat hampered by the stringent row and column layout design inherent in framesets.

Figure 12-11 shows a sample inline frame placed in a document. Note that the frame is truly "inline"—that is, completely enveloped by the document around it.

Note Inline frames are not fully supported by all user agents. Inline frames are only safe to use if you are relatively certain that your entire audience will be using an <iframe> compatible browser to view your documents. If this is not the case, you should stay away from inline frames, or code your documents to offer incompatible browsers an alternative. See Chapter 25 for more information about making your documents cross-browser compatible.

If you do decide to utilize inline frames, keep in mind that, like other frame constructs, your documents will only validate against frameset DTDs.

Inline frames are accomplished with the <iframe> tag. This tag has the following, minimal format:

```
<iframe src="url_of_content"></iframe>
```

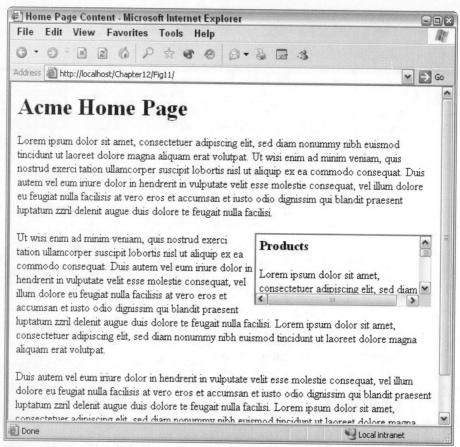

Figure 12-11: Inline frames define separate scrollable regions truly inline within the document.

The `<iframe>` tag has a handful of additional attributes. These are listed in Table 12-3.

Table 12-3
The `<iframe>` Tag Attributes

Attribute	Value(s)	Use
align	left right top middle bottom	Alignment of the frame to surrounding text
frameborder	0 = no border 1 = border (default)	Whether the frame should have a visible border

Attribute	Value(s)	Use
height	pixels %	The height of the frame
longdesc	url	A URL to a document containing the long description of the frame
marginheight	pixels	The size of the internal top and bottom margins of the frame
marginwidth	pixels	The size of the internal left and right margins of the frame
name	name_of_frame	The name of the frame (for use in scripting and otherwise referencing the frame and its properties)
scrolling	yes no auto (default)	Whether the frame should have scrollbars or not
src	url	The URL of the content to display in the frame
width	pixels %	The width of the frame

These attributes function exactly like their frame-based kin. It is recommended that you use as many attributes as possible to more closely specify how your <iframe> layout will be rendered.

The following code was used for the document displayed in Figure 12-11.

frameset.html

```
<!DOCTYPE HTML PUBLIC "-//W3C//DTD HTML 4.01 Frameset//EN"
    "http://www.w3.org/TR/html4/frameset.dtd">
<html>
<head>
  <title>Home Page Content</title>
</head>
<body>
  <h1>Acme Home Page</h1>
  <p>Lorem ipsum dolor sit amet, consectetuer adipiscing elit, sed diam nonummy
nibh euismod tincidunt ut laoreet dolore magna aliquam erat volutpat. Ut wisi
enim ad minim veniam, quis nostrud exerci tation ullamcorper suscipit lobortis
nisl ut aliquip ex ea commodo consequat. Duis autem vel eum iriure dolor in
hendrerit in vulputate velit esse molestie consequat, vel illum dolore eu feugiat
nulla facilisis at vero eros et accumsan et iusto odio dignissim qui blandit
praesent luptatum zzril delenit augue duis dolore te feugait nulla facilisi.</p>

<iframe name="productframe" src="products.html"
  height="100px" width="250px"
  align="right" frameborder="1" marginheight="5px"
  marginwidth="5px" scrolling="auto">
</iframe>
```

```
  <p>Ut wisi enim ad minim veniam, quis nostrud exerci tation ullamcorper
  suscipit lobortis nisl ut aliquip ex ea commodo consequat. Duis autem vel
  eum iriure dolor in hendrerit in vulputate velit esse molestie consequat,
  vel illum dolore eu feugiat nulla facilisis at vero eros et accumsan et
  iusto odio dignissim qui blandit praesent luptatum zzril delenit augue duis
  dolore te feugait nulla facilisi. Lorem ipsum dolor sit amet, consectetuer
  adipiscing elit, sed diam nonummy nibh euismod tincidunt ut laoreet dolore
  magna aliquam erat volutpat.</p>
  <p>Duis autem vel eum iriure dolor in hendrerit in vulputate velit esse
  molestie consequat, vel illum dolore eu feugiat nulla facilisis at vero
  eros et accumsan et iusto odio dignissim qui blandit praesent luptatum
  zzril delenit augue duis dolore te feugait nulla facilisi. Lorem ipsum
  dolor sit amet, consectetuer adipiscing elit, sed diam nonummy nibh euismod
  tincidunt ut laoreet dolore magna aliquam erat volutpat. Ut wisi enim ad
  minim veniam, quis nostrud exerci tation ullamcorper suscipit lobortis nisl
  ut aliquip ex ea commodo consequat.</p>
  </body>
  </html>
```

products.html

```
<!DOCTYPE HTML PUBLIC "-//W3C//DTD HTML 4.01 Frameset//EN"
    "http://www.w3.org/TR/html4/frameset.dtd">
<html>
<head>
  <title>Product Page Content</title>
</head>
<body>
  <h3>Products</h3>
  <p>Lorem ipsum dolor sit amet, consectetuer adipisc-
ing elit, sed diam nonummy
nibh euismod tincidunt ut laoreet dolore magna aliquam erat volutpat. Ut wisi
enim ad minim veniam, quis nostrud exerci tation ullamcorper suscipit lobortis
nisl ut aliquip ex ea commodo consequat. Duis autem vel eum iriure dolor in
hendrerit in vulputate velit esse molestie consequat, vel illum
dolore eu feugiat
nulla facilisis at vero eros et accumsan et iusto odio dignissim qui blandit
praesent luptatum zzril delenit augue duis dolore te feugait nulla facil-
isi.</p>
</body>
</html>
```

Summary

This chapter introduced the concept of frames, including the relatively new inline
frame construct. Using frames or inline frames, you can insert separately scrollable
and formatted regions inside a larger document. As with most older HTML
technologies, you should take care when choosing to use frames—in many
instances, you would be better off learning and using CSS instead.

✦　　✦　　✦

Forms

HTML's somewhat humble beginnings were receive-only; that is, the user could receive data, but was not expected to be able to send data. However, that was quickly realized as a deficiency of HTML—with the user agents being run in graphical environments with rich user interfaces, creating a similar interface for which to allow users to submit data seemed a natural extension.

Today, forms comprise a complex yet flexible framework to allow users basic controls. These controls can be used to provide input back to scripts or to submit data. This chapter delves into the particulars of HTML forms.

Understanding Forms

HTML forms simply place a handful of GUI controls on the user agent to allow the user to enter data. The controls can allow text input, allow selection of predefined choices from a list, radio or check boxes, or other standard GUI controls.

After the data is entered into the fields, a special control is used to pass the entered data on to a program that can do something useful with the data. Such programs are typically referred to as form handlers because they "handle" the form data.

The following code shows a basic HTML form whose output is shown in Figure 13-1.

```
<!DOCTYPE HTML PUBLIC "-//W3C//DTD HTML 4.01//EN"
  "http://www.w3.org/TR/html4/strict.dtd">
<html>
<head>
  <title>A Simple Form</title>
</head>
<body>
<form action="formhandler.php" method="post">
  <table cellspacing="20">
  <tr><td>
    <!-- Text boxes -->
    <p><label for="fname">First Name: </label>
```

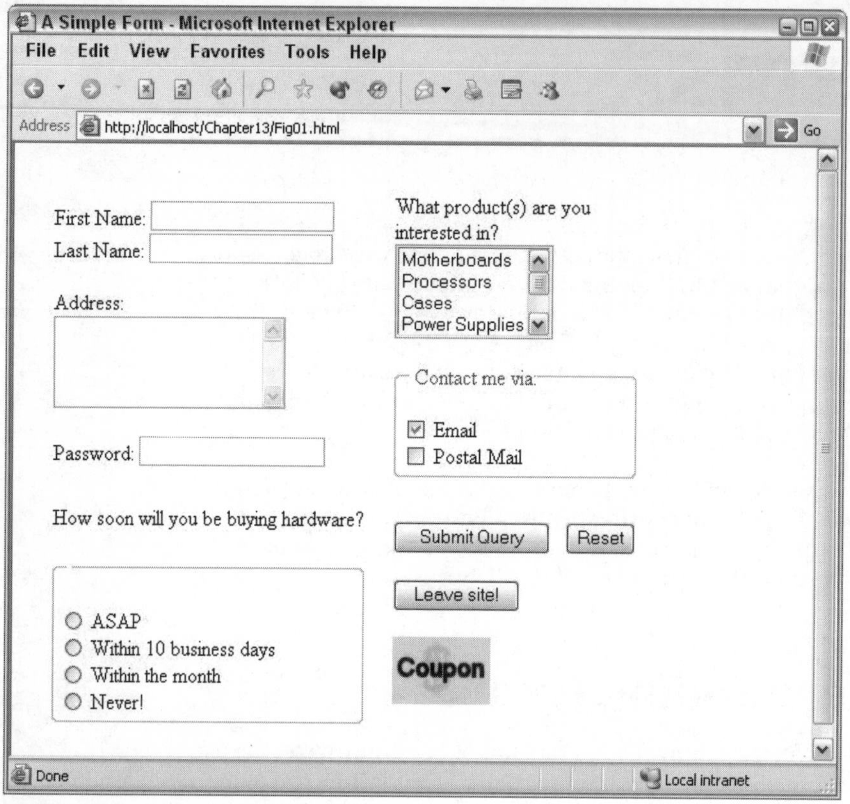

Figure 13-1: A simple HTML form.

```
    <input type="text" name="fname" id="fname"
    size="20"><br>
<label for="lname">Last Name: </label>
    <input type="text" name="lname" id="lname" size="20">
</p>

<!-- Text area -->
<p><label for="address">Address:</label><br>
  <textarea name="address" id="address"
    cols=20 rows=4></textarea>
</p>

<!-- Password -->
<p><label for="password">Password: </label>
  <input type="password" name="password" id="password"
    size="20">
</p>

</td>
<td>
<!-- Select list -->
<p><label for="products">What product(s) are you<br>
```

```
interested in? </label><br>
<select name="prod[]" id="products" multiple="multiple"
  size="4">
  <option id="MB">Motherboards
  <option id="CPU">Processors
  <option id="Case">Cases
  <option id="Power">Power Supplies
  <option id="Mem">Memory
  <option id="HD">Hard Drives
  <option id="Periph">Peripherals
</select>
</p>

<!-- Check boxes -->
<fieldset>
  <legend>Contact me via: </legend>
  <p><input type="checkbox" name="email" id="email"
      checked>
    <label for="email">Email</label><br>
  <input type="checkbox" name="postal" id="postal">
    <label for="postal">Postal Mail</label></p>
</fieldset>

</td>
</tr>
<tr>
<td>
<!-- Radio buttons -->
<p>How soon will you be buying hardware?</p>
<fieldset>
<legend></legend>
<p><input type="radio" name="buy" value="ASAP"
    id="buyASAP">
  <label for="buyASAP">ASAP</label><br>
<input type="radio" name="buy" value="10" id="buy10">
  <label for="buy10">Within 10 business days</label><br>
<input type="radio" name="buy" value="30" id="buy30">
  <label for="buy30">Within the month</label><br>
<input type="radio" name="buy" value="Never"
  id="buyNever">
  <label for="buyNever">Never!</label></p>
</fieldset>
</td>

<td>
<!-- Submit and Reset buttons -->
<p>
<input type="submit">   
<input type="reset">
</p>

<!-- Button -->
<p>
<input type="button" name="Leave" value="Leave site!">
</p>
```

```
                    <!-- Image -->
                    <input type="image" name="Coupon" src="coupon.jpg">

                    <!-- Hidden field -->
                    <input type="hidden" name="referredby" value="Google">

                 </td>
                 </tr>
                 </table>

             </form>
             </body>
             </html>
```

Note　Many form tags do not have closing tags. However, XML and its variants require that all elements be closed. If you are coding for XML or one of its variants (such as XHTML), be sure to close your tags by including the closing slash (/) at the end of tags that lack a formal closing tag.

Inserting a Form

You insert a form into your document by placing form fields within `<form>` tags. The entire form or any of the tags can be formatted like any other element in your document, and can be placed within any element capable of holding other elements (paragraphs, tables, and so on).

The `<font>` tag has the following, minimum format:

```
<form action="url_to_send_data" method="get|post">
```

The action attribute defines a URL where the data from the form should be sent to be "handled." Although you can use just about any URL, the destination should be a script or other construct capable of correctly interpreting and doing something useful with the data.

Note　Form actions and form data handlers are covered in the section, *Form scripts and script services,* later in this chapter.

The second attribute, `method`, controls how the data is sent to the handler. The two valid values are `get` and `post`. Each value corresponds to the HTTP protocol of the same name.

HTTP GET

The HTTP GET protocol attaches data to the actual URL text to pass the data to the target. You have probably noticed URLs that resemble the following:

```
http://www.example.com/forms.cgi?id=45677&data=Taarna
```

The data appears after the question mark and is in name/value pairs. For example, the name `id` has the value of `45677`, and the name `data` has the value of `Taarna`.

Note In most cases, the name corresponds to field names from the form and may relate to variables in the data handler.

However, because the data is passed in the text of the URL, it is easy to implement—you can pass data by simply adding appropriate text to the URL used to call the data handler. However, GET is also inherently insecure. Never use GET to send confidential data to a handler, because the data is clearly visible in most user agents and can be easily sniffed by hackers.

HTTP POST

The HTTP POST method passes data encoded in the HTTP data stream. As such, it is not typically visible to a user and is a more secure method to pass data, but can be harder to implement. Thankfully, HTML forms and most other Web technologies make passing data via POST a trivial task.

Additional <form> attributes

The `<form>` tag has many additional attributes. These attributes are listed in Table 13-1.

Table 13-1 <form> Tag Attributes	
Attribute	**Values**
Accept	A comma-separated list of content types that the handler's server will accept
accept-charset	A comma-separated list of character sets the form data may be in
Enctype	The content type the form data is in
Name	The name of the form (deprecated, use the `id` attribute instead)
Target	Where to open the handler URL (deprecated)

Although you may not need these attributes in simple forms, these attributes can be very useful. The `accept`, `accept-charset`, and `enctype` attributes are invaluable for processing nontextual and International data. The `id` attribute (formerly the `name` attribute) should be used to uniquely identify a form in your document, especially if you use more than one form in the same document.

Field Labels

The `<label>` tag defines textual labels for form fields. The `<label>` tag has the following format:

```
<label for="id_of_related_tag">text_label</label>
```

For example, the following code defines a label for a text box:

```
<p><label for="FirstName">First Name: </label>
<input type="text" id="FirstName" name="FirstName" value=""
size="30" maxlength="40"></p>
```

The role of the `<label>` tag is accessibility-related. Most users can rely upon the layout of your forms to determine what labels go with what fields. However, if the user agent does not have a visual component, or if the user is visually impaired, the visual layout of the form cannot be relied upon to match labels and fields. The `<label>` tag's `for` attribute ensures that the user agent can adequately match labels with fields.

Text Input Boxes

One of the most used fields of HTML forms is the simple text field. This field allows for the input of small pieces of text—names, addresses, search terms, and so on.

The text input field tag has the following format:

```
<input type="text" name="field_name" value="initial_value"
  size="size_of_field" maxlength="max_characters_allowed">
```

Although all the attributes previously listed are not required, they represent the minimum attributes that you should always use with your text boxes. The following sample text box is designed to accept a name, appears 30 characters long, accepts a maximum of 40 characters, and has no initial value:

```
<p>Name: <input type="text" name="username" value=""
  size="30" maxlength="40"></p>
```

The following code example defines a text box to accept an e-mail address. It appears 40 characters wide, only accepts 40 characters, and has an initial value of "`email@example.com`":

```
<p>Email: <input type="text" name="email"
value="email@example.com" size="40" maxlength="40"></p>
```

Password Input Boxes

The password input box is similar to the text box, but visually obscures data entered into the box by displaying asterisks instead of the actual data entered into the field. The following example displays a password field that accepts 20 characters.

```
<p>Password: <input type="password" name="password" value=""
size="20" maxlength="20"></p>
```

Caution The password field only visibly obscures the data to help stop casual snoops from seeing what a user inputs into a field. It does not encode or in any way obscure the information at the data level. As such, be careful how you use this field.

Radio Buttons

Radio buttons are groups of small, round buttons that allow a user to choose one option in a group. The name "radio" button comes from how old-fashioned radios used to be tuned—you pushed one of many buttons to tune to a preset station. When one button was pushed, the rest were reset to the out position. Like those buttons, form radio buttons are mutually exclusive—only one of the group can be set. When one is selected, the others in the group are deselected.

The radio button field has the following format:

```
<input type="radio" name="group_name" [checked="checked"]
value="value_if_selected">
```

Note that the `value` attribute defines what value is returned to the handler if the button is selected. This attribute should be unique between buttons in the same group.

The following example code defines a group of radio buttons that allows a user to select their gender:

```
<p>Gender:
<input type="radio" name="gender" value="male"> Male
<input type="radio" name="gender" value="female"> Female</p>
```

If you want a button selected by default, add the `checked` attribute to the appropriate button's tag.

Tip XML and its variants do not allow attributes without values. HTML will allow the `checked` attribute to be used with or without a value. To ensure your code remains as compliant as possible, it is suggested that you specify a checked box with the checked attribute as `checked="checked"` **instead of just** `checked`.

Check Boxes

Check boxes are small, square boxes that are used to select non–mutually exclusive choices. They are so named because, when selected, they display a checkmark (or more commonly an "X") in the box like the check boxes in paper lists.

The `checkbox` field has the following format:

```
<input type="checkbox" name="field_name" [checked="checked"]
  value="value_if_selected">
```

As you can see, other than the mutually exclusive issue, check boxes are very similar in definition to radio buttons. The following example displays a check box allowing the user to select whether they receive solicitous e-mails:

```
<p><input type="checkbox" name="spam_me" checked="checked"
value="spam_me"> Add me to your email list</p>
```

Note that the `checked` attribute can be used to preselect check boxes in your forms. Also, just like radio buttons, the value attribute is used as the value of the check box if it is selected. If no value is given, selected check boxes are given the value of "on."

List Boxes

List boxes are used to allow a user to pick one or more textual items from a list. The list can be presented in its entirety, with each element visible or as a pull-down list where the user can scroll to their choices.

List boxes are implemented using `<select>` and `<option>` tags, and optionally the `<optgroup>` tag.

The `<select>` tag provides the container for the list and has the following format:

```
<select name="name_of_field" size="items_to_show"
  [multiple="multiple"]>
```

The `<option>` tag defines the items for the list. Each item is given its own `<option>` tag. This tag has the optional attributes shown in Table 13-2.

Table 13-2	
`<option>` Tag Attributes	
Attribute	**Values**
Label	A shorter label for the item that the user agent can use
Selected	Indicates that the item should be initially selected
Value	The value that should be sent to the handler if the item is selected; if omitted, the text of the item is sent item is selected; if omitted, the text of the item is sent

An example of a minimum of `<option>` tags follows:

```
<option>Sunday
<option>Monday
<option>Tuesday
<option>Wednesday
```

```
<option>Thursday
<option>Friday
<option>Saturday
```

Occasionally, you might want to group options of a list together for clarity. For this you use `<optgroup>` tags. The `<optgroup>` tag encapsulates items that should be in that group. For example, the following code defines two groups for the preceding list of options, weekend and weekday:

```
<optgroup label="Weekend">
  <option>Sunday
  <option>Saturday
</optgroup>
<optgroup label="Weekday"
  <option>Monday
  <option>Tuesday
  <option>Wednesday
  <option>Thursday
  <option>Friday
</optgroup>
```

Different user agents display option groups differently, but the default behavior is to display the option group labels above the options to which they apply, as shown in Figure 13-2.

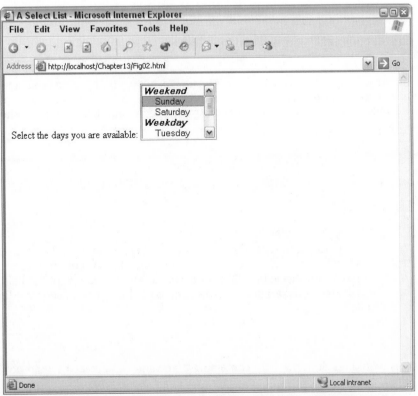

Figure 13-2: Option groups are displayed in the list as nonselectable items.

Combining all three tags to create a list would resemble the following code:

```
<p>Select the days you are available:
<select name="AvailDays" size="5" multiple="multiple">
  <optgroup label="Weekend">
    <option>Sunday
    <option>Saturday
  </optgroup>
  <optgroup label="Weekday"
    <option>Monday
    <option>Tuesday
    <option>Wednesday
    <option>Thursday
    <option>Friday
  </optgroup>
</select>
</p>
```

Large Text Areas

For large pieces of text, you can use the `<textarea>` tag. This tag can accept textual input of up to 1,024 characters and uses a multiline text box for input.

The `<textarea>` tag has the following format:

```
<textarea name="name_of_field" cols="number_of_columns"
rows="number_of_rows"></textarea>
```

Note that the `<textarea>` tag is one of the few form tags that has an open and a close tag. If you want the field to have default content, the content should be placed between the tags. For example, the following code results in the initial form shown in Figure 13-3:

```
<textarea cols="50" rows="6">
John Doe
123 Main Street
Anywhere, USA
</textarea>
```

Tip

Whatever is placed between the `<textarea>` tags appears verbatim in the text box when the form is first displayed. Therefore, it is important to carefully watch the formatting of your HTML code. For example, if you want the field to be initially blank, you *cannot* place the open and close tags on separate lines in the code:

```
<textarea>
</textarea>
```

This would result in the field containing a newline character—it would not be blank.

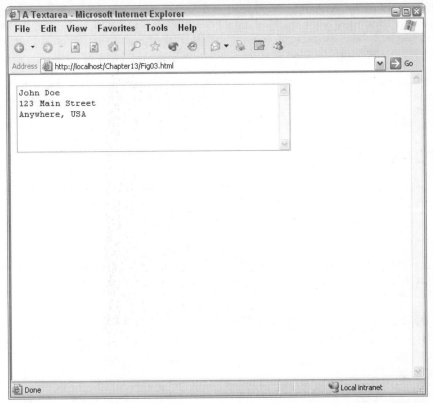

Figure 13-3: You can set a default value for the <textarea> tag by placing content between the open and close tags.

Note that the text entered into the `<textarea>` field wraps within the width of the box, but the text is sent verbatim to the handler. That is, where the user enters line breaks, those breaks are also sent to the handler. However, the wrapped text (without hard line breaks) is sent without breaks.

Note   Previous versions of HTML supported a `wrap` attribute for the `<textarea>` tag. This attribute could be used to control how text wrapped in the text box as well as how it was sent to the handler. Unfortunately, user agent support for this attribute was inconsistent—you could not rely on a browser to follow the intent of the attribute. As such, the attribute has been deprecated and should not be used.

Hidden Fields

Hidden fields are used to add data to the form without displaying it to the user. The hidden field has the following format:

```
<input type="hidden" name="name_of_field"
value="value_of_field">
```

Other than not being visibly displayed, hidden fields are like any other field. Hidden fields are used mostly for tracking data. For example, in a multipage form, a `userid` field can be hidden in the form to ensure that subsequent forms, when submitted, are tied to the same user data.

Keep in mind that hidden fields do not display on the user agent but are still visible in the code of the document. As such, hidden fields should never be used for sensitive data.

Buttons

Occasionally, you might have need for additional, custom buttons on your form. For those cases, you can use the button field. This field has the following format:

```
<input type="button" name="name_of_field"
value="text_for_button">
```

This tag results in a standard graphical button being displayed on the form. The following code example results in the button shown in Figure 13-4:

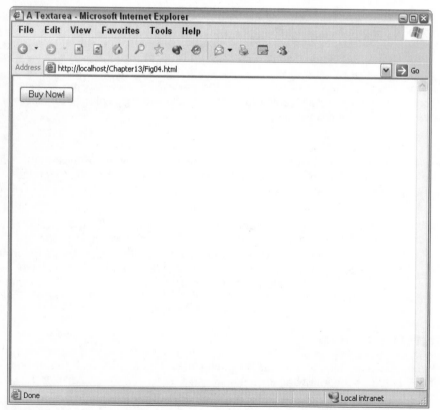

Figure 13-4: You can use the button field to add custom buttons to your form.

```
<input type="button" name="BuyNow"
value="Buy Now!">
```

Buttons by themselves, however, are useless on a form. To have the button actually do something, you will need to link it to a script via the `onclick` or other attribute. For example, the following code results in a button that, when clicked, runs the script "buynow":

```
<input type="button" name="BuyNow"
value="Buy Now!" onclick="JavaScript:buynow()">
```

Images

Images provide a graphical means to convey a message. Using the image type of the `<input>` tag you can add images to your form, an image that can be used along with other form elements to gather data. The image field has the following format:

```
<input type="image" name="name_of_field"
src="url_to_image_file">
```

However, like the button field, image fields by themselves do not provide any actual form controls. To use the image for input purposes, it must be linked to a script. The following example causes the image `buynow.jpg` to be displayed on a form. When the image is clicked, the script `buynow` is run:

```
<input type="image" name="buynow" src="buynow.jpg"
onclick="JavaScript:buynow()">
```

File Fields

File fields allow a user to browse for a local file and send it as an attachment to the form data. The file field has the following format:

```
<input type="file" name="name_of_field"
size="display_size_of_field">
```

The file field results in a text box with a button that enables the user to browse for a file using their platform's file browser. Alternately, the user can simply type the path and name of the file in the text box. Figure 13-5 shows an example of a file field in Internet Explorer.

However, in order to use this control in your forms you must do the following:

✦ Specify your form as multipart, which allows the file to be attached to the rest of the data.

✦ Use the POST, not the GET, method of form delivery.

Figure 13-5: The file field allows a user to send a local file.

This means your `<form>` tag should resemble the following:

```
<form action="form_handler" method="post"
enctype="form/multipart">
```

Submit and Reset Buttons

Submit and reset buttons provide control mechanisms for users to submit the data entered to a handler and reset the form to its default state. These buttons have the following format:

Submit button

```
<input type="submit" [value="text_for_button"] >
```

Reset button

```
<input type="reset" [value="text_for_button"] >
```

The `value` attribute for both tags is optional—if this attribute is omitted, the buttons will display default text (usually "`Submit`" and "`Reset`," but is ultimately determined by the user agent).

The submit button, when clicked, causes the form to be submitted to the handler specified in the `<form>` tag's `action` attribute. Alternately, you can use the `onclick` attribute to call a script to preprocessing the form data.

The reset button, when clicked, causes the form to be reloaded and its fields reset to their default values. You can also use the `onclick` attribute to change the button's behavior, calling a script instead of reloading the form.

Tip

Use of `onclick` to change the reset button's behavior is not recommended. Using `onclick` to cause the submit button to run a script for preprocessing is an expected process, but the reset button should always simply reset the form. If you need a button to perform some other function, use a custom button field that is appropriately labeled.

Tab Order and Keyboard Shortcuts

Two additional attributes, `tabindex` and `accesskey`, should be used with your form fields to increase their accessibility.

The `tabindex` attribute defines what order the fields are selected in when the user presses the Tab key. This attribute takes a numeric argument that specifies the field's order on the form.

The `accesskey` attribute defines a key that the user can press to directly access the field. This attribute takes a single letter as an argument—that letter becomes the key the user can press to directly access the field.

Note

Keys specified in `accesskey` attributes usually require an additional key to be pressed with the key. For example, user agents running on Windows require the Alt key to be pressed along with the letter specified by `accesskey`. Other platforms require similar keys—such keys typically follow the GUI interface conventions of the platform.

The following example defines a text box that can be accessed by pressing *Alt+F* (on Windows platforms), and is third in the tab order:

```
<p><label for="FirstName"><u>F</u>irst Name: </label>
<input type="text" id="FirstName" name="FirstName" value=""
tabindex="3" accesskey="F" size="30" maxlength="40"></p>
```

Preventing Changes

There are two ways to display information in common form fields but not allow a user to change the data—by setting the field to read-only or disabled.

You can add the `readonly` attribute to text fields to keep the user from being able to edit the data contained therein.

The `disabled` attribute effectively disables a control (usually graying out the control, consistent with the user agent's platform method of showing disabled controls) so the user cannot use the control.

The following code shows examples of both a read-only and a disabled control. The output of this code is shown in Figure 13-6.

```
<!DOCTYPE HTML PUBLIC "-//W3C//DTD HTML 4.01//EN"
  "http://www.w3.org/TR/html4/strict.dtd">
<html>
<head>
  <title>A Textarea</title>
</head>
<body>
```

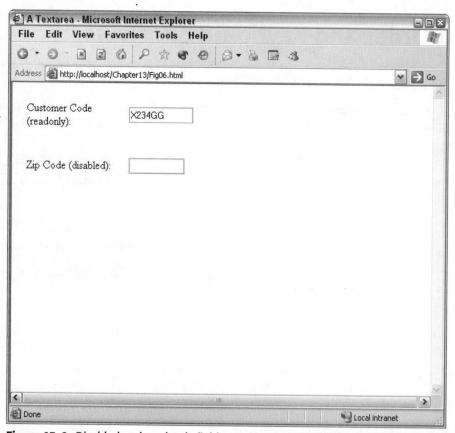

Figure 13-6: Disabled and read-only fields can be used to show data without the data being edited.

```
<form action="formhandler.php" method="post">
<table cellspacing="10" width="600">
<tr><td width="25%">
<p>Customer Code (readonly):</p>
</td><td>
<input type="text" size="12" value="X234GG"
  readonly="readonly">
</td></tr>
</table>
<tr><td>
<p>Zip Code (disabled):</p>
</td><td>
<input type="text" size="10" value=""
  disabled="disabled">
</td></tr>
</table>
</form>
</body>
</html>
```

Although the two attributes make the fields look similar on screen, the `readonly` field can be selected, just not edited. The `disabled` field cannot be selected at all.

Tip

Disabling a control that is not applicable in certain instances is common practice. For example, international addresses do not have a U.S. ZIP code. If a user indicates that they have an international address, you might decide to disable the ZIP code field so they do not enter data in that field.

You can use client-side scripts to dynamically disable controls. Use `onblur` or `onchange` attributes to call a script from fields that could change the enabled status of other fields—those scripts check the data entered and enable or disable other fields by changing the value of that field's disabled attribute. More information on such techniques can be found in Chapters 25 and 26.

Fieldsets and Legends

Sometimes, it is advantageous to visually group certain controls on your form. This is a standard practice for graphical user agents, as shown in Figure 13-7.

The `<fieldset>` tag is used as a container for form elements and results in a thin border being displayed around the elements it surrounds. For example, the following code results in the output shown in Figure 13-8.

```
<fieldset>
<p>Gender: <br>
<input type="radio" name="gender" value="male"> Male <br>
<input type="radio" name="gender" value="female"> Female</p>
</fieldset>
```

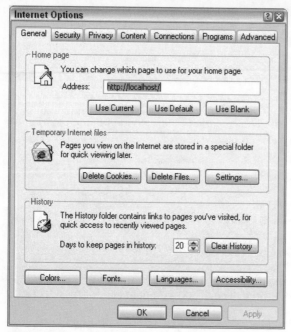

Figure 13-7: Grouping controls allows a user to better understand a form's organization. This is standard in GUI interfaces, as demonstrated in this Windows Internet Explorer dialog box.

The `<legend>` tag allows the surrounding `<fieldset>` box to be captioned. For example, the following code adds a caption to the previous example. The output of this change is shown in Figure 13-9.

```
<fieldset>
<p><legend>Gender </legend>
<input type="radio" name="gender" value="male"> Male <br>
<input type="radio" name="gender" value="female"> Female</p>
</fieldset>
```

Form Scripts and Script Services

As previously mentioned in the *Understanding Forms* section in this chapter, form data is typically passed to a data handler, a script or program that does something useful with the data.

Form handlers typically do one or more of the following actions with the form data:

✦ Manipulate or verify the data

✦ E-mail the data

✦ Store the data in a file or database

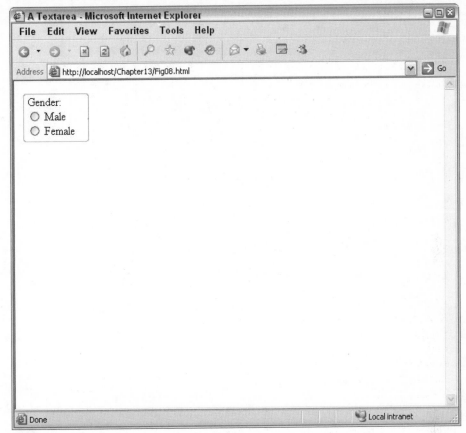

Figure 13-8: The `<fieldset>` tag can help add organization to your forms.

There are many ways to construct a form handler, but the usual method is by using a server-side programming language to create a script that does what you need to the data. Common form handlers are created in Perl, Python, PHP, or other server-side programming language.

Security is an issue that should be considered when creating form handlers. One of the earliest, most popular form handlers, `formmail.cgi`, was found to have a vulnerability that allowed anyone to send data to the script and have it e-mail the data to whomever the sender wanted. This functionality was an instant hit with e-mail spammers who still use unsecured `formmail` scripts to send anonymous spam.

Because form-handling scripts can be so diverse (performing different functions, written in different languages), it is hard to give tangible examples here. You should use a language you are comfortable with to create a form handler that does exactly what you want.

If you want a generic form handler to simply store or e-mail the data, you can choose from a few routes.

Figure 13-9: The `<legend>` tag can add captions to your fieldsets.

Download a handler

Several sites on the Internet have generic form handlers available. One of my favorites is the CGI Resource Index, `http://cgi.resourceindex.com/`. This site has several dozen scripts that you can download and use for your form handling.

Use a script service

Several services are also available that allow you to process your form data through their server and scripts. You may need such a service if you cannot run scripts on your server or want a generic, no-hassle solution.

A partial list of script services is available at the CGI Resource Index, `http://cgi.resourceindex.com/`. From the main page, select Remotely Hosted and browse for a service that meets your needs.

Summary

This chapter showed you the particulars of HTML forms. It demonstrated how to include them in your documents and what each form tag can accomplish. The next two chapters introduce multimedia content and scripting—showing you how to include both in your documents. The next part of this book (Part III) dives into the deep subject of Cascading Style Sheets (CSS).

✦　　✦　　✦

Multimedia

◆ ◆ ◆ ◆

◆ ◆ ◆ ◆

Multimedia on the Web has grown up. You can see full-length movies on the Web, watch baseball games in real time on MLB.com, watch video news bulletins on CNN, and play games with other users.

Generally, the best user experiences exist within the realm of broadband access, such as DSL and cable. Getting streaming video to work over a dialup connection is nearly impossible, but that doesn't completely rule out multimedia. However, most developers who are reaching for lofty goals in the multimedia world now target folks with fast connections—since a sufficient base of broadband connections have been installed.

This chapter examines some of the multimedia platforms most frequently used on today's Web. Many, of course, have crowned Flash as the unofficial king of multimedia, but don't discount other technologies, especially if you're developing slideshows and video presentations.

Introducing Multimedia Objects

Depending on the browser with which your users view your Web pages, multimedia can offer either a very rewarding or a very frustrating experience for your users.

For example, if your users are using Netscape 3 to view a multimedia page, chances are they'll be taking a long journey that they'll ultimately cancel. This journey will consist of numerous dialog boxes and visits to Web pages for downloading plug-ins, which are small extensions to browsers used to extend a browser's capabilities. These downloads are necessary when a browser first encounters a multimedia object, because browsers don't have native support for such multimedia as Flash, RealAudio (now known as RealOne), and so on.

In fact, you might be surprised to find out that browsers on today's market generally don't provide native support for the near ubiquitous Flash plug-in (Opera is the lone exception, but it's usually a version or so behind the latest Flash players). Instead, the plug-in for Flash needs to be installed. However, Macromedia, the developer of Flash, has made the installation process so painless that Macromedia claims that Flash is now in more than 97% of all browsers. Those figures may be inflated by Macromedia's PR machine, but there is little question that the installed base is huge. You can be assured, however, that of those who don't have the plug-ins installed, many of them have older browsers such as Netscape 3. The reason for the difference is that modern browsers make plug-in installation a snap, whereas older versions required multiple visits to different sites and often numerous forms.

Frankly, the best way to handle users with antiquated browsers is to simply bypass their multimedia options altogether, because their use of such an ancient browser is an indication that they don't care very much about the newest technology anyway. This can be done using browser-sniffing scripts.

Browser sniffing, or browser detection, is a JavaScript-based process for detecting what kind of browser a user is using to view Web pages and displaying content based on the results of these findings. Chapter 26 explains how to develop these scripts.

You can use a browser-sniffing script to send users with older browsers to HTML-only pages or write messages to their browser windows telling them they have crummy browsers (in a nice way, of course).

Keep in mind that professional-looking multimedia requires a substantial investment in either your time or money (which you'll spend to get a professional to put it together for you). A long time ago, HTML purists cringed when they saw the notorious `<blink>` tag. Today, many Web site visitors' first reaction upon seeing Flash intros is to hunt for the "Skip Intro" button on these presentations. When making a decision about whether to use a multimedia object, ask yourself the following questions:

✦ Does the multimedia object actually offer something I can't otherwise accomplish with HTML?

✦ Does it truly enhance my Web site?

✦ Will my users' browsers support the multimedia object I'm using?

✦ Do I have the resources to make a genuinely professional multimedia presentation?

If you can answer these questions in the affirmative, you're ready to go.

Your multimedia options

There are four general categories of multimedia objects:

✦ *Video clips*—are supported by such applications as RealOne Player, the Windows Media Player, or Apple's QuickTime. Generally, when a file relying on one of these programs is accessed, the multimedia doesn't appear within the browser window (although it can). Instead, it spawns a window of the player application that plays the media.

✦ *Animations*—can be generated by bit-map-based (paint) applications, such as Fireworks and Photoshop. These kinds of programs create GIF files consisting of several frames to produce an animation. Maybe you remember seeing a stack of papers in elementary school with a series of pictures, and as you flip through the stack, the image changed ever so slightly, creating an animated effect. The process is similar with animated GIFs. You see them everywhere these days, especially in banner ads. Most people consider them annoying, so use them with care and caution.

✦ *Sounds*—can come in many formats, but again, you want to use them judiciously, because you can turn off your Web site visitors with them and even get them into trouble if they're visiting your Web page from the work place.

✦ *Slide shows*—are surprisingly useful for Web sites and can be created quite easily using PowerPoint or a free slide creation tool such as the presentation creation tool in OpenOffice.org's office suite.

What about Java applets?

Java applets, although not as common as they once were, are still used occasionally by some developers. The problem with Java applets is that they rely on a Java Virtual Machine installation that has proven to result in terrible inconsistencies across platforms. The only way around this is to hire an army of programmers to produce rock solid browser-sniffing scripts. One example of a reasonably successful deployment of Java-based applets was ESPN's GameCast, but even that has moved over to Flash.

Including multimedia in your Web pages

One kind of multimedia requires no plug-ins at all and can be written directly in your HTML. This is the animated GIF, which can simply be included in an img element, like so:

```
<img src="myAnimation.gif" width="468" height="60">
```

As long as the animated GIF actually animates, you're in business.

Most other multimedia requires the use of a plug-in, although you could consider some Dynamic HTML and CSS to be multimedia; and certainly, especially with some of the transition effects available in Internet Explorer through the use of both scripting and Microsoft's proprietary extensions to CSS, multimedia effects can be accomplished this way.

 Cross-Reference Dynamic HTML and CSS effects are covered in detail in Chapter 27.

The standard way of embedding a multimedia object using HTML 4.0 is through the use of the object element. The attributes available for the element are shown in Table 14-1.

Table 14-1
Attributes of the Object Element

Attribute Name	HTML Standard and Description
archive (optional)	(HTML 4.0) A space-separated list of URIs for archives of classes and resources to be preloaded. Using this attribute can significantly improve the speed of an object
classid (optional)	(HTML 4.0) Specifies the location of the object's implementation by URI. Depending upon the type of object involved, it can be used with or as an alternative to the data attribute
codebase (optional)	(HTML 4.0) Indicates the base URI for the path to the object file. The default is the same base URI as the document
codetype (recommended)	(HTML 4.0) Specifies the content type of data expected. If this is omitted, the default is the same as the type attribute
data (optional)	(HTML 4.0) Specifies the location of the object's data. If given as a relative URI, it is relative to the code-based URI
height (optional)	(HTML 4.0) Specifies the initial height in pixels or percentages of the element
hspace (optional)	(HTML 4.0) Defines the number of pixels on the horizontal sides of the element
id (optional)	(HTML 4.0) (CSS enabled) Formats the contents of the tag according to the style id. Note: IDs must be unique within a document
name (optional)	(HTML 4.0) The name attribute assigns the control name to the element
standby (optional)	(HTML 4.0) This specifies a message that is shown to a user while the object is loading
style (optional)	(HTML 4.0) (CSS enabled) Formats the contents of the element according to the listed style
type (optional)	(HTML 4.0) Indicates the content type at the link target. Specify the type as a MIME-type. This attribute is case-insensitive
vspace (optional)	(HTML 4.0) Defines the number of pixels on the vertical sides of the element
width (optional)	(HTML 4.0) Specifies the initial width in pixels or percentages of the element.

You can also use child `param` elements within an `object` element to pass parameters to the multimedia object. These parameters are generally like little bits of helpful information that help fine-tune exactly how you want the object to behave. You can use Table 14-2 to review the `param` element's attributes.

Table 14-2
Attributes of the param Element

Attribute Name	HTML Standard and Description
Name	Specifies the name of the parameter being passed to the object
type (optional)	Specifies the MIME type of the data
value (optional)	Specifies the value of the parameter being passed to the object
Valuetype	Specifies the type of value being passed

The following example shows a Flash file embedded in an HTML document:

```
<object classid="clsid:d27cdb6e-ae6d-11cf-96b8-444553540000"
codebase="http://download.macromedia.com/pub/shockwave/cabs/f
lash/swflash.cab#version=5,0,0,0" width="120" height="600"
id="marrow" align="middle">
<param name="allowScriptAccess" value="sameDomain" />
<param name="movie" value="marrow.swf" />
<param name="loop" value="false" />
<param name="quality" value="high" />
<param name="bgcolor" value="#ffffff" />
<embed src="marrow.swf" loop="false" quality="high"
bgcolor="#ffffff" width="120" height="600" name="marrow"
align="middle" allowScriptAccess="sameDomain"
type="application/x-shockwave-flash"
pluginspage="http://www.macromedia.com/go/getflashplayer" />
</object>
```

The key to using the `param` elements is that the multimedia object must understand what the parameters mean. So, you need to either have access to some documentation about how the multimedia object works and what kind of parameters it expects, or you need to get your hands on a tool that generates the HTML for you. In the case of Flash, its movie exporting facilities take care of this for you. Listing 14-1 provides an example.

Listing 14-1: **Embedding a Flash File Using an Object Element**

```
<!DOCTYPE html PUBLIC "-//W3C//DTD XHTML 1.0
Transitional//EN" "http://www.w3.org/TR/xhtml1/DTD/
xhtml1-transitional.dtd">
```

Continued

Listing 14-1: *(continued)*

```
<html xmlns="http://www.w3.org/1999/xhtml" xml:lang="en"
lang="en">
<head>
<meta http-equiv="Content-Type" content="text/html;
charset=iso-8859-1" />
<title>marrow</title>
</head>
<body bgcolor="#ffffff">
<object classid="clsid:d27cdb6e-ae6d-11cf-96b8-444553540000"
codebase="http://download.macromedia.com/pub/shockwave/cabs/
flash/swflash.cab#version=5,0,0,0" width="120" height="600"
id="marrow" align="middle">
<param name="allowScriptAccess" value="sameDomain" />
<param name="movie" value="marrow.swf" />
<param name="loop" value="false" />
<param name="quality" value="high" />
<param name="bgcolor" value="#ffffff" />
<embed src="marrow.swf" loop="false" quality="high"
bgcolor="#ffffff" width="120" height="600" name="marrow"
align="middle" allowScriptAccess="sameDomain"
type="application/x-shockwave-flash"
pluginspage="http://www.macromedia.com/go/getflashplayer" />
</object>
</body>
</html>
```

Note the use of the deprecated embed element as a child element of the object element. The embed element is still needed for Netscape 4 and some other browsers, however, so use it if you're looking for cross-browser functionality. Keep in mind the following about the embed element:

Do not include a name attribute with the object element when using the embed element, especially if it is the same name value as that of the embed element because it could cause confusion when scripting.

Parameters are handled through the use of custom attributes, such as those shown in Listing 14-1. Notice, for example, the allowScriptAccess="sameDomain" attribute/value pair. The allowScriptAccess attribute is not actually part of the embed element. Instead, it's a special attribute that Flash understands. These custom attributes have the same functionality as the object element's param element children. Different plug-in vendors may require different configuration parameters.

The pluginspage attribute *is* an attribute of the embed element. It manages the way in which a plug-in is obtained if it isn't installed in the browser. This attribute points to a page to get the plug-in if the plug-in is not detected by the browser.

How the Eolas Lawsuit Will Affect You

As this book was being written, Microsoft was trying to deal with losing a $521 million patent infringement lawsuit filed by Eolas, a company founded by Michael Doyle, former director of the University of California academic computing center. The patent governs the use of any object included in a Web page using the embed, object, or applet elements. Although Microsoft has appealed the decision, future versions of Internet Explorer (beyond version 6) will present a pop-up window asking users if they wish to view an embedded application or media file.

This does not affect objects that use no param elements.

There are some workarounds. One, obviously, is to not include any param elements. That pretty much wipes out any hope of using Flash. Another is to embed the applications using script.

The following example shows how to create a Web page that uses DHTML to load a Microsoft Windows Media® Player control.

```
<HTML>
    <HEAD>
        <SCRIPT SRC="sample.js"></SCRIPT>
    </HEAD>
    <BODY>
        <SCRIPT>
        ReplaceContent();
        </SCRIPT>
    </BODY>
</HTML>
```

An ActiveX control can be inserted into a Web page by setting the innerHTML or outerHTML property of an existing element, or by calling document.write (which is the healthier, cross-browser method). The following script creates the Windows Media Player using document.write:

```
function ReplaceContent(){
    document.write('<OBJECT CLASSID="CLSID:6BF52A52-394A-11d3-
B153-00C04F79FAA6">');
    document.write('<PARAM NAME="URL"
VALUE="http://msdn.microsoft.com/workshop/');
document.write('samples/author/dhtml/media/drums.wav"/></OBJECT>');
}
```

Multimedia Plug-Ins and Players

There are several kinds of popular multimedia plug-ins and players. The following are the most popular:

✦ Flash

✦ RealOne

✦ Windows Media Player

✦ Adobe Acrobat Reader

Flash

Flash, which has become arguably the most prevalent multimedia format, began life as a plug-in for something called FuturePlayer. FuturePlayer was purchased by Macromedia, which has made significant refinements to the original product. Macromedia had enjoyed reasonable success with its own Shockwave format, which was quite similar to Flash files but generated by Macromedia Director. Macromedia did a good job of commingling the two formats and, eventually, Shockwave pretty much disappeared in favor of Flash. Today's Flash can display MP3-based video and sound, along with vector graphics, and can harness data sources from relational databases and XML.

In fact, Flash has become a serious application platform in its own right, enabling developers to display changing data in real time.

RealOne

RealOne is a media player that reads video and audio files. Real, Inc., the developer of RealOne, was one of the first companies to introduce the concept of streaming audio to desktops. Streaming media (audio and video) is sent in real time through special servers. If you're doing professional-level streaming media, you'll want to see if your host provider (if you're using one) offers access to a Real Audio server.

If you're planning on developing for RealOne, you can find comprehensive Software Development Kits (SDKs) and tutorials at this site: `http://www.realnetworks.com/resources/sdk/`.

You can create standards-based files that RealOne can understand by using the Synchronized Multimedia Language (SMIL), described near the end of this chapter. Figure 14-1 shows an instance of a RealOne player.

Windows Media Player

Windows Media Player has a huge installed base because it comes as part of the Windows operating system. Its functionality is virtually identical to RealOne, offering video and music playing capabilities. To properly display Windows Media Player files, you should use the ASX markup language, which is an XML-based proprietary language developed by Microsoft.

When a user clicks an ASX link, the browser spawns an instance of the Windows Media Player. For example, refer to the following link:

```
<A HREF="http://webserver/path/yourfile.asx">Link to
Streaming Content</A>
```

Figure 14-1: A RealOne player accessing the main Real portal.

This links to the following file and opens up a Media Player:

```
<ASX version = "3.0">
<TITLE> ASX Demo</TITLE>
    <ENTRY>
    <TITLE>A New Song</TITLE>
    <AUTHOR>Chuck White</AUTHOR>
    <COPYRIGHT>(c)2003 Chuck White</COPYRIGHT>
    <!-- This is a comment. Change the following path to
point to your ASF -->
        <REF HREF =
"mms://windowsmediaserver/path/mysong.asf" />
    </ENTRY>
</ASX>
```

For the specifics of what the various elements mean in an ASX file, go to
`http://msdn.microsoft.com/library/default.asp?url=/nhp/Default.`
`asp?contentid=28000411`.

QuickTime

QuickTime has distinguished itself by consistently raising the bar on video quality.
QuickTime has long been a staple in the Apple world, but its quality is so good it has
made inroads into the Wintel world, as well.

The feature set is similar to RealOne and Windows Media Player. Like RealOne, you can create media shows for QuickTime using SMIL, as shown at the end of this chapter.

Animations

There are three main categories of animations. The simplest is an animated GIF file, but even those can be time consuming, because to make a nice animation requires that you create a new image for each frame of an animation. Another category of animation is a Java-based or ActiveX animation. Java is a machine-independent language that requires that the target user have a Java Virtual Machine (JVM) installed on his or her computer. Inconsistencies in JVMs have forced most Web animation aficionados to abandon Java as an animation platform. Active X animations are even more rare, because they're limited to Windows-based Internet Explorer browsers.

This helps explain why the third category, Flash, has become so popular—along with the fact that Macromedia has created what can only be described as a genuine application environment within the Flash framework.

Creating animated GIFs

Including an animated GIF file is the easiest of all the multimedia tasks. You simply create one in a paint program that supports them, or find an inexpensive or free program that specializes in helping you create them.

All Animated GIF creation programs are different, but their essence is the same. You start off with one frame, and when you want your image to change, you create another frame to represent that change. The frames can be on a complicated timeline, or as simple as the interface shown in Figures 14-2 and 14-3, which demonstrate an animated advertising banner being created using Macromedia's Fireworks.

The animation creation software then generates an animated GIF file consisting of as many frames as you indicate. You can also set the amount of time between the frame changes, as shown in Figure 14-4.

Figures 14-5 and 14-6 show the transition between one frame of a completed animated advertising banner and another.

Keeping files sizes small

Generally, you want to keep your file sizes small, and if you're creating advertising banners, the Web sites that run your ad will probably require you to keep them small. To keep your files small, keep in mind the following tips:

✦ Use as few frames as possible.

✦ Use as few colors as you can. This is where a higher-end animation program such as Fireworks (www.macromedia.com) or DeBabelizer (www.equilibrium.com) comes in handy. They help reduce the number of colors in your animation without degrading quality.

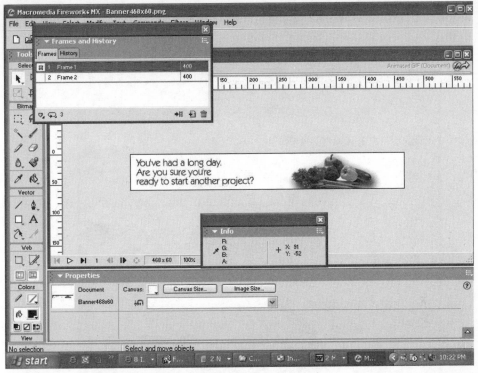

Figure 14-2: The first frame of an animation built in Fireworks.

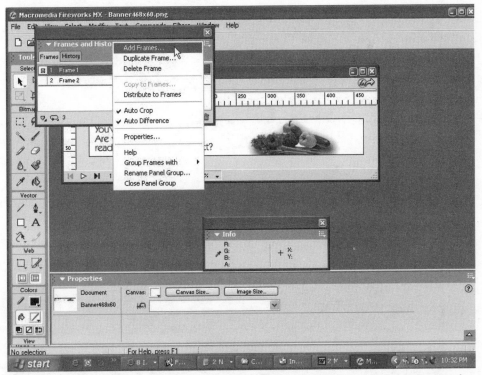

Figure 14-3: To build the second frame, you simply add the frame using the Frames and History palette.

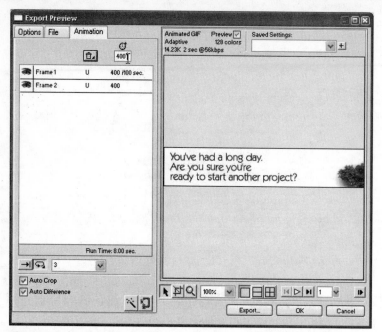

Figure 14-4: Changing the time interval between frame changes.

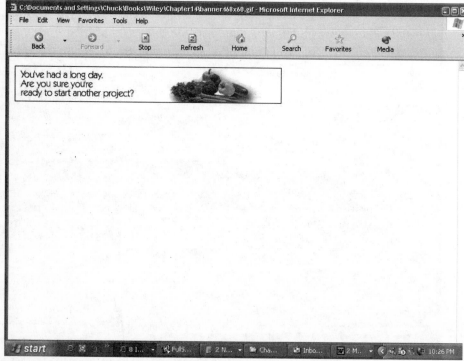

Figure 14-5: Transitioning between one frame of a completed animated advertising banner and another, part one.

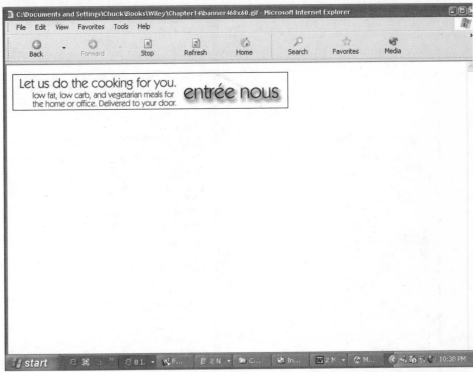

Figure 14-6: Transitioning between one frame of a completed animated advertising banner and another, part two.

Creating a Flash file

Creating a Flash file is not so easy. Flash is enormously popular because it's a very powerful tool, but in the wrong hands it can spell disaster. The Flash file format (with a .fla extension) is the starting point of a Flash presentation on the Web. Figure 14-7 shows two instances of the same Flash file side by side, each in a different stage of the animation. This kind of animation is much more sophisticated than an animated GIF, because it runs programmatically based on a scripting language similar to JavaScript named ActionScript. In the case of the animation shown in Figure 14-7 (downloadable as marrow.swf and marrow.fla), the text falls quickly into the pane to mimic someone quickly typing code. This is done through the use of an external XML file, which is simply looped through over and over again.

Done correctly, Flash is a marvelous tool, but it isn't the most intuitive program on earth, so be prepared for a bit of a learning curve if you want your Flash presentations to look professional. You've already seen how to include a Flash presentation in your HTML page in a previous explanation of how to use the object element.

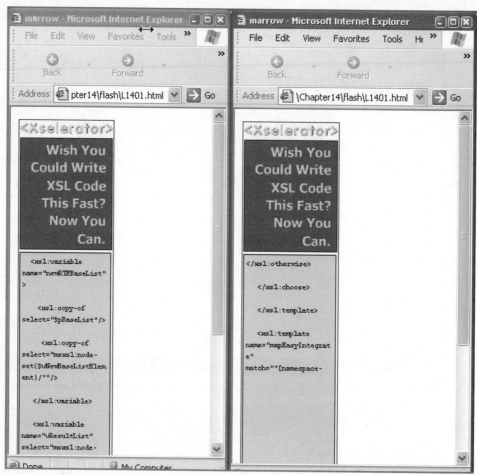

Figure 14-7: A Flash animation in action.

Video Clips

There are three major types of video:

✦ MPEG (short for Motion Picture Experts Group), which includes video versions of MP3

✦ AVI, used primarily on Windows

✦ QuickTime, originally an Apple-only format but now widely available on Windows and Apple machines

You can either link to video files or embed them directly into your Web page. Generally, it's best to give people fair warning that your Web page contains a video, so you should at a minimum link to the page that contains the embedded video, and then embed the video into that linked page. You can also embed video in presentations made with Flash MX and above (Flash MX 2004). In fact, Flash MX handles video so well that many people are turning to that as their presentation environment for video. Flash itself is not video (unless you consider the animations it creates video), but is instead a presentation platform that can include video, music, and pictures as part of the finished presentation.

To link to a video file, simply include it in an a element, as in the following example:

```
<a href="myVideo.mpg">This is a movie link.</a>
```

When a user clicks the link and has the supporting software, the video will play in the user's default media player.

You can also use the object element (and the embed element if you're targeting Netscape users), but keep in mind that there are some preferred ways of including multimedia that have already been discussed. In other words, you can embed a video, such as an mpg file, directly in your Web page, but you'll be at the mercy of whatever system setup your user has. It's better to target a specific or group of specific media players by including your video in a SMIL or ASX file (discussed later in this chapter), or each of them, then giving your users a choice of which they'd like to view. For example, you could provide a link that says, "Window Media Player Users Click Here" for ASX files, and then target QuickTime and RealOne users with SMIL documents.

Sounds

Most of us are aware of the copyright infringement issues that can accompany copying and/or distributing MP3 files. You can include sound the same way you include video, but do be careful of copyright infringement. It may not seem obvious that copying music is copyright infringement, but there is absolutely no legal haze regarding copying and *distributing* content. You can't do it without permission without expecting a lawsuit. In addition to MP3, there are four additional fairly common sound formats:

✦ Musical instrument digital interface (MIDI, pronounced "middy") is basically synthesized music. If you've ever seen those electric pianos in the store, or, better yet, you have one, you have seen a device that can generate a MIDI file. The advantage is that the files are small. The disadvantage is that if the individual making the music isn't skilled, the result will be poor.

✦ AU is a fairly low-quality but small file size sound format most often found in Java applets.

✦ Audio Interchange File Format (AIFF) is a Macintosh-based format that is now found on other platforms as well.

✦ WAV is a Windows-based sound format of reasonably high quality.

Needless to say, MP3 has surpassed these other formats by a wide margin in popularity.

You can also include background sound to an Internet Explorer page using the `bgsound` element:

```
<bgsound src="bigsounds.wav">
```

Or, in Netscape, you can use the `embed` element:

```
<embed src="bigsounds.wav" autostart="true">
```

Note   Just keep in mind that startling someone with background music when they're visiting your page is a cruel act and isn't likely to be forgiven, or rewarded with a return visit to your Web site, unless your site happens to be so heavily music-oriented that your visitors expect it.

Slide Shows

Slide shows are a nice way to distribute presentations you may have given to groups of people who might want to see the slide show you used during the presentation again. You can basically take a slide show you created for such an event and port it directly to the Web. You can create presentations from PowerPoint, which is a widely distributed slideshow presentation software tool. However, if you don't have Powerpoint and/or don't want to shell out the money for a PowerPoint license, you can use freeware such as OpenOffice. The following sections look at how to export presentations from both of these programs.

Exporting PowerPoint presentations to the Web

To create PowerPoint Presentations for the Web, you need to be certain your settings are correct. This seems like a simple enough requirement, but access to the correct settings is hidden away somewhat. In PowerPoint 2002 and PowerPoint 2003, you'll find the Web settings in two places.

You can choose your Web settings by going to Tools ➪ Options. Choose the General tab (shown in Figure 14-8). From there, choose the Web Options . . . tab.

Or, you can export your document as a Web page by going to File ➪ Save As Web Page . . . You'll see a dialog box like that shown in Figure 14-9. Instead of clicking Save, click the Publish button just under the file list in the dialog box. After clicking Publish, you'll see a dialog box like that shown in Figure 14-10. Click the Web Options button for additional options, such as which browser(s) to target, the size of your images, and so on. When you click OK, you'll return to the Publish as Web Page dialog box, which also has a browser support option (a better one, in fact, because it lets you choose all browsers). Choose the directory you want to save the files to. If you're a novice, it's best to create a new directory, and then simply upload that new

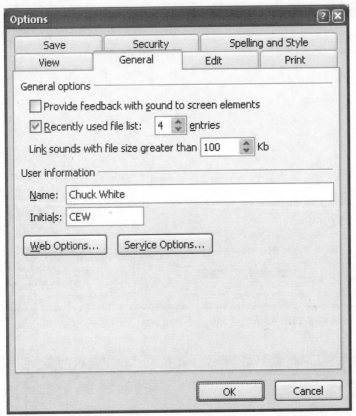

Figure 14-8: The General Options tab in PowerPoint's Options dialog box.

directory in its entirety to your server so you don't have to worry about managing files. When you're done, click Publish, and then upload the directory you saved your files to onto your server.

Following either of the two preceding methods, you should now see the Web Options dialog box, as shown in Figure 14-11.

This dialog box is your control panel for managing the way a PowerPoint presentation looks when it is delivered to the Web. It manages such settings as browser compatibility, screen size and resolution, and what format your graphics should be in.

The controls are managed through the following group of tabs, named, successively, from left to right (top bullet being left and bottom being right):

✦ General

✦ Browsers

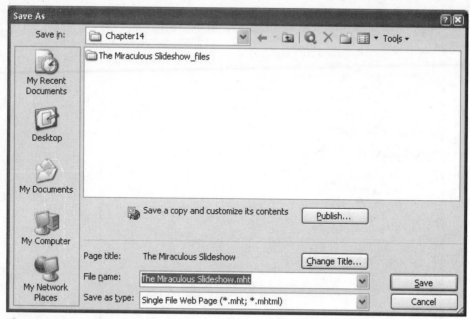

Figure 14-9: PowerPoint's Save As Web Page...dialog box.

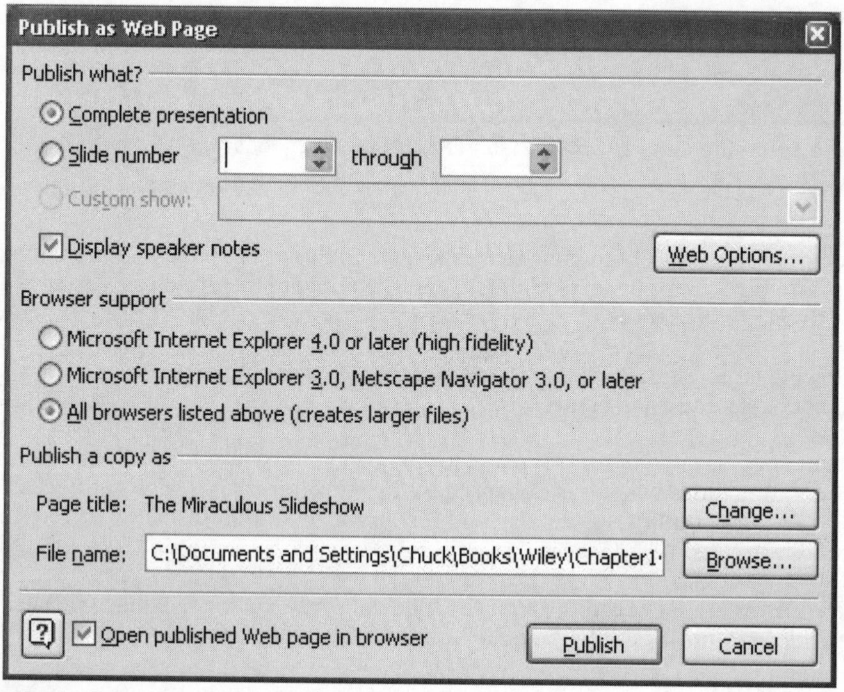

Figure 14-10: PowerPoint's Publish As Web Page dialog box.

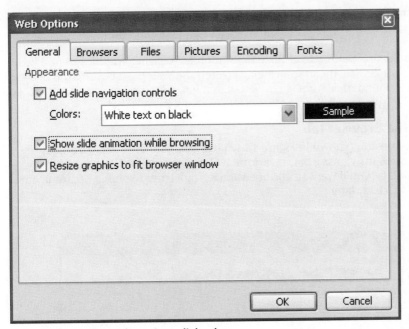

Figure 14-11: The Web Options dialog box.

- ✦ Files
- ✦ Pictures
- ✦ Encodings
- ✦ Fonts

Each of these options is briefly explained in the following sections.

Note These specific instructions pertain to the latest edition of Microsoft Office, which as this book went to press was Office 2003. The tabs in PowerPoint 2002 (part of Office 2002) are slightly different, but you can still find most of the settings described on the Web Options interface or the Publish dialog box. For example, the browser settings in PowerPoint 2002 are found on the Publish dialog box because there is no Browser tab.

Choosing options in the General tab

The General tab lets you decide on your presentation's core settings (seen previously in Figure 14-11).

If you choose to enable slide navigation controls, PowerPoint will insert the navigation controls into a small thin frame in a frame-based output. You can also enable PowerPoint animations, but you'll need to be sure your viewers can see them, and if they're running Netscape, Opera, or Safari, they probably won't. Generally, it's best to leave this unchecked unless you're on a corporate intranet that relies on MS products.

You should also be sure to choose the option for resizing graphics to fit a browser window; otherwise, the graphics may stretch the Web page beyond the browser window's boundaries, forcing users to scroll left, which most people hate to do.

Using the Browser tab

The Browser tab (shown in Figure 14-12) lets you configure how to adjust the presentation for viewing in the various Web browsers. For full downward compatibility, you'll want to choose Microsoft Internet Explorer 3.0, Netscape Navigator 3.0, or later.

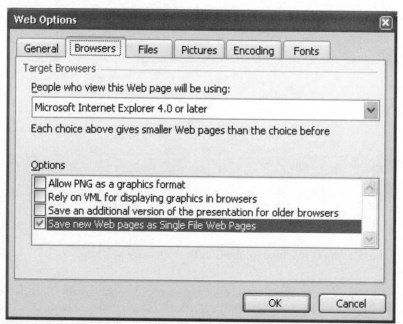

Figure 14-12: Using PowerPoint's browser tab in the Web Options dialog box.

You're also presented with options for saving graphics in Portable Network Graphics (PNG) format, and saving line art as Vector Markup Language (VML). Again, these should only be checked if you know your target audience's browsers support these formats. You can be sure that older versions of Netscape don't support PNG, and that the only browser that supports VML is Internet Explorer. PNG is a bitmap graphics format similar to GIF but capable of a much deeper range of colors. VML is an XML-based markup language for vector graphics, which are geometry-based graphics based on a Cartesian-like grid system similar to what you'll find in CAD programs and applications such as Adobe Illustrator or Macromedia Freehand. A long time ago, VML competed with Scalable Vector Graphics Language (SVG) as a standard, but the W3C chose SVG, which is also covered briefly in this chapter.

This tab has two additional options that are pretty self explanatory: Save an additional version of this presentation for older browsers and Save new Web pages as Single File Web Pages.

Changing settings in the Files tab

In the Files tab (shown in Figure 14-13) you can organize supporting files in a folder or store them within the presentation folder itself. The reference to long file names dates back to the old 8.3 DOS conventions, when file names were limited to eight characters and didn't allow for spaces.

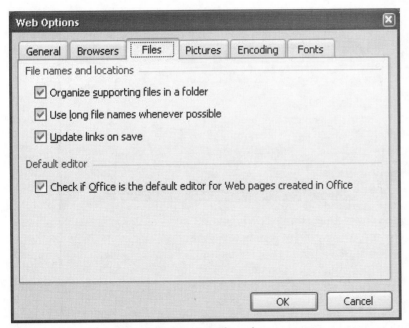

Figure 14-13: Changing settings in the Files tab.

If you choose the option Check if Office is the default editor for Web pages created in Office, you can edit the PowerPoint HTML presentation in PowerPoint itself rather than your system's default Web editor. This just means that PowerPoint will treat the file like any other PowerPoint presentation, providing you with all of PowerPoint's tools within its user interface. In other words, it's like opening up a PowerPoint presentation.

Choosing screen resolution in the Pictures tab

This one is pretty self-explanatory. The Pictures tab has one option, which allows you to choose the screen resolution. The most common screen resolution for most

Web interfaces is 800 × 600 (pixels), so that's a good one to choose if you're targeting a large cross-browser audience.

Choosing an encoding in the Encoding tab

The default on the Encoding tab (shown in Figure 14-14) is a Windows encoding, not necessarily what you want. Encodings are tricky, but simple at their core. Each letter in an alphabet, be it an English, Japanese, or Russian alphabet, is mapped to a special numeric value (after all, computers can't read—they deal with binary sets of numbers only at their core level). The problem is not all such mappings, called encodings, are the same. If you choose a Windows encoding, which was created before more standardized encodings were approved by international bodies, the potential exists that visitors to your Web site will get some funny characters. To eliminate this potential, change the default setting to Western European, as shown in Figure 14-14.

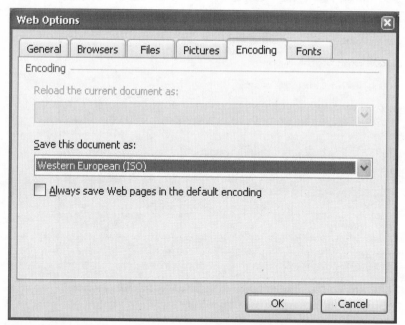

Figure 14-14: You should change the default encoding to a more Web-standardized one.

Using the Fonts tab to choose fonts

The Fonts tab allows you to use the default font character set, as well as a default proportional and fixed-width typestyle along with their point sizes. After clicking OK, you then click Publish to save your document.

Listing 14-2 shows how an HTML page generated by PowerPoint looks. Note the use of the many namespaces as represented by the xmlns namespace declarations (they look like attributes, but they're actually namespace declarations that bind elements to a specific type of application, in this case, MS Office).

Listing 14-2: Under the Hood of a PowerPoint Web Page Export

```
<html xmlns:v="urn:schemas-microsoft-com:vml"
xmlns:o="urn:schemas-microsoft-com:office:office"
xmlns:p="urn:schemas-microsoft-com:office:powerpoint"
xmlns:oa="urn:schemas-microsoft-com:office:activation"
xmlns="http://www.w3.org/TR/REC-html40">

<head>
<meta http-equiv=Content-Type content="text/html; charset=iso-8859-1">
<meta name=ProgId content=PowerPoint.Slide>
<meta name=Generator content="Microsoft PowerPoint 11">
<link rel=File-List
href="The%20Miraculous%20Slideshow_files/filelist.xml">
<link rel=Preview
href="The%20Miraculous%20Slideshow_files/preview.wmf">
<link rel=Edit-Time-Data
href="The%20Miraculous%20Slideshow_files/editdata.mso">
<title>The Miraculous Slideshow</title>
<!--[if gte mso 9]><xml>
 <o:DocumentProperties>
  <o:Author>Chuck White</o:Author>
  <o:Template>OCEAN</o:Template>
  <o:LastAuthor>Chuck White</o:LastAuthor>
  <o:Revision>3</o:Revision>
  <o:TotalTime>18</o:TotalTime>
  <o:Created>2003-11-02T03:43:46Z</o:Created>
  <o:LastSaved>2003-11-02T04:02:44Z</o:LastSaved>
  <o:Words>24</o:Words>
  <o:PresentationFormat>On-screen Show</o:PresentationFormat>
  <o:Company>The Tumeric Partnership</o:Company>
  <o:Bytes>62053</o:Bytes>
  <o:Paragraphs>6</o:Paragraphs>
  <o:Slides>2</o:Slides>
  <o:Version>11.4920</o:Version>
  </o:DocumentProperties>
  <o:OfficeDocumentSettings>
   <o:PixelsPerInch>80</o:PixelsPerInch>
  </o:OfficeDocumentSettings>
</xml><![endif]-->
<link rel=Presentation-XML
href="The%20Miraculous%20Slideshow_files/pres.xml">
<meta name=Description content="11/1/2003: The Miraculous
Slideshow">
<meta http-equiv=expires content=0>
<![if !ppt]><script>
<!--
```

Continued

Listing 14-2: *(continued)*

```
        var ver = 0, appVer = navigator.appVersion, msie =
appVer.indexOf( "MSIE " )
        var msieWin31 = (appVer.indexOf( "Windows 3.1" ) >= 0),
isMac = (appVer.indexOf("Macintosh") >= 0)
        if( msie >= 0 )
            ver = parseFloat( appVer.substring( msie+5,
appVer.indexOf ( ";", msie ) ) )
        else
            ver = parseInt( appVer )

        if( !isMac && ver >= 4 && msie >= 0 )
                window.location.replace(
"The%20Miraculous%20Slideshow_files/frame.htm"+document.locat
ion.hash )
        else if( ver >= 3 ) {
            var path =
"The%20Miraculous%20Slideshow_files/v3_document.htm"
                if ( !msieWin31 && ( ( msie >= 0 && ver >= 3.02 )
|| ( msie < 0 && ver >= 3 ) ) )
                    window.location.replace( path )
            else
                    window.location.href = path
        }
//-->
</script><![endif]>
</head>

</html>
```

Exporting OpenOffice.org presentations

OpenOffice (www.openoffice.org) is a free office suite that can read and write MS Office documents such as Word and PowerPoint. So, if you don't want to spend money for PowerPoint, you don't have to. OpenOffice is almost as good, and it's free.

The first step to exporting an OpenOffice presentation to the Web is to select File ➪ Export from the main menu. You'll then be presented with a wizard, as shown in Figure 14-15.

You can choose an existing design or create a new one. This can be somewhat confusing because the natural assumption is that you've already created your design in the slide presentation program, so why is OpenOffice asking you to create a new one? When you click Next, you find out what the application is referring to. What you are doing is deciding how you want the HTML to work. Do you want frames? Or, do you prefer to avoid frames? Those options are the first two listed in the wizard's radio buttons under the label "Publication type." You can then choose whether or not to create a title page or notes for the online version of your presentation.

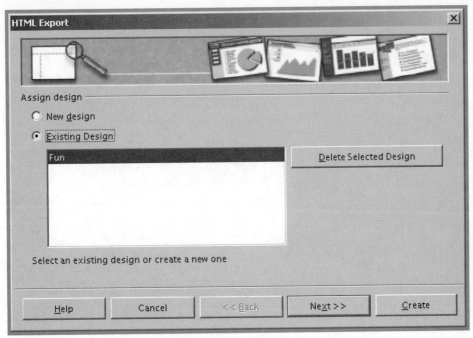

Figure 14-15: The OpenOffice HTML Export wizard.

The next two "Publication type" options are Automatic and Webcast. If you choose Automatic, the wizard changes its appearance, as shown in Figure 14-16.

The wizard changes labels from Options to Advance slide. You can allow the user to advance the slide herself by choosing the As stated in document radio button, or create an automated page that moves to the next slide automatically at a named interval by choosing the Automatic radio button.

If you choose the Webcast publication type, the wizard changes again, to a screen that looks like that shown in Figure 14-17.

You're then presented with the option of generating server-side script for Active Server Pages or by using Perl. When you choose this option, OpenOffice generates a series of Perl scripts for managing the slideshow.

The rest of the options in the HTML Export wizard are pretty self-explanatory. They allow you to choose what kind of buttons you want to include (if you've chosen to generate static HTML instead of a Webcast or server-side script), what resolution you want OpenOffice to process images, and so on.

SMIL

The Synchronized Multimedia Language (SMIL, pronounced like the word smile) is an XML-based language for presenting multimedia programs over the Web. You can

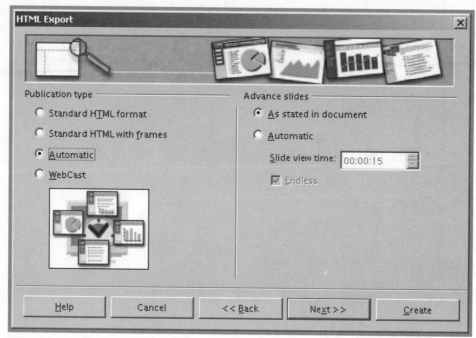

Figure 14-16: The HTML Export wizard changes its appearance depending on the Publication type you choose.

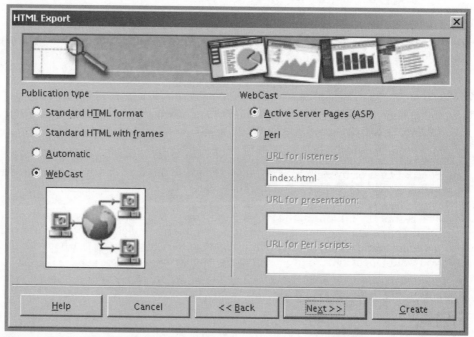

Figure 14-17: The HTML Export Wizard displays server-side scripting options when you choose Webcast.

use it to create slide shows, or as a presentation layer for media players such as RealOne or QuickTime (but not for Windows Media Player). You can hand code a SMIL document, keeping in mind XML syntax rules (closing all elements, nesting tags within one root element, quoting all attribute values, and so on). To create a SMIL presentation, follow these basic steps.

1. A source begins and ends with the `smil` element. SMIL is a case-sensitive language and always uses lowercase:

   ```
   <smil>
   [...]
   </smil>
   ```

2. SMIL documents consist of two parts, a head and body, both of which must live within the `smil` element, which is a parent element of the `head` and `body` elements.

   ```
   <smil>
    <head>
     [...]
    </head>
    <body>
     [...]
    </body>
   </smil>
   ```

3. You can also include meta tags in the head element, but you need to remember that because SMIL is based on XML, the element must include its closing tag:

   ```
   <meta name="description" content="A great show!" />
   ```

4. Next, you need to include some layout elements, within which will go the most important pieces of your multimedia show. The following code shows where to put the layout elements (in bold).

   ```
   <smil>
    <head>
     <meta name="description" content="A great show!" />
     <layout>
      <!-- layout tags -->
     </layout>
    </head>
    <body>
     <!-- media and synchronization tags -->
    </body>
   </smil>
   ```

5. You'll need to determine the screen size of your presentation. You do this with the `root-layout` element, which includes width and height attributes to determine the width and height that the media player, such as QuickTime or RealOne, should allot to its window size:

   ```
   <root-layout width="300" height="200"
                background-color="white" />
   ```

6. You can also use absolute positioning to position elements within the media player's screen. Absolute positioning in SMIL uses the same concepts as absolute positioning in Cascading Style Sheets, with a grid whose point of origin is the upper-left corner, which is 0 pixels. The following code fragment creates a *region*, which is simply a container for holding elements similar to HTML's div element. The region begins 20 pixels from the left-most portion of the media player's window, and 20 pixels from the top.

```
<head>
 <layout>
  <root-layout width="300" height="200"
       background-color="white" />
  <region id="region1" left="20" top="20"
       width="100" height="200" />
 </layout>
</head>
```

Note that the region has also been given a width and a height. Now you are able to create elements and include them within this region.

Cross-Reference

See Chapter 23 for details on how absolute positioning works.

7. The first element we'll drop into our new region is a logo, which was created in Adobe Illustrator and exported as SVG. Note that you can create an SVG image in OpenOffice.org's drawing module if you don't want to pay the licensing fees for Adobe Illustrator. Including the SVG in the document is as easy as writing an HTML img element:

```
<body>
   <img src="logo.svg" alt="Javertising!"
        region="logo" />
</body>
```

Note that you must identify in which region to place the logo. The following code creates a new region named logo for holding the logo.

```
<smil>
 <head>
  <layout>
   <root-layout width="300" height="200"
        background-color="white" />
   <region id="logo" left="20" top="20"
        width="100" height="100" background-color="white"
/>
  </layout>
 </head>
 <body>
  <img src="logo.svg" alt="Javertising!"
        region="logo" />
 </body>
</smil>
```

8. Next, save the file with a .smil file extension, then open it in an SMIL-compliant media player such as RealOne or QuickTime.

9. The resulting presentation is shown in Figure 14-18. You can put any number of media objects in place of that SVG file, such as videos and even text.

Figure 14-18: A simple SMIL-based presentation shown in RealOne.

Naturally, you're not limited to SVG; in fact, that particular graphics format has not yet really taken hold, although it still holds great promise. It's more likely you'll use a JPEG or GIF graphic, along with some video and/or audio. Table 14-3 shows the kinds of media you can use in a SMIL document and the support from the major SMIL media players. You may not have heard of GRiNS. GRiNS is a media player from Oratrix that you can find at http://www.oratrix.com/Products/G2P.

Table 14-3
Multimedia Player Support for Media Content Using SMIL

Media Tag	RealOne	QuickTime	GRiNS
GIF img	Yes	Yes	Yes
JPEG img	Yes	Yes	Yes
SVG img	Yes	No	No

Continued

Table 14-3 (continued)			
Media Tag	RealOne	QuickTime	GriNS
Microsoft Wav audio	Yes	Yes	Yes
Sun Audio audio	Yes	Yes	Yes
Sun Audio Zipped audio	No	Yes	No
MP3 audio	Yes	Yes	No
Plain text	Yes	Yes	Yes
Real text textstream	Yes	No	No
Real movie video	Yes	No	No
AVI video	Yes	No	Yes
MPEG video	Yes	No	Yes
MOV video	Yes	No	No

You've seen how to construct a basic SMIL document, and how anyone with a simple text editor can create a presentation or show. There's much more to SMIL than this, including more advanced functionality, such as media sound and video synchronization. To read more about how you can create lavish rich media using SMIL, visit the W3C SMIL Web site at: `http://www.w3.org/AudioVideo/`. Or, visit a SMIL tutorial at `http://www.w3schools.com/smil/smil_reference.asp`.

Summary

In this chapter, you learned about the following multimedia topics:

✦ Introducing multimedia objects

✦ Multimedia plug-ins and players

✦ Animations

✦ Video clips

✦ Sounds

✦ Slide shows

You were also warned that you should use multimedia with care. The most practical use for multimedia is often the simple slide show, because the demands for professionalism won't be quite as stringent. But if you dabble in such multimedia formats as Flash and video, be sure to keep a close eye on quality, because a poorly developed multimedia presentation is worse than none at all.

✦   ✦   ✦

Scripts

Standard HTML was designed to provide static, text-only documents. No innate intelligence is built into plain HTML, but it is desired, especially in more complex documents or documents designed to be interactive. Enter scripts—svelte programming languages designed to accomplish simple tasks while adhering to the basic premise of the Web; easily deployable content that can play nicely with plain-text HTML.

This chapter covers the basics of scripting and goes into the details of how to use client-side scripting in your documents.

Client-Side versus Server-Side Scripting

There are two basic varieties of scripting, client-side and server-side. As their names imply, the main difference is where the scripts are actually executed.

Client-side scripting

Client-side scripts are run by the client software—that is, the user agent. As such, they impose no additional load on the server, but the client must support the scripting language being used.

JavaScript is the most popular client-side scripting language, but Jscript and VBScript are also widely used. Client-side scripts are typically embedded in HTML documents and deployed to the client. As such, the client user can usually easily view the scripts.

For security reasons, client-side scripts generally cannot read or write to the server or client file system.

Server-side scripting

Server-side scripts are run by the Web server. Typically, these scripts are referred to as CGI scripts, CGI being an acronym for

Common Gateway Interface, the first interface for server-side Web scripting. Server-side scripts impose more load on the server, but generally don't influence the client—even output to the client is optional; the client may have no idea that the server is running a script.

Perl, Python, PHP, and Java are all examples of server-side scripting languages. The script typically resides only on the server, but is called by code in the HTML document.

Although server-side scripts cannot read or write to the client's file system, they usually have some access to the server's file system. As such, it is important that the system administrator take appropriate measures to secure server-side scripts and limit their access.

Note Unless you are a system administrator on the Web server you use to deploy your content, your ability to use server-side scripts is probably limited. Your ISP or system administrator has policies that allow or disallow server-side scripting in various languages and performing various tasks.

If you intend to use server-side scripts, you should check with your ISP or system administrator to determine what resources are available to you.

This chapter deals with client-side scripting.

Cross-Reference For more information on server-side scripting, see Chapter 28.

Setting the Default Scripting Language

To embed a client-side script in your document you use the `<script>` tag. This tag has the following, minimal format:

```
<script type="script_type">
```

The value of `script_type` depends on the scripting language you are using. The following are generally used script types:

✦ `text/ecmascript`
✦ `text/javascript`
✦ `text/jscript`
✦ `text/vbscript`
✦ `text/vbs`
✦ `text/xml`

For example, if you are using JavaScript, your script tag would resemble the following:

```
<script type="text/javascript">
```

Note

The W3C recommends that you specify the default script type using an appropriate META tag in your document. Such a tag resembles the following:

```
<META http-equiv="Content-Script-Type"
content="text/javascript">
```

Note that this does not alleviate the need for the type attribute in each <script> tag. You must still specify each <script> tag's type in order for your documents to validate against HTML 4.01.

If your script is encoded in another character set than the rest of the document, you should also use the charset attribute to specify the script's encoding. This attribute has the same format as the charset attribute for other tags:

```
charset="character_encoding_type"
```

Including a Script

To include a script in your document, you place the script's code within <script> tags. For example, consider the following script:

```
<script type="text/javascript">
  function NewWindow(url){
    fin=window.open(url,"","width=800,height=600,
    scrollbars=yes,resizable=yes");
  }
</script>
```

You can include as much scripting code between the tags as needed, providing that the script is syntactically sound. Scripts can be included within the <head> or <body> sections of a document, and you can include as many <script> sections as you like. Note, however, that nested <script> tags are not valid HTML.

Generally, you will want to place your scripts in the <head> section of your document so the scripts are available as the rest of the page loads. However, you may occasionally want to embed a script in a particular location in the document—in those cases, place an appropriate <script> tag in the <body> of the document.

Calling an External Script

If you have some scripts that you want to use in multiple documents, consider placing the scripts in an external file. You can then use the src attribute of the

<script> tag to specify that the script content can be found in that file. For example, suppose you want to include the following script in multiple documents:

```
function NewWindow(url){
  fin=window.open(url,"","width=800,height=600,
  scrollbars=yes,resizable=yes");
}
```

You can place the script in a text file on the server and specify the file's URL in the appropriate <script> tags' src attribute. For example, suppose the preceding file was stored in the file scripts.js on the server. Your script tag would then resemble the following:

```
<script type="text/javascript" src="scripts.js"></script>
```

One major advantage to external script files is that if you need to edit the script, you can edit it in one place—the external file—and the change is effected in all the files that include it.

Triggering Scripts with Events

Most HTML tags include several event attributes that can be used to trigger scripts. Table 15-1 lists these attributes and their use for triggering scripts.

Cross-Reference See Appendix A for a comprehensive list of what tags support event attributes.

Table 15-1
Event Attributes

Attribute	Trigger Use
Onclick	When item(s) enclosed in tag is clicked
Ondblclick	When item(s) enclosed in tag is double-clicked
Onmousedown	When mouse button is pressed while mouse pointer is over item(s) enclosed in tag
Onmouseup	When mouse button is released while mouse pointer is over item(s) enclosed in tag
Onmouseover	When mouse pointer is placed over the item(s) enclosed in tag
Onmousemove	When mouse is moved within the item(s) enclosed in tag
Onmouseout	When mouse is moved outside of the item(s) enclosed in tag
Onblur	When item(s) enclosed in tag have focus removed

Attribute	Trigger Use
Onfocus	When item(s) enclosed in tag receive focus
Onload	When the document finishes loading (valid only in `<body>` tag)
Onunload	When the document is unloaded—when the user navigates to another document (valid only in `<body>` tag). This event is often used to create pop-ups when a user leaves a site
Onsubmit	When a form has its submit button pressed (valid only in `<form>` tags)
Onreset	When a form has its reset button pressed (valid only in `<form>` tags)
Onkeypress	When a key is pressed while the mouse pointer is over the item(s) enclosed in the tag
Onkeydown	When a key is pressed down while the mouse pointer is over the item(s) enclosed in the tag
Onkeyup	When a key is released while the mouse pointer is over the item(s) enclosed in the tag

Note Many of the `event` attribute triggers are dependent on the element(s) to which they apply being "in focus" at the time of the trigger. For example, in an HTML form an `onmouseout` event attached to one field will not trigger unless the same field has the focus.

Event triggers have a variety of uses, including the following:

✦ Form data verification

Using `onfocus` and `onblur` attributes, each field can be verified as it is edited. Using `onsubmit` and `onreset`, an entire form can be verified or reset when the appropriate button is clicked

✦ Image animation

Using `onmouseover` and `onmouseout` attributes, an image can be animated when the mouse pointer passes over it

✦ Mouse navigation

Using `onclick` and `ondblclick` attributes, you can trigger user agent navigation when a user clicks or double-clicks an element

For example, you can create images to use as buttons on your page. Figure 15-1 shows two images for use on a button. The image on the left is used for general display, while the image on the right is used when the mouse is over the button.

Tip Users appreciate visible feedback from elements on your page. As such, it is important to always provide visible changes to navigation elements—links should have a visibly different style when moused over, as should navigation buttons.

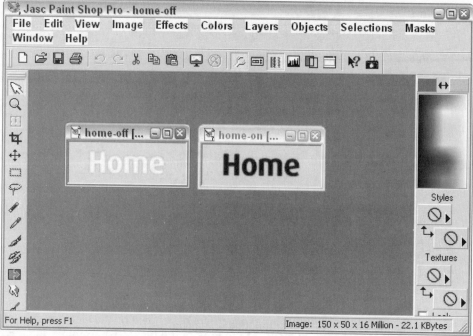

Figure 15-1: Two images for use as a button.

Combining `onmouseover`, `onmouseout`, and `onclick` events, you can easily create a button that reacts when the mouse is over it and navigate to a new page when clicked. Consider the following document that uses a few JavaScript scripts and events to create a navigation button.

```html
<!DOCTYPE HTML PUBLIC "-//W3C//DTD HTML 4.01//EN"
  "http://www.w3.org/TR/html4/strict.dtd">
<html>
<head>
  <META http-equiv="Content-Script-Type"
  content="text/javascript">
  <title>Event Buttons</title>

  <script type="text/javascript">
    // Activate the specified button
    function activate(bname) {
      imageid = bname + "button";
      aname = bname + "-on.jpg";
      document.images(imageid).src =
        aname;
    }
    // Deactivate the specified button
    function deactivate(bname) {
      imageid = bname + "button";
      dname = bname + "-off.jpg";
```

```
        document.images(imageid).src =
            dname;
    }
  </script>

</head>
<body>
<p>
<img alt="Home page" id="homebutton"
   src="home-off.jpg"
   onmouseover="activate('home')"
   onmouseout="deactivate('home')"
   onclick="document.location='home.html'"
>
</p>
</form>
</body>
</html>
```

When the document loads, the button is displayed in its inactive (off) state, as shown in Figure 15-2. When the mouse is placed over the button, the `onmouseover` event launches the JavaScript `activate` function and the button is displayed as active (on), as shown in Figure 15-3.

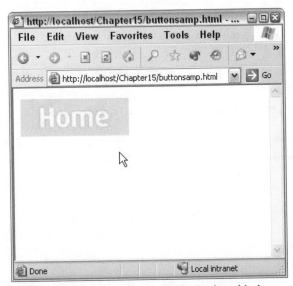

Figure 15-2: The button is initially displayed in its inactive (off) state.

When the mouse leaves the button, the `onmouseout` event launches the `deactivate` function, returning the button display to its inactive state. When the button is clicked, the `onclick` event changes the `location` property of the user agent, effectively navigating to a new page (in this case `home.html`). Note that the

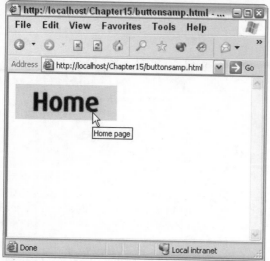

Figure 15-3: The button is changed to active (on) when the mouse is over it.

JavaScript code for the `onclick` attribute is contained directly in the value of the attribute—because the code is only one line a separate function is not necessary.

 JavaScript is covered in more detail in Chapter 25.

Hiding Scripts from Older Browsers

Not all browsers support JavaScript. Many of the older browsers are not JavaScript enabled, and some of the latest browsers may not support the scripting language you are using.

 Most modern browsers will ignore scripts of types they do not recognize.

If you are concerned about older browsers not recognizing your scripts, you will need to *hide* your scripts so that older browsers will ignore them (instead of trying to render them).

To hide your scripts, simply place them within a special set of comment tags. The only difference between normal comment tags and script-hiding tags is that the closing tag contains two slashes (//). Those two slashes enable browsers that support scripting to find the script.

For example, the following structure will effectively hide the scripts within the
`<script>` tag:

```
<script type="text/javascript">
  <!-- hide scripts from older browsers
  --- Script content ---
  // stop hiding scripts -->
</script>
```

Summary

This chapter introduced how to add basic intelligence and dynamic content to your
site view client-side scripting. You learned how to embed scripts in your documents
and how to utilize external script files. You also learned how to use event attributes
to trigger scripts from user actions.

Chapters 25 through 28 provide additional scripting content.

✦   ✦   ✦

Controlling Presentation with CSS

Introducing Cascading Style Sheets

T he first part of this book emphasized the importance of Cascading Style Sheets (CSS) and the standards migration away from hardcoded HTML and toward using styles. This part of the book, starting with Chapter 16, delves deeply into the subject of CSS.

This chapter provides an overview of what CSS is, and the next few chapters cover details about various formatting property groups and how to best use them.

CSS Overview

Cascading Style Sheets were created to provide a powerful, yet flexible means for formatting HTML content. CSS works much like style sheets in a word processing program—you define a "style" that contains formatting options that can be applied to document elements.

For example, consider the following code:

```
<!DOCTYPE HTML PUBLIC "-//W3C//DTD HTML 4.01//EN"
    "http://www.w3.org/TR/html4/strict.dtd">
<html>
<head>
  <title>A Sample Style</title>
  <style type="text/css">
    h1 { color: Red; }
  </style>
</head>
<body>
...
```

Note the <style> element inside of the <head> element. It defines one style, setting the font color of all <h1> elements to red. This is the same as using the following code throughout the document, wherever `<h1>` elements are used:

```
<h1><font color="red">Heading Text</font></h1>
```

Using the preceding method (`<font>` tags), you would need to change every instance in the document if you later changed your mind about the formatting. Using CSS requires that you change only the style definition at the top of the document to affect all `<h1>` elements.

Note CSS can be a complicated beast, especially once you get into the different selector methods, inheritance, and the complete cascade picture. However, at its core it is a very simple concept: Assign formatting attributes in one place that can be easily modified later. As you read through the chapters in Part II, keep this concept in mind and resist getting bogged down in the CSS concepts that you may not need.

Style Rules

All style rules follow the same basic format:

```
selector {  property1:  value1;  property2:  value2; ...
propertyN:  valueN; }
```

Note that the formatting of CSS rules is very exact and follows these guidelines:

- ✦ The selector is followed by the formatting property definitions, which are enclosed in braces ({ }).

- ✦ A colon separates each property/value pair. Note that values that include spaces should be enclosed in double quotes, as in the following example:

```
font-family: "Times New Roman";
```

- ✦ Each property/value pair ends with a semicolon.

Tip Technically, the last property/value pair of a style definition need not end in a semicolon. However, it is good practice to end *all* your property/value pairs with a semicolon.

The *selector* is the elements that the style should be used on. The *properties* are all formatting properties of the selected elements that should be set to the associated *values*. A very simple example of a style rule follows:

```
h1 { color: Red; }
```

The selector (h1) causes this rule to be applied to all `<h1>` elements. The color property affects the font color of matching elements—in this case, the font color is set to red.

You can specify multiple selectors to apply to the same style definition—you separate the selectors with commas. For example, if you wanted all heading tags (1 through 6) to render as red text, you could use the following definition:

```
h1, h2, h3, h4, h5, h6 { color: red; }
```

Selectors are covered in detail in Chapter 17.

Style Rule Locations

Styles can be defined within your HTML documents or in a separate, external style sheet. You can also use both methods within the same document. The following sections cover the various methods of defining styles.

Using the <style> element

The <style> element behaves like other HTML elements. It has a beginning and ending tag and everything in between is treated as a style definition. As such, everything between the <style> tags needs to follow style definition guidelines. A document's <style> section must appear inside the document's <head> section, although multiple <style> sections are permissible.

The <style> tag has the following, minimal format:

```
<style type="text/css">
... style definitions ...
</style>
```

External style sheets

You can also place your style definitions in a separate file and reference that file within the documents where you need it. When creating a separate style sheet file, you do not need to include the <style> tags, only the definitions. For example, the following is an example style sheet file named mystyles.css:

```
/* mystyles.css - Styles for the main site */
h1, h2, h3, h4 { color: blue; }
h1 { font-size: 18pt; }
h2 { font-size: 16pt; }
h3 { font-size: 14pt; }
h4 { font-size: 12pt; }
p { font-size: 10pt; }
```

You can include comments in your styles to further annotate your definitions. Style comments begin with a /* and end with a */. Comments can span several lines, if necessary.

To link an external style sheet with a document, use the `<link>` tag in the `<head>` of the document to which you want the styles applied. The `<link>` tag has the following format when used to link a style sheet:

```
<link rel="stylesheet" type="text/css"
href="url_to_style_sheet" />
```

Continuing with the `mystyles.css` style sheet example, the following `<link>` tag would link the style sheet to the document:

```
<head>
  <link rel="stylesheet" type="text/css"
  href="mystyles.css" />
</head>
```

Tip

Although external style sheets can have any valid filename, it is advisable to name your style sheets with an extension such as `.css` to easily identify what the file contains.

You can use the `<link>` tag to link any style sheet that is accessible to the user via HTTP. If your style sheet was on another server, for example, you would simply include a full form URL to the sheet:

```
<link rel="stylesheet" type="text/css"
href="http://www.example.com/styles/sales.css" />
```

Several style sheets can be linked to the same document. When that is the case they follow the cascading guidelines as covered in the section *Understanding the style sheet cascade* later in this chapter.

Style definitions within individual tags

Most HTML tags include a `style` attribute that allows you to specify styles that should directly impact the tag in which they appear. For example, if you wanted a particular `<h1>` tag to render its text in red, you could use the following code:

```
<h1 style="color: red;">Red Headline</h1>
```

The *only* advantage to using styles in this manner is to remain HTML 4.01 compliant. It is a much better practice to put your styles in a `<style>` tag or external style sheet than to code individual tags. However, sometimes you might find that nudging a particular tag individually is advantageous.

Understanding the Style Sheet Cascade

The concept behind Cascading Style Sheets is essentially that multiple style definitions can trickle, or cascade, down through several layers to affect a document.

Several layers of style definitions can apply to any document. Those layers are applied in the following order:

1. The user agent settings (typically, the user is able to modify some of these settings)

2. Any linked style sheets

3. Any styles present in a `<style>` element

4. Styles specified within a tag's `style` attribute

Each level of styles overrides the previous level where there are duplicate properties being defined. For example, consider the following two files:

mystyles.css

```
/* mystyles.css - Styles for the main site */
h1, h2, h3, h4 { color: blue; }
h1 { font-size: 18pt; }
h2 { font-size: 16pt; }
h3 { font-size: 14pt; }
h4 { font-size: 12pt; }
p { font-size: 10pt; }
```

index.html

```
<!DOCTYPE HTML PUBLIC "-//W3C//DTD HTML 4.01//EN"
  "http://www.w3.org/TR/html4/strict.dtd">
<html>
<head>
  <link rel="stylesheet" type="text/css"
    href="mystyles.css" />
  <style type="text/css">
    h1 { color: Red; }
  </style>
</head>
<body>
  <h1>A Sample Heading</h1>
  ...
```

What color will the `<h1>` heading in `index.html` be? The external style specifies blue, but the style element specifies red. In this case, the internal style takes precedence and the `<h1>` text will appear in red.

Note One advantage to cascading is that documents at different levels or from different departments can be similar, but have a slightly different look or feel to match their origin. For example, you could have a `company.css` style sheet that is linked to all corporate documents. You could also have an `hr-department.css` style sheet that adds additional definitions or replaces some of the standard corporate definitions to give HR documents a slightly different look and feel.

In addition, a document may have multiple instances of linked style sheets or `<style>` elements. In such cases, the sheets are applied in order, with subsequent definitions overriding any previous definitions.

Note that properties are only overridden when they appear multiple times. Otherwise, the styles are additive. For example, the text in the `<h1>` tag would still be rendered in 18pt type (from the external definition); only the color would change.

The CSS Box Formatting Model

CSS uses a clever metaphor for helping you specify containers (block-level elements) on your page: the box. When you define formatting for your block-level elements—whether they be paragraphs, blockquotes, lists, images, or whatever—for purposes of CSS, you are defining formatting for a box. CSS doesn't care what is in the box; it just wants to format the box.

Box dimensions

The first thing the browser does is render the block-level element to determine what the physical dimensions of the element are, given the font selected for the element, the contents of the element, and any other internal formatting instructions supplied by the style sheet. Then the browser looks at the element's padding, the border, and the margins to determine the space it actually requires on the page. Figure 16-1 shows a representation of how these measures relate to one another.

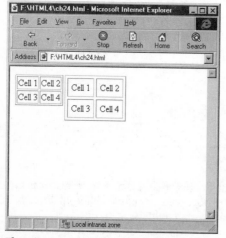

Figure 16-1: A visual representation of how margins, borders, and padding relate to each other and the element they affect.

Padding is the distance between the outside edges of the element and the border. The *border* is a line or ridge. The *margin* is the distance between the border and the outer box of the next container. How you define the padding, border, and margin is described in detail in the following sections.

Padding

You don't need to define any padding, but if you are going to define a border, then you probably want to define padding so your element doesn't look too crowded. The default for an element is no padding. Figure 26-2 shows the same table with and without padding. You can see that the one without padding looks crowded.

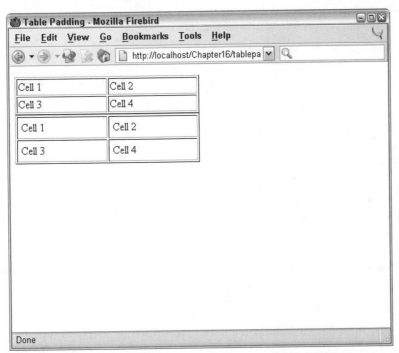

Figure 16-2: Tables with (bottom) and without padding (top).

Five properties are associated with padding. They are as follows:

1. `padding`, which gives the same padding on all sides
2. `padding-top`
3. `padding-right`
4. `padding-bottom`
5. `padding-left`

Get used to seeing the -top, -right, -bottom, and -left additions to property names. This is how all box-related properties are specified.

Suppose you want to define your paragraphs to have padding on the top, the left, and the right; you could use the following style sheet:

```
p {
   padding-top: 10px;
   padding-right: 10px;
   padding-left: 10px;
}
```

Tip Notice the liberal formatting of the style definitions in this section. As with other HTML coding, you will find it helpful to format your style definitions with liberal white space, namely line breaks and indents.

Or, you could use shorthand to write out the padding properties, as follows:

```
p {
   padding: 10px 10px 0px 10px;
}
```

You can always string the top, right, bottom, and left properties together in that order. The same shorthand works for margins and borders. Notice that no commas are used between the items in the list.

Border

The default is to have no border on elements. You can define a border in two different ways. Either you can define the width, color, and style of the border by side, or you can define the width, color, and style for the box individually. Two examples follow:

```
blockquote {
   border-width: 1pt 1pt 0pt 1pt;
   border-color: black;
   border-style: solid;
}
```

The previous example creates a black, solid border for the top, right, and left sides of the list.

```
blockquote {
   border-top: 1pt solid black;
   border-right: 1pt solid black;
   border-left: 1pt solid black;
}
```

Both these examples create the same border. The border is inserted between the padding, if there is any, and the margin, if there is any. Valid values for border style are as follows:

- ✦ none
- ✦ dotted
- ✦ dashed
- ✦ solid
- ✦ double
- ✦ groove
- ✦ ridge
- ✦ inset
- ✦ outset

Or, if you want to create a border that is the same on all four sides, you can use the border property:

```
blockquote {
   border: 1pt solid black;
}
```

Margins

Margins create white space outside of the border. Notice in Figure 26-2 that the two tables are immediately adjacent to each other. This is because neither one has margins. Margins are created with the `margin`, `margin-top`, `margin-right`, `margin-bottom`, and `margin-left` properties. They work exactly the same as the padding property described in the previous section.

CSS Levels 1, 2, and 3

There are three levels of CSS—two actual specifications and a third level in recommendation status. Notable differences exist between the two standards and the third recommendation. The main differences between the three levels are as follows:

- ✦ CSS1 defines basic style functionality, with limited font and limited positioning support.
- ✦ CSS2 adds aural properties, paged media, better font and positioning support. Many other properties have been refined as well.
- ✦ CSS3 adds presentation-style properties, allowing you to effectively build presentations (think Microsoft PowerPoint) from Web documents.

Keep in mind that you don't have to specify the level of CSS you are using for your documents, but you do have to be conscientious about what user agents will be accessing your site. Although most browsers support CSS, the level of support varies dramatically. It's always best to test your implementation on target user agents before widely deploying your documents.

Summary

This chapter introduced you to the subject of CSS. You learned what CSS is and the various methods to implement it with your documents. Lastly, you learned the major differences between the various CSS levels. The next few chapters break down the CSS properties into various sections and cover them individually.

✦　　✦　　✦

Creating Style Rules

The first step to understanding Cascading Style Sheets (CSS) is to understand how to correctly write style rules. There are two pieces to each rule: the selector, which tells the rule what elements it should apply to, and the rule itself, which does all the formatting. This chapter delves into the many levels and types of selectors and the different metrics you can use when setting style properties.

Note Half the battle with styles is remembering the syntax, selector methods, and all the property names. If you find yourself constantly working with CSS and writing definitions, you might want to invest in an editor that can do most of the work for you. An example of a program that gets the job done without unnecessary features is Macromedia Homesite (`http://www .macromedia.com`). Homesite is a basic editor that can take the tedium out of mundane tasks like style writing. Other, more full-featured programs also have helpful CSS tools. See Chapter 34 for examples of Web publishing software.

Understanding Selectors

CSS styles work by taking a definition of attributes and applying them to any tags that match the *selector* associated with the definition.

As a review, CSS style definitions follow this format:

```
selector { property1: value1; property2: value2; ...
propertyN: valueN; }
```

The selector is what browsers use to match tags in a document to apply the definition. The selector can take several different forms, offering a lot of flexibility to match almost any use of tags in a document.

Matching elements by name

The easiest selector to understand is the plain element selector, as in the following example:

```
h1 { color: red; }
```

Using the actual element name (h1) as the selector causes all those tags to be formatted with the attributes of the definition (color: red). You can also attach multiple selectors to the same definition by listing them all in the selector area, separated by commas. For example, this definition will affect all heading tags in the document:

```
h1, h2, h3, 4h, h5, h6 { color: red; }
```

Using the universal selector

The universal selector can be used to match any element in the document. The universal selector is an asterisk (*). As an extreme example, you can use the universal selector to match *every* tag in a document:

```
* { color: red; }
```

Every tag will have the color: red attribute applied to it. Of course, you would rarely want a definition to apply to all elements of a document. You can also use the universal selector to match other elements of the selector. For example, using the child/descendent matching method of selectors, you can use the universal selector to select everything between the parent and the descendent. The following selector matches any <ol> tag that is a descendent of a <td> tag, which is a descendent of a <tr> tag:

```
tr td ol { color: red; }
```

 Note   You'll find more information on child/descendent selectors in the *Matching child, descendent, and adjacent sibling elements* section later in this chapter.

However, this selector rule is very strict, requiring all three elements. If you also wanted to include descendent <ol> elements of <td> elements, you would need to specify a separate selector, or use the universal selector to match all elements between <tr> and <ol>, as in the following example:

```
tr * ol { color: red; }
```

You can use this technique with any of the selector forms discussed in this chapter.

Matching elements by class

You can also use selectors to match elements by class. Why would you want to do this? Suppose that you had two areas on your page with different backgrounds, one light and one dark. You would want the light background area to have dark text and the dark background area to have light text. You could then use the class attribute in select elements within those areas to ensure that the appropriate styles were applied.

To specify a class to match with a selector you append a period and the class name to the selector. For example, this style will match any paragraph tag with a class of darkarea:

```
p.darkarea { color: white; }
```

For example, suppose that this paragraph was in the area of the document with the dark background:

```
<p class="darkarea">Lorem ipsum dolor sit amet, consectetuer
adipiscing elit, sed diam nonummy nibh euismod tincidunt ut
laoreet dolore magna aliquam erat volutpat. Ut wisi enim ad
minim veniam, quis nostrud exerci tation ullamcorper suscipit
lobortis nisl ut aliquip ex ea commodo consequat.</p>
```

The specification of the darkarea class with the paragraph tag will cause the paragraph's text to be rendered in white.

Tip The universal selector can be used to indicate that all tags with a given class should have the style applied. For example, this style definition will apply to all tags with the darkarea class:

```
*.darkarea { color: white; }
```

However, you can also omit the universal selector, specifying only the class for the same effect:

```
.darkarea { color: white; }
```

Matching elements by identifier

Just as you can match classes, you can also match element identifiers (the id attribute). To match identifiers, you use the pound sign (#) in the selector. For example, the following style will match any tag that has an id attribute of comment:

```
#comment { background-color: green; }
```

Matching elements that contain a specified attribute

Besides class and id, you can match *any* attribute. To do so, specify the attribute and the value(s) you want to match in the selector. This form of the selector has the following format:

```
element[attribute="value"]
```

For example, if you want to match any table with a border attribute set to 3, you could use this definition:

```
table[border="3"]
```

You can also match elements that contain the attribute, no matter what the value of the attribute is set to. For example, to match any table with a border attribute, you could use this definition:

```
table[border]
```

Tip

You can combine the various selector formats for even more specificity. For example, the following selector will match table tags with a class attribute of datalist, and a border attribute of 3:

```
table.datalist[border="3"]
```

You can stack multiple attribute definitions for more specificity. Each attribute is specified in its own bracketed expression. For example, if you wanted to match tables with a border attribute of 3 and a width attribute of 100%, you could use this selector:

```
table[border="3"][width="100%"]
```

Note

Two other attribute-matching methods can be used to match a value in a space or hyphen-separated list in an attribute's value. To match a value in a space-separated list, you use ~= instead of the usual equal sign (=). To match a value in a hyphen-separated list, you use |= instead of the usual equal sign (=). For example, the following definition would match "us" in a space-separated value in the language attribute:

```
[language~="us"]
```

Matching child, descendent, and adjacent sibling elements

One of the most powerful selector methods you can use for matching elements is defining selectors that use the relationships between elements. For example, you can specify a style for italic text only when in a heading, or list items in ordered lists.

Understanding document hierarchy

All elements in a document are related to other elements. The hierarchy follows the same nomenclature as family trees—ancestors, parents, children, descendents, and siblings. For example, consider the following code and Figure 17-1, which shows a typical HTML document and its hierarchy.

```
<html>
<body>
<div class="div1">
  <h1>Heading 1</h1>
  <table>
    <tr><td>Cell 1</td><td>Cell 2</td></tr>
    <tr><td>Cell 3</td><td>Cell 4</td></tr>
  </table>
  <p>Lorem ipsum dolor sit amet, consectetuer adipiscing
  elit, sed diam nonummy nibh euismod tincidunt ut laoreet
  dolore magna aliquam erat volutpat. Ut wisi enim ad minim
  veniam, quis nostrud exerci tation ullamcorper suscipit
  lobortis nisl ut aliquip ex ea commodo consequat.</p>
</div>
<div class="div2">
  <h1>Heading 2</h1>
  <p>Lorem ipsum dolor sit amet, consectetuer adipiscing
  elit, sed diam nonummy nibh euismod tincidunt ut laoreet
  dolore magna aliquam erat volutpat. Ut wisi enim ad minim
  veniam, quis nostrud exerci tation ullamcorper suscipit
  lobortis nisl ut aliquip ex ea commodo consequat.</p>
  <ol>An ordered list
    <li>First element
    <li>Second element
    <li>Third element
  </ol>
</div>
</body>
</html>
```

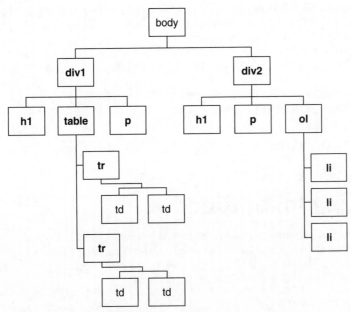

Figure 17-1: A graphical representation of the document's hierarchy.

Ancestors and descendents

Ancestors and descendents are elements that are linked by lineage, no matter the distance. For example, in Figure 17-1 the list elements under `div2` are descendents of the body element, and the body element is their ancestor.

Parents and children

Parents and children are elements that are directly connected in lineage. For example, in Figure 17-1 the table rows under `div1` are children of the table element, which is their parent.

Siblings

Siblings are children that share the same, direct parent. In Figure 17-1, the list elements under `div2` are siblings of each other. The header, paragraph, and table elements are also siblings because they share the same, direct parent (`div1`).

Selector mechanisms for hierarchies

There are several selector mechanisms to use in defining rules, specifying matched elements by their relationships to other elements.

To specify ancestor and descendent relationships, you list all involved elements separated by spaces. For example, the following selector matches the list elements in Figure 17-1:

```
div.div2 li
```

To specify parent and child relationships, you list all involved elements separated by a right angle bracket (>). For example, the following selector matches the `table` element in Figure 17-1:

```
div.div1 table
```

To specify sibling relationships, you list all involved elements separated by plus signs (+). For example, the following selector matches the `paragraph` element under `div1` in Figure 17-1:

```
table + p
```

Understanding Inheritance

Inheritance is the act of picking up attributes from one's ancestors. In CSS, all *foreground* properties are passed down (inherited) to descendent elements. For example, this definition would result in all elements being rendered in blue, because every tag in the document is a descendent of the body tag:

```
body { color: blue; }
```

Note that this is only true for foreground properties. Background properties (background color, image, and so on) are not inherited.

Inheritance is the default action unless an element has the same attribute defined differently. For example, the following definitions result in all elements, *except* for paragraphs with a notblue class, being rendered in blue:

```
body { color: blue; }
p.notblue { color: red; }
```

Instead of blue, the notblue paragraphs are rendered in red.

Attributes that are not in conflict are cumulative on descendent elements. For example, the following rules result in paragraphs with an emphasis class being rendered in bold, blue text:

```
body { color: blue; }
p.emphasis { font-weight: bold; }
```

Pseudo-classes

CSS has a handful of pseudo-classes that you can use to modify attributes of elements in your document. Pseudo-classes are identifiers that are understood by browsers to apply to a subset of elements, without the element needing to be explicitly tagged with the style. Such classes are typically dynamic and tracked by other means than the actual class attribute.

For example, there are two pseudo-classes that can be used to modify the attributes of visited and unvisited links in the document (explained in the next section). If you use the pseudo-classes, you don't have to actually specify the classes in individual links—the browser determines which links fit into which class (visited or not) and applies the style(s) appropriately.

The following sections discuss the various pseudo-classes available in CSS.

Defining link styles

A handful of pseudo-classes can be used with links (usually <a> tags). The link pseudo-classes are listed in Table 17-1.

Table 17-1 Link Pseudo-classes	
Pseudo-class	*Matches*
:link	Unvisited links
:visited	Visited links
:active	Active links
:hover	The link that the browser pointer is hovering over
:focus	The link that currently has the user interface focus

For example, the following definition will cause all unvisited links in the document to be rendered in blue, visited links in red, and when hovered over, green:

```
:link { color: blue; }
:visited { color: red; }
:hover {color: green; }
```

Note the order of the definitions; it is important. Because the link participation in the classes is dynamic, :hover must be the last definition. If the order of :visited and :hover were reversed, visited links would not turn green when hovered over because the :visited color attribute would override the :hover color attribute. The same ordering is important when using the :focus pseudo-class—place it last in the list of definitions affecting similar elements.

You can combine pseudo-classes with other selector methods, as needed. For example, if you wanted all links with a class attribute of important to be rendered in a bold font, you could use the following code:

```
:link.important { font-weight: bold; }
...
<a href="http://something.example.com/important.html"
   class="important">An important message</a>
```

The :first-child pseudo-class

The :first-child pseudo-class applies the designated style(s) to the first child element of a specified element. You can use this class to add additional space or otherwise change the formatting of the first child element. For example, to indent the first paragraph of all <div> elements, you could use this definition:

```
div > p:first-child { text-indent: 25px; }
```

The :lang pseudo-class

The language pseudo-class (:lang) allows constructing selectors based on the language setting for specific tags. This is useful in documents that must appeal to multiple languages that have different conventions for certain language constructs. For example, the French language typically uses angle brackets (< and >) for quoting purposes, while the English language uses quote marks (' and ').

In a document that needs to address this difference, you can use the :lang pseudo-class to change the quote marks appropriately. The following code changes the <blockquote> tag appropriately for the language being used:

```
/* Two levels of quotes for two languages */
:lang(en) { quotes: '"' '"' "'" "'"; }
:lang(fr) { quotes: "<<" ">>" "<" ">"; }

/* Add quotes (before and after) to blockquote */
blockquote:before { content: open-quote; }
blockquote:after { content: close-quote; }
```

The pseudo-elements `:before` and `:after` are covered later in this chapter in the *Pseudo-elements* section.

The `:lang` selectors will apply to all elements in the document. However, not all elements make use of the `quotes` property, so the effect will be transparent for most elements. The second two definitions in the preceding example add quotes to the `blockquote` element, which typically does not include quotes.

Pseudo-elements

Pseudo-elements are another virtual construct to help you apply styles dynamically to elements in your documents. For example, the `:first-line` pseudo-element applies a style to the first line of an element dynamically—that is, as the first line grows or shrinks the browser adjusts the style coverage accordingly.

The various pseudo-elements are covered in the following sections.

Applying styles to the first line of an element

The `:first-line` pseudo-element allows you to specify a different definition for the first line of elements in the document. This is shown in the following code and Figure 17-2:

```
<!DOCTYPE HTML PUBLIC "-//W3C//DTD HTML 4.01//EN"
  "http://www.w3.org/TR/html4/strict.dtd">
<html>
<head>
  <title>First-line formatting</title>
  <style type="text/css">
    p:first-line { text-decoration: underline; }
    p.noline:first-line { text-decoration: none; }
  </style>
</head>
<body>
<h1>IN CONGRESS, July 4, 1776.</h1>
<p class="noline">The unanimous Declaration of the thirteen
United States of America,</p>

<p>When in the Course of human events, it becomes necessary
for one people to dissolve the political bands which have
connected them with another, and to assume among the powers
of the earth, the separate and equal station to which
the Laws of Nature and of Nature's God entitle them, a decent
respect to the opinions of mankind requires that they should
declare the causes which impel them to the separation.</p>

</body>
</html>
```

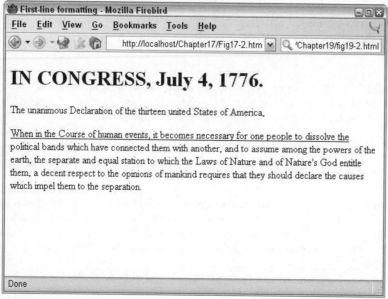

Figure 17-2: :first-line pseudo-element can be used to affect only the first line of elements.

Note   Use of the :first-line pseudo-element is somewhat hindered due to the limited range of properties it can affect. Only properties in the following groups can be applied using :first-line: **font properties, color properties, background properties,** word-spacing, letter-spacing, text-decoration, vertical-align, text-transform, line-height, text-shadow, **and** clear.

Note that the preceding code example uses classes to manage elements by exception. Since we want most paragraphs to have their first line underlined, a universal selector is defined to apply to all paragraph tags. A second selector, using a class (noline), is defined to apply to elements that have their class set to noline. This helps simplify our document—we only have to add class attributes to the exceptions instead of the rule.

Applying styles to the first letter of an element

Just as the :first-line pseudo-element can be used to affect the properties of the first line of an element, the :first-letter pseudo-element can be used to affect the first letter of an element. You can use this to achieve typographic effects such as dropcaps, as shown in the following code and Figure 17-3:

```
<!DOCTYPE HTML PUBLIC "-//W3C//DTD HTML 4.01//EN"
   "http://www.w3.org/TR/html4/strict.dtd">
<html>
<head>
```

```
<title>Drop cap formatting</title>
<style type="text/css">
   p.dropcap:first-letter { font-size: 3em;
   font-weight: bold; float: left;
   border: solid 1px black; padding: .1em;
   margin: .2em .2em 0 0; }
</style>
</head>
<body>
<h1>IN CONGRESS, July 4, 1776.</h1>
<p>The unanimous Declaration of the
thirteen united States of America,</p>
<p class="dropcap">When in the Course of human events,
it becomes necessary for one people to dissolve the political
bands which have connected them with another, and to assume
among the powers of the earth, the separate and equal station
to which the Laws of Nature and of Nature's God entitle them,
a decent respect to the opinions of mankind requires that
they should declare the causes which impel them to the
separation.</p>
</body>
</html>
```

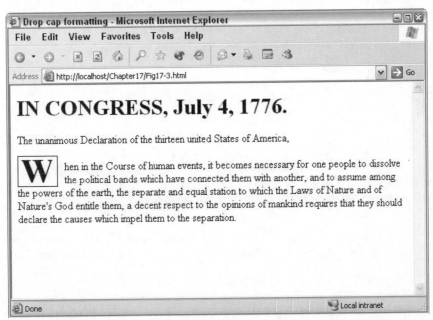

Figure 17-3: The :first-letter pseudo-element can be used to achieve effects such as drop caps.

Specifying before and after text

You can use the :before and :after pseudo-elements to autogenerate content before and after specific elements. These pseudo-elements were used in the section,

The *:lang pseudo-class*, to add quote marks to the beginning and ending of
`<blockquote>` elements:

```
blockquote:before { content: '"'; }
blockquote:after { content: '"'; }
```

Note the use of the `content` property. This property can assign specific content to
content-generating selectors. In this case, quote marks are assigned to the `before`
and `after` properties so that `<blockquote>` elements will begin and end with
quotes, as shown in Figure 17-4.

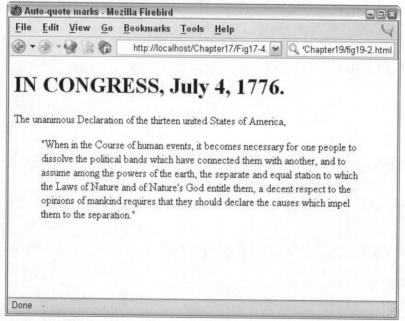

Figure 17-4: Opera supports generated content, as demonstrated by the
generated quotes around the `<blockquote>` paragraph.

Note   Many browsers do not support CSS-generated content. See Appendix B for
more information on what properties are supported by which browsers.

Generated content breaks the division of content and presentation, of which CSS is
supposed to stick to presentation. However, additional content is sometimes
necessary to enhance the presentation. Besides adding elements such as quote
marks, you can also create counters for custom numbered lists and other more
powerful features.

Cross-Reference   More information on CSS content generation can be found in Chapter 19.

Shorthand Expressions

CSS supports many properties for fine control over elements. For example, the following properties all apply to borders:

✦ border

✦ border-collapse

✦ border-spacing

✦ border-top

✦ border-right

✦ border-bottom

✦ border-left

✦ border-color

✦ border-top-color

✦ border-right-color

✦ border-bottom-color

✦ border-left-color

✦ border-style

✦ border-top-style

✦ border-right-style

✦ border-bottom-style

✦ border-left-style

✦ border-width

✦ border-top-width

✦ border-right-width

✦ border-bottom-width

✦ border-left-width

Several of these properties are shorthand properties, which enable you to set multiple properties at a time. For example, to set an element's border as shown in Figure 17-5, you could use the following definition:

```
p.bordered {
  border-top-width: 1px;
  border-top-style: solid;
  border-top-color: black;

  border-right-width: 2px;
  border-right-style: dashed;
  border-right-color: red;
```

```
    border-bottom-width: 1px;
    border-bottom-style: solid;
    border-bottom-color: black;

    border-left-width: 2px;
    border-left-style: dashed;
    border-left-color: red;
  }
```

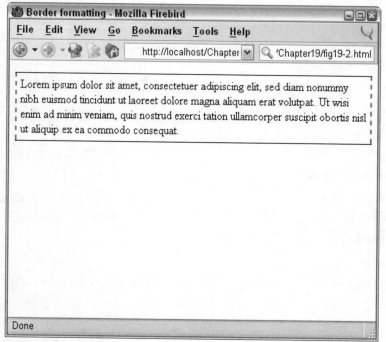

Figure 17-5: A paragraph using different borders requires multiple properties to be set.

However, you can use the `border-side` properties to shorten the definition, defining the border width, style, and color with one property:

```
p.bordered {
    border-top: 1px solid black;
    border-right: 2px dashed red;
    border-bottom: 1px solid black;
    border-left: 2px dashed red;
  }
```

You could further simplify this style by using the `border` property, which allows you to set all the sides to the same property and then list the exceptions:

```
p.bordered {
    border: 1px solid black;
```

```
    border-right: 2px dashed red;
    border-left: 2px dashed red;
}
```

The preceding definition first sets all the sides to the same width, style, and color. Then the left and right are set to their proper properties, overriding the border property's left and right side settings.

See Appendix B for more information on the various shortcuts in CSS.

Avoid overusing shortcut properties or being too ingenious in setting styles with minimal properties. Although you may save in typing, you will also decrease the legibility of your code. Take a look at the example definitions in this section— although the first example is lengthy, it leaves little to the imagination of how the border is being formatted.

Property Value Metrics

Now that you know how to apply values to properties, let's talk about the values themselves. You can specify your values using several different metrics, depending upon your needs and use.

CSS styles support the following metrics:

✦ CSS keywords and other properties, such as thin, thick, transparent, ridge, and so forth

✦ Real-world measures

- inches (in)

- centimeters (cm)

- millimeters (mm)

- points (pt)—the points used by CSS2 are equal to $1/72^{th}$ of an inch

- picas (pc)—1 pica is equal to 12 points

✦ Screen measures in pixels (px)

✦ Relational to font size (font size (em) or x-height size (ex)

✦ Percentages (%)

✦ Color codes (#rrggbb or rgb(r,g,b))

✦ Angles

- degrees (deg)

- grads (grad)

- radians (rad)

✦ Time values (seconds (s) and milliseconds (ms))—used with aural style sheets

✦ Frequencies (Hertz (Hz) and kilo Hertz (kHz))—used with aural style sheets

✦ Textual strings

Which units you use depends on which properties you are setting and what the application of the document is. For example, it doesn't make any sense to set the document's property values to inches or centimeters unless the user agent's display is calibrated in real-world measures or your document is meant to be printed.

Cross-Reference
See Chapter 24 for more information about formatting documents for printing. See the relevant chapters in Part III for examples of how to use the various metric values in properties. See Appendix B for a list of what properties support which metrics.

In the case of relational values (percentages, em, and so on), the actual value is calculated on the element's parent settings. For example, consider the following two definitions for the <i> element. Both of definitions will set the font size of all italic elements to 11pts, by specifying 1.1 times the parent's font size, or 110% of the parent's font size. The output of this code is shown in Figure 17-6.

```html
<!DOCTYPE HTML PUBLIC "-//W3C//DTD HTML 4.01//EN"
  "http://www.w3.org/TR/html4/strict.dtd">
<html>
<head>
  <title>Border formatting</title>
  <style type="text/css">
    /* Set paragraph font to 10pt */
    p { font-size: 10pt; }
    /* Set font to 1.1 * parent */
    i.def1 { font-size: 1.1em; }
    /* Set font to 110% parent */
    i.def2 { font-size: 110%; }
  </style>
</head>
<body>
  <p>Lorem ipsum dolor sit amet, <i class="def1">consectetuer
  adipiscing</i> elit, sed diam nonummy nibh euismod
  tincidunt ut laoreet dolore magna <i class="def2">aliquam
  erat volutpat</i>. Ut wisi enim ad minim veniam, quis
  nostrud exerci tation ullamcorper suscipit obortis nisl ut
  aliquip ex ea commodo consequat.</p>
</body>
</html>
```

Note
The em unit can be quite powerful because it allows you to specify a value that changes as the element sizes change around it. However, using the em unit can have unpredictable results. As such, em is best used when you need a relational, not absolute, value.

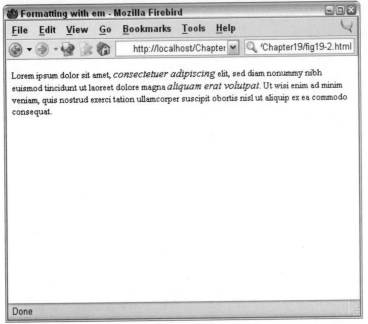

Figure 17-6: Using the em and percentage metrics, you can define elements to be a relative size, driven by the elements around them.

Summary

This chapter rounded out the basics of CSS. You learned how to construct valid CSS rules using simple and complex selectors, the role inheritance plays throughout document styles, and the different metrics you can use to specify properties.

✦   ✦   ✦

Fonts

I remember working with an award-winning print designer in Chicago who was so resistant to computers and desktop graphic software that he eventually disappeared from the industry. Good print designers have strong feelings about typography as an art form, and many of them resisted early desktop publishing tools, not so much because these tools couldn't perform, but because they ended up in the hands of a new generation of designers who, in the mind of the old school, didn't truly appreciate typography.

When print designers began to encounter Web design projects, they were aghast. Most designers don't like to compromise when it comes to the quality of their designs, and the Web is all about compromise. Discovering that the font they so carefully chose would likely not appear as they hoped but, worse, would more than likely be replaced with another font, was a traumatic experience for many traditionalists.

Today, the Web is still all about compromise. Flash hasn't changed that. Scalable Vector Graphics (SVG) haven't changed it (though they both could yet), and today's browsers certainly haven't changed it. However, there is considerably more you can do with fonts than you were able to do at one time, and some careful planning and a little extra work can give you considerable control over the way your Web pages render fonts. This chapter explores fonts, why you need to understand them, and how you can have your pages render at least close to something like you had in mind when you originally conceived your design.

Web Typography Basics

Fonts basically consist of *glyphs*, which are the actual machine-based descriptions of individual members of a font family. These descriptions are based on either a vector-based outline or a pixel-based bitmap. Each font exists on an invisible grid called an *em square*, which forms the boundaries that a font description relies on. See Figure 18-1 for a description of a glyph's properties.

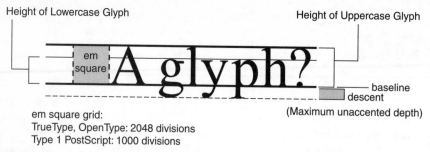

em square grid:
TrueType, OpenType: 2048 divisions
Type 1 PostScript: 1000 divisions

Figure 18-1: Glyph attributes.

As you can see in Figure 18-1, the em square determines the height boundaries that a font can meet on the grid. Print-based typefaces, such as PostScript, determine exact widths and heights by breaking the em square up into smaller pieces (1,000 pieces for PostScript, 2,048 for TrueType). OpenType, which is found on both Web-based fonts (see the section towards the end of this chapter on downloadable Web fonts), also breaks an em square up into 2,400 parcels. Machines then use these parcels as ways to exactly measure distance within an em square and the existence of different parts of a font glyph. For example, say the bottom of a g is measured within the scope of those divisions. The positioning based on those divisions is what gives each font its unique characteristics.

The wrong way to describe fonts

It may seem a little heavy-handed to say that just because the W3C has deprecated an element (meaning that the element is discontinued and is no longer part of any formal specification) you shouldn't use it. But when you realize that its use leads to extremely tedious maintenance issues, the argument suddenly seems a bit less heavy-handed. These maintenance issues arise because of the very nature of how a font element works.

You can use the font element to render font attributes. The font element has been deprecated, and you won't even find it in the XHTML 1.1 specification. The theory behind its use was that it would control the way a font looked. In practice, ghastly things happened. For example, users might set a font size to 1 that on some screens is so tiny as to be unreadable, or a font size at 3, which on a screen whose user has poor vision takes up the entire screen for a couple of words because the user's browser preferences are set with large font sizes. Still, you might work for a large site that continues to insist on using this dinosaur, so here are this element's attributes:

- ✦ SIZE=CDATA (font size adjustment)
- ✦ COLOR=Color (font color adjustment)
- ✦ FACE=CDATA (font face adjustment)
- ✦ HTML 4.0 core attributes
- ✦ HTML 4.0 internationalization attributes

You can see these attributes at work in the following example:

```
<font size="1" face="Helvetica, Arial, Verdana, sans-serif"
color="blue" lang="en-US" class=".small" style="font-family:
Times, serif;" id="confusingElement">This is an HTML
deprecated element!</font>
```

Load the code from Listing 18-1 into your browser and you'll see something similar to that shown in Figure 18-2.

Listing 18-1: **Using the Font Element to Name a Font Family**

```
<body>
     <font size="1" face="Helvetica, Arial, Verdana, sans-
serif" color="blue" lang="en-US" class=".small" style="font-
family: Times, serif;" id="ConfusingElement">This is an HTML
deprecated <span style="font-
size:28px;">element!</span></font>
  </body>
```

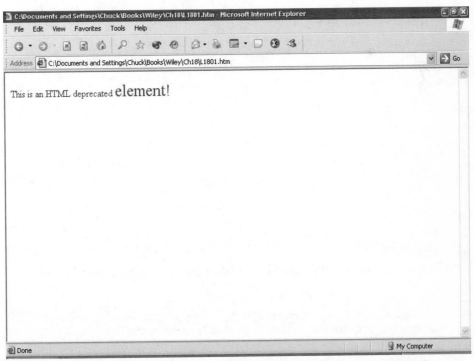

Figure 18-2: The attempt to style a string of characters using the font element fails.

You'll notice several things about Listing 18-1 and Figure 18-2. First, no matter what fonts you have installed on your system, if you're testing in a modern browser, you won't see sans-serif fonts rendered even though you call for them in the `font` element. This is because you're using a stylesheet, which overrules font element attribute information in CSS-compliant browsers. To make the font element's attributes work, you must be certain that no style sheet rules are in conflict with your intentions. So delete the style sheet information and the `class` attribute so that the font element looks like this:

```
<font size="1" face="Helvetica, Arial, Verdana, sans-serif"
color="blue" id="LessConfusingElement">This is an HTML
deprecated <span style="font-
size:28px;">element!</span></font>
```

Your browser window will now display, as shown in Figure 18-3.

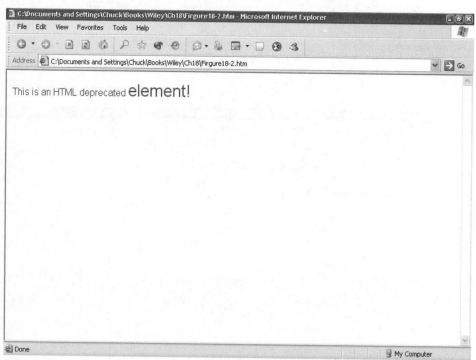

Figure 18-3: A string of characters successfully styled by using the font element.

If you name a font family with spaces between characters, you need to enclose the name in single quotes, as shown in bold in the following:

```
<font size="1" face=" 'Helvetica Narrow', Arial, Verdana,
sans-serif">This is an HTML deprecated <span style="font-
size:28px;">element!</span></font>
```

The right way to describe fonts

If you examine Figure 18-4 and Listing 18-2, which creates the screen rendered in that figure, you'll immediately see the benefits of working with the right way of managing fonts, which is CSS.

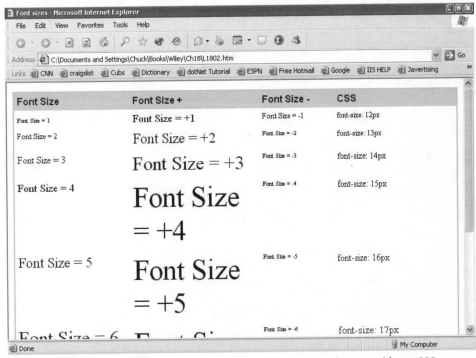

Figure 18-4: A table of different font sizes shows a lack of consistency without CSS.

Listing 18-2: Creating Font Sizes with CSS and the Font Element's Size Attribute

```
<html>
<head>
<title>Font sizes</title>
<meta http-equiv="Content-Type" content="text/html;
charset=iso-8859-1">
<style type="text/css">
<!--
.12pixels {font-size: 12px;}
.13pixels {font-size: 13px;}
.14pixels {font-size: 14px;}
.15pixels {font-size: 15px;}
```

Continued

Listing 18-2: *(continued)*

```
.16pixels {font-size: 16px;}
.17pixels {font-size: 17px;}
.18pixels {font-size: 18px;}
.sans-serif {font-family: Frutiger, Arial, Helvetica, sans-
serif;}
.sans-serif-b {font-family: Frutiger, Arial, Helvetica, sans-
serif;font-weight: 900;}
-->
</style>
</head>
<body>
<table width="100%" border="0" cellspacing="0"
cellpadding="5" style="border: #cccccc thin solid">
  <tr align="left" valign="top" bgcolor="#D5D5D5" >
    <td width="26%" valign="bottom" class="sans-serif-b">Font
Size</td>
    <td width="29%" valign="bottom" class="sans-serif-
b">Font Size +</td>
    <td width="17%" valign="bottom" class="sans-serif-
b">Font Size -</td>
    <td width="28%" valign="bottom" class="sans-serif-
b">CSS</td>
  </tr>
  <tr align="left" valign="top">
    <td><p><font size="1">Font Size = 1</font> </p></td>
    <td><font size="+1">Font Size = +1</font> </td>
    <td><font size="-1">Font Size = -1</font></td>
    <td class="12pixels">font-size: 12px</td>
  </tr>
  <!-- Additional rows of all the font-sizes here - download
actual code to view all rows -->
</table>
<p> </p>
</body>
</html>
```

Notice the consistency of the sizes in the fourth column. If you open the file in your browser and change your browser's text size settings, you'll see that the fonts in the fourth column remain the same size, whereas the sizes in the first three columns, which don't use CSS for style formatting, all vary wildly.

Hopefully, you're now convinced of the need to use CSS for styling your fonts. It's time to examine just how to do that. You can style several aspects of a font to make it bolder, italicized, add space between each character in a word, make it larger or smaller, make a font fatter or thinner, and add space between lines of text. For the syntactic details on how to use these styling capabilities, refer to Appendix B, *CSS Levels 1 and 2 Quick Reference*.

Working with Font Styling Attributes

There are several styling attributes to control such characteristics as font families, sizes, bolding, and spacing.

Naming font families using CSS

As I've shown, CSS provides a mechanism for rendering font families in a browser if those fonts are installed on a user's system. This is accomplished by creating either an inline style on an element such as a td or span element, or by creating a class rule selector within the style element. Either way, the syntax is the same, with a list of font family names, each separated by a comma, contained within a set of braces:

```
font-family {Arial, Helvetica, sans-serif;}
```

The browser will look first for the Arial font in the preceding example, then the Helvetica font, then the "default" sans-serif font, which is whatever sans-serif font the user's operating system defaults to.

If you name a font family with spaces between characters, you need to enclose the name in quotes, as shown in bold in the following:

```
.myFontClass {font-family:  'Helvetica Narrow', sans-serif}
```

In practice, it may be a good idea to use quotes even when there are no spaces between characters, because some versions of Netscape 4 have trouble recognizing font names otherwise.

Listing 18-3 shows a brief example of creating both an inline style and calling a class selector to name a font family.

Listing 18-3: Using Class Selector and Inline Style to Name a Font Family

```
<html>
<head>
<title>Font sizes</title>
<meta http-equiv="Content-Type" content="text/html;
charset=iso-8859-1">
<style type="text/css">
<!--
.myFontClass {font-family: "Helvetica Narrow", sans-serif}
-->
</style>
</head>
<body>
<p>This is an <span  style="font-family: 'Helvetica Narrow',
sans-serif">inline</span> style.</p>
```

Continued

Listing 18-3: *(continued)*

```
<p>This uses a <span class="myFontClass">class
selector</span></p>
</body>
</html>
```

The first bolded line shows a class selector named myFontClass, which is called by a span element's class attribute (the last bolded code fragment). Figure 18-5 shows the results from rendering Listing 18-3 in the browser.

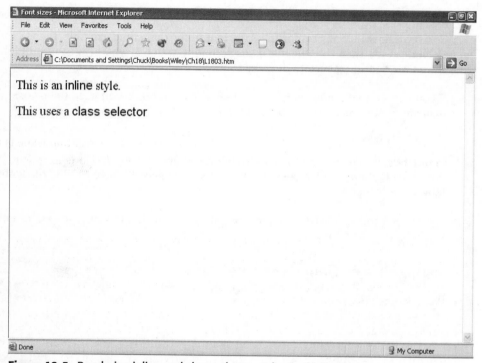

Figure 18-5: Rendering inline and class selector styles in the browser.

Understanding font families

When choosing font families for style sheets, it helps to understand some basic facts about fonts. For example, Arial and Helvetica are virtually identical. Arial is more commonly seen on Windows systems, and Helvetica on Macs and UNIX. It's best to call them both in a style sheet so that one of them will appear on a user's machine no matter what environment they're in. If you use the generic "sans-serif," you'll get the default sans-serif font on the user's system. So your best, lowest common denominator CSS font selector looks like this:

```
myFontClass {font-family: Arial, Helvetica, sans-serif}
```

Using this font will render a sans-serif font on the vast majority of modern browsers.

To understand what a font family is, consider what a font family is not. Helvetica and Helvetica Narrow do not constitute a font family, even though it's reasonable to suspect they would belong to the same family. Helvetica Narrow, by itself, is a font family. So is Helvetica, which actually refers to a basic kind of Helvetica font. Helvetica Condensed and other variations also exist.

Understanding fonts and font availability

The first thing to understand about font availability is that they probably aren't. In other words, all your best-laid plans when it comes to your design are likely to end up in complete disappointment. The reason? The fonts you name in a CSS file may, or may not, be on your users' computer systems.

There are a few ways to ensure, for example, that Arial or Helvetica will appear as expected on your Web page for most of your audience. However, other than those two fonts, it's either a crapshoot or a lot of jumping through font hoops to get your fonts to render. The reason is simple. You can ask your user's browser to display the Frutiger font, for example, but if their system doesn't have it installed, the browser will simply display the next closest thing. How the browser decides that issue is an algorithmic process based on something called the Panose system (see sidebar), but the bottom line is that your HTML/CSS does not embed any actual font information or fonts; it merely requests that the browser display a font *if* that font happens to be on the user's system.

How the Panose System Works

Panose is a system of font substitution that uses a combination of mapping software (as in software that makes calculated comparisons), a ten-digit numbering system, and a classification method to help the browser match font property values. If that fails, the browser tries to find the closest match. For example, if you name Futura Extra Bold as the only font when you name a font family using either CSS or the font element's face attribute, and the user's system doesn't have Futura Extra Bold installed, the browser will probably use something like Arial Black because both fonts are heavy, wide sans-serif fonts.

Working with font styles

In traditional HTML, you can choose whether you want your font to appear in Roman style (non-italic) font or italics by using or not using the em or i elements:

```
Emphasizing a point with the <em>em element</em> or the <i>i
element</i>.
```

The preceding code fragment results in the following in a browser:

Emphasizing a point with the *em element* or the *i element*.

If you want to really be sure even the earliest of browsers recognize your italics, em is the way to go. More importantly, it's a better choice because aural browsers should *emphasize* the contents of this element to sight-impaired users of your Web site.

For this reason, this is one of the rare exceptions to the rule of using CSS for styling over HTML elements. However, there's nothing wrong with using both. To use italics in CSS, simply include the following either inline or in a rule selector:

```
font-style: italic
```

Note Be sure to call it "italic," not "italics" with an s. You can also use `font-style: oblique`, but older versions of Netscape will not recognize it.

Establishing font sizes

Managing font size can be tricky even with CSS, but most developers seem to agree that the most reliable unit of measurement in CSS is the pixel. Managing font sizes in straight HTML, as noted earlier in the chapter, is about as inexact a science as there is, but the general rule is that it's supposed to work like that shown in Listing 18-2, provided earlier in this chapter, which shows all the available attribute values for the font element's `size` attribute. The way it's *supposed* to work, but often doesn't, is that using the plus sign (+) before a number (for example, +1 or +2) makes the font bigger relative to the default font size on the page. In production environments, this is not a reliable process. If you must use the font element's `size` attribute in your HTML (believe it or not, some large sites actually still make this a requirement), be aware that relative sizing using the plus sign before a number has inconsistent browser support, so your results will vary.

To establish size using CSS, you simply name the property in your selector or inline style rule:

```
.twelve {font-size: 12px}
H1 {font-size: xx-large}
.xsmall {font-size: 25%}
```

In the preceding code fragment, three style rules are created, each with its own font size. The first creates a relative size using pixels as the unit of measure. Never spell out the word pixels in your style definition. Always use the form px.

px is the most reliable unit of measure because it is based on the user's screen size, and the pixel resolution of his or her monitor. It also has virtually bug-free support across all browsers that support CSS.

Other relative sizes include the following:

✦ em, for ems, is based on the em square of the base font size, so that 2em will render a font twice as large as your document's base font size. Support in Netscape 4 and IE3 is awful.

✦ ex is based on the X height of the base font size, so that 2ex will render a font whose X character is twice as tall as the X character at the default, or base, font size. This is a meaningless unit in the real world, because support is either nonexistent or so poor as to make it worthless.

The next line in the preceding code fragment sets an absolute size called xx-large, although it isn't absolute among browsers, only the one browser your user is using to render the page. xx-large is part of a larger collection that includes the following possible values:

```
xx-small, x-small, small, medium, large, x-large, xx-large
```

Other absolute sizes include the following:

✦ pt for points. This is appropriate for pages that are used for printing, but is not a particularly reliable measure for managing screen-based fonts.

✦ in (inches), cm (centimeters), mm (millimeters), and pc (picas) are all rarely used on the Web, because they're designed with print production in mind.

Finally, you can create a font size using a percentage by simply adding the % character next to the actual size. This will render the font x% of the base size.

You can experiment with font sizes by modifying Listing 18-2.

Using (or not using) font variants

In theory, the CSS font-variant property lets you create fonts in uppercase that are smaller sizes in relative terms to their base size. In practice, it doesn't work very well in most browsers, and isn't worth your trouble. See the CSS reference in Appendix B for syntactical details.

Bolding fonts by changing font weight

Font weight refers to the stroke width of a font. If a font has a very thin, or light, stroke width, it will have a weight of 100. If it has a thick, or heavy, stroke width, it will be 900. Everything else is inbetween. To denote font width, you use a numeric set of values from 100 to 900 in increments of 100: 100, 200, 300, 400, and so on. Or, you can use the keywords bold, normal, bolder or lighter to set a value, which will be relative to the font weight of the element containing the font.

The keyword bold is equal to the numeric value 700. An example of using font-weight in style rules written for a style element might be as follows:

```
p {font-weight: normal}
p.bold {font-weight: 900}
```

Making font wider or thinner using font stretch

This font property is supposed to allow you to make a font look fatter or thinner. Support is nonexistent, however. The curious among you can see the CSS reference in Appendix B for syntactical details.

Line height and leading

The CSS `line-height` property is another one of those nice-in-theory properties that just doesn't pan out in the real world. The syntax is supposed to let you set the space between lines in a process that in the print world is called leading. It works fairly well in Internet Explorer, but is a mess in Netscape 4. The syntax is easy enough:

```
line-height: normal
line-height: 1.1
line-height: 110%
```

The first example in the preceding series of rules makes the line height the same as the base line height of the document. The next line makes the line height 1.1 times greater than the base line height, as does the third, except the third uses percentages as a unit of measure.

Tip

A good resource for CSS browser compatibility can be found at: `http://www.richinstyle.com/bugs/table.html`. The site doesn't include IE6, but it has a good survey of all the other browsers' support for various CSS properties, and you really want to know how things look in older browsers anyway.

Downloading Fonts Automatically

When you write HTML, you're probably well aware that when you set up an `img` element in a Web document, the image downloads into the client machine's cache, enabling the browser to display the image. This process needs to take place if the image is to be viewed. An *embedded font file* works the same way. An embedded font file is a font object that you create and embed into the page using a font creation tool such as Microsoft's WEFT, which creates embedded fonts optimized for IE5, or HexMac by HexMac, which creates embedded fonts optimized for Netscape (but downloadable to IE5 with the use of an ActiveX Control).

Dynamic font standards and options

Basically, there are two font-embedding platforms: OpenType and TrueDoc. The two font platforms differ in some ways, the most obvious being that since they both use different file types, you have to jump through some hoops to develop any kind of font compatibility across browser platforms.

The two formats also differ in how they appear on the screen. TrueDoc looks more like an image file, whereas OpenType looks more like a typeface.

OpenType

OpenType is a font distribution standard developed by Microsoft and Adobe Systems, the purpose of which is to establish a means of providing some semblance of typography to the Web using the same kind of principles involved in font metrics that can be found in such type formats as PostScript and TrueType. Font metrics describe the metrics, or measurement, of a type character's shape using an em square as the basis. The em square, as mentioned earlier, is the grid upon which a font exists and from which its width and height are calculated.

The technology is centered around the creation of a font object file, with an `.eot` extension, which is generated by a font creation tool either designed specifically for that purpose, or as an engine residing in a broader-based Web authoring program.

One such tool, WEFT, is both a standalone application and a shared component that can be licensed from its developer, Microsoft, by application developers who are building Web-authoring software. The standalone program is free and can be found at `http://www.microsoft.com/typography/web/embedding/weft/`.

Currently, only Internet Explorer (versions 4 and higher) supports OpenType.

TrueDoc

BitStream, a typeface manufacturer, makes the competing standard TrueDoc. Netscape 4.0 and higher are the only browsers that directly support TrueDoc, although BitStream makes an ActiveX control that can be used in IE5. You can find more information on TrueDoc at `http://www.truedoc.com/`.

Licensing issues

The reason font embedding has not spread more quickly across Web deployment lies not so much in the reluctance of Web authors to embrace the technology (although that's part of it), nor in the technology itself; but rather, licensing issues have slowed the pace of development, because font vendors are reluctant to invest in the development of a font only to see it distributed on Web sites without compensation.

Should you use font embedding or style sheets?

Many developers, in noticing the various squabbles in the realm of font embedding, have simply barricaded themselves from the entire affair by avoiding both platforms completely. As difficult as it might be to develop compatible pages using the two font platforms, however, you can't do any damage using them, because they rely on style sheets and `font` elements to do their work. And when they fail, they fail gracefully.

The question of deployment then becomes a question of resources, and whether or not your organization has enough of them to utilize embedded fonts as part of the production process.

How to add downloadable fonts to a Web page

The two methods of font embedding have some similarities, in that both require a tool to create the font objects that get embedded into the Web page. The obvious tool of choice for IE5 developers would be WEFT, or any other tool that generates OpenType font files. Similarly, there are tools for TrueDoc font files that create font objects with a `.pfr` extension, which is the file extension for TrueDoc files.

Syntax

When you are developing OpenType files for IE5, you use an at-rule style sheet to establish their links:

```
@font-face {
    font-family: Garamond;
    font-style: normal;
    font-weight: 700;
    src:
url(http://www.myDomain.com/myFontDirectory/GARAMON3.eot);
```

TrueDoc files are used with the `link` tag and the `fontdef` attribute:

```
<LINK REL= "fontdef"
SRC="http://www.myDomain.com/myFontDirectory/Garamond.pfr">
```

If you don't want to develop TrueDoc (PFR) files, you can work from a list of font PFR that are publicly available on the TrueDoc site. These and their full URLs are listed at the following URL: `http://www.truedoc.com/webpages/availpfrs/avail_pfrs.htm`.

If you're developing for Netscape Navigator, all you need is the `link` element's `src` attribute. If you're developing pages for IE5, you'll need to include the ActiveX Control. The ActiveX control is embedded in your page with a JavaScript file located on the TrueDoc site:

```
<SCRIPT LANGUAGE="JavaScript"
SRC="http://www.truedoc.com/activex/tdserver.js">
    </SCRIPT>
```

Put the preceding code in the `head` element of your HTML.

Summary

Here's one final argument for using CSS over the `font` element to style text. Even if you work with the largest Web site in the world, and even if stakeholders have it written in stone that your Web pages MUST work to the lowest common denominator browser, they will if you use CSS instead of the `font` element, and they won't if you use the `font` element over CSS.

This is because you can write basic HTML using HTML in its earliest purest form, and if you avoid using some of the earlier proprietary elements that began to surface after Netscape's popularity was at its peak, every browser in the world should be able to read your Web page, including text-based browsers such as Lynx.

This chapter, aside from taking a rather strong stand on using CSS over the font element, covered the following:

✦ Web typography basics

✦ Working with font styling attributes

✦ Downloading fonts automatically

The next chapter looks at text formatting, including indenting and aligning text, controlling letter and word spacing, and using text decoration such as underlines and blinking.

✦ ✦ ✦

Text Formatting

Since the Web was initially text-based and the recent push is to make Web documents more like printed matter, it is no surprise that there are many styles to control text formatting. From simple justification to autogenerated text, one of CSS's major strengths is dealing with the printed word. This chapter covers the basics of text formatting.

Aligning Text

Multiple properties in CSS control the formatting of text. Several properties allow you to align text horizontally and vertically—aligning with other pieces of text or other elements around them.

Controlling horizontal alignment

You can use the `text-align` property to align blocks of text in four basic ways: left, right, center, or full. The following code and the output in Figure 19-1 show the effect of the justification settings:

```
<!DOCTYPE HTML PUBLIC "-//W3C//DTD HTML 4.01//EN"
  "http://www.w3.org/TR/html4/strict.dtd">
<html>
<head>
  <title>Text Justification</title>
  <style type="text/css">
    p:left { text-align: left; }
    p.right { text-align: right; }
    p.center { text-align: center; }
    p.full { text-align: justify; }
  </style>
</head>
<body>
<div style="margin: 50px">
<h3>Left Justified (default)</h3>
<p class="left">Lorem ipsum dolor sit amet, consectetuer
adipiscing elit, sed diam nonummy nibh euismod tincidunt
ut laoreet dolore magna aliquam erat volutpat. Ut wisi
```

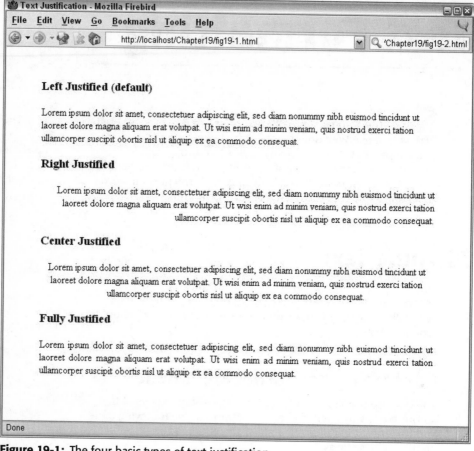

Figure 19-1: The four basic types of text justification.

```
enim ad minim veniam, quis nostrud exerci tation ullamcorper
suscipit obortis nisl ut aliquip ex ea commodo consequat.</p>

<h3>Right Justified</h3>
<p class="right">Lorem ipsum dolor sit amet, consectetuer
adipiscing elit, sed diam nonummy nibh euismod tincidunt
ut laoreet dolore magna aliquam erat volutpat. Ut wisi
enim ad minim veniam, quis nostrud exerci tation ullamcorper
suscipit obortis nisl ut aliquip ex ea commodo consequat.</p>

<h3>Center Justified</h3>
<p class="center">Lorem ipsum dolor sit amet, consectetuer
adipiscing elit, sed diam nonummy nibh euismod tincidunt
µt laoreet dolore magna aliquam erat volutpat. Ut wisi
enim ad minim veniam, quis nostrud exerci tation ullamcorper
suscipit obortis nisl ut aliquip ex ea commodo consequat.</p>

<h3>Fully Justified</h3>
<p class="full">Lorem ipsum dolor sit amet, consectetuer
```

```
adipiscing elit, sed diam nonummy nibh euismod tincidunt
ut laoreet dolore magna aliquam erat volutpat. Ut wisi
enim ad minim veniam, quis nostrud exerci tation ullamcorper
suscipit obortis nisl ut aliquip ex ea commodo consequat.</p>
</div>
</body>
</html>
```

Note that the default justification is left; that is, the lines in the block of text are aligned against the left margin and the lines wrap where convenient on the right, leaving a jagged right margin.

In addition to the four standard alignment options, you can also use text-align to align columnar data in tables to a specific character. For example, the following code results in the data in the Amount Due column being aligned on the decimal place:

```
<!DOCTYPE HTML PUBLIC "-//W3C//DTD HTML 4.01//EN"
  "http://www.w3.org/TR/html4/strict.dtd">
<html>
<head>
  <title>Table Column Justification</title>
  <style type="text/css">
    td.dec { text-align: "."; }
  </style>
</head>
<body>
  <table border="1">
  <tr>
    <th>Customer</th>
    <th>Amount Due</th>
  </tr>
  <tr>
    <td>Acme Industries</td>
    <td class="dec">$50.95</td>
  </tr>
  <tr>
    <td>RHI LLC</td>
    <td class="dec">$2084.56</td>
  </tr>
  <tr>
    <td>EMrUs</td>
    <td class="dec">$0.55</td>
  </tr>
  </table>
</body>
</html>
```

Note Columnar alignment using the text-align property is not well supported in today's user agents. You should test your target agents to ensure compliance before using text-align this way.

Controlling vertical alignment

In addition to aligning text horizontally, CSS enables you to align text to objects around it via the `vertical-align` property. The `vertical-align` property supports the following values:

✦ baseline—This is the default vertical alignment; text uses its baseline to align to other objects around it.

✦ sub—This value causes the text to descend to the level appropriate for subscripted text, based on its parent's font size and line height. (This value has no effect on the size of the text, only its position.)

✦ super—This value causes the text to ascend to the level appropriate for superscripted text, based on its parent's font size and line height. (This value has no effect on the size of the text, only its position.)

✦ top—This value causes the top of the element's bounding box to be aligned with the top of the element's parent bounding box.

✦ text-top—This value causes the top of the element's bounding box to be aligned with the top of the element's parent text.

✦ middle—This value causes the text to be aligned using the middle of the text and the mid-line of objects around it.

✦ bottom—This value causes the bottom of the element's bounding box to be aligned with the bottom of the element's parent bounding box.

✦ text-bottom—This value causes the bottom of the element's bounding box to be aligned with the bottom of the element's parent text.

✦ length—This value causes the element to ascend (positive value) or descend (negative value) by the value specified.

✦ percentage—This value causes the element to ascend (positive value) or descend (negative value) by the percentage specified. The percentage is applied to the line height of the element.

The following code and the output in Figure 19-2 shows the effect of each value:

```
<!DOCTYPE HTML PUBLIC "-//W3C//DTD HTML 4.01//EN"
  "http://www.w3.org/TR/html4/strict.dtd">
<html>
<head>
  <title>Vertical Text Alignment</title>
  <style type="text/css">
    .baseline { vertical-align: baseline; }
    .sub { vertical-align: sub; }
    .super { vertical-align: super; }
    .top { vertical-align: top; }
    .text-top { vertical-align: text-top; }
    .middle { vertical-align: middle; }
    .bottom { vertical-align: bottom; }
    .text-bottom { vertical-align: text-bottom; }
```

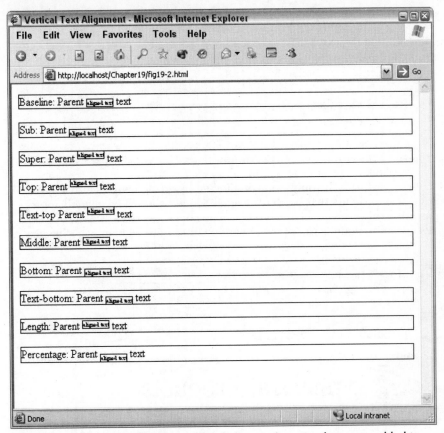

Figure 19-2: The effect of various vertical-align settings. Borders were added to the text to help contrast the alignment.

```
          .length { vertical-align: .5em; }
          .percentage { vertical-align: -50%; }
          /* All elements get a border */
          body * { border: 1px solid black; }
          /* Reduce the spans' font by 50% */
          p * { font-size: 50%; }
      </style>
  </head>
  <body>
     <p>Baseline: Parent
       <span class="baseline">aligned text</span> text</p>
     <p>Sub: Parent
       <span class="sub">aligned text</span> text</p>
     <p>Super: Parent
       <span class="super">aligned text</span> text</p>
     <p>Top: Parent
       <span class="top">aligned text</span> text</p>
     <p>Text-top Parent
       <span class="text-top">aligned text</span> text</p>
```

```
    <p>Middle: Parent
      <span class="middle">aligned text</span> text</p>
    <p>Bottom: Parent
      <span class="bottom">aligned text</span> text</p>
    <p>Text-bottom: Parent
      <span class="text-bottom">aligned text</span> text</p>
    <p>Length: Parent
      <span class="length">aligned text</span> text</p>
    <p>Percentage: Parent
      <span class="percentage">aligned text</span> text</p>
  </body>
</html>
```

Of course, text isn't the only element affected by an element's `vertical-align` setting—all elements that border the affected element will be aligned appropriately. Figure 19-3 shows an image next to text. The image has the `vertical-align` property set to middle. Note how the midpoint of both elements is aligned.

Figure 19-3: The `vertical-align` property can be used to vertically align most elements.

Indenting Text

You can use the `text-indent` property to indent the first line of an element. For example, to indent the first line of a paragraph of text by 25 pixels, you could use code similar to the following:

```
<p style="text-indent: 25px;"> Lorem ipsum dolor sit amet,
Consectetuer adipiscing elit, sed diam nonummy nibh euismod
tincidunt ut laoreet dolore magna aliquam erat volutpat. Ut
wisi enim ad minim veniam, quis nostrud exerci tation
ullamcorper suscipit obortis nisl ut aliquip ex ea commodo
consequat.</p>
```

Note that the `text-indent` property only indents the first line of the element. If you want to indent the entire element, use the `margin` properties instead.

 Cross-Reference See Chapter 20 for more information about the `margin` properties.

You can specify the indent as a specific value (1in, 25px, and so on), or as a percentage of the containing block width. Note that when specifying the indent as a percentage, the width of the user agent's display will play a prominent role in the actual size of the indentation. Therefore, when you want a uniform indent, use a specific value.

Controlling White Space within Text

White space is typically not a concern in HTML documents. However, at times you'll want better control over how white space is interpreted and how certain elements line up to their siblings.

Clearing floating objects

The `float` property can cause elements to ignore the normal flow of the document and "float" against a particular margin. For example, consider the following code and resulting output shown in Figure 19-4:

```
<!DOCTYPE HTML PUBLIC "-//W3C//DTD HTML 4.01//EN"
  "http://www.w3.org/TR/html4/strict.dtd">
<html>
<head>
  <title>Floating Image</title>
</head>
<body>
  <p><b>Floating Image</b><br>
  <img src="sphere.png" style="float: right;">
  Lorem ipsum dolor sit amet, consectetuer
  adipiscing elit, sed diam nonummy nibh euismod tincidunt
  ut laoreet dolore magna aliquam erat volutpat. Ut wisi
  enim ad minim veniam, quis nostrud exerci tation
  ullamcorper suscipit obortis nisl ut aliquip ex ea commodo
  consequat.</p>

  <p><b>Non-Floating Image</b><br>
  <img src="sphere.png">
  Lorem ipsum dolor sit amet, consectetuer
  adipiscing elit, sed diam nonummy nibh euismod tincidunt
  ut laoreet dolore magna aliquam erat volutpat. Ut wisi
  enim ad minim veniam, quis nostrud exerci tation
  ullamcorper suscipit obortis nisl ut aliquip ex ea commodo
  consequat.</p>
</body>
</html>
```

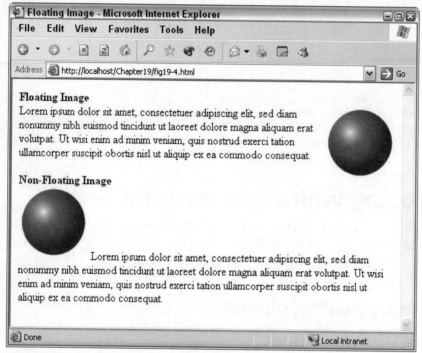

Figure 19-4: Floating images can add a dynamic feel to your documents.

Although floating images can add an attractive, dynamic air to your documents, their placement is not always predictable. As such, it's helpful to be able to tell certain elements not to allow floating elements next to them. One good example of when you would want to disallow floating elements is next to headings. For example, consider the document shown in Figure 19-5.

Using the clear property you can ensure that one side or both sides of an element remain free of floating elements. For example, adding the following style to the document in Figure 19-5 ensures that both sides of all heading levels are clear of floating elements—this results in the display shown in Figure 19-6.

```
h1,h2,h3,h4,h5,h6 { clear: both; }
```

You can specify left, right, both, or none (the default) for values of the clear property. Note that the clear property doesn't affect the floating element. Instead, it forces the element containing the clear property to avoid the floating element(s).

The white-space property

User agents typically ignore extraneous white space in documents. However, at times you want the white space to be interpreted literally, without having to result to using a `<pre>` tag to do so. Enter the white-space property.

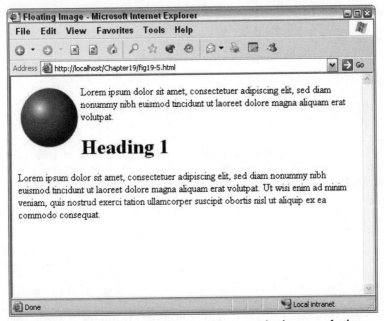

Figure 19-5: Floating images can sometimes get in the way of other elements, as in the case of this heading.

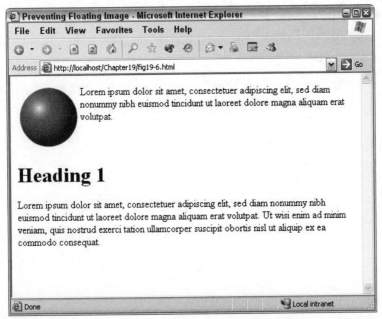

Figure 19-6: Using the `clear` property forces an element to start past the floating element's bounding box (and before any additional floating elements begin).

The white-space property can be set to the following values:

✦ normal

✦ pre

✦ nowrap

The default setting is normal, that is, ignore extraneous white space.

If the property is set to pre, text will be rendered as though it were enclosed in a <pre> tag. Note that using pre does not affect the font or other formatting of the element—it only causes white space to be rendered verbatim. For example, the following text will be spaced exactly as shown in the following code:

```
<p style="white-space:  pre;">This          paragraph's   words
  are
irregularly          spaced,      but will be rendered       as
    such
by            the            user            agent.</p>
```

Setting the white-space property to nowrap causes the element not to wrap at the right margin of the user agent. Instead, it continues to the right until the next explicit line break. User agents should add horizontal scroll bars to enable the user to fully view the content.

Controlling Letter and Word Spacing

The letter-spacing and word-spacing properties can be used to control the letter and word spacing in an element. Both elements take an explicit or relative value to adjust the spacing—positive values add more space, and negative values remove space. For example, consider the following code and output in Figure 19-7:

```
<!DOCTYPE HTML PUBLIC "-//W3C//DTD HTML 4.01//EN"
  "http://www.w3.org/TR/html4/strict.dtd">
<html>
<head>
  <title>Letter Spacing</title>
  <style type="text/css">
    .normal { letter-spacing: normal; }
    .tight  { letter-spacing: -.2em; }
    .loose  { letter-spacing: .2em; }
  </style>
</head>
<body>
  <h3>Normal</h3>
  <p class="normal">Lorem ipsum dolor sit amet, consectetuer
  adipiscing elit, sed diam nonummy nibh euismod tincidunt
  ut laoreet dolore magna aliquam erat volutpat. Ut wisi
  enim ad minim veniam, quis nostrud exerci tation
  ullamcorper suscipit obortis nisl ut aliquip ex ea commodo
  consequat.</p>
  <h3>Tight</h3>
```

```
<p class="tight">Lorem ipsum dolor sit amet, consectetuer
adipiscing elit, sed diam nonummy nibh euismod tincidunt
ut laoreet dolore magna aliquam erat volutpat. Ut wisi
enim ad minim veniam, quis nostrud exerci tation
ullamcorper suscipit obortis nisl ut aliquip ex ea commodo
consequat.</p>
<h3>Loose</h3>
<p class="loose">Lorem ipsum dolor sit amet, consectetuer
adipiscing elit, sed diam nonummy nibh euismod tincidunt
ut laoreet dolore magna aliquam erat volutpat. Ut wisi
enim ad minim veniam, quis nostrud exerci tation
ullamcorper suscipit obortis nisl ut aliquip ex ea commodo
consequat.</p>
</body>
</html>
```

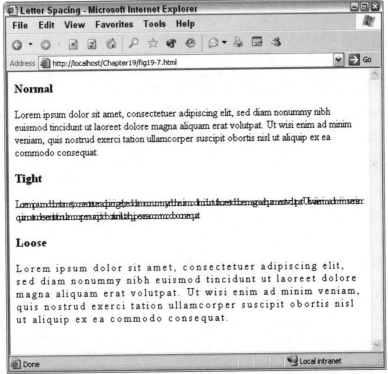

Figure 19-7: The `letter-spacing` property does exactly as its name indicates, adjusts the spacing between letters.

Note that the user agent can govern the minimum amount of letter spacing allowed—setting the letter spacing to too small a value can have unpredictable results.

The `word-spacing` property behaves exactly like the `letter-spacing` property, except that it controls the spacing between words instead of letters. Like `letter-spacing`, using a positive value with `word-spacing` results in more spacing between words, and using a negative value results in less spacing.

Specifying Capitalization

Styles can also be used to control the capitalization of text. The `text-transform` property can be set to four different values, as shown in the following code and Figure 19-8:

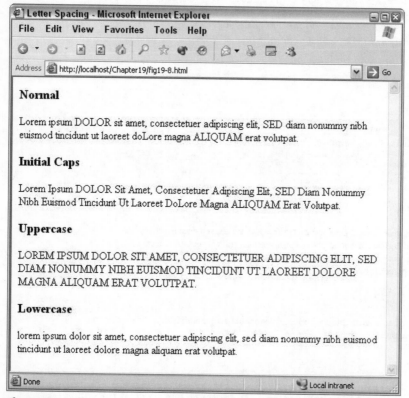

Figure 19-8: The `text-transform` property allows you to influence the capitalization of elements.

```
<!DOCTYPE HTML PUBLIC "-//W3C//DTD HTML 4.01//EN"
   "http://www.w3.org/TR/html4/strict.dtd">
<html>
<head>
  <title>Letter Spacing</title>
  <style type="text/css">
    .normal { text-transform: none; }
    .initcaps { text-transform: capitalize; }
    .upper { text-transform: uppercase; }
    .lower { text-transform: lowercase; }
  </style>
</head>
<body>
```

```
<h3>Normal</h3>
<p class="normal">Lorem ipsum DOLOR sit amet, consectetuer
adipiscing elit, SED diam nonummy nibh euismod tincidunt
ut laoreet doLore magna ALIQUAM erat volutpat.</p>
<h3>Initial Caps</h3>
<p class="initcaps">Lorem ipsum DOLOR sit amet,
consectetuer adipiscing elit, SED diam nonummy nibh euismod
tincidunt ut laoreet doLore magna ALIQUAM erat
volutpat.</p>
<h3>Uppercase</h3>
<p class="upper">Lorem ipsum DOLOR sit amet, consectetuer
adipiscing elit, SED diam nonummy nibh euismod tincidunt
ut laoreet doLore magna ALIQUAM erat volutpat.</p>
<h3>Lowercase</h3>
<p class="lower">Lorem ipsum DOLOR sit amet, consectetuer
adipiscing elit, SED diam nonummy nibh euismod tincidunt
ut laoreet doLore magna ALIQUAM erat volutpat.</p>
</body>
</html>
```

Note that there are some rules as to what `text-transform` will and won't affect.
For example, the `capitalize` value ensures that each word starts with a capital
letter, but it doesn't change the capitalization of the rest of the word. Setting the
property to `normal` will not affect the capitalization of the element.

Using Text Decorations

You can add several different effects to text through CSS. Most are accomplished via
the `text-decoration` and `text-shadow` properties.

The `text-decoration` property allows you to add the following attributes to text:

✦ underline

✦ overline (line above text)

✦ line-through

✦ blink

As with most properties, the values are straightforward:

```
<p style="text-decoration: none;">No Decoration</p>
<p style="text-decoration: underline;">Underlined</p>
<p style="text-decoration: overline;">Overlined</p>
<p style="text-decoration: line-through;">Line Through</p>
<p style="text-decoration: blink;">Blink</p>
```

The `text-shadow` property is a bit more complex, but can add stunning drop
shadow effects to text. The `text-shadow` property has the following format:

```
text-shadow: "[color] horizontal-distance
vertical-distance [blur]"
```

The property takes two values to offset the shadow, one horizontal, the other vertical. Positive values set the shadow down and to the right. Negative values set the shadow up and to the left. Using combinations of negative and positive settings, you can move the shadow to any location relative to the text it affects.

The optional color value sets the color of the shadow. The blur value specifies the blur radius—or the width of the effect—for the shadow. Note that the exact algorithm for computing the blur radius is not specified by the CSS specification—as such your experience may vary with this value.

The text-shadow property allows multiple shadow definitions, for multiple shadows. Simply separate the definitions with commas.

The following code creates a drop shadow on all `<h1>` headlines. The shadow is set to display above and to the right of the text, in a gray color.

```
h1 { text-shadow: #666666 2em -2em; }
```

The following definition provides the same shadow as the previous example, but adds another, lighter gray shadow directly below the text:

```
h1 { text-shadow: #666666 2em -2em, #AAAAAA 0em 2em; }
```

Unfortunately, not many user agents support `text-shadow`. If you want such an effect, you might be better off creating it with a graphic instead of text.

Formatting Lists

Several CSS properties modify lists. You can change the list type, the position of the elements, and specify images to use instead of bullets. The list-related properties are covered in the following sections.

An overview of lists

There are two types of lists in standard HTML, ordered and unordered. Ordered lists have each of their elements numbered and are generally used for steps that must followed a specific order. Unordered lists are typically a list of related items that do not need to be in a particular order (commonly formatted as bulleted lists).

Lists are covered in more detail in Chapter 5.

Ordered lists are enclosed in the ordered list or `<ol>` tag. Unordered lists are enclosed in the unordered list or `<ul>` tag. A list item tag (`<li>`) precedes each item in either list. The following code shows short examples of each type of list. Figure 19-9 shows the output of this code.

```
<ol>An ordered list
   <li>Step 1
   <li>Step 2
   <li>Step 3
</ol>
<ul>An unordered list
   <li>Item 1
   <li>Item 2
   <li>Item 3
</ul>
```

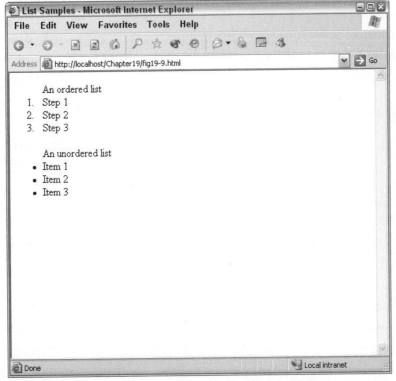

Figure 19-9: An example of an ordered and unordered list.

CSS lists—any element will do

An important distinction with CSS lists is that you don't need to use the standard list tags. CSS supports the `list-item` value of the display property, which, in effect, makes any element a list item. The `<li>` tag is a list item by default.

Note

There is a list style shortcut property that you can use to set list properties with one property assignment. You can use the list-style property to define the other list properties, as follows:

```
list-style: <list-style-type> <list-style-position>
<list-style-image>
```

For example, to create a new list item you can define a class as a list item using the display property:

```
.item { display: list-item; }
```

Thereafter, you can use that class to declare elements as list items:

```
<p class="item">This is now a list item</p>
```

As you read through the rest of this section, keep in mind that the list properties can apply to any element defined as a `list-item`.

Note   Both bullets and numbers preceding list items are known as *markers*. Markers have additional value with CSS, as shown in the *Generated content* section later in this chapter.

List style type

The `list-style-type` property is used to set the type of the list and, therefore, what identifier is used with each item—bullet, number, roman numeral, and so on.

The `list-style-type` property has the following valid values:

- disc
- circle
- square
- decimal
- decimal-leading-zero
- lower-roman
- upper-roman
- lower-greek
- lower-alpha
- lower-latin
- upper-alpha
- upper-latin
- hebrew
- armenian
- georgian
- cjk-ideographic

- ✦ hiragana
- ✦ katakana
- ✦ hiragana-iroha
- ✦ katakana-iroha
- ✦ none

The values are all fairly mnemonic; setting the style provides a list with appropriate item identifiers. For example, consider this code and the output shown immediately after:

HTML Code:

```
<ol style="list-style-type:lower-roman;">
  A Roman Numeral List
  <li>Step 1
  <li>Step 2
  <li>Step 3
</ol>
```

Output:

```
A Roman Numeral List
   i. Step 1
  ii. Step 2
 iii. Step 3
```

You can use the none value to suppress bullets or numbers for individual items. However, this does not change the number generation, the numbers are just not displayed. For example, consider the following revised code and output:

HTML Code:

```
<ol style="list-style-type:lower-roman;">
  A Roman Numeral List
  <li>Step 1
  <li style="list-style-type:none;">Step 2
  <li>Step 3
</ol>
```

Output:

```
A Roman Numeral List
   i.   Step 1
        Step 2
 iii.   Step 3
```

Note that the third item is still number 3, despite suppressing the number on item 2.

Positioning of markers

The `list-style-position` property can change the position of the marker in relation to the list item. The valid values for this property are `inside` or `outside`. The `outside` value provides the more typical list style, where the marker is offset from the list item and the entire text of the item is indented. The `inside` value sets the list to a more compact style, where the marker is indented with the first line of the item. Figure 19-10 shows an example of both list types:

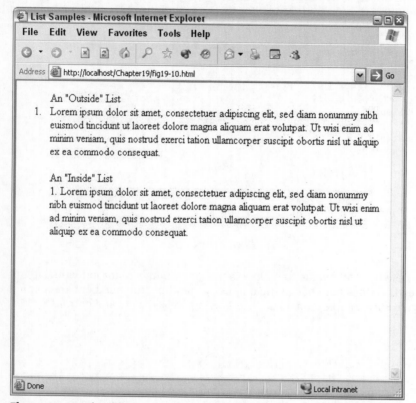

Figure 19-10: The difference between inside and outside positioned lists.

Images as list markers

You can also specify an image to use as a marker using the `list-style-image` property. This property is used instead of the `list-style-type` property, providing a bullet-like marker. You specify the image to use with the `url` construct. For example, the following code references `sphere.jpg` and `cone.jpg` as images to use in the list. The output is shown in Figure 19-11.

```
<ol>
   <li style="list-style-image: url(sphere.jpg)">
   Lorem ipsum dolor sit amet, consectetuer
```

```
adipiscing elit, sed diam nonummy nibh euismod tincidunt
ut laoreet dolore magna aliquam erat volutpat.
<li style="list-style-image: url(cone.jpg)">
Lorem ipsum dolor sit amet, consectetuer
adipiscing elit, sed diam nonummy nibh euismod tincidunt
ut laoreet dolore magna aliquam erat volutpat.
</ol>
```

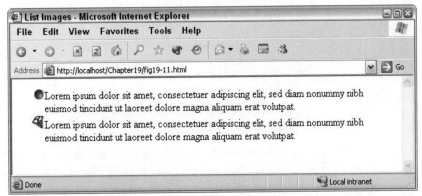

Figure 19-11: You can use images as list markers, such as the sphere and cone shown here.

Note that you can use any URL-accessible image with the `list-style-image`. However, it is important to use images sized appropriately for your lists.

Auto-generated Text

CSS has a few mechanisms for autogenerating text. Although this doesn't fit in well with the presentation-only function of CSS, it can be useful to have some constructs to automatically generate text for your documents.

Note   You can do much more with autogenerated content than is shown here. Feel free to experiment with combining pseudo-elements (covered in Chapter 17) and other autogenerated text constructs (listed with other CSS elements in Appendix B).

Specifying quotation marks

You can use the autogeneration features of CSS to define and display quotation marks. First, you need to define the quotes, and then you can add them to elements.

The `quotes` property takes a list of arguments in string format to use for the open and close quotes at multiple levels. This property has the following form:

```
quotes: <open_first_level> <close_first_level>
<open_second_level> <close_second_level> ... ;
```

The standard definition for most English uses is as follows:

```
quotes: '"' '"' """ """;
```

This specifies a double-quote for the first level (open and closing) and a single-quote for the second level (open and closing). Note the use of the opposite quote type (single enclosing double and vice versa).

Note Many browsers do not support autogenerated content.

Once you define the quotes, you can use them along with the `:before` and `:after` pseudo-elements, as in the following example:

```
blockquote:before { content: open-quote; }
blockquote:after  { content: close-quote; }
```

The `open-quote` and `close-quote` words are shortcuts for the values stored in the `quotes` property. Technically, you can place just about anything in the content property because it also accepts string values. The next section shows you how you can use the content property to create automatic counters.

Note When using string values with the content property, be sure to enclose the string in quotes. If you need to include newlines, use the `\A` placeholder.

Numbering elements automatically

One of the nicest features of using the `content` property with counters is the ability to automatically number elements. The advantage of using counters over standard lists is that counters are more flexible, enabling you to start at an arbitrary number, combine numbers (for example, 1.1), and so on.

Note Many user agents do not support counters. Check the listings in Appendix B for more information on what user agents support what CSS features.

The counter object

A special object can be used to track a value and can be incremented and reset by other style operations. The `counter` object has this form when used with the `content` property, as in the following:

```
content: counter(counter_name);
```

This has the effect of placing the current value of the counter in the content object. For example, the following style definition will display "Chapter" and the current value of the "chapter" counter at the beginning of each `<h1>` element:

```
h1:before { content: "Chapter " counter(chapter) " "; }
```

Of course, it's of no use to always assign the same number to the `:before` pseudo-element. That's where the `counter-increment` and `counter-reset` objects come in.

Changing the counter value

The `counter-increment` property takes a counter as an argument and increments its value by one. You can also increment the counter by other values by specifying the value to add to the counter after the counter name. For example, to increment the `chapter` counter by 2, you would use this definition:

```
counter-increment: chapter 2;
```

Tip You can increment several counters with the same property statement by specifying the additional counters after the first, separated by spaces. For example, the following definition will increment the chapter and section counters each by 2:

```
counter-increment: chapter 2 section 2;
```

You can also specify negative numbers to decrement the counter(s). For example, to decrement the `chapter` counter by 1, you could use the following:

```
counter-increment: chapter -1;
```

The other method for changing a counter's value is by using the `counter-reset` property. This property resets the counter to zero or, optionally, an arbitrary number specified with the property. The `counter-reset` property has the following format:

```
counter-reset: counter_name [value];
```

For example, to reset the `chapter` counter to 1, you could use this definition:

```
counter-reset: chapter 1;
```

Tip You can reset multiple counters with the same property by specifying all the counters on the same line, separated by spaces.

Note that if a counter is used and incremented or reset in the same context (in the same definition), the counter is first incremented or reset before being assigned to a property or otherwise used.

Chapter and section numbers

Using counters, you can easily implement an auto-numbering scheme for chapters and sections. To implement this auto-numbering, use `<h1>` elements for chapter titles and `<h2>` elements for sections. We will use two counters, chapter and section, respectively.

First, you need to set up your chapter heading definition, as follows:

```
h1:before {content: "Chapter " counter(chapter) ": ";
          counter-increment: chapter;
          counter-reset: section; }
```

This definition will display "Chapter *chapter_num*:" before the text in each <h1> element. The chapter counter is incremented and the section counter is reset—both of these actions take place prior to the counter and text being assigned to the content property. So, the following text would then result in the output shown in Figure 19-12:

```
<h1>First Chapter</h1>
<h1>Second Chapter</h1>
<h1>Third Chapter</h1>
```

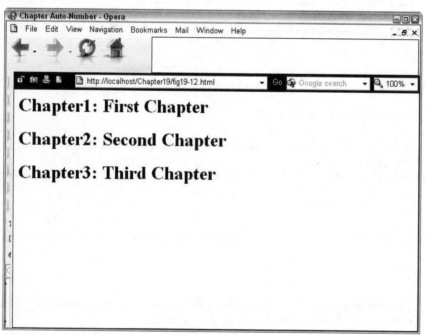

Figure 19-12: Auto-numbering <h1> elements.

The next step is to set up the section numbering, which is similar to the chapter numbering:

```
h2:before {content: "Section " counter(chapter) "."
counter(section) ": ";
counter-increment: section;
```

Now the styles are complete. The final following code results in the display shown in Figure 19-13:

```html
<!DOCTYPE HTML PUBLIC "-//W3C//DTD HTML 4.01//EN"
   "http://www.w3.org/TR/html4/strict.dtd">
<html>
<head>
  <title>Chapter Auto-Number</title>
  <style type="text/css">
    h1:before {content: "Chapter " counter(chapter) ": ";
               counter-increment: chapter;
               counter-reset: section; }
    h2:before {content: "Section " counter(chapter) "."
               counter(section) ": ";
               counter-increment: section; }
  </style>
</head>
<body>
  <h1>First Chapter</h1>
    <h2>Section Name</h2>
    <h2>Section Name</h2>
  <h1>Second Chapter</h1>
    <h2>Section Name</h2>
  <h1>Third Chapter</h1>
</body>
</html>
```

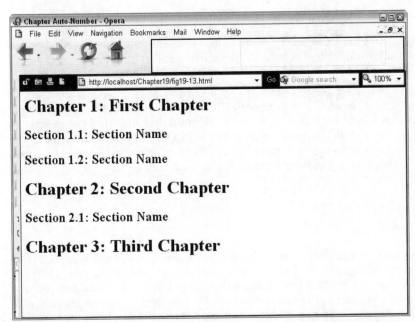

Figure 19-13: The completed auto-numbering system does both chapters and sections.

Tip   The counters should automatically start with a value of 0. In this example, that is ideal. However, if you need to start the counters at another value, you can attach resets to a higher tag (such as <body>), as in the following example:

```css
body:before {counter-reset: chapter 12 section 10;}
```

Custom list numbers

You can use a similar construct for custom list numbering. For example, consider the following code, which starts numbering the list at 20:

```
<!DOCTYPE HTML PUBLIC "-//W3C//DTD HTML 4.01//EN"
  "http://www.w3.org/TR/html4/strict.dtd">
<html>
<head>
  <title>List Auto-Number</title>
  <style type="text/css">
    li:before {content: counter(list) ": ";
               counter-increment: list; }
  </style>
</head>
<body>
  <ol style="counter-reset: list 19;
      list-style-type:none;">
    <li>First item
    <li>Second item
    <li>Third item
  </ol>
</body>
</html>
```

Note that the `<ol>` tag resets the counter to 19 due to the way the `counter-increment` works (it causes the counter to increment before it is used). So you must set the counter one lower than the first occurrence.

Tip

You can have multiple instances of the same counter in your documents, and they can all operate independently. The key is to limit each counter's scope: A counter's effective scope is within the element that initialized the counter with the first reset. In the example of lists, it is the `<ol>` tag. If you nested another `<ol>` tag within the first, it could have its own instance of the `list` counter, and they could operate independently of each other.

Summary

This chapter covered basic text formatting with CSS. You learned how to justify and align text, as well as control most other aspects of text layout. As you continue to learn CSS, you will see that the considerable information presented here barely scratches the surface of the capabilities of CSS. The next few chapters deal with particular elements and specific uses of CSS—however, it is when you use all of the capabilities together that CSS really shines.

✦   ✦   ✦

Padding, Margins, and Borders

The CSS formatting model places every element within a layer of boxes, each layer customizable by styles. This chapter introduces the box formatting model and its individual pieces—padding, borders, and margins. You learn how each is defined and manipulated by CSS.

Understanding the Box Formatting Model

CSS uses the box formatting model for all elements. The box formatting model places all elements within boxes—rectangles or squares—that are layered with multiple, configurable attributes.

Note   Box layout and formatting models have been used in traditional publishing for ages. Open any magazine or newspaper and you will see box layout in action–the headline within one box, columns of text in their own boxes, ads in boxes, and so on.

Figure 20-1 shows a typical Web page. Although the design doesn't seem too boxy, if you turn on borders for all elements you can see how each element is contained in a rectangle or square box. Figure 20-2 shows the same Web page with borders around each element.

Within each CSS box you have control over three different, layered properties:

✦ Margins—Represent the space outside of the element, the space that separates elements from one another.

Figure 20-1: A typical Web page that isn't overtly boxy in design.

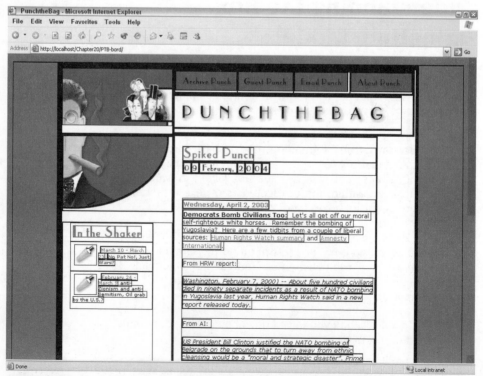

Figure 20-2: The same Web page with borders around all elements, clearly showing the box formatting model.

✦ Borders—Configurable lines inside the elements margins, but outside of the element's padding (defined next).

✦ Padding—The space between the element and the element's border.

Figure 20-3 shows a visual representation of how these properties relate.

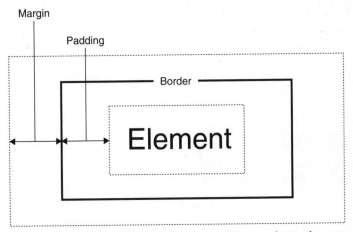

Figure 20-3: How the margin, border, padding, and actual element relate to each other spatially.

Each of these properties can be separately configured, but can also work well together to uniquely present an element.

Defining Element Margins

Margins are an important issue to consider when designing documents. Some elements have built-in margins to separate themselves from adjoining elements. However, sometimes you will find that you need to increase (or decrease) the standard margins.

For example, when using images, you may find the margin between the image and the surrounding elements too slim. An image next to text is shown in Figure 20-4. Notice that the "T" is all but touching the image.

Note that the following code was used to separate the two elements:

```
<img src="square.png" style="float: left;"><p>Text next to an image</p>
```

You can use the margin properties to adjust the space around an element. There are properties to adjust each margin individually, as well as a shortcut property to adjust all the margins with one property.

Figure 20-4: The margins on some elements are too tight, as shown by how close the text is to the image.

The `margin-top`, `margin-right`, `margin-bottom`, and `margin-left` properties adjust the margins on individual sides of an element. The `margin` property can adjust one side or all sides of an element. The margin properties all have a simple format:

```
margin-right: width;
```

The `margin` shortcut property allows you to specify one, two, three, or four widths:

```
margin: top right bottom left;
```

For example, suppose you want to set the margins as follows:

✦ Top: 2px

✦ Right: 4px

✦ Bottom: 10px

✦ Left: 4px

You could use this code:

```
margin: 2px 4px 10px 4px;
```

Tip   You don't have to specify all four margins in the `margin` property if some of the margins are to be set the same. If you only specify one value, it applies to all sides. If you specify two values, the first value is used for the top and bottom, and the second value is used for the right and left sides. If three values are given, the top is set to the first, the sides to the second, and the bottom to the third.

So let's return to the example in Figure 20-4, where the text is too close to the image. You can separate the two elements by increasing the right margin of the image, or the left margin of the text. However, you probably would not want to increase any of the other margins.

Tip There are no real guidelines when it comes to which margins to adjust on what elements. However, it's usually best to choose to modify the least number of margins or to be consistent with which margins you do change.

Adding Padding within an Element

Padding is the space between the element and its border. The configuration of the padding is similar to configuring margins—there are properties for the padding on each side of the element and a shortcut property for configuring several sides with one property.

The properties for configuring padding are: `padding-top`, `padding-right`, `padding-left`, `padding-bottom`, and `bottom`.

Note that you can use padding like a margin; increasing the padding increases the space between elements. However, you should use margins for increasing spacing between elements, and only use padding to help the legibility of the document by separating the element from its border.

Tip An element's background color extends to the edge of the element's padding. Therefore, increasing an element's padding can extend the background away from an element. This is one reason to use padding instead of margins to increase space around an element. For more information on backgrounds, see Chapter 21.

Adding Borders

Unlike margins and padding, borders have many more attributes that can be configured using CSS. You can specify the look of the border, its color, its type, and various other properties. Each of the groups of properties is discussed in the following sections.

Border style

There are 10 different types of predefined border styles. These types are shown in Figure 20-5.

Note The border type `hidden` is identical to the border type `none`, except that the border type `hidden` is treated like a border for border conflict resolutions. Border conflicts happen when adjacent elements share a common border (when there is no spacing between the elements). In most cases, the most eye-catching border is used. However, if either conflicting element has the conflicting border set to `hidden`, the border between the elements is unconditionally hidden.

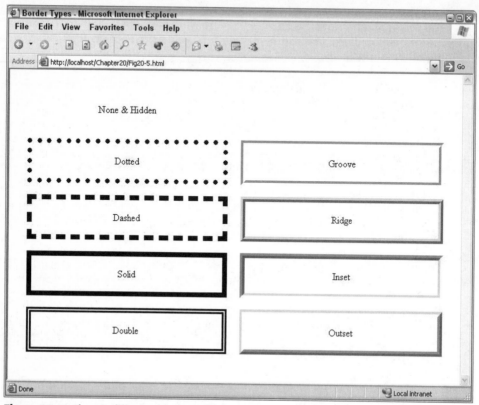

Figure 20-5: The 10 different border types.

The border-style properties include properties for each side (`border-top-style`, `border-right-style`, `border-bottom-style`, `border-left-style`) and a shortcut property for multiple sides (`border-style`). The individual side properties accept one border style value and sets the border on that side of the element to the type specified by that value. The following example sets all of the side borders of an element to `dotted`:

```
border-style: dotted;
```

The `border-style` shortcut property can set the border style for one or multiple sides of the element. Like most other shortcut properties covered in this chapter, values for this property follows these rules:

✦ If you only specify one value, it applies to all sides.

✦ If you specify two values, the first value is used for the top and bottom, while the second value is used for the right and left sides.

✦ If three values are given, the top is set to the first, the sides to the second, and the bottom to the third value.

Border color

The border color properties allow you to specify the color used for an element's borders. Like most other border properties, there are color properties for each side as well as a shortcut property that can affect multiple borders with one property.

The border color properties are: `border-top-color`, `border-right-color`, `border-bottom-color`, `bottom-left-color`, and `border-color`. The individual side properties take a single color value, while the shortcut border-color takes up to four values. Like the `border-style` property, how many values you enter determines what sides are affected by what values. (See the previous section for the rules used to apply multiple values.)

The border color properties take color values in three different forms:

✦ *Color keywords*—Black, white, maroon, and so on. See Appendix C for a list of color keywords.

✦ *Color hexadecimal values*—This value is specified in the form: `#rrggbb`, where `rrggbb` is two digits (in hexadecimal notation) for each of the colors red, green, and blue. See Appendix C for a list of color hexadecimal values.

✦ *Color decimal or percentage values*—This value is specified using the `rgb( )` property. This property takes three values, one each for red, green, and blue. The value can be an integer between 0 and 255 or a percentage. For example, the following specifies the color purple (all red and all blue, no green) in integer form:

`rgb(255, 0, 255)`

✦ And the following specifies the color purple in percentages:

`rgb(100%, 0, 100%)`

Tip

Most graphic editing programs supply RGB values in several different forms in their color palette dialog boxes. For example, take a look at the dialog box in Figure 20-6.

Border width

The actual width of the border can be specified using the border width properties. As with the other border properties, there are individual properties for each side of the element, as well as a shortcut property. These properties are: `border-top-width`, `border-right-width`, `border-bottom-width`, `border-left-width`, and `border-width`.

Note

The `border-width` shortcut property accepts one to four values. The way the values are mapped to the individual sides depends on the number of values specified. The rules for this behavior are the same as those used for the `border-style` property. See the *Border style* section earlier in this chapter for the specific rules.

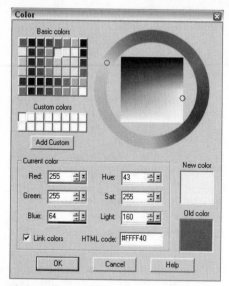

Figure 20-6: Many graphic editing programs specify colors using multiple RGB value formulas that you can cut and paste into your Web documents.

You can use the keywords `thin`, `medium`, or `thick` to roughly specify a border's width—the actual width used depends on the user agent. You can also specify an exact size using `em`, `px`, or other width/length values. For example, to set all the borders of an element to 2 pixels wide, you could use the following definition:

```
border-width: 2px;
```

The ultimate shortcut: The border property

You can use the `border` property to set the width, style, and color of an element's border. The `border` property has the following form:

```
border: border-width border-style border-color;
```

For example, to set an element's border to thick, double, and red, you would use the following definition:

```
border: thick double red;
```

Additional border properties

Two additional border properties are used primarily with tables:

✦ border-spacing—This property controls how the user agent renders the space between the borders of the cells in a table.

✦ border-collapse—This property selects the "collapsed" model of table borders.

Cross-Reference These two border properties are covered in more depth with other table properties in Chapter 22.

Using Dynamic Outlines

Outlines provide another layer around the element to allow the user agent to highlight elements. For example, Figure 20-7 shows the default outline provided by Internet Explorer when a check box label is in focus.

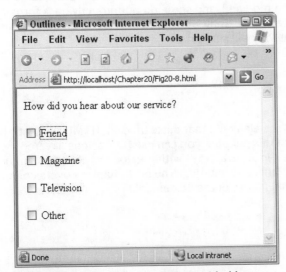

Figure 20-7: The default outline provided by Internet Explorer—shown around the Friend label.

Note Outlines are positioned directly outside the border of elements. The position of the outline cannot be moved directly, but can be influenced by the position of the border. Note that the outline does not occupy any space, and adding or suppressing outlines does not cause the content to be reflowed.

Using CSS you can modify the look of these outlines. Unlike the other properties covered in this chapter, all sides of the elements outline must be the same; you cannot control the sides individually.

The outline properties are `outline-color`, `outline-style`, `outline-width`, and the shorthand property `outline`. These properties work exactly like the other properties in this chapter, allowing the same values and having the same effects. Note that the format of the `outline` shortcut property is as follows:

```
outline: outline-color outline-style outline-width;
```

To use the outline properties dynamically, use the `:focus` and `:active` pseudo-elements. These two pseudo-elements allow you to specify that an element's outline is visible only when the element has the focus or is active. For example, the following definitions specify a thick red border when form elements have focus and a thin green border when they are active:

```
form *:focus { outline-width: thick; outline-color: red; }
form *:active { outline-width: thin; outline-color: green; }
```

Note   At the time of this writing, none of the popular Web browsers (Internet Explorer, Opera, Mozilla, and so on) handle outlines consistently or correctly. Some do not allow the outline to be modified, and some do not properly track focus or active elements. Therefore, when using outlines, it is best to extensively test your code on all platforms you will support.

Summary

The box formatting model and the elements that make up each HTML element's box is quite powerful. As you saw in this chapter, you can use the various, layered properties that make up the box in several ways within a document—from simple ornamentation purposes to advanced formatting. The next chapter covers colors and backgrounds, two additional pieces of the box model.

✦   ✦   ✦

Colors and Backgrounds

The previous chapter introduced you to the CSS box formatting model and the concept of padding, borders, and margins. This chapter extends that discussion into colors and backgrounds, two additional components of the box formatting model.

Foreground Color

The foreground color of an element is the color that actually comprises the visible part of the element—in most cases, it is the color of the font.

You can control the foreground color using the `color` property. This property has the following format:

```
color: color_value;
```

The `color_value` can be specified in any of the usual means for specifying a color:

- ✦ *Color keywords*—Black, white, maroon, and so on.
- ✦ *Color hexadecimal values*—This value is specified in the form: `#rrggbb`, where `rrggbb` is two digits (in hexadecimal notation) for each of the colors red, green, and blue.
- ✦ *Color decimal or percentage values*—This value is specified using the `rgb( )` property. This property takes three values, one each for red, green, and blue. The value can be an integer between 0 and 255 or a percentage. For example, the following specifies the color purple (all red and all blue, no green) in integer form:

  ```
  rgb(255, 0, 255)
  ```

- ✦ And the following specifies the color purple in percentages:

  ```
  rgb(100%, 0, 100%)
  ```

Tip

Most graphic editing programs supply RGB values in several different forms in their color palette dialog boxes.

For example, to set the font color to red for paragraph elements in the `redtext` class, you could use this definition:

```
p.redtext { color: red; }
```

When specifying foreground colors, keep in mind what background colors will be used in the document. It's ineffective to use red text on a red background, or white text on a white background, for example. If you have multiple background colors in your document, consider using classes and the CSS cascade to ensure that the right foreground colors are used.

Keep in mind that the user settings can affect the color of text as well—if you don't explicitly define the foreground color, the user agent will use its default colors.

Background Color

The background color of an element is the color of the virtual page that the element is rendered upon. For example, Figure 21-1 shows two paragraphs—the first has a default white background, and the second has a light gray background.

Note

Saying that the document has a default color of white is incorrect. Technically, the document will have the color specified in the rendering user agent's settings. In typical Internet Explorer installations (as shown in Figure 21-1), the color is indeed white.

To specify a background color, you use the `background-color` property. This property has a format similar to other color setting properties:

```
background-color: color_value;
```

For example, to set the background of a particular paragraph to blue, you could use the following definition:

```
<p style="background-color: blue; color: white">This
paragraph will render as white text on a blue background.</p>
```

Note that the definition also sets the color property so the text can be seen on the darker background. The result is shown in Figure 21-2.

Sizing an Element's Background

An element's background is rendered within the element's padding space—that is, inside the border of the element. For a visual example, take a look at Figure 21-3. Each paragraph specifies a slightly larger padding value (thick borders have been added to each paragraph for clarity).

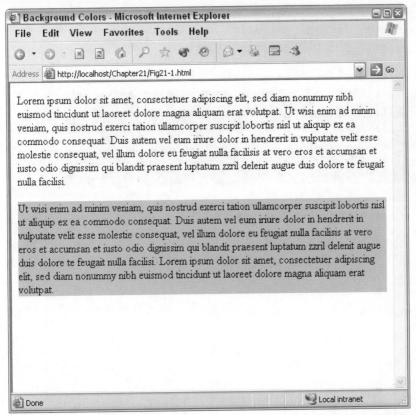

Figure 21-1: Background colors can be used to affect the color of the virtual page elements are rendered on.

Background Images

Besides using solid colors for backgrounds you can also use images. For example, the paragraph in Figure 21-4 uses a gradient image for the first paragraph (the image is shown by itself after the paragraph for comparison).

To add an image as a background, you use the `background-image` property. This property has the following format:

```
background-image: url("url_to_image");
```

For example, the paragraph in Figure 21-4 uses the following code, which specifies `gradient.gif` as the background image:

```
p { background-image: url("gradient.gif");
    height: 100px; width: 500px;
    border: thin solid black; }
```

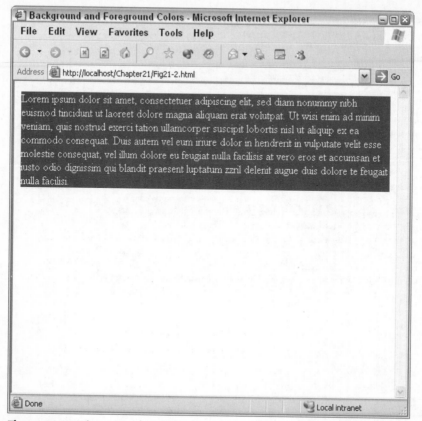

Figure 21-2: When using a dark background color, you should usually use a light foreground color.

Note

The example shown in Figure 21-4 has a few additional properties defined to help make the example. A border was added to the paragraph and image to help show the edges of the image. The height and width of the paragraph were constrained to the size of the image to prevent the image from repeating. For more on repeating and scrolling background images, see the next section.

The background image can be used for some interesting effects, as shown in Figure 21-5, where a frame image is used as text ornamentation. (Again, the image is repeated alone, with border, for clarification of what the image is.)

The following CSS definition is used for the paragraph in Figure 21-5:

```
p.catborder { height: 135px; width: 336px;
    background-image: url("cat.gif");
    padding: 80px 135px 18px 18px; }
```

This code uses several additional properties to position the text within the border frame:

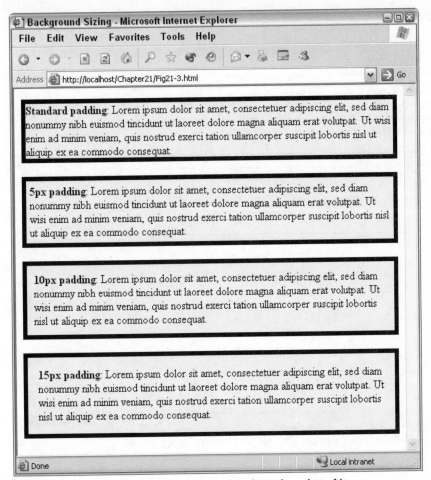

Figure 21-3: An element's background extends to the edge of its padding—sizing the padding can size the background.

✦ Explicit `width` and `height` properties specify the size of the full image.

✦ Explicit `padding` values ensure that the text stays within the box.

Repeating and Scrolling Background Images

Element background images act similarly to document background images—by default, they tile to fill the given space. For example, consider the paragraph in Figure 21-6, where the smiley image is tiled to fill the entire paragraph box.

Notice, also, how the right and bottom of the background are filled with incomplete copies of the image because the paragraph size is not an even multiple of the background graphic size.

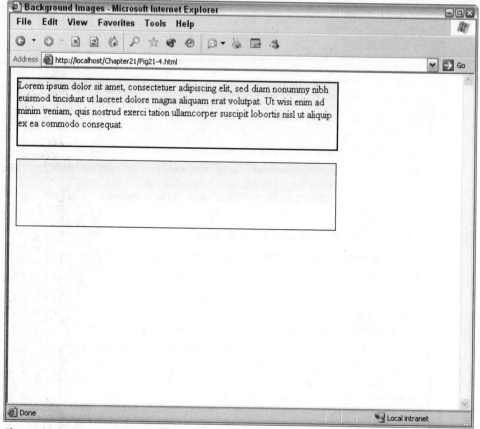

Figure 21-4: You can also use images for element backgrounds.

You can specify the repeating nature and the actual position of the background image using the background-repeat and background-attachment properties. The background-repeat property has the following format:

```
background-repeat:    repeat | repeat-x | repeat-y | no-repeat;
```

The background-attachment property has the following format:

```
background-attachment:    scroll | fixed;
```

The background-repeat property is straightforward—its values specify how the image repeats. For example, to repeat our smiley face across the top of the paragraph, specify repeat-x, as shown in the following definition code and Figure 21-7:

```
p.smiley { background-image: url("smiley.gif");
          background-repeat: repeat-x;
          /* Border for clarity only */
          border: thin solid black; }
```

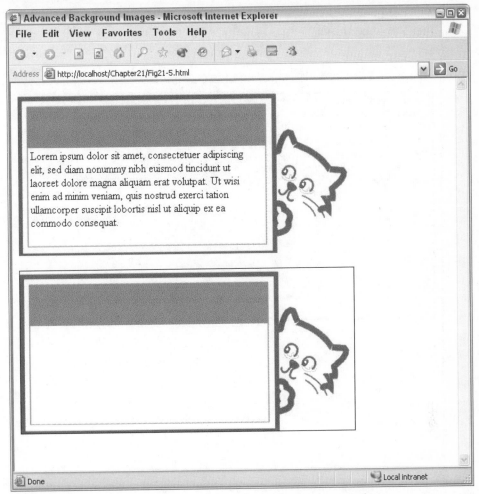

Figure 21-5: Background images can be used as textual ornamentation.

The background-attachment property controls how the background is attached to the element. The default value, scroll, allows the background to scroll as the element is scrolled. The fixed value doesn't allow the background to scroll; instead, the contents of the element scroll over the background.

The scroll behavior can be seen in Figure 21-8 where two identical elements are shown. The bottom paragraph has been scrolled a bit, and the background scrolls with the element's content.

The following code is used for the paragraphs in Figure 21-8:

```
p.smileyscroll { height: 220px; width: 520px;
        overflow: scroll;
```

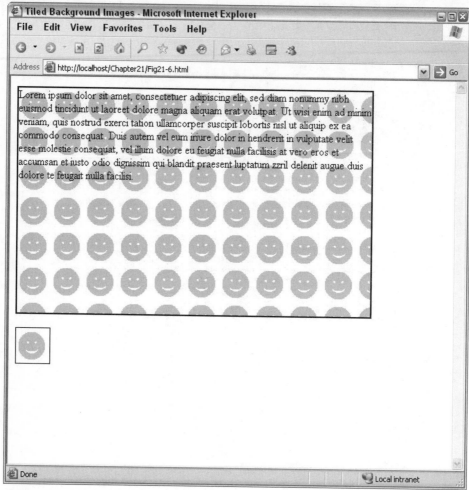

Figure 21-6: By default, background images will tile to fill the available space.

```
background-image: url("smiley.gif");
background-attachment: scroll;
border: thin solid black; }
```

Note   Notice the use of the `overflow` property in the code for Figure 21-8. This property controls what happens when an element's content is larger than the element's defined box. The `scroll` value enables scroll bars on the element so
the user can scroll to see the rest of the content. The `overflow` property also
supports the values `visible` (which causes the element to be displayed in its
entirety, despite box size constraints) and `hidden` (which causes the part of
the element that overflows to be clipped and inaccessible).

If you change the `background-attachment` value to fixed, the background image
remains stationary, as shown in Figure 21-9.

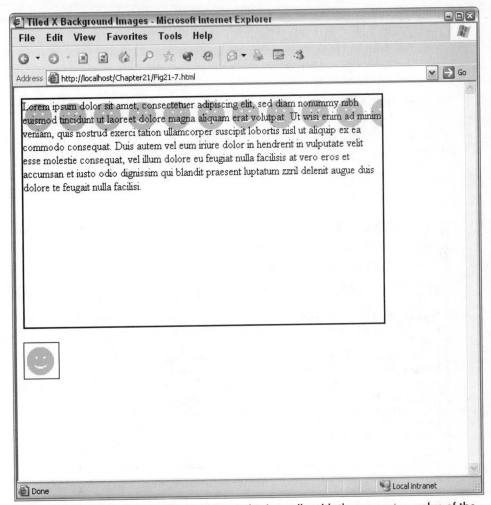

Figure 21-7: Repeating a background image horizontally with the `repeat-x` value of the `background-repeat` property

Tip   Non-scrolling backgrounds make great watermarks. Watermarks—named for the process of creating them on paper—are slight images placed in the background of documents to distinguish them. Some companies place watermarks of their logo on their letterhead.

Positioning Background Images

The `background-position` property allows you to position an element's background image. This property's use isn't as straightforward as some of the other properties. The basic forms of the values for this property fall into three categories:

✦ Two percentages that specify where the upper-left corner of the image should be placed in relation to the element's padding area

✦ Two lengths (in inches, centimeters, pixels, em, and so on) that specify where the upper-left corner of the image should be placed in relation to the element's padding area

✦ Keywords that specify absolute measures of the element's padding area

No matter what format you use for the background-position values, the format is as follows:

```
background-position:  horizontal_value  vertical_value;
```

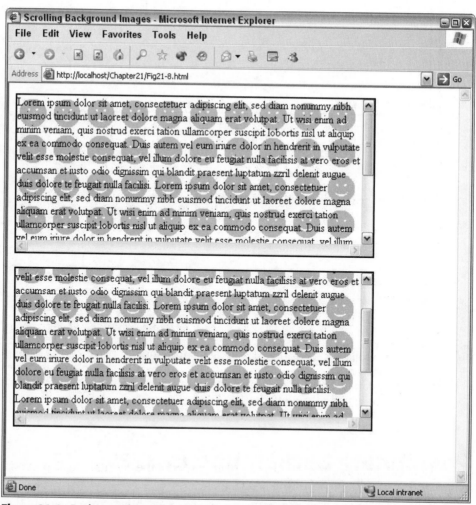

Figure 21-8: Backgrounds scroll by default, as shown by the second paragraph.

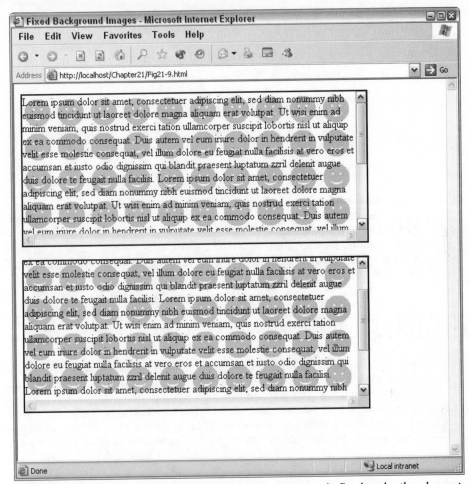

Figure 21-9: You can specify that a background image remain fixed under the element with the `background-attachment` property.

If only one value is given, it is used for the horizontal placement—the image is centered vertically. You can mix the first two formats (for example, `10px 25%`), but keywords cannot be mixed with other values (for example, `center 50%` is invalid).

The first two forms are much like the value formats used in other properties. For example, the following definition positions the upper-left corner of the background in the middle of the element's padding area:

```
background-position: 50% 50%;
```

The next definition places the upper-left corner of the background 25 pixels from the top and left sides of the element's padding area:

```
background-position: 25px 25px;
```

Several keywords can be used for the third format of the background-position property. They include top, left, right, bottom, and center.

For example, you can position the background image in the top, center of the element's padding using the following:

```
background-position: top center;
```

Or, you can position the background image directly in the center of the element's padding with the following:

```
background-position: center center;
```

> **Tip**
>
> Combining the background attributes can achieve more diverse effects. For example, you can use background-position to set an image in the center of the element's padding, and specify background-attachment: fixed to keep it there. Furthermore, you could use background-repeat to repeat the same image horizontally or vertically, creating dynamic striping behind the element.

Summary

This chapter completes the concept of a box formatting model and how it is used and manipulated by CSS. You learned about foreground colors, background colors, and background images. You learned how these components can be manipulated separately or combined for maximum formatting effect. The next chapter covers another powerful formatting tool—tables. Chapter 23 rounds out the CSS element formatting subject by showing you how to position elements using CSS.

✦ ✦ ✦

Tables

Earlier in this book, you learned how to use tables to
format documents. This chapter explains how CSS can
make a great formatting tool even better. Although many table
tag attributes still exist in the strict HTML standards, CSS
offers many advantages when formatting tables.

Defining Table Styles

Because the `<table>` tag attributes, such as border, rules,
cellpadding, and cellspacing, have not been deprecated, you
might be tempted to use them instead of styles when defining
your tables. Resist that temptation.

Using styles for tables has the same advantages as using styles
for any other elements—consistency, flexibility, and the ability
to easily change the format later.

For example, consider the following table tag:

```
<table border="1" width="200px" cellpadding="3px"
cellspacing="5px">
```

Now suppose you had four tables using this definition in your
document, and you had four documents just like it. What if you
decided to decrease the width and increase the padding in the
tables? You would have to edit each table, potentially 16
individual tables.

If the table formatting were contained in styles at the top of the
documents, you would have to make four changes. Better yet,
if the formatting were contained in a separate, external style
sheet, you would only have to make one change.

The border properties can be used to control table borders,
and the padding and margin properties can affect the spacing
of cells and their contents.

Controlling Table Attributes

You can use CSS properties to control the formatting of tables. One issue with using CSS is that some of the properties do not match up name-wise with the tag attributes. For example, there are no `cellspacing` or `cellpadding` CSS properties. The `border-spacing` and `padding` CSS properties fill those roles, respectively.

Table 22-1 shows how CSS properties match table tag attributes.

Table 22-1 CSS Properties for Table Attributes		
Purpose	**Table Attribute**	**CSS Property(ies)**
Borders	border	border properties
Spacing inside cell	cellpadding	padding
Spacing between cells	cellspacing	border-spacing
Width of table	width	width and table-layout properties
Table framing	frame	border properties
Alignment	align, valign	text-align, vertical-alignment properties

Table borders

You can use the border properties to control the border of a table and its subelements just like any other element. For example, the following definition causes all tables and their elements to have single, solid, 1pt borders around them (as shown in Figure 22-1):

```
table, table * { border: 1pt solid black; }
```

Note that we specified all tables and all table descendents (`table, table *`) to ensure that each cell, as well as the entire table, has a border. If you wanted only the cells or only the table to have borders, you could use the following definitions:

```
/* Only table cells have borders */
table * { border: 1pt solid black; }
```

or

```
/* Only table body has borders */
table { border: 1pt solid black; }
```

The results of these two definitions are shown in Figure 22-2.

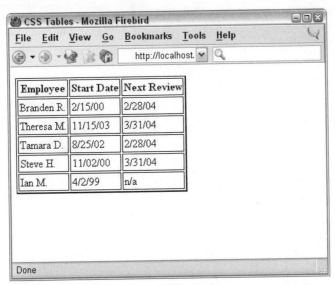

Figure 22-1: A table using CSS formatting.

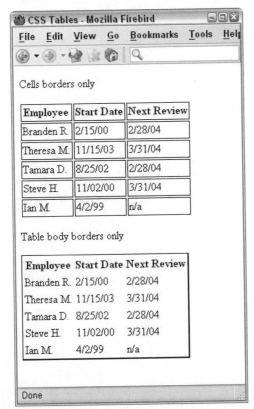

Figure 22-2: A table using selective bordering.

You can also combine border styles. For example, the following definitions create a table with borders similar to using the `border` attribute. The result of this definition is shown in Figure 22-3.

```
table { border: outset 5pt; }
td { border: inset 5pt; }
```

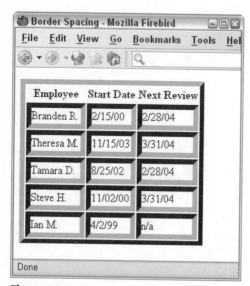

Figure 22-3: You can combine border styles to create custom table formats.

Table border spacing

To increase the space around table borders, you use the `border-spacing` and `padding` CSS properties. The `border-spacing` property adjusts the space between table cells much like the `<table>` tag's `cellspacing` attribute. The `padding` property adjusts the space between a table cell's contents and the cell's border.

The `border-spacing` property has the following format:

```
border-spacing: horizontal_spacing vertical_spacing;
```

Note that you can choose to include only one value, in which case the spacing is applied to both the horizontal and vertical border spacing.

For example, Figure 22-4 shows the same table as in Figure 22-1, but with the following `border-spacing` definition:

```
border-spacing: 5px 15px;
```

Note   Some user agents, such as Internet Explorer, disregard the border-spacing property. See Appendix B for a full list of what browsers support what properties.

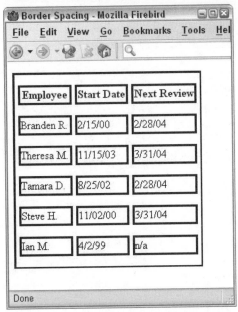

Figure 22-4: Different horizontal and vertical `border-spacing` can help distinguish data in columns or rows.

Collapsing borders

Sometimes you will want to remove the spacing between borders in a table, creating gridlines instead of cell borders. To do so, you use the `border-collapse` property. This property takes either the value of `separate` (default) or `collapse`. If you specify collapse, the cells merge their borders with neighboring cells (or the table) into one line. Whichever cell has the most visually distinctive border determines the collapsed border's look.

For example, consider the two tables in Figure 22-5, shown with their table definitions directly above them.

Notice how the borders between the table headers and normal cells inherited the inset border while the rest of the borders remained solid. This is because the border around the table headers was more visually distinctive and won the conflict between the borders styles being collapsed.

Borders on empty cells

Typically, the user agent does not render empty cells. However, you can use the `empty-cells` CSS property to control whether the agent should or should not show empty cells. The `empty-cells` property takes one of two values: `show` or `hide` (default).

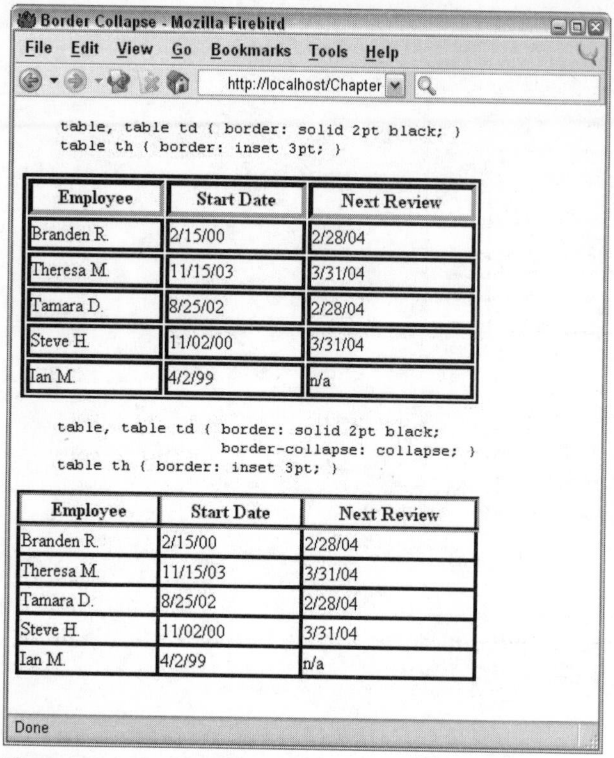

Figure 22-5: Collapsing table borders turns individual borders into gridlines between cells.

Figure 22-6 shows the following table with various settings of the empty-cells property.

```
<table>
  <tr><th>Heading</th><th>Heading</th><th>Heading</th></tr>
  <tr><td>X</td><td></td><td>X</td></tr>
  <tr><td></td><td>X</td><td></td></tr>
  <tr><td>X</td><td>X</td><td>X</td></tr>
</table>
```

Note Some user agents, such as Internet Explorer, disregard the empty-cells property. See Appendix B for a full list of what browsers support what properties.

Table Layout

The table-layout property determines how a user agent sizes a table. This property takes one of two values, auto or fixed. If this property is set to auto, the user agent automatically determines the table's width primarily from the contents of the table's cells. If this property is set to fixed, the user agent determines the table's width primarily from the width values defined in the tags and styles.

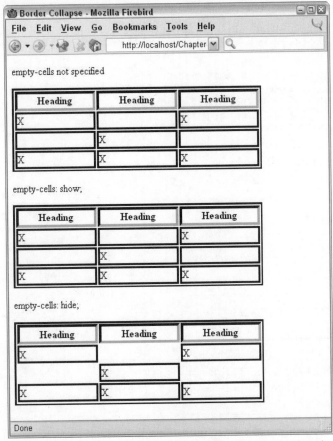

Figure 22-6: The `empty-cells` property controls whether the user agent displays empty cells or not.

Aligning and Positioning Captions

CSS can also help control the positioning of table caption elements. The positioning of the caption is controlled by the `caption-side` property. This property has the following format:

```
caption-side: top | bottom | left | right;
```

The value of the property determines where the caption is positioned in relationship to the table. To align the caption in its position, you can use typical text alignment properties such as `text-align` and `vertical-align`.

For example, the following code places the table's caption to the right of the table, centered vertically and horizontally, as shown in Figure 22-7.

```
<!DOCTYPE HTML PUBLIC "-//W3C//DTD HTML 4.01//EN"
    "http://www.w3.org/TR/html4/strict.dtd">
```

```html
<html>
<head>
  <title>Table Caption Positioning</title>
  <style type="text/css">
    table { margin-right: 200px; }
    table, table * { border: 1pt solid black;
                     caption-side: right; }
    caption { margin-left: 10px;
              vertical-align: middle;
              text-align: center; }
  </style>
</head>
<body>
<p>
<table>
  <tr><th>Employee</th><th>Start Date</th>
    <th>Next Review</th></tr>
  <tr><td>Branden R.</td><td>2/15/00</td>
    <td>2/28/04</td></tr>
  <tr><td>Theresa M.</td><td>11/15/03</td>
    <td>3/31/04</td></tr>
  <tr><td>Tamara D.</td><td>8/25/02</td>
    <td>2/28/04</td></tr>
  <tr><td>Steve H.</td><td>11/02/00</td>
    <td>3/31/04</td></tr>
  <tr><td>Ian M.</td><td>4/2/99</td>
    <td>n/a</td></tr>
  <caption>Tech Employee Review Schedule</caption>
</table>
</p>
</body>
</html>
```

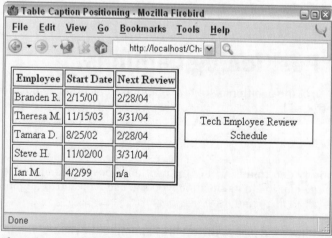

Figure 22-7: Positioning a caption to the right of a table.

Note that the table's caption is positioned inside the table's margin. By increasing the margin of the table, you allow more text per line of the caption. You can also explicitly set the width of the caption using the `width` property, which increases the margins of the table accordingly.

Summary

As you saw in this chapter, combining tables and CSS makes for a great, dynamic formatting tool for Web documents.

✦   ✦   ✦

Element Positioning

In the various chapters within this section, you have seen
how dynamic documents can be when formatted with CSS.
This chapter shows you how you can position elements using
CSS properties.

Understanding Element Positioning

There are several ways to position elements using CSS. The
method you use depends on what you want the position of the
element to be in reference to and how you want the element to
affect other elements around it. The following sections cover
the three main positioning models.

Static positioning

Static positioning is the normal positioning model—elements
are rendered inline or within their respective blocks.
Figure 23-1 shows three paragraphs; the middle paragraph
has the following styles applied to it:

```
width: 350px; height: 150px;
border: 1pt solid black;
background-color: white;
padding: .5em;
position: static;
```

Note   Several styles have been inserted for consistency
throughout the examples in this section. A border and
background have been added to the element to enhance
the visibility of the element's scope and position. The element also has two positioning properties (top and left),
although they do not affect the static positioning model.

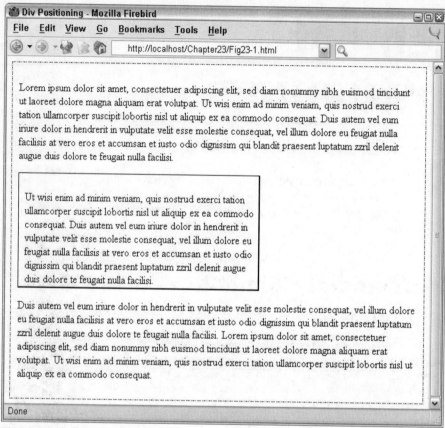

Figure 23-1: Static positioning is the normal positioning model, rendering elements where they should naturally be.

Relative positioning

Relative positioning is used to move an element from its normal position—where it would normally be rendered—to a new position. The new position is *relative* to the normal position of the element.

Figure 23-2 shows the second paragraph positioned using the relative positional model. The paragraph is positioned using the following styles (pay particular attention to the last two, `position` and `top`):

```
width: 350px; height: 150px;
border: 1pt solid black;
background-color: white;
padding: .5em;
position: relative;
top: 100px; left: 100px;
```

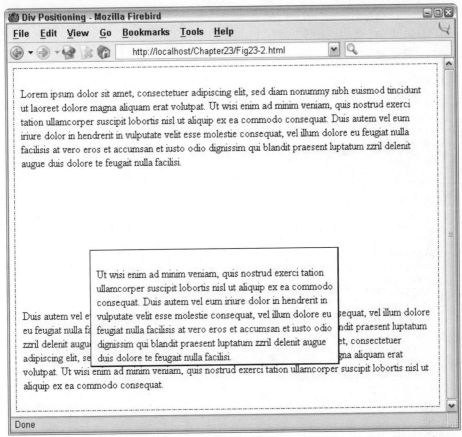

Figure 23-2: Relative positioned elements are positioned *relative* to the position they would otherwise occupy.

With relative positioning, you can use the side positioning properties (`top`, `left`, and so on) to position the element. Note the one major side effect of using relative positioning—the space where the element would normally be positioned is left open, as though the element were positioned there.

Note | The size of the element is determined by the sizing properties (`width` or `height`), the positioning of the element's corners (via `top`, `left`, and so on), or by a combination of properties.

Absolute positioning

Elements using absolute positioning are positioned relative to the view port instead of their normal position in the document. For example, the following styles are used to position the second paragraph in Figure 23-3:

```
width: 350px; height: 150px;
border: 1pt solid black;
background-color: white;
padding: .5em;
position: absolute;
top: 100px; left: 100px;
```

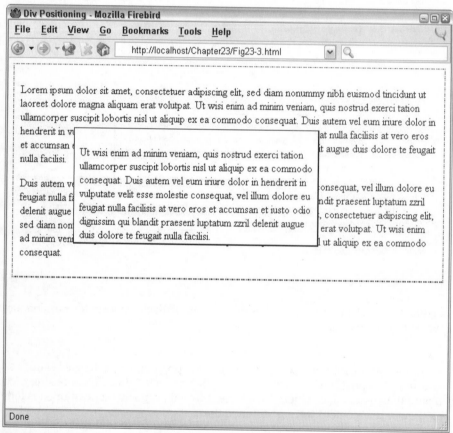

Figure 23-3: The absolute positioning model uses the user agent's view port for positioning reference.

Note that the positioning properties are referenced against the view port when using the absolute positioning model—the element in this example is positioned 100px from the top and 100px from the left of the view port edges.

Unlike the relative positioning model, absolute positioning does not leave space where the element would have otherwise been positioned. Neighboring elements position themselves as though the element were not present in the rendering stream.

Fixed positioning

Fixed positioning is similar to relative positioning in that the element is positioned relative to the view port. However, fixed positioning causes the element to be fixed in the view port—it will not scroll when the document is scrolled; it maintains its position. The following code is used to position the second paragraph shown in Figures 23-4 and 23-5.

```
width: 350px; height: 150px;
border: 1pt solid black;
background-color: white;
padding: .5em;
position: fixed;
top: 100px; left: 100px;
```

Note that when the document scrolls (Figure 23-5) the fixed element stays put.

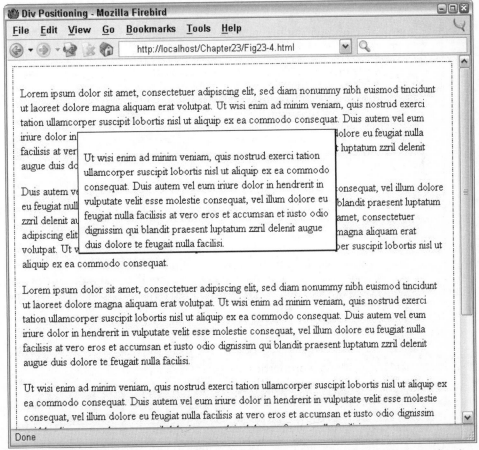

Figure 23-4: Elements using the fixed positioning model are positioned relative to the view port, much like absolute positioning.

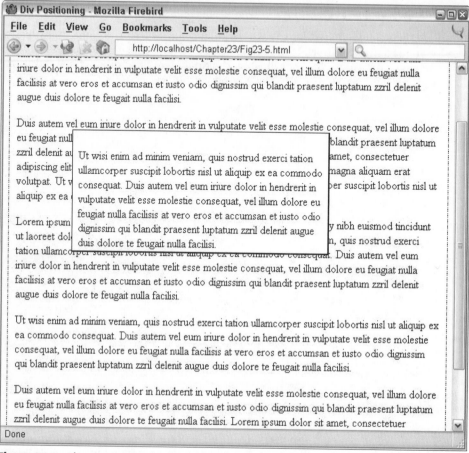

Figure 23-5: Elements using the fixed positioning model do not scroll in the view port, as shown when this document scrolls.

Note   Not all user agents support all the positioning models. Before relying upon a particular model in your documents, you should test the documents in your target user agents. The properties supported by various user agents are covered in Appendix B.

Specifying Element Position

Element positioning can be controlled by four positioning properties: `top`, `right`, `bottom`, and `right`. The effect of these properties on the element's position is largely driven by the type of positioning being used on the element.

The positioning properties have the following format:

```
side:    length | percentage ;
```

The specified side of the element is positioned according to the value specified. If the value is a length, the value is applied to the reference point for the positioning model being used—the element's normal position if the relative model is used, the view port if the absolute or fixed model is used. For example, consider the following code:

```
position: relative;
right: 50%;
```

These settings result in the element being shifted to the left by 50% of its width, as shown in Figure 23-6. This is because the user agent is told to position the right side of the element 50% of where it should be.

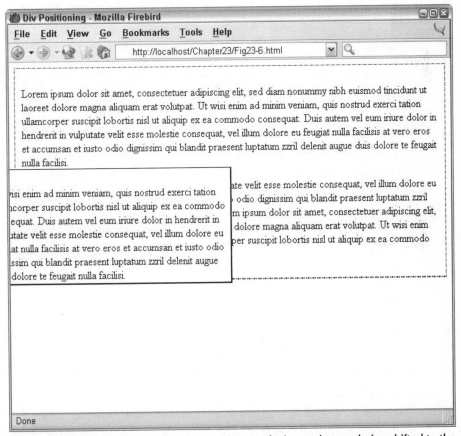

Figure 23-6: A `relative`, 50% `right` value results in an element being shifted to the left by 50% of its width.

However, if the following settings are used, the element is positioned with its right side in the middle of the view port, as shown in Figure 23-7:

```
position: absolute;
left: 50%;
```

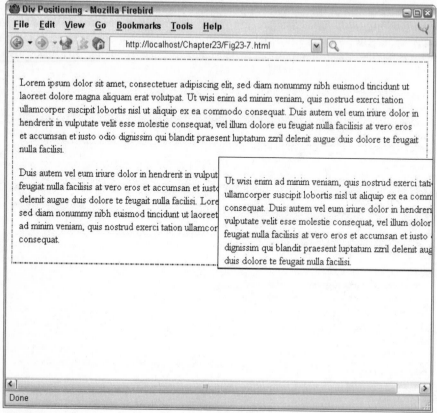

Figure 23-7: An `absolute`, 50% `left` value results in an element being shifted so its left side is in the middle of the view port.

Here, the user agent references the positioning against the view port, so the element's right side is positioned at the horizontal 50% mark of the view port.

Note   Positioning alone can drive the element's size. For example, the following code will result in the element being scaled horizontally to 25% of the view port, the left side positioned at the 25% horizontal mark, and the right at the 50% horizontal mark.

```
position: absolute;
left: 25%; right: 50%;
```

However, whichever property appears last in the definition drives the final size of the element. For example, the following definition will result in an element that has its left side positioned at the view port's horizontal 25% mark, but is 300 pixels wide (despite the size of the view port):

```
position: absolute;
left: 25%; right: 50%;
width: 300px;
```

The `width` overrides the `right` setting due to the cascade effect of CSS.

Floating Elements to the Left or Right

The other way to position elements is to *float* them outside of the normal flow of elements. When elements are floated, they remove themselves from their normal position and float to the specified margin.

The float property is used to float elements. This property has the following format:

```
float: right | left | none;
```

If the property is set to right, the element is floated to the right margin. If the property is set to left, the element is floated to the left margin. If the property is set to none, the element maintains its normal position as per the rest of its formatting properties. If the element is floated to a margin, the other elements will wrap around the opposite side of the element. For example, if an element is floated to the right margin, the other elements wrap on the left side of the element.

For example, the image in Figure 23-8 is not floated and appears in the normal flow of elements. The same image is floated to the right margin (via the style float: right) in Figure 23-9.

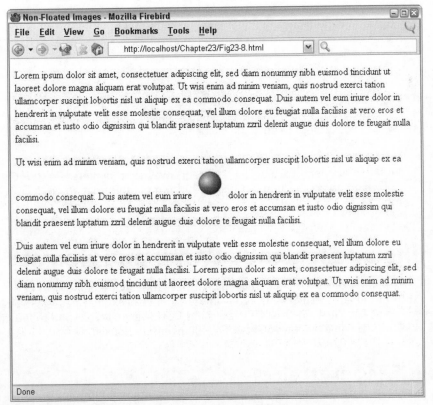

Figure 23-8: A nonfloated image is rendered where its tag appears.

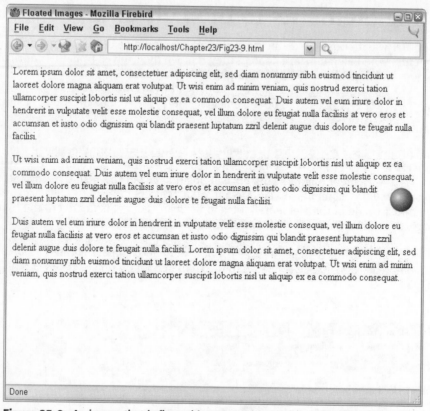

Figure 23-9: An image that is floated is removed from the normal flow and is moved to the specified margin (in this case, the right margin), and the other elements wrap on the exposed side of the element.

Cross-Reference   If you don't want elements to wrap around a floated element, you can use the clear property to keep the element away from floaters. See the *Clearing floating objects* section in Chapter 19 for more information on the clear property.

Defining an Element's Width and Height

There are multiple ways to affect an element's size. You have seen how other formatting can change an element's size—in the absence of explicit sizing instructions the user agent does its best to make everything fit. However, if you want to intervene and explicitly size an element, you can. The following sections show you how.

Specifying exact sizes

You can use the width and height properties to set the size of the element. For example, if you want a particular section of the document to be exactly 200 pixels wide, you can enclose the section in the following <div> tag:

```
<div style="width: 200px;"> ... </div>
```

Likewise, if you want a particular element to be a certain height, you can specify the height using the height property.

> **Note** Keep in mind that you can set size constraints—minimum and maximum sizes—as well as explicit sizes. See the next section for details on minimum and maximum sizes.

Specifying maximum and minimum sizes

There are properties to set maximum and minimum sizes for elements as well as explicit sizes. At times, you will want the user agent to be free to size elements by using the formatting surrounding the element, but still want to constrain the size, allowing an element to be displayed in its entirety instead of being clipped or displayed in a sea of white space.

You can use the following properties to constrain an element's size:

- ✦ min-width
- ✦ max-width
- ✦ min-height
- ✦ max-height

Each property takes a length or percentage value to limit the element's size. For example, to limit the element from shrinking to less than 200 pixels in height, you could use the following:

```
min-height: 200px;
```

Controlling element overflow

Whenever an element is sized independently of its content, there is a risk of it becoming too small for its content. For example, consider the paragraphs in Figure 23-10—the paragraphs are the same except that the second paragraph has had its containing box specified too small, and the contents fall outside of the border.

In this example the user agent (Opera) chose to display the rest of the element outside its bounding box. Other user agents may crop the element or refuse to display it at all.

If you want to control how the user agent handles mismatched elements and content sizes, use the overflow property. This property has the following format:

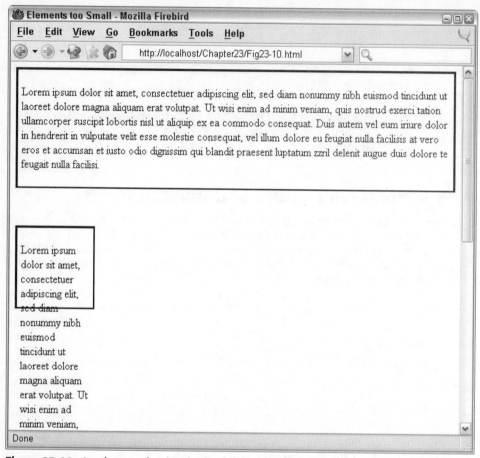

Figure 23-10: An element that is mis-sized doesn't always handle its content properly.

```
overflow: visible | hidden | scroll | auto;
```

The values have the following effect:

✦ visible—The content is not clipped, and is displayed outside of its bounding box, if necessary (as in Figure 23-10).

✦ hidden—If the content is larger than its container, the content will be clipped. The clipped portion will not be visible, and the user will have no way to access it.

✦ scroll—If the content is larger than its container, the user agent should contain the content within the container, but supply a mechanism for the user to access the rest of the content (usually through scroll bars). Figure 23-11 shows the same paragraph as in Figure 23-10, but with its overflow property set to scroll.

✦ auto—The handling of element contents is left up to the user agent. Overflows, if they happen, are handled by the user agent's default overflow method.

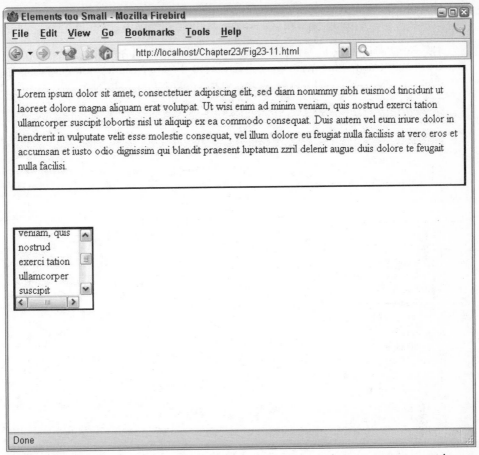

Figure 23-11: The `overflow` property set to `scroll` instructs the user agent to supply a mechanism to view the entire content (usually scrollbars).

Stacking Elements in Layers

Using CSS positioning can often lead to elements stacked on top of one another. Usually, you can anticipate how the elements will stack and leave the user agent up to its own devices regarding the display of stacked elements. At times, however, you will want to explicitly specify how overlapping elements stack. To control the stacking of elements, you use the `z-index` property.

The `z-index` property has this format:

```
z-index:   value;
```

The property controls the third dimension of the otherwise flat HTML media. Because the third dimension is typically referred to along a Z axis, this property is named accordingly (with a Z). You can think of the z-stack as papers stacked on a desktop, overlapping each other—some of the papers are covered by other pieces.

The value controls where on the stack the element should be placed. The beginning reference (the document) is typically at index 0 (zero). Higher numbers place the element higher in the stack, as shown in the diagram in Figure 23-12.

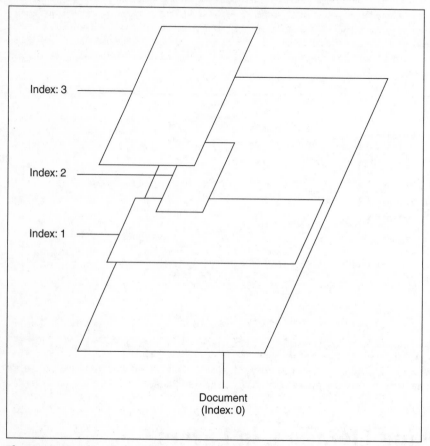

Index: 3

Index: 2

Index: 1

Document
(Index: 0)

Figure 23-12: The effect of the `z-index` property.

A practical example of `z-index` stacking can be seen in Figure 23-13. Each element is assigned a z-index, as shown in the following code:

```
<!DOCTYPE HTML PUBLIC "-//W3C//DTD HTML 4.01//EN"
   "http://www.w3.org/TR/html4/strict.dtd">
<html>
<head>
  <title>Z-index Stacking</title>
  <style type="text/css">
    .box1 { position: absolute;
        top: 25%; left: 25%;
```

```
                    width: 200px; height: 200px;
                    background-color: red;
                    color: white;
                    z-index: 200; }
        .box2 { width: 400px; height: 400px;
                    background-color: yellow;
                    z-index: 100; }
        .box3 { width: 400px; height: 100px;
                    background-color: green;
                    position: absolute;
                    top: 20%; left: 10%; color: white;
                    z-index: 150; }
    </style>
</head>
<body>
<div class="box2">
<p><b>Box 2:</b> Lorem ipsum dolor sit amet, consectetuer
adipiscing elit, sed diam nonummy nibh euismod tincidunt ut
laoreet dolore magna aliquam erat volutpat. Ut wisi enim ad
minim veniam, quis nostrud exerci tation ullamcorper suscipit
lobortis nisl ut aliquip ex ea commodo consequat. Duis autem
vel eum iriure dolor in hendrerit in vulputate velit esse
molestie consequat, vel illum dolore eu feugiat nulla
facilisis at vero eros et accumsan et iusto odio dignissim
qui blandit praesent luptatum zzril delenit augue duis
dolore te feugait nulla facilisi.</p>

<p class="box1"><b>Box 1:</b> This is text</p>

<p>Ut wisi enim ad minim veniam, quis nostrud exerci tation
ullamcorper suscipit lobortis nisl ut aliquip ex ea commodo
consequat. Duis autem vel eum iriure dolor in hendrerit in
vulputate velit esse molestie consequat, vel illum dolore eu
feugiat nulla facilisis at vero eros et accumsan et iusto
odio dignissim qui blandit praesent luptatum zzril delenit
augue duis dolore te feugait nulla facilisi. Lorem ipsum
dolor sit amet, consectetuer adipiscing elit, sed diam
nonummy nibh euismod tincidunt ut laoreet dolore magna
aliquam erat volutpat.</p>
</div>
<div class="box3">
  <p><b>Box 3:</b> This is text.</p>
</div>
</body>
</html>
```

The code uses a mix of <div> and <p> elements for diversity. Since box1's index is the highest (200), it is rendered on the top of the stack. Box3's index is the next highest (150), so it is rendered second to the top. Box2's index is the lowest (100), so it is rendered near the bottom. The document itself is recognized as being at 0, so it is rendered at the bottom of the stack.

If you change the z-index of box1 to 125, it will render under box3, as shown in Figure 23-14.

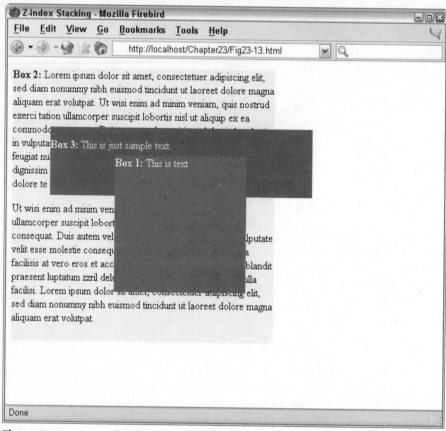

Figure 23-13: A sample of `z-index` stacking.

Tip　You can use many of the properties in this chapter for animation purposes. Using JavaScript, you can dynamically change an element's size, position, and/or z-index to animate it. For more information, see Chapters 25 and 26.

Controlling Element Visibility

You can use the `visibility` property to control whether an element is visible or not. The `visibility` property has the following format:

```
visibility: visible|hidden|collapse;
```

The `visible` and `hidden` values are fairly self-explanatory—set to `visible` (default), an element is rendered; set to `hidden`, the element is not rendered.

Note　Even though an element is hidden with `visibility`, set to `hidden` it will still affect the layout—space for the element is still reserved in the layout.

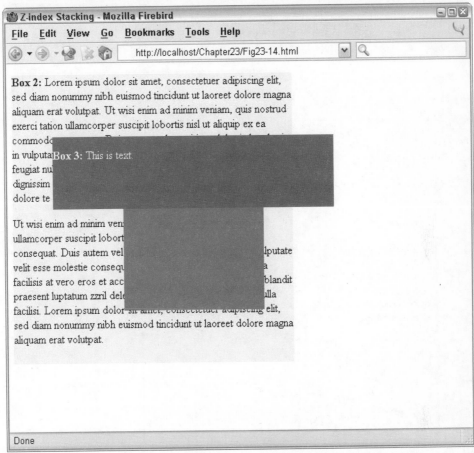

Figure 23-14: Changing an element's z-index changes its position in the stack.

The collapse value causes an element with rows or columns to collapse its borders. If the element does not have rows or columns, this value is treated the same as hidden.

For more information on collapsing borders, see Chapter 22.

Summary

HTML documents formatted with CSS can produce dramatic results. Previous chapters showed you how to format individual elements, and this chapter showed you how to position elements in all three dimensions. Chapter 24 shows you how to format your documents for printing, truly bridging online and print media.

✦   ✦   ✦

Defining Pages for Printing

Have you ever printed a Web page and been amazed at just how badly the page printed? All kinds of nasty things can happen. The most annoying is probably when the text runs off the left side of the page, but there are other annoyances, as well. The Web, after all, was originally intended as a browsing medium. And although researchers who use the Web and write simple HTML pages can always be counted on to format their HTML in a way that makes their pages suitable for printing (largely because they simply eschew bells and whistles), those of us with an eye for design tend to run into some problems.

This problem is less common on today's modern Web, partly because CSS allows Web authors to control the way a page looks in print. You might not even notice that a Web page contains very specific formatting instructions when simply viewing it in a browser, because many of the properties associated with print-based formatting are not designed to appear in the browser, but instead provide instructions as to how the printer should manage the flow of a page.

This chapter takes a look at how to use CSS to pass instructions to the printer to make your Web pages look more readable. CSS support for printed media is not particularly strong yet, but it gains with each new browser version, so it's worth taking a look at (even those CSS properties that don't yet have full browser support).

The Page Box Formatting Model

If you've ever worked with a desktop publishing platform using software such as Quark XPress, InDesign, or PageMaker, you're probably familiar with the concept of a page box, within which fits everything that must go on a page. Even if you haven't worked with desktop publishing software, you've probably seen precursors to the Web's page box formatting model in word processing packages you've used.

When you work in a word processing or desktop publishing environment, you work with finite page sizes and page margins. The CSS page box formatting model is an attempt to replicate this for browser-based media. The page box model is based on the CSS box model (introduced in Chapter 16), as shown in Figure 24-1.

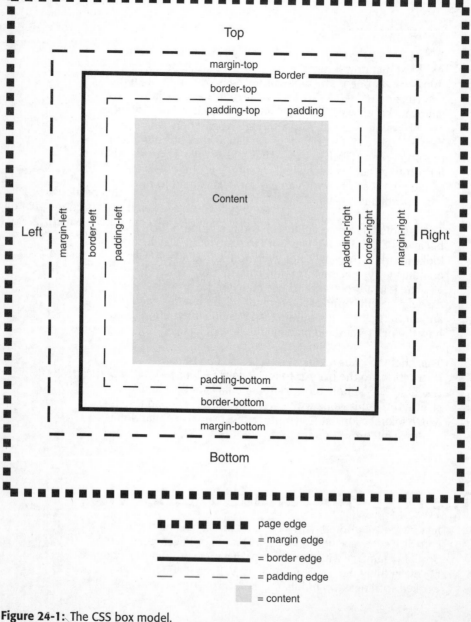

Figure 24-1: The CSS box model.

Figure 24-1 simply extends the box model to reveal two major areas:

✦ The page area, which contains all of a page's elements.

✦ The margin area, which surrounds the page area. When a page area size is specified, the margins, if any, are subtracted.

On top of the page box, the model is expanded still further to account for the difference between continuous media, as represented by a browser, and *paged* media, which consists of discrete and specific page entities. This expansion is represented by the visual formatting model, which allows transfer of the continuous media as seen in a Web browser to an actual sheet of paper or transparency (or even film).

Defining the Page Size with the @page Rule

In word processing and desktop publishing environments, you define a page size by using a dialog box within a set-up option of some kind. In CSS, you define the size of a page using the @page rule. The @page rule defines which pages should be bound to the definitions within the rule. You then use a page property within a style element or attribute to indicate which page a specific element belongs to.

Unfortunately, browser support has still not caught up to this particular CSS rule, and support is pretty nonexistent at this point. Microsoft actually does provide support for this rule, but only through the MSHTML component, which application developers use as a browser widget within their applications. Internet Explorer itself does not include support for this rule in its printing templates, which are used for print previewing and printing Web documents from the browser. If you're a programmer, you can find more information on how you can override this behavior at this address: http://msdn.microsoft.com/workshop/browser/hosting/hosting.asp.

Listing 24-1 demonstrates how the @page rule works.

Listing 24-1: Using an @page Rule to Set up Page Size

```
<style type="text/css">
<!--
@page printed{
size: 3in 3in;
margin: .5in;
page-break-after: left;
{
body, p {
    page: printed
    width: 600px;
    widows: 1;
    page-break-after: right;
}

-->
</style>
```

In Listing 24-1, a page named "printed" is defined. Then, HTML elements that are defined in the stylesheet using printed within the page property should emerge from the printer according to the specifications outlined in the @page rule:

```
body, p {
    page: printed
    width: 600px;
    widows: 1;
    page-break-after: right;
}
```

In CSS2, page selectors can be used to name the first page, all left pages, all right pages, or a page with a specific name that the rules apply to. In the case of Listing 24-1, a named page called printed was used.

Setting up the page size with the size property

The actual dimensions of the page are defined using the size property, also shown in Listing 24-1. The size property consists of two absolute values, one for the width and the other for the height. So the following translates into an 81/2 × 11 size page:

```
@page {
size: 8.5in 11in;
{
```

You can also use the following relative size values:

✦ auto is the default value and is whatever the target paper size is in your printer's settings.

✦ landscape flip flops the dimensions named in the size property so that in the previous example, the printed sheet would print out at 11 inches wide by 8 inches deep.

✦ portrait overrides the targeted media's default settings to correspond with the dimensions you set in the size property.

Setting margins with the margin property

In general, you need to be careful when using margins because they are the outermost layer of a page. If you set the margins of a body element to three inches on either side, for example, be sure to set the width of that same body element as well, or your page will look like that shown in Figure 24-2.

However, in theory, you should be able to set margins for the printed page without worrying about the body text running off to one side of the browser when you neglect to set the width of the page's other elements.

This is because margins can be set using the margin property in CSS within an @page rule. Margins were covered in Chapter 20, *Padding, Margins, and Borders*. You can set

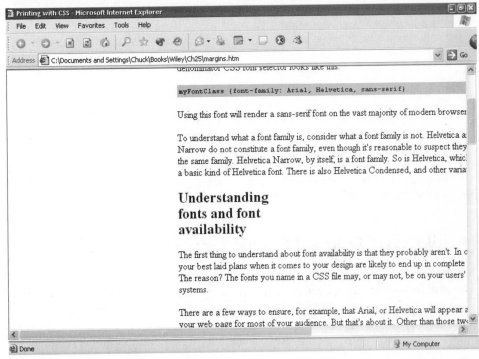

Figure 24-2: Bad margins.

the page margins, as shown in Listing 24-1, by simply using the margin property in the same manner as you use it anywhere else, as shown here:

```
@page {
size: 3in 3in;
margin: .5in;
page-break-after: left;
{
```

The margin settings should be ignored when being viewed on the Web when they're set in an @page rule. However, once again, at the time of this writing, browser support for this feature is weak.

Controlling Page Breaks

Another way to control the flow of a printed page is to force page breaks before or after named elements. There's good news here. Browser support is actually pretty decent (see Table 24-1).

You can set the page-break-before or page-break-after property in a p element, for example, to force a page break before or after all p elements. You probably wouldn't want to actually do that unless you have awfully long paragraphs, but you can create a class selector rule and apply the rule to the first or last paragraph of a page, depending on your needs, like this:

```
pagebreak
    {
    page-break-before: always;
    }
```

In this case, then, you simply apply it to a head element of a page:

```
<h2 class="pagebreak">How the Panose System Works</h2>
```

Note that you can't use page breaks within positioned elements. This means that if you have an absolutely positioned div element with a child p element and the p element has a page break assigned to it via a CSS rule, it won't work.

Using the Page-Break Properties

When your users wish to print your pages, you may want to avoid starting pages with a few lines from a paragraph that started on a previous page. The way to accomplish this is with a CSS page-break property. There are three of them:

✦ The page-break-before property specifies how a page should break after a specific element, and on what side of the page the flow should resume.

✦ The page-break-after property specifies how a page should break before a specific element, and on what side of the page the flow should resume.

✦ The page-break-inside property tells the browser how to break a page from within a box element. Actual support for this property is limited to Opera 3.5. Neither Internet Explorer nor Netscape browsers support this property.

If you don't have a lot of headings, you can set up a style rule and call a page-break property using an element's class attribute. Browser support is strongest in Opera 3.5 and above.

Using the page-break-before and page-break-after properties

The page-break-before and page-break-after properties specify how a page should break before or after a specific element, depending on which of the two properties you use, and on what side of the page the flow should resume. The CSS2 documentation provides these general guidelines:

✦ Page breaking should be avoided inside table elements, floating elements, and block elements with borders.

✦ Page breaking should occur as few times as possible. In other words, it's not a good idea to break a page with every paragraph.

✦ Pages that don't have explicit breaks should be approximately the same height.

Once again, the best support for this property is in the Opera browser.

Internet Explorer also supports page-break properties, particularly the always value. In fact, in Internet Explorer, the left and right values are treated as if they are always. In addition, Internet Explorer ignores this property when used with hr and br elements. Table 24-1 lists the values that can be used with either the page-break-before or page-break-after property.

 Caution Even though Opera is designed to support the inherit property value, some bugs have been reported on this feature indicating that Opera will often crash on pages using this value.

In Table 24-1, the browser support can be assumed to be true for versions following the one named for each specific browser, unless an inconsistency or bug is noted in the description.

Table 24-1
Page-Break-Before/After Property Values

Value	CSS Version	Description	Browsers
inherit	2	Specifies that the value should be inherited from the parent	None
auto	2	Allows the user agent (browser) to insert page breaks on an as-needed basis	IE4, Netscape 7, Opera 3.5
avoid	2	Tells the user agent to avoid inserting page breaks before or after the current element	Opera 3.5
left	2	Forces one or two page breaks to create a blank left page	IE4, Opera 3.5
right	2	Forces one or two page breaks to create a blank right page	IE4, Opera 3.5
always	2	Tells the browser or user agent to always force a page break before or after the current element	IE3, Netscape 7, Opera 3.5
""	NA	This is not a value found in the spec but is actually a value that can be used in Internet Explorer; it explicitly specifies that no property value should be used, and therefore, no page break should be inserted before the current element	IE5

Listing 24-2 shows how the page-break-before property is used in a head element (H2) to help ensure that a page starts with a head element instead of a few lines of dangling paragraph text. Figures 24-3 and 24-4 show how the effect appears in a Print Preview screen in Internet Explorer. Note that the figures represent the rendered page as it would look with all the source code intact (Listing 24-2 was snipped to save space).

Listing 24-2: Using the Page-Break-Before CSS Property

```html
<html>
<head>
<title>Printing with CSS</title>
<meta http-equiv="Content-Type" content="text/html;
charset=iso-8859-1">
<style type="text/css">
<!--
p.code {
    font-family: "Courier New", Courier, mono;
    font-size: 11px;
    background-color: #CCCCCC;
    padding: 3px;
}
.pagebreak {
  page-break-before: always;
}
.inlinecode {
    font-family: "Courier New", Courier, mono;
}
-->
</style>
</head>
<body>
<h1>Understanding Font families</h1>
<p>When choosing font families for style sheets it helps to
understand some basic facts about fonts. For example, Arial
and Helvetica are virtually identical.
<!-- Code snipped to save trees -->
</p>
<h2 class="pagebreak">How the Panose System Works</h2>
<p>Panose is a system of font substitution that uses...
<!-- Code snipped to save trees -->
</p>
<h2>Working with Font styles</h2>
<p>In traditional HTML you can choose whether you want your
font to appear in Roman style (non-italic) font or italics by
using or not using the <span class="inlinecode">em</span>
  or <span class="inlinecode">i</span> elements:</p>
<!-- Code snipped to save trees -->
<!-- More paragraphs here -->
</body>
</html>
```

Figures 24-3 and 24-4 show how the Print Preview looks before applying the page break using the `class` attribute. Note the last heading on the first page in

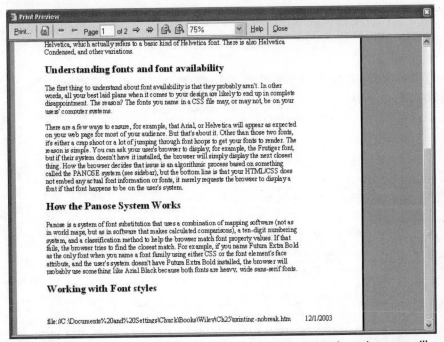

Figure 24-3: You can use your browser's Print Preview to view how the page will look in print (Page 1).

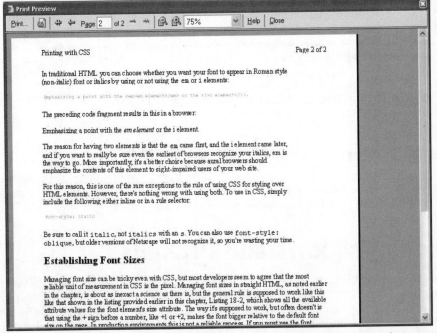

Figure 24-4: Page two of the print preview using `page-break-before` shows the break occurring on the H2 element.

Figure 24-3, which is at the end of the page and has no text under. This is because the page broke at a bad spot. Figures 24-5 and 24-6 show how the print previews look after the CSS has been fixed.

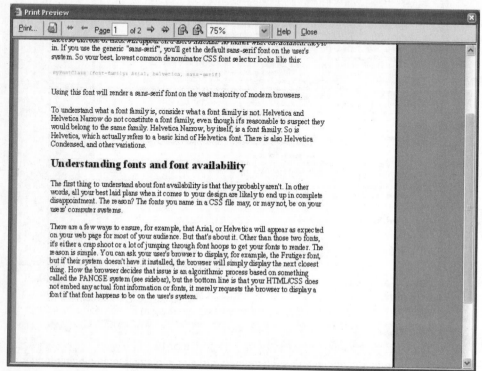

Figure 24-5: This page improves upon the page breaking in Figures 24-3 and 24-4 (Page 1).

The page break in Listing 24-2 is handled through a class selector shown in bold, which is applied to an H1 element, also in bold.

Using the page-break-inside property

You can also use a `page-break-inside` property to handle page breaks within elements (for example, if you have a very long `div` element). However, in practice, the only current browser support is in Opera 3.5 and higher.

Handling Widows and Orphans

Widows and orphans are normally tragic subjects, but CSS has provided developers an opportunity to reduce their impact. A *widow* is the number of lines at the top of a page. It can be unsightly if there is, for example, just one sentence at the top of a page before a section break. An *orphan* is similar, except it occurs at the end of a page. Again, it can be unsightly if a section or paragraph starts at the very end of

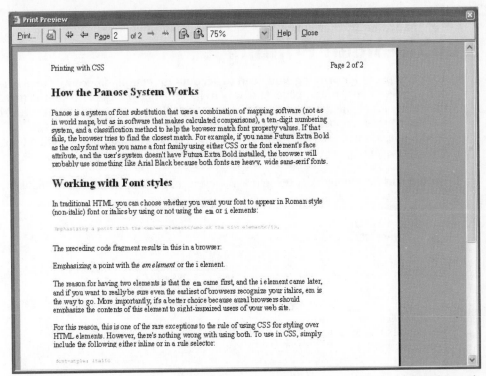

Figure 24-6: This page improves upon the page breaking in Figures 24-3 and 24-4 (Page 2).

a page and the page break results in only a line or two of text at the very end of the page.

One way to help control widows and orphans is through page-breaks. This is especially true since the two CSS properties that are relevant to widows and orphans, respectively named, conveniently enough, `widow` and `orphan`, have virtually no browser support beyond Opera.

Both of these properties have similar syntax:

```
widow: 4;
orphan: 3;
```

You name the property, then supply the value, which can either be an integer or the explicit value `inherit`, the latter of which means the element named in the style rule inherits the properties of its parent. The following sets a p element's widow to a minimum of three lines. This means that the bottom of the page must have a minimum of three lines when printing:

```
<p STYLE="orphans: 3">This paragraph must not be on the top of a page by
itself if it doesn't consist of at least three
lines.</p>
```

If it doesn't, the entire block must be moved to the next page.

Preparing Documents for Double-Sided Printing

To set up pages for printing, you need to account for margin differences on each side of a double-sided, printed page. One way to handle that would be to set the margins differently for elements you expect to appear on different pages, but that would be ugly and almost impossible to do. The only other way is to use CSS @page pseudo-classes named :left and :right, and to set the margins of each differently. But, once again, the catch is that browser support is not yet there.

For the curious among you, these pseudo-classes, working in tandem, look like this:

```
@page :left {
  margin-left: .5in;
  margin-right: .25in;
}
@page :right {
  margin-left: .25in;
  margin-right: .5in;
}
```

You can also specify style for the first page of a document with the :first pseudo-class:

```
@page { margin: 1in }
@page :first {
  margin-top: 3in
}
```

The preceding code sets all the margins at one inch, but the top margin of the first page at three inches, thus overriding the overall page margins established by the first @page rule.

Summary

As you can see, printed page management within the CSS realm still has a way to go in terms of browser support, which is why we focused most of our attention on the one area that has a comparatively high degree of support, that of page breaks. You can use page breaks to great effect, and if you expect your users to print your Web documents, there's really no reason not to use them.

The next chapter takes a look at some of the Web development tools available. You'll learn about text editing tools as well as WYSIWYG tools. You'll also see how graphic-editing programs can influence your design decisions and improve your productivity.

✦   ✦   ✦

Advanced Web Authoring

JavaScript

Up to this point, you have learned how to create static documents on the Web with HTML. However, as the Web matured from its meager beginnings, it was clear that static documents provided limitations—limitations that could be circumvented with a small level of automation. Enter scripting. *Scripting* is a simple form of programming usually used to refer to application macro languages, or in this case, to create small programs to help automate Web pages. This chapter begins the discussion of scripting by introducing the most popular scripting language on the Web, JavaScript.

JavaScript Background

JavaScript is the language of choice for the vast majority of scripting on the Web. It is supported by the two major browsers (Internet Explorer and Navigator), along with other varieties including StarOffice (`www.staroffice.com`) and Opera (`www.opera.com`). JavaScript is a relatively simple and powerful language, and is in broad enough use to make it the de facto standard for Web scripting languages.

Note VBScript is an extension of Visual Basic created by Microsoft as a competitor to JavaScript. However, Microsoft's efforts were not as widely accepted, because JavaScript was introduced to the Web developer world first. As a result, Microsoft has added complete support for JavaScript (calling it *Jscript*) to Internet Explorer, in addition to VBScript.

However, using JavaScript does have a drawback. As long as there is more than one browser, there will be more than one way of doing things. Different developers keep up with industry standards and recommendations at different rates. The result is a mess for the lowly Web author who wants to do fun and exciting things with a Web page, but doesn't want to limit their site to only those with the latest and greatest browser.

JavaScript is an object-oriented scripting language. With JavaScript, you can manipulate many variables and objects on your page. With JavaScript and the Document Object Model (DOM), you can change the value of all the properties of all the objects on your page. Because the DOM requires browsers to redraw pages in response to events, JavaScript becomes far more powerful with the DOM.

Note It's easy to confuse Java and JavaScript—after all, they appear to be closely related. Although JavaScript bases its syntax and structure on Java, the two languages are quite independent of each other and serve completely different purposes. Java is the product of Sun Microsystems, which created it as a cross-platform, object-oriented programming language. JavaScript is a product of Netscape, which developed it to enable Web developers to add programming functionality to Web pages.

JavaScript is the most widely used scripting language on the Web. Originally developed by Netscape, JavaScript has now grown beyond the realm of anything Netscape can control and is supported natively by all the major browsers. In conjunction with the DOM, you can use JavaScript to animate, display, or hide any part of your page, validate forms, and interact in other ways with the end user.

Note A standardized version of JavaScript is defined by the European Computer Manufacturers Association (ECMA, at `www.ecma.ch`), which calls their language *ECMAScript.* Netscape turned JavaScript over to ECMA in an attempt to stabilize the language and make it more widely accessible to other developers. This has not prevented Netscape or Microsoft from continuing to make their own innovations and changes outside the standards created by the ECMA.

When combined with the DOM, you can do many things with JavaScript on a Web page, including the following:

✦ *Create a dynamic form displaying relevant fields, based on information already provided.* For example, if a visitor answers *yes* to an insurance form question about whether any family members have died before age 55, a set of questions about which relatives and how they died would appear. If the answer is a *no,* the next question to appear might ask whether the visitor uses tobacco or illegal drugs. This helps to avoid such techniques as "If no, skip to question 13."

✦ *Reward certain screen interactions, such as answering a series of trivia questions correctly, by providing a congratulatory animation.* The JavaScript can both evaluate the results of the quiz and animate a still image (or a series of images) without reloading the page and without requiring additional actions by the visitor, such as clicking a "see results" button.

✦ *Sort the results of a database table based on the sort order requested by the visitor without additional server requests.* Once receiving the information from the server, the client can sort the data in useful ways utilizing JavaScript and the DOM.

Note This chapter is a very brief introduction to JavaScript. For the full story, plus lots of examples and expert advice, check out Danny Goodman's *JavaScript Bible* (Wiley Publishing, Inc). The DOM is also covered in Chapter 26.

Even with all JavaScript can do, it has limitations. JavaScript is limited to its own sandbox within the browser. JavaScript cannot manipulate files on the client computer, including creating, writing, or deleting any system files. JavaScript also cannot execute any operations outside of the browser, including launching an installer or initiating a download.

These limitations may seem like a handicap for developers, but they help to safeguard site visitors. Right now, few Web citizens fear JavaScript; because of its built-in limitations it is not perceived as a security threat. This is unlike Java and ActiveX. Many visitors have disabled the capability for their browsers to accept any of those technologies for fear of rogue programs. JavaScript would do well to avoid any similar security scare, so some modest limitations are an acceptable price.

Writing JavaScript Code

JavaScript follows a fairly basic syntax that can be outlined with a few simple rules:

✦ With few exceptions, code lines should end with a semicolon (;). Notable exceptions to the semicolon rule are lines that end in a block delimiter ({ or }).

✦ Blocks of code (usually under controls structures such as `functions`, `if` statements, and so on) should be enclosed in braces ({ and }).

✦ Although not necessary, explicit declaration of variables is a good idea.

✦ The use of functions to delimit code fragments is highly advised and increases the ability to execute those fragments independently from one another.

Data types and variables

Variables are storage containers where you can temporarily store values for later use. JavaScript, like most scripting languages, supports a wide range of variable types (integer, float, string, and so on) but incorporates very loose variable type checking. That means that JavaScript doesn't care too much about what you store in a variable or how you use the variable's value later in the script.

JavaScript variable names are case-sensitive but can contain alphabetic or numeric characters. The following are all valid JavaScript variable names:

```
Rose
rose99
total
99_password
```

Although JavaScript doesn't require that you declare variables before their use, declaring variables is a good programming habit to develop. To declare a variable in

JavaScript, you use the `var` keyword. For example, each of the following lines declares a variable:

```
var name = "Hammond";
var total;
var tax_rate = .065;
```

Variables are referenced in the script by their names—JavaScript doesn't require any characters to prefix the variable names. For example, you can reference the variable named `total` by simply using the following:

```
total
```

Calculations and operators

JavaScript supports the usual range of operators for both arithmetic and string values. Tables 25-1 through 25-4 list the various operators supported by JavaScript.

Table 25-1
JavaScript Arithmetic Operators

Operator	Use
+	Addition
-	Subtraction
*	Multiplication
/	Division
%	Modulus (division remainder)
++	Increment
–	Decrement

Table 25-2
JavaScript Assignment Operators

Operator	Use
=	Assignment
+=	Increment assignment
-=	Decrement assignment
*=	Multiplication assignment
/=	Division assignment
%=	Modulus assignment

Table 25-3
JavaScript Comparison Operators

Operator	Use
==	Is equal to
!=	Is not equal to
>	Is greater than
<	Is less than
>=	Is greater than or equal to
<=	Is less than or equal to

Table 25-4
Logical Operators

Operator	Use
&&	And
||	Or
!	Not

Handling strings

Strings are assigned using the standard assignment operator (=). You can concatenate two strings together using the concatenate operator (+). For example, at the end of this code, the full_name variable will contain "Terri Moore":

```
first_name = "Terri";
last_name = "Moore";
full_name = first_name + " " + last_name;
```

Control structures

JavaScript supports the following control structures:

✦ if-else

✦ while

✦ for

The if-else structure

The if-else structure is used to conditionally execute lines of code, depending on a condition that is usually a comparison of values.

The if-else structure has the following syntax:

```
if ( condition ) {
    ...statements to execute if condition is true...
} else {
    ...statements to execute if condition is false...
}
```

Note The else portion of the if-else structure is optional and can be omitted if you do not need to execute statements if the condition is false.

For example, consider the following code:

```
if ( state == "CO") {
    flower = "Columbine";
}
```

This code sets the flower variable to "Columbine" if the state variable is "CO". (The State flower of Colorado is the Columbine.)

The while structure

The while structure is used to execute lines of code over and over again while a certain condition is true.

The while structure has the following syntax:

```
while ( condition ) {
...lines to execute while condition is true...
}
```

For example, consider the following code:

```
while ( address.length < 20) {
    address = address + " ";
}
```

This structure will spacefill (add spaces to the end of) the address variable until it is 20 characters in length. If it is already longer than 20 characters, the structure's statements will be skipped altogether.

Tip Always ensure that your while structures include a means to change the structure's condition to false. Otherwise, you run the risk of creating an endless loop, where the while structure's statements continuously repeat without end.

The for structure

The for structure is used to execute a block of code much like the while structure. The difference is that the for structure is tailored specifically for numerical loops, usually counting a specific number of loops.

The `for` structure has the following syntax:

```
for (assignment; condition; change; ) {
  ...statements to execute while condition is false...
}
```

The assignment, condition, and change blocks of the `for` structure work together to control the number of times the statements are executed.

♦ The assignment block's code is executed at the beginning of the loop and is executed only once.

♦ The condition block provides a conditional statement. While this statement evaluates as `true` the loop continues to execute.

♦ The change block's code is executed at the end of *each* loop.

Typically, the blocks reference the same variable, similar to this example:

```
for ( x = 1; x <= 10; x++; ) {
```

In this case, the loop's execution is as follows:

♦ The variable x is set to 1 at the beginning of the loop.

♦ The value of variable x is checked—if it is less than or equal to 10, the loop's statements are executed.

♦ At the end of each loop the variable x is incremented by one, and the loop is repeated.

In short, this structure would execute 10 times.

Note The description provided here for the `for` structure is somewhat simplistic. The various blocks (referenced herein as assignment, condition, and change) can be quite complex and take various forms. The simplistic explanation here shows the most common use as a numeric counter and loop handler.

Break and continue

Two additional loop-related commands come in handy when using loops in JavaScript: `break` and `continue`.

The `break` command ends the loop, and code execution continues *after* the loop structure.

The `continue` command ends the *current iteration* of the loop, and execution continues with the next iteration of the loop.

Functions

Functions are a means of grouping code fragments together into cohesive pieces. Typically, those pieces perform very specific tasks—receiving values to execute upon and returning values to indicate their success, failure, or result.

There are essentially two types of functions, built-in JavaScript functions and user-defined functions.

Built-in functions

JavaScript has quite a few built-in functions to perform a variety of tasks. Augmenting the functions are a bunch of properties and methods that can be used with just about any object, from browser function to variable.

The scope of built-in JavaScript functions, methods, and properties is too vast to adequately convey here. However, comprehensive references can be found on the Internet, including the following:

✦ Netscape Devedge JavaScript 1.5 Guide
(http://devedge.netscape.com/library/manuals/2000/javascript/1.5/guide/)

✦ DevGuru JavaScript Quick Reference
(http://www.devguru.com/Technologies/ecmascript/quickref/javascript_intro.html)

User-defined functions

Like any other robust programming language, JavaScript allows for user-defined functions. User-defined functions allow you to better organize your code into discrete, reusable chunks.

User-defined functions have the following syntax:

```
function function_name (arguments) {
   ...code of function...
   return value_to_return;
}
```

For example, the following function will spacefill any string passed to it to 25 characters and return the new string:

```
function spacefill (text) {
   while ( text.length < 25 ) {
      text = text + " ";
   }
   return text;
}
```

Elsewhere in your code you can call a function similar to the following:

```
address = spacefill(address);
```

This would cause the variable address to be spacefilled to 25 characters:

✦ The `spacefill` function is called with the current value of `address`.

✦ The `spacefill` function takes the value and assigns it to the local variable `text`.

✦ The local variable `text` is spacefilled to 25 characters.

✦ The local variable text (now spacefilled) is returned from the function.

✦ The original calling assignment statement assigns the returned value to the `address` variable.

Note The arguments passed to a function can be of any type. If multiple arguments are passed to the function, separate them with commas in both the calling statement and function definition, as shown in the following examples:

Calling statement:

```
spacefill(address, 25)
```

Function statement:

```
function spacefill (text, spaces)
```

Note that the number of arguments in the calling statement and in the function definition should match.

The variables used by the function for the arguments and any other variables declared and used by the function are considered local variables—they are inaccessible to code outside the function and exist only while the function is executing.

Using objects

One of the most powerful uses of JavaScript is in accessing document objects. You can use this ability to check document attributes, change document contents, and more.

Cross-Reference This chapter gives only a basic introduction to objects and the document object model. For more information on objects, the DOM, and how JavaScript relates to both, see Chapters 26 and 27.

Most objects are accessed through the document's object collection. The collection is referenced through a structure of tiered objects whose structure is similar to the following:

```
document.element_in_document.sub-element_of_element
```

For example, the following statement references the `address` form field in the `info` form:

```
document.info.address
```

In order for this to work, the elements and subelements must be appropriately named in the document. For example, the form referenced in the preceding code would need name attributes for its elements:

```
<form name="info" action="handler.cgi" method="post">
<input type="text" name="address">
```

To make use of objects, you also have to understand and use properties. Properties are attributes that an object has. In real life these would be attributes such as size, color, smell, and so on. In the DOM they are attributes such as value, length, and so on.

You reference an object's properties by appending the property keyword to the object reference. For example, to reference the length of the address field, you would use the following:

```
document.info.address.length
```

Event Handling in JavaScript

You have seen the word *events* thrown around a lot in this part of the book so far. You'll remember that an event is any action taken by the visitor sitting at the browser. An event can also be caused by the browser, such as when the page finishes loading. Every mouse movement, every click of the mouse, every keystroke can generate an event. As a developer, you must decide what kinds of actions you want to take based on events. Acting on events requires `event handlers`, which are discussed later in this chapter.

Table 25-5 shows the major scriptable events.

Table 25-5 Scriptable Events	
Event	*Trigger*
Load	This event is triggered when the page is loaded
Unload	This event is triggered when the page is unloaded (usually when another page is called)
MouseOver	This event is triggered when the mouse goes over an object on the page
MouseOut	This event is triggered when the mouse is no longer over an object it was formerly over

Event	Trigger
MouseDown	This event is triggered when a visitor clicks (only the downstroke of the mouse button) on an object
MouseUp	This event is triggered when visitors release the mouse button they have depressed. Most systems handle only the mouseUp event, rather than both mouseDown and mouseUp, or only mouseDown. If visitors start to click (triggering a mouseDown), and then move the mouse off of the object (triggering a mouseOut), and then release the button (triggering a mouseUp), normally visitors don't want any action taken
Click	This event is triggered when visitors both click and release an object
DblClick	This event is rarely used in Web pages because Web pages rely on single clicks, but you can capture and act on a double-click, as well
keyPress	This event is triggered when a keyboard key is depressed and released
keyDown	This event is triggered when a keyboard key is depressed
keyUp	This event is triggered when a keyboard key is released
Focus	This event is triggered only in forms, when the cursor moves to highlight a field (either by tabbing to that field, by using a mouse to place the cursor at that field, or by using an access key to bring the focus to that field)
Blur	This event is triggered only in forms when the cursor is moved away from a field that was formerly in focus
Submit	This event is only triggered in forms when the object clicked is a `BUTTON` element with a `type` of "submit" or an `INPUT` element with a type of "submit"
Reset	This event is only triggered in forms when the object clicked is a `BUTTON` element with a `type` of "reset" or an `input` element with a `type` of "reset"
Change	This event is only triggered in forms when the contents of the object in focus are changed and then the focus leaves this object. In other words, if an input field has today's date in it and the visitor changes the date and tabs to another field or clicks another field, the change event is triggered

For example, if you wanted a particular JavaScript function to execute after a page is loaded, you could use a `<body>` tag similar to the following:

```
<body onload="javascript:runthis();">
```

This would execute the function `runthis` after the document loads.

Using JavaScript in HTML Documents

Incorporating JavaScript into your HTML documents is straightforward, and as you'd expect, handled through the use of the `<script>` element. This section details the various methods of including JavaScript in your documents.

Adding scripts with the script element

Now that you have an idea what JavaScript can do, you must understand how to insert your JavaScript into your page. HTML offers the `script` element. If you want the script to be event-driven, include the `script` element in the `head`. If you want the script to execute when the page first loads, include the script in the `body` element. You can have both types of scripts.

The basic syntax is the same as any other HTML:

```
<script language="javascript">
/* script goes here */
</script>
```

Most scripts tend to be placed directly in the Web page, but you have one other option. If your script is long or it uses functions you want other scripts to use, you can put your script into an external text file and link to it with the `script` element's `src` attribute, as shown in the following code. For JavaScript scripts, the file extension is usually JS.

```
<script language="javascript" src="/javascript/lib_date.js">
/* Perhaps a comment what the external script is for */
</script>
```

Although the most popular browsers (Navigator, Internet Explorer, Opera, and StarOffice) are JavaScript-capable, other browsers still do not support it for a variety of reasons. As a responsible developer, you should hide your scripts from non-JavaScript browsers by commenting out the contents of your script. A browser ignores any tags it doesn't recognize, so the JavaScript-challenged browser will see the `<script>` tag and ignore it; and then it will see a big, long comment (that actually contains your script) that it will ignore; and, finally, it will come to the `</script>` tag and ignore that.

```
<script language="javascript">
<!-- Hide script from incompatible browsers
...script here...
// finish hiding script -->
</script>
```

The JavaScript-capable browser, on the other hand, won't be fazed by HTML comments. It will ignore the opening HTML comment tag by accepted language convention and then process the rest of the contents as JavaScript. When it gets to the bottom, it sees a JavaScript comment marker (//) and ignores that line, which includes the closing half of the HTML comment tag.

JavaScript execution

When does JavaScript script execute? That depends on where the script is and how it's written. If a script has some effect on the initial display of the page, it should run before the page is loaded. If a script needs to be ready to run when a certain condition is met on the page, it needs to appear before the place on the page that will encounter the event. If a script needs to run in the course of loading the page, it needs to be included in the page itself.

For example, consider the following code:

```
<head>
<script language="javascript">
function currentTime() {
   var timeStr = ""; //declare an empty string
   now = Time();
   timeStr = now.getHours() + ":";
   timeStr = now.getMinutes();
   return timeStr;
}
</script>
<title>My Home Page</title>
</head>
<body>
<!-- rest of document here -->
</body>
</html>
```

This snippet declares a function called currentTime in the document's head, but it doesn't execute yet. But, once the page is loaded, any hyperlink, form or other page feature that wants to use currentTime can, because it was declared before the page was loaded. If the script was placed at the bottom of the document, the entire page would have to load before the function became available, which could create problems if the user or page tries to invoke the function before it's ready.

Tip

JavaScript is an *interpreted* language, which means it is evaluated and executed line by line. Because the JavaScript interpreter is moving through the scripts sequentially, you need to make sure that functions and other routines are declared *before* they're needed.

The choice of when the script executes is yours. If you want the script to execute when the page is finished loading, you can place it last on the page, or put it in the document's head with a reference to it in the <body> tag, as follows:

```
<BODY onload="JavaScript:currentTime()">
```

Your document can include as many scripts as you want or need in the head and body of the document, depending only on the patience of the end user to wait for the download.

Practical Examples

The uses for JavaScript are potentially unlimited. The following sections highlight a few of the more popular uses.

Browser identification and conformance

Using JavaScript you can determine what browser is being used to access your content and adjust the features of your documents accordingly. For example, you wouldn't want to use a JavaScript feature, such as `window.focus()`, with a browser that doesn't support the function. If you are using DHTML and the Document Object Model (DOM), it helps to know what browser is being used so you can determine the correct DOM model to utilize.

Cross-Reference   You can find more information on DHTML and the DOM in Chapters 26 and 27.

Typically, you can find the details of the browser in the `navigator.userAgent` variable. For example, if someone is using Microsoft Internet Explorer version 6, this variable would contain something similar to the following:

```
Mozilla/4.0 (compatible; MSIE 6.0; Windows NT 5.1;
.NET CLR 1.0.3705; .NET CLR 1.1.4322)
```

From the content of the variable, you can determine that the browser is Mozilla 4.0 compatible and, specifically, is MSIE 6.0. This variable contains a lot of information, much of it superfluous to our intent—just knowing the browser. Additional variables exist to help ferret out the information without having to parse the `navigator.userAgent` value. Some of these variables are listed in Table 25-6.

Table 25-6 Useful Browser Window Properties and Methods	
Variable	**Content**
`navigator.appName`	The formal name of the application (Microsoft Internet Explorer, for example)
`navigator.appVersion`	The version number of the browser
`navigator.platform`	The operating system the browser is running on (Linux, win32, etc)
`navigator.userLanguage`	The language the browser is using (en-us, for example)

Using if/then statements, you can provide the appropriate code for various browsers, similar to the following:

```
browser=navigator.appName
if (browser.indexOf("Microsoft")!=-1)
  {
    // Browser is MSIE, insert browser
    // browser specific code here


  }
if (browser.indexOf("Netscape")!=-1)
  {
    // Browser is vintage Netscape, insert
    // browser specific code here


  }
if (browser.indexOf("Mozilla")!=-1)
  {
    // Browser is Mozilla, insert
    // browser specific code here


  }
```

However, this method is far from fool proof because the browser itself supplies this information—many browsers masquerade as other browsers and don't report their full details. A better way to write code is to detect actual features instead of relying on the browser name to ascertain which features it supports.

You can tell if a function, method, or property exists by using an if statement. For example, to determine that window.focus is supported by the user's browser you could use a construct similar to the following:

```
if (window.focus)
  {
    // window.focus() is supported, use it
  }
else
  {
    // window.focus() is not supported,
    // use alternate method
  }
```

If you are using DHTML or otherwise making use of the DOM, you have probably noticed that different browsers implement the DOM differently. You can use the preceding method with document objects to determine the appropriate DOM model to use with code similar to the following:

```
if (document.getElementById) {
    // access DOM via getElementById
}
else if (document.all) {
    // access DOM via document.all
}
```

```
else if (document.layers) {
    // access DOM via document.layers
}
```

Note that you can determine if a browser supports DHTML at all by checking for any of the DOM models:

```
if (document.getElementById || document.all
    || document.layers)
{
    // browser can do DHTML
}
```

Tip The Quirksmode Web site (www.quirksmode.org) is an excellent source of browser compliance, quirks, and solutions.

Last modification date

Using the lastModified property of the document object, you can place the timestamp of the current document file in your document's text. For example, the following code will insert the date (in the default format: MM/DD/YYYY HH:MM:SS) wherever the code is placed in the document:

```
<script>
  document.write(document.lastModified);
</script>
```

Caution The lastModified property is problematic when used with some browsers. Always test your code on target browsers before fully deploying it.

Rollover images

Using the DOM, JavaScript can dynamically change images in the current document. This technique is commonly used with graphical buttons—you create buttons that have a different look when the mouse passes over them and use the onMouseOver event to trigger a script to change the button accordingly.

For example, suppose you created the two buttons shown in Figure 25-1. The button on the left is to be displayed when the mouse is *not* over the button, and the one on the right displays when the mouse is over the button.

The document code to handle the rollover change is shown in the following listing:

Figure 25-1: Two buttons for rollover purposes—
btnHomeNrm.jpg (left image) is the normal button, and
btnHomeHgh.jpg (right image) is the highlighted button.

```
<!DOCTYPE HTML PUBLIC "-//W3C//DTD HTML 4.01//EN"
  "http://www.w3.org/TR/html4/strict.dtd">
<html>
<head>
  <title>Rollover Sample</title>
  <script type="text/JavaScript">
    function btnHigh( btnName, hgh ) {
    // Display correct button - hgh = 0 = normal button
    //     hgh = 1 = highlight button
      var obtn = document.getElementById(btnName);
      if (hgh) {
        obtn.src = btnName + "Hgh.jpg";
      } else {
        obtn.src = btnName + "Nrm.jpg";
      }
    }
  </script>
</head>
<body>
<img id="btnHome" src="btnHomeNrm.jpg"
    border="0"
    onMouseOver="JavaScript:btnHigh('btnHome',1);"
    onMouseOut="JavaScript:btnHigh('btnHome',0);">
</body>
</html>
```

This code works by using one function called by the OnMouseOver and onMouseOut
events of the <img> element. When a user puts the mouse over the image, the
function is called with the root name of the button (btnHome) and the highlight
variable (hgh) set to 1 (highlight). The function gets the button's id via the name
(note how the <img> element's id is the same as the root name of the images) and
sets the element's src property to the highlighted image. This process is repeated
when the user removes the mouse from the element, but the highlight variable (hgh)
is set to 0 (do not highlight), and the function sets the element to the normal image.

You can use the same function for an unlimited number of buttons as long as each
uses a unique id and the same image file-naming conventions.

Tip

To actually make the button do something, add an `onClick` event to the `<img>` tag to call another function, or directly manipulate the `document.location.href` property, as in the following examples:

```
onClick="JavaScript:dosomethingelse()"
```

and

```
onClick="document.location.href='home.html'"
```

Caching images

When animating images on a page, it helps to have the images (and all their variants) already cached by the browser. This eliminates the lag caused by the server sending the image(s) to the browser and the resulting delay in the image being displayed.

To cache images, you can use a function similar to the following JavaScript function:

```
function preloadimages() {

var pictures = new Array
// List all the images to preload here
(
 "images/rdm1.gif"
,"images/rdm2.gif"
,"images/rdm3.gif"
,"images/rdm4.gif"
,"images/rdm5.gif"
,"images/rdm6.gif"
,"images/rdm7.gif"
,"images/rdm8.gif"
,"images/rdm9.gif"
);

// Load each image in array
  for (i=0;i<preloadimages.arguments.length;i++) {
    myimages[i]=new Image();
    myimages[i].src=preloadimages.arguments[i];
  }
}
```

This function creates a new image object for each entry in the `pictures` array, causing the browser to request the image from the server and cache it locally. Thereafter, any request for the image will be served from the browser's cache instead of the server, eliminating display lag.

To use this function, replace the `images/rdm...` entries with the correct URLs of the images you want to preload, and call the function from an `onLoad` event within the document, as shown in the following example:

```
<body onLoad="JavaScript:preloadimages();">
```

Note that preloading images takes just about as long as displaying the images normally. As such, little can be gained by preloading static images in the current document. However, images on subsequent pages, images used in animations, or dynamic buttons (see the previous section) are all good candidates for preloading.

Form validation

Form validation is one of the purposes most used by JavaScript. Consider the simple form shown in Figure 25-2.

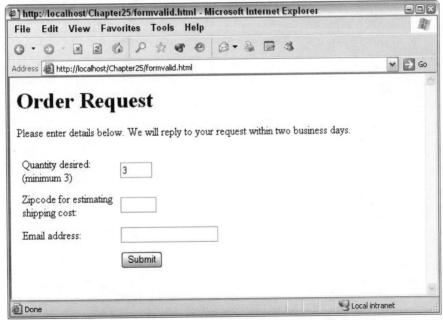

Figure 25-2: A simple form to request a quote for shipping products.

Although the form is simple, a few pieces of information should be verified before the data is accepted:

✦ The quantity should be a number and be at least three.

✦ The ZIP code should be a five-digit number.

✦ The e-mail address should resemble a valid e-mail address (include an @ and a period).

Performing complex checks on the data—such as validating that the ZIP code is authentic, not just five random numbers—isn't feasible using JavaScript. But the following document provides enough validity to weed out totally bogus data:

```
<!DOCTYPE HTML PUBLIC "-//W3C//DTD HTML 4.01//EN"
    "http://www.w3.org/TR/html4/strict.dtd">
```

```html
<html>
<head>
  <title></title>
  <script type="text/JavaScript">

    function req(myField, myLabel) {
     // Check for non-blank field
       var result = true;
       if (myField.value == "") {
         alert('Please enter a value for the "'
           + myLabel +'" field.');
         myField.focus();
         result = false;
       }
       return result;
    }

    function grThan (myField, myLabel, num) {
    // Check if field value > num
      var result = true;
      if (myField.value <= num) {
        alert('Please enter a value for the "'
          + myLabel +'" field, greater than '
          + val + '.');
        myField.focus();
        result = false;
      }
      return result;
    }

    function isInt (myField, myLabel) {
    // Check if field is an integer
      var result = true;
      if (!req(myField, myLabel))
        result = false;
      if (result) {
        var num = parseInt(myField.value,10);
        if (isNaN(num)) {
          alert('Please enter valid number in the "'
            + myLabel +'" field.');
          myField.focus();
          result = false;
        }
      }
      return result;
    }

    function validEmail(myField, myLabel) {
     // Check for "valid" email (not empty, has
     // "@" sign and ".")
       var result = false;
       if (req(myField, myLabel))
         result = true;
       if (result) {
         var tempstr = new String(myField.value);
```

```
        var aindex = tempstr.indexOf("@");
        if (aindex > 0) {
          var pindex = tempstr.indexOf(".",aindex);
          if ((pindex > aindex+1) &&
          (tempstr.length > pindex+1)) {
            result = true;
          } else {
            result = false;
          }
        }
      }
    if (!result) {
      alert("Please enter a valid email address "
          + "in the form: yourname@yourdomain.com");
      myField.focus();
    }
    return result;
  }

  function valform (myform) {
  // Validate form fields as specified below
    // Quantity > 2 (and integer)
    if ( !grThan(myform.qty,"Quantity",2) ||
        !isInt(myform.qty,"Quantity") ) {
      return false;
    }
    // Valid Zipcode
    if (!isInt(myform.zip,"Zipcode")) {
      return false;
    }
    // Valid email
    if (!validEmail(myform.email,"Email")) {
      return false;
    }
    return true;
  }
</script>
</head>
<body>
<h1>Order Request</h1>
<p>Please enter details below. We will reply to
your request within two business days.</p>
<form name="orderform"
  action="http://www.synergy-ent.com/projects/pi.php"
    method="POST"
    onSubmit="return valform(document.orderform);">
  <p>
  <table border="0" cellpadding="5">
  <tr><td>
    Quantity desired:<br>
    (minimum 3)
  </td><td>
    <input type="text" name="qty" value="3"
      size="4">
  </td></tr>
```

```
<tr><td>
  Zipcode for estimating<br>
  shipping cost:
</td><td>
  <input type="text" name="zip" value=""
    size="5" maxlength="5">
</td></tr>
<tr><td>
  Email address:
</td><td>
  <input type="text" name="email" value=""
    size="20" maxlength="30">
</td></tr>
<tr><td>
   
</td><td>
<input type="submit" value="Submit">
</td></tr>
</table>
</p>
</form>

</body>
</html>
```

This code works by using the `onSubmit` event with the `<form>` element. When the user clicks the Submit button, the event handler calls the specified function (`valform`) *before* actually submitting the form data to the specified handler. If the function returns `true`, the form data is submitted. If the function returns `false`, the form data is not submitted and the user is returned to the document.

The `valform` function steps through a handful of smaller functions to validate parts of the form. The various functions return `true` if the data is valid, `false` if the data is invalid. If all functions return `true`, the main function returns `true` as well, allowing submission of the data. If any function returns `false`, the main function also returns `false`, and the data is not submitted.

Each validation function also displays an error message if invalid data is encountered, placing the user agent focus on the offending field.

Note

The functions used here are typical of functions used to validate most form data. However, each form is different and will probably require custom functions to validate its content—although you can use this example as a template, you should create tests specifically for your data.

A comprehensive collection of form validation scripts can be found in the archives of Netscape's DevEdge site:

```
http://developer.netscape.com/docs/examples/javascript/
formval/overview.html
```

Although the code was written in 1997, it still contains a wealth of useful functions for form validation.

Specifying window size and location

By accessing the user agent's properties you can manipulate some aspects of the user's browser window. Table 25-7 lists a handful of the useful properties available.

	Table 25-7
	Useful Browser Window Properties and Methods

Property/Method	Use
window.moveTo(x,y)	Move the upper-left corner of the browser window to position x,y on the user's screen
window.resizeTo(x,y)	Resize the browser window to x pixels wide by y pixels tall
window.resizeBy(x,y)	Resize the browser window, adding x pixels to the width and y pixels to the height (negative values shrink the window)
document.body.clientWidth	Returns the current width of the browser window (in pixels)
document.body.clientHeight	Returns the current height of the browser window (in pixels)
document.body.scrollTop	Returns the number of pixels the user has scrolled down from the top of the document. Returns 0 if the vertical scrollbar is inactive (Internet Explorer and compatible browsers)
window.pageYOffset	Returns the number of pixels the user has scrolled down from the top of the document. Returns 0 if the vertical scrollbar is inactive (Netscape and compatible browsers)
document.body.scrollLeft	Returns the number of pixels the user has scrolled right, from the left edge of the document. Returns 0 if the horizontal scrollbar is inactive (Internet Explorer and compatible browsers)
window.pageXOffset	Returns the number of pixels the user has scrolled right, from the left edge of the document. Returns 0 if the horizontal scrollbar is inactive (Netscape and compatible browsers)

Note The resize methods resize the entire window of the user agent, which includes toolbars, status bars, and so on—not just the content. Several other methods and properties can be used to return information about the browser and set certain attributes, but most of them are hit or miss as far as browser compliance is concerned. You can find more information on the properties and methods at DevGuru:

```
www.devguru.com/Technologies/ecmascript/quickref/
javascript_index.html
```

You can use the code in the following example to play with some of the browser window properties and methods:

```
<!DOCTYPE HTML PUBLIC "-//W3C//DTD HTML 4.01 Transitional//EN"
    "http://www.w3.org/TR/html4/loose.dtd">
<!-- Note the use of the transitional DTD above! -->
<html>
<head>
  <title>Window Functions</title>
  <script type="text/JavaScript">
  function resetwindow() {
  // Reset window to upper left of screen
  // at a size of 500 x 400 pixels
    window.resizeTo(500,400);
    window.moveTo(0,0);
  }

  function sizeBy(x,y,smaller) {
  // Increase or decrease (if smaller)
  // size of window by x and y pixels
    if (smaller) {
      x *= -1;
      y *= -1;
    }
    window.resizeBy(x,y);
  }

  function scrollreport() {
  // Report position of both scrollbars
    var hpos, vpos;
    var hmsg, vmsg;
    if (navigator.appName ==
      "Microsoft Internet Explorer") {
      hpos = document.body.scrollLeft;
      vpos = document.body.scrollTop;
    } else {
      hpos = window.pageXOffset;
      vpos = window.pageYOffset;
    }
    hmsg = "Horz Scroll: " + hpos;
    vmsg = "Vert Scroll: " + vpos;
    alert(hmsg + "\n" + vmsg);
  }
  </script>
</head>
<body onLoad="resetwindow();">
<div style="width: 600px; height: 600px;">
  <form>
  <p><input type="button" value="Reset"
    accesskey="R"
    onClick="resetwindow();"></p>
  <p><input type="button" value="Larger"
    accesskey="L"
    onClick="sizeBy(50,50,0);">
    
```

```
    <input type="button" value="Smaller"
      accesskey="S"
      onClick="sizeBy(50,50,1);"></p>
    <p><input type="button" value="ScrollBar Report"
      accesskey="B"
      onClick="scrollreport();"></p>
    <p><input type="button" value="Close Me"
      accesskey="C"
      onClick="self.close();"></p>
</div>
</body>
</html>
```

Note The `<div>` sets a specified size for the elements in the document body to help ensure that scrollbars will appear at smaller window sizes. Note that the `accesskey` attributes for the buttons allow you to access the buttons even if you can't see them in the document window.

Frames and frameset control

You can also use JavaScript to help direct content to specific frames, if your document uses frames.

The `window.frames` property can be used to access the frames currently active in the user agent window. You can access the frame properties using two methods, by name or by position in the frameset:

```
<!-- A frameset -->
<frameset rows="25%,50%,25%">
  <frame name="frame1" src="banner.html" />
  <frame name="frame2" src="content.html" />
  <frame name="frame3" src="footer.html" />
</frameset>
// Access a frame (frame2) by name
window.frames["frame2"].location="home.html"
// Access a frame by position in frameset
// (first frame is 0, second frame is 1)
window.frames[1].location="home.html"
```

Either of the two preceding JavaScript examples will replace the content of `frame2` with that of the `home.html` document.

Tip You can use the `window.frames.length` property to determine how many child frames are currently displayed in the active user agent window.

Using cookies

The Web is largely a stateless environment. The user agent requests a page and receives a response from the server. Typically, neither entity tracks the user's state (beyond the client's concept of Back and Forward through the cache). Enter cookies, a way to save information on the user's machine that the user agent can later retrieve and use.

Note Over the years, cookies have gotten a bad reputation. The technology is not at fault, but the use of it is. Several individuals and companies have used cookies to track user *behavior* and report the data for demographic, shopping, or simply spying purposes. The heart of the cookie technology is fairly benign and can be used for very useful purposes, such as remembering what messages you have read in a forum, favorite settings for sites, and so on.

You can use the JavaScript `document.cookie` property to set and retrieve cookies. The following code shows examples of functions to set, retrieve, and delete cookies:

```
// setCookie
// Sets cookie specified by 'name' (and optionally
// 'path' and 'domain') to 'value'.
// Cookie defaults to expire at end of session,
// but can be specified to expire 'expires'
// number of milliseconds from now.
function setCookie(name, value, expires, path, domain) {
  if (expires) {
    if (expires != 0) {
      var curDate = new Date();
      var expDate = new Date(curDate.getTime() + expires);
    }
  }
  var curCookie = name + "=" + escape(value) +
      ((expires) ? "; expires=" + expDate : "") +
      ((path) ? "; path=" + path : "") +
      ((domain) ? "; domain=" + domain : "");
  document.cookie = curCookie;
}


// getCookie
// Retrieves cookie value specified by 'name' (and
// optionally 'path' and 'domain').
// Returns cookie value or null if cookie is not found.
function getCookie(name) {
  var dc = document.cookie;
  var prefix = name + "=";
  var begin = dc.indexOf("; " + prefix);
  if (begin == -1) {
    begin = dc.indexOf(prefix);
    if (begin != 0) return null;
  } else {
    begin += 2;
  }
  var end = document.cookie.indexOf(";", begin);
  if (end == -1) end = dc.length;
  return unescape(dc.substring(begin + prefix.length, end));
}
```

```
// delCookie
// Deletes cookie specified by 'name' (and
// optionally 'path' and 'domain') by setting
// expire to previous date.
function delCookie(name, path, domain) {
  if (getCookie(name)) {
    document.cookie = name + "=" +
    ((path) ? "; path=" + path : "") +
    ((domain) ? "; domain=" + domain : "") +
    "; expires=Thu, 01-Jan-70 00:00:01 GMT";
  }
}
```

Summary

This chapter introduced you to JavaScript, a simple yet effective scripting language that can automate certain aspects of your documents. You learned what JavaScript is, the language's programming conventions, how to incorporate it into HTML, and were presented with several typical examples of its use. The next few chapters extend this knowledge, showing you the magic of Dynamic HTML.

✦   ✦   ✦

Dynamic HTML

Dynamic HTML (DHTML) is a combination of standard HTML and CSS, and often JavaScript, used to create dynamic Web page effects. These can be animations, dynamic menus, text effects such as drop shadows, text that appears when a user rolls over an item, and other similar effects.

This chapter introduces DHTML by reviewing some JavaScript basics and providing a look at the Document Object Model, which allows you access to HTML elements so that you can change their properties and/or content. Examples of common DHTML techniques are provided.

The Need for DHTML

DHTML, when used correctly, can significantly enhance the user experience. DHTML was originally best known for its flashy effects, and these still exist, but their importance is questionable, and when used improperly they can be annoying for your users. Fancy text animations and bouncing balls might be fun to write, but they're not so much fun for the user. This chapter focuses on the more practical aspects of DHTML. Most of these have to do with navigation. After all, your Web site is all about the user experience. Whenever you create an enhancement to your Web site, you should always ask, "Does this improve the user experience? Can they navigate my site more easily? Read my Web page more easily?"

How DHTML Works

DHTML can work either by applying certain CSS properties, or by using JavaScript to manipulate HTML elements. When using JavaScript, DHTML takes advantage of a browser's object model, which is a tree of objects based on the element set of HTML and on the property set of CSS. When you code against that object model, you can change an element's properties, which are associated with an element's attributes. An element's attributes, in fact, are referred to as properties in a

JavaScript environment. How these properties are referred to, and what actions (methods) you can take on them, is determined by the Document Object Model (DOM).

DHTML and the Document Object Model

The DOM is a standardized process for accessing the parts of a Web page through a common application programming interface (API). What this means in practical terms is that each element in a document is accessible via script, usually JavaScript. We say "usually" JavaScript because no rule states that a language that accesses the DOM needs to be JavaScript. It can be any language, from Java (which is different than JavaScript) to C# or Visual Basic. As it turns out, though, most DOM-related activity vis-a-vis the browser is powered by JavaScript.

The standardized form of JavaScript is called ECMAScript. This is a relevant fact because usually if you confine your scripting to a combination of the W3C's Level One Core DOM and ECMAScript, you'll be pretty successful at achieving cross-browser scripting compatibility.

You can find the specification for ECMAScript at `www.ecma-international.org/publications/standards/Ecma-262.htm`.

The W3C's Level One Core DOM is basically a set of properties and methods that can be accessed from a given element. For example, one of the most ubiquitous (and dastardly, in many people's opinion) methods is the `window.open()` method, which makes it possible for advertising pop-ups to appear. The `open()` method acts upon the `window` object, which, although not an element (the DOM isn't restricted to elements), is still an object that can be manipulated by script.

Using event handlers

Notice the `onclick` attribute in the following code fragment:

```
onclick="this.style.fontSize='60px'; this.style.color='red'">
```

This tells the browser that when the user clicks the `div` element, something should happen. In this case, that something is that the following two attributes of the style element will change:

✦ `style.fontSize='60px'` tells the browser to change the font size to 60 pixels.

✦ `style.color='red'"` tells the browser to change the color to red.

The `onclick` attribute is actually an event handler. An event is something that happens, as you probably already know. A party, for example, is an event. When a human triggers the `onparty` event, sometimes that human falls down drunk. When a human triggers an `onclick` event in a browser, more benign things take place, such as text color changes, menu changes, and so on. Table 26-1 shows the common event handlers associated with JavaScript.

Table 26-1 JavaScript Event Handlers	
Event Handler	**Usage**
onAbort	Occurs when a user stops an image from loading
onBlur	Occurs when a user's mouse loses focus on an object. Focus is when the cursor is active on an object, such as a form input field. When a cursor is clicked within the field, it has focus, and when the mouse is taken out of the field, it loses focus, causing an `onBlur` event
onChange	Occurs when a change takes place in the state of an object, when, for example, a form field loses focus after a user changes some text within the field
onClick	Occurs when a user clicks an object
onError	Occurs when an error occurs in the JavaScript
onFocus	Occurs when a user's mouse enters a field with a mouse click
onLoad	Occurs when an object, such as a page (as represented by the body element) is loaded into the browser
onMouseOut	Occurs when a mouse no longer hovers over an object
onMouseOver	Occurs when a mouse begins to hover over an object
onSelect	Occurs when a user selects text
onSubmit	Occurs when a form is submitted
onUnload	Occurs when an object is unloaded

When one of these events takes place, code is executed. Many browsers have their own, custom event handlers, but if you stick with those found in Table 26-1, you'll find cross-compatibility issues much easier to solve.

It's all about objects

The other thing you should have noticed about the JavaScript code fragment you saw at the beginning of this chapter is that there is some interesting dot syntax going on:

```
style.fontSize='60px'
```

This is the key to all DHTML and working with the DOM. When script accesses an object, it does the same thing you need to do when finding objects on your computer. When you look for a file on your hard drive, you drill down a group of nested folders to find something. So the final path might look something like this:

```
C:\Documents and Settings\Chuck\Books\goodbook.doc
```

On the World Wide Web, the same thing happens:

```
http://www.mywebsite.com/2003/WORLD/index.html
```

Here, the Web server drills down a specific path that finds the document in bold. When you use JavaScript and the DOM you do the same basic thing. You begin with a top-level object, which is always the `window` object. Normally, you don't need to name that, because it's understood to just always be there. Then, you drill down to the next level. The previous code which demonstrated how to use an `onclick` event (`onclick="this.style.fontSize='60px';`) was able to circumvent this because the same object that called the event had changes (it changed itself), so we could use the `this` keyword. However, had another object been changed, you would have had to name that object's position within the hierarchy of document objects. The easiest way to do that is to be sure you use the `id` attribute (which means the HTML object must contain an `id` attribute containing a unique value), and then drill down to the object in your code. As shown in Figure 26-1, you can access most of the objects associated with a browser window using JavaScript and the DOM.

Cross-Browser Compatibility Issues

The most important caveat to exploring DHTML is that there are tons of compatibility issues. The newest iterations of Mozilla/Netscape and Internet Explorer have actually begun to come closer together, but developers working with DHTML during the height of the browser wars quickly learned that developing cross-browser DHTML was a very difficult proposition. As a result, most large professional sites eschew complex DHTML in favor of simpler cross-browser routines to improve navigation and other facets of the user experience, rather than excessive visual effects.

Browser detection

You can detect what kind of a browser a user is running by running a browser-detection script. This kind of script, along with some more finely tuned type of object detection described in the next section, is sometimes referred to as *browser sniffing*. At its simplest, a typical browser-detection script looks like this:

```
<SCRIPT LANGUAGE="JavaScript">
<!--

var bName =navigator.appName;
var bVer = parseFloat(navigator.appVersion);
if (bName == "Netscape")
```

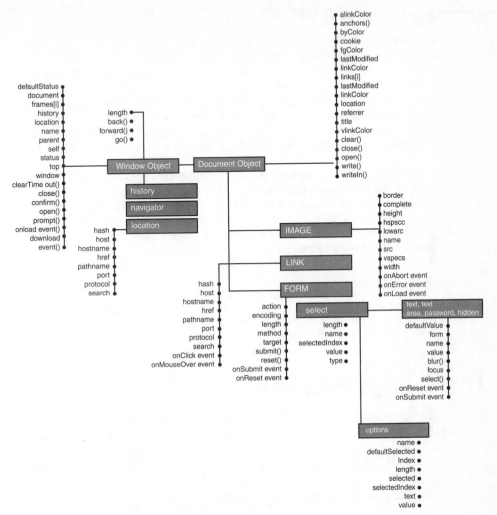

Figure 26-1: The Core Document Object Model used by ECMAScript (JavaScript).

```
   var browser = "Netscape Navigator"
else
   var browser = bName;
document.write("You are currently using ", browser, " ",
bVer, ".");


// -->
</SCRIPT>
```

Note

When using simple browser-sniffing scripts, you can replace the code in bold
in the preceding example with more complex tasks. In the next chapter, you'll
see how to work with different CSS properties based on which browser a user
is using.

Object detection

Object detection is a more precise way of browser sniffing. It examines a browser's support for various aspects of the object model. This avoids the potential for successfully checking a browser version but not checking to see if a browser actually supports a specific object property or method. For this reason, object detection is the preferred method for browser sniffing and is considered best practice. In addition, unless you've got the object model of all the different browsers memorized, it's pretty hard to know which browser supports which object. It's easier to just check and see if a browser supports a specific object's properties or methods.

The principles used in object detection are quite similar to those used in browser detection. You make use of JavaScript if statements to check a browser's support for a named object's properties or methods. If it does support the object, you execute some given code. For example, using regular expressions can be very handy in JavaScript, but not if your users' browsers don't support them. So you create a simple detection script to see if they do:

```
if (window.RegExp) {
  // execute some regular expressions
} else {
  // provide an alternative to regular expressions
}
```

DHTML Examples

This section offers a few practical examples of DHTML. The scripts you'll see are necessarily simple to get you started. There are tons of resources on the Internet for additional help, including a vast array of freely available scripts that you can customize for your own use. We'll take a look at a few of the most popular DHTML routines.

Breadcrumbs (page location indicator)

If you've ever seen a series of links at the top of a browser window with the current page's link deactivated, you've seen breadcrumbs. Breadcrumbs derive their name from the concept of a navigation trail, designed to help users know where they are relative to the page they are in. Many user interface experts consider breadcrumbs an absolute necessity. Generally, you'll find breadcrumbs most easily managed through server-side scripting, but if you don't want to deal with server-side scripting, or, if you simply don't have access to a server-side scripting engine (maybe you are simply creating some pages on your home page offered by your ISP), you can create them using JavaScript.

Writing out the code in pseudo-code

Generally, the best way to develop any code is to spell it out in pseudo-code. In other words, think about what you're trying to do in English or whatever your spoken language is. In this case, our pseudo-code looks like this:

```
Split the current URL into each folder.
For each folder
    Create a link string-based object.
Next Folder,
Combine all result string objects together using a separator
or delimiter to form a single string.
Print the string out to the browser window.
```

Using the window object to manage URLs

As I mentioned, most action using JavaScript takes place by way of the DOM, which you'll see in action in the upcoming JavaScript breadcrumb example. In this case, you'll use the window `location` property to handle the first part of your pseudo-code. The `location` property contains the current window's URL. You'll need this URL because in order to develop breadcrumbs according to the pseudo-code, you'll need to break apart the URL string and rip out each directory from it. You do this by separating each chunk of string that is delimited by a forward slash.

Therefore, the first step in creating breadcrumbs is to initialize a JavaScript variable to store the URL, as in the following example:

```
var sURL = window.location.toString();
```

Building string arrays with the split() method

Once you've got your URL string, you can use the JavaScript `split()` method to store an array of substrings from the URL string you stored in the `sURL` variable. The `split()` method splits a string according to a delimiter you name as the method's argument. It stores each substring as part of an array, indexed in character sequence. This means you don't need to initialize an array with something like this:

```
var sDir = new Array();
```

Instead, you can initialize the array by using the `split()` method:

```
var sDir=sURL.split("/");
```

Remembering that array indexes are counted beginning with 0, not 1, if your URL is `http://www.mydomain.com/mydirectory/here`, the `split()` method used in the preceding code fragment will create an array that looks like this:

```
sDir[0] = http:
sDir[1] = www.mydomain.com
sDir[2] = mydirectory
sDir[3] = here
```

Next, initialize a variable to store your output string:

```
var sOutput="";
```

Then, create a JavaScript `for` loop to loop through the array. Note that the loop looks a little different than some loops you may have seen:

```
for (y=2;y<(sDir.length-1);y++)
```

What's different about this loop? Usually, you start such a loop with y=0 (or, more often, i=0, but i is simply the name of the new loop variable and we already are using that in another part of the code, as shown in Listing 26-1). Of course, in many instances you won't start a loop at an array's zero index value, and this is one of them, because you happen to know that the first two "splits" contain parts of the string related to the protocol (http:), and we don't want that or the first / of http://, either.

Listing 26-1: **Building a Simple Breadcrumbs Header**

```
<!DOCTYPE HTML PUBLIC "-//W3C//DTD HTML 4.01 Transitional//EN">
<html>
<head>
<script language="javascript">
function Nest(x)
{
    var x=x-3;
    var sNesting="";
    for (i=0;i<x;i++)
    {
        sNesting=sNesting + "../";
    }
    return sNesting;
}
function breadcrumbs()
{
    var sDir = new Array();
    var sURL = window.location.toString();
    sDir=sURL.split("/");
    var sOutput="";
    for (y=2;y<(sDir.length-1);y++)
    {
        sOutput=sOutput + " :: <a href='" +
Nest((sDir.length-y)+1) + "index.html'>" + sDir[y] + "</a>";
    }
    document.write(sOutput);
}
</script>
<style type="text/css">
<!--
body {
    font-family: Frutiger, Verdana, Arial, Helvetica, sans-
serif;
}
.breadcrumbs {

    font-size: 10px;
}
```

```
-->
</style>
<title>Breadcrumbs</title>
<meta http-equiv="Content-Type" content="text/html;
charset=iso-8859-1">
</head>
<body>
<div id="breadcrumbs" class="breadcrumbs">
<script language="javascript">
breadcrumbs();
</script>
</div>
<div style="border: navy 1px solid; padding: 12px; width:
440px; text-align:center; margin-top:12px;">
Here is some content.
</div>
</body>
</html>
```

Listing 26-1 shows the breadcrumb code in its entirety. Note that it appends an `index.html` to each directory (shown in bold in the listing), so you might have to change that to your directory's homepage. The final result is shown in Figure 26-2.

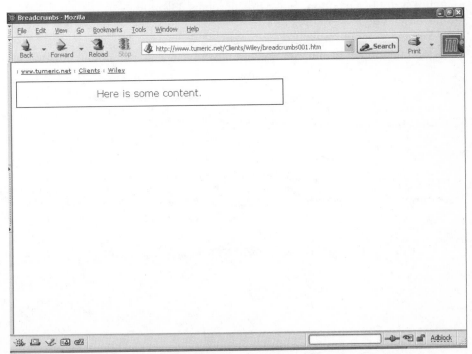

Figure 26-2: Breadcrumbs rendered in a browser using code from Listing 26-1.

If you look at Figure 26-2, you can see there is one thing about the results you might not like. It would be better to have a "dry" breadcrumb containing a nonactive link for the page the user is currently on. Accomplishing that takes some JavaScript sleight of hand, but luckily, resources are already available for you to work with, as you'll see in the next section.

Fine-tuning your breadcrumbs

One example of an Internet-based resource you can rely on for creating breadcrumbs is a GNU-based JavaScript file that is freely downloadable over the Internet, including through this book's Web site. This is a much more finely tuned example of a breadcrumb script that accounts for a large number of variables.

Note

GNU is an open source licensing model that allows you to freely distribute and modify software, with some minor legal constraints, such as giving credit to the author of the software. You can view GNU licensing terms at www.gnu.org/copyleft/gpl.html.

The file was written by Henning Poerschke of WebMediaConception.com. The downloadable file is called `js_paths.js`. The JavaScript is well documented, but you can find more information about it at http://webmediaconception.com/de/development/artikel/JS_breadcrumbs.en.html.

You'll need to make one change in the JS file you download. You will want to wrap the entire script in a function named breadcrumbs, like this:

```
function breadcrumbs() {
  //this is where the downloaded
script should go
}
```

In other words, you need to add the following line to the top of the script and a closing brace (}) to the end of the script:

```
function breadcrumbs() {
```

This turns the script into a function, which can then be called in the part of the page requiring the breadcrumbs. Listing 26-2 shows how to use it in your HTML.

Listing 26-2: **Using a Breadcrumbs JavaScript File**

```
<html>
<head>
<script language="JavaScript" type="text/javascript" src=" js_paths.js">
</script>
<title>Breadcrumbs</title>
<meta http-equiv="Content-Type" content="text/html; charset=iso-8859-1">
<style type="text/css">
```

```
<!--
body {
      font-family: Frutiger, Verdana, Arial, Helvetica, sans-serif;
}
.breadcrumbs {

   font-size: 10px;
}
-->
</style>
</head>

<body>
<div id="breadcrumbs" class="breadcrumbs">
<script>breadcrumbs()</script>
</div>
<div style="border: navy 1px solid; padding: 12px; width: 440px;
text-align:center; margin-top:12px;">
Here is some content.
</div>
</body>
</html>
```

As you can see in Listing 26-2, using the JavaScript is as simple as inserting a link to it in the head element of your HTML and calling it on the part of the page you need the breadcrumbs to display.

If you want to skip the step of giving the script a function name, you can simply import the script in the part of the page where you need the breadcrumbs to appear. Replace the bold script element in Listing 26-2 with this:

```
<script type="text/javascript" src="/js_paths.js"></script>
```

If you choose this method, don't import the JS file in the head element.

You might be wondering why to bother creating the breadcrumbs() function at all. It appears to be more work. If your Web page uses a lot of JavaScript, it's a good idea to import all your JavaScript in the page header and call functions as needed, because it gives you a more modular design. This is truer when working with a lot of JavaScript code. If you aren't using much JavaScript, you should simply use whichever method is most comfortable to you.

Rollovers

You've probably seen image rollovers and may know how to code them. This section shows you how to create rollovers using CSS. First, you'll see how easy rollovers can be with CSS that requires no scripting using the a:hover pseudo-class. Then, you'll see how to manipulate CSS properties in rollovers using JavaScript.

Creating rollovers using the a:hover pseudo-class

The easiest kind of rollover is to simply use CSS. You don't even need to use JavaScript. Instead, you can use the CSS `a:hover` pseudo-class to change the color or text size of an object. You can also change the background color or any other CSS property. This is all as simple as defining the `a:hover` pseudo-class within a stylesheet:

```
<style type="text/css">
<!--
.button {
   font-family: Verdana, Arial, Helvetica, sans-serif;
   background-color: #CCCCCC;
   padding: 3px;
   border: 1px solid;
}
a:hover {
   background-color: #FF0000;
}
-->
</style>
```

In the preceding code fragment, a button is defined in the `.button` class, and then a `background-color` property is defined for the `a:hover` pseudo-class. Whenever the `a:hover` pseudo-class is used, the properties of its target take on whatever you defined for it as soon as the user's mouse "hovers" over the object. However, you're not quite finished. Can you figure out why that CSS alone will not create the rollover on the following HTML?

```
<div><span class="button">Rollover1</span><span
class="button">Rollover2</span><span
class="button">Rollover3</span></div>
```

The `a:hover` pseudo-class works only on links, so you need to create a link for the desired effect to work. Listing 26-3 shows how to create the appropriate CSS and HTML to make the rollover effect work.

Listing 26-3: **Creating a Rollover Effect Using CSS**

```
<!DOCTYPE HTML PUBLIC "-//W3C//DTD HTML 4.01
Transitional//EN">
<html>
<head>
<title>Using the a:hover pseudo-class</title>
<meta http-equiv="Content-Type" content="text/html;
charset=iso-8859-1">
<style type="text/css">
<!--
.button {
   font-family: Verdana, Arial, Helvetica, sans-serif;
   background-color: #CCCCCC;
   padding: 3px;
   border: 1px solid;
   cursor:hand;
}
```

```
a:hover {
    background-color: #FF0000;
    text-decoration: none;
}
a {
text-decoration:none;

}
-->
</style>
</head>

<body>
<div><span class="button" title="Go to Rollover Land"><a
href="#">Rollover1</a></span><span class="button" title="Go
to Rollover Land"><a href="#">Rollover2</a></span><span
class="button" title="Go to Rollover Land"><a
href="#">Rollover3</a></span></div>
</body>
</html>
```

Note the link that is created for each button. Here, you simply assign a # identifier in lieu of a full link (but normally, of course, you'd insert a real URL). Note also that a `text-decoration` property is assigned to both the a element and the a-hover pseudo-class. This is done to avoid an underline being shown in the button. Finally, notice one additional bit of easy code that can make your links more dynamic. The `title` attribute is an underused HTML attribute that you can use on all HTML elements to add meaning to them. It's particularly useful on a elements. On browsers that support the `title` attribute, links are just that much more dynamic because when the mouse hovers over elements with title attribute values, a small "help" window, known as a *ToolTip*, appears, as shown in Figure 26-3.

Using display properties with a:hover to create rollovers

You can push the aforementioned concepts further by combining the a:hover with display properties to create genuine rollover effects. There is no JavaScript involved. They work because you can give an element a unique identifier through the id attribute and take advantage of the different kinds of styling mechanisms available to anchor tags. First, you define a div element to wrap around the a elements that serve as linked menu items, making sure to give the div element a unique identifier:

```
<div id="links">
<a href="http://www.tumeric.net/">Home<span> The Tumeric
Partnership</span></a>
<a
href="http://www.tumeric.net/Service/Default.aspx">XSL<span>
The Transformation Station is your one-stop source for gnarly
XSL Transformations.</span></a>
</div>
```

The first part of each link is displayed as a button. The second part of each link, contained in a span element, is the part that will appear below the menu item

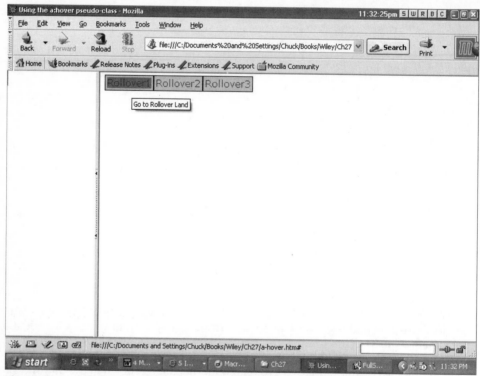

Figure 26-3: A ToolTip as rendered in a browser when the `title` attribute is used on a link.

dynamically when a user's mouse rolls over the button. This acts as a description of the link, and provides more information to the user. This is possible by declaring the following CSS rule for `div` elements with `link id` attribute values:

```
div#links a span {display: none;}
```

This tells the browser that no `span` elements contained within links that are themselves contained in `div` elements with `item id` attributes should be displayed. The `a:hover` pseudo-class can then be used to display that same `span` element's content when a user's mouse is "hovering" over the link:

```
div#links a:hover span {display: block;
    position: absolute; top: 80px; left: 0; width: 125px;
    padding: 5px; margin: 10px; z-index: 100;
    color: #AAAAAA; background: black;
    font: 10px Verdana, sans-serif; text-align: center;}
```

Change the value in bold in the preceding code to place exactly where you want your menu description to appear. You can download a running example of this from the downloadable code for this book. The file name is `cssrollover.htm`. Eric Meyer developed this and other similar CSS techniques, and a similar file and many more can be found on his Web site at `www.meyerweb.com/eric/css/edge/popups/demo.html`.

Creating rollovers using JavaScript

Creating rollovers using JavaScript can be as simple or as tedious as you wish it to be. Best practice would suggest that you should create rollovers, like any other JavaScript-based functionality, in a way that creates the least problems for the most users.

 Cross-Reference To learn how to create good old-fashioned, image-based rollovers, see Chapter 25.

You can take advantage of the narrowing gap in differences among browsers by relying on the event models of IE5/6 and Mozilla (and by extension Netscape 7). For example, the following bit of code creates a rollover of sorts that results in a JavaScript alert box display when a user mouses over a portion of text:

```
To use this rollover, <span style="color:red; cursor:hand;"
onMouseOver="alert('AMAZING!!!')">
mouse over these words</span>.
```

The result of this simple bit of code is shown in Figure 26-4.

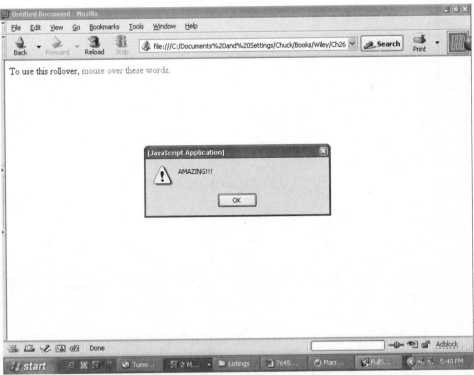

Figure 26-4: When a user mouses over a portion of text, an alert box is displayed.

Mozilla/Netscape 7 and IE5/6 allow all elements to use event handlers such as onmouseover. But because it's an attribute, browsers that don't support event handlers in all their elements will simply ignore the call to the JavaScript because they simply ignore the attribute itself. Keep this concept in mind when you're working with DHTML. In other words, try to limit the damage. The beauty of CSS is if you use it right, browsers that don't support CSS will simply ignore your styling, and the same is true for the use of event handlers in HTML. The same principle holds for CSS-based changes, even if you're using deprecated elements such as the font element (see Figure 26-5):

```
<a HREF="http://www.tumeric.net/" style="text-
decoration:none;">
<font color="#0000ff"
      onMouseOver="this.style.backgroundColor = '#cccccc'"
      onMouseOut="this.style.backgroundColor = '#ffffff'"
      title="Click Here!">The Tumeric Partnership</font></a>
```

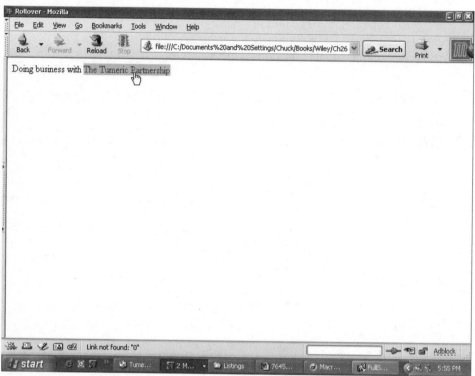

Figure 26-5: When a user mouses over a portion of text, the background color is changed.

In the old days of browser wars and incompatibilities, these examples would only work in Internet Explorer, but now they'll work in Mozilla-based browsers, too.

Note   Saying that something works in Mozilla-based browsers means browsers based on the new open source Mozilla 1.0 codebase governed by the Mozilla Public License and Netscape Public License. Mozilla versioning can be confusing, because JavaScript tests for user agents will reveal (on a Windows machine) something like this: Mozilla/5.0 (Windows; U; Windows NT 5.1; en-US; rv:1.5) for browsers implementing the Mozilla 1.0 codebase. This is because the Mozilla codebase was completely rewritten from scratch, and the old Navigator codebase was tossed into the ash heap forever.

Collapsible menus

Collapsible menus have become a staple in Web development, and you can generally avoid the hassle of creating your own from scratch by simply searching the Internet for something that is close to what you want; then make any adaptations necessary to reflect your own site's needs. Collapsible menus generally come in two styles:

✦ *Vertical menus that expand and collapse on the left side of a Web page and within a reasonably small space.* When a user clicks his or her mouse on an item, a group of one or more subitems is displayed, and, generally, remains displayed until the user clicks the main item again, which then collapses the tree.

✦ *Horizontal menus that live at the top of a page.* When a user rolls his or her mouse over an item, a group of one or more subitems is displayed, and, generally, disappears when the mouse loses focus on the item.

How they work

Generally, most collapsible menus rely on either the CSS `display` property or the CSS `visibility` property. The JavaScript used to manage these menus turns the visibility on or off depending on where a user's mouse is, or turns the display on or off to collapse or expand a menu. The difference between the `visibility` property and the `display` property is that when you hide an element's visibility, the element still takes up visible space in the browser document. When you turn the `display` property off by giving it a `none` value (`display="none"`), the space where the affected element lives collapses.

The other component to a DHTML menu is usually a JavaScript array containing all the menu items. For example, the JavaScript might contain a function for defining the menu's parameters:

```
function item(parent, text, depth) {
    this.parent = parent
    this.text = text
    this.depth = depth
}
```

When using a prewritten menu you acquire from the Internet, you'll generally want to look for a JavaScript array containing all the menu item parameters. In this case, the array would contain arguments for the previously defined function:

```
outline = new makeArray(6)

outline[0] = new item(true, 'SimplytheBest.net', 0)
outline[1] = new item(false, '<A HREF="shareware.html">Shareware &
```

```
Freeware</A>', 1)
outline[2] = new item(true, 'Scripts', 1)
outline[3] = new item(false, '<A HREF="javascripts/dhtml_scripts.html">DHTML
Scripts</A>', 2)
outline[4] = new item(false, '<A HREF="cgiscripts/cgiscripts.html">CGI
Scripts</A>', 2)
outline[5] = new item(false, '<A HREF="info/index.html">Information
library</A>', 1)
```

To edit the menu for your own purposes, you simply change the links in the array (shown in bold in the preceding code). Most menus are built using an array that's at least somewhat similar to the preceding one. Note the correlation between the first argument in the item function (parent) and the actual values used in the array. When an item's parent argument is true, instead of a link, the category of links is named and no actual link is generated. When the parent argument is false, a link is generated. Each menu you find on the Web might have a somewhat different implementation, but the general construction will be the same.

Finding collapsible menus on the Internet

As mentioned, you generally don't need to write your own menu from scratch, because so many developers have made them freely available. Instead, you can download someone else's menu and change the CSS and some of the other specifics, such as where the links go.

One common style used with vertical menus is a Windows Explorer-like menu tree. A very good example of this kind of menu can be found at www.webreference.com/ programming/javascript/trees/Example/example.htm.

You'll find an explanation of how the developer created these menus at www/ .webreference.comprogramming/javascript/trees/.

A good resource for a wide variety of DHTML menus can be found at http:// simplythebest.net/info/dhtml_menu_scripts.html.

The scripts on this site contain detailed instructions on how to use the menus on your own site. You can enter "DHTML menus" into Google to find additional menus.

Summary

DHTML can be very complex, and some very long tomes have been written on the subject. This chapter introduced the following topics:

✦ The Document Object Model (DOM)

✦ Cross-browser compatibility issues and browser detection

✦ DHTML examples such as breadcrumbs, rollovers, and collapsible menus

If you're not comfortable with scripting, you can find a wide variety of resources on the Internet for free scripts that you can adapt to your own needs with little JavaScript background. You also saw how you can avoid JavaScript altogether with some clever CSS manipulation. However, if you enjoy scripting or are already comfortable with it, you'll find that coding increasingly complex code against the Document Object Model will demonstrate that browsers can be software environments, and Web pages containers for very robust software applications.

In the next chapter, you'll see how DHTML can work more specifically with CSS. You learn more about how the DOM is used to access CSS properties, and how to display effects with no scripting.

✦   ✦   ✦

Dynamic HTML with CSS

◆　◆　◆　◆

In This Chapter

Dynamic HTML and the
Document Object Model

DHTML and CSS Properties

Internet Explorer Filters

◆　◆　◆　◆

CSS can be a powerful tool for creating dynamic pages with special effects. In this chapter, you'll see how you can change a CSS property dynamically in various browsers. You'll be introduced to Dynamic HTML, albeit briefly, as the next chapter serves as the real introduction to that concept. Here, you'll see how to access CSS properties and script them to perform tasks, such as change text colors. You'll see that every CSS property can be changed.

You'll also find that some browsers, most notably Internet Explorer, feature CSS-like syntax for creating dynamic filtered effects such as drop shadows and blurs.

Chapter 26 talked a lot about the Document Object Model (DOM) and objects, which can seem pretty daunting at first, so let's break it down to the simplest scale, that of CSS. Say you have a div element with a blue font inside it. To make the div (and its contents) accessible by script, you need to identify it somehow. You can do this using the id attribute of the <div> tag. The id attribute is available to every HTML element for this very reason. So you can write a div element like so:

```
<div id="myID" style="color:blue">I'm blue now, but I may
not be later.</div>
```

Notice that since the example uses CSS, there's no need to use the font element to color our text. Now, say you want to change the text to red. This is easy with the DOM and JavaScript, especially if you're using Internet Explorer 4 or above, because IE makes accessing the DOM just a tad easier than some other browsers do:

```
<div id="myID" style="color:blue; cursor:hand"
onclick="this.style.fontSize='60px'; this.style.color='red'">
I'm blue now, but I may not be later.</div>
```

If you load the preceding code fragment into Internet Explorer, your browser will render as shown in Figure 27-1.

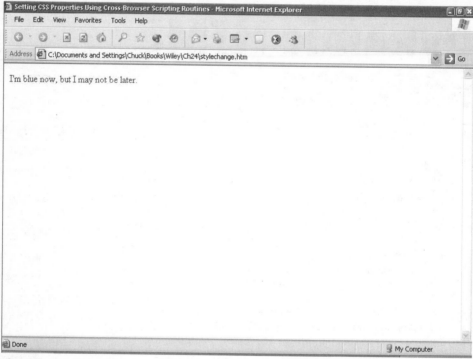

Figure 27-1: When this text styled in CSS is clicked, it will change.

Listing 27-1 shows some modification to the previous code fragment. This time, the `this` keyword isn't used because another `div` object is created, along with an `onClick` event handler for that `div` object. When the new `div` object is clicked, the text in the `div` object labeled by the `myID` attribute gets bigger and turns red.

Note   Listing 27-1 only works in IE4 and later and Mozilla/Netscape with Gecko engines (Netscape 7 and later).

Listing 27-1: Accessing an Element by Drilling Down the DOM Hierarchy

```
<html>
<head>
<title>Setting CSS Properties Using Cross-Browser Scripting
Routines</title>
</head>
<body>
<div  id="myID" style="color:blue;">
  <p>I'm blue now, but I may not be later.</p>
```

```
</div>
    <div style="width: 100px; padding: 4px; background-color:
#cccccc; border: blue outset 1px; cursor:hand">
        <div align="center"><a href="#" style="text-decoration:
none" title="Click to change font styles!"
onclick="myID.style.fontSize='60px';
myID.style.color='red'">Click
        here</a> </div>
    </div>
</body>
</html>
```

Notice in Listing 27-1 the relationship between the myID attribute and the code that is executed by the onclick event. Normally, you'll call a function from an onclick event. But you can also simply execute the script from the event handler, as well.

You can see the changes in Figures 27-2 and 27-3.

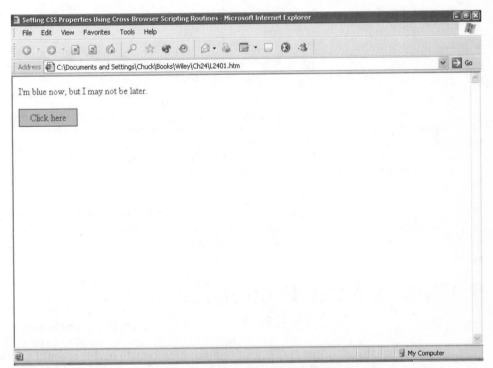

Figure 27-2: This text can be changed by clicking the Click Here button.

Cross-Reference More detailed information about function calls and other intricacies of event handling can be found in Chapter 15, *Scripts*, and Chapter 26, *DHTML*.

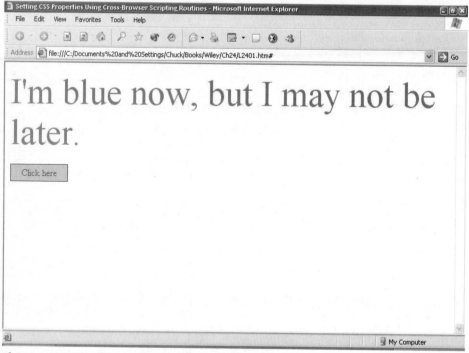

Figure 27-3: When the button is clicked, the text changes.

The solutions for changing CSS shown so far are of limited use because they rely on Gecko's and Internet Explorer's interpretation of the object model, the latter of which deviates quite substantially from that of the W3C object model. They both share the same core object model defined by the Document Object Model of the W3C. However, Internet Explorer expands on the DOM by a substantial amount.

Note For the full list of properties and methods available to the Internet Explorer object model, visit `http://msdn.microsoft.com/workshop/author/dhtml/reference/dhtml-reference-entry.asp`

DHTML and CSS Properties

What you've been seeing so far is that any object can be accessed using the Document Object Model, and one of those objects is the `style` object (in Internet Explorer). Unfortunately, as easy as the scripts you've seen so far seem to be, the real world makes things a little harder, because different browsers use different nomenclatures for their objects. For example, Gecko (the engine running current versions of Netscape) calls its stylesheet object `sheet`. On the other hand, older versions of Netscape, such as 4.0, use this kind of document traversal to access style sheet properties:

```
document.tags.p.fontSize
```

In order to account for all the differences in syntax between browsers, you need to set up browser sniffing routines which, as mentioned in the previous chapter, are chunks of code that check to see what kind of browser is accessing a Web page and executes the appropriate code. You'll see how this works in the next section.

Setting CSS properties using JavaScript

Navigator 4.x, Netscape 6, Mozilla, and Internet Explorer make CSS1 properties of elements accessible from JavaScript through their Document Object Model. However, the Navigator 4.x DOM and Internet Explorer DOM are different. They both implement parts of the W3C CSS1 standards, but they cover different areas, so JavaScript code that defines CSS1 rules on one browser won't work on other browsers. The Gecko layout engine covers all of the properties in W3C CSS1 standards.

To define CSS1 rules from JavaScript and have them work in Navigator 4.x, Netscape 6, Mozilla, and Internet Explorer, you need to do the following things:

1. Insert an empty style element into the document's `head` and give it a unique ID through the use of the `id` attribute. Then, later, you'll be able to change the properties of the style element.

2. In the `head` element, place the JavaScript for defining your CSS1 rules in a script element so it executes before the body element is loaded into the browser window. This is to make Navigator 4.x play nice, because in Navigator 4.z no "Dynamic CSS" will be rendered until you reload the page.

3. Use a browser sniffing routine as shown in bold in Listing 27-2. Note that the key aspect of this routine is a series of "if" statements. *If* the browser is Netscape 4, do one thing, and *if* the browser is IE, do another. Notice also the use again of dot syntax to access the browser name through the use of the `userAgent` property of the navigator object to determine the browser name.

On Navigator 4.x, the JavaScript is as follows:

```
document.tags.P.fontSize="25pt";
```

On Internet Explorer, the following is executed:

```
document.styleSheets["MyID"].addRule ("P", "fontSize:25pt");
```

On user agents implementing Gecko, the following statement is executed:

```
document.getElementById('tssxyz').sheet.insertRule('P @@ta { fontSize:
25pt }',
document.getElementById('tssxyz').sheet.cssRules.length )
@@ta is evaluated.
```

The final code should look something like Listing 27-2.

Listing 27-2: **Setting CSS Properties Using a Cross-Browser Script**

```
<<html>
<head>
<title>Setting CSS Properties Using Cross-Browser Scripting
Routines</title>
<STYLE ID="MyID" TYPE="text/css">
.MyClass {}
</STYLE>

<SCRIPT LANGUAGE="JavaScript1.2"><!--
function changeIt() {
NewSize = 20;
var agt=navigator.userAgent.toLowerCase();
if ( (parseInt(navigator.appVersion)==4) &&
     (agt.indexOf('mozilla')!=-1) &&
(agt.indexOf('spoofer')==-1)
&& (agt.indexOf('compatible') == -1) ) {
document.tags.H1.color="red";
document.tags.p.fontSize=NewSize;
document.classes.MyClass.all.color="green";
document.classes.MyClass.p.color="blue";
}
 else if (agt.indexOf('gecko') != -1) {
document.getElementById('MyID').sheet.insertRule('p
@@ta { font-size: ' + NewSize + ' }',

document.getElementById('MyID').sheet.cssRules.length )
document.getElementById('MyID').sheet.insertRule('.MyClass
@@ta { color: purple }',
document.getElementById('MyID').sheet.cssRules.length )
document.getElementById('MyID').sheet.insertRule('p.MyClass
@@ta { color: blue }',
document.getElementById('MyID').sheet.cssRules.length )
}
else if ( (parseInt(navigator.appVersion)>=4) &&
     (agt.indexOf('msie') != -1) ) {
document.styleSheets["MyID"].addRule ("p", "font-size:"
@@ta + NewSize);
document.styleSheets["MyID"].addRule (".MyClass",
@@ta "color:purple");
document.styleSheets["MyID"].addRule ("p.MyClass",
@@ta "color:blue");
}
}
//--></SCRIPT>

</head>
<body>
<div style="width: 100px; padding: 4px; background-color:
#cccccc; border: blue outset 1px; cursor:hand">
    <div align="center"><a href="#" style="text-decoration:
none" title="Click to change font styles!"
onClick="changeIt();">Click
    here</a> </div>
```

```
</div>
<p class="MyClass">
Here is some test script in a P element
</p>
<div class="MyClass">
Here is some test script in a P element
</div>
</body>
</html>
```

Listing 27-2 is a boilerplate of sorts. You could do a lot of different things that are relevant to specific browsers with it by replacing the code that gets executed between the braces in an if statement, as shown in bold in the following example:

```
if ( (parseInt(navigator.appVersion)==4) &&
      (agt.indexOf('mozilla')!=-1) &&
(agt.indexOf('spoofer')==-1)
              && (agt.indexOf('compatible') == -1) ) {
  //do something here
}
```

You can see in Figures 27-4 and 27-5 that clicking the Click Me button achieves the same kind of effects obtained through Listing 27-1, but this time the changes will work in most other browsers.

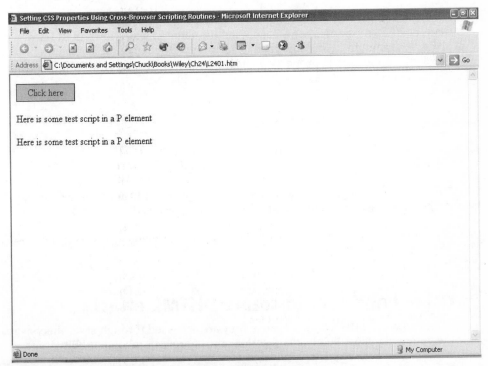

Figure 27-4: This text can be changed in different browsers.

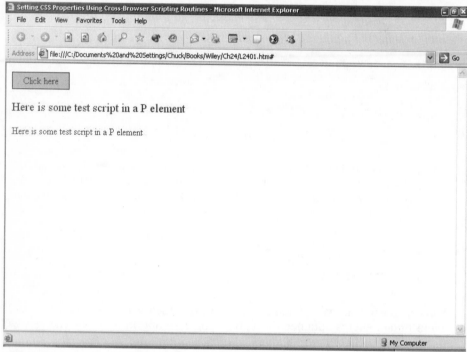

Figure 27-5: A cross-browser script lets the user change the text by clicking a button.

Generally, CSS properties are all accessed the same way as shown in the two preceding examples. CSS properties in script tend to map out in such a way that if there is a hyphen in the property name, to access the property in script you delete the hyphen and upper case the next letter, like this:

```
font-size
```

becomes

```
fontSize
```

Therefore, you can perform tasks such as change visibility and create dynamic menus quite easily by manipulating CSS scripting properties.

Cross-Reference For examples of hierarchical dynamic menus and changing object visibility, refer back to Chapter 26.

Using behaviors to create DHTML effects

Internet Explorer Behaviors, because they are accessed through style sheets, create the potential to completely avoid serious cross-browser incompatibility issues. When calling even highly complicated scripting routines, if you bind your routines to behavior selectors in style sheets, you might never need to worry about the ubiquitous JavaScript error codes that occur so often when users access your site with non-IE browsers.

Behaviors can expose the XML object model as well as a number of other models and controls, including COM and ActiveX. Yet, because they're designed to be exposed through style sheets, browsers and operating systems that don't support COM won't throw a fit when you use them, because they'll be accessed only by browsers that support the controls you are calling. This is all possible without any direct referencing to the `navigator` object, the tried and true method of redirecting those you didn't want accessing certain pages.

The syntax for a behavior looks like this:

```
.myBehavior {behavior: url(value)}
```

You may remember the syntax for other style sheet selectors that call on URLs to do their work, such as the background selector. The behavior selector operates on the same principle by binding a URL to the Web page, exposing the Web page to whatever methods and properties are residing in the URL source being referred to. Specifically, the bound source is a `scriptlet` (thus, the `.sct` extension):

```
.myBehavior {behavior: url(myScriptlet.sct)}
```

Note A scriptlet is different than an imported JavaScript because it is specific to Microsoft browsers and is designed specifically to work with behaviors.

If you are using an Active X or COM control, you would specify it as such:

```
.myBehavior { behavior:url(#myObject)}
```

In this case, `myObject` must be accessed in the HTML file by an `<OBJECT>` tag:

```
<OBJECT ID=myObject ... ></OBJECT><UL>
<DIV CLASS="myBehavior">my text, your text</DIV>
```

Internet Explorer Filters

IE includes a variety of dynamic effects in a browser-safe way that won't send browsers that don't support them crashing into a heap. The reason for this is that they use CSS-like syntax. If a browser doesn't support the syntax, the CSS code that implements a given effect is simply ignored.

What follows is a closer examination of how to apply various visual effects through IE's extension to CSS2 style sheets. None of the properties that follow are part of the CSS2 specification—rather, they are extensions that are specific to Internet Explorer beginning with IE4 and, in the case of behaviors, IE5.

Filters

If you've ever worked in a paint program you're familiar with filters and their effects. IE4 and IE have introduced them to the world of Web browsing through a set of controls that come packaged and install with the program. You can access them through style sheets, although not through CSS2 style sheets, but, instead, style sheet extensions that are compatible only with IE4 and IE. There are several kinds of filters, all of which fall into two basic categories: static and dynamic.

Static filters are visual filters that create effects such as drop shadows, transparencies, and glows. These visual filters are called static not because they can't be made dynamic (they can through just a small amount of scripting code), but because their siblings, transition filters, are dynamic effects that create an effect during a transition of some kind, such as hiding or showing a layer, or the loading of a new page into the browser. In fact, the easiest kind of filter to create is a filter that produces an effect, such as a wipe or a fade, as a page loads. The code is simply plunked into a meta tag, and therefore cannot load an error message into browsers that don't support it.

Like any other style sheet property, filters can be applied using event handlers. This can help committed developers who want to produce interesting projects for use over the Web.

It's easy to determine if a particular HTML element can react to filter effects. Generally, if the HTML element is a windowless container, you'll be able to apply a filter to it. `frame` and `iframe`, then, are out, and `div` and `img` are in. When using `div` or `span`, it is imperative that you include at least one positioning property in its definition. In other words, in its style sheet, indicate either the height or width of the `div` or `span` element, or its left and right position.

Valid HTML filter elements

The following list shows which elements you can apply filters to.

- ✦ BODY
- ✦ BUTTON
- ✦ DIV (with a defined height, width, or absolute positioning)
- ✦ IMG
- ✦ INPUT
- ✦ MARQUEE
- ✦ SPAN (with a defined height, width, or absolute positioning)
- ✦ TABLE
- ✦ TD
- ✦ TEXTAREA

✦ TFOOT

✦ TH

✦ THEAD

✦ TR

The following section begins with a look at filters with the visual filters that are applied through style sheets, followed by a look at the light and visual transition filters.

Visual filters

There are several static filter controls that come as a part of the IE package, the definitions of which follow. They're easy to use with style sheet selectors, although the actual rendering of some is better than others. Some of them, such as glow, can be quite impressive, whereas the drop shadow effect may remind you of the infamous `<BLINK>` tag. All visual filters follow the same general syntax: a CSS-like selector followed by a value consisting of the filter name and a series of its required parameters.

```
{ filter: value(parameter, parameter)}
```

alpha

You know what an *alpha channel* is, even if you think you don't. Any graphic file format that is capable of rendering a transparency or varying degrees of opacity has an alpha channel. In IE, the alpha channel sets the opacity level of an object. Using the optional `startx(y)` and `finishx(y)` values allows you to create a gradient, as in the following syntax.

```
{filter: alpha(Opacity=value, FinishOpacity=value, Style=value,
StartX=value, StartY=value, FinishX=value, FinishY=value)}
```

Valid parameter values are as follows:

✦ 0 to 100 for opacity, where 0 is transparent and 100 is opaque

✦ 0 to 100 for the optional parameter `FinishOpacity`

✦ A value of 0 (uniform), 1 (linear), 2 (radial), or 3 (rectangular) for the style parameter, which sets the gradient shape

✦ An x or y value for the `StartX`, `StartY`, `FinishX`, and `FinishY` values.

For example:

```
H1 {filter: alpha (20)}
H2 {filter: alpha (20, 100, 1, 10, 10, 200, 300)}
```

As you might have surmised, you obviously would need to set all of the gradient values if you set the `FinishOpacity` value.

blur

This filter creates a movement across the screen according to the parameters you set for it, and has the following syntax:

```
{ filter: blur(add=value, direction=value, strength=value, )}
```

Valid parameter values are as follows:

✦ The boolean values true and false for add, which tell IE whether or not to add the original image to the blur

✦ A direction value of a point of a round path around the object (the value must be a multiple of 45 within a 360-degree path)

✦ A strength value that is represented by an integer, indicating the number of pixels affected by the blur (a default of 5)

These parameters are represented in the following example:

```
H1 {filter: blur (false, 45, 20)}
```

chroma

This filter creates a transparency level out of a specific named color and has the following syntax:

```
{ filter: chroma(color)}
```

No parameters are needed with this filter—the only needed value is the color, named as a hexadecimal color. This is not a reliable filter for any image that has been subject to dithering, either as a result of antialiasing, or a reduction in the size of its color palette from 24-bit to 8-bit, including JPEG, but is rather best used on an image that was created with a Web safe color palette in the first place, as in the following example:

```
H1 {filter: chroma (#ff3399)}
```

dropShadow

This filter creates a movement across the screen according to the parameters you set for it, and has the following syntax:

```
{FILTER: dropShadow(Color=value, OffX=value, OffY=value,
Positive=value)}
```

Valid parameter values are as follows:

✦ Hexadecimal color values for color

✦ A positive or negative integer for offx and offy, which indicates how many pixels along a horizontal (x) and vertical (y) axis the drop shadow is offset

✦ A zero or nonzero value for the parameter positive, which indicates whether or not to pick up transparent pixels for the drop shadow (0, false, is yes; any other number, true, is no, because the value is actually inquiring about nontransparent pixels, so if you want a drop shadow for a fully transparent object, you should set this value to 0.)

Here is an example using some of the parameters:

```
H1 {filter: dropShadow (#336699, 8, 8)}
```

Listing 27-3 shows how to build a drop shadow, and Figure 27-6 shows how it looks rendered in a browser.

Listing 27-3: **Building a Drop Shadow Filter**

```
<html>
<head>
<title>Using a Drop Shadow</title>
</head>
<body>
<DIV style = " font-size:50px; position: absolute; top: 20; left:15;
width:440px; height: 148; font-family: sans-serif; color: #FF9966;
filter: dropShadow (#336699, 1, 1)">
Here is a drop shadow.
</div>
</body>
</html>
```

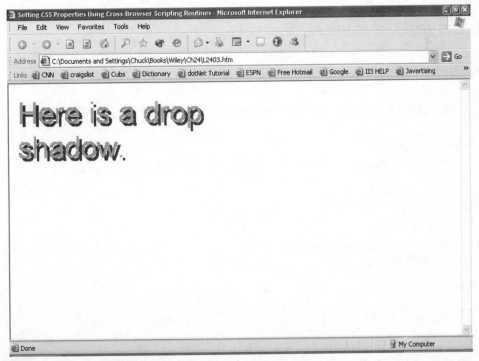

Figure 27-6: A Drop Shadow rendered in a browser.

flipV

This filter flips an object along a horizontal plane. It has the following syntax:

```
{ filter: flipV}
```

This filter takes no parameters, as reflected in the following example:

```
H1 {filter: flipV}
```

flipH

This filter flips an object along a vertical plane. It has the following syntax:

```
{ filter: flipH}
```

This filter takes no parameters, as reflected in the following example:

```
H1 {filter: flipH}
```

Glow

This filter creates a glow around the outside pixels of an object. It has the following syntax:

```
{FILTER: Glow(Color=color, Strength=strength)}
```

Valid parameter values are a hexadecimal number for the color value, and a value of 1-255 for the strength value, which represents the intensity of the glow. The following example shows a strength value of 200:

```
H1 {filter: glow (#333399, 200)}
```

gray

This filter removes the color information from an object. It has the following syntax:

```
{filter: gray}
```

This filter takes no parameters, as reflected in the following example:

```
H1 {filter: gray}
```

invert

This filter reverses the values of an object's hue, saturation, and brightness. It has the following syntax:

```
{filter: invert}
```

This filter takes no parameters, as reflected in the following example:

```
H1 {filter: invert}
```

light ()

The light filter can produce not only some fun effects, but can enhance a page visually, as well. The light filter has numerous methods you can call on for some special effects. The various methods you can call on are listed in the next sections.

addAmbient

The addAmbient filter adds an ambient light source to an object. When the light filter is first applied via a style sheet, a default addAmbient light method is applied that results in a black box. The syntax is as follows:

```
object.filters.Light.addAmbient(R,G,B,strength)
```

The parameters, in parentheses, must be in the order shown.

addCone

By naming a variety of values, you can position a cone light source to act as a kind of spotlight on a particular portion of an element or image. Here is the syntax for this filter method:

```
object.filters.Light.addCone(x1,y1,z1,x2,y2,R,G,B,strength,spread)
```

Valid cone parameters (in this order) include the following:

✦ x1 is the light's starting point, or source position on the x axis

✦ y2 is the light's starting point, or source position on the y axis

✦ z1 is the light's starting point, or source position on the z axis

✦ x2 is the light's target point, or target position on the x axis

✦ y2 is the light's target point, or target position on the x axis

Unlike many other filter calls, valid color ranges are defined as base-10 RGB ranges, rather than as hexadecimals.

```
(0-255) Red
(0-255) Green
(0-255) Blue
```

And in degrees:

```
(0-255) Strength
(0-90) Spread Angle
```

You can only add a total of three cones to one image. In some versions of IE4, even if you only add three cones, if the user clicks a fourth time, an error message is generated.

addPoint

The addPoint filter adds a more finely focused area of light to an element than the addCone method. To use this method, follow this syntax:

```
object.filters.Light.addPoint(x,y,z,R,G,B,strength)
```

changeColor

The changeColor filter changes light color using the following syntax:

```
object.filters.Light.changeColor(lightnumber, r,g,b,
zero/nonzero)
```

`lightnumber` refers to the indexed number in the collection. Zero/nonzero refers to a nonzero or zero (0) number, with zero changing the color in an increment specified in the r, g, b parameters, and a nonzero number setting the color to the value indicated.

changeStrength

This filter changes light strength. To use it, follow the syntax shown here:

```
object.filters.Light.changeStrength(lightnumber, strength,
zero/nonzero
```

A zero/nonzero value of zero (0) results in an incremental or decremental change in strength value, and a value of nonzero results in a new strength set to the value indicated.

Clear

Clear deletes all the lights from the object, and has the following syntax.

```
object.filters.Light.Clear
```

moveLight

Moves a light source to a position indicated in the method's parameters. The syntax looks like this:

```
object.filters.Light.moveLight(lightnumber, x, y, z, boolean)
```

`boolean` is a true/false operation, indicating whether the movement is absolute or relative to the source's original position. False means absolute; true means relative.

mask

Mask creates a stencil-like effect of an object by painting the object's transparent pixels and converting its nontransparent pixels into transparent ones. It has the following syntax:

```
{Filter: mask(Color=value)}
```

Valid parameter value is a hexadecimal number for the color value; which indicates the color that the transparent areas should be painted, as shown in the following example:

```
H1 {filter: mask (#333399)}
```

shadow

This shadow filter creates a border around one of its edges to simulate a shadow. It has the following syntax:

```
{ filter: shadow(color=value, direction=value)}
```

Valid parameter values are hexadecimal RGB values for color and a direction value of a point of a round path around the object (the value must be a multiple of 45 within a 360-degree path).

```
H1 {filter: shadow(#333333, 45)}
```

wave

The wave filter creates a sine wave across the vertical plane of an object. It has the following syntax:

```
{ filter: wave(add=value, freq=value, lightStrength=value,
phase=value, strength=value, )}
```

Valid parameter values are as follows:

✦ The boolean values `true` and `false` for `add` tell IE whether or not to add the original image to the filter effect.

✦ A frequency value is denoted by an integer that indicates the number of waves.

✦ A value ranging from 1-100 indicates the strength of the light being used in the filter.

✦ A phase value between 1-100 indicates the offset percentage vis-a-vis the wave.

✦ A strength value denotes the intensity of the wave represented as an integer.

You can see these parameters in the following example:

```
H1 {filter: wave (false,10, 45, 20, 50)}
```

x-ray

This filter reduces an image to a black and white format to resemble an x-ray. It has the following syntax:

```
{ filter: Xray}
```

This filter takes no parameters, as reflected in the following example:

```
{filter: xray}
```

Reveal transition filter

This is a personal favorite of mine, mostly because I am inherently lazy, and, though not actually accessed by a style sheet, you can develop a nice page transition by simply writing it in the meta tag at the beginning of a document. The revealtrans filter has the following syntax:

```
{filter: revealtrans(duration=value, transition=value)}
```

Possible values include a floating-point number as a duration value and an integer for the type of transition you want. There are several kinds of transitions an object or page can make as it reveals itself. These transitions are listed in Table 27-1.

Table 27-1 Possible Transitions	
Transition	**Value**
Box in	0
Box out	1
Circle in	2
Circle out	3
Wipe up	4
Wipe down	5
Wipe right	6
Wipe left	7
Vertical blinds	8
Horizontal blinds	9
Checkerboard across	10
Checkerboard down	11
Random dissolve	12
Split vertical in	13
Split vertical out	14
Split horizontal in	15
Split horizontal out	16
Strips left down	17
Strips left up	18
Strips right down	19
Strips right up	20
Random bars horizontal	21
Random bars vertical	22
Random	23

Two of the possible transition values are used in the following example:

```
.filter {filter: revealtrans(duration=10, transition=22)}
```

This style sheet creates a transition that can be applied to whatever HTML element takes the class name "filter." You can also apply a transition page to a page as it is loaded or as it exits the page:

```
<META HTTP-EQUIV="Page-Enter"
CONTENT="RevealTrans(Duration=5,Transition=2)">
```

Simply include this in your head tag along with any other meta tags you might have. Browsers that don't support the transition will simply ignore it. You can also write a transition that creates the effect as the browser unloads the page:

```
<META HTTP-EQUIV="Page-Exit"
CONTENT="RevealTrans(Duration=5,Transition=2)">
```

In fact, it's been my experience that this tends to work better than the pages that have the Page-Enter attribute.

Summary

This chapter introduced you to using Dynamic HTML with CSS. You discovered that each CSS property is scriptable, and that you can even create dynamic effects without script. Specifically, this chapter covered the following topics:

✦ An introduction to the Document Object Model

✦ DHTML and CSS properties

✦ Internet Explorer filters

So far, you've seen how client-side scripting, which depends on a browser's capabilities, can be used to take advantage of a browser's scripting support to make changes to Web pages on the fly. In the next chapter, you'll see how many developers remove this dependency by using server-side scripting, which allows you to create scripting routines on the server to dynamically produce HTML based on things such as user input or even user location. You'll see that when using server-side scripting, you can worry less about browser support because you generate basic HTML, and the "dynamic" qualities of Web page behavior are handled by the server.

✦   ✦   ✦

Introduction to Server-Side Scripting

Earlier in this book, you learned the ins and outs of delivering fairly static data via HTML, CSS, and related technologies. Chapters 25–27 introduced you to client-side scripting and how it can be used to automate documents. However, client-side scripting is fairly limited in scope and resources. It cannot, for example, query a database and display unique content driven by the query. Enter the world of server-side scripting—higher level programs that can run on a Web server to extend its capabilities. This chapter introduces the server-side scripting concept and the most popular options for accomplishing server-side scripting.

> **Note**
>
> Due to the complexity of the server-side scripting subject, it is outside the scope of this book to actually teach any server-side scripting. To do so would require several chapters for each different technology/language presented here. This chapter is only designed to introduce the concept and to give you the various options available for server-side scripts.

How Web Servers Work

A *Web server* is a patient program that sits on your server (that is, the physical machine dedicated to serving pages and performing other server functions) waiting to receive an HTTP request via TCP/IP.

Any server configured to handle communications via TCP/IP (the Internet's communications protocol) has ports. These aren't physical ports, like the serial port and parallel ports on the back of your computer, but they serve the same purpose. All HTTP requests come through port 80 unless the server has been configured differently. Port 80 is the default Web server port. This is how your server, which may be a file server, an applications server, and an FTP server, in addition to being a Web server, keeps it all straight.

When an HTTP request comes through port 80 to the Web server, the Web server finds the page requested, checks the permissions of the client making the request, and, if the client has the appropriate permission, serves the page. Figure 28-1 illustrates the request process.

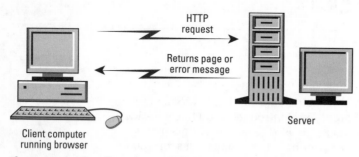

Figure 28-1: The client requests the page. Then the server evaluates the request and serves the page or an error message.

Generally, HTTP requests are anonymous. What this really means is an account has been created on the Web server for HTTP requests. When a request comes through port 80, it is assumed to come from this account. Each file on the Web server has certain permissions associated with it. If the HTTP account has adequate permission to read that page, and the page isn't otherwise protected, the Web server will serve that page.

Server-side scripting fills many gaps and can be used for the following purposes:

✦ *"Intelligent" page generation.* The contents of a page can be determined by the user—via previously established preferences, database queries, and so on.

✦ *Form verification and handling.* In Chapter 23 you learned how JavaScript can be used to do basic form validation. However, using server-side scripts the form data can be validated at a much more detailed level—data verified against database content, run through credit card processors, and so on.

✦ *Dynamic page generation.* Because most server-side scripting languages can interface with databases, generating dynamic content is fairly easy using server-side scripting. This concept is covered in more detail in Chapter 29.

You can run server-side scripts via several different methods:

✦ They can be run by specifying the script in a standard URL format, such as www.example.com/dosomething.cgi.

✦ They can be called from another script or static page by using a form action:

```
<form action="validate.cgi" method="POST">
```

✦ They can be called from another script or static page by using a link:

```
The results of the survey can be found
<a href="results.cgi">here</a>.
```

In any case, the Web server must know how to handle server-side script requests—calling a CGI page (for example, `validate.cgi`) via any method will only cause an error in the server unless it knows how to process the request.

In the case of most server-side scripts, the Web server simply turns over processing of the script to an interpreter or the operating system. The script is executed in a separate environment, able to draw upon other resources but still have its output sent to the HTTP client.

 Note The concept of using external resources to process scripts is covered in the *Common Gateway Interface* section later in this chapter.

Market-Leading Web Servers

Several different Web servers are in use today. Many of these servers are single-purpose applications, providing an HTTP interface into peripherals, applications, or appliances.

In the mainstream HTTP server world, two programs reign supreme: The Apache Software Foundation's HTTP Server (Apache) and Microsoft's Internet Information Server (IIS).

Apache

The Apache Software Foundation is a group that provides support for the Apache community of Open Source projects. Included in those projects is the Foundation's HTTP Server Project (commonly referred to as Apache). Apache gets its name from the way it was originally developed. Originally, the server was made of several components or "patches," making it "a patchy server."

Apache was one of the earliest developed Web servers and still undergoes continual development and improvement. Bug and security fixes take only days to find and correct, making Apache the most stable and secure Web server available.

Another advantage of rapid development and releases is the robust feature set. New Internet technologies can be deployed in Apache much more quickly than in other Web servers.

Apache continues to implement its features with distinct pieces, or *modules*. Utilizing a modular approach to feature implementation enables Apache to be deployed with only the amount of overhead necessary for the features you want. It also facilitates third parties developing their own modules to support their own technologies.

Apache supports almost all Internet Web technologies, including proprietary solutions such as Microsoft's FrontPage extensions. Apache supports all manner of HTTP protocols, scripting, authentication, and platform integration.

Tip   Visit the Apache module Web site (http://modules.apache.org) for information on the modules included with Apache and the registered third-party modules.

Apache is available for many platforms, including Windows, UNIX, and Linux. It is estimated that more than 70% of Web servers on the Internet are Apache servers.

IIS

Microsoft's Internet Information Server is Microsoft's answer to serving HTTP content. Developed in early 1995, IIS was designed to provide HTTP deployed content on Microsoft NT servers. Although standard Web deployed documents (HTML, and so on) were part of the IIS design, the server was created to integrate more fully into Microsoft's server products—deploying a litany of Microsoft technology.

IIS continues to evolve with each release of Microsoft's server platforms. A handful of new capabilities are included in the newest IIS versions, including the ability to act as sophisticated media servers, but the underlying structure is still HTTP deliverable content.

Note   Microsoft technologies offer a double-edged sword to the Internet. The Web owes a lot to Microsoft's development of both server and client technologies. However, some of the technologies come in proprietary packages unavailable to non-Microsoft platforms. For example, Active Server Pages (ASP) redefined interactivity on the Web, providing a near-Windows-like graphical user experience. However, ASP technology is only available on Microsoft server platforms.

Because IIS runs on Windows, controlling the server is accomplished through the use of standard Windows components and management consoles. However, as of this writing, IIS is still only available on Microsoft server platforms (NT/2000 Server/2003 Server).

The Need for Server-Side Scripting

As you saw in Chapter 25, JavaScript and other client scripting languages are very limited in the amount of resources available to the script. As a general rule, client-side scripts can only access the user agent's features (usually a very limited set of the features) and the document's content. Although such capabilities are enough for simple automation and driving dynamic formatting, such limitations leave much to be desired. More robust content requires more robust tools.

Server-side scripts are so named because they run on the server instead of in the client's user agent. As such, server-side scripts can have access to all resources that the Web server and its underlying platform (operating system and hardware) have access to. Database content, hardware peripherals, robust data storage, and more are all available to server-side scripts.

Most server scripting languages perform their magic in the background, without the user being aware that they are there. The Web server executes the script, which accesses databases, peripherals, or other servers, and passes any output from the script on to the user agent for display.

For example, point your browser at an online shopping mecca such as Amazon.com. Several different server-side scripts are responsible for the content you see on every page. Some scripts provide the advertising banners, others provide the specials of the day, while others handle the searching and browsing requests.

Server-side scripting offers another benefit that might not be readily apparent—the ability to communicate between user agents. Online Web-chat and other such services utilize server-side scripts and applications to accomplish their magic.

Server-Side Scripting Languages

Several different scripting languages are available for use on Web servers—more are appearing each day. This section describes the most popular languages and technologies in use today.

Common Gateway Interface

The Common Gateway Interface (CGI) was developed as a standard way for programs to talk to a Web server, thereby extending the server's capabilities. The CGI specification allows most programming languages to interact with Web servers. As long as a language can accomplish the following tasks, it is a viable CGI platform:

✦ Read from standard input

✦ Write to standard output

✦ Read from environment variables

Tip
Just because a programming language *can* be used to implement CGI doesn't mean that it *should* be used. There are several security concerns relating to using CGI with a Web server. Many of the more common CGI-capable languages have built-in security components and therefore are safer to use. Other, unproven languages (operating system, macro languages, and so on) can present the outside world with more access to your server and underlying file system than you intend.

The most common CGI languages are C and Perl. The former is a compiled language, that is, it needs to be converted to a binary program before it can be run. The latter is an interpreted language—interpreted languages are converted into binary programs on the fly, as they are run.

> **Note** Keep in mind that a program must output data in a form recognized by the user's interface, typically a Web browser. For example, a CGI program used to render an HTML document must pass the correct MIME type and document type definition as well as encapsulate its output in appropriate HTML tags.

Each type of programming language (compiled/interpreted) has distinct advantages and disadvantages. Compiled languages tend to be faster executing, but require the extra compilation step to be deployed. Interpreted languages are a bit slower, but provide a little more flexibility during development.

> **Note** A great online resource for CGI scripting is the CGI Resource Index (www.cgi-resources.com).

Several varieties of C are available for Windows and Linux platforms. Likewise, Perl is available for most platforms.

ASP, .NET, and Microsoft's technologies

As with most technologies, Microsoft has made several noteworthy achievements in creating tools and deployment solutions for the Internet. The latest initiative, .NET (pronounced dot-net), provides a solid platform to develop and deploy solutions over the Internet using Microsoft technology.

Microsoft's earliest contributions to the Web were in the form of Active Server Pages (ASP) and ActiveX controls. ASP is Microsoft's answer to CGI, allowing their programming languages to be used to extend a Web server's capabilities. ActiveX controls extended the interactivity possible in Web pages by providing standard, Windows-like controls for users to interact with data on the Web. An example of a complex ActiveX control is provided in Figure 28-2, which shows the interface for a popular network camera.

> **Note** ActiveX controls only loosely fit into the scheme of server-side scripting, because they are actually downloaded and used by the client instead of the server. They are mentioned here for a sense of completeness and because they provide a viable option for extending the capabilities of the Web.

For the most part, ASP operates much like standard CGI, incorporating programs to extend a server's capabilities. For example, the following code uses Visual Basic to store a value that is later output within an HTML document:

```
<%@ Page Language="VB" %>
<%
HelloWorld.InnerText = "Hello World!"
%>

<!DOCTYPE HTML PUBLIC "-//W3C//DTD HTML 4.01//EN"
    "http://www.w3.org/TR/html4/strict.dtd">
```

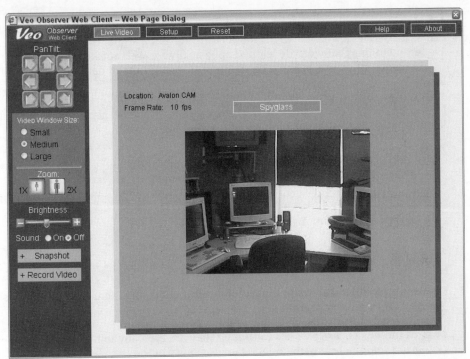

Figure 28-2: The ActiveX control used by a popular network camera to allow control of the camera over the Internet.

```
<html>
<head>
<title>Hello World ASP Sample</title>
</head>
<body>

<p id="HelloWorld" runat="server"></p>

</body>
</html>
```

This simple example only scratches the surface of the power behind ASP. More complex code could look up data in a database and present it in tabular format or perform other complex operations whose results could then be presented in HTML, using the same method as shown previously.

To use ASP (and the latest ASP.NET) requires a Microsoft Server running IIS along with the various pieces of ASP and .NET technologies. A good tutorial for getting up and running with ASP appears on the ASP101.com Web site, at www.asp101.com/lessons/install.asp.

Note   The ASP101 Web site is a great resource for all things ASP-related—tutorials, sample code, and more (www.asp101.com).

PHP

PHP is a relative newcomer to the server-side scripting arena. However, it is one of the few solutions that were developed specifically for Web automation. As such, it has the most robust set of features for presenting all kinds of data in Web-friendly formats.

Hypertext Preprocessor (*PHP* for short) is essentially a general-purpose scripting language with the following features:

✦ Based on open source technologies

✦ The capability to run before the resulting page is displayed

✦ A Perl-like structure and syntax

✦ Robust HTTP handling capabilities

✦ The capability to coexist with raw HTML in the same file

✦ Modules for interacting with other technologies, such as MySQL

Unfortunately, PHP also has some serious drawbacks, also relating to its newness and genesis as a Web programming language:

✦ Numerous security issues (although they are typically found and fixed quickly) are compounded by the relative accessibility of the language to fledgling programmers.

✦ PHP versions up through 4.3 do not have robust object handling capabilities. As such, the language is not as flexible (or, arguably, as powerful) as those languages that do have robust object-oriented programming (OOP) structures.

✦ The structure of PHP programs can be fairly loose, allowing bad programming techniques to be used where highly structured code would otherwise be used. (Note that this is also a benefit as PHP tends to be easy to learn and the concern is mitigated if the person learning PHP takes the time to learn good programming habits as well.)

The following code is an example of how PHP could be used to render the "Hello World" example shown in the ASP section, earlier in this chapter:

```
<?php
$HelloWorld = "Hello World!";

header('Content-type: text/html');
print <<<HTML
<!DOCTYPE HTML PUBLIC "-//W3C//DTD HTML 4.01//EN"
    "http://www.w3.org/TR/html4/strict.dtd">

<html>
<head>
<title>Hello World ASP Sample</title>
</head>
<body>
```

```
<p>$HelloWorld</p>

</body>
</html>
HTML;
?>
```

As with the earlier ASP example, this simple PHP example only scratches the surface of what you can accomplish with PHP. Instead of simply setting a string variable, the code could access a database and present the resulting data in a number of complex forms.

PHP is available on Windows and Linux and requires that the PHP processor be installed on the Web server (both operating system and Web server application).

> **Note** You can find several sources of information online for PHP. The best resource is the PHP Web site itself (www.php.net), which has full language documentation, sample code, and more. For more sample code, visit the PHP Resource Index, at http://php.resourceindex.com.

ColdFusion

ColdFusion by Allaire (now owned by Macromedia) is one product that greatly increases what your Web site can do without requiring any programming. Using a simple language, called Cold Fusion Markup Language(CFML), you can create powerful scripts you write right into your HTML pages. The ColdFusion server returns the script's results right into your page.

Some of the cool things you can do are as follows:

✦ Schedule the generation of a page daily, hourly, or at whatever interval you choose.

✦ Pull content off other sites and parse it into your own format. (Get permission from the site owner before you try this.)

✦ Send mail to everyone in a database from a Web page based on criteria indicated on the form on the Web page.

✦ Insert records into a database. Update a database record. Read a database for records that meet certain criteria.

ColdFusion is available for both NT and UNIX (Solaris) platforms. It works with ODBC-compliant databases. You can find out more from the Macromedia Web site (www.macromedia.com).

Summary

Web publishing has come a long way from its humble beginnings as a means of delivering static textual documents. Using various scripting technologies, browser plug-ins, and other technologies, you can deliver just about any type of content via the Web.

In this chapter, you learned how server-side scripting can be used to extend the capabilities of the Web server, tying in almost any resource available to the server, including databases, peripherals, and more.

✦   ✦   ✦

Introduction to Database-Driven Web Publishing

Although databases are not new to the computer world, only in the last few years has database-driven Web content become widespread. From real-time inventory tracking to dynamic content publishing (think online newsletters, and so on) database integration can add a lot of power to your online documents. This chapter introduces you to the concept of database-driven publishing.

Note   A full discussion and in-depth examples of database publishing are beyond the scope of this book. This chapter introduces you to the concepts and should give you enough information to get started. However, for more information on the subject you should pick up a book dedicated to the subject.

Understanding the Need for Database Publishing

As previously discussed throughout this book, pure HTML documents tend to be very static, offering little to no dynamic content. Consider the following examples:

✦ An order form presented with straight HTML cannot properly represent the vendor's stock levels, potentially allowing customers to order more product than can be shipped.

✦ An online newsletter must be manually assembled and edited in HTML. Furthermore, such online content cannot be easily searched or presented in multiple formats.

✦ Customer records, historical data, and so on cannot be manipulated, searched, or validated against other data.

However, when your documents can interact with database content, you can easily mitigate the concerns mentioned in the preceding list:

✦ The order form can represent the current stock level, alerting customers to backordered items and potential ship dates. The form can also look up shipping estimates and tax rates where applicable.

✦ The online newsletter can be edited piecemeal and assembled by running database queries against a database holding massive amounts of content. The content (even historical content) can be represented in many forms and searched for specific content.

✦ Data can be stored, retrieved, validated, and otherwise manipulated.

How Database Integration Works

HTML and client-side scripts are not equipped to access databases. Database access requires tools on the server side of the equation, typically server-side scripts or an HTTP-enabled data server.

Figure 29-1 shows a simple example of how standard HTTP requests (typically HTML documents) are served.

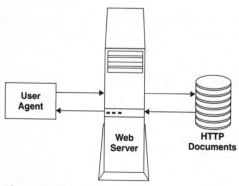

Figure 29-1: A typical HTTP request is served by the Web server.

Figure 29-2 shows an example of how a Web server can be integrated with a database using server-side scripting.

 For more information on server-side scripting, refer to Chapter 28.

Options for Database Publishing

Two methods are commonly used for database publishing: pre-generated content and on-demand content. Each method has its advantages and disadvantages, as discussed in the following sections.

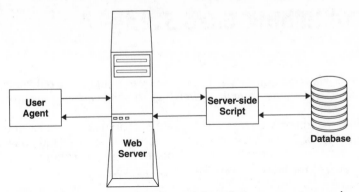

Figure 29-2: A server-side script can be relied upon to store and retrieve data from a database. The same script can manipulate the data in many ways before passing it back to the server for delivery to the requesting client.

Pre-generated content

The concept of pre-generated content relies upon background scripts being run on the server at regular intervals, generating static pages from the database content. For example, a script might run every few hours to refresh the content, allowing recent articles or prices to appear on the appropriate pages.

Pre-generated content is typically used on sites that experience a high volume of traffic, or where the content doesn't change much.

The advantage to pre-generating content is that it takes the load off of the database server, letting the Web server do what it does best, serve static HTML pages. The disadvantages are that the content isn't as timely (it's only as up-to-date as the frequency of the generating script allows it to be), and the user cannot dynamically generate the content.

On-demand content

On-demand content relies on server-side scripts to deliver the data each time a user visits a page. The scripts query the database for appropriate content and display it as required on each page. For example, a "Recent Headlines" script might run at the top of the main page, displaying the headlines of the most recent articles.

On-demand content is typically used on sites that experience a lower volume of traffic or on sites where the content changes rapidly or must be accurate up-to-the-minute.

The advantage to on-demand content is that it can be as current as the data in the database allows. The requesting scripts can also dynamically generate the content, allowing a user more control over what he or she sees. The disadvantage is that this method places more load on the scripts and database; the scripts are run and the database is accessed each time a page is requested.

Database Publishing Case Study—A Newsletter

An online newsletter is a good example to show the power of database publishing. Many such documents are online, from daily Web logs to online article repositories.

Cross-Reference For more information on Web logs, see Chapter 30. For many examples of Web logs, see the lists at Syndic8.com (www.syndic8.com) or Userland Software (www.userland.com). For online article repositories, see any number of Web sites provided by Internet.com (www.internet.com).

The concept is straightforward: take a bunch of small to large articles and present them in a logical online format. Make them presentable in various formats (by author, by date, by subject, and so on), and include a search feature for users to find content that interests them.

The manual method

A friend of mine maintained a publishing site before the golden age of Web blogging, before the numerous tools were available to aid such efforts. He used a manual system of publishing, similar to the following:

1. Daily articles would be posted at the top of the main page. This would move older articles down on the page.

2. Once a month (usually at the end of the month), the content assembled on the main page would be moved to an archive page. The archive would be named according to the month it was assembled (for example, march-04.html).

3. The main page would be cleared of article content, and a link to the new archive would be added to the navigation section.

4. The process would repeat for each month.

Figure 29-3 shows this process in a graphical format.

The database method

After a few months of performing the process outlined in the preceding section, my friend related his plight to me and we set to work implementing a database publishing system for his use. The system functioned as outlined in the following list:

1. Using a simple form, each article could be entered into the database. Each article was stored with the following data:

   • Date article was written

   • Author of article

Daily Process

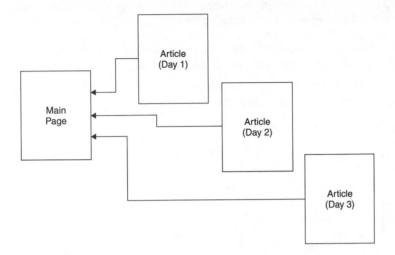

Monthly Process

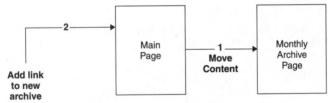

Figure 29-3: The manual process of maintaining an online newsletter.

- Subject of article
- Main text of article
- Whether the article is final or in draft form (should it be published?)

2. The main page of the site used a server-side script to retrieve the last few articles from the database and present them in their entirety.

3. A navigation bar allowed a user to visit monthly archives. The same server-side script generated all monthly archives—the month was passed as an argument and the script would retrieve only articles published in that month.

4. A full-text index was generated on each article, allowing a simple search function to be implemented for users. The user would enter search terms into a simple form—the data entered would be used in a query against the database content. Matching articles were presented on a separate page.

Tip

As previously mentioned in this chapter, many Web blogging programs exist to easily implement the system described here. However, these programs do not alleviate the need for custom server-side scripts. At times, you will need a customized system, either to augment an existing system or to replace a prefab tool. The concepts presented in this chapter also provide a decent base for building other database-enabled Web projects.

Figure 29-4 shows a graphical example of this new process.

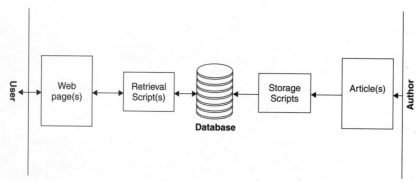

Figure 29-4: The new process places the content in a database where server-side scripts can retrieve it as necessary.

The tools

For this task MySQL was used as the database and PHP was used as the scripting language. Both technologies were well known, could be easily implemented on the Web server (Apache), and provided enough power and flexibility for the project. Also, both technologies were attractively priced—they were free. Because both are open source projects, they can be downloaded, installed, and used without the high price of other commercial solutions.

Tip

For more information on these technologies, visit their home pages. The MySQL home page can be found at www.mysql.com. The PHP home page can be found at www.php.net.

Database structure

Three MySQL tables were created to hold the article data. The first table, for authors, holds the details for various authors allowed to post articles. The second table, for categories, allows arbitrary categories to be defined and attached to articles. The third table holds the articles themselves.

Tables 29-1 through 29-3 show the configuration of the tables.

Table 29-1
The Authors Table

Column	Definition	Use
Idx	Integer, auto increment	Index for authors
Name	Character field	Name of author
Pwd	Character field	Password for author (encoded when saved in table)
Email	Character field	E-mail address of author

Table 29-2
The Categories Table

Column	Definition	Use
Idx	Integer, auto increment	Index for category
Name	Character field	Name of category
Description	Character field	Full description of category

Table 29-3
The Article Table

Column	Definition	Use
Idx	Integer, auto increment	Index for articles
Pubdate	Date field	Date article was written
Cat	Integer	Index of category that article should be attached to
Author	Integer	Index of author that wrote article
Title	Character field	Title/headline of the article
Article	Text field	The text of the article
Publish	Integer	Used as binary field (0 = draft, don't publish; 1 = final copy, publish)

The following listing shows the table definitions in MySQL:

```
CREATE TABLE 'authols' (
  'idx' int(10) unsigned NOT NULL auto_increment,
  'name' varchar(40) NOT NULL default ",
  'pwd' varchar(20) NOT NULL default ",
```

```
  'email' varchar(40) NOT NULL default '',
  PRIMARY KEY ('idx')
) TYPE=MyISAM ;

CREATE TABLE 'categories' (
  'idx' int(10) NOT NULL auto_increment,
  'name' varchar(40) NOT NULL default '',
  'description' text NOT NULL,
  PRIMARY KEY ('idx')
) TYPE=MyISAM ;

CREATE TABLE 'articles' (
  'idx' int(10) unsigned NOT NULL auto_increment,
  'pubdate' datetime NOT NULL default '0000-00-00 00:00:00',
  'cat' int(10) unsigned NOT NULL default '0',
  'author' int(10) unsigned NOT NULL default '0',
  'title' varchar(80) NOT NULL default '',
  'article' text NOT NULL,
  'publish' tinyint(1) unsigned NOT NULL default '0',
  PRIMARY KEY ('idx'),
  FULLTEXT KEY 'title' ('title','article')
) TYPE=MyISAM ;
```

Scripting basics

As mentioned earlier in this section, PHP was chosen for the server-side scripting because of its ability to interface easily with MySQL. With the MySQL functionality compiled into PHP, opening a database connection is performed with the `mysql_connect()` function:

```
$link = mysql_connect("host", "user", "password")
```

The `host`, `user`, and `password` arguments are replaced by the information necessary to access the database. In this case, the database is running on the same machine as the Web server, so `localhost` is used as the host. The user and password arguments are replaced by account credentials that have read-only rights to the database (the scripts will only retrieve info, not write it).

After a link has been established to the database, queries can be run against the data using the `mysql_query()` function:

```
$result = mysql_query($query,$link);
```

In this example, the `$query` variable contains the SQL query. The results of the query are stored in the `$result` variable. The script can then process the results and display them accordingly. For example, the following query would return the titles of all published articles in the database, sorted by their publication date:

```
SELECT title FROM articles WHERE publish = "1"

ORDER BY pubdate DESC
```

What is SQL?

Structured Query Language (SQL, generally pronounced "sequel") was developed as a means to lend consistency to database queries. The language provides keywords to accomplish standard database tasks—looking up information, storing information, replacing information, and so on. Each command given to the database is called a *query*, whether it is simply querying for information, storing info, or performing some other task.

Like most computer technologies, SQL varies a bit from implementation to implementation. The examples presented here are specific to MySQL and might be different if you are using PostgreSQL, Microsoft Access, or other SQL-compatible databases.

The basic way to look up information is via a SELECT query, in a form similar to the following:

```
SELECT   data_list FROM   table_list WHERE   conditions
```

For example, to select all customers' first and last names when the customers' address is in the 46250 ZIP code, you could use a query similar to the following:

```
SELECT first_name, last_name FROM customers
   WHERE zipcode = "46250"
```

This, of course, is provided that you have a table named "customers" that stores data in fields named first_name, last_name, and zipcode.

Adding data uses a different query, utilizing the INSERT format:

```
INSERT INTO table_list (data_list) VALUES (data_values)
```

For example, to insert a customer's data into the customer table, you might use a query similar to the following:

```
INSERT INTO customers (first_name, last_name, address, city,
state, zipcode) VALUES ("T.", "Wierzbowski", "Colonial Marine
Way", "West Hollywood", "CA", "90069");
```

As previously stated, implementations of SQL vary between applications, so you should check the documentation for your database server to determine what form of queries to use.

If this query were used in the preceding mysql_query() example, the article titles would be stored in array form in the $result database. PHP could parse the data, outputting one title per line (in HTML format) using code similar to the following:

```
print "<p> \n"; //Start the text block
while ($line = mysql_fetch_array($result, MYSQL_ASSOC)) {
  // For each returned title, output in italic font
  print "<i>$line['title']</i><br> \n";
}
print "</p> \n"; // End text block
```

The net result of this code would be a listing of the titles of all published articles, sorted by their publication date in descending order, similar to the following:

```
<p>
<i>Bush heads to Africa</i><br>
<i>Marvel movie news</i><br>
<i>Thousands of Web sites might be attacked on Monday</i><br>
<i>Miami running back re-sentenced</i><br>
<i>Charlie Chan movies banned in the USA</i><br>
<i>Riddick name change and new release date</i><br>
</p>
```

Sample scripts

By using methods similar to those described in the previous section, you can create several scripts, each of which can access the database of articles and provide the data in various forms. Some examples follow:

✦ Headlines (the title field) of the last two weeks of articles (see Figure 29-5).

✦ Articles sorted by category (see Figure 29-6).

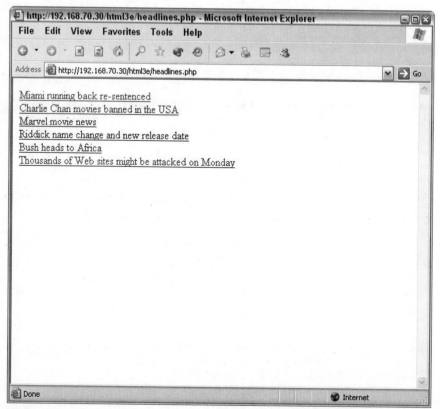

Figure 29-5: The headline script generates headlines from recent articles.

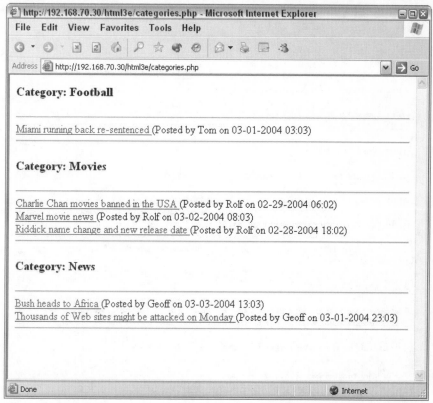

Figure 29-6: The category script generates recent article headlines sorted into their respective categories.

✦ Teasers of current articles—that is, the first 20 words of the article (see Figure 29-7).

✦ Full text of the article with links to more articles in the category or by the author (see Figure 29-8).

In addition to the standard data, the scripts also provide links to additional information. For example, the headline script outputs the headlines embedded in links to the full article script, similar to the following:

```
<a href="displayarticle.php?idx=20"> Charlie Chan movies
banned in the USA</a>
```

When a user clicks the headline, the `displayarticle` script is called to display the full article. Similar constructs can be used to link to more articles in the same category, by the same author, and so forth.

The scripts can be included in template pages via server-side includes, or the entire site can be generated via PHP, and the article scripts can be called as required.

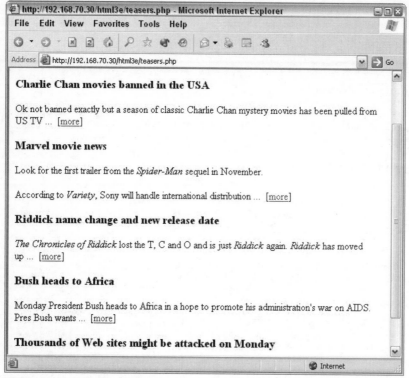

Figure 29-7: The teaser script generates short versions of articles.

Adding search capabilities

Adding a search capability to the system is remarkably easy. A full-text index is created on the `title` and `article` columns in the `article` table (see the MySQL table definition earlier in this section). This index can then be searched using textual expressions via a select query, driven by user input into a standard HTML form. Articles that match the search criteria are then displayed (generally in headline form), and the user can browse them accordingly.

Tip　Even without a full-text index the database can be easily searched via a WHERE clause in a SELECT query. For example, to find all articles that contain the text "Charlie Chan," a query similar to the following could be used:

```
SELECT idx,title,article FROM articles
   WHERE title LIKE "%Charlie Chan%"
   OR article LIKE "%Charlie Chan%"
```

This query would return all articles that contained "Charlie Chan" in their title or in the text of the article.

The other-side of the process—publishing tools

One area that has not been covered in this case study is the publishing side, that is, how do the articles get into the database to begin with? This process requires a few

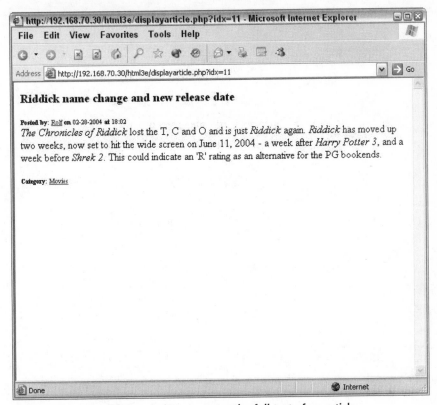

Figure 29-8: The full-text script generates the full text of an article.

additional scripts, accessible only to the authors and system administrators. The scripts allow for creation of new author records, new categories, and new articles. For security's sake, only the new article script is accessible to authors—system administrators take care of the creation of new authors and new categories.

Note   As a temporary measure, tools such as phpMyAdmin can be used to manipulate the data in a MySQL database. Figure 29-9 shows an example of phpMyAdmin in use. (You can find more information on phpMyAdmin at `www.phpmyadmin .net/`.) However, the tool is somewhat archaic in design and can be easily misused, at worst resulting in massive data loss due to a misplaced click. It's usually best to create more user-friendly tools.

An example of an article maintenance tool is shown in Figure 29-10.

Authentication and Security

Any additional technologies added to Web publishing bring additional security concerns—database publishing is no exception. You need to be concerned with when adding a database to the mix: access to the database as a whole and further restricting access for users.

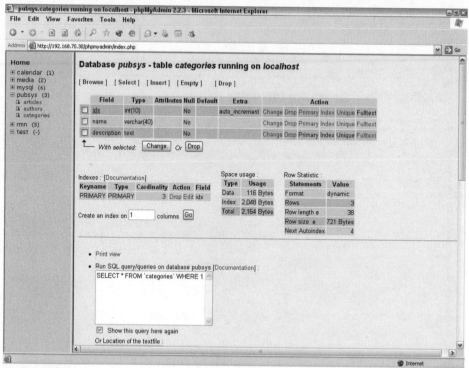

Figure 29-9: Tools such as phpMyAdmin, although not very user-friendly, can help fill gaps in database administration.

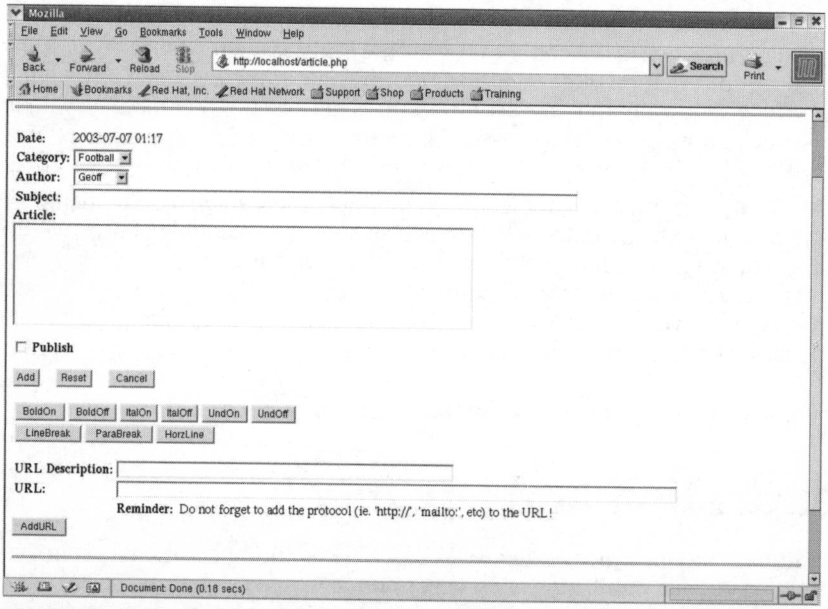

Figure 29-10: An example of an article maintenance tool that allows creation and editing of articles in the database

In the case of MySQL, access is restricted per user, as seen in the user and password fields required in the `mysql_connect()` PHP function. Each user is assigned unique rights to the data. Access can be granted or denied on a table-by-table basis.

For a publishing system it is best to create a very limited user for general use. This *user* can be used by the scripts for general query access, but have write, delete, and update access denied. This helps limit the exposure of the data; even if the general user credentials are compromised, the data can only be queried, not overwritten or deleted.

For authors you could implement a tiered security structure as follows:

✦ Protect the maintenance scripts by placing them in an area of the Web site that is only accessible by machines used by the authors or, better yet, is password-protected by the Web server.

✦ Use a unique user account (*author*) for author-level database access, granting permission to the `article` database but restricting access to the `categories` and `authors` tables.

✦ Use the `authors` table to uniquely identify each author, requiring the author(s) to log in using the credentials stored in the table. Additional code in the article maintenance script(s) can restrict authors from modifying articles that are not their own.

Note   A unique MySQL account for each author might be overkill. It adds additional database administrator overhead while only providing slight advantages. You wouldn't want to restrict individual rows in the database by author; simple script-employed, individual article security is enough.

Summary

Database publishing has been around for many years. However, only in the last few years have economical, easy-to-use tools been available to help deploy database-driven solutions. This chapter introduced you to the concept of database publishing and showed you an example of how database integration can be used to add dynamic content to your documents.

✦   ✦   ✦

Creating a Weblog

The Web has created a viable media for publishing all manner of content—providing an alternative avenue for businesses and the average Joe alike to propagate information. A recent innovation, weblogging, extends the ability to publish content online and to even syndicate the content. This chapter covers the basics of blogging.

The Blog Phenomenon

Weblogging, or blogging for short, is the latest craze on the Web. Gaining popularity in the mid-90s, almost everyone has a blog nowadays.

Blogs come in many varieties:

- ✦ The equivalent of an online diary, where the owner posts their thoughts about life, the universe, and everything

- ✦ Themed articles where the owner posts their thoughts on specific topics, such as technology, politics, religion, and so on

- ✦ News-related blogs where the owner posts aggregated news content

However, just like the desktop publishing explosion in the late '80s taught us, just because someone can access technology doesn't mean they should. As desktop publishing came of age, everyone with a computer began fancying themselves as a designer—it became quite clear that graphic design is an art that can only be aided, not replaced, by technology. Now, as blogging is reaching epic proportions, many people fancy themselves as Dave Barry-caliber writers seemingly with the assumption that the entire world cares what they think. It only takes a few moments of surfing the vast variety of blogs to ascertain just how wrong those assumptions can be.

Dave Barry is a well-known humor columnist for the *Miami Herald*. His column is syndicated in over 500 newspapers worldwide. Dave Barry actually has his own blog, which can be found at `http://weblog.herald.com/column/davebarry/`.

That said, the blog world is full of useful information. From offering a look at the daily routine of people in interesting positions to the latest electronic gadget news, several blogs are bound to interest even the most jaded reader.

The support that large corporations (such as Microsoft) are lending to blogging is a sign that blogging has come into its own and is seen as a valuable resource. Such corporations encourage their employees to blog with the intent that such activities will increase communication between employees and the tech world at large. However, in the wake of such support also come a handful of blog-related firings, companies letting employees go for inappropriate blog entries.

The real power of blogging comes in the community that has grown up around the technology. Online blogs have created a tightly knit subculture on the Web where authors read and respond to each other's articles, leave comments to articles of interest, and so forth.

The ability to leave comments on an author's blog is a double-edged sword. Although the feature allows the community to be more involved, the feature has also been used inappropriately by the spamming community. Anonymous comments containing links to other sites routinely get indexed by search engines. As such, comments on popular blogs can cause the site referenced in the comment to increase in rank in the search engine. Several tools are available to help stop blog spamming, but just like e-mail spam, nothing will completely remove it.

Another complementary technology, "Really Simple Syndication" (RSS) feeds, has helped the aggregation of blog content. RSS is an XML specification for syndicating content. It enables authors to publish their headlines or teasers for articles in a distinct format—a format that can then be read by other applications to effectively syndicate the articles.

Look for more information on RSS in the section, *Syndicating content with RSS*, later in this chapter.

Blog Providers and Software

Just as there are many topics for blog content, there are many blog providers and software to enable blogging. This section gives an overview of the more popular blogging provider/software solutions.

Userland Software

According to the Userland Software site, Userland "provides Web Content Management and creation tools for building sites that bring people together." One of the pioneers of blog technology, Userland provides several different content management and blog solutions.

Note　You can find Userland Software on the Web at: www.userland.com/.

Offered as commercial products, Userland Software's Manila and Radio Userland tools enable users to easily set up content management and aggregation sites. Manila is geared towards workgroups whose members need to share information. Radio Userland is geared toward the general blog author.

The benefit to using Userland's tools is twofold:

✦ The tools integrate into your local system, easing the pain of setting up online solutions or using Web-based solutions.

✦ Userland has built a large blogging community; using their tools connects your site to this community.

Movable Type

One of the most popular server-side blogging applications is Movable Type. Movable Type uses a series of CGI programs to publish and maintain blog content. Movable Type must be installed on a server that has Perl and either a Berkeley DB or MySQL database.

Note　You can find Movable Type's Web site at: www.movabletype.org/.

Movable Type is a very popular solution due to the following:

✦ Movable Type is highly customizable, using a flexible template system to easily publish content in a variety of formats and/or integrate into an existing site design.

✦ The large community of developers creating various plug-ins to extend the capabilities of Movable Type.

✦ The large community of bloggers who use the program.

✦ Its relative low cost (free for non-commercial use, though donations are encouraged, and $150 for commercial use license).

Movable Type uses special tags that you can embed in any HTML document to publish your content. Although Movable Type is fairly easy to install and use, it is recommended for the more technical user.

Blosxom

Blosxom (pronounced "blossom") was designed as a lightweight, feature-packed, blogging application. One of the more simple solutions for blogging, Blosxom runs as Perl CGI scripts on a variety of platforms. Using simple text files for article storage, Blosxom is designed to work with the tools you are already using—Emacs, Microsoft Word, Notepad, or other text editors.

Note   Find the Blosxom Web page at www.blosxom.com/.

Blosxom is completely Open Source, meaning that it is free for use and the source code is available for you to modify as you want or need. Blosxom also has a fairly robust plug-in architecture and an active developer community providing several plug-ins.

Although its simplicity is also its bane, Blosxom is a good middle ground between the other two solutions mentioned in this section.

Posting Content to Your Blog

Posting content to your blog is usually as easy as typing an article into the blogging application you are using. In the case of Radio Userland, you use their application; Movable Type uses Web based forms; and Blosxom uses any text editor.

Blog content varies from blog to blog and article to article, but content generally falls into one of the following categories:

✦ Generalized, original content

✦ Response to another online article or item

✦ Aggregation of information from elsewhere

In most cases, your content will contain a link to other content online or even text from the content. For example, the following is typical of a blog entry:

In his *Things I Hate* column, Joe User makes the following observation:

"This would be text from the column referenced above ..."

My feelings on this matter ... (response to above citation here)

In this example the text "Things I Hate" would be a link to the article being cited. The verbatim text is set off in quotes or uses a distinct convention to identify the text as a quote, not the citing author's work. The text then continues with the current author's text, adding to the cited article, offering a retort, or whatever.

Tip Although quoting others is a huge part of the whole blog scene, it is still very important to clearly delimit and credit other people's text. In most cases, you will want to indent the text, set it off in quotes or a special font, and make sure to include a link to the original.

Handling Comments

Most blogs also include a comment section that appears directly after the posted content. Visitors to the blog are encouraged to post comments about the articles posted there, creating the hybrid news article-public forum scheme that is a blog.

Most blogging applications support comments and allow you to configure how the comments are presented in your blog. One of the choices you will need to make is how comments are represented on your page—whether they are displayed whenever the attached article is displayed, or only available when a `comment` link is clicked.

Although most visitors understand the purpose of comments in a blog, there are still people who abuse the comments, using them to attack others, post inappropriate content, and so forth.

Thankfully, most blogging software has tools to help stop comment spam and control user posts. Check the documentation for your blogging software to determine what tools are at your disposal for displaying and managing comments.

Note Keep in mind that expressing one's views is part of the appeal of blogs. As such, you should be prepared for negativity and even direct criticism if you enable comments. You should resist the urge to delete comments you simply disagree with—but stay on top of content that is truly objectionable to help protect yourself and readers. Alternatively, you can disable comments altogether.

Using Permalinks

Most blogs include several methods to browse their content:

✦ The most recent articles are posted in descending order on the main page.

✦ Search features enable users to find articles containing content that interests them.

✦ Archives list articles by day, week, or month and have controls to move from article to article.

The advantage to having multiple methods of displaying content is that visitors to the site can choose the method that best suits their needs. However, other blog authors need one location to reference an article when linking to it from their site/blog. Enter the concept of *permalinks*, a unique URL that points directly to the article in question, usually on a page all by itself (without being buried in a navigation scheme).

You will typically see permalinks near the bottom of the text of blog articles, as shown in Figure 30-1.

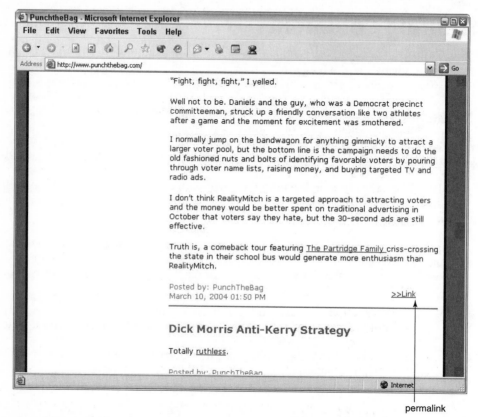

permalink

Figure 30-1: Permalinks, usually located near the end of articles, provide a unique URL to reference the article.

Sometimes blog authors use the verbatim text "permalink" to denote the location of the permalink. Other blogs, such as the example shown in Figure 30-1, note the link with a graphic or simple "link" text.

Whenever you link to another blog's content, be sure to use the permalink.

Using Trackbacks

You have seen how links are used to reference articles elsewhere, but how does the original author know about the link to his material? That dilemma was one of the reasons behind the invention and adoption of trackback technology.

TrackBack was first released as an open specification in 2002. It was released as a protocol and feature of Movable Type version 2.2 and has since been adopted by many other blogging applications.

The methodology behind trackbacks is shown in Figure 30-2. Site A posts an article that is interesting to Site B. Site B references the article on Site A and uses a trackback to let Site A know about the reference. Site B also uses trackbacks to alert other sites that may be interested in the topic—whether the interest is in the original article or the reference.

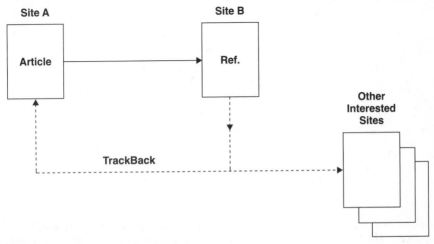

Figure 30-2: The methodology behind trackbacks.

Syndicating Content with RSS

Netscape introduced RSS in 1999 as a concept to syndicate content. At that time, RSS stood for *Rich Site Summary*. However, Netscape abandoned the concept in 2001 and UserLand Software began pioneering a similar technology as *Really Simple Syndication*. Still others refer to the RSS concept as *RDF Site Summary*.

In any case, RSS exists as a simple way to syndicate content.

Note   UserLand Software maintains quite a bit of documentation on RSS at the following Web site: http://backend.userland.com/rss.

Syndication is a means of distributing content with the intent of allowing others to publish it. Typically, syndication applies to newspaper columns, comics, and other works of art—and, generally, one derives a fee for each use.

In this case, syndication means an easy method for others to preview your content and optionally republish it. Sites such as slashdot.org, cnet.com, and others use RSS feeds to syndicate their content, as do many Weblog (blog) authors.

RSS syntax

The syntax for RSS feeds varies considerably depending on the version of RSS that you adhere to. However, the feed is usually published as an XML file with a strict syntax. For example, a typical RSS feed file might resemble the following:

```
<?xml version="1.0"?>
<rss version="2.0">
<channel>
<title>title_of_site</title>
<description>description_of_site</description>
<link>http://link.to.site</link>

<item>
<title>title_of_article</title>
<description>short_desc_of_article ...</description>
<pubDate>pubdate_in_RFC 822_format</pubDate>
<link>link_to_article</link>
</item>

<item>
...
</item>

</channel>
</rss>
```

In XML format, the file's headers spell out its content and which version of RSS is being used. The beginning of the `<channel>` section provides details about the main site, while each `<item>` section provides details about a particular article. Each feed can have up to 15 `<item>`s and is generally arranged with the newest article first and the oldest article last. As articles are added to the feed, the older articles are moved off the feed.

Publishing the feed

The XML file is made accessible via HTTP, and special applications can access the feeds and notify users when the feed is updated. For example, the open source project BottomFeeder can monitor several feeds and even seek out new feeds. Figure 30-3 shows an example of BottomFeeder in action.

Note   You can download BottomFeeder from the BottomFeeder home page at www.cincomsmalltalk.com/BottomFeeder/.

A popular Windows reader is NewsGator (http://www.newsgator.com/), which integrates into Microsoft Outlook. Several other applications can monitor RSS feeds as well, such as Trillian (www.trillian.cc/trillian/index.html). (The Pro version has a nifty news plug-in.)

These tools monitor feeds by periodically accessing the RSS feed file and informing the user when the feed file changes. The individual `<item>` blocks are usually displayed for users, who can visit the site or see the complete article by clicking the listing.

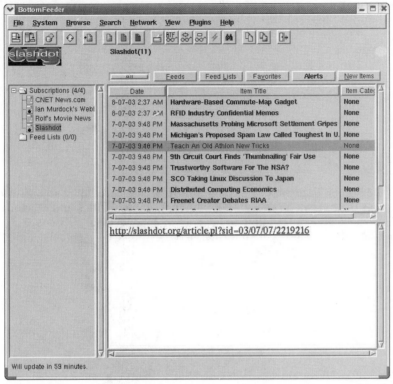

Figure 30-3: Applications such as BottomFeeder can monitor several RSS feeds.

Most blogging software will automatically create RSS feeds from your content. You still must configure how many articles will be placed in the RSS file, how long they will stay, and what information (title, teaser, and so on) is stored in the feed. See your software's documentation for details on how to configure your feed.

If your blogging software doesn't support RSS feeds natively, look for tools such as NewsIsFree (http://www.newsisfree.com/) to build your feeds.

Note   Don't forget to put a link to your feed on your site and publicize your feed through services such as http://www.syndic8.com/.

Building an Audience

The key to blog success is networking. Finding sites that serve up content in the same vein as your site and appraising them of articles they might find interesting is a good strategy. However, use common sense and moderation—don't be a bother and back off if you don't get positive responses.

Using syndication listing sites is another good way to drive traffic. Visit www.syndic8.com/ and register your site. Most blogging software sites will also include listing areas for listing your blog; doing so helps promote your site as well as the software you use.

 Cross-Reference For more tips on promoting your site, see Chapter 37.

Summary

Blogging is the hottest thing on the Web right now. Besides providing an outlet for folks to express their views on everything from their life to politics and religion, blogs also provide a great alternative to full content management systems. Blogs can be used to syndicate and aggregate information.

✦   ✦   ✦

Introduction to XML

The essence of Web development is markup, even when using a powerful visual editor such as Dreamweaver or GoLive to create markup. Markup drives everything on the Web. Without it, there would be no World Wide Web.

Markup consists of a set of rules that a document must follow in order for the software processing that document to read it correctly. The process of software reading a marked-up document is often referred to as *parsing*. If the document is not marked up correctly, the software can't parse it.

In theory, HTML was designed to maintain a strict set of markup rules, but those rules were enforced rather loosely by the Web browsing software designed to parse HTML.

The result was inconsistency, and browser vendors who added their own markup "rules" exacerbated the problem; each browser, in essence, followed its own set of rules. The `frame` element, for example, found its way into the HTML specification when it gained popularity shortly after Netscape introduced it. Browser developers raced ahead with new features, while the W3C, the organization responsible for Web standards, lagged behind.

Over the past few years, the situation has reversed, and the W3C has released a slew of specifications that vendors are having difficulty keeping up with.

One of these specifications, Extensible Markup Language (XML), was introduced by the W3C to address general inconsistencies in markup, and to add another data-centric layer to the user interface paradigm. This chapter introduces you to XML and how and when to deploy it.

The Need for XML

The Web is all about markup, but it's also about data. This is true whether the data is document-centric, such as the kind of content in a magazine or journal, or more granular, such as the kind of data extracted from a database. One problem with this type of data is that it can be difficult to extrapolate across different software environments and platforms because it has traditionally been stored in proprietary formats. What if you were able to instead develop a set of rules defining a table of text-based data and simply wrap markup around each chunk of data?

Such data could be as simple as a Web configuration file that stores settings on how a Web server is configured, such as this piece of code from a .NET web.config file:

```
<appSettings>
  <add key="DSN"
   value="server=(local);uid=guest;
   pwd=guess;Database=Realtor"/>
</appSettings>
```

Or, the data could be much more complex, derived from a large number of relational tables requiring a carefully constructed set of rules in order for the processing software to know what each element means. Many modern database systems, such as Oracle, can now be used to extract such data into sets of marked-up elements. These result in documents that can be easily shared across platforms, software environments, and even other companies and organizations, because the markup these documents are based on, XML, has consistent rules worldwide. The key to this kind of integration is the use of documents that define rules for what an element means. There isn't much good to having the following element if you don't know what the element is supposed to do:

```
<book>United</book>
```

Is it a book named *United*? Or does it refer to booking a passenger seat on United Airlines? By developing a document containing rules that describe an element's use and purpose, you can use XML to provide a human readable and machine-portable database that can be easily used among different software languages and environments. In addition, you can imagine the programming possibilities when you consider that each element in an XML document is an object that can be manipulated by JavaScript or another kind of language, such as Java or C#. This is made possible by the Document Object Model, which consists of a series of standardized methods and properties created by the W3C to access parts of an XML document using object-oriented languages.

Some specific uses for XML include the following:

✦ Use it to store data outside your HTML.

✦ Use it to store data inside HTML pages as "Data Islands."

✦ Use it to share and exchange data between incompatible systems.

✦ Use it as a data storage mechanism completely outside the HTML layer.

✦ Use it to make data available to runtime languages such as JavaScript or an object-oriented language such as Java, C#, or Basic/Visual Basic.

✦ Use it to make your data human-readable.

✦ Use it to invent new languages or plug data into an existing language (a process called transformation, which you'll see in the section on XSL).

Relationship of XML, SGML, and HTML

XML is a subset of the Standard Generalized Markup Language (SGML). So is HTML. SGML is a markup standard that asks its document creators to develop a set of rules that a processor should follow as it attempts to parse a structured document. In the case of HTML, that set of rules is called a Document Type Definition (DTD). The first HTML DTD, published by Tim Berners-Lee and Daniel Connolly, contained the most basic HTML elements—things like paragraph and listing elements. The original draft of the document defining these basic rules can still be found at `www.w3.org/MarkUp/draft-ietf-iiir-html-01.txt`.

In theory, if a Web author deviated from the rules as established by the HTML 1.0 specification, the result should have been a broken document (although browsers were expected to "fail gracefully," allowing users to at least view the content even if the content's display was ruined). This is because SGML requires strict adherence to the rules when a DTD is created. In practice, browsers, the software used to parse HTML documents, did not strictly enforce adherence to these rules.

Berners-Lee and Connolly could have created different elements for HTML rather than the ones they chose, as long as they stuck to the guidelines as established by SGML. Among those guidelines are rules that describe how an element should start (with a < character), what it should contain, what attributes it should possess, and how DTDs themselves are written. For example, in the DTD, to indicate that an element has no content, or is empty, you would include the following:

```
<!ELEMENT IMG     - O EMPTY -- Embedded image -->
```

SGML allows anyone to create a set of markup rules. The trick is getting software developers to write software that will parse a document according to your custom-made DTD. You could, for example, write a DTD that instructs a software program to emit a beep every time a link is clicked. Or, that uses a `para` element instead of a `p` element to define paragraphs. Or, as in the earlier example, you could define an element named `book` that describes a book title or refers to an airline reservation.

Note   You can view various versions of HTML DTDs at `www.hwg.org/resources/?cid=74`.

SGML is very powerful because it lets users create structured documents that are human readable and very portable across environments. For this reason, it was very popular in government circles and with companies with massive documentation needs, such as aircraft manufacturers and military contractors. Although it is still used extensively by these users, XML is replacing SGML in many cases.

With such a good system in place, why would you need XML? SGML is very complex. It isn't beyond the capabilities of most people, but it is if you don't have a lot of time, and most of us don't. So there was no payoff unless the scope of a project using SGML was large. XML was designed to be an SGML Light. It brought the power of SGML into the hands of everyone without requiring a huge investment in time. If you can remember just a few basic rules, you can start writing your XML within a few minutes. And you don't even need to write a DTD to define the elements you're creating. It helps, as you'll see later, but it isn't a requirement.

Versions of XML

There is currently only one version of XML. XML 1.0 is currently in its second edition, which simply means that the specification has undergone some minor editing and a new, cleaned-up version was released containing such minor differences from the original that not even an incremental version upgrade was considered necessary. Version 1.1 is currently in Candidate Recommendation and will presumably be released soon as a final version. There are few changes in 1.1, other than some minor Unicode-related items (you'll be learning about Unicode in the section *Understanding Encoding*).

How XML Works

XML doesn't actually do anything on its own. It's just a way to mark up text-based data. More specifically, it's a methodology for describing how a structured document should handle sequences of characters.

Getting started with XML parsers

Before you begin creating XML documents, it's a good idea to find a parser, which is software that can read an XML document. There are two kinds of parsers: validating and nonvalidating. A validating parser reads an XML document and determines if it is following the rules of a DTD. A nonvalidating parser doesn't care about validation, and only checks an XML document to be sure that the syntax is correct. A document that follows these rules is called a *well-formed* document. The obvious examples of widely distributed nonvalidating parsers are Internet Explorer and Netscape 7.0, or any of the new Mozilla-based browsers, which can be found at `www.mozilla.org/start/1.5/`.

To open an XML document in Internet Explorer 5 or later, or in Netscape/Mozilla, you simply open it using the File menu in those programs, and choose Open... Both browsers will display the XML in a tree-based format.

You can find a list of other XML parsers at `www.xml.com/pub/rg/XML_Parsers`.

Begin with a prolog

There are no pre-existing elements in XML. Most basic XML documents start with a prolog, which includes a declaration that states a document as being an XML document:

```
<?xml version="1.0"  encoding="ISO-8859-1"?>
```

The declaration must come first, before anything else, and its characters must be the first the parser encounters (no white space before that question mark). A prolog can also include a Processing instruction. A processing instruction (PI) tells the parser to pass the data it contains to another application. For example, if a prolog has a processing instruction containing a style sheet, the following PI would tell the processor to pass the named file to software that can handle the style sheet processing:

```
<?xml-stylesheet type="text/xsl" href="note.xsl"?>
```

You'll learn more about style sheets later in the chapter, in the section named *Style Sheets for XML: XSL*, but PIs are not limited to style sheet processing. They can pass all kinds of information to processors. The trick is whether the XML parser is actually capable of doing so. No rule exists to say that it must. Generally, when there is a lot of action with PIs, vendors create extensions to parsers or bundle them into larger XML processing components so that the processing is hidden. Microsoft's XML parser, MSXML, for example, contains a processing component for style sheets.

Understanding encoding

Did you notice the bolded encoding attribute in the prolog (encoding="ISO-8859-1") in the prolog example? That actually isn't an attribute; it just looks like one, but it's an important part of the XML prolog. Encoding, in fact, is a vital part to truly understanding XML. XML requires all XML parsers to handle an encoding named UTF-8. An encoding is sort of like a mapping between alphanumeric characters and the numbering system your computer understands. UTF-8 is a fairly new and comprehensive encoding that covers most languages of the world. It is based on Unicode, which is an amalgamation of various encodings such as UTF-8 and UTF-16, which is also supported by XML and is different than UTF-8 in the number of byte sequences used to store characters.

In Unicode-based encodings, for example, the capital letter A is represented by the hexadecimal number U+0041. The small letter a is represented by the hexadecimal number U+0061. Every letter and numeric character in every alphabet in the world (almost) has such a number assigned to it.

Note The U+ in the preceding examples are not part of the hexadecimal number, but characters added to show they are part of Unicode. In a Web page, you would use &0041 and &0061; instead of U+0041 and U+0061.

Each human language is a subset of the vast UTF-8 encoding attached to it. Western European languages, for example, use the ISO-8859-1 encoding, which is simply a table of mappings within UTF-8 dealing specifically with Western languages. This is important to XML development because XML is concerned with how sequences of these mapped numerical references are structured within an XML document.

Your encodings need to be consistent to successfully parse XML. If you use Windows-specific encodings, for example, you'll need to be absolutely sure that everything that interacts with Windows encodings is also a Windows encoding. This is because Windows uses a different set of tables for mapping characters to numbers than UTF-8. The Windows encoding for Latin-based languages, for example, is called Windows Code Page 1252 (sets of encodings are also called code pages). This code page, also referred to as ANSI (from the American National Standards Institute), isn't a subset of UTF-8 the way ISO-8859-1 is. Luckily, most characters happen to map out to the same numerical references in both encoding sets, but not all do. For example, the ™ character used for trademarks does not map out to the same hexadecimal number in ANSI as it does in ISO-8859-1.

Things get even more difficult when you're dealing with Chinese alphabets, because two well-established encoding mechanisms are in use for Chinese languages. For example, in Taiwan, an encoding named Big 5 is used. Its mappings are quite different than UTF-8. Even though an XML-compliant parser must be able to parse UTF-8 documents, there's nothing forcing developers to use UTF-8, and most Chinese-based Web sites don't use it. This is a critical distinction to be aware of when working internationally. A `sale` element in a Big 5 document (assuming a Chinese translation, of course) is not a `sale` element in UTF-8, because element names are dependent on their encoding.

This may seem like an awfully long explanation about something so arcane, but it is a virtual guarantee that at some point in your XML work you'll encounter a square character or question mark in output generated from XML. It usually takes people hours or days to figure out the source of these character "anomalies." You have the advantage of knowing they occur because of encoding problems. When a system doesn't recognize a character, it generally emits a square character (a border with empty space), a solid black square, or a question mark. This is invariably related to an encoding issue. Make sure encodings between output and input within your XML environment are consistent, and you should avoid these kinds of problems. You can't force a billion people to change their encodings to UTF-8, but you can develop a system in your own environment to handle Big 5 encodings, which is a lot easier to do anyway.

Well-structured XML

XML does not consist of many syntax rules, but the ones it has are very strict, and parsers that don't follow them to the letter are not considered genuine XML parsers.

Including a root element

The most basic rule is that in order to be a *conforming* or well-formed XML document (in other words, a legitimate one), it must consist of one root element. Therefore, the following is a conforming XML document:

```
<hello>world</hello>
```

You don't even have to include the XML declaration, but it's good form to do so, and is a much better way to maintain the integrity of your documents if versions should change. If you do include a declaration and you declare your XML document as an XML 1.0 document, your syntax must adhere to that version. Declarations are not required because the creators of the XML specification knew that some existing SGML and HTML document qualified as XML documents or could be easily made into XML, and didn't want those documents to fail when there was no XML declaration.

Properly nesting XML documents

In HTML, you can get away with some improper nesting, such as that shown here:

```
<b><i>Most browsers will render this</b></i>
```

In XML, all elements must be properly nested within each other, like this:

```
<b><i>All XML parsers will parse this</i></b>
```

In addition, the root element must contain the group of all the other elements. In other words, there must be one "master" element, within which all the other properly nested elements are contained. An XML parser would not correctly parse the following:

```
<html><b><i>All XML parsers will parse this</i></b>
```

This is because there is no closing tag for the `html` element. You can fix this by simply adding one, as in the following example:

```
<html><b><i>All XML parsers will parse this</i></b> </html>
```

If an element has no content, you must use a closing tag. There are two ways to do this. You can use the kind of closing tag you're used to seeing in HTML, as in the following:

```
<img src="my.gif"></img>
```

Or, you can simply include a closing slash within the element tag, as follows:

```
<img src="my.gif"/><br />
```

Note the extra space between the end of the XML name and the closing forward slash. Although this isn't necessary in XML, if you're creating HTML documents with XML syntax (known as XHTML), you'll need them or browsers won't render things such as line breaks correctly.

Maintaining case sensitivity in XML

HTML elements and attributes are case sensitive. Therefore, `<data type="bad" />` is different than `<data TYPE ="bad"/>` and `<DATA type="bad"/>`.

Using quotes in attribute values

In HTML, you can also get away with not including quotes around attributes. For example, you can write the following and a browser will render the element correctly:

```
<td colspan=2>some data</td>
```

In XML, all attribute values *must* be quoted:

```
<td colspan="2">some data</td>
```

Handling line breaks and white space in XML documents

Windows applications store line breaks as pairs of carriage return, line feed (CR LF) characters, which map out to 000D; and 000A; in XML UTF-8 using hexadecimal format. In UNIX applications, a line break is usually stored as an LF character. Macintosh applications use a single CR character to store a line break. This is an important distinction when working on large Web sites that may have source control software, which often has a translation option for handling cross-platform line-break differences when merging files between development and production environments.

Using predefined entities and entity or character references

Several entity references must be used to "escape" XML markup characters to prevent an XML parser from interpreting markup characters as XML when that is not your intent. These are called predefined entities and are shown in Table 31-1.

Table 31-1 Predefined Entities		
Entity	**Markup Equivalent**	**Unicode Value (In Decimal Format)**
<	&lt;	&#60;
>	&gt;	">
&	&amp;	"&
'	&apos;	"'
"	&quot;	""

By referring to Table 31-1, instead of writing markup like this,

```
<body>This is a left angle bracket: < </body>
```

you need to escape the < character you see in the preceding code in bold, like this (change is also in bold):

```
<body>This is a left angle bracket: &lt; </body>
```

The same steps are necessary for the other predefined entities listed in Table 31-1. Instead of using the markup shown under the heading "Markup Equivalent," you can also use the Unicode values shown in the next column.

Every character in any language you use (with a few rare exceptions involving comparatively obscure languages) can be represented by character references, which are Unicode values mapped to characters (a process described earlier). For example, if you wanted to write out the word "Foo," you could write it like this:

```
&#70;&#111;&#111;
```

Managing white space in XML

The default behavior of XML is to preserve white space. In HTML, the default behavior is to collapse white space. This means that within a p element in HTML, the following,

```
Hello
there
```

would look like this in a browser:

```
Hello there
```

However, in XML, the original line break is preserved. XML includes a special attribute that can be used within any element called xml:space. You can use this to override XML's default line breaking behavior with the following:

```
xml:space = "preserve"
```

The options available for this attribute are default and preserve. Because the default corresponds to the default mechanism that allows for line breaks, you'll rarely specifically call for that value.

Document Type Definitions

As previously mentioned, an XML document that follows the syntax rules of XML is called a well-formed document. You can also have, or not have, a *valid* document. A document is valid if it *validates* against a Document Type Definition (DTD). A DTD is a document containing a list of rules about how the structure of an XML document should appear. For example, should all contact elements contain a phone element, like this?

```
<contact>
   <name>Johnny Rude</name>
   <address>111 East Onion Ave.</address>
   <phone>1-323-456-4444</phone>
</contact>
```

The preceding code fragment is a well-formed document as it stands. However, you may wish to define rules that more clearly delineate the purpose of each element and the position of each element within the framework, or structure, of the document as a whole.

A DTD can exist either outside the XML document that validates against it or within that same document. If the DTD exists outside of the document, you must declare it within the XML document so that the XML parser knows you're referring to an *external* DTD, like this:

```
<!DOCTYPE root SYSTEM "filename">
```

In the case of the preceding contact XML, the DOCTYPE declaration would look like this (the DOCTYPE declaration is in bold):

```
<?xml version="1.0"?>
 <!DOCTYPE contact SYSTEM "contact.dtd">
<contact>
   <name>Johnny Rude</name>
   <address>111 East Onion Ave.</address>
   <phone>1-323-456-4444</phone>
</contact>
```

You need to create a separate DTD file named contact.dtd when you declare such an external DTD, and that DTD must be adhered to.

You can also declare the DOCTYPE and define its rules within the actual XML document validating against it, as in the following example:

```
<?xml version="1.0"?>
<!DOCTYPE contact [
  <!ELEMENT contact (name, address, phone)>
    <!ELEMENT name      (#PCDATA)>
    <!ELEMENT address   (#PCDATA)>
    <!ELEMENT phone     (#PCDATA)>
]>
<contact>
   <name>Johnny Rude</name>
   <address>111 East Onion Ave.</address>
   <phone>1-323-456-4444</phone>
</contact>
```

The bolded markup contains the DTD. All you need to do to create an external DTD is take the following steps:

1. Create an inline DTD first, as done in the preceding code.

2. Cut the bolded part of the code out of the XML document and paste it into a new text file.

3. Name it contact.dtd (or whatever your DTD's name really is).

Of course, creating the DTD within the validating XML document is not a necessary first step. You can create the file separately from the beginning. But doing it within the validating XML makes it easy to test if you're using an XML-enabled browser such as IE5 and later or Mozilla (and Netscape 7.xxx). When you can load the file into a browser without any errors, you can then split the DTD markup (in bold in the preceding code) into a separate file and call it `contact.dtd` (or some other name), then refer to it in the XML document as previously shown:

```
<!DOCTYPE root SYSTEM "contact.dtd">
```

DTD and XML structure is defined using the following core components of XML:

✦ Elements

✦ Attributes

✦ Entities

✦ PCDATA

✦ CDATA

Each of these is described in the sections that follow.

Using elements in DTDs

Elements are the main data-containing components of XML. They are used to structure a document. You've seen them in HTML, and the core principles are the same in HTML. An element can contain data, or it can be empty. If it is empty, it normally consists of an attribute, but that isn't a requirement. The HTML `br` and `img` elements are good examples of empty elements.

XML elements are declared with an element declaration using the following syntax:

```
<!ELEMENT name    datatype>
```

The first part of the declaration (`!ELEMENT`) says that you are defining an element. The next part (`name`) is where you declare the name of your element. The next part (*datatype*) declares the type of data that an element can contain. An element can contain the following types of data when defined by DTDs:

✦ EMPTY data, which means there is no data within the element.

✦ PCDATA, or parsed character data.

✦ One or more child elements: There is always a root element and, if the XML document defined by the DTD is to contain additional elements, the DTD must define what those elements are in the root element's declaration.

Using element declaration syntax for empty elements

Empty elements are declared by using the keyword EMPTY:

```
<!ELEMENT name EMPTY>
```

For example, to declare an empty `br` element, you would write the following:

```
<!ELEMENT br EMPTY>
```

This element would appear as follows in an XML document:

```
<br />
```

Using element declaration syntax for elements with PCDATA

Elements that don't contain any other elements and only contain character data are declared with the keyword #PCDATA inside parentheses, like this:

```
<!ELEMENT name (#PCDATA)>
```

A typical example of such an element follows:

<!ELEMENT note (#PCDATA)>

An XML parser might then encounter an actual note element that looks like this:

```
<note>This note is to warn you that not all DTDs are good
DTDs. There are bad DTDs. DTD design is more an art than a
science.</note>
```

You can see there are no elements within the note element, just text (character data).

Using element declaration syntax for elements with child elements

Elements can contain sequences of one or more children, and are defined with the name of the children elements inside parentheses:

```
<!ELEMENT name (child_name)>
```

If there is more than one element, you separate each element with a comma:

```
<!ELEMENT name (child_name, child_name2)>
```

An example, using the code you saw earlier for the contact document, might look like this:

```
<!ELEMENT contact (name, address, phone)>
```

Declaring the number of occurrences for elements

You can also declare how often an element can appear within another element by using an *occurrence operator* in your element declaration. The plus sign (+) indicates that an element *must* occur at least one or more times within an element. Therefore, if you create the following declaration, the phone element must appear at least once within the `contact` element:

```
<!ELEMENT contact (phone+)>
```

You can declare that a group of elements must appear at least one or more times:

```
<!ELEMENT contact (name, address, phone)+>
```

To declare that an element can appear zero or more times (in other words, it's an optional element), use an asterisk instead of a plus sign, as in the following:

```
<!ELEMENT contact (phone*)>
```

If you want to limit an element to zero or one occurrence, use a question mark (?) operator instead:

```
<!ELEMENT contact (phone?)>
```

The following XML would not be valid when the declaration uses a ? operator for the phone element:

```
<contact>
    <phone>222-222-2222</phone>
    <phone>222-222-2223</phone>
</contact>
```

You can also use a pipe operator (|) to indicate that one element *or* another element can be contained within an element:

```
<!ELEMENT contact (name,address,phone,(email | fax))>
```

In the preceding declaration, the sequence of name, address, and phone elements must all appear in the order shown, followed by either the email or fax elements. This means the following XML is valid:

```
<contact>
    <name>John Smith</name>
    <address>111 West Main St.</address>
    <phone>212-222-2222</phone>
    <email>west@main.com</email>
</contact>
```

However, the following XML would not be valid if validating against the same DTD:

```
<contact>
    <name>John Smith</name>
    <address>111 West Main St.</address>
    <phone>212-222-2222</phone>
    <email>west@main.com</email>
    <fax>222-222-2222</fax>
</contact>
```

As a test of what you've seen so far, look at Listing 31-1 and see if you can determine why it won't validate. What could you do to make it work?

Listing 31-1: A Nonvalidating XML Document

```
<?xml version="1.0"?>
<!DOCTYPE contact [
  <!ELEMENT contact (name, address, (address)?, city, state,
postalcode, phone, (email | fax))>
  <!ELEMENT name          (#PCDATA)>
  <!ELEMENT address       (#PCDATA)>
  <!ELEMENT city          (#PCDATA)>
  <!ELEMENT state         (#PCDATA)>
  <!ELEMENT postalcode    (#PCDATA)>
  <!ELEMENT phone         (#PCDATA)>
  <!ELEMENT email         (#PCDATA)>
  <!ELEMENT fax           (#PCDATA)>
]>
<contact>
  <name>Johnny Rude</name>
  <address>111 East Onion Ave.</address>
  <city>Big City</city>
  <state>CA</state>
  <postalcode>96777</postalcode>
  <phone>1-323-456-4444</phone>
  <fax>test</fax>
  <email>rude@rude.com</email>
</contact>
```

If you try to parse Listing 31-1 using a validating parser, you'll get an error. The reason is because there is a `fax` and an `email` element, but the DTD in bold calls for an `email` *or* a `fax` element. To fix the document, you need to remove either the `fax` or the `email` element.

Using attributes in DTDs

Attributes define the properties of an element. For example, in HTML, the `img` element has an `src` property, or attribute, that describes where an image can be found. When deciding whether something should be an element or attribute, ask yourself if the potential attribute is a property that helps describe the element in some way. Attributes shouldn't contain data with line breaks unless you're okay with those breaks being replaced with one nonbreaking space, because attributes don't render line breaks in XML.

Using entities in DTDs

Entities are used to store frequently used or referenced character data. You've already seen some of XML's predefined entities. You can also create your own. When you do that, you must declare them in your DTD. You can't, for example, simply use ` ` in an XML document. You must first declare it by defining what it means and letting the XML parser know about it. When an XML parser encounters an entity it *expands* that entity. For example, this means that the parser recognizes   as a nonbreaking space if you have defined it as such.

Using PCDATA and CDATA in DTDs

PCDATA is parsed character data, which means that all character data is parsed as XML; any starting or closing tags are recognized, and entities are expanded. Elements contain PCDATA.

CDATA is data that is not parsed by the processor. This means that tags are not recognized, and entities are not expanded. Attributes do not contain PCDATA; they contain CDATA.

XML Schemas

DTDs can be somewhat limiting. Consider, for example, the following XML document:

```
<datatypes>
<Boolean>true</Boolean>
<integer>1</integer>
<double>563.34</double>
<date>11-01-2006</date>
</datatypes>
```

As far as a DTD that might define the rules for the preceding code fragment is concerned, every element contains character data. The value for the integer element is not actually an integer, and the date isn't a date. This is because DTDs don't have mathematical, Boolean, or date types of data.

The W3C introduced another rules development methodology called XML Schema to handle richer data typing and more granular sets of rules that allow for much greater specificity than DTDs. In addition to the types of rules DTDs manage, Schema manages the number of child elements that can be used, as well as data types allowed in an element, such as Booleans and integers.

The use of datatyping is especially important because it facilitates working with traditional databases and application program interfaces (APIs) based on Java, C++, and other languages, such as JavaScript.

Working with Schemas

Now that you're familiar with DTDs, it should be fairly easy to see how their concepts extend to a greater range of datatypes. XML Schema uses XML syntax to develop rule sets, so it is actually more intuitive than the DTD syntax you saw earlier in the chapter.

Recall that an example earlier in the chapter created a simple XML document for contacts that was derived from `contact.dtd`. Let's call that XML document `contact.xml`. If you look at Listing 31-2, you can see the same principles at work in a schema. Pay particular attention to the `xs:sequence` `xs:element` children (in bold) that live in the `xs:complexType` element.

Listing 31-2: A Schema for a Contact XML Document

```xml
<?xml version="1.0"?>
<xs:schema xmlns:xs="http://www.w3.org/2001/XMLSchema"
targetNamespace="http://www.tumeric.net/schemas"
xmlns="http://www.tumeric.net/schemas"
elementFormDefault="qualified">
<xs:element name="contact">
    <xs:complexType>
      <xs:sequence>
<xs:element name="name" type="xs:string"/>
<xs:element name="address" type="xs:string"/>
<xs:element name="city" type="xs:string"/>
<xs:element name="state" type="xs:string"/>
<xs:element name="postalcode" type="xs:string"/>
<xs:element name="age" type="xs:integer" />
      </xs:sequence>
    </xs:complexType>
</xs:element>
</xs:schema>
```

In a DTD, the sequence of elements that should appear in the `contact.xml` document was defined by placing commas between elements in an element definition. In XML Schema, a sequence is defined by creating a sequence of elements in a specific order with an `xs:sequence` element. This is part of the larger definition of the XML document's root element, which is the `contact` element. Note the use of the `type` attribute in the `xs:element` element, which defines the data type.

Numerous datatypes are available. If you're familiar with the Java programming language, it might help you to know that most of the datatypes are very similar to Java datatypes. If you're not familiar with Java, Schema consists of four basic datatypes:

✦ numerical (such as integer and double)

✦ date

✦ string

✦ Booleans

Tip

You can find out the specifics of various datatypes available through XML: Schema at `www.w3.org/TR/xmlschema-2/`.

The `contact` element is a *complex type* of element because it contains other elements. If an element isn't defined by giving it child elements, it's a *simple* type of element.

To reference a schema in an XML document, refer to it like this:

```
<?xml version="1.0"?>
<contact xmlns="http://www.tumeric.net/schemas"
xmlns:xsi="http://www.w3.org/2001/XMLSchema-instance"
xsi:schemaLocation=
"http://www.tumeric.net/schemas/contact.xsd">
    <name>Johhny Rude</name>
    <address>111 East Onion Ave.</address>
    <city>Big City</city>
    <state>CA</state>
    <postalcode>96777</postalcode>
    <phone>1-323-456-4444</phone>
    <fax>test</fax>
    <email>rude@rude.com</email>
</contact>
```

The schema is referenced through a *namespace*. A namespace is represented in an XML document by a namespace declaration, which looks suspiciously like an element attribute but isn't. This is an important distinction, because when you work with an XML document's Document Object Model a namespace is part of that model, as is an attribute, so don't confuse the two. The syntax looks like this:

```
xmlns="http://www.tumeric.net/schemas"
xmlns:xsi="http://www.w3.org/2001/XMLSchema-instance"
xsi:schemaLocation="
http://www.tumeric.net/schemas/contact.xsd"
```

Only the code highlighted in bold is an attribute/value pair. The other two lines of code are namespaces, which serve as identifiers. They tell a processor that elements associated with them are unique and may have specially developed definitions. The important part of the namespace is the Uniform Resource Identifier (URI), which is what gives a namespace its unique identity. Therefore, when elements live within a specific namespace governed by a schema, they must adhere to the rules of that schema.

The first namespace in the preceding code fragment refers to a namespace established in the schema that uniquely binds the schema to a specified resource, in this case a Web site. You don't have to refer to a Web site, and the reference is not actually a physical pointer. Instead, the URI is simply an easy way to establish identity, because a Web site should be unique. It isn't guaranteed to be unique, of course, because anyone can hijack your Web site address name and use it for their own schema, but it has become fairly standard practice to do so. You could, instead of a Web site name, use a long mash of characters, as in the following example:

```
xmlns="hk45kskds-scld456ksaldkttsslae697hg"
```

The second namespace refers to the W3C's schema location so that XML processors will validate the XML document against the schema. This is necessary because you then need to call the resource you're using, in this case, a schema that can be found on the path named in the `xsi:SchemaLocation` attribute. When the processor finds the schema, it attempts to validate the XML document as the document loads. If the XML document doesn't conform to the rules you set forth in the schema definition, an error will result (assuming your parser can work with XML Schema).

XML on the Web

Many companies leverage XML on the Web by using it as part of their middle tier. For example, a database can be used to store and return data to users, but along the way that data may be converted to XML, which, in turn, is transformed using Extensible Stylesheet Language Transformations (XSLT) into HTML renderable on a browser.

XSLT has thus become an integral part of any XML deployment on the Web. To render any meaningful HTML from XML, you'll need to have at least a basic understanding of how XSLT works.

Summary

XML has played a significant role in many large Web sites during the last few years. If you are a Web development professional, there isn't any doubt that at some point, a prospective employer will ask you about it, or a current employer will want to know if you're ready to help with migration to an XML-based environment. Even if you're a freelancer or hobbyist, you'll find yourself exposed to XML frequently.

Most Web logs, for example, which are covered in Chapter 30, rely on XML to store data, and use an XML-based syntax, Rich Site Summary (RSS), for managing syndication. The list goes on. The bottom line is that you'll want to learn how to convert, or transform, XML documents into HTML. To do this, you'll need to learn something about XSLT and other XML components, which are covered in the next chapter.

✦   ✦   ✦

XML Processing and Implementations

Chapter 31 gave you a taste of what XML is like and how it works, but now it's time to figure out exactly what you can do with it. As an HTML/Web developer, you'll be processing XML so that you can generate HTML pages for the Web. Doing this requires that you understand the essential aspects of addressing an XML document. In other words, how do you access the various parts of an XML document, referred to as *nodes*, and then do something with each of those parts? This chapter explores how to process XML, heavily emphasizing the transformation language that makes it possible, Extensible Stylesheet Language Transformations (XSLT).

Processing XML

You can take various chunks of XML documents and output them into HTML. To do this, you must use the XSLT language. This is a language designed to take XML "source" documents and transform them into something else, such as HTML. But to work with XSLT, you need to have an idea how another language, called Xpath, works.

XPath

When working with XML documents you'll often work with a process that takes one or more chunks of the XML document and does something with it. The process may be one that *transforms* the XML into an HTML document so that browsers can view the XML data in a nicely formatted way, or it may be a SQL Server database that extracts bits of an XML document to dump into a query or database table. For these processes to work, you need to be able to get at certain parts of a document. Generally, the way to do that is through the use of XPath.

XPath is often associated with a host language that uses specific aspects of XPath but may expand on the core XPath framework and provide additional functionality. XSLT is a classic example of a host language for XPath. XQuery is another.

XPath, like XML, is case-sensitive, and all XPath keywords use lower case.

At the core of XPath is an expression. The result of every expression is a sequence, an ordered collection of zero or more items.

Finding information using XPath

When someone gives you an address for an important meeting and you don't know where it is, what do you do? Most likely, you employ one of those online mapping services or maybe even use a GPS service from your car. Either way, you end up with a mapping service that shows you the route to your address. This route may be a very short, simple route, or a very complex one, depending on the quality of the mapping service and where your address is in relation to your starting point. Assume for a moment that someone has given you directions from one part of San Francisco to another. You're trying to get from the 500 block of Hayes Street to 50 United Nations Plaza by car. To do this, you need to know something about the structure of the city's street layout. There is some linkage between each step of the route. Here are the basic directions:

1. Start out going North on OCTAVIA ST toward IVY ST.
2. Turn RIGHT onto GROVE ST.
3. Turn RIGHT onto HYDE ST.
4. Turn LEFT onto MARKET ST.

Notice that you can't go straight from Octavia to Hyde Street. You have to follow a specific series of steps because all of the streets in the city are connected to each other and have a relationship with one another that you must address to traverse the city.

XPath works the same way. XPath addresses an XML document, allowing you to traverse that document. Luckily, traveling around an XML document is much easier than traveling around San Francisco, because an XML document has a tree structure like that shown in Figure 32-1, whereas San Francisco streets require years of study to understand.

Locations and steps

A typical XPath expression walks along the structure of a document that relies on the development of a link between the node being searched and the root node. Break that link, and it is much more difficult to find out where you are in a document.

Note   The root node in XPath is always the document node. Don't confuse this with the root element, which is the first element encountered in an XML document.

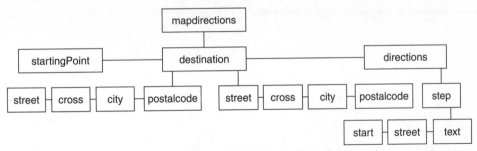

Figure 32-1: You can navigate an XML document by "walking" along a tree structure.

Consider the following path. It's not an XPath, but it looks a lot like one, as you'll soon discover:

```
C:\Program Files\Internet Explorer\Setup
```

The preceding snippet is an addressing scheme for a file management system on your hard drive (if you're on Windows).

An XPath works the same way when it traverses an XML document to help you and your cohorts find information. Consider the XML document in Listing 32-1

Listing 32-1: **Map Directions Mapped to an XML Document**

```xml
<?xml version="1.0" encoding="UTF-8"?>
<mapdirections>
    <startingPoint>
        <street>500 Hayes St</street>
        <cross/>
        <city>San Francisco</city>
        <postalCode>94102-4214</postalCode>
    </startingPoint>
    <destination>
        <street>50 United Nations Plz</street>
        <cross/>
        <city>San Francisco</city>
            <postalCode>94102-4910</postalCode>
    </destination>
    <directions>
        <step>
            <start direction="North"/>
            <street>Octavia St</street>
            <text>North, towards Ivy St.</text>
        </step>
        <step>
            <street>Grove St</street>
            <text>Turn RIGHT onto GROVE ST.</text>
        </step>
```

Continued

Listing 32-1 *(continued)*

```
<!-- XPath: /mapdirections/directions/step -->
<step>
    <street>Hyde St</street>
    <text>Turn RIGHT onto HYDE ST.</text>
</step>
<step>
    <street>Market St</street>
    <text>Turn LEFT onto MARKET ST.</text>
</step>
    </directions>
</mapdirections>
```

To extract information out of Listing 32-1 you need to start somewhere. That beginning is referred to as the *context node,* the originating node from which an XPath expression is evaluated. To find the street element representing the first step you need to get to your destination, you write an XPath that walks the XML document tree, as in the following example:

```
/mapdirections/directions[1]/step[1]/street[1]
```

The [1] in the preceding code fragment indicates the first node within a node set, so directions[1] means the first directions element. When you lead off your expression with the / character, you are indicating the document's root node. More formally, a path expression consists of a series of one or more steps separated by /, and which can, but are not required to, begin with / or // (you'll learn about the // characters later). In other words, I didn't have to lead off the preceding statement with the / character; I simply chose it to be certain that the XPath processor would begin evaluating the XML document at the root level. If you look at the directions to the destination again, you'll see that no matter where you are in your route, the starting point never changes. That starting point is like your root node. But as you progress along the route, obviously your position does change. This position along the route is your context node. From this point, any time along the route, you can change your direction. You can decide to change routes or even your final destination, but you must always begin at your current point along the route.

If you leave off the / character, the XPath processor will begin to evaluate the expression from wherever the processor was in the document at the time the statement was read; in other words, from your context node. So leading off with a / character forces the starting point of your journey to begin at the root node of the document. If you tried to access the node by providing XPath analysis software nothing more than the street element, the software would likely not find it. It would be as if a mapping tool, in giving you the directions I've been referring to, simply said, "Go to Hyde Street."

Note
The root node in XPath is always the document node, and consists of all the nodes of the entire document. Don't confuse this with the root element, which is the first element encountered in an XML document.

A street system in a city is a form of linking system. XPath also provides a consistent linking mechanism via a special notation called *location steps*. In their simplest form, location steps are simply the process of getting from one part of the tree to another, step by step, until you reach your destination. In other words, a location step is a progression through an XML document tree that begins at the context node and moves through the hierarchy in a specific direction you define in order to get to your destination.

A discussion of some fundamentals behind location steps follows to show you how you can access different nodes.

For simplicity, continuing with the idea of map directions in San Francisco, say you only need the value of the last street in the directions. You already know where you're going to end up. You can see this by scanning the document. However, the XPath processor doesn't know this and will need specific instructions on how to navigate to the last street element. There are actually a lot of ways to do that, as you will see as you move your way around XPath.

When traversing documents using location steps, you can use unabbreviated or abbreviated syntax. The unabbreviated syntax relies on something called an *axis*. An axis uses the context node, which is basically whatever your starting point is when your location step is defined, to move either forwards or backwards from the context node, or, if you prefer, up and down the XML source document tree. Figure 32-2 shows one view of this, and Figure 32-3 shows a more traditional XPath schematic of a document (both of these are based on Listing 32-1).

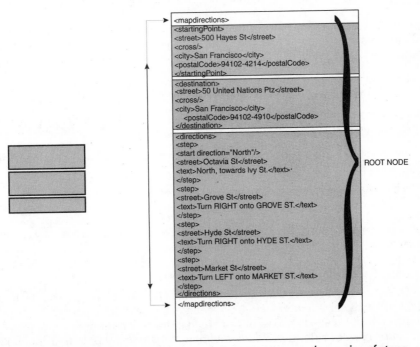

Figure 32-2: Walking up and down a document tree reveals a series of steps you can use to traverse a tree.

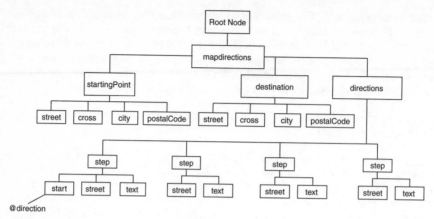

Figure 32-3: A schematic of an XML document.

A typical unabbreviated axis notation looks like this:

```
child::*
```

The axis is on the left side of the : : characters, and on the right side is a node test.

Here's an example with the XPath you need to drop into the statement in bold:

```
/mapdirections/directions[1]/step[1]/street[1]
```

If you want to access one or more of the nodes indicating a `street` value, you'll need to address your document in the same way you provide directions to someone to an address they provide:

1. The `mapdirections` node is retrieved when using `child::*` or its abbreviated syntax, `/*` or `*`.

2. The `startingPoint` node is retrieved when using `child::*/child::*` or its abbreviated syntax, `/*/*`.

3. The first step node is retrieved when using `child::*/child::*/child::*` or its abbreviated syntax, `/*/*/*`.

4. Each street node is accessed using `/child::*/child::*/child::* /street` or `/*/*/*/street`.

Each step progresses along the tree following a very specific pattern until you find your way to the one of the elements you're looking for.

Using axes for directing traffic

When you're viewing directions for an address to a city street, you are usually told to turn right or left at certain intersections. When dealing with XML documents, the direction you turn is called an axis, only instead of turning right or left, you move forward, in reverse, or sideways. When you move forward, you refer to a child axis, as you've just seen. In the `child::*` XPath, `child` is axis, the : : characters are a delimiter, and the * is a node test. The node test might be something else, such as a specific element. When you move in reverse, you refer to a parent axis, which looks like this: `parent::*`. When you move sideways, you refer to a sibling, like this: `preceding-sibling::*` or `following-sibling::*`. XPath uses a number of axes, which are listed in Table 32-1. Each kind of axis lets you traverse the document going in one direction or another.

	Table 32-1 **XPath Axes**	
Axis	**Description**	**Example**
Child	Contains the direct children of the context node when the context node is a root or element node. Used to move forward (or down) the XML document tree hierarchy	`child::*`
Descendant	Contains the descendents of the context node. This is beyond direct children, and includes children of children, and children of children of children. Used to move forward (or down) the XML document tree hierarchy	`/descendant::*`
Parent	Contains the direct parent of the context node. Used to move in reverse (or up) along the XML document tree hierarchy	`//street[parent::node() [name()='step']]`
following-sibling	Contains all sibling nodes that occur after the context node. Used for moving sideways along the same level of a document	`/step/street[following-sibling::node()[.= 'North, towards Ivy St.']]`
preceding-sibling	Contains all sibling nodes that occur before the context node. Used for moving sideways along the same level of a document	`text[preceding-sibling:: node()[.='Octavia St']]`

Continued

Table 32-1 (continued)

Axis	Description	Example
Self	This is the context node itself	self::*
descendant-or-self	Contains all descendant nodes as well as the context node itself, not including attribute or namespace nodes	descendant-or-self::someElement
ancestor-or-self	Contains all ancestor nodes, as well as the context node itself	//text[last()]/ ancestor- or-self::*
Ancestor	Contains all the ancestor nodes of the context node in reverse document order. The first node instance is the parent of the context node, the second node is the grandparent, and the third is the great-grandparent. This pattern is followed to the top of the document	/street[ancestor:: node() [name()='step']]
Following	Contains all the nodes that follow the current node, except for attribute or namespace nodes and descendent nodes	following::*
Preceding	Contains all the nodes that precede the current node	preceding::*
Attribute	Contains all the attribute nodes of the context node	attribute::myAttribute Name
Namespace	Contains the namespace nodes of the context node	namespace::*

Style sheets for XML: XSLT

As a Web developer, you'll need to be able to understand the process of transforming XML documents into HTML and other formats. This process is based on a language called XSLT. Many people call XSLT XSL, but XSL is actually a language for specifically transforming documents into a print-based XML vocabulary called XSL Formatting Objects (XSL-FO). XSLT is the engine that drives all transformations from XML to other formats, such as HTML, other XML documents with different structure, text, and XSL-FO, which in turn is often converted into PDF. This chapter focuses on XSLT.

> **Note** XSLT is often referred to as XSL. Technically, XSL is the formatting language informally known as XSL-FO, but the convention of most developers has been to refer to XSLT as XSL, even though it's really not technically correct to do so. This book refers to XSLT by its proper name/acronym.

XSLT is a complex language. You can get through the basics fairly quickly, but it can take some time to master complex tasks. This chapter introduces you to a few of the basic concepts. For further information, you should consult a book written specifically for XSLT development.

Transformation using XSLT

At its most basic, a transformation using XSLT occurs when you transform a document like this:

```
<bad>A bad document</bad>
```

to this:

```
<good>A good document</good>
```

In other words, you transform a document whenever you want to *change the markup* of an XML document into another format, such as HTML, SVG, or SMIL (just to name a few examples), or into a set of new XML elements. You can change the name of elements when you transform a document, and you can even transform the content of a document by replacing it with different content. Here's another example of a transformation from the "bad" document into something else:

```
<html>
<head>
</head>
<body>
A bad document
</body>
</html>
```

You can see the resulting document is completely different. It consists of a series of new elements, in this case HTML elements, as shown in Figure 32-4.

A transformation is generated when a special kind of software called an XSLT processor receives an XML document called a source document. The source document must be well-formed XML, because the XSLT processor works in tandem with an XML parser (which often comes bundled with the XSLT processor you're using). The XML parser reviews the XML source document, and if it decides the

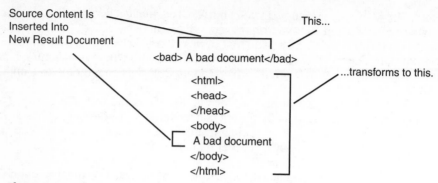

Figure 32-4: The source content is transformed into HTML.

source document is a legitimate XML document, it then passes the document along to the XSLT processor.

The XSLT processor then examines the XSLT style sheet that you write and, based on that style sheet, attempts to detect what kind of document you are trying to create. Once it can detect what kind of document you are trying to create, it then outputs the type of markup you need based on the markup instructions in your XSLT document. The output may be a series of XML elements, an HTML document, or a series of strings (called text nodes). It creates the output by using a series of elements that exist within the XSLT *namespace*.

A namespace is a mechanism that allows the definition of an XML element to be unambiguously identified within an XML document. This identification is made possible by binding an element to a Uniform Resource Identifier (a URL or URN). Namespaces are covered more thoroughly in the section titled *Namespaces are your friend—really they are* later in the chapter.

XSLT relies on XPath for addressing documents. It uses a subset of the XPath language called pattern matching to define a set of rules that a specific node should follow in order to be processed, and it uses the full XPath expression syntax to select nodes for processing (generally, but not exclusively, through an XSLT element's `select` or `test` attribute). Whenever you see the `select` attribute in an XSLT element, it's a cue that you have encountered an XPath expression.

Getting started with XSLT

If you're on Windows, running some XML through an XSLT processor is as easy as using Internet Explorer. Just be sure you're using Internet Explorer 6 (not 5 or below). Earlier versions use an antiquated, pre-1.0 version of XSL, and running the code you see in this chapter will not work in anything other than Internet Explorer 6. To use it, add a processing instruction to your XML file that you want to transform, and then load the XML file into Internet Explorer. The processing instruction should look like this:

```
<?xml-stylesheet type="text/xsl" href="foo.xsl"?>
```

You can also use the latest Mozilla builds to view style sheet-rendered XML using the same processing instruction previously shown. The advantage of using Mozilla is that it shouldn't matter what operating system you're using. It should work as well on a Mac or Linux as it does on Windows.

You can also use command-line programs such as Saxon, created by the editor of the upcoming XSLT 2.0 specification, Michael Kay, or Xalan, created by The Apache Foundation.

Note   Look for Saxon at `http://saxon.sourceforge.net/`, and look for Xalan at `http://xml.apache.org/xalan-j/`.

Both of these are Java-based XSLT processors that integrate well with Web servers such as Apache.

Outputting XML and HTML using XSLT

XSLT has built-in outputting options that make it easy to output just about any text-based output you can think of, in addition to XML. For example, you can output HTML. You can also output text. In addition, an XSLT processor automatically makes certain adjustments for the output you choose. If you choose to output XML, the XSLT processor will output an XML declaration at the top of the document that is generated, and if you generate HTML, it will create a minimum amount of meta information that becomes more detailed depending on the parameters you decide on when you develop the stylesheet. It will also convert `<br />` elements into more HTML-friendly `<br>` elements and output other HTML elements correctly, even though you need to write them within your style sheet using XML syntax.

The first thing an XSLT processor needs to know as it begins to process a source document for transformation is what kind of output to generate. This is handled by the aptly named `xsl:output` element. This element lets you decide what format your result document, which is also often called a result tree, when output to XML because of its hierarchical nature, should take. A result document/tree is simply the result of the transformation after it has made its way through the XSLT processor. There is no requirement that the result be well-formed XML. The result can be just about any text format you can think of from text to Rich Text Format.

The `xsl:output` element is a top-level element, meaning it isn't nested within any other elements. Convention also suggests that you should include it as close to the `xsl:stylesheet` or `xsl:transform` element as you can. The syntax for the `xsl:output` element looks like this:

```
xsl:output
  name = qname
  method = "xml" | "html" | "text"
  version = nmtoken
  encoding = string
  omit-xml-declaration = "yes" | "no"
  standalone = "yes" | "no"
  doctype-public = string
  doctype-system = string
  cdata-section-elements = qnames
  indent = "yes" | "no"
  media-type = string
```

The encoding attribute is important because, as mentioned in the previous chapter, you need to keep your encodings consistent between XML documents. The `method` attribute of the `xsl:output` element is also obviously important. The default is `xml`. Choosing `indent="yes"` will pretty-print your result document, meaning it will indent your results to make them easier to read.

Creating style sheets

Now that you've seen what kind of output you can generate, you need to know how to do it. At the very top of every style sheet is an element called the `xsl:stylesheet` element. You can also use the `xsl:transform` element. They both mean exactly the same thing, and provide exactly the same functionality.

This element helps establish the fact that the XML document containing the `xsl:stylesheet` element is in fact a style sheet document that should be read by an XSLT processor, as in the following example:

```
<?xml version="1.0" encoding="UTF-8"?>
<xsl:stylesheet>
</xsl:stylesheet>
```

However, just because you know it's a style sheet doesn't mean that any XML processing software will know it. XML is great for letting you create intuitive elements, but something needs to provide a hint about what exactly the `xsl:stylesheet` element does.

Namespaces are your friend—really they are

One way to identify an XML element name, or group of names, and their purpose, is by using a namespace, and binding that namespace to an imaginary friend. In this case, the imaginary friend is a URI that seems shaped like a URL, but the URI can really take on any shape at all. You'll want to form it in a way that can somehow provide a uniquely identifying characteristic to the namespace, which is why so many software developers bind their namespace to a Uniform Resource Identifier (URI) that looks like it resolves to a URL. A URI identifies a resource by way of some kind of meta information; a URL locates a resource, and a URL is itself a type of URI.

To offer a concrete example of the importance of namespaces, imagine you're an IT professional for a company that specializes in body stockings for magicians. Further, say that you wrote some software that communicated, through an XML message, to the factory floor the elements and attributes specific to these body stockings. You could use this XML document to send to some firmware some specifics about the body stockings. Perhaps you've developed some software that the machines on your factory floor use to help in the fabrication process for making hosiery, and the software has a built-in processor that looks for the namespace you've developed:

```
xmlns:xsl= "http://fancystockings.magical.com"
```

The namespace is in bold. This makes your element unique to your organization, in this case, your company, Fancy Stockings. Your namespace URI doesn't have to be a Web site. It can be anything you feel will uniquely identify your elements. So a fragment from your XML document might look like this:

```
<?xml version="1.0" encoding="UTF-8"?>
<xsl:stylesheet
xmlns:xsl="http://fancystockings.magical.com">
   <xsl:stocking type="silk" color="chartreuse">
     <xsl:fibercount>600000000001</xsl:fibercount>
   </xsl:stocking>
</xsl:stylesheet>
```

Note the use of the xsl prefix. Because you are using your own namespace, http://fancystockings.magical.com, this document has nothing to do with XSLT, even though it uses what looks to be XSLT elements.

The absolutely vital part of this document fragment is the namespace, as represented by the namespace declaration that leads off with xmlns. (Oh, a quick aside here. xmlns is not an attribute. It's a namespace declaration. This matters, because if you are searching your document for attribute nodes using XPath and expect to find your namespace, it will pull a major disappearing act. The trick to finding it will be to hunt for namespace nodes.) The namespace is shared by the imaginary software you built for the machinery on the factory floor. You design the software so that it will recognize one namespace and one namespace only, and that is the fancystockings.magical.com namespace. Interestingly enough, you don't even have to use the xsl: prefix in your XML document for your software to understand that you're working with a magician's body stocking elements. The only part that has to jive is the URI that is bound to your namespace. If you don't believe it, try doing a search and replace on all your style sheet elements after you get the hang of XSLT. Replace the xsl: prefix with anything else containing a colon at the end (in other words, any other namespace prefix). For example, you could replace xsl: with foo:, just be sure to also change the prefix bound to the namespace. The style sheet processor will recognize the style sheet as long as you have the correct namespace. And this namespace is as follows:

```
http://www.w3.org/1999/XSL/Transform
```

The only significance to this URI is the fact that an XSLT processor will recognize it. It has nothing to do with any actual network traffic, and you don't need to be connected to the Internet to make it recognizable to an XSLT processor. All you need is the software. When you add this namespace to the original style sheet document, as follows, it makes the XML document instantly recognizable to an XSLT processor:

```
<xsl:stylesheet
xmlns:xsl="http://www.w3.org/1999/XSL/Transform">
```

But when you're developing your style sheet, you could do this instead:

```
<foo:stylesheet
xmlns:foo="http://www.w3.org/1999/XSL/Transform">
```

The prefix is not the namespace; the URI the prefix is bound to is the namespace (see Figure 32-5):

```
http://www.w3.org/1999/XSL/Transform
```

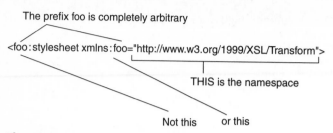

Figure 32-5: Deconstructing a namespace.

Adding versioning control with the version attribute

Now that the XSLT processor will recognize the namespace and react accordingly, the first thing it will do is scream about an error. This is because you need to include the version attribute so the processor knows which version of XSLT you are using.

> **Note** Generally, you'll use version="1.0" because, as of this writing, XSLT 2.0 has not yet been released; and it will probably be a while after it is released before production-ready XSLT processors get to market, as version 2.0 will undergo some major changes in the way data typing is handled (XSLT 2.0 will include support for data types such as integers and Booleans).

This wraps up your first style sheet. The following style sheet will return every node of a document:

```
<xsl:stylesheet version="2.0"
xmlns:xsl="http://www.w3.org/1999/XSL/Transform">
</xsl:stylesheet>
```

Because this style sheet doesn't specify any details, it will simply return all the text nodes of the document jumbled together, but it's a start. A hidden element is at play here, a template element that guarantees that something will get returned if you don't ever get around to defining your own output instructions.

Listing 32-2 shows how a typical shell for a style sheet might look. There are some elements involved you haven't been introduced to yet, but it's a good idea now to get an idea of the overall structure of a style sheet.

Listing 32-2: **An XSLT Shell**

```
<xsl:stylesheet version="1.0"
xmlns:xsl="http://www.w3.org/1999/XSL/Transform">
<xsl:output method="html"/>
<!-- or some other output method -->
   <xsl:template match="/">
      <!-- matches the root of the XML document tree -->
<html>
   <head>
   <title>My first XSLT document</title>
   </head>
```

```
    <body>
     Directions to:
      <xsl:value-of
 select="mapdirections/startingPoint/street" />
     </body>
  </html>
      </xsl:template>
  </xsl:stylesheet>
```

To view the XSLT transformation in a browser, add the following Processing Instruction to Listing 32-1, immediately underneath the XML declaration (in bold in Listing 32-1):

```
  <?xml-stylesheet type="text/xsl" href="L3202.xsl" ?>
```

If you have access to Mozilla 1.0 or higher, Netscape 7.0 or higher, or Internet Explorer 6.0 or higher, you can view the transformation in your browser. Otherwise, you'll need an XML parser and XSLT processor.

One of the keys to Listing 32-2 is the `xsl:value-of` element, which generates the *text* value of a named node from a source document. Since the value of the street element is `500 Hayes St`, that's the value inserted by the `xsl:value-of` element. You can see the result of using Listing 32-2 with Listing 32-1 as a source document in Figure 32-6.

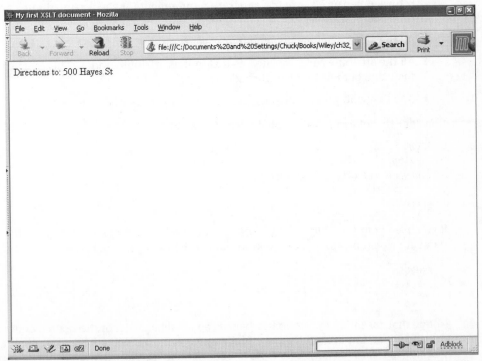

Figure 32-6: The result of transforming Listing 32-1 with Listing 32-2 as rendered in Mozilla.

Introducing templates

You may have noticed an `xsl:template` element in the brief XSLT shell shown in Listing 32-2. This is the primary rule maker that controls what kind of output is generated. The `xsl:template` element creates a rule that contains instructions about what and how to output nodes from the XML source tree. The templates themselves don't actually process anything; they merely carry the rules that tell other elements how to process results.

There is a corresponding `xsl:apply-templates` element that chooses which `xsl:template`, or rule, to apply, because you can have many rules in one document for any number of different nodes. If there is no `xsl:template` element in the style sheet, a default rule is invoked. If there is no `xsl:apply-templates` element, the template matching the root of the document is processed. You can also process templates using the `xsl:call-template` element. In that case, you define your template and give it a name using the `name` attribute, and then use the `xsl:call-template` element later to process it when the `xsl:call-template` element's name attribute matches the name attribute in the template you are calling.

When using the `xsl:apply-templates` element, the default rule, when applied, processes nodes in the following way:

✦ All the children of the root nodes are processed, or returned, to the result tree. This might seem confusing at first, since it would be normal to imagine that this means, for example, that an attribute node will automatically end up in the root tree. Indeed, it does, but only the text contained in the attribute value is returned because there is a separate requirement for the way attributes are returned.

✦ All the children of each element are also returned.

✦ All the attributes are returned as text, not as attribute nodes. This means that the value of their text is returned.

✦ No comment, processing-instruction, or namespace nodes are returned.

Consider the following source document fragment:

```
<BSR>
    <VERB value="PROCESS">PROCESS</VERB>
    <NOUN value="INVOICE">INVOICE</NOUN>
    <REVISION value="002">002</REVISION>
</BSR>
```

If you used your basically empty style sheet to process these nodes, a default template would be applied and you would get the following back:

```
PROCESS
INVOICE
002
```

Notice that essentially what comes back is an amalgamation of the textual content of the document, but in a pretty unhelpful way (imagine a 20MB source document and you can see what I mean). So a style sheet's default template generally needs your interdiction. You can stop all this default processing by adding one single instruction rule, with one very simple instruction (like the example shown in bold in the following):

```
<?xml version="1.0" encoding="UTF-8"?>
<xsl:stylesheet version="2.0"
xmlns:xsl="http://www.w3.org/1999/XSL/Transform">
  <xsl:template match="/">
    Magical pants for magical people
  </xsl:template>
</xsl:stylesheet>
```

In the `xsl:template` element in the preceding code, if you had left off the string of text "Magical pants for magical people" from the `xsl:template` and had simply done this:

```
<xsl:template match="/">
</xsl:template>
```

You would end up with an empty node set in your result document. This can be a neat trick, actually because a default template is always going to be invoked against the root node of a document. By extension, this means that, in effect, a default template is also invoked against other nodes in the source document that are children of the root node. At times, you'll find it convenient to stop the default processing of one node for some reason as a programming strategy.

A quick glance at XSLT syntax might suggest that templates are governed exclusively through the use of the `xsl:template` and `xsl:apply-templates` elements. This is a sensible conclusion, because the `xsl:template` element is such an important feature of the language, but there is a distinction between template rules, which are defined by the `xsl:template` element, and other forms of "template content." In fact, several elements contain template content. These are called *content constructors* in XSLT 2.0, and although the term isn't defined for XSLT 1.0, it fits nicely. Table 32-2 shows the content constructors available in XSLT 1.0.

Table 32-2
XSLT Template Elements

Element Name	Purpose	Parent Element(s)
xsl:comment	Generates comments into the result tree using XML comment syntax	Any content constructor; any literal result element
xsl:copy	Copies the current node to the result tree	Any content constructor; any literal result element
xsl:element	Creates an element	Any content constructor; any literal result element

Continued

Table 32-2 *(continued)*

Element Name	Purpose	Parent Element(s)
xsl:for-each	Iterates through one or more nodes and generates its content for each instance	Any content constructor; any literal result element
xsl:if	Contains instructions that will only be processed if the expression in the xsl:if select attribute is true	Any content constructor; any literal result element
xsl:message	Generates a system message to the user	Any XSLT element whose content model is content constructor; any literal result element xsl:function element
xsl:otherwise	Used in conjunction with the xsl:when statement to provide one last option in the alternatives provided by one or more xsl:when statements in an xsl:choose statement	xsl:choose
xsl:param	Establishes a parameter name and value that can be used by non-XSLT environments to pass values into the result tree and is often used in conjunction with xsl:call-template or xsl:apply-templates elements and the xsl:with-param to assign values to nodes	xsl:stylesheet xsl:transform xsl:function xsl:template
xsl:processing-instruction	Generates a processing-instruction into the result tree	Any XSLT element whose content model is content constructor; any literal result element
xsl:template	Builds a template rule for later processing by either the xsl:apply-templates element or the xsl:call-template	xsl:stylesheet xsl:transform
xsl:variable	Stores a value for use by other elements	xsl:stylesheet xsl:transform xsl:function Any XSLT element whose content model is content constructor; any literal result element

Element Name	Purpose	Parent Element(s)
xsl:when	A conditional that processes its contents when its test attribute evaluates to true	Xsl:choose
xsl:with-param	Used for assigning values to parameters when using call-template elements	xsl:apply-templates xsl:apply-imports xsl:call-template

A closer look at template rules

You can generate nodes using content constructors in four ways:

✦ By creating literal result elements

✦ By creating text nodes

✦ By creating XSLT instructions

✦ By creating XSLT extension instructions

Creating literal result elements

When you want to generate HTML or some other markup, you create something called *literal result elements*, which are elements you add directly to the processing tree. Take a look at the source document in Listing 32-3; then look at Listing 32-4 to view a transformation using literal result elements.

Listing 32-3: **A Source XML File**

```
<?xml version="1.0" encoding="UTF-8"?>
<products>
     <product>
          <name>Bert&apos;s Coffee</name>
          <date>2003-01-21</date>
     </product>
     <product>
          <name>Bert&apos;s Tea</name>
          <date>2003-02-21</date>
     </product>
     <product>
          <name>Bert&apos;s Soda</name>
          <date>2002-02-15</date>
     </product>
     <reorders>
```

Continued

Listing 32-3: *(continued)*

```
            <reorder>
                    <name>Bert&apos;s Soda</name>
                    <cost>1.99</cost>
                    <date>2002-12-15</date>
            </reorder>
            <reorder>
                    <name>Bert&apos;s Tea</name>
                    <cost>2.99</cost>
                    <date>2002-06-15</date>
            </reorder>
            <reorder>
                    <name>Bert&apos;s Coffee</name>
                    <cost>5.99</cost>
                    <date>2002-05-15</date>
            </reorder>
        </reorders>
</products>
```

Pay special attention to the literal result elements in bold in Listing 32-4.

Listing 32-4: A Transformation Using Literal Result Elements

```
<?xml version="1.0" encoding="UTF-8"?>
<xsl:stylesheet version="1.0"
xmlns:xsl="http://www.w3.org/1999/XSL/Transform">
    <xsl:output method="html" version="4.0" encoding="ISO-
8859-1" indent="yes"/>
    <xsl:template match="/">
        <html>
            <head>
                <title>Literal Result
Elements</title>
            </head>
            <body>
              <xsl:apply-templates
select="products/reorders/reorder/date"/>
            </body>
        </html>
    </xsl:template>
    <xsl:template match="date">
      <p>
        <xsl:value-of select="."/>
      </p>
    </xsl:template>
</xsl:stylesheet>
```

The result of transforming Listing 32-3 using Listing 32-4 is the following HTML:

```
<html>
<head>
<META http-equiv="Content-Type" content="text/html;
charset=ISO-8859-1">
<title>Literal Result Elements</title>
</head>
<body>
<p>2002-12-15</p>
<p>2002-06-15</p>
<p>2002-05-15</p>
</body>
</html>
```

XML Implementations

Most XML implementations you encounter as a Web developer will involve XSLT on some level, unless you're writing your XHTML from scratch. However, a few XML implementations in existence won't directly involve XSLT. For example, it's just as likely as not that your XHTML will be developed without XSLT intervention. You may also encounter Web services XML vocabularies such as Simple Object Access Protocol (SOAP), Web Services Description Language (WSDL), and Universal Description, Discovery, and Integration (UDDI). Then there are the widget-based XML vocabularies for visual interface development, such as XUL, which is an XML vocabulary for developing Mozilla skins.

XHTML

XHMTL is the newest edition of HTML released by the W3C. The plan is to eventually deprecate all versions of HTML prior to XHTML. In other words, as far as the W3C is concerned, XHTML is the current version of HTML

It's also possible to transform XHTML into another format, even HTML 4.0. The biggest difference between HTML and XHTML is that XHTML must follow the rules of XML syntax. The elements and attributes used by XHTML are basically the same as HTML, except that you must use a closing tag in an empty element, such as the br element, like this:

```
<br />
```

Note the extra space after the br characters. This is done for backwards compatibility. If you end the tag without the space (`<br/>`), older browsers won't recognize the br element. When you create XHTML from XSLT, you must specify the PUBLIC and System DOCTYPE using the xsl:output element:

```
<xsl:output  doctype-
  system="http://www.w3.org/TR/xhtml1/DTD/xhtml1-
```

```
transitional.dtd" doctype-public="-//W3C//DTD XHTML 1.0
Transitional//EN"  method="html" version="4.0" encoding="ISO-
8859-1" indent="yes"/>
```

This will generate the following:

```
<!DOCTYPE html PUBLIC "-//W3C//DTD XHTML 1.0
Transitional//EN" "http://www.w3.org/TR/xhtml1/DTD/xhtml1-
transitional.dtd">
<html>
...
</html>
```

You also need to indicate the namespace for XHTML within the `xsl:stylesheet`
element:

```
xmlns="http://www.w3.org/1999/xhtml"
```

XHTML elements are also all case-sensitive, and must be in lower case. Listing 32-5
shows an XSTL document transforming Listing 32-3 into an XHTML document.

Listing 32-5: **Creating an XHTML Document with XSLT**

```
<?xml version="1.0" encoding="UTF-8"?>
<xsl:stylesheet xmlns="http://www.w3.org/1999/xhtml"
version="1.0"
xmlns:xsl="http://www.w3.org/1999/XSL/Transform">
    <xsl:output doctype-
system="http://www.w3.org/TR/xhtml1/DTD/xhtml1-
transitional.dtd" doctype-public="-//W3C//DTD XHTML 1.0
Transitional//EN" method="html" version="4.0" encoding="ISO-
8859-1" indent="yes"/>
    <xsl:template match="/">
        <html>
            <head>
                <title>Literal Result
Elements</title>
            </head>
            <body>

                <xsl:apply-templates
select="products/reorders/reorder/date"/>
            </body>
        </html>
    </xsl:template>
    <xsl:template match="date">
        <p>
            <xsl:value-of select="."/>
        </p>
    </xsl:template>
</xsl:stylesheet>
```

Listing 32-6 (L3206.xhtml) on the books companion Web site shows the result of the transformation generated by Listing 32-5.

Cross-Reference   Appendix A provides more details on the element syntax of XHTML.

Web services (SOAP, UDDI, and so on)

One of the banes of working with multiple environments across the Web has been that it has been impossible to generate true programmatic experiences across such systems. In other words, if you want to create an executable program that works across the Internet, you have to make sure each computer accessing the program has a browser plug-in installed. Web services were introduced to try to counter that problem by allowing developers to create function calls across the network without interference from firewalls and without regard to the kinds of software environments on either the receiving or transmitting end.

This is accomplished by placing the function calls within XML-based documents using formats such as SOAP and WSDL.

XUL

XML also is finding increased use as an interface development mechanism. XUL, for example, is a language developed for Mozilla that helps build the Mozilla and Netscape interface. You can learn how to build your own custom skins for Mozilla at `http://www.mozilla.org/projects/xul/`.

Laszlo, which creates server-based Flash files, uses a similar XML-based vocabulary for building data-powered and dynamic Flash sites. You can find more information on Laszlo at `http://www.laszlosystems.com/`.

Even Longhorn, Microsoft's upcoming operating system replacement for Windows, bases its GUI on an XML syntax.

Theoretically, you could output all of these XML vocabularies using XSLT from an XML source file.

WML

You can also generate markup for mobile phones from XSLT (or from scratch) by using the WAP Wireless Markup Language Specification (WML). WML is markup that is similar in concept to HTML but with a different syntax geared specifically for small, mobile devices, such as cell phones and PDAs. You can find more information on WML at `http://www.wapforum.org/what/technical.htm`.

Summary

You can easily see the benefits of starting with one source document based on XML and generating output to HTML, PDF, WML, and even XUL or other GUI vocabularies from one source. Whenever there is a change in your content, you only need to make the change in the XML source file. You won't need to make the changes in the presentation files if you build your XSLT files correctly.

As XML has matured, more and more large Web sites have adopted it because of its flexibility. For this reason, getting a handle on at least some of the fundamentals of XSLT and XML processing in general will contribute significantly to your knowledge of how modern Web sites are built.

Now that you've spent the greater portion of the book on how to develop Web sites, it's time for deployment. Chapter 33 examines how to test and validate your pages during the staging process, which is the necessary first step before your pages and site go live.

✦   ✦   ✦

Testing, Publishing, and Maintaining Your Site

◆ ◆ ◆ ◆

◆ ◆ ◆ ◆

Testing and Validating Your Documents

After creating your documents, it is important to test them to ensure that visitors to your site will not encounter any unforeseen problems. This chapter covers the basics of testing your code, including what tools are at your disposal.

Testing with a Variety of Browsers

Despite being built on standards, no two browsers support HTML and CSS to the same degree. Some browsers don't implement certain features while others implement them, well, differently.

Note   Contrary to popular belief, Microsoft's Internet Explorer is no worse than other browsers regarding supporting standards. Even though Microsoft has created many proprietary technologies for its browser, it does a fair job of supporting the actual standards.

When coding your documents it is important to understand your expected audience and what browsers they may be using. Although Microsoft Internet Explorer has market share on its side, many people use other browsers, such as Mozilla, Opera, Konqueror, Safari, and so forth. As such, it is doubtful that everyone will be able to view your documents the way you originally intended, especially if you use some of the more esoteric features and technologies.

Make sure you test your pages on all target platforms to ensure that no show-stopping errors exist on any of the platforms. At a bare minimum, you should test on a current Microsoft (Internet Explorer) browser and a Netscape/Mozilla browser because most browsers incorporate one of these two technology bases.

Tip   For a good source of browser compatibilities, check out Brian Wilson's Index DOT Html at `www.blooberry.com/indexdot/html/index.html`.

Also, don't forget the non-computer browsers used by cell phones, PDAs, and other mobile devices. If your site will appeal to mobile device users, you should at least obtain the Software Development Kit (SDK) or emulator for each suspected platform and preview your documents accordingly.

Tip   You can use server-side and client-side scripts to adjust document behavior according to the browser being used. Typically, such scripting is only necessary to adjust other script behavior—what document object model objects are accessed and so forth.

Testing for a Variety of Displays

Many Web designers make the mistake of designing their documents for specific screen resolutions. When the document is displayed on a smaller resolution the page elements tend to jam together or break across unexpected lines.

Your documents should be suitable for many resolutions. Although most users will be running at resolutions of at least 800×600 pixels, you may have the occasional user running lower resolutions.

Always test your documents at various resolutions and color depths to look for any shortcomings.

Validating Your Code

Validating your documents' code is a very good idea. It helps double-check your document for simple errors—typos, unclosed tags, and so on—and also verifies that your code meets expected standards.

Specifying the correct document type definition

There are many ways to validate your documents, but they all rely on your documents containing a correct document type definition (DTD) declaration. For example, if you want to base your documents on Strict HTML 4.01, you would include the following DTD declaration at the top of your document:

```
<!DOCTYPE HTML PUBLIC "-//W3C//DTD HTML 4.01//EN"
  "http://www.w3.org/TR/html4/strict.dtd">
```

The `DOCTYPE` declaration informs any user agent reading the document what standard the document is based on. The information is primarily used by validation clients in validating the code within the document, but it might also be used by a display agent to determine what features it must support.

Tip   You can find a valid list of DTDs at `http://www.w3.org/QA/2002/04/valid-dtd-list.html`.

Validation tools

You can use several tools to validate your documents. Tools you have at your disposal include the following:

✦ The online W3C HTML validation tool, found at `http://validator.w3.org/`.

✦ The online Web Design Group (WDG) validation tool, found at `www.htmlhelp.com/tools/validator/`.

✦ Validation utilities built in to Web development tools such as Macromedia's Dreamweaver MX, shown in Figure 33-1.

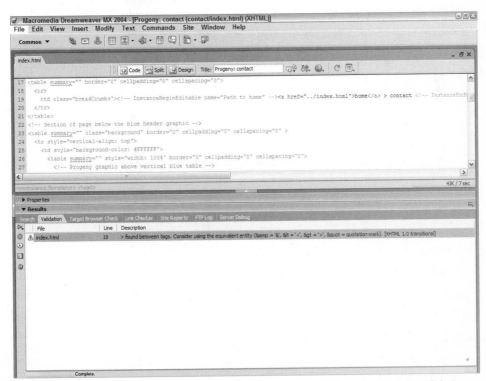

Figure 33-1: Macromedia's Dreamweaver MX includes a comprehensive code validation feature.

✦ Any of the various separate applications that can be run locally. A comprehensive list is maintained on the WDG site at http://www.htmlhelp.com/links/validators.htm.

Understanding validation output

Consider the following HTML document:

```
<!DOCTYPE HTML PUBLIC "-//W3C//DTD HTML 4.01//EN"
  "http://www.w3.org/TR/html4/strict.dtd">
<html>
<head>
  <title>Validation Test</title>
</head>
<body>
  <form action="" method="POST">
    <input name="text" type="text">
    <br>
    <input name="submit" type="submit">
  </form>
</body>
</html>
```

When this code is passed through the W3C Markup Validation Service, the following first error is returned:

```
Line 9, column 30: document type does not allow element
"INPUT" here; missing one of "P", "H1", "H2", "H3", "H4",
"H5", "H6", "PRE", "DIV", "ADDRESS" start-tag
   <input name="text" type="text">
```

Although the document looks to be conforming HTML, the validation service thinks otherwise. However, what exactly does the error mean?

In short, it means that the <input> element must be contained within a block element other than the <form> tag. Typically, the paragraph tag (<p>) is used, but you can also use <div>, a heading, <pre>, and so on.

Note   The W3C also has an online CSS validation tool, accessible at: http://jigsaw.w3.org/css-validator/. Similar to the HTML validation tool, this tool will make sure your CSS style sheet is free from typos and that all the attributes are paired with their matching styles.

Adding a paragraph container solves the problem and makes the document valid:

```
...
  <form action="" method="POST">
    <p>
    <input name="text" type="text">
    <br>
    <input name="submit" type="submit">
    </p>
  </form>
...
```

Tip When working on making a document validate, always handle the errors in order. The example in this section actually results in four separate errors, each relating to the missing block elements. Adding the preceding elements solves all four problems.

Summary

Throughout this book, you have seen how simple documents can become quite complex. From simple typos to complex structures gone awry, I'm sure you have also found your share of errors. However, it's the errors lying underneath the veneer of your documents that should concern you the most—the errors that you do not see but will affect a handful of visitors to your site. It is important to constantly test and validate your code to help alleviate these problems.

✦　✦　✦

Web Development Software

As you have seen throughout this book, Web development is an area rich in features. The Web has come a long way from its early beginnings as a text-only medium. As online documents get more complex, the tools to create them become more powerful. Although you can still create large, feature-rich sites using a simple text editor, using more complex and powerful tools can make the task much easier. This chapter introduces several popular tools that can help you create the best online documents possible.

Note   This chapter provides several recommendations on tools you should consider for online document development. However, the recommendations are just that, recommendations. Only you can decide what tools will work best for you. Luckily, most of the tools covered in this chapter have demo versions you can download and try out for a limited time. Be sure to visit the Web sites referenced for each tool to get more information and perhaps even download a trial version.

Text-Oriented Editors

Text-oriented editors have been around since the dawn of the cathode-ray tube (CRT, the technology used in most computer display screens). However, today's editors can be quite powerful and feature-rich, doing much more than simply allowing you to create text documents. This section covers the latest in text-oriented editing.

Simple text editors

Simple text editors—such as Windows Notepad or vi on UNIX/Linux—provide an invaluable service. They allow you, without intervening features, to easily edit text-based documents. As such, they are a logical addition to your Web development toolkit.

However, although you could create an entire site with one of these simple tools, there are better tools for actual creation.

Smart text editors

Smart text editors are editors that understand what you are editing and attempt to help in various ways. For example, Linux users should look into vim or Emacs and enable syntax highlighting when editing documents with embedded code (HTML, CSS, JavaScript, and so on). Figure 34-1 shows an example of a large PHP file in vim.

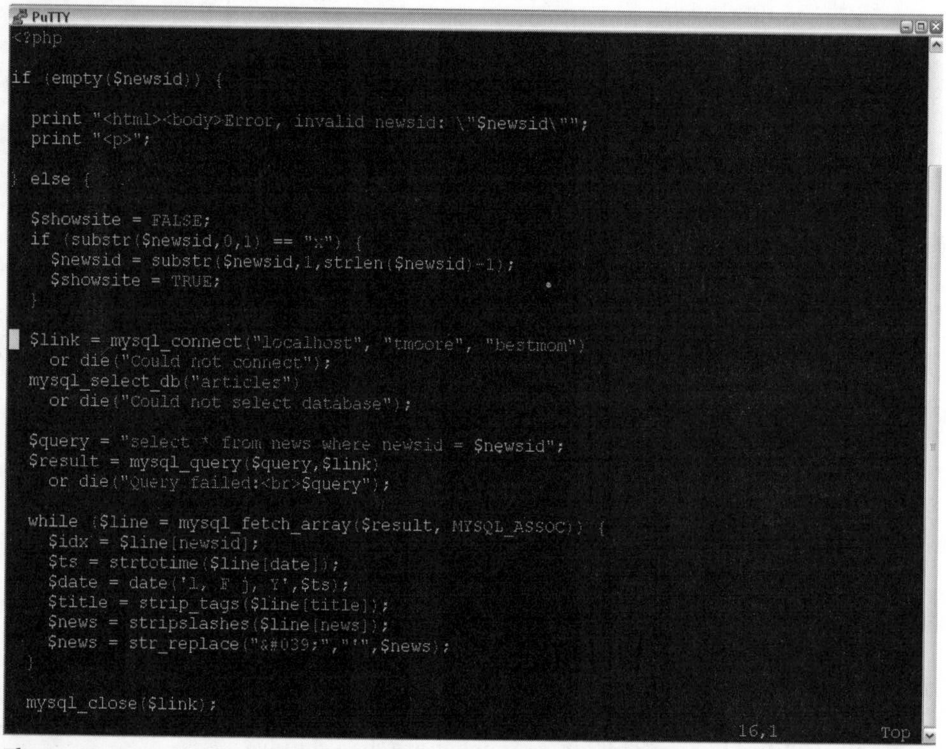

Figure 34-1: Syntax highlighting can help you avoid simple errors.

Although it may be hard to tell in the black and white Figure, various elements have been colorized to show where they begin or end. Using methods like this the editor keeps you abreast of what elements have been opened and which have been closed. For example, the editor may highlight quoted text in green. If most of the document turns green, it is likely that you forgot to close a quote somewhere. These editors also offer features such as auto-indenting, which can help you keep your documents structured.

Windows users have a few choices for smart editors, as well. My favorite is Textpad, which uses document class templates to understand the syntax of almost any coded document. TextPad is loaded with standard editor features. You can find TextPad on the Internet at www.textpad.com.

HTML-specific editors

There are a few non-WYSIWYG editors that understand HTML and provide specific features to help you code. However, Homesite (now owned by Macromedia) has always stood out from the crowd.

Homesite provides the next level of functionality for HTML editing with special tools for entering tags and their parameters, codes for entities, and more. Figure 34-2 shows the Homesite main interface, and Figure 34-3 shows a step in the wizard for creating a <table> tag.

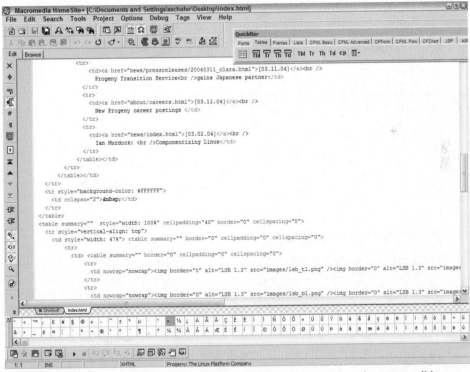

Figure 34-2: Macromedia's Homesite includes several features to make HTML editing a breeze.

Homesite includes a host of other features designed to make your coding easier. Visit Macromedia's Web site for more information (www.macromedia.com/software/homesite/).

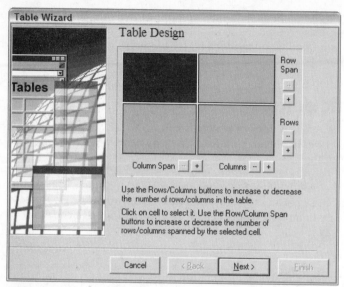

Figure 34-3: Homesite includes wizards for building more complex tags such as tables.

WYSIWYG HTML Editors

Just as *what you see is what you get* (WYSIWYG) editors revolutionized word processing, WYSIWYG HTML editors have revolutionized Web publishing. Using such tools designers can design their pages visually and let the tools create the underlying HTML code. This section highlights the three most popular visual tools available for WYSIWYG editing.

Microsoft FrontPage

FrontPage is Microsoft's Web editing tool. Although most of the Microsoft Office suite of programs can output HTML, FrontPage allows you to manage documents at the site level—creating a template design, navigation controls between pages, and more. Figure 34-4 shows the main interface of FrontPage, and Figure 34-5 shows the Web (site) view.

Earlier versions of FrontPage were known for creating non-standard HTML and catering to Microsoft Web extensions. Current versions are much better about adhering to standard code, though the program is still more feature-rich when used with other Microsoft technologies. Still, FrontPage makes a solid, economical choice for a WYSIWYG editor.

Note FrontPage is much more powerful when teamed with a Web server running Microsoft's FrontPage extensions. If you use FrontPage, it is worth your time investigating running the extensions on your Web server.

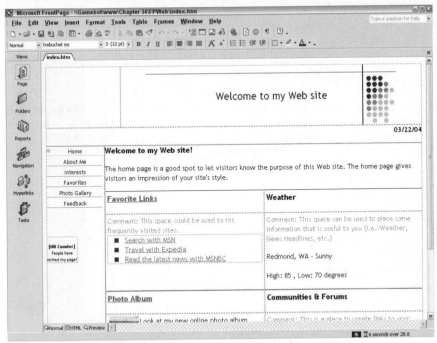

Figure 34-4: Microsoft FrontPage is a visual editor for Web documents.

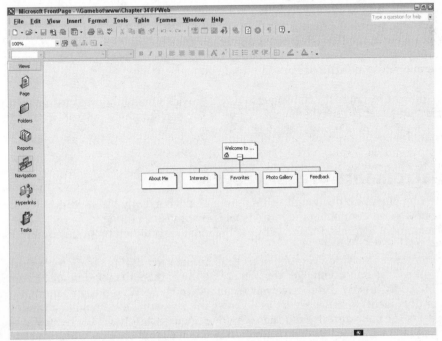

Figure 34-5: FrontPage enables you to edit related documents as a site.

You can learn more about FrontPage and download an evaluation copy from Microsoft's FrontPage site, at `www.microsoft.com/office/frontpage/prodinfo/default.mspx`.

NetObjects Fusion

NetObjects Fusion is another site-level design tool that offers WYSIWYG editing. The advantages of using NetObjects Fusion include easy management of entire sites, pixel-accurate designs, and a plethora of features that make publishing on the Web a breeze. Such features include the following:

✦ Advanced scripting support

✦ Automatic e-commerce catalog building

✦ Enhanced photo gallery support

✦ Hooks for including external pages and code

✦ Incremental publishing capability

✦ Flexible meta tag management

✦ Powerful, full-site management tools

Note   NetObjects Fusion should not be confused with Macromedia's ColdFusion product. The former is owned by Website Pros and is a WYSIWYG Web editor. The latter is owned by Macromedia and is a database integration tool for the Web.

Figure 34-6 shows the page design view of NetObjects, and Figure 34-7 shows the site layout view. In the latter you can easily create, delete, and move pages around your site—NetObjects Fusion will automatically adjust all links, navigation bars, and other references between the pages.

Besides the visual tools, NetObjects Fusion provides many ways to customize the actual code behind the documents, as well. You can learn more about NetObjects Fusion on the Web at `www.netobjects.com`.

Macromedia Dreamweaver

The king of all Web document editing programs is currently Macromedia Dreamweaver. Combining the best visual and nonvisual editing tools with several development features, Dreamweaver is the most feature-rich program covered here.

Dreamweaver provides as much or as little automation during creation of new documents as you would like. You can create the entire site in text mode, editing HTML code directly. Alternatively, you can use the WYSIWYG design editor to create your documents visually. Figure 34-8 shows Dreamweaver's main editing window, splitting the code and visual design windows. Figure 34-9 shows the results of the Target Browser Check feature, which enables you to test your code against the compatibility of specific browsers.

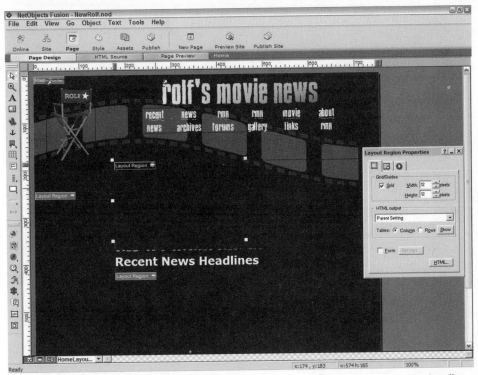

Figure 34-6: NetObjects Fusion provides a good framework for designing pages visually.

However, the feature-rich nature of Dreamweaver comes at a price—it is easily the most complicated program covered in this chapter. The learning curve for Dreamweaver can be quite steep, even to create simple sites. However, once you get used to Dreamweaver, it is easy to appreciate its powerful features.

You can learn more about Dreamweaver at www.macromedia.com/software/dreamweaver/.

Other Tools

Tools to create HTML are only half of the equation when creating online documents. You must also have tools available to do graphic editing and supply any multimedia content you use. This section covers a handful of additional tools necessary to create rich, online content.

Graphic editors

Year's ago text-only Web pages were the norm. However, today's Web is a visual feast, and your documents must incorporate as much imagery as possible to get noticed.

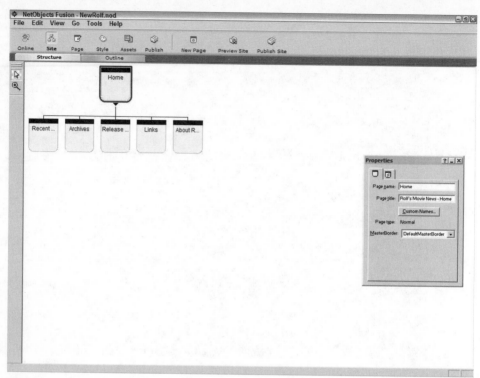

Figure 34-7: At the site level, NetObjects Fusion gives you complete control over your site's organization while behind the scenes it adjusts links between pages automatically.

Almost every operating system comes with at least one graphic editor. However, the capabilities of the included editors are quite limited and should not be relied upon for much—the same goes for graphics programs bundled with many scanners, printers, and other graphics peripherals.

In a perfect world you should consider using both a vector-based and a raster-based editing program. Vector-based editors use shapes and lines to create images, while raster-based editors use individual dots (pixels) to create images. Vector-based images are traditionally more exact and clear, but raster-based images allow for more visually striking effects. The best results can be obtained using both—use the vector tools to create solid imagery and raster tools for special effects and finishing work.

Note   Only raster-based images (specifically JPEG, GIF, and PNG images) are supported by common user agents.

Vector-based editing tools include the following:

✦ Adobe Illustrator (www.adobe.com/products/illustrator/main.html)

✦ Macromedia Freehand (www.macromedia.com/software/freehand/)

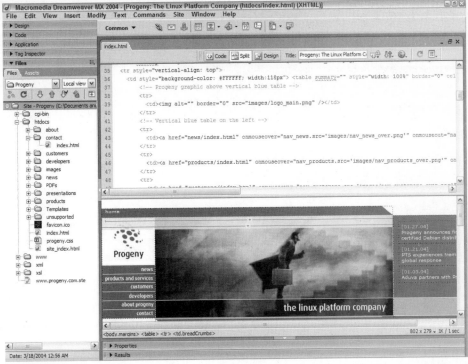

Figure 34-8: Dreamweaver's main editing window can show the code view, the design (visual) view, or both.

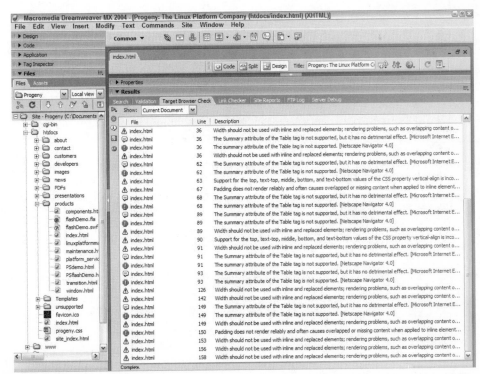

Figure 34-9: The Target Browser Check feature checks your code against the compatibility of specific browsers.

Raster-based editing tools include the following:

✦ Paint Shop Pro (www.jasc.com/products/paintshoppro)

✦ Adobe Photoshop (www.adobe.com/products/photoshop/main.html)

✦ Macromedia Fireworks (www.macromedia.com/software/fireworks/)

✦ The GIMP (www.gimp.org/)

Note   Paint Shop Pro actually supports both raster and vector editing.

Note that these tools can be quite expensive—the latest version of Photoshop is several hundred dollars. Of course, Photoshop is without equal for raster editing; no other tool provides as much power and extensibility. Paint Shop Pro is quite capable at a hundred dollars, and The GIMP provides suitable editing without a price tag (it's Open Source).

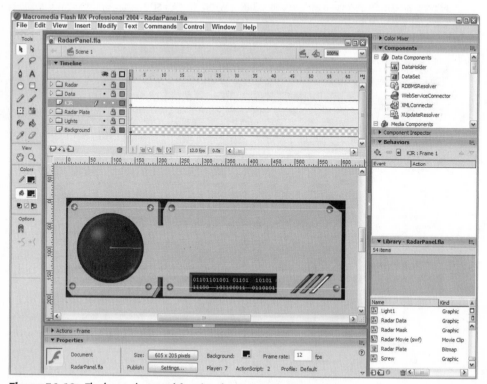

Figure 34-10: Flash can be used for simple or complex animations.

Tip Fledgling Web designers needing a handful of tools should look into Macromedia's Studio product line. The Studio series provides Dreamweaver, Flash, Freehand, and Fireworks in one comprehensive package. Learn more at: www.macromedia.com/software/studio/.

Macromedia Flash

Macromedia Flash is the latest staple for simple multimedia on the Web. Flash provides an animation platform with plenty of power via ActionScript, a flexible scripting language, and can be used for simple buttons or full-blown product demos.

Although the interface is a bit idiosyncratic, Flash is an indispensable tool for online animation. Figure 34-10 shows a Flash document in development.

The main draw of Flash is two-fold:

✦ It has become a standard on the Web that users expect.

✦ Flash can provide even complex animations in a small package (small file size).

As such, Flash is another tool you should consider adding to your collection. You can learn more about Flash at www.macromedia.com/software/flash/.

Summary

This chapter introduced several essential and powerful tools you can use to make online document creation and deployment a breeze. You saw how text editor features can help with the tedium of coding and how full-blown Web design packages can ease the creation of even large sites. Although acquiring the right tools may seem costly, consider the time you will save by using them.

✦　　✦　　✦

Choosing a Service Provider

Now that you're a seasoned developer, how do you actually find an appropriate place to publish your Web site? The answer depends on a number of different factors. If you're a family member trying to post some family business or personal information, you may want to just use the services your Internet Service Provider (ISP) offers, because they usually offer free personal Web site hosting with their Internet access plans. If you're a small business owner, you'll want something more robust, and you'll want to consider acquiring a domain name and a company that can host it on a computer that shares space with other small businesses. If you're a large operation or hope to become one, you probably want a dedicated computer of your own for your Web site.

This chapter takes a look at the options available to you.

Types of Service Providers

There are four general types of Web hosting service plans:

✦ Web publishing services provided by ISPs, or personal Web sites

✦ Shared hosting services

✦ Dedicated hosting plans

✦ Co-location

One final option is to simply set up your own computer and host the site yourself. You can do this if you have a static IP address. A DSL connection is usually fast enough to serve pages fairly quickly, as long as your traffic is reasonable (once you start getting into the 100,000 hits per day range, things could become tricky). Setting up your computer to be a Web server opens you up to a lot of security issues and can be a time-consuming task, but if you have a spare computer and want to learn the ins and outs of Web hosting, there isn't a better way.

Web publishing services provided by ISPs

A Web publishing service or personal Web hosting service is a very basic Web hosting service that is generally part of the contract agreement with your ISP. To take a real-world example, if you have an Internet access account with AOL or Earthlink, you also get some Web space as a part of the agreement. You can use this kind of account for running a business, but because domain name hosting is usually not included, it's not a great choice for serious online business transactions. A typical Web hosting arrangement with an ISP will include anywhere from 1MB to 10MB of space.

Generally, a Web site you have using such a sight will have a URL such as `http://myisp.net/~chwhite`. Most people find these kinds of hosting services sufficient for personal Web sites, but not for businesses.

Using shared hosting services

Shared hosting services are somewhat akin to renting space on a machine that is shared among several customers. This machine's Web server dedicates part of its directory structure to your account, and the host provider makes sure that the domain name you secure, such as myserioussite.com, resolves to the directory paths you have secured on the host machine.

Shared hosting sites generally feature significantly more disk space and bandwidth than a personal hosting service. Most shared hosting services also offer better support services, which generally aren't available on personal Web hosting service plans. This can include maintenance of e-mail accounts linked to the site domain name and an offering of generic server scripts and instructions on how to use them. Your data files are stored on a Web server that is shared by other Web sites, which can affect your Web site's performance if the traffic generated by other sites on the server is high. Many kinds of plans are available on any operating system. You can choose from among Apache-based Web hosting plans using Linux or UNIX operating systems, and from Microsoft-based operating systems and Web servers.

You can also choose plans that include database access. Linux-based services usually offer mySQL, and Windows-based services offer SQL Server. The databases are also shared. You are usually given read/write rights to one database from within a pretty large collection of databases. If one of the customers has extremely high traffic, this can slow the database-driven part of your Web site down, because everyone is competing for the same memory allocation.

Any shared hosting service worth signing up for will set your site up for you and provide you with simple, easy-to-follow instructions on how to upload files to the server.

Costs range anywhere from free to about $69.00 per month.

Using dedicated hosting

A dedicated host is a service provider that dedicates a computer to your Web site. No other Web sites share your computer. A dedicated communications line with a minimum bandwidth allotment may also be provided. The range of services made available by the hosting company to you can vary widely. Some will simply set up your box with a Web site already running, but they'll also let you set up the server yourself if you prefer. Because setting up a Web server can be a fairly complex task, you should only undertake it if you are comfortable with doing so. Some people prefer to just have the hosting company set the site up for them, and others like to be responsible for all aspects of their Web site's configuration.

Some dedicated host providers also offer technical services, including but not limited to the following:

✦ Script development

✦ Security development

✦ E-mail maintenance

Using co-location services

Co-location, known affectionately as co-lo, is the most expensive and most advanced kind of hosting service available. You buy your own server and store it at a facility that has access to a high-speed hub. You can choose between using telecommunication lines provided by the hosting facility and contracting directly with a telecommunications company for outside lines. Co-lo facilities maintain Network Access Points (NAPs) and usually offer extended power backup capability, climate control, and around-the-clock technical support.

Estimating Your Costs

To estimate your costs on hosting plans, you first have to decide which of the preceding plan types you wish to acquire. Then you should go to a Web site such as www.thelist.com, which provides a comprehensive list of each type of hosting service in each category. You should begin this process before you even start working on your Web site, because you'll want to incorporate these costs into your budget. Some of these costs may be absorbed by your development budget, because you may find yourself wanting to take advantage of some hosting services' development services.

Support and Service

The kinds and types of services that hosting providers offer can vary immensely. The services you choose will have a direct impact on how much money you spend.

For example, the following is a list of services you can choose from www.thelist.com when selecting a dedicated hosting services provider:

✦ *CGI forms*—A service that creates, for example, forms that mail results to you.

✦ *Design services*—Some providers offer graphic and Web design services.

✦ *Real Server*—A special server that is configured especially for multimedia streaming on the Real platform.

✦ *CGI Access*—Simply means that a CGI directory is made available on a UNIX or Linux server so that you can create Perl-based executable scripts for more dynamic server-side pages.

✦ *NT servers or UNIX servers*—You'll want to make this basic choice because development on these platforms can be quite different when working with backend applications.

✦ *MS FrontPage*—Some ISPs offer Microsoft FrontPage extensions, which are extensions installed on the Web host that are configured to communicate with Microsoft FrontPage markup.

✦ *Database support*—Expect to add between 20 and 50 U.S. dollars for database support.

✦ *Chat and/or message board software*—This option is configured by the hosting provider to allow the creation of chat sites or message board forums.

✦ *Credit card processing*—Many host providers provide Secure Sockets Layer (SSL) credit card processing services.

✦ *Access traffic logs and traffic analysis reports*—These are pretty basic and a must-have in any decent plan.

✦ *Unique DNS hosting, DNS parking*—Can include the management of DNS subdomains so that you can, for example, have a main site named www.mysite.com and have a subdomain named http://checkout.mysite.com, where the checkout is handled by a host provider's DNS configuration to resolve to your site.

✦ *E-mail auto responder, forwarding, POP SMTP processing, and list processing*—You can take advantage of numerous e-mail processing services a host provider may offer. At the most basic level, a host provider should provide you with e-mail POP and SMTP accounts that resolve to your domain name (ed@mysite.com) and offer multiple mailboxes. Most providers now also provide List Processing services so you can distribute e-mail-based newsletters and other kinds of mass mailings (but a good host provider will prevent you from sending spam).

✦ *Shell telnet access*—Telnet is a command-line (usually) utility that gives you access to your Web site's configuration tables and allows you to edit your HTML files remotely.

✦ *Redundant Internet*—Allows you to actually use more than one host provider in case one of the provider's servers goes down.

✦ *Money-back guarantee and toll-free phone support*—Self-explanatory.

✦ *Daily site backups*—Prevent you from losing data in case of a system crash.

✦ *Adult content allowed*—Many service providers do not allow adult content, and if you're compelled to go that route, it's best to work with a provider that specializes in adult content.

✦ *24-Hour Support*—This is not necessarily a given with some of the cheaper plans, but you'll find it handy when there's an outage.

✦ *VPN Support*—Provides support for Virtual Private Networks so that you can connect to another desktop from your own computer.

Bandwidth and Scalability

One of your chief considerations in choosing a host provider is whether or not the host provider can handle the traffic demands of your site. If you have a small business and aren't expecting much traffic, particularly if your business is intended to stay small (maybe you run a small flower shop or some other local business and you just want to post a Web site), you can probably get by with a shared hosting plan. You can probably get by with a shared hosting plan if you have expansion plans, too. In that case, you need to be ready for a sudden spike in traffic. If you can afford a dedicated site, you should aim for that if you have big plans. If you can't afford it, make sure your site is *scalable*.

Scalability means that you build your site so that it can rapidly absorb growth without making either your users or you suffer. One way to accomplish this is to be sure you use commonly known Web application environments, and be certain you will want to stick with them as your business grows. It's difficult and time consuming to port Active Server Pages (ASP) pages to PHP (PHP is a recursive acronym that stands for Hypertext Preprocessor) or Java Server Pages (JSP), and vice versa. Simple HTML is much easier to port, of course, but you want to maintain a good, solid organizational structure for your directories and files.

You must also take into consideration the location of your audience. If you're expecting a truly international audience, you want to be prepared to move to a hosting service that has ready access to a Network Access Point (NAP) on the Internet. This is also called a *backbone*. These are like traffic hubs on the Internet. If your site is on a backbone or has direct access to one, the site's performance will be better than if it doesn't, especially if you have international visitors.

Contracts

You can sign up with a Web hosting company for any amount of time, but pricing is usually structured so that the longer you sign up for, the better your bargain is. Typical contracts are one, three, and five years. Many Web hosting companies offer month-to-month plans, but these are usually limited to shared hosting plans.

Domain Names

Every computer that connects to the Internet is given a unique identifier called an Internet Protocol (IP) address. IP addressing is easily understood if you liken it to your phone number, which, when dialed, always manages to connect to your phone. You'll come in contact with two kinds of IP addresses when your ISP sets you up on the Internet. A *static* IP address is a permanent IP address that you always keep. More commonly, you'll get a *dynamic* IP address from your ISP. This means that the ISP assigns you a different IP address every time you log on. To host a Web site, you need a static IP address.

The Domain Name System (DNS) is used to map a name to a static IP address. Computers use these to communicate with themselves using a name (such as www.tumeric.net). When a computer requests a URL, the DNS translates that name into the corresponding IP address.

When you sign up for a Web site, one of the first things you'll have to do is determine a domain name for your site. Then, you register your domain name with a domain registrar.

Domain registrars register your domain name and hook you up to the Internet by making sure your domain name is added to a huge database of domain names that are mapped to specific IP addresses.

Note   The organization that governs this process is called The Internet Corporation for Assigned Names and Numbers (ICANN). They maintain a list of registrars at www.icann.org/registrars/accredited-list.html.

Generally, the process works like this:

1. You visit one of the accredited registrars.

2. You use the registrar's site to check and see if the domain name you wish to use is unclaimed. For example, if you wanted to start a Web site using the name ebay.com, you'd find that someone is already using that domain name. Most registrar sites maintain an easy-to-use search interface that allows you to check if the domain you want is in use, and helps you find alternative names if it is.

3. After you have successfully chosen a name, you submit it to the ICANN through the registrar's site.

4. The registrar then usually "parks" your site by assigning you an IP address on one of its servers for a small fee. You can also provide an IP address, which your hosting company should have given you when you signed up with them.

5. Have your credit card handy, because next you'll be asked to pay for the service provided by the registrar.

6. The registrar then maps the domain name to either the IP address you provided or the IP address on its server that it used to park your domain name. The mapping is then is forwarded to ICANN, and it goes into a massive database containing all the world's IP addresses and corresponding domain names.

Tip   Some Web hosting companies actually take care of this process for you, so you may be able to skip these steps. Some registrars also act as hosting services, and will try to sell you a hosting plan. Keep in mind that you're under no obligation to host your site using the services of the registrar you use to register your site.

Summary

Your choice of a Web hosting plan is directly related to what you want to achieve. If you have small plans or have a small business, there is no need to go to the expense of a dedicated machine, which is always going to cost more than a shared service, whether you host it yourself, use a co-location service, or use a Web hosting service with a dedicated hosting plan.

One thing to keep in mind is that Web hosting services are incredibly competitive. It's a buyer's market. If, after you've chosen a Web hosting option, you're unhappy with your Web hosting service, get another one.

The next chapter explains how to actually work with your host provider to upload files and build your site.

✦　　✦　　✦

Uploading Your Site with FTP

Now that you have documents to deploy on the Web, how do you actually move the files to the Web server? If you don't have an automated publishing tool (as covered in Chapter 34), you will probably use File Transfer Protocol (FTP). This chapter provides an introduction to FTP and explains how you can use it to deploy your files to a server.

Introducing FTP

File Transfer Protocol was created to easily move files between systems on the Internet. Dating back to the very early days of TCP/IP and the Internet, FTP hasn't evolved much in the years it has been in service. FTP encapsulates several functions to transfer files, view files on both sides of the connection, and more.

FTP servers use TCP/IP ports 20 and 21. These ports are unique to the FTP service, allowing a server to run a Web server (port 80), an FTP server (ports 20 and 21), as well as other services at the same time.

The FTP server sits patiently waiting for a client to request a connection on port 21. The client opens an unprivileged port greater than port 1024 and requests a connection from the server. After the connection is authenticated the client can initiate commands. When data is transferred between the client and server, the server initiates the connection, using port 20—the client uses one port higher than the port used for commands. Figure 36-1 shows a graphical representation of the connection and port arrangement.

One problem with the traditional FTP process is that the server must initiate the data connection. This requires that the server be able to access the requisite port on the client to initiate the connection. If the client is using a firewall, this could present a problem, as the firewall might prevent

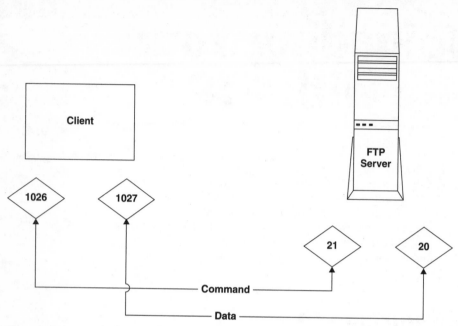

Figure 36-1: A typical FTP connection.

the server from accessing the correct port. Because the client port isn't consistent, configuring the firewall to allow access is problematic.

To solve this problem, a new mode of FTP was created. Passive mode (typically referred to as *PASV*) allows the client to initiate both connections.

Note If you are behind a firewall, you should always try to use passive mode.

FTP Clients

The first FTP clients were text-only applications. The connection is initiated and data is transferred using textual commands. The latest FTP clients employ the same graphical interface as most modern operating systems, using standard file manager-like interfaces to accomplish FTP operations.

Note Graphical FTP clients use the same methods and commands to communicate with the FTP server, but typically hide the communication from the user.

The following listing shows a typical dialog using a textual FTP client. The client initiates a connection, and the user logs in, gets a directory listing on the server, and then transfers a file. For clarity, the commands entered by the user are in boldface:

```
$  ftp ftp.example.com
Connected to ftp.example.com.
220 ftp.example.com FTP server ready.
Name: sschafer
331 Password required for sschafer.
Password: _____
230 User sschafer logged in.
Remote system type is UNIX.
Using binary mode to transfer files.
ftp> cd www
250 CWD command successful.
ftp> ls
200 PORT command successful.
150 Opening ASCII mode data connection for file list.
drwxr-xr-x  2 sschafer sschafer  4096 Jan 20 16:45 Products
drwxr-xr-x  2 sschafer sschafer  4096 Jan 16 18:41 About
drwxr-xr-x  2 sschafer sschafer  4096 Jan 6 15:16 Images
-rwxr-xr-x  1 sschafer sschafer  1571 Jan 12 17:58 index.html
drwxr-xr-x  2 sschafer sschafer  4096 Jan 15 04:16 Scripts
226-Transfer complete.
226 Quotas off
ftp>  put index.html
local: index.html remote: index.html
200 PORT command successful.
150 Opening BINARY mode data connection for index.html.
226 Transfer complete.
2095 bytes sent in 0.3 secs (3.6 kB/s)
ftp>  close
221 Goodbye.
ftp>  quit
$
```

Figure 36-2 shows a graphical FTP client accessing the same site. The client shows the file listing of the remote server. To transfer a file, the user simply drags the file into or out of the client window. Notice the underlying FTP commands and output in the lower-right corner of the application. Some graphical clients allow you to take manual control, entering spurious commands as required.

Table 36-1 shows a list of common FTP commands.

ASCII versus Binary Transfers

FTP servers support two modes of file transfers: binary and ASCII. Binary mode transfers are used when the content of the file contains higher-byte characters—characters not generally available on the keyboard. ASCII transfers are used when the content contains only lower-byte characters, such as text files.

Continued

Continued

Some FTP servers will automatically switch file modes as required, but most FTP servers require that the mode be explicitly changed. Some FTP clients will also automatically change the mode depending on the file being transferred. As a general rule, always double-check the mode being used before transferring files.

Most files can be transferred in binary mode. However, some ASCII files don't respond well to being transferred in binary format. For example, Perl scripts transferred in binary format will generally have their line breaks corrupted, creating problems for the Perl interpreter when the script is run. You might consider enabling ASCII mode when transferring text files, just in case.

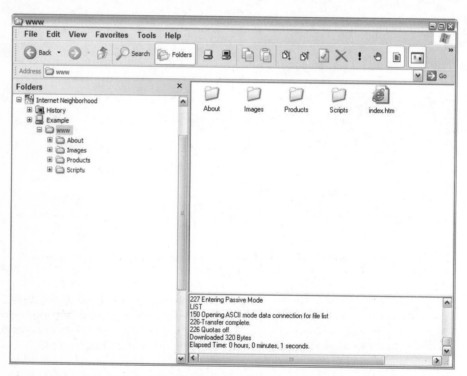

Figure 36-2: Graphical FTP clients use graphical user interface methods to transfer files.

Notable FTP Clients

Most operating systems include a textual FTP client, aptly named FTP. To use the client, type **ftp** at a command prompt. However, not all textual clients use the same commands or have the same options. Most clients support a help command—type **help** followed by the name of the command you need help with. Unfortunately, the

Table 36-1
Common FTP Commands

Command	Syntax	Use
Ascii	Ascii	Switch to ASCII mode for file transfers
Binary	Binary	Switch to binary mode for file transfers
Cd	cd *directory_name*	Change the remote directory
Close	Close	Close the current connection to the server (log off)
Get	get *filename*	Download a file from the server
Lcd	lcd *directory_name*	Change the directory on the local machine
Ls	ls [*file_spec*]	List files on the server (in the current directory)
Mget	mget *file_spec*	Download multiple files from the server
Mkdir	mkdir *directory_name*	Create a new directory on the server
Mput	mput *file_spec*	Upload multiple files to the server
Open	open *server_address*	Open a new connection to the server (prompt for username and password)
Pasv	Pasv	Enter passive mode
Put	put *filename*	Upload a file to the server
Quit	Quit	Exit the client
Rmdir	rmdir *directory_name*	Remove a directory on the server

standard help output simply tells you what the command does, not the syntax or options.

Tip

> There are many ways to place files on the Web server. The easiest, of course, is to create and edit the files directly on the server. If you are using a development product (such as those discussed in Chapter 34), you can use its features to upload your content (typically such programs use FTP to transfer files).

Quite a few graphical FTP clients are available—from $100 commercial solutions to shareware solutions. The following list is a subset of available clients:

✦ Windows clients

- FTP Voyager—This shareware client allows you to transfer files between servers, resume aborted downloads, and more. It also has a scheduler that can automatically transfer files as set times.

- CoffeeCup FTP client—This freeware client contains the usual options for graphical clients.

- CuteFTP—This popular Shareware client contains a number of features to make FTP transfers easier. It provides a download queue, macro recording, and a scheduler to automate file transfers.

- WS-FTP—This FTP client has the typical features found in other commercial solutions, but is free for certain individuals and organizations.

- Internet Neighborhood Pro—This commercial client from KnoWare, Inc. allows an FTP connection to function as a network drive mapping.

✦ Linux

- Desktop specific clients—Both K Desktop Environment (KDE) and Gnome include graphical clients specific to the desktop environment.

- Additional Open Source solutions—Many graphical FTP clients are available for Linux. Each distribution contains several you can choose from. Even more are available from various online sources.

Tip

Your Web browser can be used as a graphical client. Simply specify the FTP protocol (`ftp:`) and the server address, as in the following example:

```
ftp://ftp.example.com
```

If the server requires authentication, you will be prompted for your login information. If you want to create a shortcut to a site with authentication, you can embed the login information into the URL, as shown in this example:

```
ftp://username:password@ftp.example.com
```

Principles of Web Server File Organization

Files on a Web server typically follow a tiered organization—placing subordinate pages in subdirectories. Furthermore, supplemental files—scripts, images, and so on—are typically placed in separate directories. Figure 36-3 shows the organizational structure of a typical Web site.

Note

There really isn't anything *typical* on the Web. As such, you should use a file and directory structure that suits your needs. The examples in this chapter are just that, examples. The important thing is that you use *some* logical organizational structure in your files and directories, and be consistent.

If your site is small enough, it can be contained in one single directory. A site with many files, however, should be organized within several directories. Use your FTP client's features to create subdirectories and transfer your files into the directories accordingly.

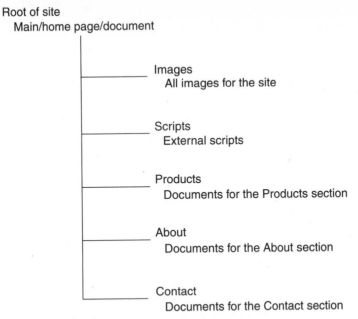

Root of site
Main/home page/document

Images
All images for the site

Scripts
External scripts

Products
Documents for the Products section

About
Documents for the About section

Contact
Documents for the Contact section

Figure 36-3: The typical organization of a Web site.

More information on organizing your content can be found in Chapter 40.

Summary

File Transfer Protocol (FTP) has been around for ages and is still the most used tool to transfer files on the Internet. This chapter introduced you to the technology behind FTP as well as some of the clients available for your use.

✦   ✦   ✦

Publicizing Your Site and Building Your Audience

Now that you've developed your site and found the appropriate place to publish it, how do you get people to find you?

You can use a number of techniques. Some of them start at the beginning, with your Web design efforts, because how you name your pages and what you include in your content can affect your page rankings in search engines.

You can also play a more direct role in search engine results by submitting your Web site's URLs to search engines and directories.

This chapter explores these options and demonstrates how some careful Web site planning can enhance your Web site's publicity.

Soliciting Links

One tried and true method is to make sure your site gets linked to by other sites. Naturally, the bigger the linking site, the better your results. When the Web was in its formative years, one of the best ways to grow a site was to get included in a "cool links" site. This same general concept still works, although such "cool links" sites now are usually more segmented because of the information glut on the Web. Although it takes a bit of effort, link building is still an important way to build awareness of your site. Acquiring a stable of sites that link to yours will also dramatically improve your page rankings in search engines such as Google.

Using link exchanges

One of the oldest methods for soliciting links is to exchange them with other Web sites. This usually takes the form of an informal arrangement between two Webmasters that is initiated when one says to another, "I'll link to your site if you'll link to mine," or simply, "Do you mind if I link to your site?" In the case of the latter, the hope upon asking a question like that is that the link will be reciprocated.

You can also use the services of banner exchange programs. These are link exchanges that allow you to place a banner ad on a network of sites. In exchange, you place a banner on your own site displaying the banner ad of sites that are members of the link exchange. The banner ads from these other sites are randomly generated as far as you're concerned—you won't know when or what site is going to be advertised on your site, so you have to accommodate that fact in your design. Most link exchange programs require that the banner be visible on the screen without a scroll down by the user.

Newsgroups

Some newsgroups are geared specifically for announcing new Web sites, and others are dedicated to topics that may be of interest to viewers of your site. You need to be extremely sensitive to newsgroup policies if you use a newsgroup to announce your site, and be sure to check out the following:

1. Carefully scour the newsgroup to see what types of posts are acceptable.

2. Seek out the group's FAQ or any other document that describes the group's policy on announcements and/or advertising.

3. Include ANNC: or ADV: in your subject header, before anything else.

4. Keep the message very short. Be sure not to post advertisements to any group unless such posts are specifically allowed by that group.

Caution   Don't, under any circumstances, post the same message to multiple groups. This is called spamming, and even if you don't have a problem with this kind of activity personally, your ISP does. If they find out you're doing it, they will probably terminate your account.

Listing Your Site with Search Engines

Submitting your URL to search engines has been a popular way to increase search engine optimization for about as long as the Web has been in existence. You can use submission agents to submit your sites to search engines, or you can do it yourself. Search engines index sites according to different criteria, so do your homework about each service before submitting your URL to the various search engines if you're doing it yourself. You can usually find a submission agent such as www.submit-it.com to do it for you for as little as $50 (U.S.). Submission agents generally take the form of Web interfaces that ask you to fill out some comprehensive forms that help describe the following about your Web site:

✦ The name of your site

✦ The URL of your site

✦ The title of your home page

✦ Your Web site's focus

✦ Your audience demographics

Then, they'll walk you through a series of potential sites to which you could submit your page based on the criteria you've selected. This is a fast way for submitting to as many as 100 search engines without requiring a visit to each one, although the submission process is still somewhat lengthy because once your "global" form is filled out, some sites will demand more information. You can expect to take between one to two hours submitting your site this way.

Some search engines, including Yahoo, charge a fee for submitting URLs to their directories, but keep in mind that results from the Yahoo directory are not the same as results from the Yahoo search engine, which is driven by Google. Yahoo maintains its own, separate, human-edited directory of sites. To be included in that directory, you must pay a fee and submit your URL to Yahoo.

If you submit your site to a large number of individual search engines yourself, get help. You can get a good overview on how to submit to individual search engines by visiting www.searchenginewatch.com/links/article.php/2156221. This Web site lists the major search directories, and how to submit to them.

You can also submit your site specifically to Google to facilitate that search engine's crawler, which is robot software that crawls the Web hunting for sites to include in the Google search database. Find this at www.google.com/addurl.html.

Facilitating Search Engine Access

You can also do a number of things to facilitate search engine access when you design your Web site, and these things are possibly even more important than going through the trouble of submitting your sites to search engines.

In fact, the whole concept of facilitating search engine access is an art called *search engine optimization*, and, if successfully deployed, can significantly enhance your page rankings in search engines such as Google and Overture.

Getting links from other sites

In the section *Soliciting Links*, you saw that there are ways to get links from other sources without spending a lot of money. The best reason for getting those links is that many search engines crawl the Web for links and tally up the results. If your site has many other sites pointing to it, this will enhance your page ranking in search engines. If you aren't having any luck getting other sites to link to you, consider building the best set of links you can find on the Web in your subject area. You'll be surprised how quickly other sites begin to link to yours, and a chain of events will occur that may lead you to a very high page ranking within just a couple of months.

Encouraging bookmarks

If you make a note on your page reminding visitors to bookmark your site if they like it, some of them actually will; and, eventually, some of them will add your link to their site. Over time, this kind of activity can result in a number of your links appearing on the Web, because people like to share links. Even Joe Schmoe's personal Web site can help your site if he includes links to your site, because search engines pay attention to who is linking to your site, so the more sites that do, the better.

Keeping your site current

If your site's content is not fresh, it's stale, and nobody likes stale content. Even if you have built a fantastic Web site full of beautiful design elements and intriguing content, users will eventually stop visiting if you don't keep the content fresh. The more compelling and timely your content is, the more often people will return and link to your site, thus improving page ranking with search engines.

Predicting users' search keywords and enhancing search retrieval

Search engines look for a common theme throughout a Web page, so it's important that the title of your page as represented in the `title` element be relevant to the subject matter of your page, and that the keywords listed in your meta tags reflect the subject and title matter.

Using the title tag to your advantage

Most search engines place the most emphasis on the title element of your Web page. A `title` element that has no meaning will be incredibly inefficient, whereas a `title` element that contains a value that has direct relevance to your Web site will begin to show almost immediate results in many search engine page rankings. This is due to a concept known as relevancy, which is part of the algorithm used by Web search engines to help determine a search result. The higher the relevancy, the better placement a page gets in a search result. You can have low traffic and still get good results from a well-named page. Plus, the title of that page is used as the first line of the search result.

Using meta tags

The Web is such a huge repository of information that it's useful to create digests of information about information. Think of an abstract in a repository of journals that describes an article or book, and you have an idea of what *meta* information is.

Meta tags involve the use of HTML's meta element. The two primary types of meta tags are Meta Descriptions and Meta Keywords.

Using Meta Description

This element is used to describe your site. Search engines use this tag to match against your title element. The better the match, the better your results will be. If your page is titled "Vintage Records—2003" and your meta description says, "Hits by Roy Orbison and other oldies," your page won't do as well as it would if your title more closely reflected the description. The Meta Description tag is written like this:

```
<meta type="description" content=" Hits by Roy Orbison and other great rock
performers from the Traveling Wilburys. This web site presents an overview and
links to the music of such musical luminaries as Roy Orbison, George Harrison,
and Tom Petty.">
```

The preceding meta tag should be on a page that has a title element that reflects the topic of your Web site, like this:

```
<title> Hits by Roy Orbison and other great rock performers from the Traveling
Wilburys.</title>
```

Using Meta Keywords

A slightly disparaged but still very effective means for creating search engine optimization patterns is to use Meta Keywords. This, like Meta Descriptions, involves the use of the meta element:

```
<meta type="keywords" content="Roy Orbison, Orbison, Tom Petty, George
Harrison, Traveling Wilburys, music, 1980s, music of the 80s">
```

The content attribute is filled by comma-delimited keywords and/or phrases. The key to making this work is to use it legitimately. If you try to fool search engines by using the same keywords repeatedly in the content attribute, search engines will ignore the tag and may even banish your site or part of your site from its database. As with Meta Descriptions, keep your keywords relevant to your page title and description.

Using the alt attribute in an img element

One of the least utilized of search optimization techniques involves the use of the img element's alt attribute. If you have a picture of Roy Orbison on a page that has content like that described in the previous sections, you should most certainly be sure that the alt attribute is used. You could write content like this:

```
<img src="orbison.gif" alt="Roy Orbison">
```

Or, you could write this:

```
<img src="orbison.gif" alt="Roy Orbison while performing with The Traveling
Wilburys">
```

Creating "Intelligent" URLs

You can also improve your search engine optimization by building "intelligent" URLs, which simply means that your URLs have relevance to the topic of the pages they point to. In our current example, this can be as simple as something like the following:

```
http://www.mymusic.com/orbison.html
```

Or, better yet, the following:

```
http://www.mymusic.com/roy_orbison.html
```

If you're working from a database, you can create relevant links by making sure that your site's URL variables contain names relevant to your site. Consider the following nonrelevant URL example:

```
http://www.mymusic.com/searchresults?12xc=Wil0rb001
```

Now compare it with the following relevant example:

```
http://www.mymusic.com/searchresults?musician=Orbison&group=Wilburys
```

Note Many search engines will reject URLs with question marks, so you may need to "encode" the question mark from the back end by replacing the question mark with a different character. Most modern back-end systems provide the facilities to handle this, but the processes are specific to the systems involved (you would handle it differently using a Java back end than a .NET back end, for example).

Using a custom domain name

Creating a custom domain name isn't as easy as it was when the Web was young, but you can still sometimes acquire a domain name that is similar to your business specialty. When you do that, users who type a URL into their address bar to "guess" a domain name may find yours. This is especially true if you have a very unique name and your customers know the name, even if they don't know how to spell it. For example, if they type the name into a Google search, there's a good chance that if they get the name wrong Google will supply alternatives by asking the user, "Did you mean xxxx?" This phenomenon has led to software companies taking on some very strange names, secure in the fact that customers who type something close to their name in a search engine's text input box will still get taken to the right page.

Strategies for Retaining Visitors On-Site

Once people have found your site, how do you keep them coming back? One way is to provide services. Such services can include chat rooms, discussion boards, and other interactive facilities.

Providing resource services

One of the best ways to both attract people to your site and keep them coming back, is to provide a service or resource that keeps people interested in your business field. For example, many of the larger software companies, such as IBM and Microsoft, maintain extensive libraries of developer information and tutorials. Whether they maintain these libraries out of altruism is only known by the executive officers of these companies, but there isn't any doubt that these kinds of sites drive traffic. If you're selling vintage records, you might want to maintain a series of articles on music, or links to musicians. If you're an insurance agent, you might want to include articles and/or links to tips on safe driving.

Maintaining a services area on your Web site will also result in links from other sites. But most importantly, it will keep your content fresh and keep visitors coming back.

Creating message boards and chat sites

Many Web hosts now offer easy-to-use message boards that you can customize for your site to match topics relevant to your Web site. This is a good way to get your Web site visitors involved in the topic areas of interest on your site. You can also find free message board software on the Internet, but configuring them can be a little tricky and usually requires a little knowledge of the back-end processes of your Web host. For example, if you're using a Web host that uses a Linux environment, you'll probably want to find free software that uses PHP as its logic engine. Similarly, if you're on a Microsoft-based environment, you'll want either an ASP-based message software solution or a .NET solution.

Many host providers also provide chat solutions, which is another way to get your visitors engaged with your site.

The Don'ts of Web Site Promotion

There are a number of things you most certainly should not do to promote your site, because they're either unethical or possibly even illegal.

Unsolicited e-mail

Hopefully, you don't need anyone to tell you what spam is or why you shouldn't be someone who engages in its use. Even though sending such bulk mailings costs the sender virtually nothing, its toll on the rest of us is substantial. And no matter what the promoters of bulk e-mail tell you, your message will not only be ignored and deleted, but your name will be tarnished if you're associated with bulk e-mail. Spamming with unsolicited e-mail typically results in e-mail servers (both the sending and receiving servers) going down under the load of a massive e-mailing, filled e-mail boxes, and wasted bandwidth.

Redundant URL submissions

As you'll see in the sections that follow, most Web site indexing services, such as Yahoo and Alta Vista, provide an online form where you can submit the address (URL) of your site to be included in their index. It's possible to submit a single site more than once, but doing so will also blacklist you with the search engines. So avoid the temptation and play by the rules to achieve the best results.

Usenet newsgroup flooding

Another form of inappropriate promotion is the spamming of newsgroups. This is similar to e-mail spamming. Most newsgroups have strict policies against spamming and will aggressively report spammers to their ISPs and/or host providers. Even groups that might once have been advertisement-friendly may now have policies against bulk e-mail advertising because spamming has become such a problem. Check with your newsgroup's FAQ to find out its policies regarding advertising.

Chat room or forum flooding

Some "marketers" have begun to use programs to flood chat rooms (particularly on AOL or IRC) with messages, or spam every user connected to that service. The message here is the same as in any other spam situation: All you'll do is annoy people and give yourself a bad name.

Summary

When developing a plan to promote your Web site, start thinking early in your development process about how you want to accomplish your goals. Incorporate your themes into your pages at an early stage to help search engines find you. This means making sure that your page titles correspond to your content. It also helps if early paragraphs in your page content contain references to your page titles and Meta Descriptions.

After your content passes the page optimization test, you can begin to submit your URLs to search engines and directories. This process should take no more than a few hours, especially if you use a service that helps you create multiple submissions to numerous sites. The final result will be increased page rankings, which translates to more visitors.

Now that you've learned how to build a great site and how to promote it, the next chapter discusses how to maintain your site to keep your visitors coming back.

✦　　✦　　✦

Maintaining Your Site

Throughout this book, you have learned how to create online content. However, once you create the content you also have to maintain it. You need to ensure your site does not contain errors, that revisions don't break links, and that you are fairly insulated from data loss. This chapter covers these topics and shows you how to perform routine maintenance on your site to minimize problems.

Analyzing Usage via Server Logs

All Web servers generate logs regarding traffic. It is important to routinely review the information in the server logs to ensure your site is not experiencing any problems you might not be aware of.

Monitoring Apache traffic

Any public Web site should have its traffic monitored. Apache does a great job of tracking all access, errors, and content it serves and storing it all in its log files. However, reading a log file—even a modest one—can be tedious and unproductive.

Thankfully, several tools are available to monitor traffic on Apache. Most tools work off the Apache log files and can be used to view retroactive traffic. The following sections cover three of the most popular open source tools—Analog, Webalizer, and Advanced Web Statistics (AWStats).

Analog
The maintainers of Analog hail it as "the most popular log file analyser [sic] in the world." Whether this claim is actually true or not, many sites all around the world use Analog. Written in C, Analog is highly portable.

The main advantage to Analog is its capability to quickly process many different log file formats. This enables Webmasters to compile data from log files on demand. Analog also supports 31 different languages.

It can display 45 different reports, including the following:

✦ Quick summaries of activities

✦ Actual hosts that connected to your site

✦ Search terms used to find your site

✦ Most common files requested

Another advantage to Analog is the amount of customization that you can add to its reports.

Analog is available for multiple platforms from the main Analog Web site (`www.analog.cx`). Binaries are available for both Linux and Windows, and full source is available if you need to compile your own copy.

Tip   Analog is one of the few log analyzers that automatically analyzes archived logs—even logs that have been compressed by a log-rotating program. By specifying a log filename with a wildcard in its configuration file, such as `access.log*`, you can instruct Analog to analyze `access.log` as well as archived logs such as `access.log.3.gz`.

Figure 38-1 shows a sample of the output from Analog.

```
Mar 2003: 16663:   810: ▬▬▬▬▬▬▬▬▬▬▬▬▬▬▬▬▬▬▬▬▬▬▬
Apr 2003: 15423:   821: ▬▬▬▬▬▬▬▬▬▬▬▬▬▬▬▬▬▬▬▬▬▬▬
May 2003: 14765:   849: ▬▬▬▬▬▬▬▬▬▬▬▬▬▬▬▬▬▬▬▬▬▬▬
Jun 2003: 14634:   862: ▬▬▬▬▬▬▬▬▬▬▬▬▬▬▬▬▬▬▬▬▬▬▬
Jul 2003:     6:     2: ▬

Busiest month: Feb 2003 (1,016 requests for pages).
```

Daily Summary

(**Go To**: Top: General Summary: Monthly Report: Daily Summary: Hourly Summary: Domain Report: Organization Report: Referring Site Report: Browser Summary: Operating System Report: Status Code Report: File Size Report: File Type Report: Directory Report: Request Report)

This report lists the total activity for each day of the week, summed over all the weeks in the report.

Each unit (▬) represents 30 requests for pages or part thereof.

```
day: #reqs: #pages:
---: -----: ------:
Sun: 18971:  1183: ▬▬▬▬▬▬▬▬▬▬▬▬▬▬▬▬▬▬▬▬▬▬▬▬▬▬▬▬▬▬▬▬▬▬▬▬▬▬▬
Mon: 20026:  1237: ▬▬▬▬▬▬▬▬▬▬▬▬▬▬▬▬▬▬▬▬▬▬▬▬▬▬▬▬▬▬▬▬▬▬▬▬▬▬▬▬▬
Tue: 20473:  1188: ▬▬▬▬▬▬▬▬▬▬▬▬▬▬▬▬▬▬▬▬▬▬▬▬▬▬▬▬▬▬▬▬▬▬▬▬▬▬▬
Wed: 20861:  1198: ▬▬▬▬▬▬▬▬▬▬▬▬▬▬▬▬▬▬▬▬▬▬▬▬▬▬▬▬▬▬▬▬▬▬▬▬▬▬▬
Thu: 21877:  1149: ▬▬▬▬▬▬▬▬▬▬▬▬▬▬▬▬▬▬▬▬▬▬▬▬▬▬▬▬▬▬▬▬▬▬▬▬▬▬
Fri: 23770:  1200: ▬▬▬▬▬▬▬▬▬▬▬▬▬▬▬▬▬▬▬▬▬▬▬▬▬▬▬▬▬▬▬▬▬▬▬▬▬▬▬▬
Sat: 19128:  1042: ▬▬▬▬▬▬▬▬▬▬▬▬▬▬▬▬▬▬▬▬▬▬▬▬▬▬▬▬▬▬▬▬▬▬▬▬
```

Figure 38-1: Sample output from Analog.

Webalizer

Webalizer is similar to Analog, providing fast processing of log files into HTML reports. Also written in C, Webalizer is highly portable, and binary versions are available for download for Windows and Linux from the Webalizer Web site (www.webalizer.com). Webalizer supports 33 different languages and has a multitude of configuration options for customizing the reports it generates.

Figure 38-2 shows a sample of the output from Webalizer.

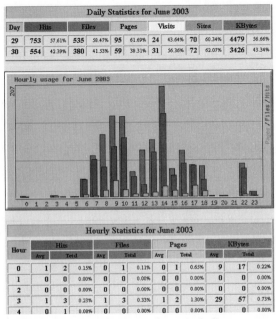

Daily Statistics for June 2003

Day	Hits		Files		Pages		Visits		Sites		KBytes	
29	753	57.61%	535	58.47%	95	61.69%	24	43.64%	70	60.34%	4479	56.66%
30	554	42.39%	380	41.53%	59	38.31%	31	56.36%	72	62.07%	3426	43.34%

Hourly Statistics for June 2003

Hour	Hits			Files			Pages			KBytes		
	Avg	Total		Avg	Total		Avg	Total		Avg	Total	
0	1	2	0.15%	0	1	0.11%	0	1	0.65%	9	17	0.22%
1	0	0	0.00%	0	0	0.00%	0	0	0.00%	0	0	0.00%
2	0	0	0.00%	0	0	0.00%	0	0	0.00%	0	0	0.00%
3	1	3	0.23%	1	3	0.33%	1	2	1.30%	29	57	0.73%
4	0	1	0.08%	0	0	0.00%	0	0	0.00%	0	0	0.00%

Figure 38-2: Sample output from Webalizer.

AWStats

Advanced Web Statistics (AWStats, www.awstats.org) is another popular open source log analyzer. AWStats is written in Perl and runs on any platform running Perl. It will run on both Apache and Internet Information Server (IIS) logs.

Note Perl is available from several different sources. You can download a copy for most platforms from CPAN (www.cpan.org). Most Linux distributions include a packaged version of Perl in their distribution, as well.

Like the other two programs, AWStats supports multiple languages (36), can be configured to read almost any log file format, and is open source, with full source code available.

AWStats runs either from the command line or from administrative pages as a CGI program. Unlike the other two analyzers just described, it is preferable to run

AWStats on a regular basis, reading the log files as they are generated instead of after the fact. The advantage to this approach is that your statistic pages are kept relatively up-to-date automatically. The downside is that AWStats wasn't written for speed, so analyzing old logs can take a while.

Figure 38-3 shows a sample of the output from AWStats.

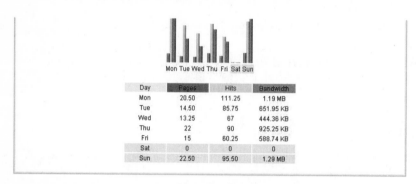

Day	Pages	Hits	Bandwidth
Mon	20.50	111.25	1.19 MB
Tue	14.50	85.75	651.95 KB
Wed	13.25	67	444.36 KB
Thu	22	90	925.25 KB
Fri	15	60.25	588.74 KB
Sat	0	0	0
Sun	22.50	95.50	1.29 MB

Hours

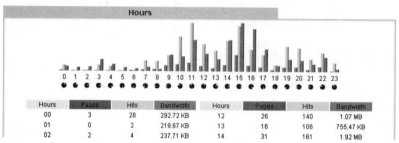

Hours	Pages	Hits	Bandwidth	Hours	Pages	Hits	Bandwidth
00	3	28	292.72 KB	12	26	140	1.07 MB
01	0	2	219.67 KB	13	16	106	755.47 KB
02	2	4	237.71 KB	14	31	161	1.92 MB

Figure 38-3: Sample output from AWStats.

Note   Several other commercial log file-analyzing programs are available, such as Webtrends' Log Analyzer series of programs (`www.netiq.com/products /log/default.asp`). However, for general use, the open source tools listed in this session work quite well.

Monitoring IIS Traffic

Unlike Apache, there don't seem to be as many freely available log analyzers for Microsoft's Internet Information Server. This is probably due to Apache's roots in the Open Source community—its specifications are freely available and the community tends to support its own.

That said, there are a few good solutions for IIS log analyzing.

✦ AWStats and Analog, covered in the preceding section on Apache, can also analyze IIS logs.

Finding the right log analyzer

All three programs covered in this session provide detailed logs that you can use to help troubleshoot your site, fine-tune your server, or just provide raw statistics. All in all, they provide fairly equal features and reporting.

How do you determine which tool is right for you?

My advice is to run at least two tools, even if you run one of them only occasionally. Running more than one helps you get a better view of your data, seeing it from multiple perspectives. Visit all the sites referenced in this section and view the sample reports to ensure that each tool provides the data you need.

Checking for Broken Links

Broken links are one of the major banes of Web sites. When you move pages or redesign your site, there is always a chance that you will break a link to another page. The various ways a link can be broken include the following:

✦ A page can be orphaned, the links to the page disappearing from referring page(s).

✦ A referring link can be mistyped or otherwise wrong.

✦ A page that is referred to might not make it to the server.

✦ A page external to your site might move or completely disappear.

Thankfully, broken links are a common problem and you have several tools at your disposal to help avoid them.

Tip

Link checkers can only check what they know about via links in documents. As such, many link checkers cannot detect totally orphaned pages. It's important to occasionally inventory the pages on your server to ensure you link to them from somewhere.

The W3C Link Checker

The World Wide Web Consortium maintains an online link checker at `http://validator.w3.org/checklink`, shown in Figure 38-4.

To use the W3C Link Checker on your site, follow these steps:

1. Put the URL to your home page in the main text box.

2. Choose the options for checking your site.

   • Use the `Summary only` option if you don't want details.

   • Use the `Hide redirects` option if you don't want to see redirect reports. You can choose to eliminate all redirect reports or only those for directories.

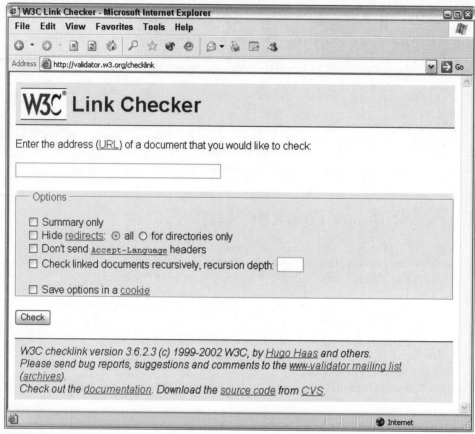

Figure 38-4: The W3C Link Checker.

- Use the `Accept-Language headers` option to control whether the Accept-Language headers are used during checking.

- To check several layers of your site, set the `recursion depth` option accordingly. Check the check box and enter the recursion depth in the associated text box.

- You can check the Save options box if you want the tool to save your settings in a cookie for later use.

3. Click the Check button to begin checking your site. The tool will display its progress as it checks your site, as shown in Figure 38-5.

Note   You can download the W3C tool and run it locally on a machine that has Perl (and required Perl modules) installed. Visit the documentation page for the checker (`http://validator.w3.org/docs/checklink.html`) for information on downloading and running the tool locally.

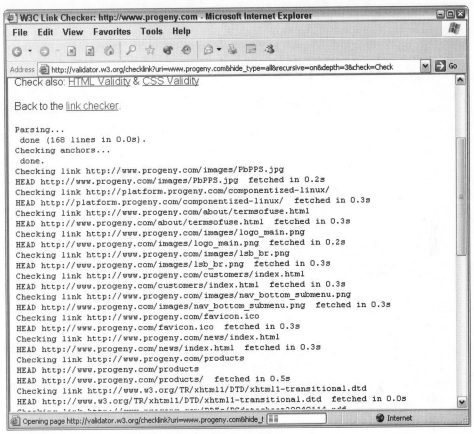

Figure 38-5: The online W3C Link Checker in action.

Checkers built into development tools

Many Web development tools have integrated link checkers that you can use while you develop your site. For example, Macromedia Dreamweaver includes a comprehensive checking feature, as shown in Figure 38-6.

Check the documentation on your favorite tool to see if it has a comparable feature.

Several Web development tools are covered in Chapter 34.

Local tools

There are several tools you can download and run locally to check links on your site. Visit your favorite software repository site (such as Tucows, www.tucows.com) to search for a suitable tool for your use.

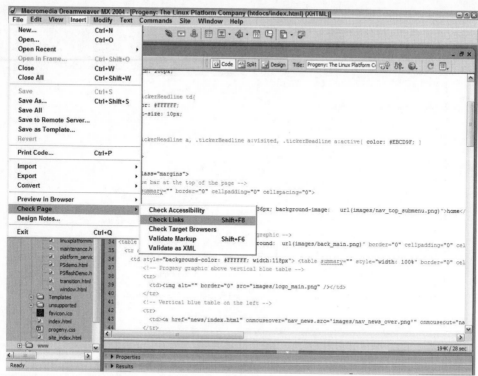

Figure 38-6: Macromedia Dreamweaver has a link checker feature built in so you can check your links as you develop your site.

Tip   Many Linux distributions come with a link-checking tool.

Watching your logs

Your server's log files can also alert you to broken links. For example, the Status Code Report shown in Figure 38-7 lists several Document not found (404) errors. These errors can be caused by broken links on your site or sites that refer to your site. By enabling more reporting details, you can usually find out what referring document had the broken link.

Responding to Feedback

Always include a feedback link on your site, typically an e-mail link to the Webmaster (you or the person generally responsible for the site). Visitors to your site can use the link to alert you to problems, provide feedback on your site, and more.

Tip   Feedback links are a target of spammers. To minimize the inconvenience of spam from feedback links, use a dedicated e-mail address (not your usual e-mail address), or obscure the address by using a form or other tool to actually perform the mailing.

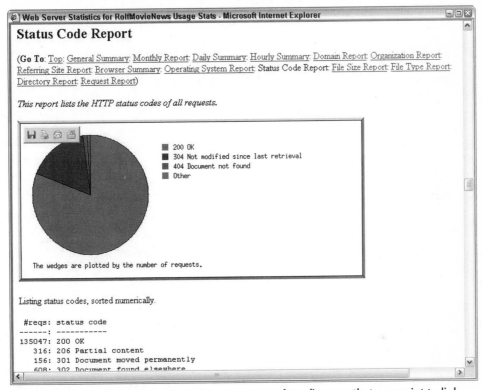

Figure 38-7: Server logs report 404 (Document not found) errors that can point to link errors inside and outside of your site.

Of course, you should always take feedback with the proverbial grain of salt—check out reported problems yourself before affecting any changes and weigh criticism (and kudos) accordingly.

Backing Up Your Data

In all areas of computing, backing up data is one of the most important tasks you can perform. Losing data, even a minimum amount, can cause many problems. To help avoid data loss, you should create and religiously follow a backup regimen. Consider the following:

✦ Keep a local, original copy of all files used on your site.

✦ Routinely copy files from your site to another location.

✦ Keep a number of past revisions of your files so you can regress changes, if necessary.

Tip   Use the archiving utility on your server (ZIP or tar) to routinely create compressed archives of your files. The copies will transfer faster and are easier to deal with in one comprehensive package.

Summary

Developing online content is only half the battle of Web publishing; maintaining the content is the other half and should be a consistent process. This chapter showed you several different tasks that should be performed on a routine basis to ensure that your site remains healthy.

✦   ✦   ✦

Principles of Professional Web Design and Development

The Web Development Process

To develop a quality Web site, you should begin to plan before you do anything else. This is true whether you're a one-person operation or a part of a large team of developers working for one of the world's monolithic sites.

Most large software and Web development houses use a functional or project requirements document and a design document for managing workflow specifics. The design document may be a part of the functional or project requirements document. After the requirements are in place, an engineering document is often created to demonstrate how the Web development team will accomplish the tasks set out in the requirements document.

This chapter explores the Web development process as a whole, focusing on the importance that planning ahead plays in the development of a successful Web site.

Challenges of Developing Large-Scale Web Sites

Many large-scale Web sites are not built from the ground up. Those that are had a plan. Those that didn't, which may very well be most of them (although there is certainly no empirical evidence for basing such a claim), now circulate many plans around to manage site updates and feature additions.

Whether you're starting a brand new site, adding a feature to a large existing site, or are a one-person operation handling all the development tasks yourself, you need to create a general attack plan based on the following steps:

1. Establish your priorities through goal and audience definition.

2. Generate a requirements analysis.

3. Produce engineering documents that meet the requirements and establish a flow for the site, or a portion of the site, to follow.

4. Choose a design theme.

5. Establish a plan for constructing the site.

6. Test and evaluate the site.

7. Market the site and track the site's usage.

8. Determine short and long-term strategies for maintaining your site.

9. Create a matrix indicating your project's progress.

These tasks are especially important when you're involved with development on very large Web sites, which will have had a lot of hands involved in development over the years. Chances are good that many of the people who belong to those hands are no longer working on the site.

Project Management Basics

One of the key ingredients in site development is *project scoping*. When you scope a project, you determine how much time your team requires to build it. Often, large sites have been cobbled together over time, and engineering teams need to strategize not only on how to make additions to a site, but how to reverse engineer existing code, especially if the site is complex.

Determining project resources is the first step you'll take in managing a Web site project. From a planning perspective, some fundamental questions need to be asked.

✦ What are your site's goals and objectives?

✦ Who's your audience?

✦ How will you speak to your audience?

✦ How will you structure your site?

✦ What will your site look like from a design standpoint?

✦ Who will handle site maintenance, and how?

✦ What is the plan for managing security policy?

Answering these questions should be a minimal first step before you begin to plan the rest of your site. You'll find that the answers to these questions will yield fundamental answers in other areas, including questions relating to functional design as well as graphic design.

The Need for Information Architecture

The next step in creating a plan for your Web site is to determine its architecture. This includes determining what kind of environment your Web site will live in. You have many kinds of server environments to choose from.Your choice will be based on a combination of factors, not the least of which includes where your expertise lies. If your strong suit is Active Server Pages (ASP) programming, you might want to avoid Java environments, and vice-versa. Of course, if you obtain a job on a Web site, you won't be making that decision unless you're running the whole show.

There are two broad categories of Web server environments: vendor-based and open source. It's normal to assume that the phrase "vendor-based Web development environments" means Microsoft, however, other software vendors also create Web development and Web server environments. The three major Web server software vendors follow:

✦ *Apache,* the leading Web server software worldwide, is from the Apache Software Foundation, and is an open source project. Open source means that the code base that runs the software is free (based on certain limitations). Because anyone can afford free, and the software itself is extremely good, it has captured nearly 70% of the Web server market, according to Netcraft.com. Apache is a good choice if you're running Java-based software on your Web server.

Note Visit Netcraft.com at `http://news.netcraft.com/archives/ web_server_survey.html`.

✦ *Sun.* If you have a Sun Microsystems system running Solaris, which is a UNIX-based operating system that runs Sun servers, you may want to consider using Sun's SunONE Web server. This Java-based Web server plays well with other Sun-based products. It only holds about a 3.5% market share, which is a steep drop from its heydays of the mid- to late-1990s. However, the most recent version of SunONE is very powerful and includes a browser-based console, which provides a GUI interface for configuring, managing, and monitoring the Web server. Security is also good, as port access is denied by default. This means access rights must be specifically granted, so you don't need to search for potential security holes.

✦ *Microsoft* holds about 25% of the share of the Web server market. It can be significantly easier to use Microsoft products, but the security issues are generally more difficult to deal with. Microsoft servers tend to be easier to compromise than Apache servers. Microsoft's Web server is called Information Services 5.0 or 6.0 (IIS 5.0 or IIS 6.0), depending on the version you are running.

Generally, if you want to run a Java-based architecture or PHP, you should probably run an Apache server. If you run ASP or .NET, you should run a Microsoft server. However, you *can* run Java-based software using Microsoft-based products, and you can also run Apache on Windows products (since Apache ports its software to multiple operating systems). If you want to run static HTML pages, pick the operating environment you're most comfortable with.

Overview of the Web Development Process

The Web development process consists of several broad steps, beginning with planning and ending with execution and maintenance. These include the following:

1. Defining your goals
2. Defining your audience
3. Developing competitive and market analysis
4. Creating a requirements analysis
5. Designing your site's structure
6. Specifying content
7. Choosing a design theme
8. Constructing the site
9. Testing and evaluating the site
10. Marketing the site

Defining your goals

The most obvious question to ask when developing a Web site is: What is it for? What are the objectives you want the site to achieve? For example, do you want to use your site to sell products, or to drive the PR process? You may want to disseminate news, or build customer service applications.

Defining your audience

Defining your audience will affect everything from the design of the site (a children's site may have lots of pastel colors or may even be a bit silly looking, whereas a science-related site will require a different design approach) to content and even navigation questions. A sophisticated audience, for example, may not need as much navigational guidance as a more general audience.

Competitive and market analysis

Discovering what your competition is doing not only helps you enhance your own market position, but can also give you solid ideas on what and what not to do on your own Web site. For example, if your competition's site consists of difficult-to-read type, you can make sure your site gets high usability ratings by making your site extremely easy to read.

Requirements analysis

Most large sites start off with something called a Project Requirements Document or Functional Requirements Document, which is a comprehensive document written in a word-processing program that contains specifications about how the Web site or a specific feature of a Web site is supposed to behave. These documents usually contain screenshots of mockups created by a team's graphic designer or graphic design department. Usually, this mockup is created in a graphics program such as Adobe Photoshop or Macromedia Fireworks (although sometimes these are broken out into separate documents called Design Requirement Documents).

A requirements document helps everyone on the team understand a Web site's expected behavior. If a part of the Web site doesn't behave according to the requirements document during testing, then a bug is filed. The bug remains open until the problem is fixed.

A list of some of the things included in requirements documents follows:

✦ Design specifications, including specific font sizes and colors

✦ Navigation specifications

✦ User experience and interaction scenarios

✦ Link behavior

✦ Page flow and page flow diagrams

✦ Usability guidelines

✦ Maintenance requirements

✦ Security policies

Often, requirements documents will be followed up by engineering requirements or execution documents that outline strategies on how the requirements will be met from an engineering perspective.

Designing the site structure

The site structure is usually defined in a requirements document. This usually involves a schematic drawing of how the Web site should flow, and which pages are parents and which are children. Figure 39-1 shows an example of a schematic for a very simple Web site containing only a few pages.

Using UML to define structure

More complex sites require more formal structure definitions. You can use flow charts, or a standardized way to create structure definitions called Unified Modeling Language (UML).

UML is a standardized modeling notation for representing software applications. You can use UML to model the way your Web application is used by each user, or the way each component behaves when interacting with other components.

Figure 39-1: Schematic for a simple Web site.

Note For an introduction to UML, visit www-106.ibm.com/developerworks/rational/library/769.html.

UML consists of two broad categories of diagrams:

✦ *Use cases* are diagrams that walk the reader through a typical user session at the Web site.

✦ *Sequential and collaboration diagrams* provide an abstract view into the relationship between the various objects in the Web site, particularly as they relate to each other. In addition to describing the navigation of a site, these diagrams focus on the application-level functionality of the site so that Java developers and other programmers working on business logic can transition quickly from concept to final production. Figure 39-2 shows a simple sequential diagram of Web functionality.

Using flow charts to define structure

You can also use your own process for creating a flow chart to define your Web site's structure. You may not have time to learn UML, or your site's team may not have the resources for it, in which case most developers simply create their own flow charts by expanding on what you saw in Figure 39-1.

You can also use software designed for creating flow charts, such as SmartDraw (www.smartdraw.com) and Visio (from Microsoft). These programs accelerate the flow-charting process by providing a drag-and-drop visual interface you use to create

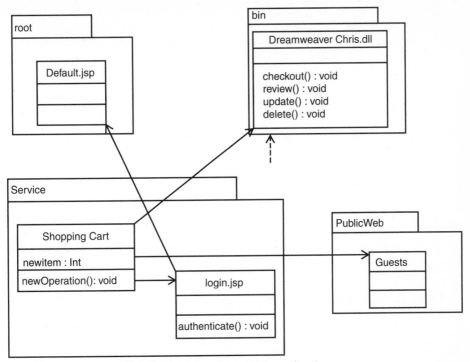

Figure 39-2: A sequential diagram showing a Web application process.

your charts and export them into graphic formats that you can use in other documents.

Specifying content

Another consideration when deciding what type of Web server software environment to choose is what kind of content you have. If you have static HTML, it doesn't matter what kind of environment you have. You can just use the one that is most comfortable to you. If you have database-driven content, you'll need to include the kind of database you expect to use in your considerations regarding a Web server environment. Several kinds of databases, including several open source varieties, are available, including the following major databases:

✦ *MySQL,* which is a popular open source database available on both Windows and UNIX/Linux servers. It's freely available at www.mysql.com and is nearly as powerful as the expensive databases from commercial vendors. If you are running a Linux box with open source Apache Web server software, this or the somewhat more powerful postgreSQL is the natural route to take for your database environment.

✦ *postgreSQL* is another open source database system that has a few more features than MySQL. You can find it at www.postgresql.org. This is also a natural choice if you're already going the open source route on Web development.

✦ *MS SQL Server* is a good choice if you know you're going to be using a Microsoft-based Web development environment. SQL Server is extremely powerful and fast, and is quite reliable. It also includes a relatively easy-to-use visual interface. It is not, however, inexpensive.

✦ *Oracle* has long been considered the standard in robust relational database systems. Oracle is a good choice if you have lots of resources, including the kind of money it takes to administer Oracle correctly. In other words, can your team afford to hire an Oracle Database Administrator (DBA)? Oracle is an expensive product with a cost based on CPU usage and the number of users that actually use the system.

✦ *DB2* is a database system developed by IBM. This is a particularly good fit if you are developing with IBM's WebSphere Web application development software, which is a Java-based Web development and deployment tool that can hook into any database, but which plays with DB2 especially well. Like Oracle and MS SQL Server, the cost of DB2 is more in line with what a large Web site can afford, and isn't the kind of investment cash-strapped organizations should consider.

Choosing a design theme

You should base your design theme on the target market analysis you perform at the opening stages of your Web site development. Sometimes your design theme will be easy. If you operate a fish store, your theme is pretty obvious. It may not be as obvious if you run a general interest site. In that case, carefully examine your market analysis and design accordingly.

If you're running a small or personal site, you can also check out predesigned templates at sites such as `http://freesitetemplates.com` and `www.templatemonster.com`.

Constructing the site

The first step in constructing a site is deciding what kind of application server environment you'll be using. An application server is somewhat like an engine that runs your Web site's logic. If you're using simple, static HTML, it doesn't matter what application server you use or whether you even have one. However, if you're interacting with a database or producing dynamic content, you'll need to work with an application server environment.

An application server lets you create dynamic content. For example, consider the following code fragment:

```
<html>
  <head>
    <title>Hello, world</title>
  </head>
  <body>
```

```
    <%= myAppServer.Write("Hello, World!")
    %>
  </body>
</html>
```

The bolded code represents a fictional application server language called WowServerPages (WSP) that has several thousand prewritten functions (methods) available to it. One of those is the `Write()` method, which simply writes text to the browser window. When the preceding code is read by the application server, it generates HTML based on the instructions it receives within special markup like that shown in bold. It then passes its results to the Web server, which sends the HTML to a user's Web browser. The user never sees this instruction and can't access it by clicking *view source* from the browser:

```
<%= myAppServer.Write("Hello, World!")
    %>
```

Only the Web application server sees it.

Virtually all application servers work this way. For example, here's the same example in a real application server environment called PHP:

```
<html>
    <head>
        <title>Hello, world</title>
    </head>
    <body>
        <?php
        echo "Hello, world";
        ?>
    </body>
</html>
```

In this case, PHP, which borrows heavily from Perl syntax, uses a method called `echo` to write text to the browser. The major application server environments available include the following:

✦ *PHP* is primarily a UNIX/Linux application server that requires a PHP parser (CGI or server module) on the machine running your Web server (or linked to a machine running your Web server). If you are running your site through a Web hosting service that is UNIX or Linux-based, ask them if PHP is installed. Most decent Web hosting service plans offer PHP as part of a basic package. You can recognize PHP pages on the Web by looking for Web sites with `.php` or `.php4` extensions at the end of file names.

✦ *Java Server Pages* (JSP) is a Java-based Web application server that requires a J2EE Java environment. You can get a free JSP-based application server called Tomcat through `www.apache.org`. JSP pages use a `.jsp` file extension.

✦ *Active Server Pages* (ASP) was developed by Microsoft and works especially well with MS SQL Server because its object model used for programming Web sites contains numerous data-binding mechanisms geared specifically to work with SQL Server, although it also works well with MySQL, because many of the data-binding processes work with any database connection. Programming ASP is based on Visual Basic. Pages written in ASP use a `.asp` file extension.

✦ *ASP.NET* has supplanted ASP and is the next-generation application server in the Microsoft world. ASP.NET allows developers to choose from a number of languages, include the new C#, VisualBasic.NET, and J#. ASP.NET pages use a `.aspx` file extension.

✦ *ColdFusion*, from Macromedia, is a commercial application server with functionality similar to the others. ColdFusion pages have a `.cfm` file extension.

Testing and evaluating the site

When your Web site is finished, you want to test it before serving it to the public. How you do that will depend on the resources of your Web development team. If your team has a lot of resources, you can set up your Web site on a testing server. This is a separate machine with Web hosting capabilities that can't be seen by the general public but provides exactly the same capabilities as your production machine, which is the machine that will actually host your publicly available site.

If your team doesn't have the kind of resources needed to make that happen, you can set up your site on a *sandbox*. A sandbox is an area on your production machine that isn't accessible to the public, which mirrors the directory structure of your Web site. For example, you may have a directory named `sandbox`, into which you would place your index and/or default html pages. Then, each of the directories in your sandbox would have the same names and files as those on your production Web site.

If your site is new, you can simply deny access to it until you're ready to go live.

To test the site, you compare the site's behavior to the requirements documents you produced at the early stages of your Web site's development. Generally, you or someone in your quality assurance (QA) team will create a use case document that is derived from the requirements document. Often, this is simply a spreadsheet with a list of use cases and cells containing expected behavior and empty cells containing actual behavior. When the expected behavior clashes with the actual behavior, a bug is filed. Then the list of bugs is submitted to the Web development team, and the site doesn't go live until the bugs are fixed.

Marketing the site

Once your site is live, you'll want to find a way to get it noticed by your target audience. In addition to the marketing tips explored in Chapter 37, *Publicizing Your Site and Building Your Audience*, you may want to try the following marketing tactics:

Throw a party and get the party publicized: When the dot-com craze was at its peak, new Web sites often threw lavish parties with well-known musicians and other talent. Those days are gone (because the days of wasteful spending have given way to more frugality and, as a result, much stronger Web sites), but you can still hold a small soiree to publicize your site to key players in your industry.

✦ Take an ad out in a trade publication geared towards your profession.

✦ Issue a press release announcing your site.

✦ Participate in e-mail discussion lists in ways that contribute to the knowledge of people on the list, and include a signature in your posts that points to your Web site.

✦ Purchase ad banners on other Web sites to announce your site.

✦ Run on-site events.

✦ Generate an e-newsletter and include a link on your Web site encouraging people to sign up for it (but don't send out the newsletter unsolicited, because that will actually do more damage than good with your prospects, who will interpret those efforts as spam).

✦ Embark on a direct e-marketing campaign.

✦ Integrating traditional marketing and sales programs into your overall plan. This may include producing brochures and spec sheets with your Web site included as part of the contact information, and will most certainly include your Web site name on business cards.

Tracking site usage and performance

Once your marketing is underway, determine its effectiveness. The first step in this process is to determine where your traffic originates. Then measure what individuals do once they get to your site. This helps you find out if one marketing approach is more effective than others.

Every Web server creates log files, which are raw data files containing information about visitors to your site. This data consists of the user's IP address, what browser the user employs, and the time of day the user came to your site.

Reading the access log file

A Web server usually has an access log file containing information formatted in the common *logfile* format that is used by most Web servers. You can purchase special software designed to parse these files and generate user-friendly graphs for your analysis. Most decent Web site hosting plans include such software with their plans. One common user access software analysis tool is WebTrends. Check with your host provider to see if they offer such software.

You can also review access logs yourself. For example, each line in an access log file represents one request, as in the following example:

```
someonesmachine_sf_someISP_hub - - [30/Aug/2004:20:01:22 - 0700]
"GET /services/index.html HTTP/1.0" 200 1223
```

In the preceding line from an access log, `someonesmachine_sf_someISP_hub` is the name of the computer that made a request for /services/index.html on the night of August 30, 2004. The 200 indicates that the request was answered successfully, and the 1223 indicates how many bytes your machine sent in response to the request.

Using a referrer log file

A referrer log keeps track of where Web users came from. This helps you find out where links to your Web site exist on other sites. For example, the following is a result from a Yahoo search resulting in a query for "fish" that leads to your site:

```
http://search.yahoo.com/bin/search?p=fish ->
/services/fish/index.html
```

You may also have a link from another site. Perhaps someone likes your pages that describe the many kinds of fish one can find in the ocean. Their link to your site may result in someone clicking the link and visiting your site:

```
http://www.someonessite/links.html ->
/services/fish/index.html
```

Using an extended log file

A personal extended log file contains a combination of access log and referrer log information. Not all Web servers generate these, but most do.

Keep in mind that log files can get quite large. Delete them from your server or copy them over to your personal computer from time to time if your Web hosting provider doesn't do that automatically for you.

Maintaining the site

Maintaining your Web site means more than just making sure it continues to work. It also means keeping your content fresh. This may mean being careful from the outset about where you place time-sensitive content. If you have time-sensitive content distributed all over the place, you'll probably lose track of some of it and it will become out of date. This is particularly true of links, which is why it's best to include a special area for hot links.

You may also want a section that includes news on your industry. You can develop your own articles, or even provide an RSS-based news feed. You can learn how to do that by visiting `www.webreference.com/perl/tutorial/8/`.

Other site maintenance tricks include simply being sure you follow some of the suggestions made in Chapter 37, particularly in regard to page titling and the use of meta information to keep your site in the eyes of search engines.

Summary

Developing a modern Web site is a multipart process. It begins with planning, because even if you have a small, one-person operation, you'll have competition for eyes. That competition is very likely to be researching and planning their Web site.

Today's Web sites have grown in sophistication because we now have so much knowledge to start with. There are many best cases out there, and a well-planned site will take advantage of what has worked in the past and leverage the knowledge gained by the 40 million or so Web sites that preceded it.

A well-planned Web site will be the final result if your Web development process consists of the following:

✦ An overview of your goals and audience

✦ An analysis of your competition and your own market

✦ An overall project management documentation including a requirements document that outlines your Web site's functional requirements

✦ Site design, construction, and testing

✦ Site marketing and tracking

The next chapter explores more closely how to develop and structure your Web site's content, including how to best approach your content from a Web writing perspective.

✦   ✦   ✦

Developing and Structuring Content

Computer monitors are not designed for long reading sessions because they have a very low pixel per inch (ppi) ratio. Hardware manufacturers are working on developing monitors with higher densities, but until they do, people are stuck with 72 pixel-per-inch and 96 pixel-per-inch computer monitors. 300 pixels per inch would be much nicer, but in the meantime, if you don't want to lose your Web site's visitors, you must be aware of how quickly they can lose patience with your site's contents. Study after study has confirmed what you'll discover in this chapter—that approximately 75% of all Web site viewers scan Web content instead of reading it. This chapter shows you how to accommodate that tendency (since you can't change it) and find ways to make the scan memorable and help your site's readers hone in on the important sections of the site.

Principles of Audience Analysis

One of the basic tenets of any writing is to know your audience. Without knowing your audience, the odds of actually communicating with your Web site visitors are nothing more than a roll of the dice. They may come away with information they want and/or need, and they may not.

Performing an audience analysis is a useful way of accomplishing a number of Web content goals, from deciding how to chunk information to determining how to manage hyperlinks. You should strive to understand your audience well so that you can communicate with them effectively.

Unfortunately, much of this analysis will be done after your site has gone live for the first time. Many Web tools exist to help generate Web site analysis, but your site must be running for it to work. Web site analysis software can give you reports on the demographics of your visitors, and provide information on how they came to your site. You can also create surveys and registration pages with forms asking users to provide information about themselves.

But how do you analyze your audience *before* your site is up and running? One way is to acquire industry reports that provide user demographics for the industry you are in. Researching general trends within your industry is valuable no matter what you're doing, whether it's building a Web site or building cars, because it helps you project trends and plan for them instead of reacting to them.

Audience analysis is an ongoing effort, as your Web site is live for a month, six months, a year, and even ten years down the road. You'll need to respond to changing demographics and emerging trends as you develop your Web site content.

Performing an Information Inventory

You should gather as much information ahead of time as you can to help organize it better. If you know your content will contain a lot of hyperlinks, for example, you should try to gather as many of them as possible before you start developing and writing content.

The same holds true for the rest of your Web site's content. If some of that content comes from a database, that information is already organized. Try to organize the rest of your content in a similar way so that it's easy for you to access and plug into your Web pages.

Chunking Information

Web readers often don't read Web material in sequence. Web pages are more like reference works than fiction, meaning that you often can't assume a reader has read one section before another. By providing information in chunks, you can help your readers quickly locate specific items of interest. Your chunks can consist of both specific content and links to supporting content or other related sites.

When organizing chunks of information, consider the following:

✦ *How will your users access your content?* Will you want to make all of your content accessible in each chunk, or will you rely heavily on hyperlinking?

✦ *Will your users want to print out your pages?* If you know your users will print out the information on your Web page, you might want to avoid chunking. If you don't know how many users will print a given page, you may want to point them to a page designed for printing or to a PDF version of the page.

✦ *How long are your pages?* Web users as a rule don't like longer pages, so the number of chunks of information per page should not be very high.

If you organize your chunks effectively, it will be obvious on your Web site, because the site itself will appear organized. This enhances the viewing experience for users, who will likely return to your site often and begin linking to it.

How Users Read on the Web

According to usability guru Jakob Neilsen, users don't read Web pages, and he provides studies to prove his point. If you think about it, you'll probably realize that you only scan Web pages, as well. With that in mind, Neilsen and others argue that the three following statements summarize user behavior regarding written content (www.useit.com/papers/webwriting/writing.html):

✦ As previously mentioned, users don't read Web pages, but scan them to focus on the few sentences that provide the information they're looking for.

✦ Users don't like long, scrolling pages and prefer brief, summary-like text.

✦ Users don't like marketing fluff (or, *marketese*, as Neilsen calls it), but actively seek out information.

Numerous studies have been released to back up Nielsen's findings. These studies show a clear pattern: Users like brevity, don't like marketing clichés, and appreciate it when you provide strong clues as to what kind of content to expect in any given chunk of text.

Developing Easily Scanned Text

Writing for the Web is not about developing clever material, but is instead about developing text that can be easily scanned by a reader searching for nuggets of information he or she can use. According to Neilsen, scannable text consists of the following characteristics:

✦ *Highlighted keywords.* These are especially useful when in the form of hyperlinks, although typeface and color variations also help.

✦ *Subheadings that have meanings, instead of subheads that try to be cute and/or clever.* If you're running a site targeted to an audience that expects that kind of writing, you obviously can diverge from Nielsen's theories (like any theory, these aren't bulletproof).

✦ *Bulleted lists that highlight key points.*

✦ *Paragraphs that consist of one idea.*

✦ *Text that uses the inverted pyramid style, starting with the conclusion.* You might want to alter this rule a bit by using a true pyramid style, but with the conclusion at the top instead of the bottom. The pyramid style is newspaper jargon that dictates that reporters write the most important sentences of an article first, and then write the remaining article by adding increasingly less relevant material.

✦ *Use half the word count (or less) you would use in conventional writing.* This doesn't need to be a hard and fast rule. You can alter it by developing comprehensive content in another area, and by providing a summary page for those users who don't want to deal with your comprehensive content; but make sure you provide a link to the more comprehensive parts.

Developing Meta Content: Titles, Headings, and Taglines

One of the most important aspects of developing content for the Web involves meta content such as titles, headings, and taglines. Meta content is content about content. It provides glimpses into the material without requiring the reader to scan the entire text.

Titles

Developing effective titles is a key part of Web content development. They help your readers understand what your topics are about. They're also excellent ways to improve search engine delivery.

See Chapter 37 for more information on how to effectively use the `title` tag to improve search engine results.

Headings

Headlines (headings) and titles should both be highly informative. Avoid superlatives and self-congratulatory text, and avoid marketing lingo. When it comes to Web content development, marketing professionals need to become information specialists. Headlines should focus on how to point users to valuable information they can use on your site. A bad headline is "Cognitive BioResearch, Inc., A Better Serum for a Better Tomorrow."

A better headline would be something like "Cognitive BioResearch, Inc.: Developers of Truth Serum for Government Officials."

This type of headline shows that the company makes a badly needed product, and it doesn't try to seduce readers with slick marketing words that mean little to most readers. Web users typically spend little time on a Web site, unless they're compelled to do so. Compelling them to do so doesn't require marketing jargon, but headlines that lure users in with a genuine promise that they'll be rewarded with timely and useful information.

Taglines

Traditionally, taglines in the marketing world have referred to the "button" line under a logo at the bottom of an ad or at the end of a commercial. A famous example of a tagline is Coca Cola's long-running "Coke is it" slogan. Tag lines are important on

Web sites, too, but their tone and purpose must be much different to be effective. On a Web site, users expect all the information they see to have some immediate relevancy. So a good tagline should be informative and begin to talk immediately about what the site does. An example of an effective tagline is from eBay's site:

> Buying new items, brand names, and collectibles on eBay is simple. Here's how it works. . .

This not only tells the Web site visitor what the site is about, but promises to immediately offer help on how to take advantage of the services the Web site offers.

The difference between taglines and headlines is that a tagline is likely to be used in many places throughout a site, whereas a headline is generally specific to one block of content.

Jakob Neilsen recommends the following when developing taglines:

> "First, collect the taglines from your own site and your three strongest competitors. Print them in a bulleted list without identifying the company names. Ask yourself whether you can tell which company does what. More important, ask a handful of people outside your company the same question.

> Second, look at how you present the company in the main copy on the home page. Rewrite the text to say exactly the opposite. Would any company ever say that? If not, you're not saying much with your copy, either."

Characteristics of Excellent Web Writing

Once you've drawn your readers in, you need to keep them. There are several general guidelines to follow, many of them established through Jakob Nielsen's usability studies. Others have cropped up over the years (when 40 million or so Web pages are up and running at the same time, there's a good chance some people have come to some conclusion about how Web development works).

Be concise

Most likely, whatever takes you 200 words to write can probably be done in 100. If your budget allows, hire a professional writer, but if it doesn't, be prepared to trim your writing thoroughly. Keep in mind the impatience of your readers, and remember that there is a good reason they're impatient—the written word on computer monitors is difficult on the eyes.

Creating easily scanned web pages

Since users are scanning your pages anyway, make it easy for them by doing the following:

✦ Use the `strong` tag or colored text (but not blue, unless it's for a hyperlink) to highlight keywords and a bold face font to highlight key points and words. Generally, readers who scan can only pick up two or three words at a time, so don't highlight entire sentences. You should also highlight words that are directly associated with topics of each page or section.

✦ Highlight words that differentiate one page from another page.

✦ Use the `em` element to render italics for figure captions or when you want to introduce a word that needs to be defined. You can also use this element to add emphasis to a specific word that doesn't warrant highlighting.

✦ When you need to highlight entire sentences, use bulleted and numbered lists, which slow down the scanning eye and draw attention to important points.

Maintaining credibility

Your Web site's credibility is absolutely crucial to your long-term success. Part of achieving credibility is avoiding marketing hype, and another part is making sure that your content is accurate. If you do make claims about your service or products, back them up somehow. One way to do that is to create informative case studies that detail how your products or services have helped others achieve specific goals that they may not have been able to reach without your help. You can also employ testimonials, but tread lightly here, and avoid falling into the trap of marketing hype. Any testimonials you use should be informative and useful.

Maintaining objectivity

Try to maintain objectivity, even though your Web site is about you, your services, or your products. You might even want to include some information about who *shouldn't* use your service or product, if appropriate. This greatly enhances your credibility with readers.

Maintaining focus and limiting verbosity

Keep your focus on your Web site by avoiding any tendency to provide unnecessary detail and by keeping paragraphs limited to one main idea. Remember that it doesn't take much for a Web site user to stray away from your Web page.

Keep a consistent style throughout your Web site. In other words, try to make sure your Web site has one "voice."

Writing in a top-down style

When a newspaper reporter develops a story, he or she will start with the most important topic and drill down as the story goes on. The reason for this dates back to the old days of newspaper printing when editors often had to snip articles wherever necessary to fit them within the space. Since these decisions were made quickly under the heat of a print deadline, reporters developed a style of article and news story writing that made the decisions on where to cut off a story easy. The details of a story were left for the end. The key points were made at the outset.

Because readers are the ultimate editors, certain aspects of this idea have been ported to the Web. You should develop your Web site in a top-down manner (also called pyramid style), because readers will also cut your story off quickly if they don't find relevant subject matter.

One difference between print pyramid style and Web pyramid style is that on the Web, you should show your conclusions first, and then begin the top-down writing style. You can mimic print articles in this way by making your headline your conclusion.

Another difference between Web and print pyramid style writing is that, as mentioned earlier, readers tend to read in chunks. This can affect the top-down approach somewhat, because you can't assume a reader has read the first part of an article.

Using summaries

It may seem unnatural to put a summary at the beginning of a section, but that's exactly where you want to put it. In fact, there's enough good writing on the Web that users actually expect to see summaries or conclusions at the beginning of paragraphs. This concept coincides with the inverted pyramid style of writing described in the previous section.

Writing for the Web

The style of your Web writing should be directly linked to the concepts you've been reading about so far in this chapter. Keep your Web content tight and focused, with an inherent respect for your reader's need to scan your Web site. You can extend this concept into your writing style.

In yet another of many studies conducted by Jakob Neilsen, 51 Web users tested five variations of a Web site using the same content, with each Web site consisting of a different writing style than the others. According to the study, "one version was written in a promotional style ("marketese"); one version was written to encourage scanning; one was concise; one had an "objective," or nonpromotional, writing style; and one combined concise, scannable, and objective language into a single site." The study found significant improvements in reader recall when sites written in promotional style were rewritten into a scannable format. In fact, although the scanning-based style Web content fared the best, all the other styles performed better than the marketese version.

Using bulleted lists

Bulleted lists are more frequently used on Web sites than on printed pages. They're generally used to explicitly detail points you're trying to make. They're an effective way to highlight larger chunks of information, because sometimes highlighting just a keyword or two isn't enough. But, if you overdo it, they lose their effectiveness. So, try to limit a bulleted list to seven items or fewer, and each page should not have more than two lists (one is better).

Using a controlled vocabulary

Now that you know the value of using keywords and meta information, it's important to know how to handle them in the body of your text. If you run amok with all kinds of synonyms for important words, you'll lose some search engine optimization benefits, because your pages will rate higher if they contain words in the content that match the keywords in your meta tags. Include in each page all possible query terms that can be used to search for the topic on your page, and then make sure those keywords appear in your meta tags.

Jargon and marketese

Jargon, especially on tech-related Web sites, can overwhelm readers who may be unfamiliar with it. If you must use jargon, be absolutely sure of your audience's ability to comprehend it, and remember that many people who are new to your field won't be familiar with expressions, words, and acronyms you became accustomed to a long time ago. If your industry is prone to jargon, even if you refrain from using it on your site, Web site visitors will appreciate a Frequently Asked Questions (FAQ) page that defines some of the jargon used by your industry.

Jargon, however, isn't as dangerous as marketing hype in place of informative text. According to Jakob Neilsen (www.useit.com/alertbox/9710a.html), "Users detested 'marketese'; the promotional writing style with boastful subjective claims ('hottest ever') that currently is prevalent on the Web."

Basic Site Components

Web sites are generally split into a number of different sections. The sections are driven by categories, and each main category may have several subcategories. A Web site will therefore consist of a category tree, with main branches that look something like this:

✦ *Company and/or organization information* contains information about the organization hosting the site. This may include subcategories containing biographies of company or organization principals, contact information, including maps, and other pertinent company data.

✦ *Frequently Asked Questions (FAQ) pages* answer commonly asked questions. These aren't necessarily questions that have been asked frequently at the time your site goes live. They may simply be questions you feel you need to address in anticipation of your users' questions.

✦ Your *home page* acts as a central hub to all the main branches to the rest of your site.

✦ *Links pages* are specifically designed to provide additional resources for your Web site visitors.

✦ *What's New pages* keep your visitors informed about additions to your site.

✦ *The table of contents* can take many forms, including a map of your site and/or well-designed menu systems.

Putting It All Together

Take a look at Figure 40-1, which is a screenshot of the company profile on the Wiley Web site found at www.wiley.com. Note the way the text on the right side of the page is sectioned off with easy-to-read section heads. The Web page also contains easy-to-find links on the left-hand side that show the part of the category tree that is relevant to the About Wiley link. Each section can be considered a branch (also called a leaf) of the main category named "About Me."

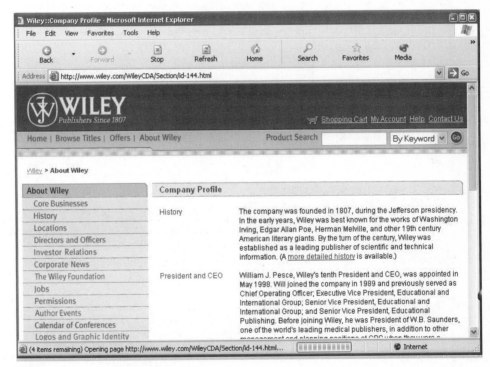

Figure 40-1: A category menu.

When you click the first leaf under About Me, Core Businesses, another group of subcategories appears, as shown in Figure 40-2.

When you click a link in the subcategory, the link for that subcategory disappears, as shown in Figure 40-3.

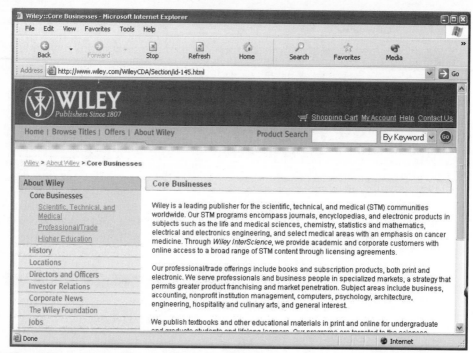

Figure 40-2: A category menu for a subcategory.

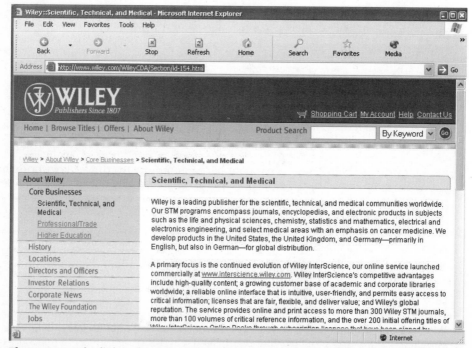

Figure 40-3: The link in the subcategory disappears when that link is visited.

The layout is organized in a way that will make sense to most visitors to the site. The focus is on easy navigation. One exercise to give yourself is to take a few paragraphs from the site (which is already well-written) and see if it's possible to improve them. Consider the following paragraph from the Company Profile page:

> Wiley is a leading **publisher** for the **scientific**, **technical**, and **medical (STM) communities** worldwide. Our STM programs encompass **journals, encyclopedias,** and **electronic products** in subjects such as **the life and medical sciences, chemistry, statistics and mathematics, electrical and electronics engineering**, and select medical areas with an emphasis on **cancer medicine**. Through **Wiley InterScience**, we provide academic and corporate customers with online access to a broad range of STM content through licensing agreements.

Notice that the preceding paragraph gets right to the point, and, in fact, acts as a summary for the rest of the paragraph. The next paragraph "drills down" to provide more detail:

> Our **professional/trade** offerings include **books** and **subscription products**, both **print** and **electronic**. We serve **professionals** and **business people** in **specialized markets**, a strategy that permits greater product franchising and market penetration. Subject areas include **business, accounting, nonprofit institution management, computers, psychology, architecture, engineering, hospitality and culinary arts, and general interest**.

The third paragraph reveals yet more detail:

> We publish **textbooks** and other **educational materials** in **print** and **online** for **undergraduate** and **graduate students** and **lifelong learners**. Our programs are targeted to the **sciences, engineering, mathematics,** and **accounting**, with growing positions in **business, education,** and **modern languages**. In **Australia,** we are a leading **publisher** for the **secondary school market**.

By this time, many readers will have moved on, not because there is something inherently wrong with the content, but simply because most users don't have the attention span to read through an entire section.

Another exercise is to review a paragraph's contents and try to pick keywords that should be entered into a meta tag, because the site currently doesn't have any. For example, the three paragraphs in our example show several possibilities for keywords, which are in bold in each paragraph. The entire following string could be pulled out of the second paragraph and be used for keywords:

```
business, accounting, nonprofit institution management, computers,
psychology, architecture, engineering, hospitality and culinary arts,
and general interest
```

The pages shown here from the Wiley site incorporate many of the concepts discussed in this chapter. It consists of a well-designed navigational structure, chunked text with well-defined highlight points, and succinct inverted pyramid-style copy. Your own Web site will have its own special needs. You can learn a lot by reviewing other sites, not only for what they're doing right, but what they may be doing wrong. As you review what other sites do, take the time to see if you can determine what areas you'd improve on. Make some notes, and then begin to apply these principles to your own site.

Summary

Did you read this whole chapter? Or, did you read the first few paragraphs and skip on down to this summary? If you did skip down to the summary, remember that this book has the advantage of being on a printed page. Your Web site has no such advantage. It is subject to the whims of your users, who will be predisposed to skip much of your content, not because they're lazy or too rushed, but because looking at the printed word on a computer screen is hard on the eyes.

You want to do everything you can to make your user's experience more enjoyable and fruitful. The next chapter, *Designing for Usability and Accessibility*, explores the concepts of taking your user's browsing experience to a higher level. It's an important chapter because it addresses issues affecting individuals who may have difficulty accessing your site because of vision problems or other difficulties. Today's Web sites must not only be easily navigated and easy to read, but must be accessible. Chapter 41 explores how to achieve accessibility and some of the laws associated with this topic.

✦   ✦   ✦

Designing for Usability and Accessibility

Many of the principles of usability and accessibility are the same. For example, making your Web site consistent and easily navigated is not just common sense, but a key tenet in usability and accessibility. But accessibility takes the concepts a step further to take into account people with disabilities. Making your Web site easy to use is a key ingredient to your success. Early planning for both of these concepts means the difference between spending just a little time on usability and accessibility and spending a lot of time on it.

Usability Analysis Methods

Consider using the following usability analysis methods when planning your site:

✦ *Hire an analyst.* You can hire an analyst who is an expert on Web site usability to compare your site to current usability standards. This can be useful in identifying usability issues but relies on the strengths, or lack of strengths, of the analyst.

✦ *Use focus groups.* You can bring in focus groups that share your target demographic and ask them to work with your Web site under closely monitored conditions that record every kind of issue that occurs. The idea is to acquire as much feedback as possible about such issues as navigation, site functionality, and overall Web site usability. Most focus groups consist of 10 to 20 participants. You can also set up smaller, more intimate labs with four or five participants.

✦ *Post surveys on your site to obtain responses from a larger sample size than focus groups can offer.* This is obviously the route to go if you're short on cash because smaller Web sites can likely not afford focus groups. Typical questions should focus on the usability of the site, including such topics as navigation, ease of purchase (if a shopping component exists on your site), and so on. The statistical sampling of respondents is not quite as accurate as a focus group might be, but this is offset somewhat by a larger sample size, which will at least reveal common problems. If a large majority of survey respondents tell you the navigation on your site is troublesome, it probably is.

✦ *Perform server log analysis.* You can examine your Web site's server requests made by real users to a Web site to review server performance and which pages visitors visit. A number of software programs make reviewing your Web server logs easy and productive. These analysis tools help analyze basic performance such as document requests and the routes people take to get to your site, but they can't make any real quantitative or qualitative analyses on user motivation and experience or your Web site's usability.

✦ *Employ data-driven site analysis.* You can spend some extra money and perform data-driven site analysis that reviews events from users as they occur. These events are more detailed than simple Web server logs and include such things as how a user works with forms on your site—which selections they make from form selection boxes, how many characters are used to fill out a form text field, and so on. This can improve the usability of your site's Web forms and enable you to perform what is known as *hill climbing*, which is a technique that lets you make incremental improvements to your Web site based on user input over a period of time.

How People Use the Web

It may sound like a ridiculous question, but one of the things to be asking yourself when setting up your Web site is, "How do people use the Web?" This is an important usability question, because it makes us explore the human experience with the Web.

Most developers are in a hurry. Time to market is always a consideration, even with the largest Web sites, some of which have intense production schedules that don't leave as much room for quality control as one might prefer. When a Web site doesn't perform as expected, the user experience suffers, and a potential regular visitor may be lost. If a form doesn't work, especially after a user enters a lot of information, that user is going to think hard about visiting again.

If anyone is in more of a hurry than developers, it's users. Web users use Web sites as if they're in a hurry even if they're not. Something about Web sites makes users impatient. You have to design and construct your site with that in mind, and remember to keep the user experience as painless as possible.

Principles of Web Site Usability

How do you make a Web site painless? You avoid distractions, make your pages error-free (test, test, and test again), make your Web site well organized and logical, and provide lots of navigational cues to help your users on their journey.

Consistency and ease of use are the order of the day. Some Web usability experts even recommend that you copy the design of the most successful sites. While that is probably an extreme nod towards usability, do study the successful sites and try to find out what it is about them that makes them successful. In the meantime, read on for details on the theories and best practices that are prevalent today.

Usability Issues

Usability is not just about convenience and the lack of errors that should be the hallmark of your Web site. In the long run, it means you must also be aware of your users' comfort level and disabilities. If you take care to make sure your Web site is usable for people with disabilities, you can be sure that the site will be usable for others.

Advertising

Advertising is a necessary evil for many sites that depend on revenue to stay afloat, but there are some obvious things to avoid:

- ✦ Looping animations simply drive people crazy and are as bad as the old `blink` tag.

- ✦ Pop-up ads. Usability studies show that not only are they not particularly effective, but that they instill negative feelings towards Web sites that use them.

- ✦ Flash interstitials are Flash-based ads that dance across the screen or pop up in front of content the reader is trying to read. They are often difficult for users to close, because there is no standard for closing them. Using these is tantamount to asking your Web visitor to leave.

If you need to use advertising, consider creative ways to do so. Maybe you can find a sponsor for your site that will add a tagline at the end of all your articles with a link to the sponsor site. Or, you can use unobtrusive banner ads. The main thing to remember is to use advertising with care.

Animation, multimedia and applets

The biggest thing to remember about animation and applets is you should use with extreme caution. If that sounds familiar, it's because you just read that same thing about advertising. That's no coincidence, as much online advertising is animated. For example, is there a business reason for using a Flash animation, or are you just tempted by them because they're cool. Keep in mind, one of the most frequently clicked links on a Flash presentation is "Skip Intro." If you're absolutely compelled to use animation, be sure they don't loop (repeat over and over). In addition, avoid scrolling text and anything in the `marquee` or `blink` elements.

Another annoyance for many Web site users is an opening sound that turns on when you visit a site. This can be especially troublesome in work environments. Users may feel a genuine business need to visit your site during business hours and may in fact be doing business for their company through your Web site, but if sound or music greets them when visiting, they may flee. Worse, they may feel embarrassed for having initiated your musical background and never return.

Color and links

Most usability studies suggest that white backgrounds are easiest on the eyes. Black backgrounds tend to be more difficult. Maintain current standards when establishing the colors for your links: links to pages that have not been visited by the user are blue; links to previously seen pages are purple or red. Some usability experts maintain that you should not deviate from the underlining method of linking, but more and more developers are finding that text simply highlighted in blue combined with a `a:hover` CSS style definition that changes the color when a user's mouse hovers over the text doesn't negatively affect usability and may even improve it.

You should also avoid giving archived items new URLs. When designing your site structure, design it in a way that stories can be stored in a specific directory permanently, and maintain the link to that site indefinitely.

Maintaining consistency

Make sure you have common layout for your all of your Web pages and be sure that the location of your title, logo, navigation, and content are all consistent from page to page. In addition, your navigational links and/or menus should be placed within the first screen your Web user encounters on any given page so they don't have to scroll to find the links.

Contents

The first screen fold, which is the first screen users see, is the most important, because it's what determines whether or not users will remain on your site. If the first screen takes a long time to download and doesn't immediately specify pertinent information to the user, users will never go to a second screen.

Drop-down menus

You can create drop-down menus using JavaScript to conserve space. Drop-down menus can be very helpful if they're done right. But often drop-down menus don't work, they flicker, or the user has to get the mouse over just the right menu at just the right spot to make it work. If you use drop-down menus, make sure they're airtight.

Fonts and font size

Fonts should be readable. That sounds obvious, but many of today's sites have very small type. This is a strain on anyone with vision that isn't excellent, which is a large proportion of any population. Generally, serif typefaces are easier to read than sans-serif.

One general survey of the Web found that a majority of sites use 12-point fonts (size= 3) for most written content. Check out the survey at `http://psychology` `.wichita.edu/surl/usabilitynews/3S/font.htm`.

The same study also rated the best fonts for reading times and ease.

Whatever you do, be consistent. Don't change your site's font. If the stories on one page are Times or serif, all of them should be.

Using frames

Frames were once highly popular with Web site designers, but never with users. They can cause fundamental problems with your Web site's navigation, especially with older browsers (which are admittedly becoming less of an issue as users upgrade). Note that the functionality of frames can be easily duplicated by using server-side includes. All major Web site servers support a scripting language capable of using server-side includes, so in today's modern Web environment the excuses for using frames are gone.

Including graphics

Graphics should be related to what you or your Web site offers, rather than acting as eye candy. Of course, having eye candy that speaks to what your Web site does is perfectly fine, but creating flashy imagery, especially that found from stock images (which means someone else may be using the same thing) can be detrimental. Also, be wary of download times. Optimize your graphics wherever possible. Long download times resulting from large images (in number of bytes, not necessarily screen size) can prompt visitors to quickly scan for faster sites.

You'll often see thumbnails that lead to larger images on many sites. This is a good compromise between the need for graphics and the need for fast download time, but be careful not to resize the image using the `img` element's attributes. You need to resize an image in your graphics editor before bringing it into your Web page.

Headings

Always use headings when developing headlines, because they're structured for that purpose and are interpreted by accessibility software (software for aiding disabled persons) correctly as headlines, whereas a CSS-styled sentence with large type will not be interpreted as a headline by such software. If you don't like the space between an `H1` element and a paragraph, try to become accustomed to it. Your Web site viewers are fine with it.

Horizontal scrolling

Avoid forcing the user to scroll horizontally by using flex tables, which are tables that use widths based on screen size. For example, the following table will take up100% of the screen, and content will collapse and expand when a user resizes the window. See Figures 41-1 and 41-2 for examples to see how a flex table can influence the way content looks in a resized window.

```
<table width="100%" border="0" cellspacing="0"
cellpadding="0">
  <tr>
    <td>Even though this is a very long line, it will collapse when the
browser window is resized. This is because you have a width that is relative
to the size of the browser window, instead of a set width of, for example 100
(width="100") pixels.</td>
  </tr>
</table>
```

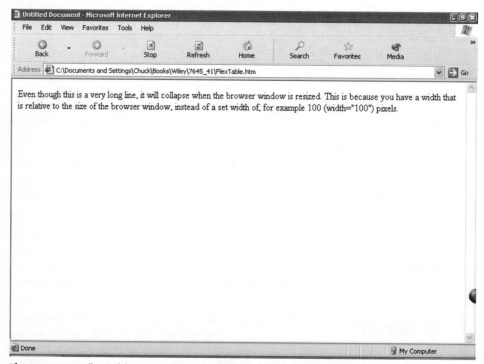

Figure 41-1: A flex table as rendered in a full-sized browser window.

JavaScript

We can't tell you not to use JavaScript because virtually every major site uses it, but we can tell you that if your JavaScript produces errors your visitors will flee. It's absolutely essential that your JavaScript be airtight. If you use JavaScript, get a good debugger. The newest versions of the Mozilla browser, which is free, contain excellent JavaScript debugging tools.

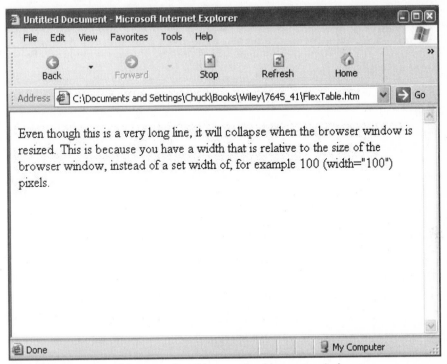

Figure 41-2: A flex table as rendered in a re-sized browser window.

Legibility

Making sure your Web site is legible is another important aspect to usability. Areas of concern to you should include the following:

✦ *Line length.* Keep your sentences short. Keep your paragraphs short. Keep everything short. People are in a hurry. You don't want them to leave in mid-sentence.

✦ *Novice versus expert users.* Keep in mind that not all your users are experts. It's possible that your some of your visitors have been surfing the Web for a very short period of time. Some people still double-clickWeb site links. Keep these users in mind as you prepare your site.

✦ *Page length.* Generally, your Web pages still shouldn't force readers to scroll down very far, although usability studies are showing that today's Web users are more willing to scroll than before. It's still a good idea to keep Web content chunked (as discussed in the previous chapter), and to keep each chunk on a separate page. Hyperlinks are a very good tool and make extremely long pages unnecessary.

✦ *Page width.* Users don't like to scroll right, so don't make them. Use flex tables if you want to be sure users won't have to scroll right (flex tables use widths of percentage-based units instead of pixel based units).

✦ *Personalization.* Users have been shown to be willing to register to a site if they can have some customized preferences. If you can drop a cookie that greets your Web visitor the next time he or she visits your site, you'll improve your chances of obtaining return visits.

Searches

If your site has a lot of pages (100 pages or more is the hard and fast rule, but if you have 50 pages or more you should consider it), you should include a search box on your main (home) page with the word "search" next to it. You don't even need to develop your own search engine to create a search tool. Google offers a free search utility that you can plug into your own site. Another free tool is Atomz (www .atomz.com). Both of these services search your site and return results specific to your site only.

Sitemaps

Provide a link to a sitemap that maps out all the major areas of your Web site. This map can appear on its own page and usually consist of category trees showing all of your site's categories and major subcategories.

Sitemaps can double as tables of content, and some Web sites place them directly on their home page and use them as their primary navigation tool.

URL length

Try to keep the length of your URLs as short as possible. If you work with server-side queries and updates, this advice can come in conflict with the way action=post and action=get attribute/value pairs work with forms. The post value should generally be reserved for updating databases, rather than simply querying them. This is because the browser caches form data and will ask the users if they want to reload a page when they hit the back button and later return to a page that results from a database query. This can be annoying to users and can be avoided by using the get value in a form action attribute when performing such tasks as simple database queries. The downside of using get is that the query shows up in the browser's URL address window. You need to decide which of those two situations is worse. If you're updating data, you should always use post.

Taglines

Conventional wisdom in today's Web world is that all Web sites should have a tagline that identifies what the owner of a Web site does. It doesn't need to be more than one line, although it needs to be clear and, as mentioned in the preceding chapter, should not consist of marketing hype. It's better to say something like, "Sellers of antique Edwardian furniture," than "The best antique furniture in the world." Be as specific as possible in as few words as possible and allow your visitors to move on, hopefully to another section on your site.

Windows 1252 character set

The bottom line on this character set is, don't use it unless you're absolutely sure everyone reading your site is an American or Western European using the Windows operating system. Use the encoding that is appropriate for your Web site's audience. Most Western encodings should look like this:

```
<meta http-equiv="Content-Type" content="text/html;
  charset=iso-8859-1">
```

The Need for Accessibility

How do you feel about shutting out 20% of all Web surfers from your site from the moment you go live? If you don't account for individuals with disabilities when you start up a Web site, that's exactly what you're doing. According to the National Institute on Disability and Rehabilitation, 19.4% of noninstitutionalized civilians in the United States had a disability in 1996. That comes out to 48.9 million people. Nearly half were considered to have a severe disability (www.infouse.com/disabilitydata/p4.textgfx.html).

Nine percent of all Web users have a disability, half of whom are blind or visually impaired, according to a study by Georgia Tech University (www.gvu.gatech.edu/user_surveys/).

If that doesn't convince you of the need for adapting to accessibility guidelines, here are a few more reasons to think about. By creating a Web site with high usability standards, you accomplish the following:

✦ You demonstrate good citizenship by not discriminating against people with disabilities.

✦ You reduce the risk of litigation, costly settlements, unfavorable publicity, and potential loss of business.

✦ You appeal to baby boomers in the U.S., a large and aging market segment that will be a contributing factor to the overall growth of disabled people in the United States as they enter into late adulthood.

✦ You gain an edge on an important market, because nearly 10% of all American Web users are disabled, along with approximately 750 million people worldwide. These people have an income of more than $188 billion U.S. dollars.

✦ You comply with federally regulated guidelines and best practices, as governments all over the world have enacted laws and regulations mandating Web site accessibility.

✦ You provide access to wireless devices.

Accessibility Mandates

If you're not motivated to improve accessibility by the inherent kindness in your heart or by the hard numbers of lost market share, there are always laws to consider. The United States, for example, has laws on the books that can make certain kinds of Web sites, especially those that have business with the Federal government, liable for criminal and civil damages if they don't comply with certain laws and regulations.

Americans with Disabilities Act

Although technically only Web sites associated with the federal government (including contractors) need to comply with the Americans With Disabilities Act (ADA), any Web site that doesn't follow its mandates may be potential targets for lawsuits. Those are the legal justifications for operating an accessible Web site. There are obvious moral and ethical considerations, as well.

There are a number of considerations when designing for ADA compliance. For example, use colors, fonts, and graphics with restraint by following these guidelines:

✦ Avoid the use of more than two or three colors (not including white) and three font sizes (which is just good design, anyway).

✦ Use bold and italic sparingly (for titles and occasional emphasis), and avoid underlining plain text (people often mistake underlined plain text as a link).

✦ Since 8–12% of the population is color blind, be careful with colors, and be sure to provide good contrast between text and the Web page background. The truth is, nothing is better than black on white when it comes to readability.

✦ Minimize the use of textured backgrounds, and when using them, keep them at a low contrast, especially when mixing font and link colors on a colored background.

✦ Avoid animations, especially looping animations, which can be a sufficient enough distraction to people with some learning disabilities that they may find your Web pages unreadable.

International

Additional U.S. and international guidelines and laws exist regarding accessibility, including the Telecommunications Act (Section 255) of 1996 in the United States, the Information Society Europe Action Plan, and the Beijing Declarations on the Rights of People with Disabilities established by the UN.

In addition, the W3C has established the Web Content Accessibility Initiative. By following the rules established by the W3C, you go a long way toward ensuring you'll be in compliance with the growing amount of international law regarding Web accessibility.

Web Content Accessibility Initiative (W3C)

The W3C's Web Accessibility Initiative (WAI) provides a comprehensive Web site containing substantial amounts of information and resources regarding ways to make your Web site more accessible. The WAI publishes guidelines for browsers, Web authors, and authoring tools, and sponsors education and outreach efforts aimed at enhancing developer knowledge and sensitivity to the issue.

A number of disabilities can affect a user's ability to access your Web page. These include the following:

✦ Visual disabilities

✦ Hearing disabilities

✦ Mobility-related disabilities

✦ Cognitive and learning disabilities

Accommodating visual disabilities

Individuals who are blind, have low vision, or color blindness have a very difficult time accessing your site if you don't accommodate them. Poor vision can render the sharpest, cleanest, and most impressive-looking Web designs completely unusable.

The one device most users take for granted, the mouse, is virtually worthless to a person with low or no vision because it requires hand-eye coordination. Images are useless on a Web page to someone with a visual impairment if you don't offer text values for them in an img element's alt attribute.

Similarly, you should make use of tabindex attributes to help users with disabilities make selections, because the computer's Tab key is used to move the focus to the item that needs to be selected. The tabindex attribute lets you customize the tabbing sequence by letting you assign indexed values to a form element. For example, in the following code fragment the first element is chosen, then the next, when the user hits the tab button:

```
<form action="this.htm" method="get">
<input name="input1" type="text" tabindex="1"><br>
<input name="input2" type="text" tabindex="1">
</form>
```

The default behavior of form widgets is that the tab index is based on the appearance in document order of each widget. The tabindex attribute allows you to override that behavior. When a device such as a screen reader tracks the user's tabbing, it alerts the user with a spoken voice that the user has found the item. This helps a user keep track of his or her place on a page. Instead of clicking the mouse, the user presses the Enter key to make a selection.

These are all things you can do easily to help your Web users enjoy your site. You should focus on using traditional HTML markup, such as em and strong elements, instead of b and i elements to emphasize points in your markup, because visual assistance software will often handle them better. You should also use one of the headline elements, such as H1, to create headlines. If you use style sheets and regular text, visual assistance software will likely not interpret markup that isn't wrapped in h1 or h2 (and so on) elements as headlines. This is an important consideration, as many designers like to avoid headline elements because of the gap between a headline and the headline's associated text content.

Providing access to the hearing-impaired

Individuals with hearing disabilities will not get anything out of your auditory masterpieces, so they'll need a way to extract textual information from them. To accomplish this, you can employ closed captioning, blinking error messages, and transcripts of the spoken audio that your users can download.

Helping users with mobility disabilities

People with physical impairments that substantially limit movement and motor controls generally find the mouse and other input devices difficult to work with and require the use of devices designed to assist the user. For example, an assistive device can allow the user to enter a key sequence to reboot a computer, instead of relying on the Ctrl+Alt+Delete key combination. You can't do too many things as a Web designer to address the needs of individuals with mobility disabilities, but by making your Web site accessible in general, you help the users' assistant devices work better.

Addressing those with cognitive and learning disabilities

Providing sensible organization and navigation is an important way to assist people with cognitive or learning disabilities. If someone has dyslexia, for example, providing a consistent navigational framework provides reminders about how to move around the site. You can alleviate short-term memory disabilities by providing an audio version of a Web page that a Web page user can listen to while reading the page.

Tools you can use

Most of the barriers people with disabilities face can be eliminated, especially if you incorporate accessibility into your Web site at the onset.

A number of tools help you help disabled users access your site. Making yourself aware of these tools and understanding how to develop your HTML accordingly will have a significant positive impact on your users. Among these tools are the following:

✦ Magnifiers

✦ Screen readers

✦ Closed captioning

✦ Keyboard enhancements

✦ Highlighting software

Table 41-1 shows a series of HTML tools you can use to help your Web pages interact with the tools disabled people use with their computers.

Table 41-1 HTML Techniques for Enhancing Accessibility	
Tool	*Technique to Use for Accessibility*
Applets, plug-ins, and non-HTML content	Provide links to accessible applets, plug-ins, and other non-HTML content, or provide alternative content
Blinking, moving or flickering content	Avoid causing content to blink, flicker, or move
Cascading Style Sheets	Be certain your Web pages are readable without style sheets
Color and contrast	Ensure that all information conveyed with color is also conveyed in the absence of color
Forms	Make forms accessible to assistive browsing technology
Frames	Create a title for each `frame` element and frame page, and be sure each frame has an accessible source
Graphs and charts	Summarize the content of each graph and chart, or use the `longdesc` attribute to link to the description or data: `<img src="/images/test.gif" style="width: 400px; height: 200px; border: none;" alt="Pie chart of honest politicians in 2004" longdesc="http://www.mywebsite .com/politicians.html">`
	Continued

Table 41-1 *(continued)*

Tool	Technique to Use for Accessibility

	Or, you can provide a hidden link that a voice browser will pick up, but would be invisible in a conventional browser on a page with a white background color:
	
	`<span style="font-size: 1pt; color: White;"><a href="`
	`http://www.mywebsite.com/politicians.html"`
	`title="Link to a pie chart showing number of`
	`honest politicians circa 2004">d</a></span>`

Image maps	Try to avoid server-side image maps. If you must use them, provide matching text links. You should rely on client-side image maps wherever possible, and use alternative text for image map hot spots. If a server-side map is needed, provide equivalent text links
Images and animations	Use the `alt="text"` attribute to provide text equivalents for images. Use `alt=""` for images that do not convey important information or convey redundant information
Multimedia	Provide captions and/or transcripts of important audio content. Provide transcripts or audio descriptions of important video content
Scripts	If script-based Web site content is not accessible, provide alternative content
Skip to main content	Offer alternatives to navigation links on content pages so that users aren't forced to deal with long navigation widgets. They should be able to skip directly to the page's main content
Table headers, tables	Use the `th` element to mark up table heading cells
Text-only page	Provide a text-only page with equivalent information or functionality when accessibility can be created in other ways
Timed responses	Be careful with session time outs, so that users with disabilities aren't forced to rush through a series of forms
Verify accessibility	Test your Web site's accessibility using available tools such as Bobby

Using forms and PDF

Online forms should have a Telecommunications Device for the Deaf (TDD) phone number available so that persons with disabilities can call your company or organization instead of worrying about how to fill out an online form. Even PDF files can be made accessible using a new "Make Accessible" command that creates a specially tagged PDF file that can be read by screen readers.

Checking accessibility using a validation service

After you're finished with your Web site and feel comfortable that you've made your Web site accessible, you can validate your site using a third-party tool. One such tool is called Bobby (`http://bobby.watchfire.com/bobby/html/en/index.jsp`).

Summary

Don't look at establishing solid usability and accessibility as a burden. By ignoring this issue, you're cutting off a huge segment of potential Web visitors. If you consider these issues early in your planning, you'll be able to accomplish your goal with a surprising small amount of work. On the other hand, if you ignore usability and accessibility and find yourself either suddenly enlightened later or forced into implementing accessibility later on, you'll find it expensive and time-consuming. Your best bet is to start now.

✦ ✦ ✦

Designing for an International Audience

Even though this book is written in English, chances are it will be translated into other languages. From a Web site perspective, if your site is only in English, you may eliminate a huge portion of your potential world market. This chapter takes a look at some options for improving your reach to the world's population.

Principles of Internationalization and Localization

Most Web pages are written in English, but only 5% of the world's population uses English as their first language. Many Web sites are responding to this reality by implementing *localization*, which is the process of creating several mirrored Web sites in different languages. By simply including Japanese, Chinese, German, French, Swedish, and Portuguese into your Web site, you're suddenly speaking to a clear majority of the world's population. Obviously, this isn't an option for small sites or for companies or organizations that haven't yet developed the resources for reaching an international audience, but localization is something you should consider as soon as it is practical.

Introduction to Web Internationalization Issues

The first step in dealing with internationalization and localization is determining your target audience. You will need to find out how many international visitors view your site, and whether targeting them is feasible.

You may only need to translate a portion of your site, but translation is obviously an essential first ingredient to localization. Setting aside translation resources is an important early step in your localization efforts.

Translating your Web site

More goes into localization than simply translating from one language to another. One of the more famous examples of how direct translation can actually hurt you is the well known "Got Milk?" campaign, which according to translation experts at The RWS Group (`www.translate.com`) translates to "Are you lactating?" in Spanish, which is most likely not the desired message.

 Tip　You can acquire free localization software from The RWS Group at: `www.translate.com/locales/en-US/index.html?init_page=default`.

For this reason, you should try to find native speakers of any language you are translating to. This can be an expensive proposition, and may not be an option if you run a small site that is only marginally profitable. But if you have already made the decision to localize, it's important to do it right.

You can also use online translation services at such Web sites as `www.etranslate.com`, which claims to have 6,000 translators worldwide. There are also service bureaus specializing in translation services, such as the well-known language services company, Berlitz.

If you're on a tight budget but you need to localize some content, you can try one of the machine-based translation services available, such as those used by some search engines to provide on-the-fly translation of Web pages. One such option is Systran's Babel Fish, which can be found via AltaVista at `http://world.altavista.com/tr/`.

This free service lets you translate a block of text. This is most helpful if your pages are simply written (without slang) and technical in nature, rather than creative or humorous. Humor often doesn't translate well to other languages. Dry and technical documents translate well when you need to rely on less expensive translation methods.

On the opposite end of the spectrum are translation software environments for large-scale enterprise systems by companies such as Idiom, Inc., (`www.idiominc.com/`), which offers a global content management system that enables users to use template-driven translation modules. A typical implementation allows translators to replace text values (contained within XSLT variables or parameters, for example) with localized content. These kinds of systems are not inexpensive, but they are very efficient and help streamline the localization process, as well as provide accountability in large-scale operations.

Understanding Unicode

Unicode is a standard developed by The Unicode Consortium for processing the world's alphabets in a consistent way. The Unicode Consortium is made up of universities, research institutes, companies, and other interested parties dedicated to creating an international standard for the way languages are represented to computers. Unicode consists of a vast number of tables each containing numerical references to an alphanumeric character. For example, the English letter A is represented by the hexadecimal number 0041 and the decimal number 65. Every character in nearly every written language in the world is represented in Unicode, as shown in Table 42-1, which shows the starting and ending hexadecimal-based numerical references for each encoding.

Table 42-1
Alphabets Represented in Unicode

Start Code	End Code	Block Name
\u0000	\u007F	Basic Latin
\u0080	\u00FF	Latin-1 Supplement
\u0100	\u017F	Latin Extended-A
\u0180	\u024F	Latin Extended-B
\u0250	\u02AF	IPA Extensions
\u02B0	\u02FF	Spacing Modifier Letters
\u0300	\u036F	Combining Diacritical Marks
\u0370	\u03FF	Greek
\u0400	\u04FF	Cyrillic
\u0530	\u058F	Armenian
\u0590	\u05FF	Hebrew
\u0600	\u06FF	Arabic
\u0900	\u097F	Devanagari
\u0980	\u09FF	Bengali
\u0A00	\u0A7F	Gurmukhi
\u0A80	\u0AFF	Gujarati
\u0B00	\u0B7F	Oriya

Continued

Table 42-1 *(continued)*		
Start Code	*End Code*	*Block Name*
\u0B80	\u0BFF	Tamil
\u0C00	\u0C7F	Telugu
\u0C80	\u0CFF	Kannada
\u0D00	\u0D7F	Malayalam
\u0E00	\u0E7F	Thai
\u0E80	\u0EFF	Lao
\u0F00	\u0FBF	Tibetan
\u10A0	\u10FF	Georgian
\u1100	\u11FF	Hangul Jamo
\u1E00	\u1EFF	Latin Extended Additional
\u1F00	\u1FFF	Greek Extended
\u2000	\u206F	General punctuation
\u2070	\u209F	Superscripts and subscripts
\u20A0	\u20CF	Currency symbols
\u20D0	\u20FF	Combining marks for symbols
\u2100	\u214F	Letterlink symbols
\u2150	\u218F	Number forms
\u2190	\u21FF	Arrows
\u2200	\u22FF	Mathematical operators
\u2300	\u23FF	Miscellaneous technical
\u2400	\u243F	Control pictures
\u2440	\u245F	Optical character recognition
\u2460	\u24FF	Enclosed alphanumerics
\u2500	\u257F	Box drawing
\u2580	\u259F	Block elements
\u25A0	\u25FF	Geometric shapes
\u2600	\u26FF	Miscellaneous symbols
\u2700	\u27BF	Dingbats
\u3000	\u303F	CJK symbols and punctuation

Start Code	End Code	Block Name
\u3040	\u309F	Hiragana
\u30A0	\u30FF	Katakana
\u3100	\u312F	Bopomofo
\u3130	\u318F	Hangul Compatibility Jamo
\u3190	\u319F	Kanbun
\u3200	\u32FF	Enclosed CJK letters and months
\u3300	\u33FF	CJK Compatibility
\u4E00	\u9FFF	CJK Unified Ideographs
\uAC00	\uD7A3	Hangul syllables
\uD800	\uDB7F	High surrogates
\uDB80	\uDBFF	High private use surrogates
\uDC00	\uDFFF	Low surrogates
\uE000	\uF8FF	Private use
\uF900	\uFAFF	CJK Compatibility Ideographs
\uFB00	\Ufb4F	Alphabetic presentation forms
\uFB50	\uFDFF	Arabic Presentation Forms-A
\uFE20	\uFE2F	Combining Half Marks
\uFE30	\uFE4F	CJK Compatibility Forms
\uFE50	\uFE6F	Small Form Variants
\uFE70	\uFEFF	Arabic Presentation Forms-B
\uFF00	\uFFEF	Halfwidth and Fullwidth Forms
\uFEFF	\uFEFF	Specials
\uFFF0	\uFFFF	Specials

Unicode tables are called code pages, and each one serves a specific set of languages. Each code page consists of a table of numerical references to each letter. Each row in Table 42-1 represents a code page. Each code page, in turn, consists of several rows of numerical reference values mapping each character of the alphabet defined by the code page. You could write the following in your HTML using one of the Unicode encodings, such as UTF-8, and a modern browser would render it as "Hello World":

```
&#72;&#101;&#108;&#108;&#111;&#32;&#87;&#111;&#114;&#108;&#100;
```

To get a handle on how this works, let's examine a code page most of us are familiar with, Basic Latin.

Basic Latin (U+0000 - U+007F)

All nations in America, most European nations, most African nations, as well as Australia and New Zealand all use the Latin encoding. In Unicode, the Latin encoding is broken down into different parts. The most basic is called Basic Latin. Only a few languages can be written entirely with a Basic Latin encoding. You generally need to incorporate additional Latin encodings because Basic Latin consists of only characters between 0 and 7F (hexadecimal). When you are using UTF-8 as your encoding, all of these Latin encodings are automatically included as part of the UTF-8 encoding. In fact, Unicode-based UTF-8 includes most of the world's written languages.

ISO-8859-1

If you are working on Web sites for Western audiences, you will most likely use ISO-8859-1, which, although not officially a subset of UTF-8, does map out to the Latin Basic and Latin Extended A Unicode sets.

This character encoding contains many of the numerical references included in the US-ASCII encoding (ISO/IEC 646), which is not actually a part of the Unicode standard and predates it. Certain numeric references in ASCII are not defined by the Unicode Standard. In addition, certain numeric references are different in Macintosh-based code pages and Windows-based code pages, which is why you'll sometimes encounter problems when transferring files between the two platforms. Unicode and ISO-defined encodings are defined by different international bodies. The Unicode standard, as previously mentioned, is defined by The Unicode Consortium, whereas ISO encodings are defined by International Organization for Standardization (ISO). In addition, the code pages used by Macintosh and Windows in earlier days, although based on ASCII, actually had a few small variations that were incompatible with each other. For example, the decimal-based code point (another word for numerical reference) for the "registered" mark (®) are different for Macintosh and Windows encodings (168 and 174, respectively), and is 174 in Unicode.

Luckily, the most familiar encoding to Western HTML developers, ISO-8859-1, is a subset of Unicode and can be used safely because most modern browsers now support Unicode. Although ISO-8859-1 is not part of the Unicode standard, the two bodies governing both standards have worked together to standardize the models to avoid driving everyone crazy.

The entire set of ISO-8859-1 numeric references can be found at `http://www.w3 .org/MarkUp/html3/latin1.html`.

Table 42-2 shows the entities you are likely to encounter as an HTML developer. If your encoding is UTF-8, you can use the decimal references, but for compatibility with older browsers you should use HTML entities, because many older browsers don't support Unicode.

Table 42-2
ISO-8859-1 HTML Entities

Description	Decimal-based Code Value	HTML Entity	Character as it appears on Web Page
quotation mark	&#34;	&quot;	"
Ampersand	&#38;	&amp;	&
less-than sign	&#60;	&lt;	<
greater-than sign	&#62;	&gt;	>
nonbreaking space			
inverted exclamation	&#161;	&iexcl;	¡
cent sign	&#162;	&cent;	¢
pound sterling	&#163;	&pound;	£
general currency sign	&#164;	&curren;	¤
yen sign	¥ ¥	¥ ¥	¥
broken vertical bar	&#166;	&brkbar;	&brkbar;
section sign	§ §	§ §	§
umlaut (dieresis)	&#168;	¨ ¨	¨
Copyright	&#169;	&copy;	©
feminine ordinal	&#170;	&ordf;	ª
left angle quote, guillemotleft	&#171;	&laquo;	«
not sign	&#172;	&not;	
soft hyphen	&#173;	&shy;	
registered trademark	&#174;	&reg;	®
macron accent	&#175;	&macr;	¯
degree sign	&#176;	&deg;	°
plus or minus	&#177;	&plusmn;	±
superscript two	&#178;	&sup2;	²
superscript three	&#179;	&sup3;	³
acute accent	&#180;	&acute;	´
micro sign	&#181;	&micro;	µ
paragraph sign	&#182;	&para;	

Continued

Table 42-2 *(continued)*

Description	Decimal-based Code Value	HTML Entity	Character as it appears on Web Page
middle dot	&#183;	&middot;	•
Cedilla	&#184;	&cedil;	˛
superscript one	&#185;	&sup1;	¹
masculine ordinal	&#186;	&ordm;	º
right angle quote, guillemotright	&#187;	&raquo;	»
fraction one-fourth	&#188;	&frac14;	¼
fraction one-half	&#189;	&frac12;	½
fraction three-fourths	&#190;	&frac34;	¾
inverted question mark	&#191;	&iquest;	¿
capital A, grave accent	&#192;	&Agrave;	À
capital A, acute accent	&#193;	&Aacute;	Á
capital A, circumflex accent	&#194;	&Acirc;	Â
capital A, tilde	&#195;	&Atilde;	Ã
capital A, dieresis or umlaut mark	&#196;	&Auml;	Ä
capital A, ring	&#197;	&Aring;	Å
capital AE diphthong (ligature)	&#198;	&AElig;	Æ
capital C, cedilla	&#199;	&Ccedil;	Ç
capital E, grave accent	&#200;	&Egrave;	È
capital E, acute accent	&#201;	&Eacute;	É
capital E, circumflex accent	&#202;	&Ecirc;	Ê
capital E, dieresis or umlaut mark	&#203;	&Euml;	Ë
capital I, grave accent	&#204;	&Igrave;	Ì
capital I, acute accent	&#205;	&Iacute;	Í
capital I, circumflex accent	&#206;	&Icirc;	Î
capital I, dieresis or umlaut mark	&#207;	&Iuml;	Ï

Description	Decimal-based Code Value	HTML Entity	Character as it appears on Web Page
capital Eth, Icelandic	&#208;	&ETH;	&Dstrok;
capital N, tilde	&#209;	&Ntilde;	Ñ
capital O, grave accent	&#210;	&Ograve;	Ò
capital O, acute accent	&#211;	&Oacute;	Ó
capital O, circumflex accent	&#212;	&Ocirc;	Ô
capital O, tilde	&#213;	&Otilde;	Õ
capital O, dieresis or umlaut mark	&#214;	&Ouml;	Ö
multiply sign	&#215;	&times;	X
capital O, slash	&#216;	&Oslash;	Ø
capital U, grave accent	&#217;	&Ugrave;	Ù
capital U, acute accent	&#218;	&Uacute;	Ú
capital U, circumflex accent	&#219;	&Ucirc;	Û
capital U, dieresis or umlaut mark	&#220;	&Uuml;	Ü
capital Y, acute accent	&#221;	&Yacute;	Ý
capital THORN, Icelandic	&#222;	&THORN;	Þ
small sharp s, German (sz ligature)	&#223;	&szlig;	ß
small a, grave accent	&#224;	&agrave;	à
small a, acute accent	&#225;	&aacute;	á
small a, circumflex accent	&#226;	&acirc;	â
small a, tilde	&#227;	&atilde;	ã
small a, dieresis or umlaut mark	&#228;	&auml;	Ä
small a, ring	&#229;	&aring;	å
small ae diphthong (ligature)	&#230;	&aelig;	æ
small c, cedilla	&#231;	&ccedil;	ç

Continued

Table 42-2 *(continued)*

Description	Decimal-based Code Value	HTML Entity	Character as it appears on Web Page
small e, grave accent	&#232;	&egrave;	è
small e, acute accent	&#233;	&eacute;	é
small e, circumflex accent	&#234;	&ecirc;	ê
small e, dieresis or umlaut mark	&#235;	ë ë	ë
small i, grave accent	&#236;	&igrave;	ì
small i, acute accent	&#237;	&iacute;	í
small i, circumflex accent	&#238;	&icirc;	î
small i, dieresis or umlaut mark	&#239;	&iuml;	ï
small eth, Icelandic	&#240;	&eth;	ð
small n, tilde	&#241;	&ntilde;	ñ
small o, grave accent	&#242;	&ograve;	ò
small o, acute accent	&#243;	&oacute;	ó
small o, circumflex accent	&#244;	&ocirc;	ô
small o, tilde	&#245;	&otilde;	õ
small o, dieresis or umlaut mark	&#246;	&ouml;	ö
division sign	&#247;	&divide;	÷
small o, slash	&#248;	&oslash;	ø
small u, grave accent	&#249;	&ugrave;	ù
small u, acute accent	&#250;	&uacute;	ú
small u, circumflex accent	&#251;	&ucirc;	û
small u, dieresis or umlaut mark	&#252;	&uuml;	ü
small y, acute accent	&#253;	&yacute;	ý
small thorn, Icelandic	&#254;	&thorn;	
small y, dieresis or umlaut mark	&#255;	&yuml;	ÿ

One of the nastiest encoding problems occurs with the trademark symbol. Different encodings use different numeric representations for it, and Macintosh and Windows platforms treat it differently. The easiest way to deal with this problem is to simply use good old-fashioned HTML: `<SUP><SMALL>TM</SMALL></SUP>`

Latin-1 Supplement (U+00C0 - U+00FF)

The Latin-1 Supplement also contains values from ISO-8859-1. The characters in this Unicode block are used for the following languages:

- ✦ Danish
- ✦ Dutch
- ✦ Faroese
- ✦ Finnish
- ✦ Flemish
- ✦ German
- ✦ Icelandic
- ✦ Irish
- ✦ Italian
- ✦ Norwegian
- ✦ Portuguese
- ✦ Spanish
- ✦ Swedish

It extends the Basic Latin encoding with a miscellaneous set of punctuation and mathematical signs.

Latin Extended-A (U+0100 - U+017F)

Once you roam past Latin-1 Supplement in Unicode, you begin to veer away from ISO-8859-1, as well. There are specific ISO encodings for different Latin languages. You can find the names of these encodings here:

```
http://developer.apple.com/documentation/macos8/TextIntlSvcs/
TextEncodingConversionManager/TEC1.5/TEC.b0.html
```

Or, you can simply guarantee the incorporation of these encodings by using UTF-8. The characters in this Unicode block are used in the following languages (among others):

- ✦ Afrikaans
- ✦ Basque

- ✦ Breton
- ✦ Catalan
- ✦ Croatian
- ✦ Czech
- ✦ Esperanto
- ✦ Estonian
- ✦ French
- ✦ Frisian
- ✦ Greenlandic
- ✦ Hungarian
- ✦ Latin
- ✦ Latvian
- ✦ Lithuanian
- ✦ Maltese
- ✦ Polish
- ✦ Provencal
- ✦ Rhaeto-Romanic
- ✦ Romanian
- ✦ Romany
- ✦ Sami
- ✦ Slovak
- ✦ Slovenian
- ✦ Sorbian
- ✦ Turkish
- ✦ Welsh

Latin Extended-B and Latin Extended Additional

The characters in this block are used to write additional languages and to extend Latin encodings. These characters include seldom-used characters such as the bilabial click, which looks like this: ⊙ . By the time you march into this territory, you should definitely be using UTF-8.

Constructing Multilanguage Sites

Encoding your pages in UTF-8 may at first seem like a good idea if you are doing a lot of localization, but some problems exist with taking that course. Mixing encodings can cause problems, so if your site is only going to be viewed by users reading with

Western languages, it's fine to use ISO-8859-1, because it's essentially a subset of UTF-8. The other problem is that many sites in countries such as China don't use Unicode at all. For example, many Chinese sites use Big 5, which is a Chinese encoding not incorporated into Unicode.

Summary

There are two main considerations when localizing your site. The first is obvious—how to accomplish the necessary translations to make things work correctly. The second, more subtle consideration involves managing the way your encodings behave so that the actual display of text works in a way you expect. Encoding is a complex subject, but it's important to understand when dealing with internationalization. If at the end of the day it all seems overwhelming, one key point to keep in mind is avoid mixing encodings. This one action on your end will avoid a lot of misery. The Chinese Big 5 encodings, for example, are simply not compatible with Unicode. So avoid sending an XML document encoded in UTF-8 through an XSLT style sheet that outputs Big 5. The same is true for ASCII. Avoid using ASCII encodings in your Web pages altogether; instead, use ISO-8859-1, and then be consistent in that use.

The next chapter takes a look at security issues in Web development. Today, hackers play an increasingly nefarious role in Web site development. Chapter 43 will help you consider some steps you can take to thwart them.

✦   ✦   ✦

Security

Throughout this book, we have tried to emphasize security, bringing up issues when appropriate along with potential solutions. However, you need to be aware of some global security issues so you can proactively protect your server and documents. This chapter covers many of those issues.

Understanding the Risks

Putting content on the Web is fairly simple, yet the security risks of doing so can be numerous and complex. This section highlights some of the more common risks and, where applicable, suggests solutions.

Theft of confidential information

One of the major risks of the Internet is theft of information. Whether it be information of a personal nature to yourself, your company, or personal information you have gathered and stored about others.

The easiest solution to prevent theft of confidential information is not to provide any access to it. Although that isn't always practical, you should be especially careful with other people's information.

Tip   Personal data on others can be a huge liability if you are not careful. Before creating online solutions, such as merchant services, consider the liabilities of doing so—especially when receiving and storing information such as credit card numbers. Consider using a service that will bear that responsibility and liability.

Vandalism and defacement

One of the latest trends in cyber hacking is vandalism and defacement. Just as in the real world, vandals can wreak havoc on your site—changing documents, creating virtual graffiti, and more.

Denial of service

Denial of service (DOS) attacks are attempts (and usually successes) at overloading a server with bogus requests. The volume of requests keeps the server from replying to legitimate requests and, in some cases, can even crash the server.

The attacks can originate from distinct hacker locations, or from unsuspecting computers that have been infected with viruses that spawn the attacks. The intent is simple: stop the target site from being able to perform its normal tasks.

Some of the largest DOS attacks were leveled against the SCO Web site in December 2003 and January 2004. The attack shut down many of the SCO servers for two days. The attack originated from computers all over the Internet that had been infected by the MyDoom virus.

Unfortunately, DOS attacks can have unexpected results, as the massive traffic can affect other sites or even entire sections of the Internet.

Loss of data

Loss of data is straightforward and involves data files being damaged or deleted from a server. Loss of data can also result from interruptions in service or the loss of communication with other systems or customers that causes data to not be stored in the first place.

Data loss can be slight or catastrophic. Data that is routinely backed up can usually be restored without much lasting impact. However, data that doesn't get stored at all, or data that isn't routinely backed up cannot be replaced. Such losses can even result in loss of assets if the loss affects other resources.

Loss of assets

Many attacks on Internet servers result in loss of assets, which ties to actual revenue. Such attacks could result in the following:

✦ DOS attack that results in a loss of sales (due to a server being unavailable to take orders)

✦ Loss of proprietary product data

✦ A situation that requires large amounts of technical resources to solve, costing actual money and time as technicians work on the situation

All of the cases in the preceding list result in a loss of assets, whether hard assets (money) or soft assets (people, time).

Loss of credibility and reputation

Victims of attacks stand to lose a lot more than data or assets—their credibility and reputation are also at stake. Losing either of those attributes creates a domino effect that could cause even more losses.

Customers who can't access a site due to a DOS attack may not return to give the site their business. Customers also are leery of sites that are victims of break-ins or data theft, fearing that their information (contact info, credit card info, and so on) might fall into the wrong hands.

Even sites that fully recover their resources and assets after an attack might never recover their credibility and reputation.

Litigation

Unfortunately, litigation in cyberspace is still in its infancy. Because the U.S. legal system works on precedent and there aren't many cyberspace precedents set, the system doesn't have the necessary background to make educated decisions. A side effect of this lack of precedents is that the legal system tends to move cautiously, as any decision will set precedent for later issues.

This doesn't deter litigation in cyberspace, but it does complicate it.

Furthermore, most crime that takes place on the Internet takes place through proxies. For example, DOS attacks are usually carried out via unsuspecting computers that were infected by worms or viruses. Also, most hackers perform their work by logging into one site and using that site to log into their target. The result is that a lot of unsuspecting people are held accountable for actions that they did not commit and inherit the burden of proving their innocence.

In short, litigation on the Internet and other computer-related areas is still a tricky business. As such, it behooves anyone using the Internet or who runs a server to employ as much caution and security as possible.

Web Site Security Issues

Now that we have covered most of the general risks, let's examine risks and solutions specific to the Web.

File permissions

A good understanding of the underlying file system on any system you use is essential to maintaining a secure system. Insufficient permissions will cause problems for your visitors—overly generous permissions can expose critical information you would rather not reveal.

When deploying a Web site, consider what rights and file ownership is truly necessary. Whenever possible assign rights to the Web server instead of general users. For example, on a Linux system where the Apache server runs as user www-data, the following permissions may be enough for your documents:

```
rwxr-x---   your_user_id www-data    filename
```

In the preceding example, the file is owned by your user ID, with read, write, and execute permissions. The group ownership is set to the user ID that the Web server runs under. The group permissions only allow read and execute, the minimum permissions necessary for the server to serve the file.

> **Note** Permissions on Windows platforms are a bit more complex and need to be managed via the IIS Windows MMC.

Unused but open ports

Any open port on a server presents a vulnerability that could be exploited. As such, it's important to only have the ports open that you really need. First and foremost, shut down and even uninstall any services that you don't need. For example, if you don't need an FTP server, don't even install one.

The next step is to perform a port scan on your system to see what ports are open that you may not know about. There are many ways to perform a port scan, including the following:

✦ Use your browser and visit one of the online port scanners, such as the one at DSL Reports (`www.dslreports.com/scan`) or the Shields Up scanner at Gibson Research (`www.grc.com`).

✦ Use a scanner application such as Nmap from insecure.org (`www.insecure.org/nmap/`).

✦ Use a telnet application to probe certain ports for activity. For example, the following command will attempt to connect via the SMTP port (25) of the local machine:

```
telnet localhost 25
```

CGI scripts

Common Gateway Interface (CGI) scripts are common targets for hackers. Many CGI scripts are poorly written from a security perspective, allowing savvy hackers to exploit them in various ways. Some exploits were fairly benign, such as using the `formmail` CGI script on a server to send anonymous e-mail (typically spam). Other CGI exploits are very dangerous, allowing hackers admin access to your server.

Whenever using CGI scripts, consider the following:

✦ Don't overly expose your CGI scripts. Avoid calling them where they will show in the browser's address bar with explicit arguments.

✦ Use CGI scripts from reputable sources and do some research into any security issues regarding the scripts you use.

✦ Use intelligent file ownership and permissions with your scripts (see the *File permissions* section earlier in this section). Assign rights to the Web server user instead of the world, and protect your CGI directories from browsing.

✦ Follow the same rules with your scripts that you do with your operating system and applications—audit their logs and update them as necessary to avoid issues.

Buffer overflows

Buffer overflows are widely used exploits. The concept of a buffer overflow is fairly simple: force an application to accept more data than it expects, causing it to overwrite other data in memory with specific data. For example, consider the following:

1. An application calls a subroutine, placing the address of the calling code on the memory stack so it can return after execution.

2. The subroutine's data is also mapped via the stack.

3. An exploit creates an overflow in the data area, causing new data (a new return address) to be written as the subroutine's return address.

4. The subroutine returns to the new address, typically accessing previously placed rogue code, a privileged command prompt, or other exploitable environment.

This is only one example of how a buffer overflow exploit can be used. The cure for such exploits is to keep your software up-to-date, as most exploits are fixed quickly after they are found. Monitoring security updates and patches for your system is critical to avoiding this issue.

Compromised systems

There is no easy cure for a compromised system. Once the system has been compromised you can never be truly sure of the extent of the compromise.

Typically, the following steps are the only recourse:

1. Isolate the system

2. Take stock of the damage, perhaps finding the method used to compromise the system

3. Back up any salvageable data

4. Reinstall the system from scratch, avoiding the component(s) that were compromised the first time

Tip

It's also good practice to inform fellow system administrators of the compromise, especially those administrators of systems closely tied to the compromised system.

Overview of Web Security Methods

The previous sections covered specific risks and solutions. This section covers preventative solutions—things that you can do on an ongoing basis to ensure you stay on top of security issues.

Drafting a comprehensive security policy

The first step to security is understanding and enforcing a strict and comprehensive policy. Start with a list of what you absolutely need your server to be able to do and pare down the list to the bare essentials, keeping track of any connections to the outside world that your server will require.

Once you know the requirements for your system, document what software you will need to accomplish the requirements and what additional security issues each additional piece of software could create (what ports will be exposed, and so forth).

Decide what user accounts you will require and what permissions are necessary for each. Most operating systems have defaults for server software; these defaults have been tested and should be used whenever possible.

This process simply creates your "to do" list of security concerns. Next, you must document actual policies and procedures—the most important part of the process. I suggest that for any questions you have on documenting specific policies and procedures you seek advice from experts, such as the following:

✦ CERT (www.cert.org) is one of the largest, most organized, and experienced security organizations.

✦ The SANS (SysAdmin, Audit, Network, Security) Institute (www.sans.org) is another highly respected security community.

Checking online security warnings

Many sites online publish security advisories, such as the following:

✦ Antivirus software vendor sites (www.mcafee.com, www.symantec.com, and so on)

✦ Microsoft's security site (www.microsoft.com/security/)

✦ Linuxsecurity.com publishes most of the security advisories for Linux (www.linuxsecurity.com/advisories/).

✦ Linux distribution sites (www.debian.org, www.redhat.com, and so on)

Most operating system vendors monitor security issues on an ongoing basis and provide automated methods to deploy security patches. Windows users should enable the Windows update service. Linux users should use `up2date` (Red Hat), `apt` (Debian), or other automated update service.

Excluding search engines

Excluding certain files and directories from search engine crawlers can help keep your system secure by hiding potentially hazardous files from the search engine. This keeps the same files from being discovered by hackers using a search engine such as Google.

Most search engines look for a file named `robots.txt` when indexing files on a site. You should place this file on the server's root; it contains instructions for search engines. The `robots.txt` file follows this format:

```
User-agent:    agent_name
Disallow:      file_or_directory_spec
Disallow: ...
```

You can use the name of the agent you want to disallow or an asterisk (*) for all agents. You can specify as many `Disallow` sections as necessary, each specifying a different directory or specific file. Note that if you specify a directory, all subdirectories of that directory are also disallowed.

A typical `robots.txt` file might resemble the following:

```
User-agent: *
Disallow: /tmp
Disallow: /images
Disallow: /cgi-bin
Disallow: /private.html
```

More information on `robots.txt` and other methods for directing search engines can be found on The Web Robot Pages (`www.robotstxt.org/wc/robots.html`).

Using secure servers

Secure servers offer another layer of security via encrypted data streams between the server and the client. Typically referred to as Secure Socket Layer (SSL), this layer can be implemented on many Internet-enabled applications—Web servers, e-mail servers, and so on.

Secure servers protect against eavesdroppers, hackers that intercept the communication between the user and server to obtain login information, personal data, credit card information, and so on.

Various servers implement SSL in various ways. In each case, you will need a certificate for use with your server. A certificate is an electronic document that is *signed* by a trusted authority, representing that the owner of the certificate is who they say they are. It's a means of providing ID to users of your site and saying "you can trust me because I am who I say I am."

There are quite a few certificate authorities, some more trusted than others. You can even sign your own certificates, though the result isn't worth much for convincing end users to trust you.

Tip   Thawte is a good place to start if you need a signed certificate. (`www.thawte.com/`)

Summary

Although it's a tangled and difficult subject, security is a topic you cannot ignore if you decide to put any content online. You can choose to manage security passively or proactively—this chapter provided details for both. However, being proactive is the best alternative, helping your content and sites stay free from being compromised.

✦   ✦   ✦

Privacy

Privacy is one of the most important considerations in the minds of many Web site visitors, so it should be at the forefront of every Web developer's concerns, as well. Although many people are now becoming more comfortable with the notion of data collection and credit card transactions, most people expect some kind of sign or label on a Web site indicating that a site is trustworthy. They also want to know you won't disseminate your information to third parties without their approval, especially in light of the spam epidemic that is bringing the e-mail system to its knees. This chapter takes a look at privacy issues and what you can do to create privacy policies that your Web site visitors will be comfortable with.

Understanding Privacy

What exactly is privacy? Whenever you visit a Web site, there's a good chance you'll have a cookie written to your hard drive that will record some information about you. Most people have given up trying to prevent this because disabling cookies makes the majority of sites that contain personalization functionality useless. In return for this, consumers now expect to see privacy policies on a Web site and assurances that those policies are actually being implemented.

Privacy Legislation and Regulations in the United States

Privacy laws in the United States are not very strong. Instead, companies and organizations have adopted self-regulating policies and procedures, as you'll see later in this chapter. However, there are a few U.S. laws you should be aware of:

✦ The Children's Online Privacy Protection Act

✦ The Electronic Communications Privacy Act (ECPA)

✦ The Patriot Act

✦ The Fair Credit Reporting Act

How much these impact you depends on a number of factors. For example, if your Web site is geared towards children, your privacy policy descriptions and implementations need to be rock solid.

The Children's Online Privacy Protection Act

The Children's Online Privacy Protection Act (COPPA) was put into effect April 21, 2000. It was created to oversee the collection of personal information from children under 13. According to the Federal Trade Commission (FTC), which enforces the act, "The new rules spell out what a Web site operator must include in a privacy policy, when and how to seek verifiable consent from a parent, and what responsibilities an operator has to protect children's privacy and safety online."

As the overseer of this act, the FTC evaluates whether the subject matter and content of your site suggests that your Web site is geared towards children. Such content can include the following:

✦ The ages of models used in online photography

✦ The makeup of visual or audio content

✦ Advertising

✦ Whether or not animation or other features are geared toward children

It's safe to say that if your site has a lot of cartoons and puzzles, the FTC will consider your site to be one that is aimed towards children.

The intent behind the act is to make sure that you maintain easy access to a privacy policy on children's sites, including your home page and wherever you collect personal information from children. The privacy link can't be one of those links you see at the bottom of Web pages using tiny font sizes, but must actually be prominent. The FTC actually advises you to use a *larger* font for these links.

The actual notice, which should be clearly understandable by children in the target market for your Web site, must contain the following information:

✦ The name and contact information of any party that collects information from children. This includes address, telephone number, and e-mail address.

✦ The type of information actually collected and how the information is collected, including if that information is collected through cookies or other passive means.

✦ How you intend to use the personal information, including any marketing and/or contest plans, or whether or not the information is available via a chat room.

✦ Your Web site's policy and intent on disclosure of collected information. You must disclose the kinds of businesses that have access to this information, why it's being passed along, and whether or not these third parties will honor the same privacy policies outlined on your site and in COPPA.

✦ A statement that a child's parent or guardian can refuse to permit the disclosure of information to a third party and that as a Web site operator you won't try to collect any more information than is absolutely necessary for successful participation in an activity that you claim requires the collection of this information.

✦ A policy that allows a parent or guardian to review any information on the site and refuse collection or use of the information you collect.

The law is designed to protect the rights of children and to prevent some of the more malicious behavior that can crop up when information gathering on children takes place, so the last thing you'll want to worry about is how compliance with the act will impact the design of your Web site. Instead, before you even consider collecting information from children, ask yourself if you really need to.

Electronic Communications Privacy Act

The ECPA was enacted in 1986 and prohibits unlawful access of electronic content, as well as disclosure of electronic content as it may apply to the privacy rights of individuals. The law covers a variety of wire and electronic communications services, which is defined by the law as "any transfer of signs, signals, writing, images, sounds, data, or intelligence of any nature transmitted in whole or in part by a wire, radio, electromagnetic, photo electronic, or photo optical system that affects interstate or foreign commerce." In addition to discouraging unlawful access to electronic communications (think wiretaps), the law also prevents government agencies from requiring disclosure of electronic communications without following a protocol such as the gathering of search warrants, and so on. The newer Patriot Act of 2001 has superseded some aspects of this law.

The Patriot Act of 2001

The Patriot Act of 2001 has become a rallying cry among civil liberty groups involved with Web privacy, particularly the Electronic Frontier Foundation. The act is a rather massive tome (300 plus pages) that was passed shortly after the events of September 11, 2001. Generally, however, this act shouldn't affect your Web site development, unless you're contracting with some foreign governments that may be considered friendly to terrorists or may be known to harbor them. If this is the case, you should review the documentation of the act, as well as the EFF's take on the situation at the following URL:

```
www.eff.org/Privacy/Surveillance/Terrorism/
20011031_eff_usa_patriot_analysis.php
```

You can review the law itself in PDF format here:

    www.dhs.gov/dhspublic/interweb/assetlibrary/hr_5005_enr.pdf&e=7417

Fair Credit Reporting Act

If you've ever obtained a credit card you've been impacted by the Fair Credit Reporting Act, which requires that credit bureaus provide access to consumers' credit reports and provides an opportunity to dispute them, which is where you come in. If a consumer disputes a blemish you've created on their credit report, you are required to respond to inquiries credit bureaus make on their behalf.

Privacy Legislation and Regulations in the EU

You may find that you are in compliance with laws in the United States, which really aren't very strong in the privacy arena, but have run afoul of standards in the European Union.

The European Union considers privacy a fundamental right, and has codified this general philosophy into law, whereas the political culture in the United States leans towards a general distrust of government that predates the Revolutionary War. Thus, the approach in the United States is largely hands-off, and is a combination of watered-down legislation, administrative regulation, and industry self-regulation.

The EU Directive on the Protection of Personal Data governs electronic communications as it pertains to information gathering and prohibits the transfer of data to any non-EU nation that doesn't meet European privacy standards.

The EU directive requires that any personal information gathered from its Web site visitors comply with the following:

✦ Collected for specified, explicit, and legitimate purposes, and in a way that is both fair and lawful under the eyes of each European Union member nation.

✦ Bears a direct relation to the activity that prompts the information gathering and does not exceed reasonable standards in regards to how much information is gathered.

✦ Maintained and updated accurately and with expirations that reflect the actual need for retaining the records.

Although the United States may seem to lag behind the EU in legislating privacy, it actually leads in areas of self-regulation, and many companies and organizations adhere to stringent privacy policies. In fact, most companies include a privacy policy in a link at the footer of their Web sites that details specific information about a company's privacy policy.

Voluntary Solutions

As previously mentioned, the United States tends to have less stringent laws regarding polices than the EU, but generally companies and organizations, especially those with substantial sites, carry privacy notices anyway. One of the most important guidelines to emerge in recent years that can help organizations develop a policy "template" is the Platform for Privacy Preferences Project from the World Wide Web Consortium (W3C), which incorporates many of the procedures developed for the EU's Directive on the Protection of Personal Data.

Platform for Privacy Preferences project

The Platform for Privacy Preferences (P3P) is a specification developed by the W3C that helps a Web site develop and implement privacy policies in a standardized way and provide these policies in a machine readable format. Not surprisingly, the specification relies on XML, which is very handy because it means your policy development can be both simple and easy to transmit.

The specification can be found at `www.w3.org/TR/2004/WD-P3P11-20040210/`.

If you look at the specification, you'll see it contains a number of XML elements so you can create policies such as that shown in this example from the W3C Web site:

```
<META xmlns="http://www.w3.org/2002/01/P3Pv1">
 <POLICY-REFERENCES>
    <POLICY-REF about="/P3P/Policies.xml# first">
       <COOKIE-INCLUDE name="*" value="*" domain="*"
    path="*"/>
    </POLICY-REF>
 </POLICY-REFERENCES>
</META>
```

P3P general syntax

Like any XML, the case of the elements is important, so it's not `policy` or `Policy`, it's `POLICY`. If you look at Listing 44-1, you can see that the XML vocabulary used for P3P is very intuitive.

Listing 44-1: **An Example of a P3P Policy Generated in XML**

```
<POLICIES xmlns="http://www.tumeric.net/P3P">
 <POLICY name="YourAssurance"
     discuri="http://www.tumeric.net/P3P/policies.aspx"
     opturi=" http://www.tumeric.net/P3P/preferences.html"
     xml:lang="en">
  <ENTITY>
   <DATA-GROUP>
   <DATA ref="#business.name">InfoExample</DATA>
   <DATA ref="#business.contact-info.postal.street">400 Data Base
```

Continued

Listing 44-1 *(continued)*

```
Avenue</DATA>
      <DATA ref="#business.contact-info.postal.city">San Francisco</DATA>
      <DATA ref="#business.contact-info.postal.stateprov">CA</DATA>
      <DATA ref="#business.contact-info.postal.postalcode">94112</DATA>
      <DATA ref="#business.contact-info.postal.country">USA</DATA>
      <DATA ref="#business.contact-info.online.email">me@tumeric.net</DATA>
      <DATA ref="#business.contact-info.telecom.telephone.intcode">1</DATA>
      <DATA ref="#business.contact-info.telecom.telephone.loccode">415</DATA>
      <DATA ref="#business.contact-info.telecom.telephone.number">1111111</DATA>
    </DATA-GROUP>
  </ENTITY>
  <ACCESS><contact-and-other/></ACCESS>
  <DISPUTES-GROUP>
   <DISPUTES resolution-type="independent"
     service="http://www.PrivacyGuaranteed.org"
     short-description=" PrivacyGuaranteed.org">
     <IMG src="http://www. PrivacyGuaranteed.org/logo.gif"
alt="PrivacyGuaranteed&amp;logo"/>
     <REMEDIES><correct/></REMEDIES>
   </DISPUTES>
  </DISPUTES-GROUP>
  <STATEMENT>
   <CONSEQUENCE>
     We do this because we are good corporate citizens and we don't want
     to get in trouble in Europe.
   </CONSEQUENCE>
   <PURPOSE><admin/><develop/></PURPOSE>
   <RECIPIENT><ours/></RECIPIENT>
   <RETENTION><stated-purpose/></RETENTION>
   <DATA-GROUP>
    <DATA ref="#ex.data.aspx"/>
    <DATA ref="#ex.http.useragent"/>
   </DATA-GROUP>
  </STATEMENT>
  <STATEMENT>
   <CONSEQUENCE>
     We use this information when you register on our site.
   </CONSEQUENCE>
   <PURPOSE><current/></PURPOSE>
   <RECIPIENT><ours/></RECIPIENT>
   <RETENTION><stated-purpose/></RETENTION>
   <DATA-GROUP>
    <DATA ref="#user.name"/>
    <DATA ref="#user.postal"/>
    <DATA ref="#user.telephone"/>
    <DATA ref="#user.login.id"/>
    <DATA ref="#user.login.password"/>
     <CATEGORIES><register/></CATEGORIES>
                            _____*#
   </DATA-GROUP>
  </STATEMENT>
 </POLICY>
</POLICIES>
```

Listing 44-1 shows a limited number of STATEMENT elements, but you can use one for every instance of data collection that exists on your Web site. Each instance is described by a STATEMENT element and abstracted using a CONSEQUENCE element.

P3P processes

P3P is currently in Working Draft, which means you can expect changes in its syntax. However, it is still a useful guide in developing privacy policies. For example, just perusing the specification's table of contents reveals an outline that reflects much of what you've learned in this chapter about both the European approach to privacy and the American approach to privacy regarding information gathering on children (the two of which are quite similar). The core steps in implementing P3P will by now look familiar:

1. Identify the *Entity* (using the ENTITY element)—who you are and how a user can contact you.

2. Disclose where your policy lives on your site using the discuri attribute of the POLICY element

3. Provide assurances that you are doing what you say by naming the entities that are providing proof of your claims, using the DISPUTES element.

4. Provide information on the kind of data you are collecting and how you are collecting it using the DATA-GROUP element.

Because P3P is based on XML, a P3P policy can be embedded in a Web Services Description Language (WSDL) document such as that shown in bold in Listing 44-2.

Listing 44-2: **Incorporating a Generic P3P Attribute in a WSDL File**

```
<?xml version="1.0"?>
  <definitions xmlns="http://www.w3.org/2003/11/wsdl"
    xmlns:foospace="http://www.tumeric.net/webservice"
    xmlns:somens="http://example.org/myservice-types"
    xmlns:p3p="http://www.w3.org/2004/02/P3Pv11"
    xmlns:soap="http://www.w3.org/2003/06/wsdl/soap12"
    xmlns:xs="http://www.w3.org/2001/XMLSchema"
    targetNamespace=" http://www.tumeric.net/webservice">
  <documentation>
  How to use a P3P generic attribute in a WSDL file
  </documentation>
  <types>
    <xs:import
   namespave='http://www.tumeric.net/webservice'/>
  </types>
  <interface name="fooface">
    <operation name="foo_ops"
    pattern="http://www.tumeric.net/wsdl">
```

Continued

Listing 44-2 *(continued)*

```
        <input message="somens:commentReq"/>
        <output message="myntypes:commentResp"/>
    </operation>
  </interface>

  <binding name="Binding" interface="foospace:fooface">
    <soap:binding protocol="http://www.w3.org/2003/05/soap/bindings
    /HTTP/"/>
  </binding>

  <service name="Service" interface="foospace:fooface"
    p3p:p3p="http://www.tumeric.net/p3p.xml">
    <endpoint name="Endpoint1" binding="foospace:binding">
     <soap:address
      location="http://www.tumeric.net/webservice" />
    </endpoint>
  </service>
</definitions>
```

Listing 44-2 uses a "generic" attribute that can be embedded into other XML vocabularies. You can then develop an XSLT style sheet to transform the file into HTML.

Generating P3P files the easy way

Nobody would be too surprised to find out that you don't want to learn a new vocabulary just to generate some private policies. Luckily, several P3P editors are available that will generate the files for you:

✦ IBM P3P Policy Editor (www.alphaworks.ibm.com/tech/p3peditor)

✦ PrivacyBot.com (www.privacybot.com)

✦ For Japanese language sites, Iajapan's Privacy Policy Wizard
(http://fs.pics.enc.or.jp/p3pwiz/p3p_en.html)

✦ P3PEdit (http://policyeditor.com)

✦ Customer Paradigm's P3P Privacy Policy Creation
(www.customerparadigm.com/p3p-privacy-policy3.htm)

These save you the trouble of learning the new syntax, however, it does help to have a general understanding of how the syntax works, because you may find yourself editing small portions of a completed file in a text editor after the file has been completed and uploaded to your server.

Certification and seal programs

A number of privacy and certification sites will guarantee the authenticity of software downloads coming from your site and provide assurances to users of your site that your Web site adheres to the highest privacy and trust standards. These include the following:

✦ TRUSTe. "TRUSTe Privacy Seals are committed to abiding by a privacy policy that gives users notice, choice, access, security, and redress with regard to their personal information," according to the company's Web site at `www.truste.org`. The company offers seals for demonstrating compliance with the American Children's Online Privacy Protection Act, EU guidelines, and health-based privacy issues.

✦ The Better Business Bureau Online Privacy Seal demonstrates compliance set for businesses wishing to adhere to Better Business Bureau standards (`www.bbbonline.org/privacy`).

✦ E-Safe is a fee-based service that provides privacy certification seals to Web sites that meet its privacy guidelines (`www.e-safecertified.com`).

✦ Guardian eCommerce Security provides ratings and an approval program for Web sites (`www.guardianecommerce.net`).

✦ Privacy Secure, Inc. runs a credit check on your company or organization (or your client's, if you're developing as a vendor), reviews any complaints with the Better Business Bureau, and reviews your online payment system (`www.privacysecure.com`).

✦ PrivacyBot.com, in addition to helping you create P3P-based privacy policy files, registers your site and offers a "Trustmark" that indicates compliance with established privacy trends (`www.privacybot.com`).

✦ SecureBiz provides an Online Privacy Seal (`https://securebiz.securelook.com`).

✦ Web Trust provides Web site auditing services (`www.cpawebtrust.org`).

✦ Verisign provides layers of security and authentication for secure Web sites (`www.verisign.com`) and generates seals of authenticity for software downloads from your Web site.

Model Privacy Policy Pages

To help guide you on your way to developing policy pages, consider reviewing some that already exist. As previously mentioned, most major Web sites carry privacy policies on their Web sites and almost always link them in the footers of their Web pages. Review policies created by large companies and organizations to gain ideas for your own site. The Federal Government of the United States maintains a best case Web site for developing privacy policies for U.S. government Web sites and contractors for the U.S. government at the following URL:

```
www.whitehouse.gov/omb/memoranda/m99-18attach.html
```

Summary

You can probably see a similarity between privacy guidelines and law in the United States regarding children, privacy policy in Europe regarding everybody, and the approach the W3C and independent privacy consultants take. Generally, the privacy model dictates that you provide access to your policies through easy-to-find links, provide assurances that your policies are actually being implemented, justify their use, and identify the type of data you gathered and what you intend to do with it.

Most organizations don't wait for legislation or bad publicity before developing privacy guidelines and procedures. They simply implement them from the beginning. You'll find that doing so helps clarify both your mission and intent to the public. By making your Web site "trustworthy," you'll get more business, especially if you mean business.

✦　　✦　　✦

Appendixes

HTML 4.01 Elements

Parent elements are indicated only where there is a limited set of associations (for example, `<td>` within `<tr>`, or `<area>` inside `<map>`). When no parent relationship is expressed, the "classification" of an element is provided as a general category that is used by other elements to describe their contents. This is distinct from the "display" information, which expresses how browsers render the element (see `http://www.w3.org/TR/REC-CSS2/sample.html` for the results of an investigation into modern browsers' rendering styles).

Let's examine the first part of the `<isindex>` reference.

This element is deprecated, which means that the HTML 4.01 Transitional DTD defines it, but the Strict DTD does not.

It is an empty element, with no content and no closing tag.

It renders inline, so it can be surrounded on both sides by text. However, it is classified as a block element, which means that it can only be contained by elements that allow block content. `<p>` is a prime example of an element that *cannot* act as the parent for `<isindex>` because `<p>` can only contain elements classified as inline.

XHTML

To create HTML that is XHTML-compliant, 4.01 elements and attributes must follow XML rules.

+ Empty elements must either have a closing tag or use the XML empty element syntax, as in the following example:

```
<img src="/images/logo.png" alt="Our logo">
</img>
```

To support older browsers, the empty element syntax should include a space before the trailing slash, as in the following example:

```
<img src="/images/logo.png" alt="Our logo" />
```

✦ Because XML is case-sensitive, all elements and attributes must be lowercase.

✦ Attribute values must always be quoted.

✦ Minimized attributes are not allowed. Attributes that do not take a value must be given a value equal to the name of the attribute, as in the following examples:

- `<input checked="checked" />`
- `<select multiple="multiple">`

Alphabetical List of the Elements

a

Context	
Purpose	Insert a hyperlink
Start/End Tag	Required/Required
Display	Inline
Classification	Inline
Content	Inline and text

Attributes		
Required	**Optional**	**Deprecated**
	charset = "encoding"	targeet="frame"
	type = "MIME type"	
	name = "anchor name"	
	href = "URL"	
	hreflang = "language code"	
	rel = "forward link type"	
	rev = "reverse link type"	
	accesskey = "key"	
	shape = (rect|circle|poly|default)	
	coords = "coordinates"	
	tabindex = "sequence value"	
	onfocus = "script"	
	onblur = "script"	

General

- ✓ Core (id, class, style, title)
- ✓ Internationalization (lang, dir)
- ✓ Standard Events (see end of appendix)

Usage	
Tip	Any type of URL may be used here.

Example

`<a href="http://www.google.com/">Google search engine</a>`

abbr

Context	
Purpose	Indicate the enclosed text is an abbreviation
Start/End Tag	Required/Required
Display	Inline
Classification	Inline
Content	Inline and text

Attributes	

General

- ✓ Core (id, class, style, title)
- ✓ Internationalization (lang, dir)
- ✓ Standard Events (see end of appendix)

Usage	
Tip	Use the `title` attribute to express the unabbreviated text. Stylesheets can be used to subtly highlight abbreviations.

Example

`<abbr title="Incorporated">Inc.</abbr>`

acronym

Context	
Purpose	Indicate the enclosed text is an acronym
Start/End Tag	Required/Required

Continued

Display	Inline
Classification	Inline
Content	Inline and text

Attributes

General

- ✓ Core (id, class, style, title)
- ✓ Internationalization (lang, dir)
- ✓ Standard Events (see end of appendix)

Usage

Tip	See <abbr> for usage tips.

Example

<acronym title="HyperText Markup Language">HTML</acronym>

address

Context

Purpose	Provide information about the author
Start/End Tag	Required/Required
Display	Block
Classification	Block
Content	<p>, inline, and text.

Attributes

General

- ✓ Core (id, class, style, title)
- ✓ Internationalization (lang, dir)
- ✓ Standard Events (see end of appendix)

Usage

Tip	Always sign your work.

Example

<address>John Doe (<a href="mailto:jd@mydomain.com">jd@mydomain.com</a>)
</address>

applet (deprecated)

Context	
Purpose	Incorporate a Java applet
Start/End Tag	Required/Required
Display	Block
Classification	Inline
Content	Any block, inline, and text; any `<param>` elements must come first

Attributes		
Required	**Optional**	**Deprecated**
width = "pixels or relative"	codebase = "URI"	
height = "pixels or relative"	archive = "URI, . . . "	
	code = "applet.class"	
	object = "serialized object"	
	alt = "description"	
	name = "locator"	
	align = (top|middle|bottom|left|right)	
	hspace = "pixels"	
	vspace = "pixels"	

General

✓ Core (id, class, style, title)

  Internationalization (lang, dir)

  Standard Events (see end of appendix)

Usage	
Tip	Use `<object>` instead.
Example	

`<applet code="tic-tac-toe.class" width="500" height="500">Play tic-tac-toe!</applet>`

area

Context	
Purpose	Describe a client-side image map
Start/End Tag	Required/Forbidden

Continued

Parent	\<map>
Content	Empty

Attributes		

Required	Optional	Deprecated
alt = "description"	shape = (rect|circle|poly|default)	target = "frame"
	coords = "length, length"	
	href = "URL"	
	nohref	
	tabindex = "sequence value"	
	accesskey = "key"	
	onfocus = "script"	
	onblur = "script"	

General

✓ Core (id, class, style, title)

✓ Internationalization (lang, dir)

✓ Standard Events (see end of appendix)

Usage	
Tip	The code for client-side imagemaps can be generated by imagemap editors. Don't forget the `alt` attribute, to make the map accessible to non-graphical clients.

Example

See \<map>

b

Context	
Purpose	Bold text
Start/End Tag	Required/Required
Display	Inline
Classification	Inline
Content	Inline and text
Attributes	

General

✓ Core (id, class, style, title)

✓ Internationalization (lang, dir)

✓ Standard Events (see end of appendix)

Usage	
Tip	Be careful to close this element properly, and don't overlap with similar tags like <i>. Nest them instead.

Example	
This is bold, <i>this is bold italic</i>.	

base

Context	
Purpose	Specify an absolute URL for use when evaluating relative URLs elsewhere in the document
Start/End Tag	Required/Forbidden
Parent	<head>
Content	Empty

Attributes		
Required	**Optional**	**Deprecated**
href = "URL"		target = "frame"

Usage	
Tip	If you use this element, use it consistently, to make it easier to remember to change the <base> element in all documents when they are moved.

Example	
<base href="http://www.mydomain.com/sample/">	

basefont (deprecated)

Context	
Purpose	Set the default font, size, and color for the entire document
Start/End Tag	Required/Forbidden
Classification	Inline
Content	Empty

Attributes		
Required	**Optional**	**Deprecated**
size = "font size"	id = "unique id"	
	color = "color value"	
	face = "typeface, typeface"	

Continued

Usage	
Tip	Use CSS instead by assigning style to the body tag.

Example

`<basefont face="Arial, Helvetica" color="blue" size="10">`

bdo

Context	
Purpose	Override the default text direction
Start/End Tag	Required/Required
Display	Inline
Classification	Inline
Content	Inline and text

Attributes		
Required	**Optional**	**Deprecated**
dir = (rtl|ltr)	lang = "language code"	

General

✓ Core (id, class, style, title)

   Internationalization (lang, dir)

   Standard Events (see end of appendix)

Usage	
Tip	Any element that supports the internationalization attributes can define the `dir` attribute, making this tag unnecessary.

Example

`<bdo dir="ltr">`Here's some English embedded in text in another language requiring a right-to-left presentation.`</bdo>`

big

Context	
Purpose	Display text in a large font
Start/End Tag	Required/Required
Display	Inline
Classification	Inline
Content	Inline and text

Attributes

General

- ✓ Core (id, class, style, title)
- ✓ Internationalization (lang, dir)
- ✓ Standard Events (see end of appendix)

Usage

Tip	Be careful to close this element properly, and don't overlap with similar tags like <i>. Nest them instead.

Example

<big>This is large, this is large and italic.</big>

blockquote

Context	
Purpose	Denote an extended quotation
Start/End Tag	Required/Required
Display	Block
Classification	Block
Content	Block, inline, and text

Attributes		
Required	**Optional**	**Deprecated**
	cite = "URL"	

General

- ✓ Core (id, class, style, title)
- ✓ Internationalization (lang, dir)
- ✓ Standard Events (see end of appendix)

Usage

Tip	Browsers will typically indent the contents. For an inline quote, you may use <q>, but be warned that all versions of Internet Explorer up to and including 6.0 do not properly support <q>.
	The 4.01 specification indicates that <blockquote> is deprecated and should be handled via stylesheets, but it is supported in 4.01 strict , XHTML 1.0, and XHTML 1.1.

Continued

Example

```
<blockquote
cite="http://www.archives.gov/national_archives_experience/declaration_transcript.html"
>
```

   When in the Course of human events, it becomes necessary for one people to dissolve the political bands which have connected them with another, and to assume among the powers of the earth, the separate and equal station to which the Laws of Nature and of Nature's God entitle them, a decent respect to the opinions of mankind requires that they should declare the causes which impel them to the separation.

```
</blockquote>
```

body

Context	
Purpose	Provide a container for all the text and elements that appear onscreen within the browser window
Start/End Tag	Optional/Optional
Display	Block
Parent	<html>, <noframes> (in the frameset DTD only)
Content	Block, inline, and text

Attributes		
Required	**Optional**	**Deprecated**
	onload = "script"	background = "image URL"
	onunload = "script"	bgcolor = "background color"
		text = "text color"
		link = "link color"
		vlink = "visited link color"
		alink = "selected link color"

General

- ✓ Core (id, class, style, title)
- ✓ Internationalization (lang, dir)
- ✓ Standard Events (see end of appendix)

Usage	
Tip	Treat the start and end tags as required, not optional.
Example	
See <html>	

br

Context	
Purpose	Insert a line break
Start/End Tag	Required/Forbidden
Classification	Inline
Content	Empty

Attributes		
Required	**Optional**	**Deprecated**
		clear = (left|all|right|none)

General

✓ Core (id, class, style, title)

Internationalization (lang, dir)

Standard Events (see end of appendix)

Usage	
Tip	This is purely for presentation, and as such can almost always be replaced with margin style attached to semantic markup.

Example
This is one line. This is the next.

button

Context	
Purpose	Create a button in a form
Start/End Tag	Required/Required
Display	Inline
Classification	Inline
Content	Any block, inline, and text

Attributes		
Required	**Optional**	**Deprecated**
	name = "form name"	
	value = "form value"	
	type = (button|submit|reset)	
	disabled	

Continued

tabindex = "sequence value"	
accesskey = "key"	
onfocus = "script"	
onblur = "script"	

General

✓ Core (id, class, style, title)

✓ Internationalization (lang, dir)

✓ Standard Events (see end of appendix)

Usage

Tip	If you want to specify the text on the button face, use this element instead of <input>.

Example

<button name="submit" value="submit" type="submit">Feed me, Seymour<img src="/images/plant.gif" alt=""></button>

caption

Context

Purpose	Define a caption for a table
Start/End Tag	Required/Required
Display	Inline
Parent	<table>
Content	Inline and text

Attributes

Required	Optional	Deprecated
		align = (top|bottom|left|right)

General

✓ Core (id, class, style, title)

✓ Internationalization (lang, dir)

✓ Standard Events (see end of appendix)

Usage

Tip	This element may be used only as the first child of a <table> element.

Example

See <table>

center (deprecated)

Context	
Purpose	Align contents in the center of the enclosing block
Start/End Tag	Required/Required
Display	Block
Classification	Block
Content	Block, inline, and text

Attributes	

General

- ✓ Core (id, class, style, title)
- ✓ Internationalization (lang, dir)
- ✓ Standard Events (see end of appendix)

Usage	
Tip	This is equivalent to <div align="center"> (deprecated) or <div style="text-align: center">.

Example

```
<body>
  <center>This text is centered.</center>
...
```

cite

Context	
Purpose	Indicate that the contents are the title of a cited text
Start/End Tag	Required/Required
Display	Inline
Classification	Inline
Content	Inline and text

Attributes	

General

- ✓ Core (id, class, style, title)
- ✓ Internationalization (lang, dir)
- ✓ Standard Events (see end of appendix)

Continued

Usage	
Tip	Typically rendered in italics.
Example	
<cite>Leaves of Grass</cite> by Walt Whitman	

code

Context	
Purpose	Identify the enclosed text as computer code
Start/End Tag	Required/Required
Display	Inline
Classification	Inline
Content	Inline and text

Attributes	

General

- ✓ Core (id, class, style, title)
- ✓ Internationalization (lang, dir)
- ✓ Standard Events (see end of appendix)

Usage	
Tip	Typically rendered in monospace. For a block of code, use <pre>.
Example	
In Java, the <code>toString()</code> method is handy for debugging.	

col

Context	
Purpose	Identify columns within a table for customization
Start/End Tag	Required/Forbidden
Parent	<colgroup>, <table>
Content	Empty

Attributes		
Required	**Optional**	**Deprecated**
	span = "number of columns"	
	width = "column width"	
	align = (left|center|right|justify|char)	

char = "alignment character"

charoff = "alignment char offset"

valign = (top|middle|bottom|baseline)

General

✓ Core (id, class, style, title)

✓ Internationalization (lang, dir)

✓ Standard Events (see end of appendix)

Usage	
Tip	This tag and <colgroup> are designed to provide a central place to apply attributes to all the cells in a column. Be warned, however, that most browsers do not support this properly, and thus CSS is recommended instead.

Example

See <table>

colgroup

Context	
Purpose	Groups semantically related column descriptors
Start/End Tag	Required/Optional
Parent	<table>
Content	0 or more <col> elements

Attributes		
Required	**Optional**	**Deprecated**
	span = "number of columns"	
	width = "column width"	
	align = (left|center|right|justify|char)	
	char = "alignment character"	
	charoff = "alignment char offset"	
	valign = (top|middle|bottom|baseline)	

General

✓ Core (id, class, style, title)

✓ Internationalization (lang, dir)

✓ Standard Events (see end of appendix)

Continued

Usage	
Tip	This tag and <col> are designed to provide a central place to apply attributes to all the cells in a column. Be warned, however, that most browsers do not support this properly, and thus CSS is recommended instead.

Example	
See <table>	

dd

Context	
Purpose	Identify a definition in a definition list
Start/End Tag	Required/Optional
Display	Block
Parent	<dl>
Content	Block, inline, and text

Attributes	

General

✓ Core (id, class, style, title)

✓ Internationalization (lang, dir)

✓ Standard Events (see end of appendix)

Usage	
Tip	There can be multiple definitions for each term (<dt>). There can also be multiple terms for each definition.

Example	
See <div>	

del

Context	
Purpose	Indicate part of a document that has been deleted
Start/End Tag	Required/Required
Display	Block or inline, depending on the content
Parent	Any element within (and including) <body>
Content	Any block, inline, and text (but cannot contain block content when used as an inline element)

Attributes		
Required	**Optional**	**Deprecated**
	cite = "URL"	
	datetime = "ISO date"	

General

- ✓ Core (id, class, style, title)
- ✓ Internationalization (lang, dir)
- ✓ Standard Events (see end of appendix)

Usage	
Tip	<del> and <ins> are unusual. They can operate either as inline or block elements, and can appear anywhere inside the <body> element.

Example

<p>Our <acronym>CEO</acronym> is <del>Jack Mann</del><ins>Barbara Smith</ins>.</p>

dfn

Context	
Purpose	Identify the enclosed text as the defining instance
Start/End Tag	Required/Required
Display	Inline
Classification	Inline
Content	Inline and text

Attributes	

General

- ✓ Core (id, class, style, title)
- ✓ Internationalization (lang, dir)
- ✓ Standard Events (see end of appendix)

Usage	
Tip	See <dl> for a definition list.

Example

<dfn>anime</dfn> refers to a distinctive Japanese tradition of cartoon animation.

dir (deprecated)

Context	
Purpose	Originally intended for multi-column directory listings, it is rendered like <ul>.
Start/End Tag	Required/Required
Display	Block
Classification	Block
Content	<li> elements that are constrained to contain inline content only

Attributes		
Required	**Optional**	**Deprecated**
	compact	

General

- ✓ Core (id, class, style, title)
- ✓ Internationalization (lang, dir)
- ✓ Standard Events (see end of appendix)

Usage	
Tip	Use <ul> instead.

Example

```
<dir>
  <li>This is</li>
  <li>a very short</li>
  <li>list.</li>
</dir>
```

div

Context	
Purpose	Provide structure for a group of elements
Start/End Tag	Required/Required
Display	Block
Classification	Block
Content	Block, inline, and text

Attributes		
Required	**Optional**	**Deprecated**
		align = (left|center|right|justify)

General

- ✓ Core (id, class, style, title)
- ✓ Internationalization (lang, dir)
- ✓ Standard Events (see end of appendix)

Usage	
Tip	<div> (a block) and <span> (an inline) provide a convenient grouping mechanism for applying CSS style. Use the `class` attribute for the CSS selectors.

Example

```
<style type="text/css"> <!--
  .dictionary dt {
    font-style: italic;
  }
  .section {
    border-top: thin groove black;
  } -->
</style>

<div class="section dictionary">
  <dl>
    <dt>tenebrous</dt>
    <dt>tenebrious</dt>
    <dd>Dark and gloomy.</dd>
    <dt>tertiary</dt>
    <dd>Third.
    </dd>
  </dl>
</div>
```

dl

Context	
Purpose	Create a definition list
Start/End Tag	Required/Required
Display	Block

Continued

Classification	Block
Content	<dt> and <dd>

Attributes		
Required	**Optional**	**Deprecated**
		compact

General

- ✓ Core (id, class, style, title)
- ✓ Internationalization (lang, dir)
- ✓ Standard Events (see end of appendix)

Usage	
Tip	This typically renders with the definition(s) rendered below and to the right of the term(s).

Example

See <div>

dt

Context	
Purpose	Identify a defined term in a definition list
Start/End Tag	Required/Optional
Display	Block
Parent	<dl>
Content	Inline and text

Attributes

General

- ✓ Core (id, class, style, title)
- ✓ Internationalization (lang, dir)
- ✓ Standard Events (see end of appendix)

Usage	
Tip	There can be multiple definitions (<dd>) for each term. There can also be multiple terms for each definition.

Example

See <div>

em

Context	
Purpose	Mark text as emphasis
Start/End Tag	Required/Required
Display	Inline
Classification	Inline
Content	Inline and text

Attributes

General

✓ Core (id, class, style, title)

✓ Internationalization (lang, dir)

✓ Standard Events (see end of appendix)

Usage

Tip	Usually rendered in italics. If bold is desired instead of italics use <strong>.

Example

There are <em>three</em> rooms, not two.

fieldset

Context	
Purpose	Group thematically related elements in a form
Start/End Tag	Required/Required
Display	Block
Classification	Block
Content	<legend> as first child; after that block, inline, and text in any order

Attributes

General

✓ Core (id, class, style, title)

✓ Internationalization (lang, dir)

✓ Standard Events (see end of appendix)

Usage

Tip	Useful for accessibility.

Example

See <form>

font (deprecated)

Context	
Purpose	Define presentational style for text
Start/End Tag	Required/Required
Display	Inline
Classification	Inline
Content	Inline and text

Attributes		
Required	Optional	Deprecated
	size = "font size"	
	color = "color"	
	face = "typeface"	

General

✓ Core (id, class, style, title)

✓ Internationalization (lang, dir)

   Standard Events (see end of appendix)

Usage	
Tip	Use CSS instead.

Example

<p>For Christmas, decorate your web pages in <font color="red">red</font> and <font color="green">green</font>.</p>

form

Context	
Purpose	Create a form for user input
Start/End Tag	Required/Required
Display	Block
Classification	Block
Content	Transitional DTD: Block, inline, and text
	Strict DTD: Block and <script>

Attributes	

Required	Optional	Deprecated
	action = "URL"	
	method = (GET|POST)	
	enctype = "MIME type"	
	accept = "MIME type"	
	name = "form name"	
	onsubmit = "script"	
	onreset = "script"	
	accept-charset = "charset"	

General

✓ Core (id, class, style, title)

✓ Internationalization (lang, dir)

✓ Standard Events (see end of appendix)

Usage

Tip In the 4.01 strict DTD form elements like <input> are not allowed as direct children of a form. Those elements must be enclosed in block elements like <fieldset>, <p>, and <div>.

Example

```
<form action="http://www.mydomain.com/cgi-bin/handle-input.cgi" method="POST">
  <fieldset>
    <legend>Personal data</legend>
    <label for="name">Name: </label><input id="name" type="text" size="30" name="Name">
  </fieldset>
  <fieldset>
    <legend>Billing data</legend>
    <label for="creditcard">Credit card: </label>
    <input id="creditcard" type="password" size="18" name="Credit">
  </fieldset>
  <div>
    <input type="submit">
  </div>
</form>
```

frame

Context	
Purpose	Describe the content for a single frame of a page
Start/End Tag	Required/Forbidden
Display	Block
Parent	<frameset>
Content	Empty

Attributes		
Required	**Optional**	**Deprecated**
	longdesc = "URL"	
	name = "frame name"	
	src = "URL"	
	frameborder = (1|0)	
	marginwidth = "number of pixels"	
	marginheight = "number of pixels"	
	noresize	
	scrolling = (yes|no|auto)	

General

  ✓ Core (id, class, style, title)

    Internationalization (lang, dir)

    Standard Events (see end of appendix)

Usage	
Tip	To use frames, declare your document to comply with the 4.01 frameset DTD.

Example

See <frameset>

frameset

Context	
Purpose	Define frame sizes and positions
Start/End Tag	Required/Required
Display	Block

Parent	<html>
Content	<frameset>, <frame>, <noframes>

Attributes		
Required	**Optional**	**Deprecated**
	rows = "height, height…"	
	cols = "width, width…"	
	onload = "script"	
	onunload = "script"	

General

✓ Core (id, class, style, title)

Internationalization (lang, dir)

Standard Events (see end of appendix)

Usage

Tip	To use frames, declare your document to comply with the 4.01 frameset DTD.

Example

```
<frameset rows="40, 25%, *">
  <frame src="header.html" name="header">
  <frame src="navbar.html" name="navbar">
  <frameset cols="20%, *">
    <frame src="left-navbar.html" name="left">
    <frame src="content.html" name="main">
  </frameset>
  <noframes>
    <body>Warning: this site expects a browser that understands frames.</body>
  </noframes>
</frameset>
```

h1, h2, h3, h4, h5, h6

Context	
Purpose	Mark the enclosed text as a heading, ranging from most prominent (<h1>) to least prominent (<h6>)

Continued

Start/End Tag	Required/Required
Display	Block
Classification	Block
Content	Inline and text

	Attributes	
Required	Optional	Deprecated
		align = (left|center|right|justify)

General

- ✓ Core (id, class, style, title)
- ✓ Internationalization (lang, dir)
- ✓ Standard Events (see end of appendix)

	Usage
Tip	<h1> should be reserved for the title of a document, due to its prominence. If text should be prominent, but it isn't technically a heading, consider using a <div> element with CSS to define the size and font weight.

Example

<h1>Document Title</h1>

<h3>Introduction</h3>

<p>…</p>

<h3>Conclusion</h3>

<p>…</p>

head

	Context
Purpose	Enclose document metadata
Start/End Tag	Optional/Optional
Parent	<html>
Content	<title> (required), <isindex> (deprecated), <base>, <script>, <style>, <meta>, <link>, <object>

	Attributes	
Required	Optional	Deprecated
	profile = "URI"	

General		
	Core (id, class, style, title)	
✓	Internationalization (lang, dir)	
	Standard Events (see end of appendix)	

Usage	
Tip	As with <body>, to be compliant with XHTML treat the open and close tags as required instead of optional.

Example

<head>

  <meta http-equiv="Content-Type" content="text/html; charset=ISO-8859-4">

  <title>Bryology Directory: Page 3</title>

  <link rel="previous" href="page2.html">

  <link rel="next" href="page4.html">

  <link rel="stylesheet" type="text/css" href="/style/global.css">

  <meta name="keywords" content="bryophyte, bryology, bryologist, moss, liverwort, hornwort">

</head>

hr

Context	
Purpose	Insert a line break
Start/End Tag	Required/Forbidden
Classification	Block
Content	Empty

Attributes		
Required	**Optional**	**Deprecated**
		align = (left|center|right)
		noshade
		size = "pixels"
		width = "pixels or relative"

General

  ✓ Core (id, class, style, title)

Continued

✓ Internationalization (lang, dir)

✓ Standard Events (see end of appendix)

Usage	
Tip	Styling <hr> with CSS is problematic due to pronounced differences between browsers. You may wish to use borders with CSS in place of <hr>.

Example
<h1>My Document</h1>
<hr>
<p>...</p>

html

Context	
Purpose	The master element containing the entire document
Start/End Tag	Optional/Optional
Parent	None
Content	<head> and either <body> or <frameset>

Attributes

General
Core (id, class, style, title)
✓ Internationalization (lang, dir)
Standard Events (see end of appendix)

Usage	
Tip	It is poor form to not include the start and end tags.

Example

```
<html>
 <head>
  <title>Hello, Web</title>
 </head>
 <body>
  <p>Just a small document.</p>
 </body>
</html>
```

i

Context	
Purpose	Italic text
Start/End Tag	Required/Required
Display	Inline
Classification	Inline
Content	Inline and text

Attributes	

General

  ✓ Core (id, class, style, title)

  ✓ Internationalization (lang, dir)

  ✓ Standard Events (see end of appendix)

Usage	
Tip	If the goal is emphasized text, consider <em> instead to convey the semantics. Conversely, don't use <em> when you just want italics.

Example

See <b>

iframe

Context	
Purpose	Create an inline subwindow in which can be inserted another document
Start/End Tag	Required/Required
Display	Block
Classification	Inline
Content	Any block, inline, and text

Attributes		

Required	**Optional**	**Deprecated**
	longdesc = "URL"	
	name = "locator"	
	src = "URL"	
	frameborder = (1|0)	

Continued

> marginwidth = "pixels"
>
> marginheight = "pixels"
>
> scrolling = (yes|no|auto)
>
> align = (top|middle|bottom|left|right)
>
> height = "pixels or relative"
>
> width = "pixels or relative"

General

✓ Core (id, class, style, title)

Internationalization (lang, dir)

Standard Events (see end of appendix)

Usage	
Tip	This tag is not defined in the strict DTD, and it is not well supported in browsers other than IE. Consider <object> instead.

Example

```
<iframe src="sample.html" scrolling="auto" width="50%" height="300">
   See <a href="sample.html"> for an illustration of this concept. <!-- Fallback text -->
</iframe>
```

img

Context	
Purpose	Insert a graphic
Start/End Tag	Required/Forbidden
Display	Inline
Classification	Inline
Content	Empty

Attributes		
Required	**Optional**	**Deprecated**
src = "URL"	longdesc = "URL"	align = (top|middle|bottom|left|right)
alt = "description"	name = "name"	border = "pixels"
	height = "pixels or relative"	hspace = "pixels"
	width = "pixels or relative"	vspace = "pixels"
	usemap = "URL"	
	ismap	

General

- ✓ Core (id, class, style, title)
- ✓ Internationalization (lang, dir)
- ✓ Standard Events (see end of appendix)

Usage	
Tip	Always use the `alt` attribute to enhance accessibility. If the image is entirely irrelevant to a non-graphical browser, such as spacer images or other visual fluff, use an empty string as the value

Example

See <button>

input

Context	
Purpose	Accept user input within a form
Start/End Tag	Required/Forbidden
Display	Inline
Classification	Inline
Content	Empty

Attributes		
Required	**Optional**	**Deprecated**
	type = (text|password|checkbox| radio|submit|reset|file|hidden| image|button)	align = (top|middle|bottom|left|right)
	name = "form name"	
	value = "form value"	
	checked	
	disabled	
	readonly	
	size = "character width"	
	maxlength = "max width"	
	src = "URL"	
	alt = "description"	
	usemap = "URL"	

Continued

ismap

tabindex = "sequence value"

accesskey = "key"

onfocus = "script"

onblur = "script"

onselect = "script"

onchange = "script"

accept = "MIME type, ..."

General

✓ Core (id, class, style, title)

✓ Internationalization (lang, dir)

✓ Standard Events (see end of appendix)

Usage	
Tip	The purpose of some attributes varies between input types.

Example

See <form>

---

ins

Context	
Purpose	Indicate part of a document that has been inserted
Start/End Tag	Required/Required
Display	Block or inline, depending on the content
Parent	Any element within (and including) <body>
Content	Any block, inline, and text (but cannot contain block content when used as an inline element)

Attributes		
Required	Optional	Deprecated
	cite = "URL"	
	datetime = "ISO date"	

General

✓ Core (id, class, style, title)

✓ Internationalization (lang, dir)

✓ Standard Events (see end of appendix)

Usage	
Tip	<del> and <ins> are unusual. They can operate either as inline or block elements, and can appear anywhere inside the <body> element.

Example	
See <del>	

isindex (deprecated)

Context	
Purpose	Create a single-line text input field for server-enabled searches
Start/End Tag	Required/Forbidden
Display	Inline
Classification	Block
Content	Empty

Attributes		
Required	**Optional**	**Deprecated**
	prompt = "prompt message"	

General

  ✓ Core (id, class, style, title)

  ✓ Internationalization (lang, dir)

    Standard Events (see end of appendix)

Usage	
Tip	Use a form instead.

Example
<isindex prompt="Search this site">

kbd

Context	
Purpose	Mark text as user input
Start/End Tag	Required/Required
Display	Inline

Continued

Classification	Inline
Content	Inline and text

Attributes	

General

- ✓ Core (id, class, style, title)
- ✓ Internationalization (lang, dir)
- ✓ Standard Events (see end of appendix)

Usage	
Tip	Usually rendered in monospace. For semantically similar content, see <code>, <samp>, and <var>.

Example
<p>In your browser's location bar, type <kbd>www.mydomain.com</kbd>.</p>

label

Context	
Purpose	Associate text with a form control
Start/End Tag	Required/Required
Display	Inline
Classification	Inline
Content	Inline or text

Attributes		
Required	**Optional**	**Deprecated**
	for = "control id"	
	accesskey = "key"	
	onfocus = "script"	
	onblur = "script"	

General

- ✓ Core (id, class, style, title)
- ✓ Internationalization (lang, dir)
- ✓ Standard Events (see end of appendix)

Usage	
Tip	This is very valuable for accessibility purposes. If the for attribute is not defined, the associated form control must be embedded in the <label> element.

Example

See <form>

legend

Context	
Purpose	Title for related form content
Start/End Tag	Required/Required
Display	Inline
Parent	<fieldset>
Content	Inline and text

Attributes		
Required	**Optional**	**Deprecated**
	accesskey = "key"	align = (top|bottom|left|right)

General

- ✓ Core (id, class, style, title)
- ✓ Internationalization (lang, dir)
- ✓ Standard Events (see end of appendix)

Usage	
Tip	Enhances accessibility by providing an explanation for the grouping of form content.

Example

See <form>

li

Context	
Purpose	Define an item in a list
Start/End Tag	Required/Optional
Display	Block
Parent	<ul>, <ol>, <dir>, <menu>
Content	Block, inline, and text

Continued

Attributes		
Required	**Optional**	**Deprecated**
		type = (1|a|A|i|I|disc|square|circle)
		value = "sequence number"

General

- ✓ Core (id, class, style, title)
- ✓ Internationalization (lang, dir)
- ✓ Standard Events (see end of appendix)

Usage	
Tip	The `value` attribute is intended to be replaced by automatic numbering in CSS, but support for that is currently spotty.

Example

See <ol>

link

Context	
Purpose	Describe an inter-document relationship
Start/End Tag	Required/Forbidden
Parent	<head>
Content	Empty

Attributes		
Required	**Optional**	**Deprecated**
	charset = "character set"	target = "frame"
	href = "URL"	
	hreflang = "language"	
	type = "MIME type"	
	rel = "relationship"	
	rev = "reverse relationship"	
	media = "media type"	

General

- ✓ Core (id, class, style, title)
- ✓ Internationalization (lang, dir)
- ✓ Standard Events (see end of appendix)

Usage	
Tip	Defining navigation links in a set of documents with meaningful linear navigation can dramatically enhance usability in those browsers that understand them.

Example	
See <head>	

map

Context	
Purpose	Create a client-side image map
Start/End Tag	Required/Required
Display	Inline
Classification	Inline
Content	Block and <area>

Attributes		
Required	**Optional**	**Deprecated**
name = "name"		

General

- ✓ Core (id, class, style, title)
- ✓ Internationalization (lang, dir)
- ✓ Standard Events (see end of appendix)

Usage	
Tip	Use <area shape="default"> to provide a fallback for the entire region, but make it the last <area> in the list or it will be the only one interpreted.

Example

```
<map name="site-overview">

 <area shape="rect" coords="10, 30, 70, 110" href="books.html" alt="Books for sale">

 <area shape="circle" coords="130,114,30" href="music.html" alt="Music online">

 <area shape="default" nohref alt="Site overview">

</map>
```

menu (deprecated)

Context	
Purpose	Create a single-column menu list
Start/End Tag	Required/Required
Display	Block
Classification	Block
Content	<li> elements that are constrained to contain inline content only

Attributes		
Required	**Optional**	**Deprecated**
	compact	

General

- ✓ Core (id, class, style, title)
- ✓ Internationalization (lang, dir)
- ✓ Standard Events (see end of appendix)

Usage	
Tip	Use <ul> instead.

Example

```
<menu>
  <li>...</li>
</menu>
```

meta

Context	
Purpose	Describe properties of a document
Start/End Tag	Required/Forbidden
Parent	<head>
Content	Empty

Attributes		
Required	**Optional**	**Deprecated**
content = "metadata value"	http-equiv = "HTTP header"	target = "frame"
	name = "metadata key"	
	scheme = "identifier"	

General	
	Core (id, class, style, title)
✓	Internationalization (lang, dir)
	Standard Events (see end of appendix)

Usage	
Tip	Any character encoding should be the first `<meta>` tag in the `<head>` element.

Example

See `<head>`

noframes

Context	
Purpose	Provide content for browsers that do not display frames
Start/End Tag	Required/Required
Display	Block
Classification	Block
Content	`<body>` (when used inside `<frameset>`), block, inline, and text

Attributes		
Required	**Optional**	**Deprecated**
	longdesc = "URL"	
	name = "frame name"	
	src = "URL"	
	frameborder = (1|0)	
	marginwidth = "number of pixels"	
	marginheight = "number of pixels"	
	noresize	
	scrolling = (yes|no|auto)	

General	
✓	Core (id, class, style, title)
✓	Internationalization (lang, dir)
✓	Standard Events (see end of appendix)

Continued

Usage	
Tip	Most commonly used as the last tag in a <frameset>, this may also be used in documents incorporated into a frame.

Example	
See <frameset>	

noscript

Context	
Purpose	Provide content for browsers that do not support scripting
Start/End Tag	Required/Required
Display	Block
Classification	Block
Content	Block, inline, and text

Attributes	

General

- ✓ Core (id, class, style, title)
- ✓ Internationalization (lang, dir)
- ✓ Standard Events (see end of appendix)

Usage	
Tip	If a script on the page provides important information, offer an alternative mechanism for obtaining the information.

Example	
See <script>	

object

Context	
Purpose	Incorporate an external media object such as an applet, movie, or image
Start/End Tag	Required/Required
Display	Block
Classification	Inline
Content	Block, inline, and text; any <param> elements must come first

	Attributes		
Required	**Optional**		**Deprecated**
	declare		align = (top|middle|bottom|left|right)
	classid = "URI"		border = "pixels"
	codebase = "URI"		hspace = "pixels"
	data = "URL"		vspace = "pixels"
	type = "object MIME type"		
	codetype = "code MIME type"		
	archive = "URI,…"		
	standby = "Load message"		
	height = "pixels or relative"		
	width = "pixels or relative"		
	usemap = "URI"		
	name = "form name"		
	tabindex = "sequence value"		

General

✓ Core (id, class, style, title)

✓ Internationalization (lang, dir)

✓ Standard Events (see end of appendix)

Usage

Tip	Nested <object> tags provide a fallback mechanism.

Example

```
<!-- Try, in order: an applet, a movie, an image, and if all else fails, some text. -->

<object title="Explore campus" classid="java:campusStroll.class"
codetype="application/java">

 <param name="startLocation" value="adminBldg">

 <object data="across-campus.mpeg" type="application/mpeg">

  <object data="campus-map.gif" type="image/gif">

    Please visit <a href="http://www.myschool.edu/campus/">our campus overview</a>
for a map and more details.

  </object>

 </object>

</object>
```

ol

Context	
Purpose	Create a numbered ("ordered") list
Start/End Tag	Required/Required
Display	Block
Classification	Block
Content	One or more <li> elements

Attributes		
Required	**Optional**	**Deprecated**
		type = (1|a|A|i|I)
		compact
		start = "start with number"

General

- ✓ Core (id, class, style, title)
- ✓ Internationalization (lang, dir)
- ✓ Standard Events (see end of appendix)

Usage	
Tip	Use CSS to define the numbering style.

Example

```
<ol style="list-style-type: lower-roman">
  <li>First item</li>
  <li>Second item</li>
</ol>
```

optgroup

Context	
Purpose	Group related <option> elements inside <select>
Start/End Tag	Required/Required
Parent	<select>
Content	One or more <option> elements

Attributes		
Required	**Optional**	**Deprecated**
label = "category label"	disabled	

General

✓ Core (id, class, style, title)

✓ Internationalization (lang, dir)

✓ Standard Events (see end of appendix)

Usage	
Tip	Future versions of HTML may allow for nested `<optgroup>` elements.

Example

See `<select>`

option

Context	
Purpose	Define an item in a selection list in a form
Start/End Tag	Required/Optional
Display	Inline
Parent	`<select>`, `<optgroup>`
Content	Text

Attributes		
Required	**Optional**	**Deprecated**
	selected	
	disabled	
	label = "shorter label"	
	value = "form value"	

General

✓ Core (id, class, style, title)

✓ Internationalization (lang, dir)

✓ Standard Events (see end of appendix)

Usage	
Tip	The value for the `label` attribute should be an extension of any enclosing `<optgroup>` `label`. The `<option>` contents should be the full name of the item.

Example

See `<select>`

p

Context	
Purpose	Define a paragraph of body text
Start/End Tag	Required/Optional
Display	Block
Classification	Block
Content	Inline and text

Attributes		
Required	**Optional**	**Deprecated**
		align = (left|center|right|justify)

General

✓ Core (id, class, style, title)

✓ Internationalization (lang, dir)

✓ Standard Events (see end of appendix)

Usage	
Tip	Using an empty <p> element to introduce a blank line is strongly discouraged.

Example

<p>Four score and seven years ago our fathers brought forth on this continent a new nation, conceived in liberty, and dedicated to the proposition that all men are created equal.</p>

param

Context	
Purpose	Provide run-time settings for an object
Start/End Tag	Required/Forbidden
Parent	<object>, <applet>
Content	Empty

Attributes		
Required	**Optional**	**Deprecated**
name = "property name"	id = "unique document id"	
	value = "property value"	
	valuetype = (data|ref|object)	
	type = "MIME type"	

Usage	
Tip	When used, this tag should be the first child of <object> or <applet>.

Example
See <object>

pre

Context	
Purpose	Define a block of text with preserved white space
Start/End Tag	Required/Required
Display	Block
Classification	Block
Content	Most inline tags and text

Attributes		
Required	**Optional**	**Deprecated**
		width = "number of characters"

General

- ✓ Core (id, class, style, title)
- ✓ Internationalization (lang, dir)
- ✓ Standard Events (see end of appendix)

Usage	
Tip	Using this tag does not eliminate the need to escape & and < characters.

Example

```
<pre>
There once was a man from Nantucket,

Who kept all of his cash in a bucket,

    But his daughter, named Nan,

    Ran away with a man,

And as for the bucket, Nantucket.

</pre>
```

q

Context	
Purpose	Mark in inline quotation
Start/End Tag	Required/Required
Display	Inline
Classification	Inline
Content	inline and text

Attributes		
Required	**Optional**	**Deprecated**
	cite = "URI"	

General

- ✓ Core (id, class, style, title)
- ✓ Internationalization (lang, dir)
- ✓ Standard Events (see end of appendix)

Usage	
Tip	Browsers must render enclosing quotation marks (but IE does not). See also <blockquote> for longer quotes.

Example

<p>Who said <q>A fool and his money are soon parted</q>?</p>

s (deprecated)

Context	
Purpose	Strike-through text
Start/End Tag	Required/Required
Display	Inline
Classification	Inline
Content	inline and text

Attributes	

General

- ✓ Core (id, class, style, title)
- ✓ Internationalization (lang, dir)
- ✓ Standard Events (see end of appendix)

Usage	
Tip	Use CSS instead: `text-decoration: line-through`.
Example	
See <strike>	

samp

Context	
Purpose	Identify computer output
Start/End Tag	Required/Required
Display	Inline
Classification	Inline
Content	inline and text

Attributes	

General

- ✓ Core (id, class, style, title)
- ✓ Internationalization (lang, dir)
- ✓ Standard Events (see end of appendix)

Usage	
Tip	Typically rendered in a monospace font.
Example	
Wait until you see <samp>fatal error</samp> on the screen; then panic.	

script

Context	
Purpose	Contain a script
Start/End Tag	Required/Required
Classification	Inline (but can also be contained in <head>)
Content	Text

Attributes	

Continued

Required	Optional	Deprecated
type = "MIME type"	charset = "character encoding"	language = " language name"
	src = "URL"	
	defer	

General

✓ Core (id, class, style, title)

✓ Internationalization (lang, dir)

✓ Standard Events (see end of appendix)

Usage	
Tip	Hide your script within comment tags so that it won't be displayed by older browsers. Some browsers end comments at the first > character, so escape any occurrences of that character using the syntax of the scripting language if possible.

Example

```
<script type="text/javascript">
 <!--
 document.write("This could easily be statically defined text!");
 -->
</script>
<noscript>
 This could easily be statically defined text (and is!)
<noscript>
```

select

Context	
Purpose	Define a selection of form items
Start/End Tag	Required/Required
Display	Inline
Classification	Inline
Content	One or more of <optgroup> and/or <option>
Attributes	

Required	Optional	Deprecated
	name = "form name"	
	size = "visible rows"	
	multiple	
	disabled	
	tabindex = "sequence value"	
	onfocus = "script"	
	onblur= "script"	
	onchange = "script"	

General

✓ Core (id, class, style, title)

✓ Internationalization (lang, dir)

✓ Standard Events (see end of appendix)

Usage

Tip   In the absence of a pre-defined default option (through the `selected` attribute), browser behavior varies. Always define a default selection.

Example

```
<form action="http://www.mydomain.com/cgi-bin/handle-input.cgi">
 <p>
 <select name="moss">
  <optgroup label="Hypnum">
   <option label="strigosum" value="hypnum-strigosum">Hypnum strigosum</option>
   <option label="strumiferum" value="hypnum-strumiferum">Hypnum strumiferum
</option>
   <option label="strumosum" value="hypnum-strumosum">Hypnum strumosum</option>
  </optgroup>
  <optgroup label="Lembophyllum">
   <option label="porotrichoides" value="lembophyllum-porotrichoides">Lembophyllum
porotrichoides</option>
   <option label="vagum" value="lembophyllum-vagum">Lembophyllum vagum</option>
  </optgroup>
 </select>
 </p>
</form>
```

small

Context	
Purpose	Display text in a small font
Start/End Tag	Required/Required
Display	Inline
Classification	Inline
Content	inline and text

Attributes	

General

- ✓ Core (id, class, style, title)
- ✓ Internationalization (lang, dir)
- ✓ Standard Events (see end of appendix)

Usage	
Tip	Be careful to close this element properly, and don't overlap with similar tags like <b>. Nest them instead.

Example

<b>This is bold, <small>this is small and bold</small>.</b>

span

Context	
Purpose	Generic inline container
Start/End Tag	Required/Required
Display	Inline
Classification	Inline
Content	inline and text

Attributes	

General

- ✓ Core (id, class, style, title)
- ✓ Internationalization (lang, dir)
- ✓ Standard Events (see end of appendix)

Usage	

Tip	<div> (a block) and <span> (an inline) provide a convenient grouping mechanism for applying CSS style. Use the `class` attribute for the CSS selectors.

Example

See <strike>

strike (deprecated)

Context	
Purpose	Strike-through text
Start/End Tag	Required/Required
Display	Inline
Classification	Inline
Content	inline and text

Attributes	

General

- ✓ Core (id, class, style, title)
- ✓ Internationalization (lang, dir)
- ✓ Standard Events (see end of appendix)

Usage	
Tip	Use CSS instead – `text-decoration: line-through`.

Example

<p><span style="text-decoration: line-through">This</span>, <strike>This</strike>, and <s>This</s> should render the same.</p>

strong

Context	
Purpose	Strong emphasis
Start/End Tag	Required/Required
Display	Inline
Classification	Inline
Content	inline and text

Continued

Attributes

General

- ✓ Core (id, class, style, title)
- ✓ Internationalization (lang, dir)
- ✓ Standard Events (see end of appendix)

Usage

Tip	Typically rendered in bold.

Example

`<p><em>Stop</em>, or I'll say <strong>stop</strong> again!</p>`

style

Context

Purpose	Define styles to be used in a document
Start/End Tag	Required/Required
Parent	<head>
Content	Text

Attributes

Required	**Optional**	**Deprecated**
type = "MIME type"	media = "type, …"	
	title = "label"	

General

- ✓ Core (id, class, style, title)
- ✓ Internationalization (lang, dir)
- ✓ Standard Events (see end of appendix)

Usage

Tip	For styles common to multiple documents, consider using an external stylesheet referenced by <link> instead.

Example

See <div>

sub, sup

Context	
Purpose	Subscripted (<sub>) or superscripted (<sup>) text
Start/End Tag	Required/Required
Display	Inline
Classification	Inline
Content	Inline and text

Attributes	

General

- ✓ Core (id, class, style, title)
- ✓ Internationalization (lang, dir)
- ✓ Standard Events (see end of appendix)

Usage	
Tip	It is difficult to render non-trivial mathematical text in HTML; MathML helps to address the problem.

Example

<p>The amount of energy gained by converting water (H₂O) to energy would follow Einstein's <tt>E = mc²</tt> equation.</p>

table

Context	
Purpose	Create a table
Start/End Tag	Required/Required
Display	Block
Classification	Block
Content	An optional <caption>, zero or more <col> or <colgroup> tags, optional <thead> and <tfoot>, and at least one <tbody> (which has optional start and end tags).

Attributes		

Required	**Optional**	**Deprecated**
	summary = "description"	align = (left|center|right)
	width = "pixels or relative"	bgcolor= "color"

Continued

border = "pixels"

frame = (void|above|below|hsides|
lhs|rhs|vsides|box|border)

rules = (none|groups|rows|cols|all)

cellspacing = "pixels or relative"

cellpadding = "pixels or relative"

General

✓ Core (id, class, style, title)

✓ Internationalization (lang, dir)

✓ Standard Events (see end of appendix)

Usage

Tip   Use the `summary` attribute to describe the structure
                           and content for speech and Braille browsers.

Example

<table rules="cols" summary="Lists the current office-holders in various nations; first column is those nations, second is the president, third is the prime minister">

<caption>Selected Governments in the Americas and Europe</caption>

<colgroup span="1" align="left">

<colgroup><col align="center"><col align="center"></colgroup>

<thead>

  <tr><th scope="col">Country</th><th scope="col">President</th>

      <th scope="col">Prime Minister</th></tr>

</thead>

<tfoot>

 <tr>

  <th scope="row">Governments Represented</th>

  <td>3</td><td>1</td>

 </tr>

</tfoot>

<tbody>

 <tr>

  <td scope="row">Argentina</th>

  <td>Eduardo Alberto Duhalde</td><td></td>

 </tr>

```
  <tr>
    <td scope="row">France</th>
    <td>Jacques Chirac</td><td>Jean-Pierre Raffarin</td>
  </tr>
  <tr>
    <td scope="row">United States</th>
    <td>George W. Bush</td><td></td>
  </tr>
  </tbody>
</table>
```

tbody

Context	
Purpose	Define the body of a table separate from any header or footer
Start/End Tag	Optional/Optional
Parent	<table>
Content	<tr>

Attributes		
Required	**Optional**	**Deprecated**
	align = (left|center|right|justify|char)	
	char = "alignment character"	
	charoff = "pixels or relative"	
	valign = (top|middle|bottom|baseline)	

General

- ✓ Core (id, class, style, title)
- ✓ Internationalization (lang, dir)
- ✓ Standard Events (see end of appendix)

Usage	
Tip	Using <thead>, <tfoot>, and <tbody> allows browsers to intelligently place the header and footer of a table if the table spans multiple pages.

Example

See <table>

td

Context	
Purpose	Define a table cell
Start/End Tag	Required/Optional
Parent	<tr>
Content	Block, inline, and text.

Attributes

Required	Optional	Deprecated
	abbr = "abbreviation"	nowrap
	axis = "category,..."	bgcolor = "color"
	headers = "idref,..."	width = "pixels or relative"
	scope = (row|col|rowgroup|colgroup)	height = "pixels or relative"
	rowspan = "number"	
	colspan = "number"	
	align = (left|center|right|justify|char)	
	char = "alignment character"	
	charoff = "pixels or relative"	
	valign = (top|middle|bottom|baseline)	

General

- ✓ Core (id, class, style, title)
- ✓ Internationalization (lang, dir)
- ✓ Standard Events (see end of appendix)

Usage	
Tip	If a cell acts as both header and data, use <td> instead of <th>.
Example	
See <table>	

textarea

Context	
Purpose	Create a multiline text entry box
Start/End Tag	Required/Required
Display	Inline

Classification	Inline
Content	Text

Attributes		
Required	**Optional**	**Deprecated**
rows = "number"	name = "form name"	
cols = "number"	disabled	
	readonly	
	tabindex = "sequence value"	
	accesskey = "key"	
	onfocus = "script"	
	onblur = "script"	
	onselect = "script"	
	onchange = "script"	

General

✓ Core (id, class, style, title)

✓ Internationalization (lang, dir)

✓ Standard Events (see end of appendix)

Usage	
Tip	Use <input type="text"> to create a one-line text box.

Example

<textarea rows="6" cols="50" name="comments">Replace this text with any comments you have.</textarea>

tfoot

Context	
Purpose	Create a table footer
Start/End Tag	Required/Optional
Parent	<table>
Content	<tr>

Attributes

Continued

Required	Optional	Deprecated
	align = (left|center|right|justify|char)	
	char = "alignment character"	
	charoff = "pixels or relative"	
	valign = (top|middle|bottom|baseline)	

General

- ✓ Core (id, class, style, title)
- ✓ Internationalization (lang, dir)
- ✓ Standard Events (see end of appendix)

Usage	
Tip	<tfoot> must precede <tbody>

Example	
See <table>	

th

Context	
Purpose	Define a table header cell
Start/End Tag	Required/Optional
Parent	<tr>
Content	Block, inline, and text

Attributes		
Required	**Optional**	**Deprecated**
	abbr = "abbreviation"	nowrap
	axis = "category, ..."	bgcolor = "color"
	headers = "idref, ..."	width = "pixels or relative"
	scope = (row|col|rowgroup|colgroup)	height = "pixels or relative"
	rowspan = "number"	
	colspan = "number"	
	align = (left|center|right|justify|char)	
	char = "alignment character"	
	charoff = "pixels or relative"	
	valign = (top|middle|bottom|baseline)	

General

- ✓ Core (id, class, style, title)
- ✓ Internationalization (lang, dir)
- ✓ Standard Events (see end of appendix)

Usage

Tip	Providing an abbreviation via the `abbr` attribute allows speech renderers to provide that abbreviation before each data cell. Use the `scope` attribute to specify the data cells to which this header applies.

Example

See <table>

---

thead

Context	
Purpose	Create a table header that browsers can place intelligently when dealing with long tables
Start/End Tag	Required/Optional
Parent	<table>
Content	<tr>

Attributes

Required	Optional	Deprecated
	align = (left|center|right|justify|char)	
	char = "alignment character"	
	charoff = "pixels or relative"	
	valign = (top|middle|bottom|baseline)	

General

- ✓ Core (id, class, style, title)
- ✓ Internationalization (lang, dir)
- ✓ Standard Events (see end of appendix)

Usage

Tip	Using <thead>, <tfoot>, and <tbody> allows browsers to intelligently place the header and footer of a table if the table spans multiple pages.

Example

See <table>

title

Context	
Purpose	Provide a caption for the document that is typically not directly rendered as part of the page
Start/End Tag	Required/Required
Parent	\<head\>
Content	Text

Attributes	
General	

      Core (id, class, style, title)

✓ Internationalization (lang, dir)

      Standard Events (see end of appendix)

Usage	
Tip	Provide a meaningful title to make search results easier to decipher and help a user orient him/herself.

Example

See \<head\>

tr

Context	
Purpose	Define a row in the table
Start/End Tag	Required/Optional
Parent	\<thead\>, \<tfoot\>, \<tbody\>
Content	\<th\>, \<td\>

Attributes		
Required	**Optional**	**Deprecated**
	align = (left|center|right|justify|char)	bgcolor = "color"
	char = "alignment character"	
	charoff = "pixels or relative"	
	valign = (top|middle|bottom|baseline)	

General

✓ Core (id, class, style, title)

✓ Internationalization (lang, dir)

✓ Standard Events (see end of appendix)

Usage	
Tip	If the first column is a header, use <th scope="row"> for that cell.
Example	
See <head>	

tt

Context	
Purpose	Monospaced ("teletype") text
Start/End Tag	Required/Required
Display	Inline
Classification	Inline
Content	Inline and text

Attributes	

General

- ✓ Core (id, class, style, title)
- ✓ Internationalization (lang, dir)
- ✓ Standard Events (see end of appendix)

Usage	
Tip	Typically renders like <code>, <kbd>, <samp>, and <var>, but conveys no semantic information.
Example	
<p>The top row of letters on a computer keyboard is <tt>qwertyuiop</tt>.</p>	

u (deprecated)

Context	
Purpose	Underline text
Start/End Tag	Required/Required
Display	Inline
Classification	Inline
Content	Inline and text

Continued

Attributes		

General

✓ Core (id, class, style, title)

✓ Internationalization (lang, dir)

✓ Standard Events (see end of appendix)

Usage	

Tip   Use CSS instead -- `text-decoration: underline`.

Example

`<p><span style="text-decoration: underline">This</span> and <u>This</u> should render the same.</p>`

ul

Context	
Purpose	Create a bullet list
Start/End Tag	Required/Required
Display	Block
Classification	Block
Content	One or more <li> elements

Attributes		
Required	**Optional**	**Deprecated**
		type = (disc|square|circle) compact

General

✓ Core (id, class, style, title)

✓ Internationalization (lang, dir)

✓ Standard Events (see end of appendix)

Usage	

Tip   Use CSS to define the bullet style.

Example

```
<ul style="list-style-type: square">
  <li>One item</li>
  <li>Another item</li>
</ul>
```

var

Context	
Purpose	Indicate an instance of some replaceable value, such as a variable or argument to a program
Start/End Tag	Required/Required
Display	Inline
Classification	Inline
Content	Inline and text
Attributes	

General

✓ Core (id, class, style, title)

✓ Internationalization (lang, dir)

✓ Standard Events (see end of appendix)

Usage	
Tip	Typically renders as monospaced text.
Example	

`<p>Set the <var>CLASSPATH</var> environment variable to run a Java application.</p>`

Event Attributes
Standard Events

The standard event attributes:

Attribute	Triggered By
onclick	Pointer button was clicked
ondblclick	Pointer button was double clicked
onmousedown	Pointer button was pressed down
onmouseup	Pointer button was released
onmouseover	Pointer was moved into
onmousemove	Pointer was moved within
onmouseout	Pointer was moved away
onkeypress	Key was pressed and released
onkeydown	Key was pressed
onkeyup	Key was released

Other Events

Less-common event attributes:

Attribute	Triggered By
onload	Document has been loaded
onunload	Document was been removed
onblur	Element lost focus
onfocus	Element gained focus
onreset	Form was reset
onsubmit	Form was submitted
onchange	Form element value changed
onselect	Text in a form field has been selected

Other Common Attributes
Core Attributes

Attribute	Description
id	ID value unique to this document
class	Space-separated list of classes useful for selecting this element for style and other purposes
style	Local style information
title	Advisory title, typically rendered by a graphical browser when the pointer is over the element

Internationalization Attributes

Attribute	Description
lang	Language code for this element's contents
dir	Direction (ltr or rtl) for the text

CSS Properties

This appendix provides a laundry list of sorts of CSS properties with which you may need to be familiar at some point.

Browser Support

Historically, CSS support in browsers has been erratic. To help developers and browser implementors navigate these troubled waters, the W3C has issued a CSS 2.1 specification that reflects a survey of modern browsers; this appendix is drawn from that specification.

For additional information about property support, go to www.blooberry.com; it's a valuable resource. Brian Wilson has posted the results of his extensive testing of some of the major browsers (Internet Explorer, Netscape, and Opera).

For many properties, it is sufficient to determine whether they are supported by your target browsers, but, particularly for the positioning properties, testing on as many browsers as reasonable is highly recommended. You have at least four modern rendering engines to consider:

✦ Internet Explorer for Windows

✦ Gecko (as seen in Mozilla, Netscape 6/7, and several other browsers)

✦ Konqueror (the browser re-used by Apple as Safari)

✦ Opera

Note   Internet Explorer 5.2 for the Macintosh is apparently different (and significantly more standards-compliant) from the then-current Windows versions, but has been abandoned by Microsoft and supplanted by Safari.

Key to the Property Summaries

Regardless of whether a CSS property is automatically inherited, the value `inherit` is always valid, and thus is not repeated for each property in this appendix.

Examples have not been provided for the many properties that allow for only one value and will always be represented as `<property-name>:<value>`. Exceptions are made for cases where the value may be open-ended or otherwise ambiguous.

The value `<length>` is shorthand for a number followed by "pt", "em", or "ex", for points, em-units, or ex-units. `<percentage>` is shorthand for a number followed by a percent sign; typically this is a percentage of the enclosing box size or current font size, but the context is indicated where it may be ambiguous or not obvious.

The color mnemonics defined by the CSS specification are as follows:

✦ aqua

✦ black

✦ blue

✦ fuchsia

✦ gray

✦ green

✦ lime

✦ maroon

✦ navy

✦ olive

✦ orange

✦ purple

✦ red

✦ silver

✦ teal

✦ white

✦ yellow

Color codes are taken from the RGB color model, and are represented as hexadecimal, base 10, or percentage values:

✦ #f0f or #ff00ff

✦ rgb(255, 0, 255)

✦ rgb(100%, 0%, 100%)

Background and Color Properties

color

Purpose	Specify the foreground color of an element
Inherited	Yes
Values	Color code or mnemonic
Default	Defined by browser
Used In	All elements
Example	{color: #C0C0C0} or {color: red}

background

Purpose	Shorthand method for background properties
Inherited	Yes
Values	See values for background-color, background-image, background-repeat, background-attachment, and background-position
Default	See individual properties
Used In	All elements
Example	{background: url("picture.gif") repeat fixed}

background-attachment

Purpose	Define whether the background image is fixed in the viewport or scrolls
Inherited	No
Values	scroll, fixed
Default	scroll
Used In	All elements

background-color

Purpose	Specify the background color of an element
Inherited	Yes

Continued

Values	Color code or mnemonic
Default	Transparent
Used In	All elements
Example	{background-color: #C0C0C0} or {background-color: red}

background-image

Purpose	Insert a graphic in an element's background
Inherited	Yes
Values	<url>
Default	None
Used In	All elements
Example	{background-image: url ("/images/bg.jpg")}
Tip	The URL may be any of the usual forms: relative and absolute, with or without a server name and protocol scheme

background-position

Purpose	Define the position of a graphic in an element's background
Inherited	No
Values	top left, top center, right top, left center, center, right center, bottom left, bottom center, bottom right <percentage> <percentage> (expressing the distance from the left and top) <length> <length> (from the left and top)
Default	0% 0%
Used In	All elements
Example	{background-position: top center} {background-position: 50% 0%} {background position: 48pt 60pt}

background-repeat

Purpose	Specify whether the background image is tiled
Inherited	No
Values	repeat-x, repeat-y, repeat, no-repeat
Default	repeat
Used In	All elements

Box Properties

border

Purpose	Shorthand method for border properties
Inherited	No
Values	See values for border-width, border-style, and border-color.
Default	See individual properties
Used In	All elements
Example	`{border: 1pt inset blue}`

border-color

Purpose	Shorthand method for border colors
Inherited	No
Values	Colors for border-top, border-right, border-bottom, and border-left
Default	The value of the `color` property
Used In	All elements
Example	`{border-color: red}`
Tip	If one value is provided, it applies to all four borders. If two, then the first will apply to top and bottom, the second to left and right. If three: top, right/left, bottom. If four: top, right, bottom, left.

border-{bottom|left|right|top}-color

Purpose	Specify a border side color
Inherited	No

Continued

Values	Color code or mnemonic
Default	The value of the `color` property
Used In	All elements
Example	`{border-right-color: red}`

border-style

Purpose	Shorthand method for border styles
Inherited	No
Values	Styles for border-top, border-right, border-bottom, and border-left
Default	none
Used In	All elements
Example	`{border-style: double solid}`
Tip	See `border-color` for the rules on how different numbers of values apply.

border-{bottom|left|right|top}-style

Purpose	Specify a border side style
Inherited	No
Values	none, hidden, dotted, dashed, solid, double, groove, ridge, inset, outset
Default	none
Used In	All elements
Example	`{border-top-style: ridge}`

border-width

Purpose	Shorthand method for border widths
Inherited	No
Values	Widths for border-top, border-right, border-bottom, and border-left
Default	medium
Used In	All elements

Example	{border-width: thin}
Tip	See border-color for the rules on how different numbers of values apply.

border-{bottom|left|right|top}-width

Purpose	Specify a border side width
Inherited	No
Values	thin, medium, thick, <length>
Default	medium
Used In	All elements
Example	{border-left-width: 2em}

border-{bottom|left|right|top}

Purpose	Shorthand method for border styles
Inherited	No
Values	Styles for border-width, border-style, border-color
Default	See individual properties
Used In	All elements
Example	{border-left: 2em solid blue}
Tip	See border-color for the rules on how different numbers of values apply.

height

Purpose	Specify the height of an element
Inherited	No
Values	<length>, <percentage>, auto
Default	auto
Used In	Block, inline-block, and replaced elements
Example	{height: 50%}
Tip	A percentage value is calculated relative to the containing element.

max-height

Purpose	Specify the maximum height of an element
Inherited	No
Values	\<length\>, \<percentage\>, none
Default	none
Used In	Block, inline-block, and replaced elements
Example	{max-height: 8em}
Tip	A percentage value is calculated relative to the containing element

min-height

Purpose	Specify the minimum height of an element
Inherited	No
Values	\<length\>, \<percentage\>
Default	0
Used In	Block, inline-block, and replaced elements
Example	{min-height: 2pt}
Tip	A percentage value is calculated relative to the containing element

width

Purpose	Specify the width of an element
Inherited	No
Values	\<length\>, \<percentage\>, auto
Default	auto
Used In	Block, inline-block, and replaced elements
Example	{width: 25%}
Tip	A percentage value is calculated relative to the containing element

max-width

Purpose	Specify the maximum width of an element
Inherited	No

Values	<length>, <percentage>, none
Default	none
Used In	Block, inline-block, and replaced elements
Example	{max-width: 25em}
Tip	A percentage value is calculated relative to the containing element

min-width

Purpose	Specify the minimum width of an element
Inherited	No
Values	<length>, <percentage>
Default	0
Used In	Block, inline-block, and replaced elements
Example	{min-width: 10pt}
Tip	A percentage value is calculated relative to the containing element

margin

Purpose	Shorthand method for margin widths
Inherited	No
Values	Widths for margin-top, margin-right, margin-bottom, and margin-left
Default	0
Used In	All elements except for grouping table elements (such as <tr> and <colgroup>).
Example	{margin: 3em 2em}
Tip	See border-color for the rules on how different numbers of values apply

margin-{bottom|left|right|top}

Purpose	Specify a margin side width
Inherited	No

Continued

Values	\<length>, \<percentage>, auto
Default	0
Used In	All elements except for grouping table elements (such as \<tr> and \<colgroup>)
Example	{margin-left: 5em}
Tip	When deciding whether to use margin or padding, it is helpful to visualize a border around the element: space inside the border is padding, outside is margin

padding

Purpose	Shorthand method for padding widths
Inherited	No
Values	Widths for padding-top, padding-right, padding-bottom, and padding-left
Default	0
Used In	All elements except for grouping table elements (such as \<tr> and \<colgroup>)
Example	{padding: 3em 0}
Tip	See border-color for the rules on how different numbers of values apply

padding-{bottom|left|right|top}

Purpose	Specify a padding side width
Inherited	No
Values	\<length>, \<percentage>, auto
Default	0
Used In	All elements except for grouping table elements (such as \<tr> and \<colgroup>)
Example	{padding-left: 5em}
Tip	When deciding whether to use margin or padding, it is helpful to envision a border around the element: space inside the border is padding, outside is margin

Display Properties

clip

Purpose	Define an element's clipping region
Inherited	No
Values	auto—No clipping
	rect(\<top\>, \<right\>, \<bottom\>, \<left\>)—Border offsets
Default	auto
Used In	Absolutely positioned elements
Example	`{clip: rect(auto, 30px, 40px, auto)}`
Tip	The above example indicates that the clipping should be performed 30px to the right of the left border and 40px below the top border

cursor

Purpose	Define the mouse pointer appearance while over an element
Inherited	Yes
Values	\<url\>, auto, crosshair, default, pointer, move, {e|ne|nw|n|se|sw|s|w}-resize, text, wait, help, progress
Default	auto
Used In	All elements
Example	`{cursor: url(/images/pointer.png), crosshair}`
Tip	Any number of URLs may be provided; the browser will try each in order until it finds one that it supports. In the above example, if the pointer image doesn't work, crosshair will be the fallback.
	In practice, only IE seems to behave properly; Netscape and Safari will neither use the URL nor proceed to successive items in the list

display

Purpose	Specify the rendering class in which this element belongs
Inherited	No
Values	inline, block, list-item, run-in, inline-block, table, inline-table, table-row-group, table-header-group, table-footer-group, table-row, table-column-group, table-column, table-cell, table-caption, none
Default	inline
Used In	All elements
Tip	This property is most commonly used in HTML to remove an element from the document flow. See also the `visibility` property It can also be used to categorize XML elements so that browsers know how to handle them

outline

Purpose	Shorthand method for outline properties
Inherited	No
Values	See values for outline-color, outline-style, outline-width
Default	See individual properties
Used In	All elements
Example	`{outline: red groove thin}`
Tip	Outlines are very similar to borders, with key differences: the outline occupies no space in the flow model, and it reflects the content (and thus may not be a rectangle)

outline-color

Purpose	Set a color for an outline
Inherited	No
Values	<color>, invert
Default	invert
Used In	All elements
Tip	Invert tells the browser to perform a color inversion on the normal background color

outline-style

Purpose	Specify a style for an outline
Inherited	No
Values	Same as border-style (except hidden is not legal)
Default	none
Used In	All elements

outline-width

Purpose	Specify a width for an outline
Inherited	No
Values	Same as border-width
Default	medium
Used In	All elements

overflow

Purpose	Specify whether content should be clipped when it overflows its container
Inherited	No
Values	visible, hidden, scroll, auto
Default	visible
Used In	Block and replaced elements
Tip	scroll should result in a scrollbar regardless of whether the content overflows. auto is browser-defined

visibility

Purpose	Specify whether an element should be visible
Inherited	Yes
Values	visible, hidden, collapse
Default	visible
Used In	All elements
Tip	Setting an element to hidden does not remove it from the document flow; use display: none to achieve that

Font Properties

font

Purpose	Shorthand method for font properties
Inherited	Yes
Values	Values for these properties: font-style, font-variant, font-weight, font-size, line-height, and font-family
	Additional values (representing system fonts): caption, icon, menu, message-box, small-caption, status-bar
Default	See individual properties
Used In	All elements
Example	`{font: 14pt Arial, Helvetica, sans-serif bold}`
Tip	Note that the commas are only used to express a list for the `font-family` property; other values are not comma-separated

font-family

Purpose	Define preferred font and fallbacks
Inherited	Yes
Values	family or generic (serif, sans-serif, cursive, fantasy, monospace)
Default	Determined by browser
Used In	All elements
Example	`{font-family: "Times Roman", sans-serif}`
Tip	Use quotes for any font that requires two or more words. Conversely, don't use quotes around the generic family names; to do so indicates that the name refers to a specific font family

font-size

Purpose	Specify a font size
Inherited	Yes
Values	\<length\>, \<percentage\>, or one of:
	Absolute: xx-small, x-small, small, medium, large, x-large, xx-large
	Relative: larger, smaller
Default	medium
Used In	All elements

font-style

Purpose	Specify the face for the current font
Inherited	Yes
Values	normal, italic, oblique
Default	normal
Used In	All elements

font-variant

Purpose	Allow for a small capital font
Inherited	Yes
Values	normal, small-caps
Default	normal
Used In	All elements

font-weight

Purpose	Determine weight (boldness)
Inherited	Yes
Values	normal, bold, bolder, lighter, 100 (lightest), 200, 300, 400 (equivalent to normal), 500, 600, 700 (equivalent to bold), 800, 900 (darkest)
Default	normal
Used In	All elements

Positioning Properties

Using these properties in place of tables for layout enhances accessibility and maintainability, but requires care and extensive testing due to browser quirks.

bottom, left, right, top

Purpose	Specify an offset from one edge of a positioned element's reference box
Inherited	Yes
Values	<length>, <percentage>, auto

Continued

Default	auto
Used In	Positioned elements
Tip	A positioned element is one whose position property is defined to something other than the default, static.

clear

Purpose	Declare whether an element will forbid floating elements to either side
Inherited	No
Values	none, left, right, both
Default	none
Used In	Block elements

float

Purpose	Float an element to the left or right, allowing text to flow around it to the other side
Inherited	No
Values	none, left, right
Default	none
Used In	All elements

position

Purpose	Determines whether an element flows with the text (static), occupies a fixed position (absolute or fixed), or is offset from the position it would occupy were it static (relative).
Inherited	No
Values	static, relative, absolute, fixed
Default	static
Used In	All elements
Tip	The difference between fixed and absolute is that a fixed element will not scroll.
	The next box after a relative element will flow as if the previous one were static. Elements that are absolute or fixed are not part of the document flow at all.

z-index

Purpose	Specify the position of an element in a three-dimensional stack (back to front)
Inherited	No
Values	auto, <integer>
Default	auto
Used In	Positioned elements
Example	{z-index: 3}
Tip	Use this when boxes may overlap to define which boxes are closer to the front. Smaller numbers are further away from the user; negative values are allowed

Text Properties

direction

Purpose	Define the direction (right to left, or left to right) of the contained text
Inherited	Yes
Values	ltr, rtl
Default	ltr
Used In	All elements

line-height

Purpose	Specify the distance between the baselines of each line of text in an element
Inherited	Yes
Values	normal, <number> (multiple of the font height), <length>, <percentage> (of the font height)
Default	normal
Used In	All elements
Example	{line-height: 2.5} and {line-height: 250%} are equivalent

letter-spacing, word-spacing

Purpose	Add to the default spacing between characters (letter-spacing) or words (word-spacing)
Inherited	Yes
Values	normal, <length> (to be added to the normal spacing)
Default	normal
Used In	All elements

text-align

Purpose	Control horizontal alignment of inline content
Inherited	Yes
Values	left, right, center, justify
Default	left (unless `direction` is `rtl`)
Used In	Block elements

text-decoration

Purpose	Add decorations (such as strikethrough) to text
Inherited	No
Values	none, underline, overline, line-through, blink
Default	none
Used In	All elements
Tip	Browsers are permitted to ignore the `blink` value (and developers are encouraged to do the same)

text-indent

Purpose	Indent the first line of text
Inherited	Yes
Values	<length>, <percentage>
Default	0
Used In	Block elements

text-transform

Purpose	Change case
Inherited	Yes
Values	capitalize, uppercase, lowercase, none
Default	none
Used In	All elements
Tip	The `capitalize` value will only transform the first character of each word. Both `uppercase` and `lowercase` affect all characters

unicode-bidi

Purpose	Describe how to handle embedded text per the Unicode bidirectionality (bidi) algorithm
Inherited	Yes
Values	normal, embed, bidi-override
Default	normal
Used In	All elements

white-space

Purpose	Control white space handling
Inherited	Yes
Values	normal—Collapse white space, break lines as needed
	pre—Don't collapse whitespace, break only at explicitly line breaks
	nowrap—Collapse whitespace, suppress line breaks in the source
	pre-wrap—Don't collapse whitespace, break lines as needed
	pre-line—Collapse whitespace, break lines as needed and as found in the source
Default	normal
Used In	All elements

vertical-align

Purpose	Control the vertical position of an element relative to the current text baseline
Inherited	No
Values	baseline—Match the baseline with the element's parent's
	middle—Place the vertical midpoint at the parent's baseline
	sub—Subscript
	super—Superscript
	text-top—Top of the box should align with the top of the parent's font
	text-bottom—Bottom of the box should align with the bottom of the parent's font
Default	baseline
Used In	All elements

List Properties

list-style

Purpose	Shorthand method for list styles
Inherited	Yes
Values	Styles for list-style-type, list-style-position, list-style-image
Default	See individual properties
Used In	Elements with `display: list-item`
Example	`{list-style: upper-roman inside}`
Tip	These styles can often be used to preserve list semantics while changing the appearance instead of using elements to create an ad hoc list

list-style-image

Purpose	Replace the bullet in an unordered list with a graphic
Inherited	Yes
Values	<url>, none
Default	none
Used In	Elements with `display: list-item`

list-style-position

Purpose	Place the list-item marker (bullet or number) relative to the content
Inherited	Yes
Values	inside (the content box), outside (same)
Default	outside
Used In	Elements with `display: list-item`

list-style-type

Purpose	Specify the marker style
Inherited	Yes
Values	disc, circle, square—Glyphs for unordered content
	decimal—Decimal numbers
	decimal-leading-zero—Decimals padded with initial zeroes
	lower-roman—Lowercase roman numerals
	upper-roman—Uppercase roman numerals
	lower-latin/lower-alpha—Lowercase letters
	upper-latin/upper-alpha—Uppercase letters
	lower-greek—Lowercase Greek letters
	georgian—Georgian numbering
	armenian—Armenian
Default	outside
Used In	Elements with `display: list-item`

Table Properties

border-collapse

Purpose	Indicate whether table elements should have overlapping or separate borders
Inherited	Yes
Values	collapse, separate
Default	separate
Used In	Table and inline-table elements
Tip	Use `border-spacing` to define the amount of separation

border-spacing

Purpose	Shorthand method for border widths
Inherited	Yes
Values	<length>
Default	0
Used In	Table and inline-table elements
Example	{border-spacing: 2pt}
Tip	Only applicable if border-collapse is set to separate

caption-side

Purpose	Place a table's caption at the head or foot
Inherited	Yes
Values	top, bottom
Default	top
Used In	Table elements

empty-cells

Purpose	Show or hide backgrounds and borders of empty table cells
Inherited	Yes
Values	show, hide
Default	show
Used In	Table elements
Tip	If an entire row is composed of empty cells and this attribute is set to hide, the net effect should be comparable to display: none

table-layout

Purpose	Select a table generation algorithm
Inherited	No
Values	auto—Scan the entire table before determining the horizontal layout
	fixed—Decide on the horizontal layout after the first row

Default	auto
Used In	Table elements
Tip	If a row after the first has more columns than previously seen, the behavior is undefined

Generated Content

No version of Internet Explorer supports any of these properties. Opera is the only major browser that supports all of them.

content

Purpose	Generate content for `:before` and `:after` pseudo-elements
Inherited	No
Values	normal—No content
	\<string>—Text to be inserted
	\<uri>—An external resource
	\<counter>—Content generated from counter() or counters()
	attr(\<attribute name>)—The value of the attribute by that name on this element
	open-quote/close-quote—Values from the `quotes` property
	no-open-quote/no-close-quote—No content, but appropriately adjusts the level of nesting for quotes
Default	normal
Used In	`:before` and `:after` pseudo-elements
Example	acronym:after {content: " (" attr(title) ")"}

counter-increment

Purpose	Increment a counter for use by `counter()` or `counters()`
Inherited	No
Values	\<identifier> \<optional integer>, none
Default	none
Used In	All elements
Example	{counter-increment: section}

counter-reset

Purpose	Reset a counter for use by `counter()` or `counters()`
Inherited	No
Values	<identifier> <optional integer>, none
Default	none
Used In	All elements
Example	`{counter-reset: section -1}`

quotes

Purpose	Define pairs of open and close quote strings for use by the content property
Inherited	Yes
Values	<open quote string> <close quote string>
Default	Browser defined
Used In	All elements
Example	`{quotes: '"' '"' '"' '"'}`

Printing Properties

page-break-{after|before|inside}

Purpose	Insert a page break after (or before, or inside) the element
Inherited	No
Values	auto—Neither force nor forbid
	always—Mandatory page break
	avoid—Encourage the browser to not insert a page break
	left—Insert one or two page breaks so that the remaining content will start on a left page
	right—Insert one or two page breaks so that the remaining content will start on a right page
Default	auto
Used In	Block elements

orphans, widows

Purpose	Specify the minimum number of lines from a single paragraph that must be left at the bottom (orphans) or top (widows) of a page
Inherited	Yes
Values	<integer>
Default	2
Used In	Block elements

Aural Properties

These are not supported by any of the major browsers, and are deprecated as of CSS 2.1. A similar but incompatible speech module is under development for CSS 3.

azimuth

Purpose	Separate voices by position on a virtual stage
Inherited	Yes
Values	<angle>, left-side, far-left, left, center-left, center, center-right, right, far-right, right-side, behind, leftwards, rightwards
Default	center
Used In	All elements

cue

Purpose	Shorthand method for cue properties
Inherited	No
Values	See values for cue-before and cue-after
Default	See individual properties
Used In	All elements

cue-after, cue-before

Purpose	Provide a sound to be played before or after the element
Inherited	No
Values	<url>, none
Default	none
Used In	All elements

elevation

Purpose	Separate voices by altitude on a virtual stage
Inherited	Yes
Values	<angle>, below, level, above, higher, lower
Default	level
Used In	All elements

pause

Purpose	Shorthand method for pause properties
Inherited	No
Values	See values for pause-before and pause-after
Default	See individual properties
Used In	All elements

pause-after, pause-before

Purpose	Define a pause before or after the element
Inherited	No
Values	<time>—Number of seconds (s) or milliseconds (ms)
	<percentage>—Relative to the inverse of the speech-rate property
Default	0
Used In	All elements

pitch

Purpose	Specify the frequency of the speaking voice
Inherited	Yes
Values	<frequency>, x-low, low, medium, high, x-high
Default	medium
Used In	All elements

pitch-range

Purpose	Specify the variation in average pitch
Inherited	Yes
Values	\<number\> between 0 and 100
Default	50
Used In	All elements

play-during

Purpose	Provide a background sound
Inherited	No
Values	\<url\> [mix, repeat]—If mix, continue to play any parent's sound, otherwise replace. If repeat, start the sound over if it is too short
	auto—Continue to play the parent's sound (rather than re-start it if inherited)
	none—Silence; stop the parent's sound
Default	auto
Used In	All elements

richness

Purpose	Specify the brightness of the voice
Inherited	Yes
Values	\<number\> between 0 and 100 (the higher the number, the more the voice will carry)
Default	50
Used In	All elements

speak

Purpose	Determine whether this element will be spoken
Inherited	Yes
Values	normal—Speak normally
	none—Suppress rendition
	spell-out—Speak one character at a time
Default	normal
Used In	All elements

speak-header

Purpose	Define whether the relevant table header information should be spoken before each cell
Inherited	Yes
Values	once, always
Default	once
Used In	Elements that have table header information

speak-numeral

Purpose	Define whether numbers should be spoken as individual digits or as words
Inherited	Yes
Values	digits, continuous
Default	continuous
Used In	All elements

speak-punctuation

Purpose	Define how punctuation should be rendered
Inherited	Yes
Values	code—Speak the punctuation
	none—Pause appropriately
Default	none
Used In	All elements

speech-rate

Purpose	Specify the rate of speech
Inherited	Yes
Values	<number>—words per minute
	x-slow, slow, medium, fast, x-fast, faster, slower
Default	medium
Used In	All elements

stress

Purpose	Determine the amount of inflection
Inherited	Yes
Values	<number> between 0 and 100
Default	50
Used In	All elements

voice-family

Purpose	Request specific voices
Inherited	Yes
Values	<specific voice>, <general voice>
Default	Browser dependent
Used In	All elements

volume

Purpose	Define the median volume
Inherited	Yes
Values	<number>—0 to 100
	<percentage>—relative to the inherited value
	silent—no sound at all
	x-soft—0
	soft—25
	medium—50
	loud—75
	x-loud—100
Default	medium
Used In	All elements

Index

Continued

Continued